VIOLENCE IN ISLAMIC THOUGHT FROM EUROPEAN IMPERIALISM TO THE POST-COLONIAL ERA

Legitimate and Illegitimate Violence in Islamic Thought
Series Editors: István Kristó-Nagy and Robert Gleave

This three-volume series examines the promotion and condemnation of violence in Islamic thought from the earliest period of Islam to the present day. Asking how violence has been justified by Muslims in the past and in the present, these studies show how violence has been legitimised, normalised or censured by Muslims, tracing the history of the argumentation across time and between regions and traditions. The stale media debate about Islam as a violent or non-violent religion is here rejected in favour of a nuanced approach which examines a variety of intellectual disciplines and literatures, examining how violence was processed by Muslim thinkers, such as scholars of law and religion, historians, poets and artists, through time. The result is a striking variety of approaches to violence, and a diversity of conceptions of legitimate and illegitimate violent acts. The series aims to alter how the relationship between violence and Islam is characterised both within and outside of academia.

Volume 1: Violence in Islamic Thought from the Qur'ān to the Mongols

Volume 2: Violence in Islamic Thought from the Mongols to European Imperialism

Volume 3: Violence in Islamic Thought from European Imperialism to the Post-Colonial Era

edinburghuniversitypress.com/series/livit

VIOLENCE IN ISLAMIC THOUGHT FROM EUROPEAN IMPERIALISM TO THE POST-COLONIAL ERA

✦ ✦ ✦

EDITED BY
MUSTAFA BAIG AND
ROBERT GLEAVE

The Legitimate and Illegitimate Violence in Islamic Thought Project
(www.livitproject.net) funded by the RCUK Global Uncertainties Programme,
administered through the Economic and Social Research Council

EDINBURGH
University Press

In memory of our fathers:
Ahmad Nisar Beg (1944–2019)
Geoffrey Roger Gleave (1933–2008)

Edinburgh University Press is one of the leading university presses in the UK. We publish academic books and journals in our selected subject areas across the humanities and social sciences, combining cutting-edge scholarship with high editorial and production values to produce academic works of lasting importance. For more information visit our website: edinburghuniversitypress.com

Edinburgh University Press Ltd
The Tun – Holyrood Road
12 (2f) Jackson's Entry
Edinburgh EH8 8PJ

First published in hardback by Edinburgh University Press 2021

Typeset in JaghbUni by
Servis Filmsetting Ltd, Stockport, Cheshire

A CIP record for this book is available from the British Library

ISBN 978 1 4744 8550 0 (hardback)
ISBN 978 1 4744 8851 7 (paperback)
ISBN 978 1 4744 8553 1 (webready PDF)
ISBN 978 1 4744 8552 4 (epub)

CONTENTS

Dates, Abbreviations and Online References viii
List of Illustrations ix
Acknowledgements x

1. VIOLENCE IN ISLAMIC THOUGHT: METHODOLOGICAL ISSUES AND PROBLEMATIC CATEGORIES 1
Robert Gleave

PART I. VIOLENCE AND ISLAM: METHODOLOGICAL CONCERNS

2. IL/LEGITIMATE VIOLENCE IN MODERN ISLAMIC THOUGHT: A MINORITY REPORT ON MUSLIM VIOLENCE 17
Bruce Lawrence

3. THE LURE OF JIHĀD: POST-TRADITIONAL HISTORIES OF VIOLENCE IN THE ISLAMIC WORLD 39
William Gallois

PART II. RESISTANCE AND COLONIALISM: SOUTH ASIAN CONTEXTS

4. FROM CLIENT TO REBEL? THE PHILOSOPHER FAŻL-I ḤAQQ KHAYRĀBĀDĪ, HIS RISĀLA GHADARĪYA AND THE EVENTS OF 1857 75
Sajjad Rizvi

5. ALTERNATIVE RESISTANCE TO THE BRITISH RAJ: AḤMAD RIḌĀ KHĀN'S LEGAL AND SOCIOPOLITICAL FATWAS 99
Mustafa Baig

6. A ṬĀLIBĀN LEGAL DISCOURSE ON VIOLENCE 123
Jan-Peter Hartung

PART III. JUSTIFYING VIOLENCE

7. BUᶜITHTU BIᵓL-SAYF: *JIHĀD*, MONOLATRY AND THEONOMY IN MODERN SALAFISM 163
Daniel Lav

8. AL-QĀᶜIDA'S POST-ARAB SPRING JIHAD: CONFIRMATION OR RE-EVALUATION? 186
Joas Wagemakers

9. THE ARAB REVOLUTIONS AND JIHADISM 210
Farhad Khosrokhavar

10. THE LOGIC OF THE CONQUEST SOCIETY: ISIS, APOCALYPTIC VIOLENCE AND THE 'REINSTATEMENT' OF SLAVE CONCUBINAGE 225
Omar Anchassi

11. 'NAY, WE OBEYED GOD WHEN WE BURNED HIM': DEBATING IMMOLATION (*TAḤRĪQ*) BETWEEN THE ISLAMIC STATE AND AL-QĀᶜIDA 249
Mathias Ghyoot

PART IV. COMMUNICATING VIOLENCE

12. VIOLENCE AND POLITICAL MOBILISATION IN THE DISCOURSE OF MUQTADĀ AL-ṢADR 291
Sarah Elibiary

13. MANAGING VIOLENT CONFLICT: HUDNA AND TAHDIʾA, BEYOND A STRATEGIC PAUSE 315
Beverley Milton-Edwards

14. NOTES ON SOME JIHADIST POEMS 334
András Hámori

15. THE 'OTHER' IN THE DISCOURSE OF HAMAS AND HIZBULLAH 347
Atef Alshaer

16. CONCLUDING REMARKS: VIOLENCE IN ISLAMIC THOUGHT 362
Robert Gleave

Bibliography 366
Index 408

DATES, ABBREVIATIONS AND ONLINE REFERENCES

All sole dates are according to the Christian (*milādī*) calendar. When in pairs, the dates are ordered *hijrī qamarī/milādī*. When alone, there is a specific reference of *qamarī* date (AH) and *hijrī shamsī* date (SH). The various editions of the *Encyclopaedia of Islam* (published by Brill) are abbreviated to *EI1*, *EI2* and *EI3* in the notes, with full online references (with weblinks) given in the bibliography. *Encyclopaedia Iranica* (various publishers, but available online) is abbreviated to *EIr* in the notes, with full online references given in the bibliography. Given the variety of languages used in original and secondary source material in this volume, we have had to take a more pragmatic view to transliteration. Where Arabic or Persian is the principal language of source material in a chapter, the author has used *EI* conventions; where Turkish predominates, then again, *EI* conventions are used; in those cases where Urdu and Pushto sources occupy the main research base, the authors have used standard transliteration systems for these sources, whilst maintaining *EI* conventions for the Arabic or Persian sources used. A characteristic feature of the materials for studying violence in modern Islamic thought is the rise of online publication as the preferred method of distribution. Inevitably, this material is ephemeral and subject to change. The now conventional 'accessed on' dates have been omitted from the footnotes, primarily in order to avoid making already substantial footnotes overlong. A note on accessed dates is given in the Bibliography (p. 366). All online material was checked by the editors at the time of going to press (January 2020); some links had already become defunct, and in these cases the last 'accessed date' as carried out by the editors should be taken as the last date of availability of any particular resource.

ILLUSTRATIONS

FIGURES

1 *FATWĀ* JUSTIFYING IMMOLATION ISSUED BY IS'S COUNCIL FOR RESEARCH AND FATWAS 253

2 SOME WORKS JUSTIFYING THE LEGALITY OF IMMOLATION RELEASED BY AL-GHURABĀʾ LI-L-ʿILĀM AND AL-WAFĀʾ 255

TABLES

1 CITATIONS OF SCHOLARS IN *AL-SABĪ: AḤKĀM WA MASĀʾIL* 243

ACKNOWLEDGEMENTS

The last volume of the *Violence in Islamic Thought* series presents us with the opportunity to acknowledge the contribution of all those involved in the various projects which have sponsored these volumes. The *Legitimate and Illegitimate Violence in Islamic Thought* (www.livitproject.net), funded by the ESRC and the AHRC as part of their 'Global Uncertainties' research programme from 2010 to 2013, enabled the first of a series of conferences on violence in Islamic thought, out of which this series of volumes emerged. Dr István Kristó-Nagy, the research fellow on that project and now a colleague in the Institute of Arab and Islamic Studies in Exeter, co-edited the first two volumes and provided much intellectual sustenance along the way to the third volume. The *Islamic Reformulations* project (2012–16), funded by the same bodies, had not only Dr Mustafa Baig (co-editor here) as its research fellow, but also Dr Sarah Elibiary (contributor here), now of the School of Oriental and African Studies. Finally, the *Understanding Shari'a* project (2016–19), funded by HERA, provided additional support for the final stage of the project, and benefited from the presence of Dr Omar Anchassi (a contributor here), now of the University of Edinburgh. It has been a rather special series of emerging researchers who have contributed to the decade-long project, and we hope that this provides some additional talent to the next generation of scholars. The successive administrators on all these projects, Ms Jane Clark, Ms Pam Navran and Ms Sarah Wood, have all ensured the smooth running of conferences and workshops where research ideas were tested and refined. They may not contribute directly to volumes such as these, but the books would not exist without them.

We should thank all the participants over the course of the project who came to the LIVIT conferences and workshops. Even when they did not contribute to the volumes, their intellectual contribution shines through in the studies within the volumes. These include Dawood Hamzah Adesola, Asma Afsaruddin, Saud Al-Sarhan, Amira Bennison, Jonathan Brown, Richard Bulliet, David Cook, Faisal Devji, Jean-Pierre Filiu, Edmund Herzig, Jonathan Githens-Mazer, Abdullah Hamidaddin, Thomas Hegghammer, Konrad Hirschler, Stephen Humphreys, Jens Kutschner, Ella Landau-Tasseron, Christian Lange, Franklin Lewis, Emma Loosley, Mohammed Mojahedi, John Nawas, Ruud Peters, Gabriel Reynolds, Martin Riexinger, Devin Stewart, Maria Subtelny, David Thomas, Deborah Tor, László Tüske and Hayrettin Yucesoy. We remember our two dear colleagues who have passed away during the life of the projects, Michael Bonner and Leonard Lewisohn.

Finally, we should thank Edinburgh University Press, and in particular the indefatigable Ms Nicola Ramsey. We have not always been the most speedy of series editors. She has kept the faith when many would have lost it, and her service and care reflects the values of EUP more generally. We are very grateful for having had the opportunity to work with the Press on these projects.

CHAPTER

1

VIOLENCE IN ISLAMIC THOUGHT: METHODOLOGICAL ISSUES AND PROBLEMATIC CATEGORIES

*Robert Gleave**

This volume, the final instalment of the series *Violence in Islamic Thought*, continues both the research focus and the working methods of the previous two collections. At the inception of the series, we set out to examine something called 'violence' in relation to something called 'Islamic Thought'. Both terms – 'violence' and 'Islamic Thought' – can (and have been) subjected to problematisation in these volumes, and also, more extensively, in the wider field.[1] The studies in the first two volumes have led us to working definitions of our

* University of Exeter

1. On the issues relating to the definitions of violence, see the classic study of Robert Wolff ('On Violence', *The Journal of Philosophy* 66.19 (1969), 601–16). Further research since Wolff, from various disciplinary backgrounds, includes Johan Galtung, 'Cultural Violence', *Journal of Peace Research* 27.3 (1990), 291–305)), Robin Fox, 'The Inherent Rules of Violence', in *Social Rules and Social Behavior*, ed. P. Collett (Oxford, 1977), pp. 32–49, Beatrice Hanssen, *Critique of Violence: Between Poststructuralism and Critical Theory* (London, 2000) and Randall Collins, *Violence: A Micro-sociological Theory* (Princeton, 2008). On what is and what is not 'Islamic', see the now influential contribution of Shahab Ahmed, *What Is Islam? The Importance of Being Islamic* (Princeton, 2016), but for the context of Ahmed's work, see Talal Asad, *Genealogies of Religion: Discipline and Reasons of Power in Christianity and Islam* (Baltimore, 1993), Norman Calder, 'The Limits of Islamic Orthodoxy', in *Intellectual Traditions in Islam*, ed. Farhad Daftary (London, 2000), pp. 66–86 and the useful educational collection of Jamal J. Elias (ed.), *Key Themes for the Study of Islam* (Oxford, 2010); and what counts as 'thought' in the context of the study of intellectual history, see (of course) Quentin Skinner, 'Meaning and Understanding in the History of Ideas', *History and Theory* 8.1 (1969), 3–53; and for a useful review and summary, see K. R. Minogue, 'Method in Intellectual History: Quentin Skinner's Foundations', *Philosophy* 56 (1981), 533–52.

fields of enquiry. First, let us examine 'violence': my colleague and co-editor of the first two volumes, István Kristó-Nagy, composed the following working definition of violence in the introduction to the first volume: 'any detrimental act performed by a living being against a living being'.[2] Of course, this (like any working definition) can be broken down and deconstructed: detrimental in what sense? Can one not be violent towards non-living things? Can one be unintentionally violent? And if not, and since intentionality only be ascribed to living 'beings', then non-living 'things' cannot, in truth, be violent? As Kristó-Nagy puts it, '[w]hen a stone is shattered by another stone, it is just movement and change',[3] not violence. Consider this passage from *Philosophical Investigations*:

> Look at a stone and imagine it having sensations. – One says to oneself: How could one so much as get the idea of ascribing a sensation to a thing? One might as well ascribe it to a number! – And now look at a wriggling fly, and at once these difficulties vanish, and pain seems able to get a foothold here, where before everything was, so to speak, too *smooth* for it.[4]

A working definition aims to allow the reader to get a foothold on the term and its utility for deeper study. Describing a volcano as erupting 'violently' or a pan of water boiling 'violently' are poetic; here the adverb functions to mean 'similar to, but not the same as a violent act of a living being against another'. By extension, any cultural product – be it poetry, visual representation, theological or legal argumentation or historical chronical – can valorise or promote detrimental acts performed by one living being against another. To the extent that they do this, they too can be labelled 'violent'.

We should not, though, let the legitimate process of terminological problematisation paralyse all meaningful investigation.[5] There will be hard cases, but hard cases can make for bad working practices. That a term's working

2. Istvan Kristó-Nagy, 'Introduction', in *Violence in Islamic Thought from the Qur'an to the Mongols*, eds R. Gleave and I. Kristó-Nagy (Edinburgh, 2014), p. 3.
3. Kristó-Nagy, 'Introduction', p. 3. To be fair, Kristó-Nagy himself recognises there may be an issue, as the violent desecration of a corpse seems to a legitimate use of the word, but, I could add, perhaps only because the corpse was once a living being.
4. L. Wittgenstein, *Philosophical Investigations* (Oxford, 1953), para. 284 (emphasis in original).
5. That definitions drive certain forms of argumentation is, of course, undeniable (see Douglas Walton, 'Arguing from Definition to Verbal Classification: The Case of Redefining "Planet" to Exclude Pluto', *Informal Logic* 28.2 (2008), 129–54); this would render all acts of definition fundamentally argumentative.

definition produces instances which test it, revealing its limitations, if you like, does not render meaningless all instances of the term's use – that, after all, is the purpose of a 'working definition'. I am, then, quite content for there to be dissatisfaction with Kristó-Nagy's working definition;[6] using it has not, I would argue, led to a mis-categorisation of the historical events described in these volumes, nor any elements of theories or ideologies described in the cultural output of premodern Islamic civilisations. Nothing, I would argue, has been called violent in these volumes when it does not deserve the term. In reference to the collection 'between your hands', so to speak, the actions, historical events, theories and ideas scrutinised by contributors here also all qualify as 'violent' under our working definition. In all this, the definition can be said to have done its job – which is to frame an enquiry and enable detailed conversations.

A similar thing can be said regarding our other principal parameter – namely, 'Islamic Thought'. Above, I alluded to 'cultural products', glossing this with poetry, visual representation, instances of theological or legal argumentation or historical chronicles. This is not an exhaustive list of the elements that we have considered 'Islamic Thought'. As already mentioned in the previous volumes, this is a term which we have taken to have a wide remit, and some may be unhappy, as it gives the impression that the 'religious' perspective is all-pervasive. Van Gelder mentions this in his examination of sexual violence in Jarīr's poetry – he explores the 'Islamic' judgement on this obscene verse.[7] We have not, generally, been interested in using the term as a badge of religious orthodoxy (we would not wish to engage in arguing one cultural artefact is 'properly' Islamic, whilst another is not). In as much as it forms part of the literary output of Islamic civilisation, I work on the basis that it deserves the term 'Islamic'. Jarīr's obscene poetry, along with the other instances described in this series, deserve the term 'Islamic' not because they are religious, but because they are a product of the Islamic milieu. Just because (some of the) the *ʿulamāʾ* of the past would not have approved of this cultural product, does not mean we implicitly accept their judgement: they should not be the arbiters of our terminological usage. Furthermore, we should not be trapped by a particular version (northern European, Protestant, Colonial, etc.) of what does (or does not) count as a 'religious' phenomenon:

6. Oliver Leaman, 'Review of R. Gleave and I. Kristó-Nagy (eds), *Violence in Islamic Thought from the Qur'an to the Mongols*' *Journal of Qur'anic Studies* 18. 3 (2016), 124–7.
7. G. Van Gelder, 'Sexual Violence in Verse', in *Violence in Islamic Thought*, eds R. Gleave and I. Kristó-Nagy, *Violence in Islamic Thought*, pp. 175–90.

intellectual dissatisfaction with these limited notions of 'religion' are now commonplace in the secondary literature.[8]

In this series, we would have been happy to use an alternative, such as Islamicate, but that term, like many others, suffers from two immediate drawbacks. First, in the academic field of the study of Islam, simply using 'Islamicate' ties one into a certain methodological approach, and any project would face the same raft of criticisms which the Hodgsonian approach itself attracts.[9] We are not yet at a stage where the term 'Islamicate' has created its own space separate from its Chicago origins. Second, Islamicate is often greeted with bafflement outside the field ('so you mean "Islamic", yes?'); the term is yet to gain currency in the wider humanities and social sciences, and it has almost no meaning to the general public. We rejected its use for our series title, though by doing so, we were not aiming to imply a criticism of the framework in which it is employed. As the introductory comments to the previous two volumes show, we are influenced by Hodgson's approach in various ways.

Since the first volume in this series was published, the latest wave of self-examination in Islamic Studies has prompted methodological reflection on the terms 'Islam' and 'Islamic' (along with cognate terms like 'Muslim'). Many academics identify as Islamicists – namely, scholars of Islamic Studies – but the frame of reference is under constant review.[10] The field, it has been argued, has almost unconsciously adopted a methodological privileging of the textual tradition of the scholarly elite (the *ʿulamāʾ*, the *udabāʾ*, the *umarāʾ*, the *kuttāb*, etc.); and within that tradition, theology, law and Qurʾānic exegesis have occupied predominant positions. The reaction has been to broaden Islamic Studies to include the study of Muslim religious society, and at a more granular level, the everyday practice of Muslims.[11] There has been a refocusing of the field, taking into

8. See the various contributions in Thomas A. Idinopulos and Brian C. Wilson (eds), *What is Religion? Origins, Definitions, and Explanations* (Leiden, 1998) and, more recently, specifically on how Islam and Islamic law was framed under nineteenth century conceptions of religion in a colonial context, see J. Stephens, *Governing Islam: Law, Empire, and Secularism in Modern South Asia* (Cambridge, 2018).
9. Hodgson's project is summarised in Edmund Burke, 'Islamic History as World History: Marshall Hodgson, "The Venture of Islam"', *International Journal of Middle East Studies* 10.2 (1979), 241–64.
10. Most of the discussion focused around Shahab Ahmed's work cited above, but see also the collection C. Dorroll (ed.), *Teaching Islamic Studies in the Age of ISIS, Islamophobia, and the Internet* (Bloomington, 2019).
11. B. Geer, 'Training Scholars to Study Non-Scholarly Life', in Dorrell (ed.), *Teaching Islamic Studies*, pp. 35–49, and Syed Rizwan Zamir, 'Rethinking the Academic Study of the "Ulamā" Tradition', *Islamic Studies* 53.3/4 (2014), 145–74.

account experiences in the past, and anthropological and sociological approaches to the study of Islam in the present. One might call this a turn to 'subalternaity'.[12] Within this disciplinary context, our conception of 'Islamic Thought' is broader than those who have used the term in the past; nonetheless, it has to be conceded, our focus in this series remains, to a large extent, elite (and possible, elitist). The cultural products which constitute the purview of Islamic thought used here (and studied in this series of volumes) certainly include the usual suspects of theology, law and Qurʾānic exegesis. But for us, Islamic thought stretches beyond them to other literary forms, not always considered examples of 'Islamic Thought' *per se* – poetry, chronicles and historiography and literature. One might think these literary forms should not be considered 'Islamic' thought, since much of the time they appear quite humanist in orientation. We have also gone beyond literature – embracing visual art and architecture as instances of 'Islamic Thought': our argument for such inclusions is that these cultural forms propose ideas about violence and its legitimacy, even if they are not in the standard format of written/oral, linear argumentation. They therefore form legitimate subjects of study in a book series on *Violence in Islamic Thought.*

In this sense, what counts as 'Islamic' (and, come to think of it, what counts as 'thought' also) is, for us, an inclusive category. Some might feel uneasy with our attempt to 'Islamicise' all aspects of the cultural output of Muslim communities through time; but, for me at least, this is only an issue if one takes a narrow view of what the 'Islam' element of 'Islamic' means. We take a relatively expansive (and pragmatic) view – Islam (with its adjective 'Islamic') is not a marker of a 'religion' in the sense used by the early pioneers in the religious studies field:[13] it is not a set of doctrines against which ideas and practices can be measured to uncover their 'Islamic' authenticity. Instead, whilst the diversity of Muslim experience over time cannot be denied, there is a common cultural frame of reference – an awareness of a shared history, if you like – which enables us to cast our net quite wide when we conceive of what is (and what is not) 'Islamic

12. The term, from Gramsci onwards, has gained popularity as a category of analysis, with the most widely cited reference being Spivak's 'Can the Subaltern Speak?', available in revised form, in R. Morris (ed.), *Can the Subaltern Speak?: Reflections on the History of an Idea* (New York, 2010), pp. 21–78.
13. Ninian Smart, 'Religious Studies in the United Kingdom', *Religion* 18 (1998), 1–9. The notion of 'religion' as a recent invention of particular forms of Western discourse (both academic, societal and political) is most influentially proposed by Wilferd Cantell Smith, *The Meaning and End of Religion: A New Approach to the Religious Traditions of Mankind* (New York, 1962); it has, of course, been regularly critiqued and reinterpreted – see, for example, Talal Asad, 'Reading a Modern Classic: W. C. Smith's "The Meaning and End of Religion"', *History of Religions* 40.3 (2001), 205–22.

Thought'. In this, our method chimes with the ideas of those for whom a critique of the field has become a major academic preoccupation. At the same time, there is no escaping the elite perspective inherent in the subjects of our collections. The producers of 'Islamic Thought' (under our conception) are primarily intellectuals, litterateurs, jurists and theologians. Even when this is extended to include artists and architects, these are societal strata usually called (not unproblematically, one can add) 'Muslim elites'. These cultural producers have, and have had, privileged status, created out of patronage and the acquisition of skills (literary or otherwise). To an extent, our focus is a product of the surviving historical record – the evidence for the work of elites has survived from the past in greater volume. But it is also an unavoidable consequence of our choice of topic: we have set out to study how violence has been discussed, processed, conceptualised and assessed in the cultural products of Muslim societies. Such a task will inevitably create a data set which is, in premodern societies, the product of the patronised intelligentsia. In defence, we can but plead awareness of the limitations, but also would argue that to frame the task otherwise would make unwieldy what are already extensive terms of reference.

Given these parameters, the collection of studies presented here on *violence* in 'modern' *Islamic thought* is both a continuation of these working methods, but also exhibits some novel developments. A few general observations are worthy of mention. First, considering the studies presented here, there is clearly a greater engagement with the methodological issues raised by a study of Islam and violence (see, for example, Chapter 2, Lawrence, and Chapter 3, Gallois). This may reflect the bent of the contributors, but it also indicates the perceived need for commentators – be they academics or those in the public domain more broadly – to take on board the methodological context for any study of this topic. It seems that the relationship between Islam and violence in the modern period is particularly problematic, and therefore some contributors feel the need to clarify their methodological framework at the outset, perhaps in order to avert potential misunderstandings. Numerous studies have demonstrated that the connection between Islam and violence, made in the popular imagination, has formed an element of the more extreme instances of Islamophobia.[14] One can debate the causes for the ease with which this connection came to prominence: it seems likely that it has its roots in medieval European stereotypes of Islam linked with the superiority of Christian culture.[15] And yet, the equation: Christianity–non-violent/Islam–violent

14. See the contributions to the collected volume: N. Massoumi, T. Mills and D. Miller (eds), *What is Islamophobia?: Racism, Social Movements and the State* (London, 2017).
15. John V. Tolan, *Saracens: Islam in the Medieval European Imagination* (New York, 2002).

was only one element here, as the negative medieval stereotypes were not dependent on Islam's supposed association with violence; given the violence of the time, such a simple equation might appear unconvincing even to the most blinkered of medieval commentators. More importantly, these stereotypes do not come out of some sort of advocacy of non-violence, but are embedded in the notion that Islam is politically threatening to the imagined fortress of Christendom, that it was fundamentally heretical, and that Islam is the religion of the irrational heathen. All these elements might be rolled up with references to Islam's barbarism (the acts of Muslims become, in synecdochic manner, the acts of Islam itself), but the violence is only occasionally evil *per se*; rather, it is evil when employed for illegitimate ends. It would be beyond our scope here to chart the rise to popularity of the notion that violence is a harm or a negative, 'essentially' (using Aristotelian terms). I am referring here to the idea that, even when the end is justified, the violence required to achieve this end is still, somehow, regrettable; at some point, it becomes common in European moral discourse to argue that violence is an evil in and of itself, diminished but not obliterated by the justice of the end cause.[16] For sure, the essential 'badness' of violent acts was not invented in the modern period (the idea exists in both Islamic and European Christian intellectual traditions). Nonetheless, the justificatory preoccupation with acts which might be classed as 'violent', the constant weighing of ends and means and the near ubiquitous use of 'violent' as a negative qualifier – these are all elements which make violence a peculiarly 'modern obsession', as Bessel describes it.[17]

To follow this argument further, the assumption that violence is always regrettable (even when justified) could be seen as an inescapable element of the so-called liberal tradition (keying into ethical and diplomatic principles of non-aggression between both nations and individuals).[18] If so, then the structure of modern moral and political discourse demands that violence, *ab initio*, be considered a negative. As discussed below, it is the almost unemotional manner in which violence and its aftermath are culturally processed in Islamic thought that has fed into a supposed special connection between Islam and violence (see the contributions concerning Islamic State legal thinking – Chapter 10 – Anchassi, and Chapter 11 – Ghyoot, where refusal to bow to the supposed 'Western' forms a fundamental element of the Jihadist rhetoric). Those commentators (usually, but not always, non-academics) who wish to portray Islam as an irredeemably

16. H. Popitz, 'Violence', in *Phenomena of Power: Authority, Domination, and Violence*, eds A. Göttlich and J. Dreher (New York: Columbia University Press, 2017), pp. 25–51.
17. R. Bessel, *Violence: A Modern Obsession* (New York, 2015).
18. See Stephen L. Carter, 'Must Liberalism Be Violent? A Reflection on the Work of Stanley Hauerwas', *Law and Contemporary Problems* 75 (2012), 201–19.

violent religion usually work on the supposition that their audience find all forms of violence morally repugnant – even if violence is sometimes morally justified also. They might pursue this line of argumentation for a combination of, say, political, psychological, cultural and religious reasons. In doing so, of course, such argumentation is based on a number of (usually unspoken) assumptions. These include, but are not limited to, the following: (1) that there is a unified item known as 'Islam' which can be assessed as violent or not; (2) that Islam, in this essentialised form, consists mainly of a set of beliefs (i.e. a 'religion' in the Victorian sense of the term), which have a straightforward causal relationship with the practice of Muslims; (3) that these beliefs can be easily obtained from the literature of Muslim scholars through the ages, and thereby assessed as to their 'violent' nature against an independent (and uncontroversial) yardstick; (4) that these beliefs can be best deduced from a certain textual corpus, beginning with choice citations from the Qurʾān, and ending with supposedly unequivocal statements by jurists. Of course, all these assumptions can be questioned: are they really reliable, research-based grounds on which to construct any analysis? But that is not my point here. Rather, these assumptions have a certain contemporary reasonableness when discussing Islam which makes their employment in the public discourse, particularly in Europe and North America, feasible. In time, I would argue, they have become almost axiomatic. The dubiousness of these assumptions, of course, explains why academics (myself included) squirm when posed the much-asked question: 'is Islam inherently violent?'[19]

It is, perhaps, the refusal of some premodern (and modern) Islamic cultural forms to be sentimental about violence which might appear out of kilter with supposed 'modern' sensibilities. The cultural forms studied in this series of volumes (from theology to miniatures) do not appear to show an overriding concern around the moral evaluation of violence. This is not surprising in one sense – why might one expect the medieval Islamic cultural world to be more or less 'peaceful' than other premodern cultural worlds? That such an absence of concern in premodern works is used to assert the Islam–violence linkage could be the result of certain ingrained notions that Islam is different. To argue that Hinduism is irretrievably violent since Krishna called for war might be unsustainable (particularly given the pioneering of non-violence by Mohandas Gandhi);[20] however, the use of premodern Muslim legal texts as representatives

19. See D. Ansorge, 'Is it Essentialism to Claim that Some Religions Foster Violence – and Some Do Not?', in *Islamic Peace Ethics: Legitimate and Illegitimate Violence in Contemporary Islamic Thought*, ed. H. Shadi (Baden-Baden, 2017).
20. On the other hand, that religion generally, Hinduism included, is particularly connected with violence in the modern period, see R. King 'The Association of "Religion" with

of 'authentic' violent Islam is commonplace. Such thoughtless anachronism and essentialism are somehow more plausible in the public domain (if not in the academic world) in relation to Islam. Why do some popular commentators feel they have unfettered permission to be anachronistic and essentialist in relation to Islam? Possible explanations include the perception that Islam is so divergent from the European tradition that the normal rules of historical analysis do not apply (the perception of Islamic exceptionalism, sometimes encouraged by analyses internal to the tradition).[21] There is also the notion that numerous Muslim actors in the modern world claim to act for 'Islam' (in toto) and make regular reference to the past (Golden Age, *al-salaf al-ṣāliḥ, al-Rashidūn*, Prophetic/Companion precedent, etc.) when justifying their contemporary ideologies. By actively seeking the judgement of history, some Muslim thinkers supply a perceived permission to activate essentialist and anachronistic modes of argumentation in European and North American public discussions, and occasionally also in the academic context.

To break the artless Islam–violence connection, one might turn to the intellectual tradition of Islamic scholarship. As the studies in these volumes have shown, premodern Islamic thought is hardly a reservoir of non-violent counter examples. Poets and litterateurs, historians and philosophers were quite willing to participate in the rhetorical justification of violence – and this feature continues into the modern period (see Chapter 4, Rizvi). From my own area of specialism, the *fiqh* tradition is not a particularly useful evidence base for a rejection of the connections between Islam and violence. Premodern *fiqh* works present violent acts as justified or otherwise according to an assessment framework which is distinctly 'un-modern' – that is, by appealing to texts and their interpretation, sources and modes of argumentation which are often quite unconvincing to those outside the tradition (and, in the more recent past, to quite a few inside it also). In *fiqh*, there is no moral squeamishness around, say, the violent punishment for criminals of the specific *ḥudūd* crimes; in *fiqh*, one rarely gains a sense that amputation, lashings and execution are somehow regrettable, even when justified. Punishments are triggered when certain evidentiary requirements are met; one would not expect a moral discourse of regret to enter into discussions around the mechanics of punishment. The same can be said of the *fiqh* regulations around *jihād*, the treatment of rebels and the maintenance of public order. It is perhaps typified by the resistance of the *fiqh* tradition to removing retaliatory

Violence: Reflections on a Modern Trope', in *Religion and Violence in South Asia: Theory and Practice*, eds J. R. Hinnells and R. King (London, 2007), pp. 226–57.

21. See, for example, J. Bowen, *Can Islam Be French?: Pluralism and Pragmatism in a Secularist State* (Princeton, 2010).

rights to the victims of violence: that individuals, rather than the state, regulates – and in many cases carries out – the punishment of criminals means that violence, though limited by the state, is not monopolised by it. In the Islamic *fiqh* tradition, the state does not have a Weberian style absolute monopoly on the legitimate use of force: individuals have a divinely sanctioned right to retaliate in kind for an act of violence against them. All this makes for a framework for the discussion of violent acts which does not marry up so well with the supposed contemporary moral consensus. Even the most 'fundamentalist' of movements – Jihadist or otherwise – are largely bound by the established rules of intellectual engagement with the religious sources. Qur'ānic phrases which have always been understood as legitimising violent acts, and which appear unacceptable in a contemporary setting, cannot just be rejected by Muslim intellectuals. They must be accommodated and explained, with historicisation being a common tactic ('what applies then does not apply now'). But such accommodation leaves the door ajar for the reintroduction of an 'unacceptable' practice, should the correct conditions be met. The very possibility of, say, amputation punishments being 'Islamically' justified is enough for some commentators to declare the whole tradition to be morally base. As discussed later in this chapter, it could be argued that many contemporary Muslim reform movements, from the 'moderate' to the *jihādī*, have been influenced by the unsentimental portrayal of violence in the *fiqh* tradition, and hence discuss (and pursue) violence in terms alien to the common moral categories of Western thought. The heartless, remorseless violence of some *jihādī* movements supposedly reflects the uncompromising detachment of the Islamic legal tradition.

The descriptions of violent punishments in *fiqh* might, in fact, reveal a negative view of violence: *fiqh* writers go to great pains to outline when and how violent punishment is justified, and when it is not. There is no free for all in a properly regulated *jihād*, and the permission to retaliate in kind for violent transgressions does not provide permission for vigilantism. *Ḥudūd* punishments are highly regulated in premodern Islamic legal discourse.[22] The jurists would not set these restrictions unless they viewed violence as a morally circumscribed commodity – to be used sparingly and only within a robust legal framework (see Chapter 5, Baig). This sort of nuance gives a richer picture, of course, but it does not solve all the problems. First, this shaded explanation is not always easy to convey to a wider audience. Second, it does not eliminate the ominous, detached nature of the language used to justify violence in *fiqh* works, which is such useful

22. R. Gleave, 'Crimes Against God and Violent Punishment in *al-Fatawa al-Alamgiriyya*', in *Religion and Violence in South Asia*, eds Hinnells and King, pp. 83–106.

copy for columnists. Some of the practices justified in premodern *fiqh* works make even the most determined Islamist uncomfortable, and this is particularly evident in the studies in this volume (see Chapter 6, Hartung, and Chapter 7, Lav). Any investigation of violence in modern Islamic thought has to deal with the fact that this *fiqh*-style detached mode of expression (though not, necessarily, the *fiqh* genre itself) has been adopted by almost all contemporary Islamist movements with their sights on political or legal change in the Muslim world. This partly explains why the international political demand made of movements such as Hamas to renounce violence is always going to be religiously difficult. It would mean abandoning the tradition of Islamic legal thinking, and it is precisely the stripped-down notions of Sharīᶜa drawn from that tradition that most Islamist groups hope to implement. The restoration of the Sharīᶜa (in terms loosely related to Islamic law found in *fiqh*) is the main rallying call of such movements.

The studies in this volume demonstrate, then, that *fiqh* modes of discourse (though not necessarily *fiqh* itself) have had a strong influence on the argumentation style found in much contemporary Muslim literature. There are other forms of argument, for sure (on Hizbullah and Hamas's rhetorical strategies, see Chapter 15, Alshaer); nevertheless, the primacy of legal justification in relation to violence is, arguably, most evident in the more intellectual reflections of the *jihādī* movements. *Jihādī* movements do have non-*fiqh* based cultural expressions: there is poetry, along with more emotive cultural products (see Chapter 14, Hámori). But when engaging in the register of justification (rather than simple encouragement to act), Islamists and *jihādī*s alike often turn to legal-style reasoning (see Chapter 12, Elibiary). Even when reacting to movements in which 'Islam' is not the main rallying point – such as the so-called Arab Spring – Jihadist groups frame their response through these lenses (on this, see Chapter 8, Wagemakers, and Chapter 9, Khosrokhavar). Breaking out of these justificatory frameworks has not (generally speaking) been achieved by such movements, in part because these types of argument have an authenticity which is difficult to replicate elsewhere. *Fiqh* discourse has a popular rhetorical power which many Islamic movements for change are eager to harness (see Chapter 13, Milton Edwards). The manner in which *fiqh* works (and by extension much contemporary Muslim discourse) discuss violent acts is, on an initial assessment at least, quite irreconcilable with the emotional and moral assessments of violence in European and North American public discussions. This was seen most dramatically and tragically in the employment of *fiqh* argumentation for the killing, enslavement and subsequent sexual violence in the literature of the Islamic State group. This is uncomfortable news for some commentators who wish to portray the Jihadists as entirely outside of the established (read: acceptable) Islamic tradition. The studies contained in this volume indicate that there are, as with all individual movements, distinctive elements to the *jihādī* ideologies. However (as pointed out), there is ample possibility for them to employ the premodern *fiqh* tradition in order to demonstrate their continuity with the past. This is not to say Jihadism is the natural inheritor of premodern Islamic thought; simply that they cannot be excluded from that consideration merely because they are politically unacceptable in the post-9/11 context. The disconnect of 'Muslim' and 'Western' discussions of violence is particularly acute in the modern period; in part, because of the increase in global connectivity, but also because the dominance of essentialising methods of argumentation are proving extremely resistant to challenge. The result is that the studies in this volume appear more 'religious' in the sense that violence and its justification in many modern settings is framed in terms which are unquestionably 'Islamic' – namely, argumentation based around the fulfilment of Islamic legal requirements.

Taking all this into consideration, these studies on violence and modern Islamic thought reflect the context in which academics now do Islamic Studies – and this means that this collection has some distinctive features when compared with the first two volumes. Three main concluding observations can be made here. First, the greater level of methodological engagement here than in the previous volumes reflects a perceived need to define parameters of debate and limit conclusions: some authors directly address the issues of defining 'Islam', 'Islamic Thought' and violence, and I have participated in this exercise in this introduction. This methodological awareness is, surely, the product of a contemporary context in which the Islam–violence relationship is both commonplace and deeply intellectually unsatisfactory. Academics are rightly concerned not to be misunderstood here, as the stakes are high. The methodological precision displayed by some authors in this volume reflects a desire to establish the purely academic basis of their analysis. It becomes essential if the individual is to counter the accusation of either being too apologetic, or slipping into Islamophobia. Another prompt, though, for this methodological awareness must be the range of materials now available for analysis – apart from literary tomes, one has Internet sites, social media outlets, pamphlets and leaflets and media-reported political declarations. With such source variety, the discriminating researcher will need to employ a more nuanced methodological toolbox in order to properly understand the superfluity of information available. The second observation relates to a greater focus on the intersection of political and religious ideas in modern Islamic thought. Of course, violence is, to an extent, an act of public concern (even when it is perpetrated in private), and hence political discussions are unavoidable. Nonetheless, whilst one hesitates to make a generalisation, it can be said that most contemporary intellectual movements in Islam are underpinned by political projects (few could be characterised as purely 'religious', if such a judgement was possible). Therefore, discussion of their ideas in relation to violence (or, indeed, any other topic) will unavoidably take a political turn. This may have been true in the premodern period as well; in the contemporary period, though, European and North American political rhetoric has been based on a separation of religion from politics, making the explicit confluence of these two spheres in modern Islam particularly noteworthy. Inevitably, this catches the eye of academic researchers. Finally, academics working on the relationship between Islam and violence in the modern period are doing so in the context of the post-9/11 War on Terror, the rise of Jihadism and the counterterrorism/deradicalisation programmes of governments around the world. There is the sponsorship of Islamic political theology by some governments in which Islam as a 'religion of peace' (that is non-violent) is promoted, in order to counter the Islam–violence media portrayal.[23] Whether this is an appropriate response, or is in any sense backed up by robust academic research, is highly debatable. It is, however, an element of the context in which independent academic research on Islam and violence is carried out, and some argue that academics have a duty to break the perceived connection of Islam and terrorism. There has been, for example, a vigorous debate around whether one should use the term 'Islamic' to describe the infamous Iraqi and Syrian based movement 'Islamic State' (formally known as ISIS, or Daesh). Alternative locutions, such as 'the so-called Islamic State' or 'the Islamic State Group', are now employed in political and media pronouncements, with the evident aim of distinguishing 'Islam' from the group's actions.[24] The general underpinning notion of the research here is that for the term 'Islamic' (in the series title 'Violence in Islamic Thought') to have any academic grounding, it cannot be based on the (albeit laudable) theological pronouncement that 'Islam does not promote violence'. The studies in this volume demonstrate, then, that studying violence in 'modern' Islamic thought involves not only the academic issues of research into the early and middle periods (laid out in the previous two volumes of the series); it faces a series of new contextual challenges, which explains the slightly different flavour of the chapters in this volume.

23. See the studies in R. Pennington and H. Kahn, *On Islam: Muslims and the Media* (Bloomington, 2018).
24. Even Ahmed, whose project seeks to emphasise a diverse vision of cosmopolitan Islam, has to concede that 'as long as the Muslim actor is making his act of violence meaningful to himself in terms of Islam—in terms of Pre-Text, Text, or Con-Text of Revelation—then it is appropriate and meaningful to speak of that act of violence as Islamic violence.' Ahmed, *What is Islam?*, p. 452.

PART I

. . .

VIOLENCE AND ISLAM: METHODOLOGICAL CONCERNS

CHAPTER

2

IL/LEGITIMATE VIOLENCE IN MODERN ISLAMIC THOUGHT: A MINORITY REPORT ON MUSLIM VIOLENCE

*Bruce Lawrence**

OVERVIEW OF MAJOR ISSUES AND THEORISTS

Modern Islamic thought concerns both Muslims and those who reflect on the nature of Islam, whether Muslim or non-Muslim. As a non-Muslim Western academic, I have long reflected on the relationship of Islam to violence. In an earlier monograph I anticipated the gaps in understanding between Muslims and others that predated, but then increased, after the first Gulf War (1991), and more recently I co-edited an anthology that examined numerous theoretical and practical engagements with violence, in and beyond Muslim contexts.[1]

The question I have repeatedly asked is: can Islam and violence be thought, understood and analysed if we ignore the colonial prism? Whether violence is deemed to be legitimate or illegitimate depends on a prior assessment of who has the authority to label violence as legitimate or illegitimate in the twenty-first century. A presentist view rules out or ignores history, but the colonial prism requires an historical prolegomenon to any consideration of violence, its justification or its consequence.

By the colonial prism, I mean the long period of European exploration and then rule over many parts of the world beyond Europe. The history of the

* Duke University

1. The monograph was *Shattering the Myth: Islam beyond Violence* (Princeton, 1998), the anthology *On Violence: A Reader*, with Aisha Karim (Durham, 2007). For research into the topic of minority issues, especially but not solely with reference to Indonesia and Egypt, I am indebted to the Carnegie Corporation, and for support I received as a Carnegie Scholar of Islam (2008–10).

Americas is one chapter of that story, oft told and well known, but another chapter, less well known but equally important, concerns large parts of Asia and Africa, some with Muslim majority, others with Muslim minority, subjects. It began in the fifteenth century and continued till the mid-twentieth century. Independence did come to most polities, but only after WWII and only after thirty of the forty-one Muslim majority states had experienced some form of colonial rule, direct or indirect, prior to independence.

It is impossible to overstate the importance of European rule and its long-term consequence – for history, commerce, education, culture and, of course, religion. The geopolitical frame of empire pervades, and in what follows I will pursue the question of Islam and violence by first revisiting the larger question of religion and ideology as they have shaped by European antecedents and influences.

RELIGION, IDEOLOGY AND VIOLENCE

Alas, the line demarcating religion from ideology is so thin as to be almost invisible, especially in theoretical studies about Islam and violence. Let me etch the three tangents of violence that pertain to post-colonial Muslim polities in Asia and Africa:

1) Structural violence

The asymmetric relation between Europe and Africa–Asia, including majority and minority Muslim states, was itself a form of violence. Let us call it structural violence, with human agents/perpetrators. Well known, and much debated, is the argument from Edward Said about the complicity of Orientalists as scholars with European policymakers as colonial agents. Both the thesis and its critique have evoked many scholarly, as well as popular, books.[2] What is less well charted, or discussed, however, is the role of languages, empires and nations in mapping the framework for thinking about Islam and violence. Major languages are English and French, major empires are British, American and French (with Dutch, Italian and Russian less emphasised) and the nations of paramount importance remain the UK, France and the US (though the role of Russia in Central Asia and the Caucasus, as also Chinese engagement with Hui and Uigur Muslims in Northwest China, cannot, and should not, be ignored).

2. See, for example, Robert Irwin, *Dangerous Knowledge: Orientalism and Its Discontents* (London, 2006).

2) Definitional violence

Structural violence elides with definitional violence. Here, instead of material shifts or economic strategies or military conquests, we must look at language, and its use or misuse, in a colonial context. Where do we find the colonial legacy in definitional studies of Islam and violence? It is, above all, in the reflex to make of religion the defining feature of minorities and majorities. This is not an Orientalist subterfuge; it is a marketable ideology, of European origin, that has found broad acceptance beyond European actors, leaders or publics. It is a policy feature of most Muslim majority states: they define themselves first and foremost by religion. So commonplace is it to think of Islam as the sole religion (whether in KSA or Kuwait or Afghanistan) or as the majority religion (as in Egypt or Bangladesh or Indonesia) that few question either its origin or viability.

Yet the twinning of Islam and identity does have a history. As Peter van der Veer, following Marcel Mauss, noted, 'nationalism may be the religion of modern society', but at the same time, 'when religion becomes a defining feature of the nation, it is transformed in a certain direction'.[3] Amartya Sen has specified the problem even more acutely. He has noted that the propensity of the British, but also Americans, is to 'focus only on religious classification. In addition to neglecting other important ideas and interests that motivate people's actions, it also has the effect of amplifying, in general, the voice of religious authority.'[4] Amin Maalouf has made a similar argument for Francophone societies, although Maalouf lays the responsibility squarely on the individual to rethink competing identities. 'Each of us has two heritages', he asserts,

> a 'vertical' one that comes to us from our ancestors, our religious community and our popular traditions, and a 'horizontal' one transmitted to us by our contemporaries and by the age we live in. It seems to me that the latter is the more influential of the two, and that it becomes more so every day. Yet this fact is not reflected in our perception of ourselves, and the inheritance we invoke most frequently is the vertical one.[5]

And so definitional violence, along with structural violence, has amplified the public, ideological significance of religion in general and Islam in particular.

3. Peter Van Der Veer, *Nation and Religion* (Princeton, 1999), pp. 19–20.
4. Amartya Sen, *Identity and Violence* (New York, 2006), p. 14.
5. Amin Maalouf, *In the Name of Identity: Violence and the Need to Belong* (New York, 2000), p. 107.

This aspect of violence is all the more difficult to trace because it has become a taken-for-granted moniker of identity in public discourse, allegedly between state, politics and civil society, but, in effect, constructing and confirming a public sphere where religion – from the state, of the state and for the state – monitors acceptable belief and action. In short, the post-colonial nation-state projects a neo-orthodoxy within national borders. That condition has been challenged, but not subverted, in the Internet age. During the past two decades, while jurisdiction over territorial or definitional borders has become more porous, and open to redefinitions of taken-for-granted categories as also the networks supporting and/or enforcing them, state actors have still found ways to project their authority online, as well as in real time.

3) Locational violence

Both structural and definitional violence also depend on location. It is not only what happened, and how one defines what happened, it is also from where you speak – or look or feel or live – that determines how you react to what happened in the aftermath of colonial rule and a series of independence movements from mid-1940s to 1970s. Theories of violence are not the same in the north and the south. If we look at the modern nation-state as a legacy of colonial rule from the nineteenth–mid twentieth century, and then consider post-colonial or neo-colonial thinking from 1962 to now, we find that the majority of the sources for thinking about violence and Islam are European.

As long ago as 1988, Ernst Gellner asserted bluntly: 'cultures are not cognitively equal', and one must recognise 'not merely the diversity but also the inequality of belief systems, as well as the great discontinuities of human history'.[6]

Gellner was right. He was arguing neither as a cultural elitist, nor as a Western triumphalist. He was asserting that there is, whether we recognise it or not, a hierarchy of cultures, as also belief systems, and any sound scholarship will confront, not avoid, its own hierarchical presuppositions. He also could have added: there is a hierarchy *within* cultures and belief systems. Who gets to speak for Africa or Asia? Who is deemed to be the spokesperson for Islam or for the global Muslim community?

There is always a hierarchy of value, sometimes acknowledged, but often discounted or ignored. In 2014 we need to reread and rethink Gellner's ancient but salutary warning: cultures, like belief systems, exhibit hierarchy and within

6. Ernest Gellner, 'The Stakes in Anthropology', *The American Scholar* Winter (1988), 29–30.

culturally valorised belief systems there are also hierarchies. In the case of Islam, they reflect the dominant values not just of Muslims, but also of those who study Islam. Figures like Tariq Ramadan and Yūsuf al-Qaraḍāwī (both considered in this chapter) are part of the Euro-American circuit because they project their voices on the Internet in English as well as Arabic (or in Ramadan's case, in French and English as well as Arabic). And most of those who speak about Islam presuppose that it is first and foremost an Arab religion, to which Arabic speakers have special insider access, while others for whom Arabic is a secondary language, or only a ritual language, are lesser, and also less important, Muslims.

AN ALTERNATE HIERARCHY OF VALUE: MALEK BENNABI

It is not just non-Arabic speaking Muslims who are devalued. Lower down the hierarchy of value, prestige and authority are those who speak in French or represent a Francophone perspective not easily translated into English, Arabic or any 'universal' language of the Internet age. Chief among them, I argue, is Malek Bennabi. Malek Bennabi (1905–73) trained as an electrical engineer in Paris, and has received a renewed focus in Algeria as both an Islamic loyalist and a radical modernist. After his studies in Paris, Bennabi could not return to Algeria immediately after the 1962 revolution because of his pro-Islamic stance, and so lived in Egypt for a time before returning to Algiers, where he held weekly salons, or open meetings, in both Arabic and French until his death in 1973.

Bennabi serves as a counterpoint to political Islam, with its focus on the public domain of government and governance, alliances and rivalries, interests and strategies. Nor does Bennabi advocate the slippery project known as the Islamisation of knowledge. Instead of making modernity Islamic, he advocates revisiting, and revitalising, the roots of Islamic civilisation. Bennabi focuses on the religious principle at the heart of every civilisational endeavour, but especially Islam. It is not enough to be Muslim. *One must be a reasoning, rational subject*; in short, a thinking individual.

And the quest for a thinking individual – at once reflective and self-critical – circles back to Arendt. For one must also ask: what kind of reason does the individual pursue – is it metaphysical, moral or purely instrumental? For Arendt, 'Thought' must be moral/metaphysical, not instrumental, Thought. Arendt indicts not just Eichmann, but those who put him on trial for accepting instrumental Thought, confusing morality with conformity. In the creation of Nazi Germany, and every totalitarian state, it is the shield of conformity that strips the human being of Thought, leaving only the shell of reason, which amounts to accepting whatever is state law as morally obligatory. There is no individual thinking, only political conformity – the opposite of Thought.[7]

Bennabi is also opposed to blind conformity. He advocates precisely the kind of moral rather than instrumental reasoning that Arendt had prized consistently from her earliest writings. To the extent that one relies on moral principles, in Bennabi's view, it is only through a ceaselessly probing endeavour to connect with first principles. It is the moral Islamic person who embodies the distinctive aesthetic sensibility that has everywhere marked the greatness of Islamic civilisation. It is neither bureaucracies nor business ventures that evoke the hope of the future for Islamic creativity. True creativity requires instead 'deep knowledge of the structures of professions, of the workings of productive organizations, attention to detail and method, diligence and perseverance in application'. Such dedication to the creative spirit is not incidental or additive; it is foundational and necessary. It must precede 'the successful transplantation of modern economies into the post-colonial Muslim world'.[8] Education at all levels is the key to this rhetorically abstract yet morally profound agenda.

In effect, Bennabi tries to walk the tightrope between authenticity and modernity. He acknowledges the superiority of European/Western culture in the public sphere, but at the same time projects the resilience of Islamic norms, and the opportunity for Islamic values, to supplement, not replace, the instruments of a high-tech, post-industrial and post-colonial world.

LESSONS FROM BENNABI

So what are the lessons we can learn from Bennabi? It is neither location in the Maghrib nor in Europe that determines one's outlook but bi-location, the experience of two worlds, the imperial world of Europe and the colonial world of North Africa, and the awareness of which defines one's primary identity, orientation and worldview. 'Post-colonialism in Algeria', notes the Argentinian/American semiotician Walter Mignolo,

> is not the same as post-colonialism in France [. . .] Bennabi's reflections before, during, and after the eight years of the Algerian war transcended the events and brought the discussion back home to Algeria, rather than letting it remain in Paris, counting in France's history.

7. Seyla Benhabib, *Another Cosmopolitanism* (New York, 2006), pp. 37–8.
8. Ali Allawi, *The Crisis of Islamic Civilization* (New Haven, 2009), pp. 72–3.

Bennabi's views could be compared to those of Camus or Sartre, but, in fact, they were more similar to Fanon's, albeit in a religious not a racial trajectory. Both Fanon and Bennabi experienced Europe, especially its higher education in the humanities and sciences, but remained grounded in Africa. 'The meaning of the Algerian war in France', as Mignolo notes, 'was embedded in the history of France and European imperialism, while the meaning of the Algerian war in Algeria was imbedded in the history of North Africa and the enduring histories of colonialism'.[9]

Though Bennabi was a conceptual idealist, he was constrained by psychological realism. Algeria after independence remained a colonised country; it could not be truly free until it faced the burden of its colonial past, which included the susceptibility to be colonised. For that lingering susceptibility, Bennabi coined a new term, *colonisabilite* – the disposition to be colonised or to remain bound by colonial ways of thinking. In order to reverse the uncritical acceptance of norms, values and concepts from the dominant French (or British or American) power, one had to revisit the colonisation of knowledge. In short, one had to reconstruct a new edifice of civilisation.

The practical outcome is *jihād fikrī*, or intellectual struggle. Its appeal is to a new generation of Muslims, but it also seeks to evoke a new programme: not Islamism or secularism but cosmopolitanism from below, the ability to move in several worlds, confirming dignity but also allowing for difference. No one should underestimate the need for all Muslims, but especially the younger generation, who are the most numerous, to do more than seek employment or education or residence abroad. To remain in their countries of birth, Generation D Muslims, those born to the Internet, Facebook and Twitter, must find dignity from the wellspring of culture. Along with opportunities generated by effective economic reform, there must also be a radical effort to engage cosmopolitanism as a Muslim project, and I want to argue that must begin with minorities.[10]

9. Walter Mignolo, author of *The Darker Side of Western Modernity* (Durham, 2011), pp. 97–8. See also the review of Bennabi in Mohamed El-Tahir El-Mesawi, 'Religion, Society, and Culture in Malik Bennabi's Thought', in *The Blackwell Companion to Contemporary Islamic Thought*, ed. Ibrahim M. Abu-Rabi' (Oxford, 2006).
10. Rainer Baubock, in calling for a new global citizenship, places the rights for transnational minorities at the heart of his project: Steven Vertovec and Robin Cohen (eds), *Conceiving Cosmopolitanism: Theory, Context, and Practice* (New York, 2002/2007), pp. 127–36, but all his examples, as also the frame of his argument, is Europe-specific, and the case of minorities beyond Europe, whether Africa or Asia, is not mentioned, much less examined or analysed.

TWO CASE STUDIES IN MINORITY CITIZENSHIP APPLYING BENNABI BEYOND NORTH AFRICA: KRISTENS IN INDONESIA, COPTS IN EGYPT

If cosmopolitanism is to succeed as a project in majority Muslim countries, it has to be traced through the narratives of actual minorities in twenty-first century polities. Arendt had noted that minorities were created by the treaties that brought into being new nation-states after WWI, with the treaties of Sevres (1920) and Lausanne (1923), but there were other minorities that existed in age-old polities, Egypt and Indonesia, and in this case they are not Muslim minorities but non-Muslim minorities in Muslim majority countries: Protestants and Catholics in Indonesia, Copts in Egypt. They have been ignored in much of the discussion about what constitutes legitimate or illegitimate violence in contemporary Islamic thought, and my effort today is not just to redress the balance, but to indicate the theoretical gain in expanding the numeric and geographic boundaries of the Muslim world.

Instead of focusing on major figures, authors (usually male) and their texts (usually in high academic language, whether French, English, Arabic or Persian), I want to look at scenarios. Let me be clear about what happens when one shifts the focus from political theory to local contexts; one must be very clear about the new hierarchy of value. Locational violence has to be replaced with nativist empathy: engaging others while retaining one's own distinctive outlook, values and interests. The pragmatics of belonging requires that people be anchored in places, and place in the twenty-first century means citizenship. If citizenship is a social goal, it must also be an analytical category.

To simplify its centrality for examining violence in Islam, whether legitimate or illegitimate, let us first note the need to cluster. It was Ludwig Wittgenstein who best articulated how names cluster: they exhibit family resemblances. According to Wittgenstein, you cannot pin a word down to a single referent or meaning without linking it to other words. Descriptions associated with a name do not become synonyms of that name, but linked names do clarify identifying traits, each amplifying the other. Just such a clustering, one that stops short of mutual convergence but allows for expansive inference, is needed to understand *citizenship* in the Muslim world. To account for the cumulative power of citizenship in nation-states we need not just one but several related concepts. Citizenship presupposes at least two other terms: *coloniality* or the colonial experience of European rule in many parts of Asia and Africa, but also, equally, *constitutions*, the structure without which the modern nation-state lacks both coherence and confidence. Coloniality, together with constitutionalism, accents the historical trajectory of the modern nation-state.

If one ignores history and adopts only a presentist lens, in looking at citizenship across the globe in the twenty-first century, one misses the historical difference emerging from the sustained colonial presence in much of Africa and Asia. What was made of that presence differed, from continent to region to nation, but the process itself has to be foregrounded, as does its principal institutional legacy: constitutions. Hamid Enayat's seminal text on Shīʿī and Sunni political thought in the twentieth century places constitutionalism at the heart of its inquiry in talking about both Iran and Sunni polities. In all cases citizenship became the crucial issue at stake in constitutional debates and their implementation.[11]

Constitutional citizenship also declares, and then regulates minority–majority relations. Any notion of violence – legitimate or illegitimate – has to look at the fate of citizens; of course, those in the majority, but also those distinguished by race, language, place or religion, and deemed to be minorities. It is the state, and its instruments, that confer both majority and minority status. Let us look at a putative Citizen Ahmad. Citizen Ahmad is at once empowered and limited by constitution making, not because he is a Muslim citizen, but because his status as Muslim or non-Muslim, believer or atheist, is determined by the state and its role in drafting, publishing, maintaining and enforcing constitutional provisions. Among the crucial state-derived devices for differentiating constitutional duties and rights is majority or minority designation. Part of the ambiguity of Citizen Ahmad's belonging depends on whether or not he is a majority or minority member of the polity where he is accepted as a citizen.

Citizen Ahmad also functions as a citizen-believer in *the public square*. Private belief or collective praying is fine, but it does not diminish the need for public square participation and, above all, overlapping consensus. Overlapping consensus in the public square, while necessary, is also imperfect. It always reflects, to quote March,

> various asymmetrical power relations and the ways in which the interests of women, racial minorities, sub-national ethnic and linguistic groups, native populations, *and* religious minorities may not be fully protected by traditional liberal conceptions of equal citizenship on an individual basis.[12]

11. Hamid Enayat, *Modern Islamic Political Thought* (London, 1982), p. 127. I recognise that not everyone accepts the functional equivalence of these neologisms in several Muslim contexts, but I think that such arguments miss the way that decoloniality can accept the name, but alter the substance, of political instruments. It is the affective not the lexical distinction which is paramount.
12. Andrew F. March, *Islam and Liberal Citizenship: The Search for an Overlapping Consensus* (New York, 2009), pp. 17–18 (emphasis in original).

The key notion of belonging comes at the end of this long rhetorical question: equal citizenship on an individual basis. Equal citizenship is not a privilege conferred; it is an ongoing and unending struggle. Instead of a once-and-for-all victory secured by independence, citizenship requires a sustained effort long after independence from colonial rule. It also assumes that one can find, and then practice, reasonable pluralism – that is, the willingness to mark difference as an agonistic rather than antagonistic loyalty. Its bedrock element is goodwill: the commitment of oneself and one's community to find *overlapping consensus through public square exchange.*

Citizen Ahmad – the fictional yet real post-colonial Muslim who becomes the member of an Afro-Asian nation-state modelled on European antecedents – is defined both by his state and his faith, but how does one link constitutional pluralism, a juridical category, with reasonable pluralism, a social practice? The answer is: not easily. And for that very reason, the link is essential if 'ordinary' believers are to find common cause, or overlapping consensus, in a diverse society.

There must be multiple Citizen Ahmads for overlapping consensus to be achieved, sustained and productive in societies where Muslims are either a majority or a minority constituency. They must transform the colonial legacy of constitution making; they must use the public square as the primary, necessary venue for the exercise of citizenship rights. Citizenship, far from a right to be conferred, remains a goal to be pursued. It is at once a belonging (marked by passports and benefits for education, health, housing), but also a longing (a longing to be equal to other compatriots, regardless of demographic, linguistic, locational, gender or religious difference). To escape the noose of *colonisabilite*, identified by Bennabi, one must combine belonging with longing, never satisfied with the status quo, yet also realising its sustained power.

Tariq Ramadan underscored the paradox of twin loyalties when he observed:

> Let us consider the social dimension (of salvation): living together as citizens. This is where the relationship between our personal belief and the beliefs of our fellow citizens is critical [. . .] the public sphere can help you protect yourself from any dogmatic, social position. Within a democratic society, what may be a dogmatic theological position cannot be imposed as a dogmatic social or political view. In this way, the public sphere enables anyone to believe that she or he has the truth while respecting the equal rights and opportunities (of all citizens) within that society.[13]

13. Foreword to Mohammad Hassan Khalil (ed.), *Between Heaven and Hell: Islam, Salvation and the Fates of Others* (New York, 2013), p. xii.

Ramadan here enshrines the goal of liberal democracy: equal rights and similar opportunities for all citizen believers. His goal may be admirable, but is it possible? It faces two major roadblocks to actual ground-level realisation: 1) individuals do not act by themselves, but often in response to authoritative figures within their local, national or transnational community, at the same time that 2) neither the state nor religious institutions are neutral bystanders; they do not remain innocent onlookers to the public sphere. They have partisan interests, and these interests shape, but also often limit, the openness of public square debate. They support the public square, while also preventing it from functioning as an equal opportunity forum.

And so why does the existence and the language of constitutions matter? Is constitutional pluralism a mere juridical sleight of hand? The US Constitution is not exceptional. It resembles other liberal constitutions that also accent the singularities characteristic of the modern nation-state. Perhaps the most instructive comparison is with the Republic of India. In both the US and India, there remains a chorus of those who believe that parallel singularities, each reinforcing the other, are required for a successful nation-state: single language, whether English or Hindi, single religion, whether Hinduism or Protestant Christianity, and single culture/society, whether caste hierarchy or liberal individualism.[14]

In other words, while the experience of the US and India are marred in their actual function, both states do make major constitutional claims that reflect an ideal common to Egypt and Indonesia. In both Muslim majority polities the modern state is inseparable from the constitutions that underwrite, and also channel, the dominant ethos. Swayed by Muslim majorities, each strives to be

14. I am here summarising the much longer argument of Sudipta Kaviraj: '[In post-1948 India] there was a significant conflict between two forms of the nationalist imagination of an "Indian" identity on which future state would be based—which could be designated as homogenizing and pluralist. Curiously, Congress leaders claimed that the new nation-state could not be viable without a homogenizing vision of Indianness around a single language (Hindi), single religion (Hinduism), and a single culture (accenting Hindu norms & values). All the pedagogic powers of the new state should be directed, in their view, towards producing a nationalist sentiment of this kind. This view was successfully contested by a radically different vision of Indianness which saw *diversity as a resource, rather than a weakness*; and which argued in favor of a federal constitution that accommodated the traditional conventions of regional autonomy and division of political authority. Being an Indian was viewed as a second-order identity that did not cancel out regional cultural identities of Bengalis or Tamils, but subsumed them within a structure that encouraged enriching exchanges between them. The new constitution, meticulously discussed over two years, eventually accepted the second view of Indian identity and translated that into the animating principle of the legal structure. It augured an Indian version of cultural pluralism.' Sudipta Kaviraj, 'Post-colonial State' (online).

democratic while also acknowledging, and often privileging, Islamic loyalty. The difficulty in each case revolves around interpretation of Sharīᶜa, and here again it is religion overloaded as a determinant of identity that holds sway in the marketplace of ideas.

THE INDONESIAN CASE

Of the two cases, Egypt is the more prominent, especially after the Arab uprisings of 2010 to the present, but the Indonesian case is more complex than the Egyptian, and so I begin with it.

In Indonesia, the debate about religious citizenship has been framed by competitive tropes; substantive Sharīᶜa versus formal Sharīᶜa. This dyad is itself a variation of the familiar distinction between contextual and textual approaches to Islamic authenticity. For those who uphold the formal/textual approach, it is the original texts – Qur᾽ān, *ḥadīth* and juridical tradition – that have an invariant meaning. That meaning must be applied in the twenty-first century as it was in the seventh century; anything less is not authentically Islamic, but deviant, corrupt innovation. For substantivists or contextualists, by contrast, the first point of reference is the contemporary period – today's world, with its structures, instruments, resources and challenges. The nation-state may be new, yet it is the pervasive structure of political representation on a global plane in the twenty-first century. All other modalities, including those offered by law, scripture and tradition, must be translated within its purview. They must address the double threshold of contemporary polities: constitutionalism and the public square.

But the debate is more than a legal knot or juridical stand-off between divergent notions of Sharīᶜa and public law. In Metro Jakarta, the public square has been expanded to include religious issues, and above all, discussion of religious identity, in twenty-first century Indonesia. It is an issue that dominates headlines in Jakarta, but any account must begin with the New Order in 1966, and examine the changes that it augured, in religion as in other aspects of contemporary Indonesia.

'Although the New Order professed neutrality in dealing with state-sanctioned religions', observes a noted scholar,

> it meddled extensively in religious affairs. One of the regime's first actions was to ban hundreds of mystical (*kebatinan*) sects regarded as left-wing, or offensive to mainstream Muslims. The government also prohibited public expressions of Chinese religion, as well as the import of literature written in Chinese characters. Chinese Indonesians were encouraged to convert to Buddhism or Christianity.

Consider the options presented to believer citizens:

> The state required citizens to profess one among five state-recognized religions: Islam, Protestantism, Catholicism, Hinduism and Buddhism. Even the adherents of these religions were subject to new state regulations, such as the requirement that all religions, including Hinduism and Buddhism, be monotheistic.[15]

Religion by itself, however, is not the decisive or major explanatory variable. The vast majority of Indonesians – 87 per cent – are Muslim, mostly Sunni and Shāfiᶜī in their outlook, yet 10 per cent are also Christian, with 7 per cent Protestant and 3 per cent Catholic. There are also smaller numbers of Buddhists, Hindus and Confucians. But Christians are not listed as a single religion. They instead registered as Kristen or Protestant, distinct from Katolic or Catholics.

It remains unclear how the New Order (1966–98) differed from the Old Order, insofar as both orders used ideologues to control and direct the message of Pancasila for their own benefit. 'Pancasila', according to one seasoned observer,

> was originally formulated and explained by Soekarno in a speech in 1945. Later, in 1958, he gave a series of public lectures explaining it again. These lectures stand as virtually the total negation of the New Order's interpretation of Pancasila. While Soekarno connected democratic consultation, national unity, internationalism, social justice and monotheism to the major revolutionary upheavals in human history, the New Order ideologues distilled these principles to little more than the idea of obedience to authority.[16]

One should not be surprised that efforts by New Order officials to sponsor interreligious dialogue rarely reached beyond superficial speechmaking. In effect, Indonesian religious discourse was beset by a zero-sum or war game mentality in which every gain for one religious group was seen as a loss for another. The Suharto government either could not or would not advance a social framework in which both Christians and Muslims might achieve their goals. Instead they preferred that all groups remain dissatisfied and dependent on it as a broker.

How can one move beyond the zero-sum, war game mentality? Part of what is needed is a new discourse. As Ulil Abshar Abdalla, another leading and

15. Robert W. Hefner in Theodore Friend (ed.), *Religion and Religiosity in the Philippines and Indonesia: Essays on State, Society, and Public Creeds* (Washington, DC, 2006), pp. 41–2 (abbreviated).
16. Max Lane, *The Unfinished Nation: Indonesia before and after Suharto* (London, 2008), p. 294, fn. 4.

endangered spokesman for 'liberal Islam', has argued, one must de-ideologise Islam and offer a de-ideologised Islam that does not compete with the official Pancasila ideology,[17] while from the Christian side, there have been, and should be, the kind of broad gauged engagement of issues that reflect boundaries, intrinsic to all religions, yet also explore shared beliefs and common interests. In effect, they signal Christian efforts to shape a theology of religious pluralism that will guide social engagement. It embodies what Ashis Nandy, the major social critic of contemporary India, has underscored as a fundamental distinction – the distinction between religion as faith and religion as ideology.[18]

What is needed, above all, are more non-governmentally sponsored Christian and Muslim efforts to make a shared concern for social justice a primary religious goal, and then to register and give wide publicity to the prospects of mutual gains through cooperation. In other words, the public square needs to have not a reduced but an expanded religious register, one where multiple voices can be heard in a dialogue marked by civic or confessional reason.

Yet religious identity eludes a single comprehensive definition. One has to chart discourse concerning the varying elements of Indonesian Muslim identity (differences between *santri* and *abangan*, reformist and orthodox), as well as significant differences between Catholic and Protestant discourse in relation to both family law and religious education. More is at stake in the formation of an Indonesian identity than simply the role of Islam in society. Especially crucial is the role of international Islam, and Islam as an international identity, as well as Christian evangelical networks, pervasive in Southeast Asia as elsewhere since the official end of the Cold War in 1991.

17. See his brief but insightful essay, Ulil Abshar Abdalla, 'Rethinking Indigenous Islam', *Afkar* 1 (2008), 100–5. Another more elaborate effort to explore this option is set forth in March (*Islam and Liberal Citizenship*, pp. 212–21). March raises the crucial question regarding scriptural precedents: what Qurʾānic verses permit Muslims to consider all fellow citizens as equal partners not merely tolerated others in a pluralist polity mandated by constitutional provisions? One way out is to cite Meccan surahs that are inclusive in their appeal, e.g., Q42:15 and Q22:68–9, deferring all salvific reckoning till the Day of Judgement. In sum, no human being, however devoutly Muslim, can preclude the possibility of salvation for another, specifically, a monotheist other, one devoted to the One God, the God of Abraham, Isaac and Ishmael.
18. See Ashis Nandy, 'The Politics of Secularism and the Recovery of Religious Tolerance', in *Secularism and its Critics*, ed. Rajeev Bhargava (Delhi, 1998), pp. 321–44. Nandy is at once a revisionist and a traditionalist, arguing that it is 'from the traditions and principles of religious tolerance encoded in the everyday life associated with the different faiths of India, that one will have to seek clues to the renewal of Indian political culture' (Nandy, 'The Politics of Secularism', pp. 336–7), not least through the promotion of agonistic rather than antagonistic approaches to religious difference.

Nowhere is the international reach of a hard-wired Islamic identity more evident than in the dire issues facing those deemed to be an unacceptable minority *within* Islam – namely, the Ahmadiyya. Much has been written about them,[19] but the major issue, seldom discussed, is the constitutional protection of Freedom of Religion. It is that provision that runs counter to the New Order, and now Reformasi (1998 to the present) project to continue agama/adat as mainstream 'official' religion, trumping any interior deviations or so-called heresies. In other words, as one astute observer has signalled, freedom of religion is not tantamount to freedom of religions, since the majority group – in the nation-state as a whole, but also within each 'official' religion – can regulate who counts as a 'true' believer.[20]

It is tempting to say that there already is an Indonesian model of combining authenticity with modernity, traditional cultures with modern structures, religious pluralism with confessional integrity, allowing sectarian difference without spurring religious warfare. But as the case of the Ahmadiyya demonstrates, there are still internal battles to be waged and won before Indonesian voices, both Christian and Muslim, can become more prominent in the discourse on Muslim and Christian national identity elsewhere in the region, as well as in international discourse on inter-religious dialogue and religious identity.[21]

On the one hand, an enormous internal variety among Indonesians confirms the importance of religion, but also its oblique impact on everyday life. Though the government monopolised religious options, individual citizens were acutely aware of the significance of both government action and media portrayal for inter-religious relations. The attention to ethnic or primordial ties vied with religion as a marker of identity and also outlook.

Indeed, since religious identity never stands apart from other identity markers, how does it compete against, or elide with, other identities? In Indonesia the convergences invoked draw on neither a collective memory nor a public will that is unanimous or even consensual, despite the touted strength of *pancasila* as a robust integrating slogan for an island nation with a myriad of languages, ethnic groups and local identities.[22]

19. No footnote text supplied.
20. Cited and summarised from Peter Beyer, 'Constitutional Privilege and Constituting Pluralism: Religious Freedom in National, Global, and Legal Context', *Journal for the Scientific Study of Religion* 42.3 (Sept. 2003), 333–9.
21. One of the clearest statements regarding the Ahmadiyya comes from the online journal *Inside Indonesia*. See http://insideindonesia.org/content/view/14/29 for Munawar Ahmad, 'Faith and Violence: The Islamic Sect Ahmadiyah Has Been Under Official Pressure and Violent Attack'.
22. So diverse is Indonesia ethnically that while the official number of ethnic groups is said to be 300, a major human rights advocate, Habib Chirzin, stated that the actual number

The real challenge, therefore, is not numbers, but process. About Indonesia, it could be said that nation formation is still an ongoing process from Aceh to Papua, with far more stability and continuity needed than just the brief fifteen years that have elapsed since the Reformasi era (1998–), but it can also be said that secession remains a back burner issue – for Aceh as well as for West Papua.

In the Phil-Indo Archipelago, the symbolic as well as numerical power of a majority will continue to demand for itself rights reflecting its 'superior' status. Bennabi's project to look for a moral Thought that is metaphysically supple and non-conformist, applied in the public square and accepted by broad segments of society, is still an elusive ideal. Just how elusive is made clear when we examine another Muslim theorist, Talal Asad. Writing about Muslim minorities in Western Europe, Asad noted that:

> Muslims in Europe should be able to find institutional representation as a minority in a democratic state that consists only of minorities. For where there are only minorities, the possibilities of forging allegiances between them will be greater than in a state with a majority presiding over several competing minorities.[23]

Laudable though it might be to have 'a model nation of minorities', not just in Western Europe but also in Indonesia, where there are far more minorities than in Europe, the project remains utopian. No, it is not just utopian, it is unattainable; and so one must continue the stretch between belonging and longing, not a closure for minorities, but the only viable path ahead beyond unabated, and often unchecked, violence.

EGYPT

The same indeterminate conclusion might seem also warranted in the case of Egypt. Indeed, since 2010, the case for Egypt may even be worse for freedom of speech, civil liberties and minority rights than Indonesia, as was certainly the message in a 2013 article from the widely circulated weekly, *The Chronicle of Higher Education*.[24]

is 1173! (He made this statement at a seminar held at Le Méridien Hotel, Jakarta, for the Religion–Society Dialogue, 13 March 2009).

23. Talal Asad, *Formations of the Secular – Christianity, Islam, Modernity* (Stanford, 2003). p. 178.
24. Titled 'Islamic Fundamentalists Challenge Academe' on the 3 April 2013 cover, it was retitled 'Islamist Movements Challenge University' on the inside flap. Though it claims

Despite the headline horrors from Cairo, there are structural issues that still give salience to the major points of my analysis; one must look beyond headlines, even while absorbing and addressing their roster of concerns. A highbrow publication, *The Chronicle of Higher Education*, is read by most academics, and quite a few policymakers. What it reports is recycled, either by direct quote or inference, in numerous other reports on Egypt. It also is detailed at a level that most background stories or crisis-focused dispatches are not. The focus is on Islamists, never defined but assumed to be the bad guys. 'Islamist groups and preachers', we are told,

> espouse a conservative interpretation of Islam that limits free speech and the rights of minorities and women. Islamists have been active for decades, and Islam permeates Egyptian public life and institutions. Academics tread carefully in matters pertaining to religion. But now some Egyptian scholars also worry that the rise of Islamist parties and groups is leading to greater intimidation and censorship. (Especially worrisome is) the country's new, Islamist-drafted Constitution (which) requires that laws be scrutinized by religious scholars, criminalizes blasphemy, and enjoins the state and society to protect ill-defined 'traditions and values'.

The writer then goes on to assess Egypt's Al-Azhar University. Though one of the most venerable institutions of Islamic learning in the world, it is now embroiled in such debates. The university has long sought to integrate Islamic teachings with the ambitions of a modern scientific university. After the ouster of the dictator Hosni Mubarak, many on the campus had hopes of reversing decades of educational decline and making the university once again a beacon of knowledge. Islamists in Egypt have granted Al-Azhar a prominent role in the new Constitution, giving its religious scholars the authority to vet laws. But the Islamists have also been caught on tape discussing how to sideline Al-Azhar's leadership, raising concerns that they plan on taking over and radicalizing the institution. Now it has become a bellwether in the region's struggle between Islamist fundamentalists and moderate scholars.

And the article proceeds to evaluate the tug of war between secular and religious forces.

to compare Tunisia and Egypt, it reports about Egypt in greater depth; see http://chronicle.com.proxy.lib.duke.edu/article/Islamic-Fundamentalists/138183/ (last accessed on 6 January 2014). All citations that follow are derived from the online version of this issue of *The Chronicle of Higher Education*.

> The value of education was bolstered by religious principles for centuries, yet starting in the late 19th century, Arab countries established secular education systems, in part because they believed that traditional religious education couldn't meet the needs of the modern state. In the 1960s, the Egyptian government brought the Islamic university under its control and added secular subjects and degrees to its offerings.

And then several scholars from Al-Azhar are cited on both sides of the debate about secular curriculum versus religious values, even in the advanced professional schools that focus on medicine, engineering and agriculture. 'The university', we are told, wants to add new courses in information technology, sociology, or foreign languages to religious degrees. But such changes are extremely sensitive. When it started small foreign-language programmes sponsored by the US Embassy and the British Council, the educational and cultural arm of the British government, an Islamist member of Egypt's parliament attacked one such language centre as a place where students were taught 'depravity and dancing, to have relations with girls and drink alcohol, and bad morals that contradict Islamic Shariah'. But we are never told about ripostes to this attack, nor are we told about either instruments of foreign presence and pressure in Egypt. It is as though Kansas and Mississippi were the only states representing science-religion debates in the USA, and we do not hear about California or Oregon, or interest groups that cross state, and also national, boundaries.

The epitome of this insular reporting, with a too glibly dichotomous view of Egypt, the Arab world and higher education, comes in a quote from the Carnegie Middle East Center, based in Beirut. Of course, the Lebanese public can make sense of what is going on in Egypt, and the Carnegie Middle East Center is uniformly respected, but some generalisations do not stand the test of pragmatic scrutiny. 'Religious teaching', we are told, 'doesn't encourage analytical thinking and is sometimes to the detriment of pluralistic norms or other religious beliefs', according to Muhammad Faour, a scholar at the Carnegie Middle East Center, in a recent report on religious education and pluralism in the Arab world. But what does the rest of this report say? It can be found online.[25] And in the

25. See http://www.isn.ethz.ch/Digital-Library/Publications/Detail/?lng=en&id=157114, where the PDF, a slim 19-page report, can be downloaded. Of course, there are multiple violations of religious freedom, many of them involving minority rights, in contemporary Egypt. Most of them are described in the annual report from the United States Commission on International Religious Freedom. For its roll call of incidents from the past year (2013), see http://www.refworld.org/docid/51826efff.html, but does this remain the only approach to religion, citizenship and issues of public square parity in

same report Muhammad Faour highlighted an initiative for reforming religious education; its sponsors were Al-Azhar, Coptic leaders and a few academics. Such a bold, far-reaching initiative could be potentially transformative. Why did this initiative find no mention, and also why does all reform have to be state-sponsored? The critical self-consciousness espoused by Bennabi must stem from civil society, not just the state. What he projects for Algeria could, and should, be said for Egypt, and among those leaders in Egypt who support progressive thinking is the head of Al-Azhar. The grand imam of Al-Azhar, Ahmad El-Tayyeb – who also heads the mosque and a network of schools and research centres – has a doctorate in Islamic philosophy from the Sorbonne. He has supported reforms at the university and issued documents aligning Islamic principles with human rights, women's rights and democracy, including the 2012 educational reform initiative.

Even more critical than a review of the tone or content of the above article is an assessment of the prospect for Egypt's Coptic, Muslim and Bahai minorities.[26] Egypt, structurally and historically, is at once similar to Indonesia, yet entirely different. For over a century, and in part due to the nature of British occupation (never mentioned in the above article), Copts have been engaged in the public life of Egypt as citizens with different ideological, political and cultural affiliations than their Muslim compatriots, but it is also the Coptic Church that has served as spokesman on behalf of the Copts, to the extent that religious affiliation became, and remains, the main marker of Coptic identity, not Egyptian citizenship.

Today the Coptic Church – both its leaders and laity – are conflicted about what they can, or should, derive from participation in the Egyptian public square. In the past decade many Egyptian Copts demanded equality between themselves and Muslims. They asked for more citizenship rights and for protection against discrimination, whether legal or social or both. During debates in 2006 regarding Constitutional Amendments, some public Coptic figures went as far as requesting the demotion of Sharīᶜa, removing it as the basis of legislation for the Egyptian Constitution. Similar arguments have also been made during the current debate about how to modify the Egyptian Constitution in the aftermath of the Arab Spring. Copts should be an equal and integral part of Egyptian society,

contemporary Egypt? The argument of this essay is: no. For accessed dates of online resources, see the Bibliography and the accompanying note, p. 366.

26. For a further assessment of Copts, Ahmadis and Bahais, beyond the brief comments offered here, please see Bruce B. Lawrence, 'Citizen Ahmad Among the Believers: Salvation Contextualized in Egypt and Indonesia', in *Between Heaven and Hell*, ed. Mohammad Hassan Khalil (Oxford: Oxford University Press, 2013), pp. 299–305.

but that adjustment requires a prior change in the Egyptian Constitution; it must be derived from secular rather than Islamic legal sources.

This plea, however, needs to be placed in a broader context of Muslim–Christian relations during the past sixty years. How have their Muslim compatriots reacted to Copts as equivalent heirs of Egyptian history and co-beneficiaries of its constitutional system of governance? Are they in fact, and not just in theory, equivocal citizens of the same creed-blind polity? The Egyptian jurist, Yūsuf al-Qaraḍāwī, remains a voice of demurral. The fiery media cleric, with deep ties to the Muslim Brotherhood, struggles to see hope for non-Muslims within the citizen structure of the modern Egyptian state, but it is not a hope that is either well defined or consensually supported. Al-Qaradāwī's discourse barely rises above the level of 'mere' tolerance. In a major fatwa he addresses the subject of whether Jews and Christians should be regarded as 'infidels' in Islam. Instead of tackling the issue of salvation, the question al-Qaradāwī poses is: what conduct can be deemed most appropriate to the believer when he must engage unbelievers in the public square? Al-Qaradāwī presupposes that there is no religious commonality. After citing several verses from the Qur'ān, al-Qaradāwī concludes: 'The Muslim's conscience is at ease and he finds no conflict between his conviction in the unbeliever's unbelief and the demand to be just and equitable towards him.'[27]

But there are sources for gauging the tone of minority citizenship prospects in Egypt other than the voices of *fiqh* (Islamic jurisprudence) exponents, whether from a physical or a virtual pulpit. These voices all crowd into a government-monitored public square. While Citizen Ahmad and Citizen Naguib – his iconic counterpart for those who are Copts – share membership in a single nation-state, one must recognise the gap in public instruments for each community; there continue to be many downsides to Egyptian politics, society and economy since Mubarak was deposed in February 2011. Yet one constant that is often undervalued is the huge, vibrant public square of Cairo. Multiple institutions represent, project and also contest each other, offering competitive perspectives on religion–state relations generally and on Muslim–Copt relations in particular. Censorship remains a grave, ongoing issue, but it has not reversed the Egyptian propensity for airing opposition views in the public arena.

Yet no matter how expansive the review of topics, issues and responses, one conclusion remains inescapable: there are multiple, always competitive and often contradictory ways of thinking about Muslim–Christian relations in contemporary Egypt, at home and abroad. While Copts do have a distinctive role in

27. al-Qaraḍāwī as quoted in March, *Islam and Liberal Citizenship*, p. 214.

Egyptian history and society, they have yet to become fully empowered citizens, and arguably they are less secure today than their counterparts in Reformasi Indonesia.

CONCLUSION

In my view, the lack of functional equality does not condemn minorities to second-class citizenship, much less eternal perdition in either Indonesia or Egypt. At the very least, the constitution in each country will continue to be the referent of possible options for minorities as also majorities, at the same time that public square debate must probe beyond the plethora of shibboleths and screeds, as well as media reports, that too often mark Coptic–Muslim relations in Egypt or Muslim–Christian relations in Indonesia. Citizenship is always and everywhere a work in progress. No nation-state in the twenty-first century has reached the plateau of full equality, with a level playing field on liberty and the pursuit of happiness, not even the USA. For Egypt and Indonesia, there are two diametrically opposite views. One is resolutely dystopic, the other modestly hopeful.

A dystopic perspective equates minority status with perpetual, and perpetually degrading, marginalisation. Yet, despite the current public policy despair about the Muslim world, I would like to close with a counter-intuitive hopeful option. Might there not be a cosmopolitan canopy persisting, enduring and even becoming more secure in the Phil-Indo Archipelago? And at the same time might Copts, beyond the present turmoil, distress and destruction, find reciprocity if not equality sustainable in twenty-first century Egypt? The weathervane of hope derives not from the metropole, but from the local profiles of religiously subaltern communities. They may be majority or minority. They may be Copts and Muslims in Alexandria or Kristens or Katolics in dialogue with Muslim Javanese partners on TV, the Internet and even Facebook (where Indonesia boasts the world's third largest pool of Facebook users), but nowhere will they be in full accord with their counterparts – either co-religionists or compatriots or both – in government or in mainstream media.

And every community will be in part measured by a more vibrant, broadly dispersed public square, where faces can be seen, voices heard and views debated and disseminated. It is not just a local but also a transnational and global process of connectivity. Paramount, though difficult to measure, for all minorities will be the scope and scale of overseas immigrant networks, as well as externally funded NGOs. Perceptions of nationhood will depend on mechanisms for citizenship in both Egypt and Indonesia. It is impossible to assess the boundary between legitimate and illegitimate acts of violence, but if violence is structural as well as episodic, as I have argued it is, then the shift toward a more transparent, and accessible, notion of citizenship rights in both majority Muslim countries will open a small window. Its fleeting rays of light appear amid clouds of ambient murkiness, yet they bode well for creating opportunities that echo distributive justice, not just preventing crimes by applying punitive justice.

The proximate goal must always be a modus vivendi. It can never be more than a social comity that contains without reducing difference. While comity is not the same as equality, it is, I argue, the most pragmatic goal of minority citizenship in both Indonesia and Egypt. Far from a perfect prospect, it is still a better fate than many other minorities, whether religious, cultural, ethnic or linguistic, face in those parts of Asia and Africa where diversity is not constitutionally recognised and where public squares remain closed portals. Citizen Ahmad must be vigilant but also patient, a citizen as much as a believer. Neither utopian nor dystopic, his future, like that of his differently Muslim or non-Muslim compatriots, rests on the everyday solidarity of collective goodwill, fuelled by shared longing for an elusive reciprocity. More than concurrent citizenship, it offers agonistic equality expressed in the public square and mediated in private acts of civility and kindness.

CHAPTER

3

THE LURE OF JIHĀD: POST-TRADITIONAL HISTORIES OF VIOLENCE IN THE ISLAMIC WORLD

*William Gallois**

This chapter argues that notions of *jihād* should be rethought in histories of Muslim peoples, especially in the colonial period, when concentrations on religiously sanctioned violence occlude other forms of Islamic resistance to European empire. Additionally, scholars ought to reflect more on the way in which discussions, and the practice, of *jihād* played an integral part in enabling the European project of nation-state building in the Arab–Islamic worlds of the nineteenth and twentieth centuries.

In dividing behaviour strictly into categories of the rightful and the illegitimate, proponents of the *jihādī* tradition operated with binaries which mirrored, and mapped on to, European expansionary ethics which stressed the beneficence of empire and viewed categories of geography and the human as being strictly divisible into binaries of selves and others, Europe and the Islamic world. In contrast, quieter, more local forms of resistance to the hegemony of European power, which ran the risk of being accused of quietism, often drew quite explicitly on the centrality of notions of justice in the Islamic ethical tradition, and in so doing developed a more effective critique of the hollow morality of civilisational imperialism.

These are Michel de Certeau's 'displaced histories', Ann Laura Stoler's 'disabled histories', 'stammers' which are 'not given the due of a narrative at all', found in the interstices of the archive, written out of the central narratives of historical meaning which describe encounters between Muslims and Europeans

* University of Exeter

in the formation of the modern imperial world.[1] Whereas histories from both the Western and Arab worlds stress processes of conquest and violent struggle in the nineteenth century, the contemporary significance of other forms of resistance merit 'placing' in history and a recognition of their 'enabling' qualities. The manner in which such ideas and practices shifted and developed over time is especially interesting in this case, for it is arguable that late twentieth- and twenty-first century understandings of *jihād* owe less to the 'tradition' than to a 'post-traditional' form of ethics which builds on the insights studied here in the disabled, local forms of thought which was resistant to European domination.[2] Put more concretely, present-day justifications of violent resistance to the power and governmentality of the modern Western state depend less on traditional understandings of the purpose of *jihād* than they do on precisely the kinds of descriptions of the suffering enjoined upon Muslims which we find in the displaced traditions of the past (when discussions of whether violence was justified placed little or no stress on the suffering victims of foreign invaders).

Grounded in the analysis of previously ignored archival evidence, this article privileges the lives of Muslims over the history of those texts which offered normative propositions as to how believers ought to conduct their lives. It rejects the notion that the tradition can be used as a means to index the morality and sincerity of Muslims in the past, and it develops an original set of interlocking arguments grounded in a rejection of the primacy of *jihād* in histories of Muslim violence and resistance. In exploring other modes of Muslim being, it shows the ways in which *jihādī* cultures were of productive value to European empires and the complex genealogies of current ideas of *jihād*, which wrench themselves away from the tradition, whilst appropriating one strand of justice-based critiques of violence.

Forms of *jihād* served in the co-production of new forms of nation and state in the Islamic world alongside the embodied violence of European invaders. Both parties' stress on the spatial organisation of territory, which stressed the unifying governmental power of a nation or state, served to diminish the spatial strength and particularity of societies which had combined organic interchange between profoundly local forms of governance, whilst being networked into enriching patterns of long-distance trade and knowledge.

1. Ann Laura Stoler, *Along the Archival Grain: Epistemic Anxieties and Colonial Common Sense* (Princeton, 2010), pp. 19–20.
2. See Selim Deringil, 'The Invention of Tradition as Public Image in the Late Ottoman Empire, 1808–1908', *Comparative Studies in Society and History* 35.1 (1993), 3–29, and Eric Hobsbawm and Terence Ranger (eds), *The Invention of Tradition* (Cambridge, 1983).

The chapter begins with an introduction of its Algerian case study and the figure of ᶜAbd al-Qādir, before moving on to explore the limits of *jihād* as an explanatory category, and thence as a mode of response to the new forms of violence introduced into the Islamic world by modern Europeans. It asks why the *jihād* of ᶜAbd al-Qādir has become reified and calcified in the production of historical knowledge in both the Arab–Islamic world and the West from the nineteenth to the twenty-first centuries, before looking in depth at the ways in which that *jihād* served the interests of European imperialists, most particularly in the creation of new forms of national space in places such as 'Algeria'. The final sections of the chapter then recuperate and analyse the lives of other Muslims in the early Algerian colony, revealing the ethical and strategic differences between such plural understandings of the idea of resistance and the manner in which these accounts recognised the revolutionary and novel qualities of French violence in Algeria.[3]

ʿABD AL-QĀDIR

This chapter concentrates on a case study of Algeria in the period 1830–47, arguing that the language and idea of *jihād* hides as much as it reveals when deployed as a means of understanding the lives of Muslims in a newly colonised state. Just as the narrative conventions of the genre of military history often tend to occlude the violent realities and suffering enjoined in colonial encounters, the focus of scholars on the impassioned, Islamic resistance of ᶜAbd al-Qādir in Algeria has tended to entrench a story of civilisational warfare best understood through religious frames.

The examples of Algeria and ᶜAbd al-Qādir are of world historical significance given the novelty, for both parties, of the new form of encounter which was enjoined in North Africa in the 1830s and the role the French invasion played in beginning a retrenchment of territories under Muslim rule. It has been claimed that more has been written about the Emir (*amīr*) than any other figure in modern Arab history,[4] while the meaning and significance of his *jihād* have been divined so as to comprehend those deeper structural shifts in both the Western and Arab–Islamic worlds of which it was emblematic. As Bennison writes:

3. I should like to thank Gavin Murray-Miller, Sajjad Rizvi, Rob Gleave, István Kristó-Nagy and Rudolph Peters for their help with this chapter.
4. Houari Touati, 'L'émir 'Abd al-Qâdir et les enjeux de la biographie', *Studia Islamica* 2 (2011–12), 5.

It has long been recognised that ʿAbd al-Qādir stood on the cusp of two worlds, that of the Maghribī past and its modern colonial future. His *jihād* responded to both and can be seen, rather like a coin, as possessing two faces: one which would have been comprehensible to Muslims in the area for many centuries and one which reflected the dilemmas facing many Muslims in the dār al-islām in their ambiguous encounter with western modernity.[5]

The extent to which ʿAbd al-Qādir can be said to be the originator of a new or modern form of *jihād* is, however, questioned by scholars such as Woerner-Powell:

> ʿAbd al-Qādir is typically assimilated into a 'modern' historical moment by the (variously teleological) narratives of globalised colonialism, declining Muslim influence, and anti-colonial nationalism. It is not self-evident that ʿAbd al-Qādir saw history in those terms, however [. . .] As has been suggested above, it was to be characteristically modern developments which were later to weaken the strand of Mālikī thought which ʿAbd al-Qādir propounded [. . .] There seems little justification for thinking that ʿAbd al-Qādir was prescient of these developments, and therefore little reason not to read him as sincere in his interpretation of his duties as an observant Muslim – especially since he adhered to his interpretation in respect of incidents where these weakened his strategic standing.[6]

While this chapter concurs that ʿAbd al-Qādir's *jihād* displayed a remarkable lack of prescience as to the significance of new forms of European governance and governmentality in the Islamic world, it will strongly question the idea of the Emir's 'sincerity' and the strategic move which follows ʿAbd al-Qādir's self-ascribed sincerity to suggest that he himself embodied *the* Islamic tradition. Instead, it will contend that plural Muslim readings of this new world can be found in the early Algerian colony. It might be argued that such moves reflect a broader tension in historical studies of Islam, which instinctively begin from the premise that the religion is both universal and possessed of a singular tradition, especially when deviations from that tradition are cast as forms of moral and theological dilution or corruption.

---

5. Amira Bennison, 'Abd al-Qādir's Jihād in the Light of the Western Islamic Jihād Tradition', *Studia Islamica* 2 (2011–12), 69.
6. Tom Woerner-Powell, "'Abd al-Qādir al Jazā'irī, Migration and the Rule of Law: "A Reply to Certain Persons of Distinction"', *Studia Islamica* 2 (2011–12), 119–20. See also Jean-Louis Marçot, 'Abd el-Kader et la modernité' *Studia Islamica* 2 (2011–12), 177–202.

The singularity of ᶜAbd al-Qādir's account of *jihād* is, of course, also belied by the radical shifts seen in his vision of the world propounded later in his life in France and Syria. There, most notably in the *Kitāb al-mawāqif*, the Emir came to reject the idea of minor, or armed, *jihād* (*al-jihād al-saghīr*) in favour, as Brower notes, of 'the major, internal or spiritual *jihād* (*al-jihād al-akbar*)', following the quite distinct, and centuries-old, Sufi line of *jihādī* interpretation.[7] As the massive literatures on ᶜAbd al-Qādir reveal, he has always served as a form of palimpsest or a blank canvas onto which the preoccupations of different historical moments can be inscribed.[8]

It ought also to be added that a more sympathetic reading of ᶜAbd al-Qādir's *jihād* could be elaborated which stressed forms of continuity between his early armed resistance to the French in Algeria and his later period of quietist contemplation in Syria. If both moments are viewed as expressions of 'ascetic piety', following Sizgorich's analysis of the origins of *jihād*, it might be claimed that the early ᶜAbd al-Qādir was engaged in a quite classical form of 'boundary demarcation and communal identity-formation' of a nature which Sizgorich suggests lay central to an early Islamic culture which borrowed from Christian antecedents.[9] The Damascene texts might then be read as being expressive of another facet of this ascetic urge, articulating a form of religious sacrifice analogous to other ascetic traditions, such as those of Zen Buddhism, which combine the ethos of the warrior with the contemplative life of the garden and the temple. Yet, if this reading has merits, it also poses the tough question as to whether the resistance in Algeria could in any sense be seen as a struggle against one's self (*nafs*).

This dilemma seems to be alluded to in the *Kitāb al-mawāqif* when ᶜAbd al-Qādir reflects on the disputed *hadīth* in which Prophet Muhammed contrasted the value of the greater, spiritual *jihād* over the lesser, worldly, material struggle. Perhaps recalling his earlier life in Algeria, ᶜAbd al-Qādir observed that:

> The fact that the Prophet categorised combat against an external enemy as a form of minor *jihād* is perfectly understandable if we recognise that not all who are

7. Benjamin Brower, 'The Amîr 'Abd Al-Qâdir and the "Good War" in Algeria, 1832–1847', *Studia Islamica* 2 (2011–12), 52.
8. Leading Brower helpfully to suggest that 'the central issue raised by 'Abd al-Qâdir's variable relationship to jihad is how it shows that jihad has been subject to critical reinterpretation like any other intellectual tradition. Therefore, as both social practice and doctrine, jihad has to be historicized to be properly understood.' Brower, 'The Amir', p. 52 (and see p. 55).
9. Thomas Sizgorich, *Violence and Belief in Late Antiquity: Militant Devotion in Christianity and Islam* (Philadelphia, 2009), pp. 13–15.

plunged into combat are real combatants. In essence, hypocrites, libertines and wrongdoers struggle against the enemy, alongside the pious.[10]

In other words, since we humans cannot determine the motives which lie in men's hearts, we are unable to ascertain whether armed *jihād* is truly being enacted as a form of spiritual struggle, or for baser motives. 'All who fight the wicked enemy are to be congratulated', he continues, 'though not all who are killed in combat are martyrs', for only God's knowledge of the connection between men's thoughts and deeds might determine who has truly been martyred (which in itself has implications in terms of the development of post-colonial forms of *jihād*, which build on ideas from colonial struggles).[11] Intriguingly, ᶜAbd al-Qādir even went on to essay the idea that all violence ought to be rejected on humanitarian and theological grounds, for: 'The Prophet qualified the struggle against enemies as the minor *jihād* [. . .] because the aim of combat is not to destroy and annihilate the creatures of God; to demolish that which God built and to devastate His lands.'[12] We await detailed readings of the Emir's work which can explore further these connections and disjuncts between his early life and his later writings.[13]

THE LIMITS OF JIHĀD AS AN EXPLANATORY CATEGORY

Why might the idea of *jihād* be questioned as a central analytic category in histories of the modern Islamic world? There is, after all, little doubt that a thematic concentration on *jihād* has been elucidatory in the manner in which common ties have been identified which connect the situations of Muslims in places as geographically diverse as West Africa, the Caucasus, Wahhābī Arabia, India and Algeria at the end of the eighteenth and the beginning of the nineteenth century.[14]

The manner, however, in which a *jihādī* shorthand serves as a nexus of discussions of both war and violence in the Islamic tradition is reductive and analytically more fragile than may first appear to be the case. Evidence provided for

10. 'Abd al-Qādir al-Djazā'irī, *Le Livre des Haltes (Kitāb al-Mawāqif)*, ed. Michel Lagarde, 3 vols (Leiden, 2000) I, p. 192.
11. Ibid.
12. Ibid., p. 193.
13. The Barthesian notion of the 'Death of the Author' might be intriguingly explored in this fashion.
14. For an interesting comparison between ᶜAbd al-Qādir and his contemporary in the Caucasus Imam Shamil, see Austin Jersild, *Orientalism and Empire North Caucasus Mountain Peoples and the Georgian Frontier, 1845–1917* (Montreal, 2002).

centring histories around ideas of *jihād* is, of course, textual, and it tends to come from a narrow corpus of texts which are accorded a special importance in Islamic Studies because they discuss the ethical character of certain modes of behaviour in the light of broader canons of jurisprudential and theological writing.[15] When the question is posed, by, say, a ruler to a cleric, 'would it be just to enjoin *jihād* in this set of circumstances?', a gift seems to be offered to the scholar, for just as a king or a commander asks for the morality of his actions to be read in the light of the tradition, so the scholar is also able to follow a parallel path in which bodies of contextual knowledge can be deployed so as to ascertain how thinking about violence sat within, and often developed, the canon of Islamic thought.

As this chapter will try to show, texts about violence are just that: texts. Writing about the morality of violence may govern and regulate the practice of violence in a particular place and time, but it may not. It may, in fact, describe only a portion of the kinds of violence or modes of defence against violence which are staged, or it may even be profoundly illusory in cloaking the distinct realities of violence at that moment. Furthermore, as is the case with military histories more generally, the language of *jihād* encourages a concentration on elite personalities, as though the contours of war and violence can be read through the delineations of combat as they are described by political and religious leaders.

Curiously, the rigidities of such *schemæ* tend to exclude actors who we might think would be inescapable in narratives of war and violence. Firstly, they tend to erase the victims of violence from the historical record, paying relatively little interest to the specific kinds of suffering imposed on civilian populations and the ways in which damage is wrought to individuals, collectivities and the social and cultural fabrics of which they form parts. This subaltern absence is paired with an equally unusual sense that we gain only glimpses of those who brought novel kinds of violence to Islamic societies at this key moment in which new forms of domination were introduced by Western powers. This void – in which the French lie relatively undescribed in Algerian *jihādī* texts – mimics the absence of 'the Algerian', both in French reportage from the early period of the conquest and later Western imperial and military histories, whose human focus tends to centre on Europeans as actors who made new worlds in empires.

This mere sketching of both aggressors and victims in both French and Islamic narratives is important because we are denied a sense of the kinds of dialogues which were enjoined by these groups in the new setting of the colony, which matters greatly because on one side (the French) a conviction developed

15. See also Khaled Abou El Fadl, *Rebellion and Violence in Islamic Law* (Cambridge, 2001), as well as Gabriele Marranci, *Jihad Beyond Islam* (London, 2006).

that specifically violent forms of conversation were most appropriate with the interlocutors they encountered in North Africa. Furthermore, the modes of historical judgement which are applied to such situations are curiously lopsided; in that codes of religiously derived ethics are applied to the analysis of Muslim violence, without there being any sense that Christian (or lay) morals ought to be used as a means of understanding or critiquing European violence.

As Temimi has written, the goal of 'decolonising' the history of the Maghreb involves the adoption of a new mindset, new structures, a new spirit and a realisation that existing modes of explanation tend unswervingly to follow the logics of the texts, leading actors and ideas of the period they study. In making such claims, Temimi was primarily implicating European modes of history, and those North African texts which followed them, but the same could also be said for the stress on *jihād* in Islamic histories and our need for

> [n]ew studies, analyses and interpretations [which] need to be undertaken of texts which are already well-known, because colonial history [. . .] has stressed the prejudices, the injustices, the pressures and the positions of the Governor Generals or the colonists of which she is the heir. Too often, those who were defeated are always in the wrong and their words are always tainted with falsehood, mistakes, exaggerations and fanaticism.[16]

THE LIMITS OF JIHĀD AS AN ISLAMIC MODE OF RESPONSE TO VIOLENCE

One of the chief limitations of *jihād* as an Islamic mode of response to European aggression in Algeria was the fact that it could so easily be construed as a form of 'fanaticism' – a holy war or a 'guerre sainte' as the French called it – which could be exploited by the armée d'Afrique as a means of persuading politicians and publics that they were engaged in a new form of just crusading on the Barbary Coast.[17] In a situation where the invasion of an Arab land was broadly perceived as being unpopular, economically wasteful and perhaps pointless, the government and the army's need for an Orientalised foe of the most classical kind was well served by self-proclaimed *jihādī*s such as ᶜAbd al-Qādir.

Yet while the manner in which his *jihād* was conceived of as being politically advantageous by the French was lost on ᶜAbd al-Qādir, it was well understood by

16. Abdeljelil Temimi, *Le Beylik de Constantine et Hadj 'Ahmed Bey (1830–1837)* (Tunis, 1978), p. 10.
17. See, for instance, Jennifer E. Sessions, *By Sword and Plow: France and the Conquest of Algeria* (Ithaca, 2011).

many of his Muslim contemporaries who deployed a much broader range of strategies of coexistence and resistance, many of which were also grounded in Islamic picturings of the world. The complexities and varieties of such positions tend, however, to become lost in histories, in which the simplicity of a struggle between two foes, two cultures and two ideas holds great narrative appeal. It is almost as though our desire to begin the narration of a form of national struggle between France and Algeria, which will last more than 130 years, blinds us to the reality that the early colony witnessed a much more confusing encounter between, on the one hand, the violent structural clarity of the modern European nation-state and, on the other, an 'Islamic space' which included overlapping zones of cultures, languages, tribes, empires and religious communities, but nothing that approximated the nation-state. Even then, we might note that the situation of the Algerian colony was sufficiently precarious for its first decade and a half that there was no certainty that it would become a permanent French possession.

It is in this context that we can point to texts and figures – such as Hadj Ahmed Bey of Constantine and Hamdan Khodja – whose accounts of the meetings of peoples in Algeria concentrated precisely on the specific and new forms of violence deployed against Algerians, those French actors who directed such attacks and the identities and suffering of their victims. Equally, we can read 'along the grain' of the colonial army's own records to find much evidence of the great variety of (subaltern) Muslim responses to this revolution in their world and quite specific contentions that *jihād*, as it was conventionally understood, was often perceived to be a source of harm for Muslims.[18]

Studies of the varieties of forms of indigenous response to European violence, as opposed to the concentration on *jihād*, also move towards the norms of the history of violence as a field. Its comparative studies of violence across a range of global settings and times focus equally on victims and perpetrators, drawing on theory, especially from anthropology, to conceptualise themes such as structural violence, the violence of modernity and varieties of genocidal thought and practice, which would seem to be valuable in studying a setting such as colonial Algeria.[19] In particular, such work stresses the dialogic character of

18. Stoler, *Along the Archival Grain.*
19. See, for example, Ben Kiernan, *Blood and Soil: A World History of Genocide and Extermination from Sparta to Darfur* (Yale, 2007); Leo Kuper, 'Genocide: Its Political Use in the Twentieth Century', in *Genocide: An Anthropological Reader*, ed. Alexander Laban Hinton (Oxford, 2002); A. Dirk Moses (ed.), *Empire, Colony, Genocide: Conquest, Occupation, and Subaltern Resistance in World History* (New York, 2008); Benjamin Brower, *A Desert Named Peace: The Violence of France's Empire in the Algerian Sahara, 1844–1902* (New York, 2009); Olivier Le Cour Grandmaison, 'Conquête de

communicative violence in empire and has begun to interrogate the connections between European beliefs about Arab violence and the reinscription of certain modes of retributive violence on Arab bodies.[20]

THE REIFICATION OF JIHĀD AND THE EMIR ʿABD AL-QĀDIR

Drawing on Temimi's idea, we might say that ᶜAbd al-Qādir's role in the early history of the Algerian colony was reified in multiple and interlocking ways, with his importance stressed by the French invaders, by colonial historians, by later generations of Maghrebi historians and, of course, by ᶜAbd al-Qādir himself, who conceived of his elevation as a form of national saviour to be central to his political and military strategy. That this project of salvation should be read as being *jihādī* was quite unsurprising, for ᶜAbd al-Qādir was a classic practitioner of 'Islamic violence', as it is understood in academic literatures, obsessed with the legitimacy and illegitimacy of political violence, whilst being almost oblivious to the new forms of violence brought by Europeans and the inherent violence of the modern colonial nation-state. Indeed, in something of a revolutionary and quite un-canonical fashion ᶜAbd al-Qādir sought to wrest control of 'Algeria' from the control of France even before this new and artificial polity had been fully conquered by the nationalising European force.

Precisely because ᶜAbd al-Qādir located the violence of his project within the Islamic tradition, we find a considerable concentration on his letters on *jihād* with clerics such as the Moroccan 'Alī b. ᶜAbd al-Salām al-Tuṣullī (d. 1842), and an imputation of ideological sincerity as compared with other Algerians' actions, which were less obviously framed by theological discussions. As Cook notes:

> He had to confront the question of how to lead a Muslim army to fight a legitimate jihad against the infidel when a large percentage of his troops believed in or tacitly accepted practices that were non-Muslim. Since ᶜAbd al-Qadir sought to found a Muslim state [. . .] he used the process of fighting to educate his largely tribal followers.[21]

l'Algérie: la guerre totale', in *Le massacre, objet d'histoire*, ed. David El Kenz (Paris, 2005); Ussama Makdisi and Paul A. Silverstein (eds), *Memory and Violence in the Middle East and North Africa* (Bloomington, 2006); Abdelmajid Hannoum, *Violent Modernity: France in Algeria* (Cambridge, MA, 2010); Olivier Le Cour Grandmaison, *Coloniser: exterminer: sur la guerre et l'état colonial* (Paris, 2005); Robert Muchembled, *A History of Violence from the End of the Middle Ages to the Present* (London, 2012).

20. William Gallois, *A History of Violence in the Early Algerian Colony* (London, 2013).
21. David Cook, *Understanding Jihad* (Berkeley, 2005), p. 85.

Such distinctions between the legitimate and considered character of ᶜAbd al-Qādir and the 'tribal' peoples of Algeria can be found across the literature, from the nineteenth-century to the twenty-first, from French texts to those from the Maghreb, from History to Islamic Studies. To all it seems plain that in the period of the so-called First Algerian War, following the French Conquest of 1830, European invaders were chiefly opposed by ᶜAbd al-Qādir, an implacable Islamist foe who enjoined holy war against them.

French and European historians have always found their texts easily structured around an antagonism between ᶜAbd al-Qādir and the French, most especially his nemesis Governor General Bugeaud. As Jacques Frémeaux remarked:

> In their opposition to the conquest of their country, local populations fell back on their age-old ideology of *Jihad* [. . .] The enemy was defined above else as a Christian [. . .] a member of a radically foreign community, with whom it was impossible to mix without endangering one's own beliefs, traditions and institutions, and whom it would be even more dangerous to obey. Thus religious legitimacy was to be crucial to all who sought to unite the inhabitants of the Regency capable of ensuring their independence.[22]

Such ideas depended upon the structures of thought found amongst the colonial occupiers of the 1830s, as we see in Charles-Robert Ageron's approving citation of General Duvivier's remark that 'Abd el Kader was Emir because liberty herself had conferred upon him her sword. He is a historical figure and History will ceaselessly evoke his name as he is never forgotten'.[23] For Ageron, therefore, Abd el-Kader was 'the personality whom Algerians could look to as their national hero'.[24] Frémeaux notes that this valorisation and historicisation was quite apparent in the views of many French officers, who in seeing Abd el-Kader as a 'great foe' accorded him 'real respect; even admiration at times'.[25] Bugeaud himself spoke of Abd el-Kader's 'genius', whilst his 'ultimate defeat did nothing but elevate his status still further', not least since this apparently intractable foe would later be awarded the grand-croix de la Légion d'honneur from France for his defence of Christians in Syria, and would fail to support the great Algerian rebellion of 1871 (in other words, when the Emir's politics had been reversed so

22. Jacques Frémeaux, *La France et l'Algérie en guerre: 1830–1870, 1954–1962* (Paris, 2002), p. 64.
23. Abdelkader Boutaleb, *L'Emir Abd-el-Kader et la formation de la nation algérienne: De l'Emir Abd-el-Kader à la guerre de libération* (Algiers, 1990), p. iii.
24. Boutaleb, *L'Emir*, p. iii.
25. Frémeaux, *La France*, p. 88.

as to stress the primary duty of the protection of the vulnerable and the illegitimacy of armed resistance on behalf of Muslim populations).[26]

Later Algerian politicians and historians also drew strength from the story of their ancestor's resistance against the colonial power in their own struggles against the French and their forging a new Algerian nation based upon the Emir's precedent.[27] As Touati wrote: '[I]n search of an archetypal hero, there was no way that Algerian nationalists could leave ᶜAbd al-Qâdir held hostage by colonial history'.[28] Works such as Mohammed-Cherif Sahli's *Abdelkader, le chevalier de la foi* (1946) and Kateb Yacine's *Abdelkader and Algerian Independence* (1948)[29] established 'ᶜAbd al-Qâdir as the founding father of the nationalist movement'; a 'heroic Hegelian', in Yacine's words, who strode a world-historical stage.[30] If Napoleon I had 'ended history' in Hegel's eschatological vision; who was to say that History and the course of human affairs had not begun again with ᶜAbd al-Qâdir?

On gaining independence in 1962, Touati notes that the curious foundational text on the Emir adopted by the new state was the hundred-year-old biography *The Life of Abdel Kader, ex-Sultan of the Arab of Algeria* by the British military officer Charles-Henry Churchill, 'which in place of the bravely defeated religious fanatic of colonial history, substituted the portrait of a statesman at war with his campaigns, his mode of administration, his plans of reform, and his principles of government'; in other words, as Touati notes, 'a precursor of the modern Algerian state'.[31]

Even much more recent work which seeks to critique the structures of Algerian history follows such patterns, as we see in Abdelmajid Hannoum's remark that: 'In all Algerian wars – from those of Abd el-Qader – to the ones of the FLN – religion was the motor and the battle cry against colonial domination and its ideology of modernity.'[32]

26. Ibid., pp. 160–1. On the Damascene years, see Michel Lagarde, ''Abd al-Qādir al-Jazā'irī et sa vision akbarienne du monde', pp. 203–22; and Michel Chodkiewicz, *The Spiritual Writings of Amir Abd el-Kader* (Albany, 1995).
27. See Abdallah Laroui, *The History of the Maghrib: An Interpretive Essay* (Princeton, 1977).
28. Touati, 'L'émir', p. 21: 'Le nationalisme algérien en quête d'éponyme ne pouvait laisser tenu en otage par la doxa coloniale.'
29. Kateb Yacine, *Abdelkader et l'indépendance algérienne* (Alger, 1983 [Algiers, 1948]). See Touati, 'L'émir', pp. 21–4; Brower, 'The Amîr', pp. 43–4.
30. Brower, 'The Amîr', pp. 43–4.
31. Touati, 'L'émir', pp. 22–3.
32. Hannoum, *Violent Modernity*, p. 10.

This dual stress on both ᶜAbd al-Qādir and the (classically interpreted) religious character of his resistance to the French is even more apparent in Islamic Studies, with its valorisation of the documentary record left by ᶜAbd al-Qādir and his correspondents, which revealed not only his own theories and practice of *jihād*, but the questions he asked of religious authorities across the Islamic world to establish the rightfulness of his struggle: was it legitimate to fight fellow Muslims who aided the invader? Could pacts and treaties be justified as short-term aims? Did Muslims have an obligation to emigrate from the *Dār al-Hārb* to the *dār al-islām*? Did the status of a sultan trump that of an Emir in the battle to expel the French from North Africa? At moments of relative weakness, the French army also appealed to 'the tradition', sending the Arabic-speaking Léon Roches to Kairouan, Cairo and Mecca to gather opinions which might justify their rule on religious grounds, contesting their foe's capacity to speak for a universal Islamic position.[33]

Hence we have Michael Bonner's comment in *Jihad in Islamic History* that:

> Jihad had a role in the first responses to this [post-1798] colonial domination. These were often attempts to build new structures within societies that were still relatively free of the invaders' influence, conforming to patterns that we have seen [. . .] in the premodern history of Islam. An example is the resistance to the French after their arrival in Algeria in 1830.[34]

And, even more strikingly, Richard Bonney's remark in *Jihād from Qur'ān to bin Laden*, describing '[t]he prototype of the anti-colonial *jihād*: the *jihād* of ᶜAbd al-Qādir in Algeria'.[35]

This textual record induces an underlying sympathy for ᶜAbd al-Qādir in works such as Cook's *Understanding Jihad*, in which the existence of such writings serves as the basis of the assertion that:

> ᶜAbd al-Qadir's questions reveal him to have been a thoughtful and ethical person, who saw in *jihād* a warfare distinguished by its virtue and righteousness, rather than a warfare seeking to achieve victory at any cost. Unfortunately, al-Tusulli's formulaic answers ignore the character of ᶜAbd al-Qadir and his genuine concern for his Muslim subjects.[36]

33. Schefer, p. 34, pp. 38–9.
34. Michael Bonner, *Jihad in Islamic History: Doctrines and Practice* (Princeton, 2006), pp. 156–7.
35. Richard Bonney, *Jihād from Qur'ān to bin Laden* (London, 2004), p. 182.
36. Cook, *Understanding Jihad*, p. 86.

Even nuanced political readings, such as that of Rudolph Peters, instinctively assume that ᶜAbd al-Qādir was the natural lead on the stage and the Muslim actor *primus inter pares*, but also that other Algerian Muslims ought to be held accountable to a different moral scale; *viz* his remark that:

> His main problem was in keeping his state together. The centrifugal forces that were inherent in his attempts to centralize the state apparatus and to do away with the privileges of the *makhzan* tribes and the *turuq*, showed themselves in the defection of some tribes and in individual or collective collaboration with the enemy. Rivalling *turuq* either cooperated with the French or denounced ᶜAbd al-Qādir for having concluded treaties with the enemy.[37]

The chief problem with such moral judgements and their identification of the principled heart of Islamic resistance to European conquest is that they pay scant heed to the political realities of Algeria in the 1830s and '40s. They originate in a reading which takes at face value ᶜAbd al-Qādir's claims to stand as a form of saviour of the people of Algeria and a belief that his appeals to tradition and external religious authority elevated him above other actors; alongside a misplaced certainty that he always followed such advice and acted in a religiously principled fashion:

> When he was in power, he tried as much as possible to act in agreement with the prescriptions of the *sharī'ah*. He preached a fundamentalist Islam, emphasizing monotheism (*tawhid*) and violently denouncing polytheism (*shirk*). He strongly condemned innovations (*bida'*) and especially the worship of saints.[38]

Yet the reality of the situation, amply documented in French and Algerian archival records, was that ᶜAbd al-Qādir was no more principled than any other political actor in this confused environment. He also 'collaborated' with the 'enemy', frequently accepting arms from the French, pacting with them, agreeing to eliminate local rivals at the behest of the invader if it suited his own interests. It ought also to be stated that ᶜAbd al-Qādir treated the French as legitimate equals in his dealings with them, and while he sought to exploit their presence for his own political ends in the void created by the expulsion of the Ottomans, it was also the case that, unlike many Algerians, ᶜAbd al-Qādir ignored much that was going on around him, failing to appreciate the effects of French governance on

37. Rudolph Peters, *Islam and Colonialism: The Doctrine of Jihad in Modern history* (The Hague, 1979), p. 56.
38. Peters, *Islam and Colonialism*, p. 55.

the peoples of Algeria. Far from being motivated by, as Cook would have it, a 'genuine concern for his Muslim subjects', ᶜAbd al-Qādir was driven by a political project of controlling and unifying Algerian space, whose chief beneficiary was France. This secular or 'realist' reading of ᶜAbd al-Qādir was brilliantly laid out by Danziger, when he noted that:

> The key to Abd el-Kader's successes lay in his ability to use existing forces, institutions and beliefs for the furtherance of resistance to the French and for internal consolidation. Despite his religious upbringing and the sincerity of his Islamic convictions, Abd el-Kader was, above all, a political leader. Abstract religious principles usually gave way to considerations of state.[39]

Such claims encourage us to look beyond the rhetoric of *jihād* – as al-Azmeh and others have done in other historical contexts[40] – so as to try to understand whose political interests were served by a mode of speech which claimed a form of moral primacy by reference to its canonical and theological heritage.

THE GIFT OF JIHĀD

It is hard to overstate how productive the idea of '*la guerre sainte*' was to those French politicians and soldiers who promoted the cause of the continued occupation of Algeria through the 1830s and 1840s, especially those who insisted that only military colonialism could serve as a form of government in such dangerous lands. To such men, ᶜAbd al-Qādir's proclamations of *jihād* could be read literally and presented as such to more sceptical French publics, serving to stress the 'civilisational' clash of the imperial encounter in Algeria and in support of the army's ever-increasing demands for troops and political control over France's new territories. Thus in January 1840, it was reported that 'ᶜAbd al-Qādir would not stop in his attempts to whip the tribes up into a state of holy war',[41] whilst in the summer of that year,

> the Emir, following the fall of Miliana and having read in the newspapers of the planned French expedition in the province of Oran, had sent a series of letters to the emperor of Morocco and the Bey of Tunis so as to try to persuade them not

39. Raphael Danziger, *Abd al-Qadir and the Algerians: Resistance to the French and Internal Consolidation* (New York, 1977), xiii, p. 212.
40. Aziz al-Azmeh, 'Mortal Enemies, Invisible Neighbours: Northerners in Andalusi Eyes', in *The Legacy of Muslim Spain*, ed. Salma Jayyusi (Leiden, 1992), pp. 259–72.
41. Service Historique de la Défense (hereafter SHD), Vincennes, 1 H 67, 2 January 1840.

> only to supply him with weapons, money and men, but also to declare war on France in the name of supporting Islam.[42]

Yet French power well understood that such proclamations were reflective only of one aspect of their relationship with ᶜAbd al-Qādir', for at the very moment when the Emir had declared a holy war on the invaders, French soldiers also noted that ᶜAbd al-Qādir had, in fact, promised a warm welcome, freedom and respect to any Christians who travelled across his territory.[43] More commonly, the French mocked ᶜAbd al-Qādir's pretensions to power and the idea *jihād* played in this picture of the world. In November 1839, for instance, Soult, the French Prime Minister and architect of its Algerian policy, wrote to General Valée to warn that 'you should be ready for all the Muslims to unleash a holy war', whilst contending that such intimidation was a sign of the Emir's 'powerlessness', believing that he had no true desire to restart a war with the French.[44] Months later, General Valée posed the stark question as to whether the French should 'push ᶜAbd al-Qādir to sign a new treaty or whether it would be better to destroy the *Amīr*'.[45] By June 1842, Bugeaud tellingly wrote to Soult that 'all is well right across the land. The rule of ᶜAbd al-Qādir has been shaken, for this chief, formerly at the head of a nation [. . .] is today accompanied by just a few horsemen [. . .] The war is over' ('La guerre serieuse est donc fini').

This was not to say that ᶜAbd al-Qādir, and the ideas he represented, did not continue to retain a certain strategic usefulness. In spite of the 'war' being over – if it had ever begun – Soult and Bugeaud continued to stress the potential dangers posed by *jihād* as a means of maintaining a force of more than 100,000 men in Africa. Yet Bugeaud's correspondence from this period (January 1843) revealed a quite different private stance, in which his righteous public anger that the dangers posed by ᶜAbd al-Qādir should never be underestimated was replaced by a pragmatic, realist tone in his dealings with the Emir. 'Hadj 'Abd al-Qādir', he wrote to him, according him his honorific title,

> I read with interest the second letter which you sent via your servant Ben Durand, whom I authorized to travel through the country so as to settle accounts, though not to speak of making peace, since my government prohibits me from dealing with you and having any form of contact other than war.[46]

42. SHD 1 H 70, 28 July 1840.
43. SHD 1 H 68, 2 April 1840.
44. SHD 1 H 64, 18 (Abd el-Kader to Valée), 19 (Soult) November 1839.
45. SHD 1 H 67, 25 January, 14, 15 February (Valée) 1840.
46. SHD 1 H 88, Bugeaud to Abd el-Kader, 9 January 1843.

This was, of course, the very same government to whom Bugeaud railed against any diminution of the idea of the threat posed by ᶜAbd al-Qādir, for his capacity to rule Algeria as the head of a militarised colonial state was dependent on metropolitan centres of power being convinced of Algeria being imperilled by the Emir. This sense was helped, perhaps just as cynically and self-consciously, by ᶜAbd al-Qādir, who in turn wrote 'Au grand des armées françaises, au capitaine des soldats de Tissu, dans le Royaume d'Alger, le Général Bugeaud' – precisely that which Bugeaud wished to communicate to his superiors, for in asserting that '[i]n making war against France, we have the sole intention of following our laws and our religious duties', the Emir played the role of the native chieftain ineluctably driven to oppose the infidel invaders.[47]

What was especially striking and tragic about this situation was the manner in which ᶜAbd al-Qādir failed to grasp the complexities of French strategy, the value his *jihād* played in validating the occupation and, critically, the brute realities of French policy, which became grounded in the idea that any tactics were morally justified in the Algerian theatre of conflict. This *naïveté* was apparent in his appeals to the French King and his belief that the increasing brutality of the occupation was somehow at odds with metropolitan policy; that it was an aberration which would be stamped out when it was realised that the civilizing mission was failing. He expressed such views at the precise moment when the so-called 'restrained occupation' had ended, when legalism (which suggested that Algerians merited the same legal treatment as metropolitan Frenchmen) had long been abandoned, while much of this had happened precisely because of the manner in which ᶜAbd al-Qādir had framed the conflict in Algeria. In April 1839 he wrote to Louis Philippe:

> Sultan of France, your military representatives seem to desire no more than combat and conquest, though I feel sure that such a system is not your own. You have certainly not come to Africa to exterminate her people, nor to chase them from their homeland. Instead, you wished to bring them the benefits of civilisation. Rather than coming to enslave them, you wished for them to enjoy those liberties which are the very basis of your nation.[48]

47. SHD 1 H 88, Abd el-Kader, January 1843. + the religious duty to end 'injustice', repeated many times. See also Jennifer E. Sessions, *By Sword and Plow*, p. 164.
48. 'Lettre de l'Emir Abdelkader à Louis-Philippe (roi de France)' in: http://rabahnaceri.unblog.fr/lettres-a-lire/lettre-de-lemir-abdelkader-a-louis-philippe-roi-de-france/ (accessed 30 August 2014).

Speaking, he believed, as the head of one nation to another, ᶜAbd al-Qādir' implored the French King to restrain his generals and their depiction of him as 'an ambitious and fanatical enemy', so that both rulers might be able to concentrate on 'our mutual civilizing projects'.

The significance of these remarks lies not only in the Emir's misapprehension of the nature of European power (as opposed to negotiations one might have had with Algeria's Ottoman overlords), but his fundamental failure to recognise that the revolutionary violence of the invader was a key feature of France's civilising mission. Exterminatory policies emerged partly from a determination to quell resistance to the conquest, but they were also a function of the French belief that such assaults were a necessary evil in a realm where *razzias* and *jihād* were understood by Algerians to be ideologies of complete violence which might be used to combat internal and external enemies. It was, in fact, this French adoption of the 'razzia' as a form of counter-*jihād* which induced precisely the kinds of horrific violence which ᶜAbd al-Qādir trustingly believed might disappear if only France's rulers knew how the morality of their conquest was being undermined by soldiers in the colony.[49]

THE TRAP OF THE NATION

As we have seen, ᶜAbd al-Qādir's *jihād* was built around a conviction that he was the leader of a 'nation' and that this status afforded him the possibility of negotiating with the King of France. The idea of the nation was central to this ideology, for only if ᶜAbd al-Qādir could be seen to be the legitimate ruler of a group of Muslims could he be their defender.

The problem, however, with this 'nationalising' *jihād* was that, like *jihād* more generally, it served French interests rather more than it did Algerians. ᶜAbd al-Qādir led only one (inchoate) group in the territory from which the French would make 'Algeria', and in following their invention and spatialisation of a new nation, he provided practical and ideological support to the creation of the colony, leaving aside his willingness to pact with France so as to eliminate local rivals as a means of enhancing the power of the two 'national' forces in the land.

Bennison is surely right that the national model which ᶜAbd al-Qādir sought to mimic was that of Morocco, describing the Emir's rise to power 'as an attempt

49. A detailed account of the manner in which French troops appropriated the idea of the 'razzia', or *ghazwa*, and transformed it into structural and punitive forms of violence can be found in Gallois, *A History of Violence*.

to replicate the 'Alawī sharifian *jihad* state'.[50] However, in seeking to recreate such an idea across Algeria, which had not had Morocco's history of a centrifugal national power, one might argue that ᶜAbd al-Qādir's national vision was as revolutionary as France's idea of the consolidation of disparate geographic, ethnic and cultural zones into a single imperial territory. While they cohered in their chief aim, ᶜAbd al-Qādir, understandably, could not conceive of what the modern European state was becoming in the nineteenth century, with a form of reach and power quite unlike other forms of political organisation known to Europeans or Africans. In effect, ᶜAbd al-Qādir proposed the creation of a nation without a state, whilst the French were ultimately determined to establish a state without a nation (for Algeria would become incorporated into the French national space).

However abstract such discussions may seem, they mattered a great deal to the disparate peoples over whom these powers fought in the 1830s and '40s. In contrast to the manner in which contemporary Islamists stress the suffering of Muslim communities as the basis of their *jihād* (or, indeed, the Emir's protection of Christians in Syria), ᶜAbd al-Qādir's politics were based on a calculation of power, rather than an ethic of justice. His appeals to clerics did not tend to stress the wrongs done to his co-religionists, but focused instead on the potential political legitimacy of the nation he led, with which he sought to supplant French rule.

The question as to who belonged to the community of people represented by the Emir was a critical one, for ᶜAbd al-Qādir's national *jihād* operated with a novel political unit which was both smaller than those empires which had claimed to represent the *umma*, or the interests of all Muslims, yet much larger than the regional, tribal and confederal units to which most Muslims in Algeria had owed allegiance before the arrival of the French.

This variety of political forms undoubtedly induced a sense of confusion with regard to how Europeans might be repelled, and explains the instinctive appeal to some of ᶜAbd al-Qādir's concentration of Muslim power. However, it is critical to recall both that some 'Algerians' believed that they could find ways of living under an overarching European imperial government, just as they had done under the Ottomans, and that still more rejected ᶜAbd al-Qādir's strategy of national *jihādī* resistance (and negotiation) as a means of combating the invader.[51]

50. Amira K. Bennison, *Jihad and its Interpretations in Pre-colonial Morocco: State-society Relations during the French Conquest of Morocco* (London, 2002), p. 13.
51. Furthermore, such discussions are important in the sense that they are preludes to many later debates on who is included and excluded and how they are represented in the Arab and Islamic nation-state.

Existing studies, nonetheless, focus relentlessly on the question as to whether ᶜAbd al-Qādir can be adjudged to be, in Marcel Émerit's words, 'the founder of Algerian nationhood', and the role which such narratives can play in the stories that an independent Algeria tells about and to itself.[52] A romantic nationalism is exemplified by Mahfoud Kaddache's *L'Emir Abdelkader* (1982), in which he writes of the ways in which ᶜAbd al-Qādir seized on sentiments of national feeling already alive in the land:

> ['the official view that the Emir had been able'] to discern in the hearts of the people, where he had felt the stirrings of liberty and dignity, the will to fight. Born on Algerian soil, raised in respect for his faith and fidelity to his country, possessed of the greatest sense of dignity and honour, Abd el-Kader responded to his people's call. The country, invaded and threatened, required the Jihad [. . .] The Nationality, the defence of the State into which the Nation had formed itself, the organisation of an armed Resistance infused by Algerian national feeling, were the goals of the Emir's policy.[53]

Writing in a newly socialist state, Mostafa Lacheraf went still further in *Algérie, Nation et Société* (1965), King notes, for he 'qualifies Abd el-Kader's resistance as doubly revolutionary. The Emir aimed both to liberate territory by means of the mobilization of the population for war; and to destroy the inauspicious, anti-nationalist and anti-social power of the great landed and merchant families.'[54] And at that same moment in France, René Gallisot argued that it would be perverse to refuse Abd el-Kader the title of nationalist, given that 'the French soldiers who directed the war in Algeria were not incorrect . . . when they spoke of a nation which would not agree to lose its independence, and of Abd el-Kader as the leader of the Arab nation.'[55] Others, however, such as Gabriel Esquer, Claude Martin, David C. Gordon and B. G. Martin,[56] have questioned what Gellner critically described as the idea of ᶜAbd al-Qādir as the 'the precursor of nation and state-building'.[57] In his survey on the topic, King himself suggests that:

52. Cited in Touati, 'L'émir 'Abd al-Qâdir', p. 19.
53. John King, 'Abd el-Kader and Arab Nationalism', in *Problems of the Middle East in Historical Perspective – Essays in Honour of Albert Hourani*, ed. John Spagnolo (Oxford, 1996), p. 134.
54. Ibid.
55. Ibid., p. 135.
56. Ibid., pp. 135–6.
57. Ernst Gellner, 'Rulers and Tribesmen', *Middle Eastern Studies* 15.1 (1979), 106.

> While a broad spectrum of Algeria's peoples had been ready and willing to answer the call to a jihad, they were equally willing to relapse into a pragmatic acceptance of the course of events when, without a charismatic leader with the force of character and intellect to bind them together, the jihad no longer seemed possible.[58]

For King, therefore, 'his aim was consciously religious rather than nationalistic',[59] while Pouillon agrees that 'Abd el Kader's understanding of 'territory' is 'a distinctly pre-modern one based on religious affiliation rather than ethnicity, land, and formal borders'.[60] Bennison, furthermore, contends that

> ᶜAbd al-Qadir's understanding of the notion [of nationhood], even late in his life, was vague at best and subsisted with his commitment to Islamic reformism of a universalist colour, and his geo-political engagement in an area which frequently encompassed the Rif mountains and other parts of the 'Alawī sultanate but only rarely included eastern Algeria, previously the eastern Beylik of Constantine.[61]

Yet what connects all such accounts, whether they argue for or against the idea of ᶜAbd al-Qadir as the father of the Algerian nation, is that they concentrate on ideas the Emir had about the world and his presumed agency and ability to make those thoughts real. They bear almost no relation (other than in Bennison) to the concomitant reality of the French forging of a new national space called 'Algeria' and the role which ᶜAbd al-Qadir's actions and policies played in the making of something which was at the same time a construct and a set of realities which had profound effects on the lives of the peoples of Algeria.

They also tend to ignore that which was destroyed in the move to statehood, for as Bennoune notes, 'most early colonial historians, tended to exaggerate the political fragmentation of pre-colonial Algeria in order to prove that the country had "never formed a nation"',[62] instead concentrating on the institution of the tribe, so as to assign 'themselves a "civilising mission" in a "tribal-stateless" society'.[63] Both Bennoune and Hermassi, however, stress that

58. King, 'Abd el-Kader', p. 141.
59. Ibid.
60. Woerner-Powell, ''Abd al-Qādir', p. 97. François Pouillon, 'Abd el-Kader, icône de la nation algérienne', in *La guerre d'Algérie dans la mémoire et l'imaginaire*, eds A. Dayan Rosenman and L. Valensi (Paris, 2004), pp. 87–102.
61. Bennison, ''Abd al-Qādir's Jihād', pp. 79–80.
62. M. Bennoune, *The Making of Modern Algeria 1830–1957* (Cambridge, 1988), p. 18.
63. Ibid., p. 19.

this binary of (civilised) nation and (primitive) tribe ignored the quite different structure of social and economic organisation in the Maghreb, in which spaces were connected by 'pre-capitalist marketing networks, religious institutions and pilgrimage'.[64] Above all, it was the trade routes and the marketplaces of the region that wove together communities, which might be culturally and socially distinct, yet whose prosperity depended on forms of spatial organisation that combined local forms of independence and national and transnational forms of interdependence. As Hermassi notes: 'The marketplace, strategic as it was for exchange, was also instrumental in cementing social relationships for an otherwise dispersed and fragmented population.'[65]

It was to be the European destruction of these marketplaces and the complex human ecology they supported which ultimately secured French dominance over Algerians; a form of spatial conquest in which the autonomy and agency of the local disappeared in the imposition of a rigid form of national spatiality that contrasted markedly with the flexible strength of indigenous organisation of space.

THE SPATIALITY OF JIHĀD

Writing about the Moroccan Emperor at this moment, Bennison observes that: 'Although Mawlay ᶜAbd al-Rahman did not publicly disavow the *jihād*, he started to view holy war as a spatially bounded rather than universal obligation and opposition to this view as rebelliousness.'[66] Precisely the same claim may be made with regard to ᶜAbd al-Qādir, especially in the famous Moroccan 'betrayal' of 1846, in which the Emir castigated the emperor's failure to support his cause, writing to an Egyptian scholar: 'Please give us your answer concerning the legally abominable deeds of the Moroccan Sultan, deeds that one does not expect from any person, let alone from notables.'[67] While ᶜAbd al-Qādir may have sought to present the community of Muslims as corresponding to the community of Muslims who followed his rule, in reality the emperor's choice of non-intervention against the French, as a means of protecting the lives of his subjects, was no more 'national' than the actions of ᶜAbd al-Qādir. Whilst, in Bennison's eyes, the Emir saw himself as a successor to his purificatory ancestors, the Almoravids and the Almohads, who had built empires upon the

64. Ibid., p. 18.
65. Ibid., p. 231.
66. Bennison, *Jihad*, p. 13.
67. Peters, *Islam and Colonialism*, p. 60.

return to religious orthodoxy over the tribal comforts of *'asabiyya*, the Moroccan Emperor saw an covetous and rapacious rival, and one whose actions endangered the safety and independence of his subjects.[68]

More generally, his epistolary explorations of the ethics of *jihād* reveal a writer for whom a realist, national politics superseded all other logics. Thus, in 1843, ᶜAbd al-Qādir 'gained no satisfactory answer as to whether Muslim collaborators with the French could be considered "apostates"',[69] ignoring his own years of 'collaboration'; whilst in 1839, a letter to Louis-Philippe had revealed precisely the extent of such a politics of mutuality, as the Emir had asked: 'In Oran why do I continue to see the chiefs of the Douars and the Smalas, when you had promised their extradition to France?'[70]

It is imperative, therefore, that we look to the lives and stories of those other 'Algerians', many of whom, such as the followers of Ahmed Bey, denounced the politics of ᶜAbd al-Qādir:

> The son of Mohiéddine has sown disorder in the land and amongst Muslims. He has cannons, he has raised an army, yet he decapitates Muslims, steals their herds and hands their goods to the French. It is in their interests that he has subdued the country [. . .] he has turned against us, sending gifts of friendship to the Bey of Tunis as a means of encircling us and expelling us from our lands. He hopes to direct a part of his army either to massacre or expel us, though we cannot leave these lands. We fear these Bedouins of Africa, allied to the French.[71]

The textual record left by the Bey of Constantine and his followers shares much with other Muslims' accounts of life in the early colony, which focus more on the consequences of French rule – and ᶜAbd al-Qādir's *jihādī* resistance – on the peoples of the land. Herein lies a critical difference of approach between the principlist writings of the Emir, which explored the motives and morals of *jihād*, with the consequentialist stress of other, less regarded texts and writers. One set of writings index actions against a set of moral ideals, whilst the others concentrate on the blunter realities of lived existence.

68. Bennison, ''Abd al-Qādir's Jihād', pp. 72–3.
69. Bonney, *Jihād*, p. 182. See also Woerner Powell, ''Abd al-Qādir', p. 119, in which he notes that his writing 'argues that material support for non-Muslims engaged in warfare against Muslims is illicit and warrants punitive reprisals'.
70. 'Lettre de l'Emir Abdelkader à Louis-Philippe (roi de France)' in: http://rabahnaceri.unblog.fr/lettres-a-lire/lettre-de-lemir-abdelkader-a-louis-philippe-roi-de-france/ (accessed 10 April 2015).
71. Temimi, *Le Beylik de Constantine*, p. 266.

Thus, in the archival record, we find many instances of Muslims describing what they saw as the impolitic and dangerous character of ᶜAbd al-Qādir's *jihād*. In July 1839 the French noted that having encouraged *jihād*, the Kabyles were disgusted by the manner in which this cloaked ᶜAbd al-Qādir's 'rapacity and ambition'.[72] Arab tribes were of the same opinion, contending that the Emir preached 'holy war' in an immoderate fashion, asking: 'why we should give you our money when you are simply bringing us war?'[73] Later that year, ᶜAbd al-Qādir once again proposed a holy war to the Kabyle tribes around Bougie, 'though in vain at the present time' as the French noted, while the start of the following year brought news that he never ceased in his attempts to foment '*la guerre sainte*'.[74] 'The Arabs', one French note from February 1838 read, 'are deeply unhappy with the behaviour of the Emir on their behalf, and they wish to fight a war of revenge against him'.[75]

In March and April 1839, reports from Mascara indicated that ᶜAbd al-Qādir had gathered the chiefs of the region in order to levy 'such outrageously inflated taxes that none had been willing to pay such sums'.[76] In fact, the "population of Cherchell had refused to pay and had revolted when the Emir had threatened to destroy their town"', which in turn had inspired Tedjini, of Ain Mahdi, to challenge ᶜAbd al-Qādir's right to represent the tribes of the desert. As tended to happen at such moments when the fragile set of alliances which constituted ᶜAbd al-Qādir's seeming power began to crack, 'a tribe who had hitherto been loyal to the *Amīr* made peace with France'.

Such reports lead us to question both the extent of the Emir's political legitimacy and Cook's claim that he was driven by his 'genuine concern for his Muslim subjects'. Such sovereign concern certainly did not extend to Berbers, who instinctively resented the revolutionary qualities of ᶜAbd al-Qādir's agglomeration of power as much as they did France's complementary forging of a national space. As Danziger notes, Berber tribes were right to intuit that such threats were intertwined, for as the Emir wrote to the French in January 1838: '[T]hese people [in the vicinity of Blida] do not understand anything and are like ruffians. They were never under the domination of the former kings . . . These tribes are the Berbers.'[77]

72. 1 H 63 – 2 – 7, 14 July 1839.
73. SHD 1 H 63, report from Daumas, 7 July 1839.
74. SHD 1 H 66, 5 December 1839; SHD 1 H 67, 2 January 1840.
75. SHD 1 H 54, 28 February 1838.
76. SHD 1 H 61, 2, 10, 24, 31 March; 6, 13 April 1839.
77. Danziger, *Abd al-Qadir*, p. 203.

The focus of studies of violence in the early Algerian colony should look, therefore, not only at ᶜAbd al-Qādir's *jihād*, but at local reactions to novel forms of French violence, generating quite different histories of the period, both of the experiences of indigenous Muslim and Jewish populations of the Maghreb and the ways in which their faith informed and did not inform the forces which were in the process of revolutionising their world.

In other places I have written extensively about the variety of violence practiced by the French and the ways in which they sanctioned and legitimated ever-increasing forms of atrocity to the point of genocide.[78] The striking feature of such documents and texts is the manner in which they focus on the consequences of the meeting of two peoples, revealing the rather insular focus of ᶜAbd al-Qādir's *jihād* and his particular view of the world, which was something of a theoretical enterprise that sought to impose the reality of statecraft, doctrine and morality upon the world at a time when the lives of the peoples of North Africa were changing in radical and tragic ways.

OTHER MUSLIMS, OTHER STORIES

There is a need, therefore, for histories of the early colony to explore the heterogeneity of Islamic responses to the novel encounter with the violence of the modern European state and to investigate the ways in which such plural responses also drew on the rich traditions of Islamic thought.

The work of Hamdan Khodja is critical in this regard, for in spite of the fact that he has generally been viewed as being a secular writer, it is arguable that his thought was more grounded in the canons of Islamic ethical thought than a more outwardly pious figure such as ᶜAbd al-Qādir. Best known for his *The Mirror: A Historical and Statistical Glimpse of the Regency of Algiers*, published in both Arabic and French in 1833, Khodja's *Miroir* was offered to Europeans as a means of seeing the great gap which existed between the purported morals of a mission of 'civilizational imperialism' and the base realities of the brutal character of the occupation of Algeria.[79]

Khodja had been a leading official and landowner under the Ottomans and had originally offered to act as an intermediary with the French, as he had done with the Maghreb's previous overlords. In contrast to the Emir, it was his analysis of the consequences of French rule and the entirely new kinds of suffering

78. Gallois, *A History of Violence*; William Gallois, 'Genocide in Nineteenth-Century Algeria', *Journal of Genocide Research* 15–1 (2013), 69–88.
79. Hamdan Khodja, *Le Miroir: Aperçu historique et statistique sur la Régence d'Alger* (Paris, 1985 [1833]).

which were enjoined on his people which drove him to write *Le Miroir* and, working for the Bey of Constantine, to begin a campaign of ethical resistance against the savagery and injustice of this new form of dominion. While it is true that in communicating with European audiences, Khodja was able to adopt a language of enlightened liberalism which seemed quite 'secular', his writings' stress on ideas of justice and non-maleficence are grounded in the core values of the Islamic ethical tradition. Indeed, Khodja's consequentialist stress on the terrible impact of French rule on civilian populations and the failure of the invader to avoid harming local peoples and the absence of a sense of justice from their own moral compass might suggest that we ought to view ᶜAbd al-Qādir as a more political, secular thinker and Khodja as a more authentically Islamic figure. It was Khodja after all whose emphasis on non-maleficence drew on the *hadīth*, which demands 'let there be no infliction of harm or reciprocating of harm', whilst, as we have seen, the community of Muslims which the Emir sought to protect was drawn around those tribal and ethnic groups who were loyal to his national prerogative.

For Khodja and the Bey of Constantine, who he moved to serve as the last indigenous power whom he believed might be able to protect the populations of the land, a civilisational battle had begun in Algeria, which saw two different forms of ethics in conflict, as well as two peoples. Khodja's duty was to reveal the untruths concealed in France's civilisational offer and to appeal to the value of his own civilisational traditions as a means of critiquing the violence of the colony, which was both structural and atrociously immediate. As he wrote to the Ottoman ambassador in Paris in July 1835:

> The French have burned the houses and the shops of Algeria. They have destroyed the roads under the pretence of widening them. They have spent five years seizing the goods of the Muslim peoples [. . .] We have to consider that our possessions are lost and, consequently, our situation is dire. Agriculture, which was the basis of our wealth, no longer exists; our trade is equally destroyed, and the safe roads which would afford a chance to trade are no longer there.[80]

Appealing to the British parliament, Ahmed Bey continued:

> What are their ambitions for our country, which they suggest they came to modernise, to bring justice and to overcome barbarism? Today we can reply that we

80. Temimi, *Le Beylik de Constantine*, p. 232.

are sure that the barbarism and injustice which they practice are more odious and hateful than any injustice or barbarism previously known here.[81]

For Khodja and Ahmed Bey, unlike ᶜAbd al-Qādir, ethics needed to be grounded in the description and critique of the effects of the actions of one set of people upon another. Unlike the Emir, they well understood the idea of competing or prioritising ethics in the Islamic tradition, for it was not enough to claim the primacy of one ethical value without considering which other moral virtues might be relegated or ignored in such concentration. Their sense of ethics was evidently grounded in the twin ideas of non-maleficence (especially the duty of the powerful not to do harm to the weak) and justice (which also described a world where care was taken that harm be avoided), whilst ᶜAbd al-Qādir's ethics were clearly grounded in a sure sense of beneficence – in the conviction that he could do good for his people and land, and that he knew how to do this. Ethics of beneficence are often characterised by strong sets of binaries which divide the world into the good and the bad and a sense that other ethical priorities lie subsumed within the overarching beneficent goal. It should, perhaps, not seem surprising that an equal and complete stress on beneficence could also be found in the French 'colonial mind', with its rigid sense of certainty that the merits of civilisational imperialism excused brutal forms of rule.[82]

Khodja and Ahmed Bey well understood the terrible consequences of such thought for the people of Algeria. For them, as Djeghloul remarks, a long-lasting, dark 'colonial night'[83] had begun, in which the future-oriented goal of an imagined new civilised society in North Africa could be used as a means of justifying the burning of houses, the destruction of roads and the quelling of peoples and cultures. That the chief form of resistance to the French was built upon a mirroring of such European moral thought and logics was a double tragedy, for those who would suffer in such an absolutist world were the peoples of Algeria.

Intriguingly, if we look beyond ᶜAbd al-Qādir's *jihād*, we find a broader diet of Muslim responses to European rule, much of which draws on the justice-centred approach seen in Khodja and Ahmed Bey. This included a form of steadfastness that was able to draw on faith which could see beyond the immediate horrors brought by the French to imagine a better future world. As one tribe wrote to the French in June 1841, they would never be terrorised into submission by the army's razzias, asserting that: '[W]e are no means ruined because you

81. Ibid., p. 230.
82. William Gallois, 'Dahra and the History of Violence in Early Colonial Algeria', in *The French Colonial Mind*, 2 vols, ed. Martin Thomas (Lincoln, 2012).
83. Abdelkader Djeghloul, 'Introduction to Hamdan Khodja, "Le Miroir"', p. 32.

have burned our harvests and cut down our trees [. . .] even if you stay here for a century, all of your tricks will do us no harm'.[84]

Such a steadfast conviction of faith, or *Istiqāma*, was complemented by an innate sense of tolerance displayed by many groups and, indeed, preachers, such as the reports of an influential Iraqi cleric, a follower of ᶜAbd al-Qādir al-Jīlānī (founder of the Qādiriyya Sufi order to which ᶜAbd al-Qādir belonged and from which he drew legitimacy), who had travelled the country preaching tolerance between Muslims and Christians.[85] Even tribes who were amongst the most recalcitrant of foes, such as the Banī ᶜĀmir (Beni Amer), would 'offer the French couscous, which was eaten by a stream whilst discussing the benefits which might come from a peace',[86] and reading through the archival records of the period, there is a sense that many Muslims adopted a position commonly found in Meccan fatwas on *jihād* from the later nineteenth century, where they would not fight if they believed that resistance would fail and cause more harm than good.[87] Such a view was also espoused (in 1847) by Mawlay ᶜAbd al-Raḥmān, who, as Bennison notes, came to share the view of 'the Wazzāniyya-Tayyibiyya brotherhood, that the viciousness of the French onslaught rendered jihād against the "infidel" too dangerous to be permissible'.[88] Even earlier than this, as Brower reveals:

> During the hajj of 1841 (1256 AH), a group of Algerian pilgrims called a meeting in Mecca with religious notables led by Sayyid Mahmūd al-Kîlânî, shaykh of the Qâdiriyya Sufi order of Baghdad. They wanted to know if ᶜAbd al-Qâdir's jihad was legitimate, and a cause that they were obliged to follow. Al-Kîlânî knew ᶜAbd al-Qâdir well, having hosted him and his father for several months in Baghdad in the 1820s when the two came to pay homage at the tomb of 'Abd al-Qâdir al-Jîlânî (founder of the Qâdiriyya Sufi order to which both men were affiliated). Nevertheless, he issued a fatwâ condemning the amîr's struggle and absolving Algerians of the obligation to make war on the French. In the Baghdad shaykh's reasoning, the jihad had to have the possibility of success for it to be legitimate, and he did not see this hope for Algerians against the French.[89]

Equally, even those who seemed to be most implacably opposed to French rule, such as Berkani, were willing to make treaties with them and to follow the path

84. SHD 1 H 76, 19, 20 June 1841.
85. SHD 1 H 51, 9 August 1837. Intriguingly, the French believed the preacher to be Jīlānī himself (b. 1077 – d. 1166 CE).
86. SHD 1 H 80, February 1842.
87. Peters, *Islam and Colonialism*, p. 62.
88. Bennison, ''Abd al-Qādir's Jihād', p. 88.
89. Brower, 'The Amir', p. 85.

of negotiating peace found in the Islamic tradition. In doing so, they would use religious language as a means of invoking the God of the *Ahl al-Kitāb* to speak to the idea of a form of sovereignty under a shared God (and what matters here is not Berkani's failure to establish any form of *dār al-islām* under French rule, nor the undoubted incomprehension and rejection of such offers on the part of France, but the aspirations which drove Berkani to describe the world in this way). As he wrote to the French army in July 1842:

> I will keep myself to myself. I will not get mixed up in anything. I shall not work against the execution of any of your orders. Do not listen to the words of those Demons who accuse me of going against your orders. God gives his approval to good works! All will be returned and come back to God! He directs us on the right path![90]

Importantly, even ᶜAbd al-Qādir's own *jihād* incorporated such pacting with the French, and he, too, was wont to invoke a shared deity to sanction such arrangements, writing to Louis-Philippe in 1839 of 'a system designed to ensure the wellbeing of populations which God has assigned to our shared protection'.[91]

Other Islamic responses to French occupation included *hijra*/emigration, which ᶜAbd al-Qādir explored in his writing, and which became more prevalent in the second half of the nineteenth century, when the effects and permanence of French rule were more commonly perceived.[92] And, connected to the notion of steadfastness, a Mahdist tendency was apparent, strongly critiqued by writers on *jihād* such as Peters, who noted:

> In some cases this belief [of a return which will bring justice] has been consciously used in order to produce this effect and keep the population quiet. Thus, during ᶜAbd al-Qādir's war against the French in Algeria, the leaders of a rival order, the Tayyibiyyah *tarīqah*, who wanted to undermine ᶜAbd al-Qādir's position, employed the *Mahdī* belief in this sense and issued the following proclamation: Be patient, Muslims, for the day of deliverance is coming. Hold fast for the arrival of he who cannot be resisted, who will return the armies of the impious back to the sea which vomited them upon our shores.[93]

90. SHD 1 H 83, Berkani to Bugeaud, translated by Léon Roches, 20 July 1842.
91. 'Lettre de l'Emir Abdelkader à Louis-Philippe (roi de France)' in: http://rabahnaceri.unblog.fr/lettres-a-lire/lettre-de-lemir-abdelkader-a-louis-philippe-roi-de-france/.
92. See also Bonney, *Jihād*, p. 181.
93. Peters, *Islam and Colonialism*, p. 42. The translation of the French text is my own.

Here again, an assumption is evidently made which establishes *jihād* as both an authentically Islamic mode of resistance and one which should be accorded a form of moral primacy, arguably replaying the structures of beneficent thought apparent in the 1830s.

Returning to Ahmed Bey's entreaties, it is apparent that the beneficent *jihādī* nation-building project of ᶜAbd al-Qādir was opposed by a quite different, religiously inspired vision for the future, which was grounded in Islamically conceived ideas of justice and freedom, providing an opportunity for the peoples of Algeria to break away from the domination of colonial power, whether Ottoman or French. The scale of support for this very different project was apparent in, for instance, the letter written to the British parliament in January 1834 by Ahmed Bey and the 'community of Constantine', with its 2,246 signatories, including 'the notables of Constantine, the heads of the great families, intellectuals, teachers, the Ulema, and leading Bedouins'.[94]

As Ahmed Bey wrote on the new taxes which the French imposed on local populations:

> Our religion teaches us that we should levy the harvest *ashur* for the Muslim *Beit-ul-māl*, while the *gharāma* and the *corvée* (municipal taxes) were imposed on us by the Turks. The population has been impoverished by these injustices; these laws without a basis in the Qur'an. And since God has rejected these taxes for many reasons, I should not want to inflict them on the population, for they would bring me ill fortune on the day of judgment. As our religion insists, the *ashur* should be used for the utility of the people and not in the service of Sultans. I cannot impose these taxes through force and savagery, so why should I now impose them for others' [French] gain when I have rejected raising such taxes for my own profit? My first response to the arguments advanced by [the French commanders] Bourmont and Clauzel is therefore to stress the contradictions in their acts and their words.[95]

Central to the struggle of Ahmed Bey, Hamdan Khodja and others, therefore, was a form of moral resistance to the injustices of French domination, which themselves built on the structures of Ottoman colonial governance. Such resistance was grounded in religion, yet it did not instinctively locate *jihād* as the most authentically Islamic response to the new contours of European imperial oppression. On a strategic level, one might argue that its resistance grounded

94. Temimi, *Le Beylik de Constantine*, pp. 227–30.
95. Ibid., pp. 214–15.

in ethical critique was as ineffective as the Emir's *jihād*, but there is a scholarly imperative to describe the character of such engagement, not least since it too drew heavily on Islamic traditions as a means of asserting its legitimacy, and because it too would become constitutive of patterns of Muslim thought and behaviour throughout the duration of the colony and more generally in the colonised Islamic world in the modern period.

CONCLUSION

Jihād makes sense of times of war, but just as the narrative conventions of military history seem to make sense of violence in the Western canon, we ought to be more suspicious of the ways in which we use such shorthands to think about the past. This is especially true of the notion of *jihād*, where actors such as ᶜAbd al-Qādir sought to connect their actions to the tradition through literatures of *jihād* and appeals to religious authorities. Such trails of evidence have the potential to deny the voice and agency of other Muslims whose engagements with colonists may have been far less self-conscious, may not have been theorised on the page, yet may also have drawn on important facets of Islamic tradition and, indeed, innovated and developed new ethics of engagement with others. A concentration on canonical texts and figures, especially those who indexed their readings of such changing worlds to the tradition, ought to be supplemented by historical forms of reconstitution, in which other Muslim responses to imperialism and modernity are read outside the genre of *jihād*.[96]

The Algerian tragedy of the nineteenth century was not the defeat of ᶜAbd al-Qādir, but his lack of realisation of the horrors brought by the French, which was well understood by Algerians who suffered, especially the Kabyles, but also by other Muslim voices, such as Hamdan Khodja and Ahmed Bey. Such writers used the Islamic tradition to critique the moral character of this new colonial experiment, in which suffering was enjoined on those for whom ethics of justice and non-maleficence predominated, wrought by forces whose actions were underpinned by exculpatory ideas of beneficence, which were arguably shared both by the French invaders and by Jihadists such as ᶜAbd al-Qādir.

Historians of the modern Islamic world therefore need to move away from the idea that *jihād* was necessarily a uniquely authentic mode of religiously inspired response to the revolutionary changes imposed by European colonists.

96. See, for example, Julia Clancy-Smith, *Rebel and Saint: Muslim Notables, Populist Protest, Colonial Encounters, Algeria and Tunisia (1800–1904)* (Berkeley, 1997); Beshara Doumani, *Rediscovering Palestine: Merchants and Peasants in Jebel Nablus 1700–1900* (Berkeley, 1995).

It was one mode of action, but it was grounded no more in tradition than many other responses, some of which ably critiqued the human consequences of the moral bluntness of *jihādī* strategies, which tended to play into the hands of Europeans who were looking for Muslim foes and narratives which stressed the simplicity of a civilisational conflict between Christians and Muslims, the moral conquest of the savage and despotic native.

Ideas of *jihād* such as that of ᶜAbd al-Qādir also mirror European understandings of the world in spatial terms, for in contrast to other Muslim responses to the invasion, which stressed a duty of care either to local communities of Muslims or to the *umma* more generally, the Emir's *jihād* wrestled with the French over control of a national space, which was arguably as revolutionary as the new forms of punitive and genocidal violence brought by the French to Algeria. This is evidently not to say that all forms of modern *jihād* are necessarily national, nor that they always provide tacit support to the military logics of foreign invaders (though many do), for conceptions and enactions of *jihād* change over time. Nonetheless, we ought to think more about the qualities of *jihād* that were constitutive in the building of new forms of space and world-building which we currently impute wholly to new European arrivals in Muslim lands in the nineteenth century.

Such debates matter, of course, precisely because they are not simply historical, but because they also connect to the structuring of the world which continues to our present. Resistance to the autocratic militarised national state in twenty-first century Algeria, whose rulers are the heirs to Bugeaud and the French generals of the 1830s, has been bloodily concentrated on *jihādī* logics which themselves are the heirs of the ideas of ᶜAbd al-Qādir; yet quite different forms of resistance grounded in critiques of injustice, emigration and steadfastness also merit being described in ways which stress the richness of their historical traditions in Algeria and their groundings in Islam.

The difference of such traditions can be conceptualised as being both spatial and temporal: spatial in the sense that they prioritise the local and the people found there; temporal in the sense that they operate with disrupted and disruptive notions of history, in which things change in ways which are both continuous and sometimes discontinuous (though the past is rarely appealed to as a resource, as routinely tends to be the case in *jihādī* writing). Cultures of *jihād*, by contrast, tend to operate with rigid spatial and temporal *schemae*, in which the difference of the local is subsumed within transnational notions of Islamic space (hence ᶜAbd al-Qādir's appeals to scholars in Egypt, Morocco and Mecca), and a flattened understanding of time, in which morality can be judged and indexed against Muslim norms. Brower is right that cultures of *jihād* ought to be historicised, but the reality of the practice of *jihād* is that many of its advocates tend to imagine it to be the expression of an eternal form of truth and duty.

As Tyan writes of *jihād* in the *Encyclopaedia of Islam*: 'The notion stems from the fundamental principle of the universality of Islam: This religion, along with the temporal power which it implies, ought to embrace to whole universe, if necessary by force.'[97] Faced by the radical difference of the world in the early nineteenth century, where Muslims now faced a new form of power which sought 'to embrace the whole universe, if necessary by force', traditional conceptions of *jihād* were therefore peculiarly unworldly and unproductive as modes of defending the lives of Muslim subjects. While *jihād* could be conceived of as a mode of temporal resistance which rejected the historical, civilisational logic of European invaders, Islamic cultures also provided many other forms of temporalities, which were deployed, by groups such as the Berbers, as distinct forms of resistance and protection. In doing so, such groups focused on the local rather than the universal or the transnational, enacting a form of 'greater *jihād*', which had at its core a notion that the locus of the Islamic world could be located in the groups of people found within it, whose lives merited protection from the unique and new forms of threat which imperilled the lives of these children, women and men.[98]

As has been seen in the case of ᶜAbd al-Qādir, the norms of *jihād* run up against the facts of the world just as much as they did for Ahmed Bey or Hamdan Khodja, so the scholarly error made in many studies of *jihād* is to imagine that the outward desire to connect behaviour to eternal norms necessarily imbues certain behaviours with unusual ethical force. Instead, studies of *jihād* ought to pay more attention to the intricate relationship between ideas and actions in encounters such as those found in early colonial Algeria.

97. Tyan, 'Djihād', *EI2*.
98. The historical significance of these battles over space and time continues to this day, as we see in work such as Wael Hallaq's *The Impossible State* (New York, 2012). As Lama Abu Lodeh's review observes – *International Journal of Middle East Studies* 46.1 (2014), 216–18 – contemporary critiques of the Western imposition of forms of modern statehood in the Islamic world often lead thinkers such as Hallaq to valorise the eternal, aspirational qualities of an 'impossible' normative Muslim 'state', when perhaps de-universalised understandings of Muslim history and community, drawn from the world rather than the text, might offer other forms of resources which we could draw from the histories of Muslims.

PART II

. . .

RESISTANCE AND COLONIALISM: SOUTH ASIAN CONTEXTS

CHAPTER

4

FROM CLIENT TO REBEL? THE PHILOSOPHER FAŻL-I ḤAQQ KHAYRĀBĀDĪ, HIS *RISĀLA GHADARĪYA* AND THE EVENTS OF 1857

*Sajjad Rizvi**

The revolts of 1857 in North India and the various '*jihād*' movements against the onset of British colonial rule, the transition from informal to formal empire, have become the focus of some recent scholarly attention, not least following the publication of William Dalrymple's *The Last Mughal* and Ayesha Jalal's *Partisans of Allah: Jihad in South Asia.* At the heart of the conflict was the most intense violence, not just the discursive othering of the opponent, but the most brutal subjection, resisting further British encroachment and then the most intense repression, which established a tone for the advent of the imperium. One of the most interesting questions on the process and events concerns less the question of religious motivation or the role of religious identity in mobilisation and activity (as few would deny the role of communal identity and belonging in political mobilisation, even as part of a complex matrix of reasons for action), but rather the role and attitude of the old Mughal service élites to the shifting realities of power politics in North India. Many of the contemporary accounts suggest that the upheavals of 1857 and the establishment of formal British Empire constitutes a 'world turned upside down', in which power relationships, legitimacy and self-justifications needed to be rethought and renegotiated. To interrogate the question of how this old élite, which emerged mostly from the culture of the *qaṣbas* of Avadh and Rohilkhand and was formed by the pedagogical and moral modes of the curriculum that is called the *dars-i niẓāmī*, adapted to British power, I want to consider the case of the philosopher–jurist–theologian–'rebel' Fażl-i

* University of Exeter

Ḥaqq (Faḍl) Khayrābādī (d. 1861).[1] His family had served the Mughals and the British in various administrative positions, but it seems that in the turmoil and developments of 1857, Khayrābādī sided with the rebels and may have issued a fatwa of *jihād*, rallying the Mughal cause. Later, on the Andaman penal colony he wrote about his role and justification for the revolt in a famous tract known as the *Risāla-yi ghadariyya*, one of the more learned accounts of the events that was smuggled off the islands and only fully made its appearance in the public sphere during the significant epoch of the emergence of independence in South Asia. His role seems to have won him condemnation to exile, where he died in 1861. What role did he play, if any, in the violence and in construction of the justification for a violent response to the British?

However, other accounts of the events in Delhi suggest a rather more reluctant rebel. That of an élite servant who was not quite trusted by more activist and radical voices, a person concerned about violating the contracts and ties of obedience and obligation that define service, coming as he did from a scholarly class which had already embraced the exigencies of British rule. The account does not mention a fatwa, nor does the religiously focused critique of the British say anything of his previous service. The conservatism of his class background, as well as his theological training in the Sunni Ḥanafī Māturīdī tradition, which tended to distrust resistance theories, do not exactly constitute the necessary potential for a rebel to be.[2]

Locating Khayrābādī within the context of various accounts of 1857, I examine his apology and arguments for revolt, and consider whether his role, contrasted not least with his close friends – the famed Urdu poets Ghālib and Shēfta – portray the predicaments of his class of administrators and intellectuals, demonstrating, to an extent, the culmination and defeat of the intellectual enterprise of what some scholars have termed the 'Delhi renaissance', a cultural and intellectual flourishing of those associated with the hybrid Delhi College.[3]

1. I am grateful to the discussants at the conference for their engagement. I would also like to thank Margrit Pernau and Aparna Vaidik for their close reading and valuable comments. Any stubborn mistakes and outlandish claims that may persist are unequivocally my responsibility. For a useful study of this *qaṣba* culture, albeit from a slightly later period, see Mushirul Hasan, *From Pluralism to Separatism: Qasbas in Colonial Awadh* (New Delhi, 2004).
2. More generally on quietism and the law of rebellion in Sunni developed traditions, see Khaled Abou El Fadl, *Rebellion and Violence in Islamic Law* (Cambridge, 2001), pp. 234–94.
3. The term seems to have been coined by C. F. Andrews in his study *Zaka Ullah of Delhi* (Cambridge, 1929), p. 45 – I owe this reference to Margrit Pernau. It was popularised in Gail Minault, 'Sayyid Ahmad Dehlavi and the Delhi Renaissance', in *Delhi Through the*

Were these intellectuals bright and cultured but ineffective and unaccustomed to the subjective violence of resistance and warfare, as lampooned so deliciously by Munshī Prēmchand (in his short story *Shaṭranj kē khilāṛī*, filmed as the *Chess Players*)?[4] Or did they understand the objectivity and practice of violence and the need to act and perform, as well as think, compose and teach?

On 29 January 2012, marking the 150th anniversary of his execution, the Muslim Students' Organisation organised a seminar in honour of 'the great patriot and freedom fighter' Fażl-i Ḥaqq Khayrābādī at Ghulam Momin College in Bhiwandi, near Mumbai.[5] A number of Muslim intellectuals and academics, including Dr Khwaja Ekram of Jawaharlal Nehru University, addressed the audience, and celebrated Khayrābādī for being the first one to issue a fatwa of *jihād*, symbolically from the Jama Masjid in Delhi, against the British in 1857 and for his efforts in the anti-colonial struggle. Other speakers stressed his role as a major scholar whose example was worth emulating. A number of other Muslim organisations and national media outlets did the same in the months that preceded and followed, including the leading national Muslim university Jamia Millia Islamia in Delhi on 18 September 2011.[6] Across the border in Pakistan, a number of events were also organised to celebrate him as a 'martyr in the cause of freedom' (*shahīd-i āzādī*), but even as a martyr, rather anachronistically, for the cause of Pakistan, fitting within a nationalist historiography that sees a linear progression from Muslims engaged in the revolt in 1857 to partition and the creation of Pakistan as a Muslim state in 1947.[7] Khayrābādī thus became an

Ages: Essays in Urban History, Culture and Society, ed. R. E. Fryekenberg (New York, 1986), pp. 289–98.

4. This short story was one of the works that Prēmchand (d. 1936) wrote in both Hindi and Urdu versions and first appeared in 1924, just as one phase of the nationalist struggle for independence failed. The film was made by Satyajit Ray (d. 1992) in 1977 as another struggle for democracy failed with Indira Gandhi's declaration of the emergency that culminated in that year.
5. 'Allama Fazle Haq Khairabadi Seminar in Bhiwandi Mumbai by MSO of India': http://sunninews.wordpress.com/2012/01/31/allama-fazle-haq-khairabadi-seminar-in-bhiwandi-mumbai-by-mso-of-india.
6. http://noorifoundation.com/index.php?option=com_content&view=article&id=131:allama-fazle-haq-convention-at-jamia-millia-islamia-university-new-delhi&catid=11:news-flashes. For accessed dates of online resources, see the Bibliography and the accompanying note, p. 366.
7. http://www.youtube.com/watch?v=tnvfCGm8g_c is a good example of this. The best and most recent revisionist account of the creation of Pakistan which stresses the political and secular nationalism of the movement in the name of a religious community and even dares to compare it to the creation of the other famous secular state for a religious community established in the middle of the twentieth century – Israel – is Faisal Devji, *Muslim Zion:*

unambiguous *jihādī*, whose service to the Mughals and to the British was easily forgotten in the presentist desire to discover continuity in the anti-imperialist struggle of the *ᶜulamāᵓ*, common especially among Deobandis in present-day South Asia.[8] As *qāᵓid-i inqilāb* or *qāᵓid-i jang-i āzādī* (Leader of the Revolution or Leader of the War of Independence), his role prefigures that of Jinnah as liberator of the Muslim nation; the modern barrister's role as *qāᵓid-i aᶜẓam* (the Great Leader) acts as a culmination in a Whiggish conception of the emergence of a Muslim nation-state.[9] Instrumentalising figures of the past for present concerns of identity is very much a feature of nationalist agendas; history is, thus, the collective repository of people's cultural memory and not just a series of inky scrawls on paper.[10] In the Indian context, the debate became centred on the contribution of Muslims to the cause of Indian nationalism: at a seminar in Jubilee Hall in Hyderabad in India, graced by a number of politicians on 29 May 2011, speakers called upon the Union government to recognise and celebrate the role of Muslims in the struggle for independence.[11] In an earlier stage of nationalist fervour, during the Khilafat Movement, Fażl-i Ḥaqq remained an inspiration for learned Muslim activists struggling against the British, such as the Deobandis

Pakistan as a Political Idea (London, 2013), a book that would appall those present at the rally.

8. Cf. Muhammad Qasim Zaman, *The Ulama in Contemporary Islam: Custodians of Change* (Princeton, 2002), pp. 11–14, 21–59; Iqbal Husain, *Religion and Ideology of the Rebels of 1857* (Delhi, 2013). A good example of a triumphalist Pakistani nationalist account is Syed Moinul Haq, *The Great Revolution of 1857* (Karachi, 1968), in which it is the Muslim resistance of the old élites sparked by the zeal of the Shah Walīullāh movement that led the surge for independence; cf. Muḥammad Saᶜīdur-Raḥmān ᶜAlawī (ed.), *ᶜAllāma Fażl-i Ḥaqq Khayrābādī aur jihād-i āzādī* (Lahore, 1987).
9. See the short pamphlet published in India: Yāsīn Akhtar Miṣbāḥī, *Qāᵓid-i inqilāb: ᶜAllāma Fażl-i Ḥaqq Khayrābādī* (Maleagaon, n. d.). For an excellent revisionist – or perhaps one should say 'Cambridge school' – correction to this teleological and rather Islamised version of Jinnah as father of the nation, see Ayesha Jalal, *The Sole Spokesman: Jinnah, the Muslim League, and the Demand for Pakistan* (Cambridge, 1985).
10. For some useful studies of how history is invoked and used in contemporary South Asia, see Daud Ali (ed.), *Invoking the Past: The Uses of History in South Asia* (Delhi, 1999); Raziuddin Aquil and Partha Chatterjee (eds), *History in the Vernacular* (Delhi, 2008); Prachi Deshpande, *Creative Pasts: Historical Memory and Identity in Western India, 1700–1960* (New York, 2007); Vinay Lal, *The History of History: Politics and Scholarship in Modern India* (Delhi, 2003); Romila Thapar, *Somnatha: The Many Voices of a History* (New Delhi, 2004); Romila Thapar, *The Future of the Indian Past* (New Delhi, 2004).
11. http://www.siasat.com/english/news/due-recognition-demanded-muslim-freedom-fighters'-role.

ᶜUbaydullāh Sindhī (d. 1944) and ᶜAbd al-Raḥīm Popalzai (d. 1944).[12] In this sense, he ushered in a nationalist pantheon of religious figures and intellectuals.

William Dalrymple's book *The Last Mughal* and debates in India on the 150th anniversary of 1857 have raised the question of religious motivation in the revolt. Dalrymple draws a parallel between the world of 1857 and today: Muslims in South Asia have a choice between two paths – a tolerant Sufism, as espoused by the benign Bahādur Shāh Ẓafar (d. 1862) who opposed all language of *jihād* and was a reluctant rebel, and the Wahhābī-inspired Jihadism of those who later founded the 'Wahhābī-like' Deoband madrasa.[13] Nowhere does one find a more nuanced understanding of how the British administration in India objectified the religiously rebellious other as 'Wahhābī', a process that was then adopted by Muslim élites as well.[14] Regardless of whether the theology of the Wahhābī movement concurred with the puritanical, literalist and reformist programme of Ibn ᶜAbd al-Wahhāb (d. 1792), the simple conflation of the two in effect alienated the rebels in India as harbingers of a foreign and 'radical' Islam that was not authentically of India – the land of syncreticism, peace and, later, non-violence.[15] Dalrymple also repeats the platitude about the need to learn from history if we are not destined to relive its mistakes.[16] It is difficult to see how the language of *jihād* raised in Delhi in 1857 has a direct connection with the present beyond the simple coincidence of a word – in fact, Asma Afsaruddin's recent work suggests that we need to be far more careful about the term and the reality that corresponds not least when simplistically projecting contemporary desires onto a classical text in order to search for justifications and explanations.[17] Contexts shift and change, even if the language of anti-imperialism seeks to

12. Muhammad Qasim Zaman, *Modern Islamic Thought in a Radical Age: Religious Authority and Internal Criticism* (Cambridge, 2012), pp. 223–34.
13. William Dalrymple, *The Last Mughal* (London, 2006), pp. 485–6. For a work that unequivocally connects modern Jihadism to the nineteenth-century Wahhābī movement against British rule in India, see Charles Allen, *God's Terrorists: The Wahhabi Cult and the Hidden Roots of Modern Jihad* (London, 2006), which attempts to discern 'patterns of behaviour, successes and failures from which lessons might be drawn'.
14. For some indicators on this, see Margrit Pernau, *Ashraf into Middle Classes: Muslims in Nineteenth-Century Delhi* (New Delhi, 2013), pp. 278–83, and Seema Alavi, *Muslim Cosmopolitanism in the Age of Empire* (Cambridge, MA, 2015), pp. 273–4, 285–6.
15. Cf. Asim Roy, *Islam in History and Politics: Perspectives from South Asia* (New Delhi, 2008).
16. For a useful review, see David Washbrook, 'Popular History Versus Academic History', in *Revisiting 1857: Myth, Memory, History*, eds S. Gooptu and B. Majumdar (Delhi, 2007), pp. 3–11.
17. Asma Afsaruddin, *Striving in the Path of God: Jihad and Martyrdom in Islamic Thought* (New York, 2013).

bolster its authenticity by recourse to excavating precursors in the past. Even if the motivations of 1857 might not have been religious, the responses in some cases were: modernists embraced British rule and the need for Islam to accommodate new learning, technology and culture, as exemplified in Sayyid Aḥmad Khān (d. 1898) and his Aligarh circle and articulated in the epic poem *Musaddas madd u jazr-i Islām* of Ḥālī (d. 1914); scripturalists insisted, on the other hand, upon a strict return to the faith of the Deoband movement; whilst others still reverted to a neo-traditionalist affirmation of popular religion associated with Aḥmad Riżā (Riḍā) Khān Barēlvī (d. 1921).[18] Most academic accounts of 1857 do not focus on religious motivation – even the seeming trigger of the fat in the cartridges is not stressed as a pivotal event; there is little evidence that the sepoys were primarily outraged by being commanded to perform acts that violated their religious and caste taboos.[19] But fundamentally, it seems that interpretations of 1857 have gone full circle, starting with religion, moving onto national fervour, then economic realities and finally returning to religion, because of the return of that category to our explanatory framework in the present.[20] Contemporary accounts, the wish to read indigenous sources, to subalternise one's reading of history in the search for new voices and perspectives, suggest that religion is meaningful, but also highly manipulative and open to manipulation. The events of 1857 were neither simply a war of independence nor a *jihād*. It was not the last hurrah of the old Indian (Mughal related) élites, nor a series of peasant or class struggles.[21] What one can see in the series of incidents and events that led to the

18. David Lelyveld, *Aligarh's First Generation: Muslim Solidarity in British India* (Princeton, 1978); *Hali's Musaddas: The Flow and Ebb of Islam*, trans. Christopher Shackle and Javed Majeed (Delhi, 1997); Barbara Metcalf, *Islamic Revival in British India: Deoband, 1860–1900* (Princeton, 1982); Usha Sanyal, *Devotional Islam and Politics in British India: Ahmad Riza Khan Barelwi and his Movement, 1870–1920*, new edn (New Delhi, 2010).
19. A useful summary of that literature and the ways in which 1857 is memorialised was the collection of articles published in 2007 in the leading journal *Economic and Political Weekly* – reprinted as *1857 Essays from the Economic and Political Weekly* (Hyderabad, 2008). For another study that focuses on 1857, see Soofia Siddique, 'Remembering the Revolt of 1857: Contrapuntal Formations in Indian Literature and History' (unpublished PhD dissertation, School of Oriental and African Studies, University of London, 2012) – I am grateful to Margrit Pernau for alerting me to this work. On the memorialisation of 1857 and some of the events and texts that I discuss in this article, see Pernau, *Ashraf into Middle Classes*, pp. 209–37.
20. John Mickelthwait and Adrian Woolbridge, *God is Back: How the Global Rise of Faith is Changing the World* (London, 2009); Mark Lilla, *The Stillborn God: Religion, Politics, and the Modern West* (New York, 2008); cf. Alister Chapman et al. (eds), *Seeing Things their Way: Intellectual History and the Return of Religion* (Notre Dame, 2009).
21. Cf. Biswamoy Pati (ed.), *The Great Rebellion of 1857 in India: Exploring Transgressions,*

declaration of formal British Empire is all and every one of these phenomena. Our present-mindedness thus acts both as an obstacle, as well as a meaningful prism. History excavates the cultural memory of communities, but also exemplifies the concerns and political and intellectual foci of the present. At the heart of these modern anxieties lies the coupled 'problematic' of religion and violence, even in the face of polemics back and forth that wish to decouple them or to insist on the essential confluence of the two.[22] It has become a commonplace to identify religion with violence; as the philosopher Hent de Vries puts it:

> Violence, in both the widest possible and the most elementary senses of the word, entails any cause, any justified or illegitimate force, that is exerted – physically or otherwise – by one thing (event or instance, group or person, and perhaps, word and object) upon another. Violence thus defined finds its prime model – its source, force and counterforce – in key elements of the tradition called the religious. It can be seen as the very element of religion.[23]

Slavoj Žižek's wonderful polemic on violence urges us to take the self-reflection a further step. He distinguishes between 'subjective' violence – an exertion of one upon the other that is considered to be a violation, a perturbation, of the normal state of affairs, such as one man stabbing another – and objective violence that is inherent in normality, structures of power and convention.[24] The objective is constituted both by our language and our economic and political systems, and of particular concern is ideological violence. Žižek writes:

> We live in a society where a kind of Hegelian speculative identity of opposites exists. Certain features, attitudes and norms of life are no longer perceived as ideologically marked. They appear to be neutral, non-ideological, natural,

Contests, and Diversities (London, 2010); Sabyasachi Bhattacharya (ed.), *Rethinking 1857* (New Delhi, 2007). The 150th anniversary of 1857 led to a huge memorial literature, a key feature of which has been the desire to allow the texts to speak for themselves and to provide a large set of contexts for making sense of the events – regional, national and international. For the former, see Pankaj Rag, *1857: The Oral Tradition* (Delhi, 2010), and for the latter, Crispin Bates et al. (eds), *Mutiny at the Margins*, 7 vols, (New Delhi/London, 2013).

22. A thoughtful – and well-evidenced and argued – case for the decoupling is William Cavanaugh, *The Myth of Religious Violence* (New York, 2009).
23. Hent de Vries, *Religion and Violence: Philosophical Perspectives from Kant to Derrida* (Baltimore, 2002), p. 1. I set aside for the moment the essential and ritualistic argument of René Girard, *Violence and the Sacred*, trans. J. Gregory (Baltimore, 1977).
24. Slavoj Žižek, *Violence* (London, 2009), pp. 1–2.

> common sense. We designate as ideology that which stands out from this background: extreme religious zeal or dedication to a particular political orientation. The Hegelian point here would be that it is precisely the neutralisation of some features into a spontaneously accepted background that marks out ideology at its purest and at its most effective. This is the dialectical 'coincidence of opposites': the actualisation of a notion or an ideology at its purest coincides with, or more precisely, appears as its opposite, as non-ideology. *Mutatis mutandis*, the same holds for violence. Social-symbolic violence at its purest appears as its opposite, as the spontaneity of the milieu in which we dwell, of the air we breathe.[25]

Violence may therefore lie in our very conceptual frameworks, our assumptions about citizenship and mutuality, in tolerance and liberalism, in power and coercion. Tolerant reason as articulated in liberal outrage against the atrocities of the rebels is one such example. However, it merely suffices to recognise that violence is not just the illegitimate actions and words of the other, but also embedded in the self. The violence of 1857 extended beyond the fighting, the killing and the brutality of the combatants: it extended to discourses and the developing institutions and structures of imperial power in Delhi.

Given the present ambiguities of violence and its legitimation in South Asia, and the wider question of *jihād* as an instrument of struggle, it is timely to reconsider the life of Fażl-i Ḥaqq Khāyrābādī between *jihād* against the British and the concerns of an élite member of the waning Mughal service class. The anxiety that the ambiguity of the acts of a hero raise for us should not detract from a consideration of how one justifies violence – and a fatwa of *jihād* is a discursive form of violence that leads to subjective violence.

Muḥammad Fażl-i Ḥaqq was born in Khayrābād, a *qaṣba* of Avadh in Sitapur district near Lucknow, in 1212/1797 into a family of scholars originating from Iran who claimed descent from the second caliph (hence, Fārūqī).[26] He grew up in Delhi, and studied rational disciplines (in particular, philosophy – *ḥikma*) with his father Fażl-i Imām (d. 1244/1828), who was the East India Company's first *ṣadr al-ṣudūr* in Delhi.[27] He also audited *ḥadīth* with Shāh ᶜAbd al-ᶜAzīz

25. Žižek, *Violence*, p. 31.
26. Sayyid Aḥmad Khān, *Āthār al-ṣanādīd*, ed. Khalīq Anjum (Delhi, 2003), II, pp. 88–107; Raḥmān ᶜAlī, *Tadhkira-yi ᶜulamāʾ-yi Hind (Tuḥfat al-fuḍalāʾ fī tarājim al-kumalāʾ)*, ed. Yūsuf Bēg Bābāpūr (Qum, 2012), p. 207; Intiẓāmullāh Shahābī, *Mawlānā Fażl-i Ḥāqq aur ᶜAbd al-Ḥaqq Khayrābādī* (Badaun, n. d.), pp. 3–11. The best and most complete account of his life (not devoid of hagiography) is Salmā Sayhūl, *ᶜAllāma Fażl-i Ḥaqq Khayrābādī* (Lahore, 2001).
27. Sayhūl, *Fażl-i Ḥaqq*, p. 35, suggests that his father entered the service of the East India

(d. 1239/1824), the leading figure of the Madrasa-yi Raḥīmiyya and son of Shāh Walīullāh (d. 1176/1762); he was famous as the first person on the cusp of empire to declare India to be *dār al-ḥarb*, which had clear implications for how best to engage with the new British presence (with hostility and violent resistance) and whether the legitimacy of a series of normative Muslim legal practices could be justified.[28] The hagiographies suggest that he had completed his studies by the age of thirteen in 1810; it is a common scholarly trope to emphasise the precocious nature of his learning.[29] He entered the service of the East India Company like his father in 1816, and became the *sar-rishta-dār* serving the British resident at Delhi as a liaising magistrate (and developing a friendship with the future King Abū Ẓafar). Khayrābādī – or, in particular, his father's house – was a pivot of the intellectual circles of the Delhi renaissance that included poets and scholars such as Ṣadr al-Dīn Khān 'Āzurda' (d. 1868, who had studied with his father), Imām-Bakhsh 'Ṣehbāʾī' (d. 1857), Nawāb Muṣṭafā Khān 'Shēfta' (d. 1869), who was also an important patron at his estate in Jahangirabad, Asadullāh Khān 'Ghālib' (d. 1869) and Muʾmin Khān 'Muʾmin' (d. 1851).[30] It was with the latter that he

Company in 1800 as a mufti and rose up the ranks to *ṣadr al-ṣudūr*; cf. Sayyid ᶜAbd al-Ḥayy Ḥasanī, *Nuzhat al-khawāṭir wa-bahjat al-maṣāmiᶜ wa-l-manāẓir* (Rae Bareli, 1991), VII, p. 374; Raḥmān ᶜAlī, *Tadhkira-yi ᶜulamāʾ-yi Hind*, pp. 203–4; Khān, *Āthār al-ṣanādīd*, II, pp. 87–8.

28. On Shāh ᶜAbd al-ᶜAzīz, see Raḥmān ᶜAlī, *Tadhkira-yi ᶜulamāʾ-yi Hind*, pp. 153–4; for an albeit rather critical account, see Saiyid Athar Abbas Rizvi, *Shāh ᶜAbd al-ᶜAzīz: Puritanism, Sectarian Polemics and Jihād* (Canberra, 1982), especially p. 96 on the link with Fażl-i Ḥaqq. The fatwa was, of course, somewhat more nuanced and recognised economic exigencies and the politics of the period; for a translation of it and a useful discussion, see Mahmood Ahmad Ghazi, *Islamic Renaissance in South Asia 1707–1867: The Role of Shah Wali Allah and his Successors* (Islamabad, 2002), pp. 172–6. For the original text of the fatwa, see Shāh ᶜAbd al-ᶜAzīz, *Fatāwā ᶜazīziyya* (Delhi, n. d.), I, p. 17.
29. The court records that Fażl-i Imām requested leave in that year to attend a wedding in his home town possibly of one of his sons – see Margrit Pernau and Yunus Jaffrey (eds), *Information and the Public Sphere: Persian Newsletters from Mughal India* (New Delhi, 2009), p. 77 for the date of 23 June 1810.
30. Natalia Prigarina, *Ghalib* (Karachi, 2000), p. 119; Amar Farooqui, *Zafar and the Raj: Anglo-Mughal Delhi c. 1800–1850* (New Delhi, 2013), pp. 23–6. A number of these figures played a role in 1857 – see Intiẓāmullāh Shahābī, *Ghadar kē chand ᶜulamāʾ* (Delhi, 1979), pp. 4–57 (on Ṣehbāʾī, Khayrābādī, Āzurda, Shēfta); ᶜAbd al-Raḥmān 'Parvāz' Iṣlāḥī, *Muftī Ṣadr al-Dīn Āzurda: ḥayāt, shakhṣiyyat, ᶜilmī aur adabī kārnāmē* (New Delhi, 1977), pp. 16–20, 59–66; Khwāja Muḥammad Ḥāmid, *Imām-Bakhsh Ṣehbāʾī* (Lucknow, 1982); ᶜAlī Sardār Jaᶜfarī, *Nawāb Muḥammad Muṣṭafā Khān 'Shēfta'* (Lahore, 1999); Shīma Majīd, *Shēfta: ik muṭālaᶜa* (Karachi, 2005); Ikrām Barēlvī, *Ḥakīm Muʾmin Khān 'Muʾmin': shakhṣiyyat aur shāᶜirī* (Karachi, 2003); Tawqīr Aḥmad Khān, *Muʾmin Khān 'Muʾmin'* (Delhi, 2007); Khān, *Āthār al-ṣanādīd*, II, pp. 55–73 (Āzurda),

would often play chess. It was also through these figures that his circle intersected with key scholarly elites involved in the Delhi College's new experiments mixing traditional and modern learning – Ṣehbāʾī taught Persian there from 1842 on Āzurda's recommendation, and Ghālib was offered a post.[31] Despite some of them getting caught up in the revolt in 1857, they all had, at times, either posts or pensions with the informal British Empire. In this sense, Fażl-i Ḥaqq's complicated relationship with the British was indicative of his wider circle.

Even while acting as a magistrate, he continued to teach students, and it was in that role that people came to him to complain about the 'Wahhābī' theology of Shāh Ismāᶜīl (d. 1831) and urged him to respond.[32] During the Wahhābī movement and *jihād* of Shāh Ismāᶜīl, he opposed him on theological grounds, condemning the *Taqwiyyat al-īmān* (Strengthening the Faith), as well as his views on the possibility of God creating another seal of the prophets (the issue of *imkān al-naẓīr*), and even issued a fatwa against him in 1825, *Taḥqīq al-fatwā fī ibṭāl al-taghwā* – arguments that were rooted in his training in the rational disciplines of the *dars-i niẓāmī*.[33] At the heart of the controversy was the centrality of the ontological status of the Prophet and the devotion that most Muslims felt to him; in that sense, the Wahhābīs, in the name of a return to pristine faith, signalled a radical discontinuity with Muslim traditions, while the learned classes like Fażl-i Ḥaqq defended not only their scholastic interest, but also the popular piety of the masses. That his position (and his actions) in effect also defended the British presence demonstrates how British policy often drew upon a reinforcement of traditional religion in informal empire. Theological and political controversy in this sense coalesced. It was these rather loyalist views which led to the cooling

175–87 (Ṣehbāʾī), 190–201 (Muʾmin); Bashīr al-Dīn Aḥmad, *Wāqiᶜāt-i dār al-ḥukūmat-i Dihlī* (Delhi, 1990), II, pp. 423–4 (Ṣehbāʾī), 424–9 (Muʾmin), 430–6 (Shēfta).

31. Margrit Pernau (ed.), *The Delhi College: Traditional Elites, the Colonial State, and Education before 1857* (New Delhi, 2006); Mawlawī ᶜAbd al-Ḥaqq, *Marḥūm Dillī kālij* (Delhi, 1989); Iṣlāḥī, *Āzurda*, pp. 33–8.
32. On Shāh Ismāᶜīl, see Khān, *Āthār al–ṣanādīd*, II, pp. 80–4; Shāh Ismāᶜīl responded to the critique in a short treatise later known as *Yak-rūzī*.
33. Fażl-i Ḥaqq Khayrābādī, *Taḥqīq al-fatwā fī ibṭāl al-taghwā yā shafāᶜat-i Muḥammad*, with Urdu translation of Muḥammad ᶜAbd al-Ḥakīm Qādirī (Lahore, 2000), and Fażl-i Ḥaqq Khayrābādī, *Imtināᶜ al-naẓīr* (Lahore, 2000). This encounter has become the centre of modern Deobandī–Barēlvī polemics in Pakistan – see, for example, in his favour, Rāja Ghulām Muḥammad, *Imtiyāz-i ḥaqq: Fażl-i Ḥaqq Khayrābādī aur Ismāᶜīl Dihlavī kē siyāsī kirdār kā taqābulī jāʾiza* (Lahore, 1979). For a discussion of the *imtināᶜ al-naẓīr* issue, see Sayhūl, *Fażl-i Ḥaqq*, pp. 84–93; Ayesha Jalal, *Partisans of Allah: Jihad in South Asia* (Cambridge, MA, 2008), pp. 80–1; Barbara Metcalf, *Islamic Revival in British India: Deoband, 1860–1900* (Princeton, 1982), pp. 65–6; Sanyal, *Devotional Islam and Politics*, pp. 249–64; SherAli Tareen, *Defending Muḥammad in Modernity* (Notre Dame, 2020).

of relations and outright polemics with Muʾmin, who supported the theological and political position of Shāh Ismāʿīl, as well as disagreements with Ghālib.[34] He encouraged his friend Ghālib to write a poem criticising the Wahhābī position that the creation of another final prophet was not impossible – Khayrābādī took the view that the creation of another Muḥammad was as impossible as God's creating his peer or another deity or, indeed, as God lying. In doing so, he drew upon his training in theology and especially in logic; the question of whether God could send another seal of the prophets was not only to become of critical political and religious significance in North India with the Aḥmadī movement, but rather, in theological terms the hypothetical was reminiscent of the classical debate on whether God could lie.[35] Ḥālī records the disagreement between Ghālib and Khayrābādī on the issue of the Wahhābīs and their theology.[36] Khayrābādī's request of Ghālib to write a poem attacking the views of Shāh Ismāʿīl rather backfired; he was not too impressed when the result, while aesthetically pleasing, held out the possibility of a possible world in which another Prophet – and a final one at that – might be created. While it is unlikely Ghālib held the theological views of the Wahhābīs – his own attachment to Shīʿism was well known, despite Ḥālī's protestations – it does signal his ability in philosophy and the crafting of metaphysics in poetry.[37] It was as if the hypothetical modal logic of Khayrābādī – for which he was famed – clashed with a more speculative possible worlds non-binary (perhaps Buddhist influenced?) logic of Ghālib, even if we might hesitate before ascribing to the poet philosophical positions for which conventions at the time did not arise.[38]

34. Ralph Russell and Khurshidul Islam, *Ghalib: Life and Letters* (New Delhi, 1994), p. 43; Prigarina, *Ghalib*, pp. 122–3; Jalal, *Partisans of Allah*, p. 108; Khān, *Muʾmin*, pp. 21–2, 34–5; Barēlvī, *Muʾmin*, p. 30. Muʾmin was already associated with the Shāh Walīullāh circle and actually named by Shāh ʿAbd al-ʿAzīz – see Barēlvī, *Muʾmin*, p. 18.
35. For a useful background discussion on God and lies in classical Islamic theology, see Sophia Vasalou, 'Equal Before the Law: The Evilness of Human and Divine Lies in ʿAbd al-Jabbār's Rational Ethics', *Arabic Sciences and Philosophy* 13.2 (2003), 243–68. Another work that backgrounds the significance of the *imkān al-naẓīr* issue is Marion Katz, *The Birth of the Prophet Muḥammad: Devotional Piety in Sunni Islam* (London, 2007).
36. Alṭāf Ḥusayn Ḥālī, *Yādgār-i Ghālib* (Kanpur, 1898), pp. 79–82; Russell and Islam, *Ghalib*, p. 33.
37. This is the sixth *mathnawī* of his Persian collection, and plays on the ambiguities of the language.
38. One startling speculation for why Ghālib might have eschewed a binary logic due to the influence of Buddhist logic upon him is articulated by Gopi Chand Narang, *Ghālib: maʿnī-āfirīnī, jadaliyyātī waḍaʿ, shunyatā aur shiʿriyyāt* (Lahore, 2013), pp. 77–84. My theoretical approach to texts remained committed to a form of soft conventionalism, modifying Skinner.

Neither Khayrābādī's family background (his father and uncle, as well as his two brothers, were in British service) nor his actions in this early period suggested a rebel in the making.[39] Yet we have documents of him complaining about the arrogance and demands of his British employers in 1816 and 1818, as well as a petition that he wrote to Akbār Shāh II in 1827 complaining of the economic decline of the realm and the influence of the British in destroying local commerce, a theme to which he returned in his later reflection upon the revolt of 1857.[40] British employment in Delhi does, however, seem to have afforded Khayrābādī the time to teach and write. It was in this period that he made his name as a philosopher and theologian, penning *marginalia* on various theological works, an influential *marginalia* on *al-Ufuq al-mubīn* of Mīr Dāmād (d. 1631) and another one on the metaphysics of *al-Shifā*ʾ of Ibn Sīnā (d. 1037) – a key text of the higher philosophical curriculum.[41] His pivotal role in the intellectual history of Islamic philosophical traditions in North India awaits a study. These works later became the central curricular texts of a rational training in the *dars-i niẓāmī* in decline in the colonial period, as attested to by their many printings and manuscripts copies in scholarly collections around South Asia.[42] A widely sought figure, his training and expertise in philosophy was perhaps peerless in his time.

39. Muḥammad Ayyūb Qādrī, 'Mawlānā Fażl-i Ḥaqq Khayrābādī: dawr-i mulāzamat', in *Mawlānā Fażl-i Ḥaqq Khayrābādī: ik taḥqīqī muṭālaʿa*, ed. Afżal (Afḍal) Ḥaqq Qarshī (Lahore, 1992), pp. 17–19.
40. Jamal Malik, 'Letters, Prison Sketches and Autobiographical Literature: The Case of Fazl-e Haq Khairabadi in the Andaman Penal Colony', *Indian Economic and Social History Review* 43 (2006), p. 85; for the petition, see Maḥmūd Aḥmad Barkātī, *Fażl-i Ḥaqq Khayrābādī aur san sattāvan* (Karachi, 1987), pp. 91–4, and also Sayhūl, *Fażl-i Ḥaqq*, pp. 385–92.
41. Asad Ahmad, 'Logic in the Khayrābādī School of India: A Preliminary Exploration', in *Law and Tradition in Classical Islamic Thought: Studies in Honor of Professor Hossein Modarressi*, eds Michael Cook et al. (Basingstoke, 2012), pp. 227–43; Asad Ahmad, 'The *Shifā*ʾ in India I', *Oriens* 40 (2012), pp. 1–24.
42. On the *dars-i niẓāmī*, see Jamal Malik, *Islamische Gelehrtenkultur in Nordindien: Entwicklungsgeschichte und Tendenzen am Beispiel von Lucknow* (Leiden, 1997), pp. 522–35; Francis Robinson, 'Ottomans-Safavids-Mughals: Shared Knowledge and Connective Systems', *Journal of Islamic Studies* 8 (1997), 152–6; Francis Robinson, *The ʿUlama of Farangi Mahall*, pp. 48–50, 248–51; Qamaruddīn, *Hindustān kī dīnī darsgāhēn* (New Delhi, 1996), pp. 345–52; on pedagogical disciplines, texts and authors, see Muftī Riżā (Riḍā) Anṣārī, *Bānī-yi dars-i niẓāmī ustād al-hind Mullā Niẓāmuddīn Muḥammad Farangī-Maḥallī* (Aligarh, 1973), pp. 257–65; Jamīl Aḥmad, *Ḥarakat al-taʾlīf bi-l-lugha al-ʿarabiyya fī al-iqlīm al-shimālī al-hindī* (Karachi, n. d.), pp. 17–22; Alṭāf al-Raḥmān Qidwāʾī, *Qiyām-i niẓām-i taʿlīm* (Lucknow, 1924); Barbara Metcalf, *Islamic Revival in British India: Deoband, 1860–1900* (Princeton, 1982), pp. 16–45; Muhammad Umar,

In 1827, his father resigned his post in favour of his student Ṣadruddīn Āzurda (d. 1868), Khayrābādī's friend, and soon after, in 1828, died. In the same year, Khayrābādī's son ᶜAbd al-Ḥaqq, the true heir of his philosophical career, was born. Benefitting from the patronage of the heir to the Mughal throne, Abū Ẓafar Bahādur (who became king in 1837), Khayrābādī continued in British service, but became embroiled in investigating corruption and gambling cases in May 1830 (which led to counter-accusations against him); with the rise of anti-British feeling (perhaps exacerbated by the Wahhābī movement and the various wars on the frontier which the Mughal elites and their princely *foederati* bankrolled in the north–east and the north–west), he resigned in 1831.[43] We can still place him in Delhi in 1832, as he was instrumental in the editing of Ghālib's first Urdu divan, a process in which he encouraged discarding two-thirds of the poetic compositions, and demonstrating the respect in which Ghālib held him in matters of aesthetics.[44] In his letters, Ghālib lamented Khayrābādī's decision to leave and put it down to Delhi being incapable of honouring its intellectuals:

> Be it known that the ineptitude of the authorities who do not know men's worth has come to the pitch where that man of unparalleled learning . . . Muhammad Fazl-i Haq has resigned and so released himself from shame and degradation. Take Maulvi Fazl-i Haq's knowledge and learning and wisdom and character and reduce them all a hundredfold; then measure this hundredth part of them against this post in the civil courts; the post would even then be less than these qualities merited . . . The day Maulvi Fazl-i Haq left Delhi I cannot describe what the people of the city felt. The heir apparent to the throne of Delhi sent for him to bid farewell. He took a shawl from his personal apparel and laid it upon his shoulders . . . What a distracted Ghalib wants of you is that you should write in shining words the news of Maulvi Fazl-i Haq's leaving Delhi and of the heir apparent's

Islam in Northern India in the Eighteenth Century (Delhi, 1993), pp. 259–305; Ḥabīb al-Raḥmān Maẓāhirī Khayrābādī, *Tadhkirat al-muṣannifīn: Dars-i niẓāmiyya aur dars-i ᶜāliyya aur tamām ᶜarabī niṣābōn mēñ shāmil jumla kutub kē muṣannifīn kā mukammal taẕkira* (n. p., n. d.); Muḥammad Ḥanīf Gangōhī, *Ẓafar al-muḥaṣṣilīn bā-aḥwāl-i muṣannifīn, yaᶜnī ḥālāt-i muṣannifīn-i dars-i niẓāmī* (Deoband, 1996); Akhtar Rāhī, *Taẕkira-yi muṣannifīn-i dars-i niẓāmī* (Lahore, 1978).

43. Pernau and Jaffrey, *Information and the Public Sphere*, pp. 244, 264, 270. The First Afghan War, for example, was implicated in the conflict in the north-west and the support for the Wahhābī cause; on this, see William Dalrymple, *The Return of a King: The Battle for Afghanistan* (London, 2013).
44. Ḥālī, *Yādgār-i Ghālib*, p. 113; Russell and Islam, *Ghalib*, p. 48; Prigarina, *Ghalib*, p. 127.

grief and of the sorrow in the hearts of the people of the city, and put it into print in *Aina-i Sikandar* and so put me in debt to your kindness.[45]

Leaving Delhi, he entered the service of the Nawab Fayż (Fayḍ) Muḥammad Khān of Jhajjar (a small principality west of Delhi), whose brother Nawab Ḥasan ᶜAlī Khān had previously requested entrance to Delhi to meet him on 2 February 1830, according to court records,[46] and then the Raja of Alwar. He was also briefly in Saharanpur, where his brother Fażl-i ᶜAẓīm was in British service (having served as William Fraser's secretary in Delhi for ten years before), and also in Tonk (on the invitation of Nawab Amīr Khān), where the interest in the intellectual disciplines, as evinced by the many manuscripts that survive in the library there today, drew him for a few days. From 1840 to 1848, he was in Rampur (teaching and acting as a magistrate) and wrote *al-Hadiya al-saᶜīdiyya fī-l-ḥikma al-ṭabīᶜiyya* as a new school-text in natural philosophy for his son, but dedicated to the Nawab Muḥammad Saᶜīd Khān (d. 1855), as well as *al-Jins al-ghālī fī sharḥ al-jawhar al-ᶜālī* on atomism and *al-Rawḍ al-mujawwad fī ḥaqīqat al-wujūd* on ontology, autographs of which still survive in the Raza Library in Rampur.[47] The *Hadiya* is a broadly Avicennan text that follows the *Physics* of *al-Shifāʾ*, but also engages in the commentary culture on the physics in the *Hidāya* of al-Abharī (d. 1263) that was central to the philosophical curriculum of the *dars-i niẓāmī*. This time allowed him to train his son, ᶜAbd al-Ḥaqq, whose association with Rampur remained. He was a close confidant (and teacher) of the Nawab Yūsuf ᶜAlī Khān (d. 1865) to whom he recommended his friend Ghālib at the beginning of 1857.[48] He then moved to Lucknow, and until the annexation of 1856 held the office of *ṣadr al-ṣudūr* – i.e. the chief judge at the court appointed by the British, suggesting that he never broke his ties with service to them. His association with these various princes linked him to the revolt (the only one of his patrons who remained loyal to the British was the Nawab of Rampur). His travels constitute the rather standard itinerary of a major intellectual in search of a patron and students (much like other figures, such as ᶜAbd ᶜAlī Baḥr al-ᶜUlūm, the son of the founder of the *dars-i niẓāmī* curriculum,

45. Russell and Islam, *Ghalib*, pp. 66–7; Prigarina, *Ghalib*, pp. 213–14.
46. Pernau and Jaffrey, *Information and the Public Sphere*, p. 196.
47. Asad Ahmed, 'Arabo-Islamic Physics in the Pre-Modern Period: The *Hadiya Saᶜīdiyya* of Faḍl-i Ḥaqq Khayrābādī', in *The Oxford Handbook of Islamic Philosophy*, eds Sabine Schmidtke and Khaled el-Rouayheb (Oxford, 2017); cf. my forthcoming, 'Calibrating Empires of the Mind: Natural Philosophy in the *dars-i niẓāmī*'. The autograph codex that includes the two texts is MS Raza Library Rampur 3459.
48. Russell and Islam, *Ghalib*, p. 117; Prigarina, *Ghalib*, p. 282.

who died in 1810 and had various patrons in Avadh, Rohilkhand, on the Carnatic coast, and in Hyderabad). Some of his service was to Mughal successor states and sometimes to the mediating British institutions in those places; at this time, the British still had use for those of his class with his skills. Did he think that situation might be changing?

When the revolt broke out, Fażl-i Ḥaqq was in Alwar and seems to have remained there until the death of Raja Bane Singh on 15 July. It is therefore unlikely he went to Delhi immediately and most probably arrived there on 16 August and presented himself to the king, becoming one of four civilian members of the revolutionary council and directly representing the king.[49] On the prompting of the rebel leader Bakht Khān, he allegedly issued a fatwa of *jihād* along with the rebel cleric Mawlawī Aḥmadullāh Shāh Fayżābādī (Fayḍābādī, d. 1858), his friend Āzurda and a number of leading clerics, and was active in rebel activities in clashes outside Delhi with the forces of Avadh around the Queen Mother Hazrat Mahal.[50] But a number of rebels were not convinced by his actions, and some suggested that he advised the king against rebellion – certainly, Bahādur Shāh himself seems to have been rather reluctant.[51] Ḥakīm Aḥsanullāh Khān, a leading courtier of Bahādur Shāh whose pro-British sympathies were clear, wrote a short account of the events, which were then transcribed and translated by the British after they retook Delhi. That account suggests that the king, whilst acting as the leader of the revolt, was somewhat reluctant to act decisively. However, that did not save Bahādur Shāh, who was condemned like Fażl-i Ḥaqq. Aḥsanullāh Khān's account – and it would make sense if it had been tampered to implicate him – presents the philosopher as a willing and urgent rebel, inciting the king to fund the rebel army, lauding its bravery and insisting that funds should be levied for the war effort from the notables in the vicinity of Delhi with whom he already had good relations, like the Raja of

49. Sayhūl, *Fażl-i Ḥaqq*, p. 58; Prigarina, *Ghalib*, p. 289. For a hagiographic assessment of his role in the revolt that celebrates it, see Maḥmūd Aḥmad Barkātī, *Fażl-i Ḥaqq Khayrābādī aur san sattāvan* (Karachi, 1987).

50. Jalal, *Partisans of Allah*, pp. 119–22; Shahābī, *Ghadar kē chand ᶜulamāʾ*, p. 37; ᶜAbd al-Shāhid Khān Shīrwānī, 'Introduction', to Khayrābādī, *Risāla ghadariyya [al-Thawra al-Hindiyya]*, trans. ᶜAbd al-Shāhid Khān Shīrwānī as *Bāghī Hindustān* (Lahore, 1974), p. 156; Haq, *The Great Revolution*, p. 194. Husain, *Religion and Ideology*, pp. 179–80 claims that he 'openly preached jihad', already disgruntled from the time of the annexation of Avadh, and issued the fatwa – but he cites no source. Rizvi, *Shāh ᶜAbd al-ᶜAzīz*, p. 96 also mentions Āzurda's signature of the fatwa.

51. Ḥakīm Aḥsanullāh Khān was widely distrusted as an English spy – even loyalists recognised this. See the account of Munshī Jīwan Lal in *Two Native Narratives of the Mutiny in Delhi*, trans. Charles T. Metcalfe (Delhi, 1974), pp. 92, 101, 107.

Alwar and the Nawab of Jhajjar.[52] At the same time, a number of authors like Imtiyāz ᶜAlī ᶜArshī have argued that Khayrābādī did not issue any such fatwa; they point to the fatwa issued in the rebel gazette *Ṣādiq al-akhbār* on 26 July 1857, which did not have Khayrābādī's signature but contained signatures of many loyalist *ᶜulamāᵓ* including his friend Āzurda, and in fact suggest that some witnesses claimed that he only arrived in Delhi on 16 August and not in May, as others have written.[53] This same fatwa is cited by a number of other later authors including Iṣlāḥī that also do not mention Khayrābādī.[54] Other witnesses and later recorders like Sayyid Aḥmad Khān deny that he ever issued a fatwa – and even describe the 26 July fatwa as a forgery engineered by the rebel commander Bakht Khān, although in this testimony, one cannot preclude Sayyid Aḥmad's desire to de-legitimise the revolt in his attempt to placate his British masters in the post-revolt period.[55] Most of Khayrābādī's biographers argue that his role in the revolt was due to his concern for protecting 'Islamic values', which he saw being eroded in society, and his desire to provide the leadership morally, intellectually and spiritually, which he thought was the prerogative of the *ᶜulamāᵓ*.[56] He was tried and convicted primarily on the charge of issuing the fatwa for *jihād*. His patron's son, ᶜAbd al-Raḥmān Khān the Nawab of Jhajjar, was executed.[57]

After the revolt in Delhi was crushed in September, he fled to Lucknow where he allegedly joined the rebels, and returning to his hometown of Khayrābād, he was arrested on 30 January 1859 and sentenced to exile on 22 February.[58] His

52. Ḥakīm Aḥsanullāh Khān, 'Memoirs', trans. S. Moinul Haq, *Journal of the Pakistan Historical Society* 6 (1958), part 1, 25. On the importance of the vizier as indicated by a loyalist, see Khān, *Āthār al-ṣanādīd*, II, pp. 45–6.
53. Imtiyāz ᶜAlī ᶜArshī, *Majmūᶜa-yi maqālāt*, ed. Fażl-i Ḥaqq Qarshī (Lahore, 1970), p. 97 – this article was first published in August 1957 in the journal *Taḥrīk* in Delhi; Munshī Jīwan Lāl, *Two Native Narratives*, p. 196 on his arrival on 16 August at court. For an extensive discussion, see Barkātī, *Fażl-i Ḥaqq Khayrābādī*, pp. 67–88, and ᶜAbd al-Shāhid Khān, 'Introduction', to Khayrābādī, *Bāghī Hindustān*, pp. 22–36.
54. Iṣlāḥī, *Āzurda*, pp. 77–9.
55. Malik, 'The Case of Fazl-e Haq Khairabadi', p. 87. Sir Syed Ahmed Khan, *Asbāb-i baghāwat-i Hind: An Essay on the Causes of the Indian Revolt* (Agra, 1859), pp. 7–8; Sir Syed Ahmed Khan, *The Causes of the Indian Revolt Written by Syed Ahmed Khan Bahadur by his Two European Friends* (Benares, 1873), p. 9. Khān's statement can also be seen as an expression of his anti-clericalism and his attempt to procure a major intellectual figure for his intellectual path.
56. Shahābī, *Mawlānā Fażl-i Ḥaqq*, pp. 10–11.
57. Rosie Llewellyn-Jones, *The Great Uprising in India, 1857–58* (Woodbridge, 2007), p. 40.
58. Dalrymple, *The Last Mughal*, p. 458n discusses briefly his condemnation, but does not engage in the debate about motivations, intentions and meaning of his involvement.

library was confiscated and removed to Calcutta, whence he was deported to the Andaman penal colony, a space of confinement whose history was coeval with the suppression of the revolts and the establishment of formal empire in India.[59] Ghālib, who had not supported the *jihād* or the revolt, wrote melancholically at the beginning of 1859 about the situation in Delhi and lamented the prosecution and condemnation of his friends including Khayrābādī, who was exiled, and Muṣṭafā Khān Shēfta, a Rohilla notable of their circle, who was condemned to nine years in prison.[60] Many of the figures in the Delhi renaissance around Khayrābādī were conflicted by the revolt, between the desire to regain old glories and power, but distrust of a revolt that would accelerate the process of their disenfranchisement. Different accounts are given of Khayrābādī's time in prison – he allegedly continued to teach there, and penned the famous account of the revolt and his apology, to which we will turn shortly.[61] His son ᶜAbd al-Ḥaqq's petition for his release apparently arrived too late; he died at Port Blair on 12 Ṣafar 1278/20 August 1861.

Khayrābādī's text was originally written in Arabic and later translated into Persian and Urdu, given the title *al-Thawra al-hindiyya* in Arabic, *Risāla-yi ghadariyya* in Persian, and when it was finally published, significantly, in Bijnor in 1947 by ᶜAbd al-Shāhid Khān Shirwānī with an Urdu translation and study, *Bāghī Hindustān*, partly sponsored by Abū al-Kalām Āzād (d. 1958).[62] The links

Rather bizarrely, Raḥmān ᶜAlī in *Tadhkira-yi ᶜulamā'-yi Hind*, p. 207, mentions him being exiled to the 'island of Rangoon', clearly confusing the Andaman penal colony with the exile of the Mughal King.

59. On the Andaman penal colony as a space of the British imperial imaginary othering resistance, see Aparna Vaidik, *Imperial Andamans: Colonial Encounter and Island History* (Basingstoke, 2010), pp. 50–60.
60. Russell and Islam, *Ghalib*, pp. 153–5. For a useful discussion of different approaches of the major poets of the Delhi renaissance to 1857, see Rakhshanda Jalil, 'Reflections of 1857 in Contemporary Urdu Literature' in *Mutiny at the Margins. New Perspectives on the Indian Uprising of 1857 Volume I: Anticipations and Experiences in the Locality*, ed. C. Bates (New Delhi, 2013), pp. 120–31. Recently, Masood Ashraf Raja has argued that we ought to read Ghālib's public and rather political diary of the events of the revolt, *Dāstānbū*, as articulating a subtle critique and resistance to the new British imperial presence, due to its focus upon the marginalisation and effacement of the old Mughal (Muslim) élite of Delhi – see his *Constructing Pakistan: Foundational Texts and the Rise of Muslim National Identity* (Karachi, 2010), Ch. 1. For a different take on Dāstānbū, see C. M. Naim, 'Ghalib's Delhi: A Shamelessly Revisionist Look at Two Popular Metaphors', *Annual of Urdu Studies* 18 (2003), 3–24.
61. Shahābī, *Ghadar kē chand ᶜulamā'*, pp. 39–40.
62. Shirvānī, 'Introduction', to Khayrābādī, *Bāghī Hindustān*, pp. 49–55, on the process leading to publication, including Āzād's role. For studies, see Saiyid Zaheer Husain

made with the struggle for independence are clear. The text was supposedly smuggled out of the prison by his companion Mawlawī ᶜInāyatullāh Aḥmad Kākorvī (d. 1863), and retained by Khayrābādī's son ᶜAbd al-Ḥaqq (d. 1898), whose own service to the British might explain the reason why it was not published by him, given the harsh condemnation of them – he had received the title of *Shams al-ᶜulamāʾ* from Lord Dufferin (1884–8).[63] This somewhat spurious provenance of the text might lead to questioning the authenticity of the attribution to Khayrābādī.[64] However, there is some evidence of the limited circulation of the text: Abū al-Kalām Āzād claims that his father Khayr al-Dīn (d. 1908) had a copy in Mecca – a centre where many a Muslim religious exile from British rule settled – and the younger Khayrābādī might have taken it there.[65] Khayr

Jafri, 'The Indigenous Discourse in the Rebels' World of 1857: An Analysis of Three Documents', in *The Great Uprising of 1857: Commentaries, Studies, and Documents*, eds Syed Najmul Raza Rizvi and Saiyid Zaheer Husain Jafri (Delhi, 2009), pp. 115–20; Jamal Malik, 'Letters, Prison Sketches and Autobiographical Literature: The Case of Fazl-e Haq Khairabadi in the Andaman Penal Colony', *Indian Economic and Social History Review* 43 (2006), 77–100; Iqbal Husain, 'Fazle Haq of Khairabad: A Scholarly Rebel of 1857', *Indian History Congress, Proceedings of the Forth-Eighth Session*, Goa University, Bambolim, 1987 (Delhi, 1988), pp. 355–65, reprinted in his *Religion and Ideology of the Rebels of 1857*, pp. 178–87; Claire Anderson, *The Indian Uprising of 1857–8: Prisons, Prisoners, and Rebellion* (London, 2007), pp. 17–18.

63. The somewhat problematic manuscript history is the reason for some doubts about the attribution to Khayrābādī of the text raised by Nādim Sītāpūrī in 1961 – see Ayyūb Qādrī, *Jang-i āzādī 1857* (Karachi, 1976), pp. 437–48.
64. Other texts written in Port Blair did make it back to the mainland, such as the account of Mawlānā Muḥammad Jaᶜfar Thānesarī called *Tawārīkh-i ᶜajīb* or *Kālā-pānī* penned in 1879 and first published in 1885 in Delhi. Thānesarī was associated with the Wahhābī movement (he wrote a hagiography of Sayyid Aḥmad 'shahīd') and was convicted in 1863 for his role in the 'Ambala Conspiracy'. He spent eighteen years from 1866 on the penal colony. The text has been published a number of times; I consulted the Lahore Sang-e-Meel printing of 1981. The whole text was apparently translated in 1964. A partial translation and study by S. Kamal Abdali is 'Muhammad Jafar Thanesari: Kala Pani or Tavarikh-e ᶜAjib', *Annual of Urdu Studies* 26 (2011), 167–216. Other studies of the text are Satadru Sen, 'Contexts, Representation and Colonized Convict: Maulana Thanesari in the Andaman Islands', *Crime, Histoire & Société* 8.2 (2004), 117–39, and Alavi, *Muslim Cosmopolitanism*, pp. 331–67. The comfort of Thānesarī's life on the Andamans suggests that the stories of Fażl-i Ḥaqq's good relations with the governor and liberty to teach and study are not incredible.
65. Saiyid Zaheer Husain Jafri, 'The Indigenous Discourse in the Rebels' World of 1857: An Analysis of Three Documents', in *The Great Uprising of 1857: Commentaries, Studies, and Documents*, eds Syed Najmul Raza Rizvi and Saiyid Zaheer Husain Jafri (Delhi, 2009), p. 123.

al-Dīn, according to some sources, had been a student of Khayrābādī.[66] In 1914, the *Tadhkira-yi ᶜulamāʾ-yi Hind* of Raḥmān ᶜAlī mentions a *Taʾrīkh-i ghadar-i Hindustān.*[67] Khayrābādī wrote his account during his imprisoned exile on Andaman. He describes himself as heartbroken (*dil-shikasta*), forlorn (*ḥasrat-kashīda*) and afflicted (*muṣībat-zada*) in his state.[68] He complains of his imprisonment, his treatment and speaks thus of himself:

> He is dejected, lonely and forlorn, subjected to drudgery, exiled from his home and country. He is distressed, afflicted, and in exile, made to suffer and separated from his family and children. The tyrant oppresses and maltreats him, keeps his family and neighbours from him and isolates him. The tyrant has imprisoned him, coerced him, depressed him by putting all sorts of hardships because of his zeal and uprighteousness for the faith and for Islam and for his reputation as one of the most famous and learned scholars.[69]

Why did he come to be in this state?

> This was due to the painful event (*wāqiᶜa fāziᶜa*), which has rendered the cities and towns desolate and made them targets of disastrous intentions and brought down misfortunes upon the inhabitants. It was a calamity that turned nobles into beggars and the destitute, and kings into prisoners and slaves.[70]

Part of his lament about the revolt seems to be his sense of the loss of status and respect for scholars of the service class like himself. There is, thus, little sympathy with the majority of the rebels. The British response to the revolt was to bring, at least in the short term, an end to the patronage of old style Muslim scholars and even to forgo ventures such as the Delhi College, which came to a temporary stop.

Why did the revolt come about? Khayrābādī argues that informal British Empire was highly interventionist. They wished to abase the rulers and notables,

66. Sayhūl, *Fażl-i Ḥaqq*, p. 70.
67. Mawlawī Raḥmān ᶜAlī, *Tadhkira-yi ᶜulamāʾ-yi Hind* (Lucknow, 1914), p. 165; Raḥmān ᶜAlī, *Tadhkira-yi ᶜulamāʾ-yi Hind*, pp. 207.
68. Khayrābādī, *Bāghī Hindustān*, p. 252; Khayrābādī, 'The Story of the War of Independence, 1857', *Journal of the Pakistan Historical Society* 5 (1957), 25–6.
69. Khayrābādī, *Bāghī Hindustān*, pp. 252–3; Khayrābādī, 'The Story of the War of Independence', p. 27.
70. Khayrābādī, *Bāghī Hindustān*, pp. 253–4; Khayrābādī, 'The Story of the War of Independence', p. 28.

to abolish hierarchy, to destroy the faiths of the land and to covert people to Christianity. They manipulated markets, destroyed local agriculture and prevented the ability of people to earn a livelihood. They also realised that education was an important tool of conquest, setting up their own schools and destroying traditional institutions and madrasas.[71] Conquest was thus commercial, intellectual and political. Then comes the famous claim that the British attempted to destroy the faith of their Indian sepoys by forcing them to chew on cow and pig fat (while loading their rifles) and that this loss of fidelity to their orthoprax traditions led to their embrace of evil, killing their betters, women and children.[72] At this stage, this sounds like a condemnation of the rebellious sepoys. Certainly, he does not shy away from condemning the excesses of the rebels or their folly. He recognised the objective violence of British imperial interventionism, as well as the subjective, and transgressive, violence of the sepoy rebels. The hierarchy that he defended was no less a subjugation of subjects in the empire and in itself a form of objective violence.

Khayrābādī suggests that the king was a reluctant rebel incapable of controlling the rebels, who included members of the royal family.[73] He is also rather critical of the king's inability to act decisively.[74] Then comes the mention of the fatwa of *jihād* of which he approves – and suggests that the *ᶜulamāᵓ*, a member of whose class he was, provided proper leadership:

> There arose a party of strong and brave Muslims for jihad and fighting after having asked for a fatwa from the pious *ᶜulama'* and their declaration that jihad had become obligatory in accordance with the fatwas of the authoritative imams.[75]

While the text is an apology written in exile in prison, one would still expect him to mention his own role in the fatwa and as a trained scholar taking up the

71. Khayrābādī, *Bāghī Hindustān*, pp. 254–6; Khayrābādī, 'The Story of the War of Independence', pp. 28–9. Even Syed Ahmed Khan complained about the unfettered preaching of the mission as a cause of the revolt – see *Asbāb-i baghāwat-i Hind*, p. 15, *The Causes of the Indian Revolt*, pp. 18–19.
72. Khayrābādī, *Bāghī Hindustān*, p. 257; Khayrābādī, 'The Story of the War of Independence', p. 30.
73. Ibid.
74. Syed Ahmed Khan goes further and says that the king's deposition was a relief to the people of India – see *Asbāb-i baghāwat-i Hind*, p. 6,;*The Causes of the Indian Revolt*, p. 7.
75. Khayrābādī, *Bāghī Hindustān*, p. 258; Khayrābādī, 'The Story of the War of Independence', p. 31.

leadership of the revolt. But he does not do so – even if he does not disapprove of the language of *jihād*.

Khayrābādī consistently uses the language of religious difference: the British forces are Christians and are supported by base Hindus and by apostate Muslims, while the rebels are loyal Muslims who adhere to the dictates of their faith.[76] They are *ghāzī-mujāhids* who seek the felicity of martyrdom, and fight against overwhelming odds.[77] The use of religious discourse is perhaps unsurprising given his training, and certainly one should not underestimate the importance of religious discourse in the mobilisation of the rebellion in 1857. He continues by describing the British as duplicitous, relying upon the duplicity of some of those close to the king, like his treacherous vizier (*al-ᶜāmil al-khawwān*) Ḥakīm Aḥsanullāh Khān, not named, who switches sides and helps the British.[78] The rebels are let down by their simple-minded and treacherous leaders (*al-khawān al-sufahāʾ*). Importantly, he portrays himself as an innocent caught up in the events in Delhi, endangered by both sides, even though his presence in Delhi was by invitation (that is to say, their treachery extended to the violation of the etiquette of hospitality).[79] Nevertheless, as the British took the city on 20 September, he left around five days later, as he says. From Delhi, he proceeded to Avadh, and he describes the revolt there led by the queen. Once again, the rebels are divided, and once again treachery and infidelity is the cause of defeat. Khayrābādī writes:

> They left the Queen and her son alone in the palace. Many of their supporters, officials of the state and servants of the government, betrayed them although they had originally come to help and support them, to protect and maintain their property and honour. They broke their pledges and promises and exchanged infidelity (*kufr*) for faith (*īmān*). They acted as hypocrites and favoured the Christians, joined them and helped them achieve victory.[80]

76. Syed Ahmed Khan also uses the language of religious distinction, but without the concomitance of conflict – see *Asbāb-i baghāwat-i Hind*, pp. 6, 15, 32–6; *The Causes of the Indian Revolt*, pp. 7, 19, 39–43. Similar language of religious difference is used in Thānesarī's *Kālā-Pānī*.
77. Khayrābādī, *Bāghī Hindustān*, p. 250; Khayrābādī, 'The Story of the War of Independence', pp. 32–3.
78. Khayrābādī, *Bāghī Hindustān*, p. 265; Khayrābādī, 'The Story of the War of Independence', p. 35.
79. Khayrābādī, *Bāghī Hindustān*, p. 267; Khayrābādī, 'The Story of the War of Independence', p. 36.
80. Khayrābādi, *Bāghī Hindustān*, p. 275; Khayrābādī, 'The Story of the War of Independence', p. 43.

Once again, the treachery of her agents and representatives is the key factor in the British victory. The complete defeat is sketched in apocalyptic terms – notables are debased, even old women come out to fight, and they are all mercilessly treated by the victorious British. He considered the illegitimacy of the annexation of Avadh – an act of British betrayal in 1856 – to be compounded by the actions of the rebels in the former princely state. Khayrābādī addresses his own arrest:

> After a few days, a Christian officer sent for me from my house, put me in prison and subjected me to torture, causing me great pain. He entrusted my case to a cruel and haughty officer, who had no sympathy for those seeking justice. Then putting me in chains, he sent me to the capital of the Kingdom [Calcutta], which had by then become the abode of ruin and destruction. Two apostates, who were by nature quarrelsome, and had previously had disputations with me on the Quran, had informed on me. They had insisted on taking Christians as friends and exchanged infidelity for faith.[81]

Khayrābādī sees himself as a victim of a miscarriage of justice, and drawing upon his judicial experience, he charges his captors with the folly and injustice of accepting unreliable witnesses. But he locates his misfortune within the wider arbitrary nature of British justice post-revolt. These comments are significant – and would have been received as such – given his prominence in the British and Mughal justice systems prior to 1857. The British desire to turn the world upside down was facilitated by the revolt: the key feature was the infidelity of the world. He continued to lament his treatment:

> Thus the Christians punished me with imprisonment by fabricating falsehoods and deceptive devices against me; they shifted me from one prison to another and inflicted injury upon injury. They continuously added to my grief and pain, deprived me of my shoes and dress, and clad me in rough and coarse clothes. They snatched from me my good and soft bedding, and gave me a highly uncomfortable one, which looked as if it were a thorn bush or a burning ember. They left me with neither pitcher nor bowl, and gave me insufficient meals to eat. They made me drink hot water and I was thus given hot drinks instead of the love of close friends. In spite of old age and weakness, every moment I was subjected to humiliation and insults.[82]

81. Khayrābadī, *Bāghī Hindustān*, pp. 288–9; Khayrābādī, 'The Story of the War of Independence', p. 51.
82. Khayrābādī, *Bāghī Hindustān*, pp. 289–90; Khayrābādī, 'The Story of the War of Independence', p. 52.

He complains of the diseases and misfortunes that he suffers, but thinking of others worse off, he enters a religious passage of praising God and being patient and cites the example of many prophets, such as Job, Noah and, of course, Muḥammad.[83] Lest we forget, this is an *apologia* at the heart of which lies his saintly *mujāhid* personage, crafted in his own narrative. Ultimately, his account is supposed to be a warning that should evince lessons (*ᶜibra*) for the need to keep the faith and to be loyal.[84] This call to loyalty is double-edged: to the Mughal Emperor or to the new Queen-Empress? The anxiety over the loyalty of Muslims in the aftermath of 1857 led to the apologetics of Sir Sayyid Ahmed Khan, Syed Ameer Ali, as well as the concerns of colonial administrators such as William Hunter, and one might consider the account – or perhaps the version that was released and made its way back to the Indian mainland – as a subtle defence of the new British imperium. Khayrābādī completes his account by seeking deliverance and hope from God, since there was no hope from humans or freedom from the prison, penning a few odes (*qaṣāʾid*).[85] The text thus seems to have been written from Andaman and before there was any sense of release – though whether he was even aware of the efforts of his son is unclear.

Both ᶜArshī and Malik suggest that the British made a mistake; the real rebel they were seeking was Khayrābādī's namesake, Mīr Fażl-i Ḥaqq Shahjahānpūrī, who was a major rebel cleric and is mentioned in accounts and in the fatwa of 26 July 1857. But he seems to have been killed in action in 1858. Clearly, much of the post-revolt judicial process was curtailed and people summarily condemned and often executed – no *habeas corpus*, no due process. Khayrābādī was not mindful of being a rebel – but was a member of a service class that was finding it difficult adjusting to the new realities of more formal British Empire in India, even while his son had no such problems serving loyally and being instrumental in the key institution of cooperation that the Delhi College designed to perpetuate the formation of that old service class for the British. It might seem odd that a chess-playing philosopher, versed in poetry, engaged in theologically remote debates on hypotheticals and an agent for British justice could become a rebel. He may not have justified violent *jihād* in response to the British through the infamous fatwa, but his own account – which it seems is reasonable to attribute to him – suggests someone whose discomfort with the actions of upstart rebels and traitors in the midst did not detract from his approval of violent resistance

83. Khayrābādī, *Bāghī Hindustān*, pp. 295–6; Khayrābādī, 'The Story of the War of Independence', p. 55.
84. Khayrābādī, *Bāghī Hindustān*, p. 293.
85. Ibid., pp. 299–328. The English account, which is somewhat abbreviated anyway, does not translate the poetry.

to both the subjective and objective violence of British imperialism. The case of Khayrābādī demonstrates that the learned old Mughal service class were never just closeted intellectuals or apolitical religious figures, but socially engaged and politically active. They considered their learning and religious credentials as qualifications to intervene in the public domain; in fact, knowledge was, to cite an old maxim, not worthy of the name if it did not produce relevant action.

CHAPTER

5

ALTERNATIVE RESISTANCE TO THE BRITISH RAJ: AḤMAD RIḌĀ KHĀN'S LEGAL AND SOCIOPOLITICAL FATWAS

*Mustafa Baig**

خدا نے آج تک اس قوم کی حالت نہیں بدلی
نہ ہو جس کو خیال آپ اپنی حالت کے بدلنے کا

God has not till today changed the state of those people
Who do not themselves have the thought to change their own state.[1]

Studies on the thought of Muslim jurists toward British rule in India are still lacking. There are works that address Islamic jurisprudence from the perspective of British attempts to manage and implement Islamic law,[2]

* University of Exeter

1. Although commonly attributed incorrectly to Muhammad Iqbal (1877–1938) and sometimes Alṭāf Ḥusayn Ḥālī (1837–1914), the couplet is by Mawlānā Ẓafar ʿAlī Khān (1873–1956), which is a form of *naẓm al-manthūr* (versification of prose, reverse of *ḥall al-manẓūm* – 'unravelling the necklace') or 'creative poetic translation' (*tarjama manẓūm takhlīqī*) of the partial verse of the Qurʾān (13.11) in Urdu (although the Qurʾān is neither poetry nor prose). This verse was a fixture on the front page of the highly influential anti-colonial newspaper he ran, *Zamīndār*. His poetry is often suffused with religiously motivated political sentiments addressing the condition of Muslims of the time. For more, see G. H. Ẓulfiqār, *Mawlānā Ẓafar ʿAlī Khān: ḥayāt, khidmāt wa-āthār* (Lahore, 2005); G. Minault, 'Urdu Political Poetry during the Khilafat Movement', *Modern Asian Studies* 8.4 (1974), 459–71 (particularly pp. 463–94).
2. See, for example, M. R. Anderson, 'Islamic Law and the Colonial Encounter in British India', in *A SOAS South Asian Reader*, eds D. Arnold and P. Robb (London, 1993), pp. 165–85 (republished by *WLUML*, Occasional Paper No. 7, June 1996); R. Peters, *Crime and Punishment in Islamic Law: Theory and Practice from the Sixteenth to the Twenty-First Century* (Cambridge, 2005), pp. 109–25; S. A. Hussain,

but less from the viewpoint of traditionally educated Islamic jurists of that era.[3]

In what follows, I will examine four fatwas from one of the most prominent jurists of British India, Imām[4] Aḥmad Riḍā (Riżā/Rażā) Khān (1856–1921), who lived during the British Raj and belonged to the Ḥanafī School of jurisprudence – the dominant school followed in India. For the most part, the study will not look at particular areas of substantive law, but will focus firstly on his position toward the fundamental question of non-Muslim British rule in India in terms of its implications for India's designation as Muslim or non-Muslim territory, and following that, what kind of policies or mechanisms of resistance should be adopted to non-Muslim colonial rule.[5]

Through an analysis of his fatwas, it will be shown that he almost always takes a distinctive position on questions of Muslims living under non-rule, *jihād* against the rulers, emigration away from the land, supporting the nigh collapsing Ottoman Empire as a caliphate and an absolute boycott of the British. In observing his opposing judgments to many scholars of the day, this study will demonstrate how a theologically-centric jurist addressed these issues in a manner that questions common understandings of the categories of *jihād*, emigration (*hijra*) and the territorial distinctions of *dār al-Islam* (land of Islam) and *dār al-ḥarb* (which I generally define as land of non-Muslims, rather than literally, as an abode of war). It further argues that one's attitude (and resistance) toward non-Muslim (colonial) rule cannot be measured by subscribing, merely, to calls for '*jihād* against the enemy' or migration away to a non-Muslim land, regardless of

'Anglo-Muhammadan Law', in *The Oxford Handbook of Islamic Law*, eds A. R. Emon and R. Ahmed (Oxford, 2018), pp. 537–50. On the impact on Islamic law of the 'the jural colonization of India and South-East Asia' see W. Hallaq, *Sharīʿa: Theory, Practice, Transformations* (Cambridge, 2009), pp. 371–95.

3. There are a series of works written as a digest of 'Mohammedan law'/'Anglo-Mohammaden' law. Some were written by Muslims, such as Syed Ameer Ali, who wrote *Student's Handbook of Mahommedan Law* (Calcutta, 1892 (first edition)), based on his Tagore lectures. Others were by non-Muslims such as Roland Wilson, who wrote a challenge to his lifelong rival Ameer Ali, *Anglo-Muhammadan Law* (London, 1895 (first edition)). Aḥmad Riżā Khān was not the Ameer Ali type of lawyer–judge–jurist, but a traditionally trained one and had no association with British courts, as will be observed below. For more on Ameer Ali, see N. Chatterjee, 'Law, Culture and History: Amir Ali's Interpretation', in *Legal Histories of the British Empire: Laws, Engagement and Legacies of Islamic Law*, eds S. Dorset and J. McLaren (Oxford, 2014), pp. 45–59.
4. He is given the title *imām* because he is regarded an authority in matters of religion, particularly among his followers.
5. There are, of course, other settings where Muslim scholars responded to colonial rule. See below.

how popular the appeal of such calls are. There is work on Aḥmad Riżā Khān's role in these issues from a historical perspective.[6] I have set out to take an 'Islamic Studies' approach, which is to focus on the precise modes of argumentation of an Islamic jurist–consult writing fatwas in this politically turbulent time for Muslims.[7] I also explore his positionality within the architecture of his own Sunni intellectual and Ḥanafī legal tradition, with regards to issues of 'continuity and change' within those structures of authority.[8] This is observed in the political and social force found in (some) of the fatwas, responsive to the times and driven by the jurisprudence. The observations consequently have the aim to expand the conceptualisation of fatwa writing. Before exploring these fatwas, some background context is in order.

BACKGROUND TO THE MUNITY OF 1857

Muslim presence in South Asia is as early as Islam itself, with Arab traders visiting the Malabar Coast via the Arabia Sea even in the pre-Islamic era. Muslim traders in the region are perhaps linked to the story of an Indian king converting to Islam and presenting gifts to the Prophet;[9] political authority, nevertheless, actually begins with the 17-year-old Muḥammad b. al-Qāsim's (d. 715)[10] conquest of the Sindh and Multan regions along the Indus River in 711–12.[11] Other

6. The seminal work in the English language is by U. Sanyal, *Devotional Islam & Politics in British India: Ahmad Riza Khan Barelwi and His Movement, 1870–1920* (Delhi, 1996).
7. For more on the Islamic Studies approach and the associated problematisations, see R. Gleave's opening chapter in this volume.
8. Following the line of argument in Wael Hallaq's *Authority, Continuity and Change* (Cambridge, 2001) and expressed by the likes of Norman Calder and Sherman Jackson.
9. Abū Saᶜīd al-Khudrī reports: '[A] king from India presented the Prophet with a bottle of pickle that had ginger in it. The Prophet distributed it among his companions piece by piece. I also received a piece to eat.' Muhammad al-Ḥākim al-Nīshāpūrī, *al-Mustadrak ᶜalā al-Ṣaḥīḥayn* (Beirut, 2002), IV, p. 150. The accounts mentioning the traders connect the conversion to the witnessing of the splitting of the moon miracle. There are different versions, and the link between them and between the *ḥadīth* is not clear. For some examples of these traditions, see T. W. Arnold, *The Preaching of Islam*, Sh. Muhammad Ashraf, (Lahore, 1979 (first published in 1896)), pp. 216–220; M. T. Titus, *Indian Islam* (Oxford, 1930) pp. 36–9.
10. For more modern personalities, I have given the year of birth and death, as it provides contextual reference to the present discussion, which is not quite the same for premodern personalities.
11. Some of the early sources which are consulted for this are al-Balādhurī's *Futūḥ al-buldān*, the *Chachnāma* (otherwise called *Fatḥ-i nāma Sindh*) and al-Bīrūnī's *Tārīkh al-Hind.* On *Chachnama*, see M. A. Asif, *A Book of Conquest: the Chachnama and Muslim Origins in*

significant Muslim rulers were the Ghaznavids (977–1186) and the five dynasties of the Delhi Sultanate (1206–1526) before the last sultan was defeated by Babūr (d. 1530), who established the Mughal Empire in 1526.[12] It was not long after though that the East India Company – a trading company set up by the British to compete with the trading posts set up by other European countries in India – established its first permanent base in 1612, the date which marked the beginning of British presence in India. With the death of the last great Mughal Emperor, Aurangzeb (ᶜĀlamgīr) in 1707 (under whose rule Mughal power reached its greatest geographical extent), the Empire was already suffering from disintegration and the emperors that followed became increasingly powerless while British political presence swelled – not to mention the huge gains made by Maratha invasions that resulted in them controlling vast parts of the Indian subcontinent by the end of the eighteenth century.

The East India Company had increased political activity in the 1750s, and after the victory in the Battle of Plassey over the Nawab of Bengal and his French allies in 1757, the Company gradually began to formally administer its expanding territory as it largely displaced other European powers from the region.[13] Along with political expansion, fears of religious interference were paramount:

> The establishment of British power in India and its subsequent expansion in the first of the nineteenth century, had an adverse effect upon Muslims. For the Hindus it was merely a change of masters; for the Muslims, however, it was quite different and dramatic. Not only did they lose political power, but they also felt that their cultural identity was at stake with the introduction of English as the official language in 1838 and the education policy. This, coupled with Christian missionary activities, convinced some Muslims that the real objective behind

South Asia (Cambridge, MA, 2016). For a good overall history, see A. Schimmel, *Islam in the Indian Subcontinent* (Leiden, 1980).

12. For a wide-ranging account, see A. Schimmel, *The Empire of the Great Mughals: History, Art and Culture* (London, 2004).
13. For details, see W. Dalrymple, *The Anarchy: The Relentless Rise of the East India Company* (London, 2019). While Indian Muslims had sought help from the Ottomans against Portuguese threats on the pilgrimage route to the Two Sacred Sanctuaries and trade routes to Mediterranean ports (which Sulayman the Magnificent (d. 1566) attempted to drive away), and Mughal rulers in periods had sought alliances or corporation with Ottoman sultans (notwithstanding intellectual links), regional rulers in fragmented India such as Tipu Sultan, the Tiger of Mysore (d. 1799), asked for assistance to fight British domination (as well as to receive Caliphal investiture), and in the case of Sultan Ali Raja of Malabar it was also to seek financial help from the 'Caliph of the Muslims' to fight the British. A. Özcan, *Pan-Islamism: Indian Muslims, the Ottomans and Britain, 1877–1924* (Leiden, 1997), pp. 6–15.

the introduction of English and a new education policy was to convert them to Christianity.[14]

While different causes are given for the lead up to the great 1857 Mutiny[15] (with the most popular yet in appearance relatively trivial, of a rumour concerning rifle cartridges greased with beef (offensive to Hindus) or pig's fat (offensive to Muslims) that sepoys had to bite off), the growing, accumulative offense and humiliation Muslims felt toward their religious and political standing is repeated in the interpretations of events by historians.

For the followers of Aḥmad Riżā Khān, the most celebrated scholar leading up to the 1857/8 uprisings was the great *ma*ᶜ*qūlī-uṣūlī*/theologian–philosopher–jurist al-ᶜAllāma Faḍl al-Ḥaqq (Fażl-i Ḥaqq) Khayrābādī (1791–1861). A master of all the Islamic sciences, he belongs to a family (and school) of pre-eminent masters/teachers (*mudarris*) and pedagogic articulators of the *dars-i niẓāmī* tradition, that added texts to its highly selective curriculum and penned commentaries on works in the various disciplines. He was also a Sufi and dedicated in his intellectual efforts in containing and refuting the 'Wahhābī' ideas of Shāh Ismāᶜīl (1779–1831).[16] Concurrently, political activity in the region intensified and became more violent with the growing dissatisfaction of British rule. Bahādur Shāh Ẓafar (1775–1862) of the Mughal dynasty – an accomplished poet, devout Sufi and religious man, rather than a man of political ambition – was proclaimed as Mughal Emperor of India (at 81 years of age) in Delhi, and the majority of rebellious rulers and states paid allegiance to him. The British moved swiftly in their attempts to suppress the rebellion. Scholars to the present day, particularly those associated with Aḥmad Riżā Khān's line of thought, give an account that Khayrābādī delivered a speech of great ardour and fervour in the Jāmiᶜ Masjid of Delhi, calling for the support of Bahādur Shāh Ẓafar and the eradication of British rule; and following the speech a fatwa was issued by Khayrābādī which called for *jihād* against the British.[17] Muslim and Western scholars have mentioned (and in some cases argued for) the leading role of Khayrābādī in the

14. A. Özcan, *Pan-Islamism*, p. 13.
15. Later also referred to as the First Independence War, with the independence of 1947 referred to as the second.
16. He wrote works such as *Imtinā*ᶜ *al-naẓīr* in refutation of the idea that another person like (*mithl*) the Prophet can exist and *Taḥqīq al-fatwā fī ibṭāl al-taghwā* regarding intercession through the Prophet.
17. Other scholars associated with the issuance of the fatwa and the independence movement include: Mufti Ṣadr al-Dīn Āzurda Dehlavī, Mawlānā Aḥmadullāh Shāh Madrāsī, Mawlānā Fayż (Fayḍ) Aḥmad Badāyūnī, Mawlānā Sayyid Kifāyat ᶜAlī Kāfī and Mufti ᶜInāyat Aḥmad Kākōrvī. Yāsīn Akhtar Miṣbāḥī, *ᶜAllāma Fażl-i Ḥaqq Khayrābādī aur*

'call for *jihād*',[18] whereas other scholarship has cast doubt on the heroic role presented in the aforementioned lines.[19] In any case, the British did eventually suppress, violently and mercilessly, the various uprisings by 1858. Delhi was in ruins with its population driven out for weeks, and major mosques were occupied by British troops; the Jāmiᶜ Mosque of Delhi was given back to Muslims only after five years. Along with his colleagues, Khayrābādī was exiled and sent to the Cellular Jail (*Kālā Pānī*) in the Andaman Islands, where many of them met their death. Bahādur Shāh was exiled to Rangoon, and his two sons and a grandson were shot dead by Major William Hodson at the 'Bloody Gate' (*khūnī darwāza*) and publicly displayed.[20]

After the 1857 Mutiny (or War of Independence, as natives often refer to it), Company rule ended, and India was thereafter ruled directly by the British Crown as a colony of the United Kingdom until the independence of India and Pakistan in 1947.

AḤMAD RIḌĀ KHĀN AL-BARAYLAWĪ (BARELWI)

Aḥmad Rizā Khān was born in Bareilly in the northern Indian region of Rohilkhand one year before the 1857 Revolt, so his early years saw the cruelty of its aftermath. He was born into a scholarly family and completed his studies at the age of thirteen. In the same year he wrote his first fatwa,[21] and his father, being so delighted at the young boy's answer, assigned him as a *muftī* tasked to issue fatwas. He went on to write a total of at least 6,847 fatwas in his lifetime.[22] It is said that he authored around a thousand books, but it is not easy to account

1857 kā inqilāb (ᶜAllāma Fażl-i Ḥaqq Khayrābādī and the 1857 Revolution) (New Delhi, 2007).

18. Examples include Schimmel, *Islam in the Indian Subcontinent*, p. 188; F. Robinson, *The 'Ulama of Farangi Mahall and Islamic Culture in South Asia* (London, 2001), p. 190. For a robust argument and refutation see Rājā Ghulām Muḥammad, *Imtiyāz-i Ḥaqq: Fażl-i Ḥaqq Khayrābādī aur Ismā'īl Dihlawī kē siyāsī kirdār kā taqābulī jā'iza* (Lahore, 1978), particularity pp. 25–50.
19. See S. Rizvi's article in the present volume that addresses this: 'From Client to Rebel? The Philosopher Fażl-i Ḥaqq Khayrābādī, his Risāla Ghadarīya and the Events of 1857'; and also J. Hartung, 'Abused Rationality? On the Role of *maᶜquli* Scholars in the Events of 1857/1858', in *Mutiny at the Margins: New Perspectives on the Indian Uprising of 1857*, ed. C. Bates (New Delhi/London, 2014), V, pp. 139–46.
20. For more, see W. Dalrymple, *The Last Mughal: Fall of a Dynasty, Delhi 1857* (London, 2007).
21. On the issue *raḍāᶜ* (milk kinship).
22. The number of published in his fatwa collection, the full title of which is *al-ᶜAṭāyā al-nabawiyya fī al-fatāwā al-riḍawiyya* (*The Prophetic Bestowals in the Riḍawī Fatwas*

for them all from the published works available, even by including the fatwas that can be considered monographs or epistles. Many in India consider him to be the greatest Ḥanafī authority after Ibn ᶜĀbidīn of Syria (d. 1784–1836), especially his supporters (who are sometimes referred to as Baraylawīs/Barelwis) that give him the titles *Aᶜlā Ḥaḍra/Ḥażrat* (the loftiest noble) and *imām ahl al-sunnah*. His legal and theological prowess was not lost on the ᶜ*ulamāʾ* of the *ḥaramayn* (Two Sacred Sanctuaries), who glowingly praised him in different avenues. His poetry and writings on, and defence of, the status of the Prophet's prophetological nature and Sunni-Sufi beliefs/practices present another example of countless scholars who were experts in jurisprudence and practitioners of Sufism, himself belonging to the Qādiriyya order.[23]

He, like Fażl-i Ḥaqq Khayrābādī before him, to whose teaching lineage he belongs, was a strong critic of Wahhābī ideology. As Khayrābādī had refuted Shāh Ismāᶜīl in *Imtināᶜ al-naẓīr* and pronounced *takfīr* on him (declaring him an apostate) with a fatwa of *kufr* on thirteen grounds in his *Taḥqīq al-fatwā*, Aḥmad Riżā Khān in his fatwa lists seventy counts of *kufr*, but stops short of declaring him an apostate.[24] The Deobandi scholar Khalīl Aḥmad Anbehtavī (d. 1927) wrote *al-Barāhīn al-qāṭiᶜa* in defence of Shāh Ismāᶜīl, who wrote on the possibility of God lying,[25] and Aḥmad Riżā Khān wrote a rebuttal fatwa titled 'Subḥān al-Subbūḥ'.[26] Hence, Aḥmad Riżā Khān is seen as the religious–intellectual heir to Khayrābādī as the Deobandis are viewed as the successors of Shāh Ismāᶜīl.

Aḥmad Riżā Khān's collection of fatwas spans twelve volumes; the newer edition extends to thirty (thick) volumes containing treatises and epistles not found in the original, as well as Urdu translations of Arabic and Persian text.[27] By a study of its pages, one is struck at the sheer breadth of topics and depth

(shortened to *Fatāwā riżawiyya*)) (Lahore, 1991–2005). This thirty-volume edition is in use here.

23. An early comprehensive biography is by his student and *khalīfa* in his Sufi order Ẓafar al-Dīn Bihārī written in 1938, *Ḥayāt-i aᶜlā ḥażrat* (Lahore, 2003). Also, Sanyal, *Devotional Islam & Politics in British India*.
24. 'Al-Kawkab al-shahābiyya fī radd abī-l-wahhābiyya', *Fatāwā riżawiyya* XV, pp. 167–237. Also 'Sall al-suyūf al-hindiyyaᶜalā kufriyyāt bābā al-najdiyya', XV, pp. 239–57.
25. Maḥmūd Ḥasan of Deoband wrote a similar work on God being capable of lying called *Juhd al-Muqill*.
26. The fatwa (like the above 'al-Kawkab al-shahābiyya') is actually a *risāla* (epistle) rather than a short fatwa; the full title of which is 'Subḥān al-subbūḥ ᶜan 'ayb kadhib maqbūḥ', XV, pp. 311–450 and is followed by 'Dāmān-i bāgh-i subḥān al-subbūḥ', XV, pp. 451–63. He refutes Shāh Ismāᶜīl and the Deobandis in many places and on a number of different issues that separated his group of scholars from the Deobandis.
27. The latest edition is in thirty-three volumes with the extra three volumes serving as an index.

of erudition, reflecting his mastery of the various disciplines in the Islamic sciences. The *istiftāʾ* (question) is normally unredacted, along with the name of the *mustaftī* (questioner), address (sometimes partial) and date of the question.[28] The longer fatwas (and other works) tend to have chronogrammatic titles, so the date can be determined by a sum of the numerical values of the *abjad* letters (*ḥiṣāb al-jumal*).

TERRITORIAL STATUS OF BRITISH INDIA

Among the main issues of contention was the territorial classification of British India. The debates began as early as 1803 (promoted by General Lord Lake's Capture of Delhi) with a fatwa by Shāh ʿAbd al-Azīz (1746–1824, son of Shāh Walīullāh (1703–62), uncle of Shāh Ismāʿīl and teacher of Fażl-i Ḥaqq Khayrābādī) declaring areas administered by the East India Company as *dār al-ḥarb*[29] – legally designated non-Muslim land. Apparently, the fatwa was written for a specific economic context without any political intent, yet was employed later with categorical import in a newer context of intensified antagonism to the British,[30] which saw the emergence of various political movements, such as the Khilafat and Hijrat Movements after the 1857 Mutiny.

The Khilafat Movement was a pan-Islamic, political protest campaign launched by Muslims in British India to support the waning Ottoman Empire, while advocating 'non-cooperation' with the British. The Hijrat (emigration) Movement was born out of the Khilafat Movement and included some of the foremost campaigners for Khilafat, such as the ʿAlī brothers (Shawkat and Muḥammad) and Abū al-Kalām Āzād, who issued a fatwa ordering Muslims to migrate to the Muslim land of Afghanistan.[31] Some connected to the movement cited the fatwa of Shāh ʿAbd al-Azīz that India was now *dār al-ḥarb*, which as a corollary meant, according to them, one of two options is incumbent: *jihād* in *dār al-ḥarb* or emigration away from it. This binary understanding of territorial

28. For further information, see M. K. Masud, 'The Significance of *Istiftā*' in the *Fatwā* Discourse', *Islamic Studies* 48.3 (2009), 341–66.
29. Shāh ʿAbd al-Azīz, *Fatāwā ʿazīzī* (Delhi, 1907), I, pp. 16–17.
30. M. N. Qureshi, *Pan-Islamism in British Indian Politics: A Study of the Khilafat Movement, 1918–1924* (Leiden, 1999), pp. 176–7.
31. M. Baig, 'Operating Islamic Jurisprudence in Non-Muslim Jurisdictions: Traditional Islamic Precepts and Contemporary Controversies in the United States', *Chicago-Kent Law Review* 90.1 (2015), 79–110 (particularly pp. 81–8). M. K. Masud, 'The Obligation to Migrate', in *Muslim Travellers, Pilgrimage, Migration and the Religious Imagination*, eds D. F. Eickelman and J. Piscatori (London and Berkeley, 1990), pp. 29–49.

designation, however, is simplistic and does not take into account the nuances and complexities associated with the *dār al-Islam/dār al-ḥarb* 'distinction'.[32]

ᶜAbd al-Bārī Farangī Maḥallī (1878–1926), hailing from the Farangī Maḥall *ᶜulamā*ᵓ and prominent stalwart of the Khilafat and Non-cooperation Movement, was among the few that split from the movement on the question of *hijra*, arguing that the fatwa of Shāh ᶜAbd al-Azīz had been misinterpreted, because in no part does he advocate emigrating from Hindustān.[33] This understanding of the fatwa appears to be correct, because if it had intended to have such an effect, it would have materialised in the immediate aftermath; there was no such emigration movement or movement of *jihād* against the British at that time.[34]

Nevertheless, the force of the emigration campaign that was coupled with the warm invitation of the Afghanistan Emir (then king) Amānullāh Khān (r. 1919–29) and the promise of a good life he offered, led tens of thousands of enthusiastic Indian Muslims to leave '*dār al-ḥarb*' for Afghanistan in 1920 (with the additional aim to mobilise for *jihād* against the British from there). It turned out to be a misery and tragic disaster, not holding the promise of the world they imagined from the Emir's words. Many perished, and many others returned to the '*dār al-ḥarb*' they left.[35] Aḥmad Riżā Khān had criticised it at the time, saying it was a ploy by Hindus to buy up their lands cheaply (which actually did happen) and take possession of mosques and shrines. In fact, he said that an exodus (*hijra ᶜāmma*) away from *dār al-islām* is illicit (*ḥarām*). Mosques and Muslim graveyards will be desecrated; women, children and the weak face annihilation. What more, he says, could your Hindu enemy desire for his enemy?[36] Aḥmad Riżā Khān's fatwa (that he wrote earlier) is unequivocal in declaring that India is legally *dār al-Islam* and not *dār al-ḥarb*, despite the fact it was no longer ruled by Muslims. Similar determinateness cannot be found in the positions of his strongest opponents of the Deobandi variety.

> The *fatawa* of the Deobandi ᶜulama, on the other hand, were ambiguous and contradictory. Muhammad Qasim Nanotawi, for instance, considered India

32. See M. Baig, 'Operating Islamic Jurisprudence in a Non-Muslim Jurisdictions', pp. 88–90.
33. ᶜAbd al-Bārī parted from the view of earlier scholars of the Farangī Maḥall who did advocate *hijra*. He was himself accused of believing in it and having contradictory positions, although his activism and writings against it shows otherwise. For more on the Farangī Maḥall scholars, see Robinson, *The 'Ulama of Farangi Mahall*.
34. In fact, he permitted his nephew to work in the service of the British and did not pursue anti-British activities in his writings or otherwise.
35. There are examples of other Muslims emigrating from colonial rule, such as in Algeria in the 1850s where a couple of thousand emigrated to Tunisa.
36. ᶜAbd al-Ḥakīm Sharaf Qādirī, *Andhere sē ujālē tak* (Lahore, 1985), pp. 204–6.

daru'l-harb for the obligation of hijrat, but *daru'l-Islam* for the purpose of usury transactions. Rashid Ahmad Gangohi's decrees have the same ring of confusion and at best are non-committal. By 1898, he was definitely preaching loyalty to the British. Indeed, at one point, he called himself 'an obedient [servant] of the *sarkar*'. Ashraf Ali Thanawi preferred to call British India *daru'l-Islam*, and Mahmud Hasan believed India was both *daru'l-harb* and *daru'l-Islam*, depending on whether or not the Muslims enjoyed religious freedom. The *ᶜulama* of al-Nadwa – principally Shibli Nuᶜmani – advised the Indian Muslims to remain loyal to their rulers in accordance with the dictates of the Qur'an and *sunnat*.[37]

In 1298 of the Hegira calendar (most probably corresponding to 1881),[38] Aḥmad Riżā Khān is asked the question (along with two other questions) on whether India is *dār al-ḥarb* or *dār al-Islam*. As he often does, and especially when the *mustaftī* (questioner) requests it, he makes a full exposition of the matter with the title: 'Iᶜlām al-aᶜlām bi-anna hindūstān dār al-Islam' ('Mountains of Knowledge on the fact that India is *dār al-Islam*').[39] He looks into the matter in a deeper juridical sense and assesses what it takes, juridically, for a state to change its territorial status. He argues that according to the Ḥanafī School, India is classed as *dār al-Islam*, because Abū Ḥanīfa and the *ṣāḥibayn* (Muḥammad al-Shaybānī and Abū Yūsuf) agree on the one condition that would render *dār al-Islam* as *dār al-ḥarb*, and that is that the laws of *shirk* (*kufr*) are publicly and officially enforced there and not a single law of Islam remains implemented. Aḥmad Riżā Khān states that this is certainly not the case in India and lists the following practices that Muslims are able to perform in the current environment: the Friday prayer, *ᶜīd* prayers, the call to prayer (*adhān*), the (lower, second) call to announce the commencement of prayer (*iqāma*), the congregational prayer and other marks of the Sharīᶜa that are practised publicly, without difficulty. He also lists inheritance laws, marriage, milk kinship, divorce, waiting period for divorced/widowed women (*ᶜidda*), revocable divorce, dowry, annulment of marriage on wife's request (*khulᶜ*), matrimonial expenses (*nafaqa*), raising of children, ancestry, gift, religious endowments, bequeaths, right of pre-emption (*shufᶜa*) and many other matters from among the *muᶜāmalāt* of the Muslims

37. Qureshi, *Pan-Islamism*, p. 179. On Deoband, see B. Metcalfe, *Islamic Revival in British India: Deoband, 1860–1900* (Princeton, 1982).
38. The dates of the *istiftā'* are given (always) in the hegira date. Only the year is given here, and unless it was written in Muḥarram of that year (which would mean 1880), then it corresponds to 1881.
39. Mountains of knowledge referring to the great scholars he cites. Aḥmad Riżā Khān, *Fatāwā riżawiyya* XIV, pp. 105–30.

that are settled and adjudicated according to Islamic law. He says that obtaining fatwas from the respected *ᶜulamāᵓ* and to act and rule upon them is even required for the British rulers: 'with the praise of God (*bi-ḥamdillāh*), such is the grandeur and dominion of the Sharīᶜa that even those who oppose it (Hindus, Magians, Christians) are caused to accept obedience to it'.[40]

Although the jurists generally state that satisfying this first condition is sufficient, two further conditions are stipulated by Abū Ḥanīfa, and that is that no other Muslim countries border the land and that not a single Muslim or *dhimmī* remains there in peace with their original covenant of security (*amān*) between them and the non-Muslim sovereign.[41] The jurists state that the opposite of the condition is required for a state to turn from *dār al-ḥarb* to *dār al-islām* – in other words, it is sufficient for a country to become *dār al-islām* if only a few laws of Islam are implemented therein. He then displays his own legal mastery, detailing objections and possible objections that could be raised, and then answers each one of them. For much of the remaining fatwa, he begins answering in the first person (*aqūlu*), switching to Arabic entirely from Urdu.[42]

One objection raised by some of his contemporaries was that if even some of the laws are non-Islamic, it is enough to render a country *dār al-ḥarb*. As well as showing how this view was inaccurate according to the texts of the legists, he states that in countries today, and in fact before today, we see the laws of *kufr* implemented where neglectful Muslim rulers have failed to implement the Sharīᶜa. 'They have allowed the *dhimmī* community to flourish, contrary to the rules of the Sharīᶜa, which accords them an inferior status.' He quotes a quatrain of Ibn ᶜĀbidīn (*al-mawlā al-shāmī* – the Syrian Master, as he calls him here) that is a sarcastic lamentation of the troubling state of the times:

أحبابنا نوب الزمان كثيرة   وأمر منها رفعة السفهاء
فمتى يفيق الدهر من سكراته   وأرى اليهود بذلة الفقهاء

O' dear friends! The afflictions of the time are many,
bitter than that is the elevation of the foolish [to high positions].
When will the era awake from its intoxicated state,
and I see the Jews humiliated to the level of the jurists.[43]

40. Aḥmad Riżā Khān, *Fatāwā riżawiyya* XIV, p. 106.
41. He provides multiple references from Ḥanafī classics to outline what the *fiqh* states on this matter.
42. Aḥmad Riżā Khān, *Fatāwā riżawiyya* XIV, p. 109.
43. Aḥmad Riżā Khān, *Fatāwā riżawiyya* XIV, p. 111, referencing Ibn ᶜĀbidīn's *Radd al-Muḥtār*. 'Jews' here is a metonym for non-Muslims. *Al-yahūd wa-l-naṣārā* (Jews and

He goes on to say how some tyrannical rulers have favoured the innovations (*bidᶜāt*) of non-Muslim leaders and adopted them in their own countries, such as taking oaths from witnesses, taxes, customs tax,[44] levying false and illicit (*bāṭil*) types of gains/tax on wealth and persons (*ᶜalā al-amwāl wa-l-nufūs*) and other types of false laws (*al-aḥkām al-bāṭila*). 'It has to be admitted that these disturbing and detestable affairs are present in Muslim countries.' Therefore, those countries cannot be classed as *dār al-ḥarb* where both Islamic and non-Islamic laws are present; this means that for a country to be classed as *dār al-ḥarb*, the entirety of laws therein must be non-Islamic. 'Hence it has been made clear that those countries which have both types of laws—some of *kufr* and some of Islam, as is the case with our country (India)—will not become *dār al-ḥarb*.'[45] He then continues to answer other possible objections on the religio–legal status of India as *dār al-islām*.

Answering the question in such detail is also important for the fact that determining the territorial status of India impacts upon other issues, such as the practice of usury and the injunction of migration. He admonishes those who consider India to be *dār al-ḥarb*, accusing them of justifying ways to engage in the consumption of usury,[46] following this up with quotes from Qurᵓānic verses and Prophetic traditions that speak of the vileness of those that engage in usurious activity and the severe punishment that will be accorded to them in the hereafter. He also asks why such people have never even had the thought to emigrate if they consider the country as *dār al-ḥarb*, 'instead they take the joys of usury and with comfort remain resident in the native land'. This fatwa was written before the Afghanistan migration of 1920, so it does not directly address that event; nonetheless, his classification would have different implications for *jihād* and emigration.[47]

That fatwa led to accusations of him being pro-British by the Central Khilafat Committee and the Jamᶜiyyat al-ᶜulamāᵓ-i Hind. Labelling him as a

Christians) are often mentioned together to denote non-Muslims (as well as People of the Book – see below), but in poetic short form the first phrase is used (or it may reflect the debased standing of Jews in Europe). The sarcasm here is that he is not *actually* in expectation of the scholars being *at least equally* degraded as non-Muslims, so it can be described rhetorically as *al-taᶜrīḍ yataḍammanu al-mubālagha* (allusion that constitutes exaggeration). It appears that later the poet Rashīd al-Hāshimī (1885–1943) adapted this in his poem.

44. A customs tax levied on goods by the government for crossing a certain point.
45. Aḥmad Rižā Khān, *Fatāwā rižawiyya* XIV, pp. 111–12.
46. On usury in *dār al-ḥarb*, see Baig, 'Operating Islamic Jurisprudence in Non-Muslim Jurisdictions', p. 96.
47. As stated earlier, to see *dār al-ḥarb* simply as territory of war (against which only a hostile relationship is possible), as much of the popular and academic literature does, is misinformed.

British agent persists in popular polemics to this day (and this probably links back to those first charges). Other than neglecting an actual reading of his fatwas on the topic (and the obvious disingenuousness and bias often found among polemicists), a study of the second question in the above fatwa shines a light on other corners of his thought. He is asked a question about whether or not Jews and Christians (*yahūd wa-naṣārā*) in the present age are considered People of the Book (*ahl al-kitāb*). Although the questioner does not specifically ask about the British Indian context, one can assume that the questioner and the *muftī* are aware that the answer to the first question (above) is connected to this next question.[48]

Aḥmad Riżā Khān responds (in the context of *dār al-Islam*) by stating that some scholars have held the opinion that if the People of the Book commit polytheism (*shirk*) by believing that Jesus is God, for example, then they are not classified as such, on account of not being (true) monotheists. It would not be permitted to marry such women or consume their slaughter as they do not fall under the ruling (*ḥukm*) of *ahl al-kitāb* (about whom the Qur'ān states it is permissible), but rather under the category of polytheists (*mushrikūn*). Although the other jurists do not hold this view, they say it is permitted, but it is either mildly reprehensible (*makrūh tanzīhī*)[49] or that it is better (*awlā*) not to do so.[50] He states his own opinion that it is safest and cautionary for one to avoid Christian women when it comes to marriage and meat for consumption, exhorting: 'It is not for the cautious person to become involved in the differences of the *ᶜulamā'*'; 'It is not for the sensible one to engage in such an action which on the one hand is not favourable and on the other hand is explicitly illicit.'[51]

There are also other fatwas where he is very critical of Christians. The point is that in the British Indian context of 'Christian' rulers (albeit not *Christian* rule),

48. The first question would also have a bearing on the next, as the jurists state that marriage to a *kitābiyya* (woman of Scripture) is not permitted in *dār al-ḥarb*, because of the dominance of the non-Muslims in that territory over Muslims (and rather than influencing the wife toward Islam, the opposite would happen to the husband and children).
49. Ibn ᶜĀbidīn, *Radd al-muḥtār*, cited in *Fatāwā riżawiyya* XIV, p. 115.
50. Ibn al-Humām (d. 1457), *Fatḥ al-qadīr*, cited in *Fatāwā riżawiyya* XIV, p. 122.
51. He says that while he had this thought in mind, he found, 'by the grace of God!', the same point mentioned in a classical legal text, *Majmaᶜ al-anhur*. It states that 'it is necessary for the rulers in our land to halt people from consuming the slaughter of Christians because in our times the Christians clearly state that they believe Jesus to be the Son of God, and at the same time no necessity (*ḍarūra*) can be established [to consume their slaughter]', so caution is an obligation (*wājib*) because of the difference of opinion that exists among the scholars. ᶜAbd al-Raḥmān Shaykhzāde (d. 1667), *Majmaᶜ al-anhur sharḥ multaqā al-abḥur* I, p. 328, cited in Aḥmad Riżā Khān, *Fatāwā riżawiyya* XIV, p. 122.

he makes no attempt to approximate the two religious traditions by drawing on commonalities or privileges accorded to the People of the Book in the Qurʾān, let alone appease the British from a faith standpoint.

In addition, the anecdotal evidence displays his attitude in practice toward the British. In one instance (in 1916), he refuses to attend a British court,[52] despite the commencement of a trial. He would intentionally affix stamps bearing the face of Queen Victoria on letters and postcards upside down.[53] He gave *waṣiyya* (testamentary directive) two hours before passing away that any monetary notes or coinage exhibiting the face of the king (George V) be thrown out.[54]

SOCIAL-POLITICAL ENGAGEMENT/DISENGAGEMENT

As mentioned above, the Khilafat Movement was organised around gathering support for the Ottoman Sultan and, as the name suggests, recognising him as a caliph of the Muslims. The movement gained widespread support, and Aḥmad Riżā Khān responds to it, not uncharacteristically, in a lengthy fatwa dated 1339 (corresponding to 1920/1), stretching to almost seventy pages.[55] The question (*istiftāʾ*) does not contain details of the questioner or the date, which suggests he may have set the question up in order to weigh in and pronounce his verdict (not uncommon for *muftī*s to do) on the fundamental cause of the movement, unless it was sent anonymously.[56] In his response he argues that the position of *khalīfa*, in the legal–terminological sense, can only belong to members of the Prophet Muahmmad's Quraysh tribe. This is proven by *mutawātir ḥadīth* – words of the Prophet reported by mass transmission of successive, concurrent chains – and the consensus (*ijmāᶜ*) of Companions (*ṣaḥāba*), Successors (*tābiᶜūn*), the Sunnis

52. On the courts, see Anderson, 'Islamic Law and the Colonial Encounter in British India'.
53. Some of these are still preserved today. It is perhaps ironic that on his seventy-fifth passing-away anniversary, the Indian government issued a commemorative stamp in honour of Aḥmad Riżā Khān on 31 December 1995 with a picture of the complex and dome of the *dargāh* (shrine), and title: 'Ala Hazrat Barelvi'. The stamp can be seen at https://www.istampgallery.com/ala-hazrat-barelvi/. For accessed dates of online resources, see the Bibliography and the accompanying note, p. 366.
54. This is also to not deter angels from entering a place in which animate objects/articles are displayed; there is the added severity of this being the British monarch. The text mentions 'king', so it is presumably George V (r. 1910–36), unless the currency was (also) bearing the faces of previous monarchs. See *Fatāwā riżawiyya* XIV, p. 13 (introduction by ᶜAbd al-Ḥakīm Sharaf al-Qādirī).
55. That is in the new edition. 'Dawām al-ᶜaysh min al-aʾimma min quraysh' ('The Lasting of Life for the *imāms* to be from the Quraysh'), *Fatāwā riżawiyya* XIV, pp. 173–238.
56. That is without addressee or address. As a matter of course, the name and addresses are maintained in the published fatwas.

(*ahl al-sunnah*) and general agreement (*ittifāq*) of Muslims down the centuries. 'No one differs on this except the *khawārij* [Seceders] and some of the *muᶜtazila* [known as 'rationalists'].' The words sultan, Emir, *imām*, *wālī* (ruler/governor) and king may be used for non-Qurayshī rulers, but not *khalīfa* or commander of the faithful (*amīr al-muʾminīn*), unless it is used customarily (*ᶜurfan*), which is of no consequence.[57] In building the edifice of his argument, Aḥmad Riżā Khān seeks to establish doctrinal certainty and close down any room for disagreement on the matter (within Sunnis), a style of argumentation found in his other fatwas. However, as with some of those issues he debates, the matters are not always as unified and unambiguous as he presents, particularly with the use of historical precedent in this case.[58]

As for the 'majestic sultanate of the Ottomans', as he describes it, it is an individual obligation (*farḍ ᶜayn*) to sincerely wish it well, as it is to wish every Muslim organisation and individual well (according to the *ḥadīth* he cites), as well as give support and assistance through prayer when needed. To offer assistance through finance and *deeds* is, on the other hand, a communal obligation (*farḍ kifāya*), and that follows the principle that 'obligations are according to the ability one has to perform them'. After quoting the Qurʾānic verse that 'God does not burden a soul except what it can bear',[59] the crucial line follows that a poor person is not obligated to give financial help, and an incapable person is not obligated to give physical help, therefore the ruling of *jihād* and fighting will not

57. Aḥmad Riżā Khān, *Fatāwā riżawiyya* XIV, pp. 174–5.
58. Along with proofs from theological and legal works, he adds to his fatwa historical reinforcement that there is no proper historical precedent of rulers referring to themselves as caliphs. On the contrary, he provides many examples, particularly from the Abbasid era, of dynastic sultans acknowledging the Abbasids universally as titular caliphs. 'Even in India, the rulers were subordinate to the caliphate in Baghdad [. . .] Non-Qurayshī rulers, whether Turks, Mughal or Pathans did not make a claim for the caliphate'. *Fatāwā riżawiyya* XIV, p. 174. This, however, is questionable, as the Ottomans did assume the title of caliph, and the Mughals had at times seen themselves as subordinate to them. There are also scholars such as al-Ghazālī (d. 1111) al-Dawwānī (d. 1502) that did not cite the Quraysh lineage as a condition for the caliphate. Shāh Walīullāh had referred to the Ottoman sultan as *amīr al-muʾminīn*. See H. A. R. Gibb, 'Some Considerations of the Sunni Theory of the Caliphate', in *Studies on the Civilisation of Islam*, eds S. J. Shaw and W. R. Polk (Boston, MA, 1962), pp. 141–50; Özcan, *Pan-Islamism*, pp. 2–10; Qureshi, *Pan-Islamism*, pp. 14–17. A more in-depth study of the fatwa may see some of these points addressed. There are details on the issue in other fatwas such as 'Nābigh al-nūr ᶜalā suʾālāt jabalfūr' (Jabalpur) in *Fatāwā riżawiyya* XIV, pp. 141–71 (although the fatwa is published in incomplete form).
59. Q2:286.

be given for Indian Muslims. This is regardless of whether that Muslim king is a Qurayshī or not.

The remainder of the fatwa is aimed at refuting the leaders of the Khilafat Movement, ᶜAbd al-Bārī Farangī Maḥallī and Abū al-Kalām Āzād (who is mockingly called *Mister* Āzād), with hermeneutic arguments and laying bare logical flaws and inconsistencies in their positions.

An important component of the Khilafat Movement was its ties to the Gandhi-led Non-Cooperation Movement (*tark-i muwālāt*) that picked up pace in 1920, following the calamitous *hijra*, from which the advocates of that call among the Khalifat Movement managed to absolve themselves of blame. It was headed on the Muslim side again by Āzād and ᶜAbd al-Bārī. They campaigned on the view that independence from the British could be achieved through Muslim–Hindu unity and non-violent non-cooperation with the British. In August 1920, the Jamᶜiyyat al-ᶜulamāʾ-i Hind issued a fatwa supporting the Indian National Congress's proposed boycott of courts, legislative councils, schools, foreign goods and so on. A question (*istiftāʾ*) is put to Aḥmad Riżā Khān in connection to Āzād's call for the Islamia College in Lahore to stop accepting government grants from the British, because doing so constitutes *muwālāt* (intimate/close friendship or loyalty) with non-Muslims, which the Qurʾān forbids.[60] In his fatwa titled *al-Maḥajja al-muʾtamina fī āyāt al-Mumtaḥina*[61] (dated 14 Ṣafar 1339/October 1920), he engages in an exegesis of the Sūrat al-Mumtaḥina verses understood by the 'non-cooperation scholars' to be the Qurʾānic basis for calling the boycotts (*muqāṭaᶜāt*).

He makes a clear distinction between *muwālāt* and simple *muᶜāmalāt* (human relations and dealings). The latter are permitted in Islamic law with all non-Muslims except apostates (*murtadd*). The *dhimmī* (non-Muslim subject in Muslim land) is equal to the Muslim in *muᶜāmalāt* and all forms of transactions are permitted also with the non-*dhimmī*, as long as such commodities are not sold that could be used in support of war or be a cause of dishonour to Islam. He argues how even marriage with a Scriptuary woman (*kitābiyya*) has been permitted in essence (*fī nafsī*),[62] considering it is legally categorised as belonging to 'contracts' (*muᶜāmalāt*). One (i.e. Muslim states) can make peace (*ṣulḥ*) with

60. See as examples Q60:1, Q4:139, Q4:144, Q5:51. The twin concepts of *al-walā wa-l-barāʾ* (association and disassociation/loyalty and disavowal) features in much of the modern discourse around *jihād*, particularly among contemporary Salafism.
61. *Fatāwā riżawiyya* XIV, pp. 419–26.
62. This term here is important because otherwise it would appear to be inconsistent with how he expressed his position in the earlier cited fatwa that emphasised much caution in marrying women from *ahl al-kitāb*. Hence, he says 'in essence' it is permitted.

them, as long as it not based on making the licit illicit and vice versa. Similarly, one can partake in a treaty and contract with them, and it is obligatory (*farḍ*) to fulfil whatever licit contract is made with them, and deception or breaking the contract is illicit (*ḥarām*).[63] He provides references from Ḥanafī texts that enable Muslim rulers to appoint non-Muslim judges to adjudicate among non-Muslims.[64] Al-Shaybānī has said that a Muslim ruler or army chief is permitted to exchange gifts with an adversarial king in both *dār al-Islam* and *dār al-ḥarb* (but it will be distributed as spoils if other Muslims are present).[65]

He goes on to say how it is surprising that the advocates of non-cooperation do cooperate and continue to use facilities such as the railway, the telegraph and the postal system, all of which benefit government revenues. He asks why are such things not considered to be among the *muᶜāmalāt* by these people? The difference, he says, is that by taking aid from the British, one is gaining wealth, while in using their services, one is giving wealth away to them. He remarks how strange it is that in this boycott it is permissible to profit them, but it is illicit to make profit from them. 'What remedy is there for this inverted logic? But then what is one to say of this community who has not only turned Sharīᶜa on its head but the essence of Islam as well!'[66]

He elaborates on his above comment by stating that they have called *muᶜāmalāt* with the British illicit, but have themselves actually engaged in *muwālāt* with the polytheist Hindus in their calls for Muslim–Hindu unity and brotherhood, calling it an obligation and even a tenet of faith. They have accepted Hindus as their guides (*hādī*) and leaders (*imām*), they make the mosques a place of mourning for their deaths, pray for their forgiveness and hold their funeral prayers there. They even state that those who do not participate in their movement have committed *kufr* – whereas, he retorts, 'this is in fact *muwālāt*, this is what is illicit, this is what is *kufr* and this is what is heresy'.[67]

Aḥmad Riżā Khān did not advocate *jihād* against the British, nor did he join calls for a complete boycott of the British in the manner that the Non-cooperation Movement campaigned for. This does not mean he had no alternative vision of his own, because he had, nonetheless, responded to a question posed on 19 Rabīᶜ al-awwal 1331/February 1913 (some years earlier than the above fatwas)

63. Baig, 'Operating Islamic Jurisprudence in Non-Muslim Jurisdictions'.
64. Ibn ᶜĀbidīn, *Radd al-muḥtār* VI, p. 71, cited in *Fatāwā riżawiyya* XIV, p. 423.
65. Ibn Māza al-Bukhārī (d. 1219), *al-Muḥīt al-burhāni fī fiqh al-nuᶜmānī*, cited in *Fatāwā riżawiyya* XIV, p. 423.
66. *Fatāwā riżawiyya* XIV, p. 425.
67. Ibid. Related discussions can be found in his 'Nābigh al-nūr', cited in *Fatāwā riżawiyya* XIV, pp. 141–71, among other places.

about 'what should do the Muslims do today?' and 'what is the way to help the Turks?'[68] His fatwa, titled 'Tadbīr falāḥ wa-najāt wa-iṣlāḥ' (Measures for [Delivering] Prosperity, Salvation and Reform), begins by citing the Qura'nic verse presented (in poetic form) as an epigraph above, 'God does not change the condition of a people until they change what is in themselves', followed by a verse encouraging optimism, which is to not lose hope in God's mercy.[69] In order to bring about meaningful change in the Muslim world, whether in Turkey or India, Muslims in India first needed to focus on themselves in order to reach a position where they can be of influence. A significant part of his answer lays out a four-point plan to weaken economic dependence on non-Muslims and hence strengthen the Muslims financially:

1) Muslims should refrain from using the British-run courts (except where necessary); instead they should adjudicate among themselves. This would also save them millions of rupees in stamp duties and legal fees that have been destructive for house upon house.[70]
2) Muslims should only trade with each other. This way the wealth would circulate within the community and trade and craftsmanship would grow to the point that they would eventually become self-reliant. This would replace the current state of exchanging a quarter kilo of silver for fifty grams of copper that Europeans and Americans simply manufacture into the shape of a watch, for example.
3) The wealthier Muslims should fund economic development. The affluent Muslims in large cities such as Bombay, Calcutta, Rangoon, Madras, Hyderabad and elsewhere should open banks for their fellow Muslims. While usury is explicitly prohibited, there are a hundred ways to earn profit that are detailed in the books of Islamic law.[71] It would financially benefit Muslim bankers, as well as benefit their Muslim brethren in need. Such a programme would halt the selling off of land (in desperation) to the Hindu trading caste (*baniya*) and wealth would instead remain in the hands of Muslims.
4) The utmost imperative is for Muslims to educate themselves in their religion

68. The brief question mentions that further documentation has been attached to the *istiftā*ʾ but they are not published.
69. Aḥmad Riżā Khān, *Fatāwā riżawiyya* XIV, pp. 142.
70. As noted earlier, refusing to attend a court trial is a step he took himself, so this is not mere exhortation.
71. He draws attention to a monograph/fatwa of his own on the topic called *Kifl al-faqīh al-fāhim fī qirṭās al-darāhim*.

> in order to become more knowledgeable and practicing. He asserts that religion (*dīn*) was, of course, the most important thing they had but they had neglected it in pursuit of other goals and reduced its role to its current weak state. 'It is the mighty religion that was the supreme foundation (*aṣl-i a*ᶜ*ẓam*) for them, to whose rope earlier Muslims held onto with steadfastness, which elevated them to exalted heights and established their glory in the four corners of the earth . . .'; '. . . It placed crowns on the heads of paupers.' Neglecting this threw the later Muslims into degradation.[72]

The mighty religion (*dīn-i matīn*) is tied to the knowledge of religion (*'ilm-i dīn*) and addressing the 'blind', he says that 'what you consider progress is actually sheer decline and what you consider honour is severe humiliation'. He then goes on to elaborate on the plan by providing mechanisms for its implementation.

In addressing the second point he says that people of noble descent consider craftwork and trading as dishonourable, and consider humiliating employment, being knocked around and obtaining illicit work as a source of pride and respect. Even when they do trade, they do not even have the sense to buy from their own people; although it could be a little more expensive, the profit will at least go to their Muslim brother. In observing the Europeans, he points out that they would never buy goods that are equal or even better in quality, but rather take inferior goods from their own. The state of sellers is such that a Hindu will take an *ānā* (¹/16 of a rupee) in profit and the Muslim gentlemen is not satisfied with a *chawannī* (a quarter),[73] even when his goods are not equal to that of the Hindu.[74]

He elaborates on the third point, saying most of the rulers are concerned with their lifestyles that do not accord with the Sharīᶜa. In dances and lewdness they can waste thousands to enhance their personal profile (done in the name of the state) and find it unthinkable to spend a small amount to save the life of a dying brother.

> How can those who have learnt business from the Hindu trading caste be attentive to permissible ways of making a living? What concern do they have with religion and what interest do they have in the rulings of Allah and the Messenger?

72. *Fatāwa riżawiyya* XV, pp. 144–5.
73. The two are among old Indian/Pakistani currency, demonetised in the last few decades.
74. Comparing the business strategy of Muslims and Hindus, he says: 'The Hindu knows the principles of trading that the less the profit margin he sets, the more he gets; the Muslim gentleman wants to obtain all his profits from a single buyer. Out of desperation, the poor customer will end up buying from the Hindu.'

> Circumcision made them Muslim and [consuming] the meat of cows has maintained their Muslim status.

After accusing them here of being Muslim in name only, he sarcastically rebukes them saying: 'they will not have to die, nor be presented to the One Almighty and nor be accountable for their deeds!'

The state of the fourth, he bemoans, is unspeakable. 'They have come to believe that secular education is the absolute Provider (*razzāq muṭlaq*).' After all the difficulties that it comes with (in its perusal), job prospects are low, and if one manages to find work then it is a degrading job. Even if they gradually earn some worldly respect, it may still be very degrading according to the sacred law. Notwithstanding this, there is no time to learn the religion and distinguishing between good and bad. The result, he observes, is that they consider religion an object of ridicule and see their fathers and forefathers as backwards, wild, uncivilised and stupid. Such ideas of so-called progress, he iterates, are a fallacy.

He analogises what he sees as the level of stupidity found among people with an individual wanting to treat an illness, but he maintains its causes: 'These are the causes that led you to humiliation and allowed foreign nations to smirk at you.' He remarks how the rallying cries around nationalism reverberate, which is another expression for wanting to 'remove the rope of Islam from their necks in order gain "freedom"'. Although this freedom, he maintains, is actually 'the restriction of extreme submissiveness' – a living example of which can be found in the fresh events that befell the Turks.

He appeals to those informed (*ahl al-raʾī*) to organise events in which people are encouraged to adhere to these four points, and he challenges that if things still do not change for the better, then one is entitled to complain. In using the Qurʾānic words 'God does not change a condition of people until they change what is in themselves' as the base-verse of his fatwa, he believes that such a course of action will anticipate the glad tidings of God – which is the change they are seeking. He ends the section with a prayer: 'O our Lord, open our eyes and show us your favoured way, for the sake of the sun of the Messengers, the moon of Madina.'[75]

CONCLUSION

A number of points emerge from his writings on the tumultuous times of British India and the wider Muslim context of the Ottoman Empire. The theme of longing for the former glory of Muslims permeates his 'political' fatwas, especially the

75. *Fatāwa riżawiyya* XV, pp. 145–7.

last one discussed. The words of poet Amīr Khusraw (d. 1325), composed in Delhi in 1289, portray India as the home of true Islamic life:

> Happy be Hindustan with its splendour of religion,
> where the Sharīᶜa enjoys perfect honour and dignity.
> In learning now Delhi rivals Bukhara;
> Islam has been made manifest by the rulers.
> From Ghazna to every shore of the ocean,
> you see Islam in its glory everywhere.
> Muslims, here, belong to the Ḥanafī creed,
> but sincerely respect all the four schools.
> They have no enmity with the Shafiᶜīs and no fondness for the Zaydīs;
> with heart and soul are they devoted to the path of the community and the *sunna*.
> It is a wonderful land, producing Muslims and favouring religion,
> where even the fish comes out of the stream as a Sunni![76]

Six hundred years later in 1879, in the same city of Delhi, the poet Ḥālī (1837–1914) complains of the destitute situation of the Muslims in India and the lost resplendence of earlier times:

> For now our every deed ignoble shows
> Our actions are the meanest of the low,
> The fair name of our fathers is eclipsed,
> Our every step disgrace the place we dwell.
> Dishonoured is the honour of the past,
> Arabia's greatness is beyond recall . . .[77]

The stark contrast between the two may not be entirely reflective of the reality, but juxtaposing the two reflects the sentiments and imagination of Aḥmad Riżā Khān and many others, particularly because of the strong emphasis on Sunni doctrine in the first poem that Aḥmad Riżā Khān spent his career defending, along with a lifetime spent expounding Ḥanafī jurisprudence. Despite the emotions exuding from some of his writings, his arguments are theology-centric, built upon the texts of authorities of the Sunni tradition that he adheres to.

This sheds further light on the nature of fatwas and fatwa writing: it is an

76. Schimmel, *Islam in the Indian Subcontinent*, p. 1. Punctuation and typology has been slightly adapted.
77. Schimmel, *Islam in the Indian Subcontinent*, p. 1.

enterprise that is not restricted to what is often considered as the (purely) legal, even in terms of the traditional areas that comprise works of Islamic jurisprudence, but it can, and does, expand to cover social, political, moral and even economic guidance. As these fatwas are found in the chapter of *siyar/jihād*, the examples here reveal that the subjects covered under '*jihād*' move far beyond warfare and fighting the enemy.[78] The fatwas presented provide a window into the social reality the questioner and the *muftī* were faced with. In responding to the questions, he gives practical micro-economic solutions (with the intended effect of growing into a macro-economic model). Nevertheless, the intersection of law and society remains constant as the *muftī*'s deliberations are unremittingly grounded in Sharīᶜa.

He was (and is) accused of having pro-British views, but he was, in fact, neither pro-British nor pro-Hindu; he was anti both. The reasons for this are, again, that his theological considerations are front and centre, as well as the fact that both, as he sees, pose a similar level of threat for the weak Muslims in India. Not enjoining *jihād* does not imply he is anti-*jihād* or pacifist. War can only take place if it is legitimate and through proper legal mechanisms. Nor does it mean he is a quietist withdrawn from political affairs. His writings contain activism, but he is not the rebel advocating a *jihād* against the British. In this sense, he is not the warrior, like Emir ᶜAbd al-Qādir al-Jazāʾirī (1808–83) fighting the French or the 'Lion of the Desert' ᶜUmar al-Mukhtār (1858–1931) against the Italians; Aḥmad Riżā Khān did not die a martyr for the cause. The experiences, however, and the degree of brutality vary, prompting different responses. That is not to say the oppression of the British should be underestimated.[79] They were not *muftī*s as he was, and his activism is found through the influence of his pen. There is an interesting contrast to be made with other scholars, such as the Javanese scholar and founder of the Nahdlatul Ulama, Hasyim Asy'ari (Hāshim b. Ashᶜarī, 1875–1947), who did issue a fatwa of *jihād* against the Dutch, although, again, the circumstances are not the same. Hence, any assessment of '*jihād* versus no *jihād*' should not simply group scholars/activists in one camp or the other, but should account for the regional conditions that inform their judgements.[80] References to Khayrābādī in Aḥmad Riżā Khān's writings

78. M. Baig, 'The Non-Violent Aspects of *kitab al-jihad*', in *Twenty-first Century Jihad: Law, Society and Military Action*, eds E. Kendall and E. Stein (London, 2015), pp. 97–111.
79. See, for example, W. Dalrymple, *The Anarchy*; S. Tharoor, *Inglorious Empire: What the British Did to India* (London, 2017).
80. Asy'ari's role appears to be more akin to the (perhaps somewhat mythologised) Khayrābādī. The former issued fatwas of *jihād* as an individual obligation on every Muslim (*farḍ ᶜayn*) in 1945 against the Dutch during the Indonesian War of Independence

on the British are missing – conspicuously, one might add. Khayrābādī may not have issued the *jihād* fatwa or been the leading figure in the 1857 Revolt, but if it was believed to be the case then as it is now, citing Khayrābādī would not be conducive to Aḥmad Riżā Khān's fatwa of *jihād* not being incumbent against the British. It may well be that he was unsure of Khayrābādī's role or it may be the manner in which he disagrees with figures he revers from his intellectual–educational heritage is to remain silent.[81] In support of this claim, the opposing view he holds to Shāh ᶜAbd al-Azīz on the territorial status of India can be cited as a clearer example. He disagrees with him, but does not mention that fatwa and his disagreement on the issue in his own fatwa. It may be out of reverence or to not entangle himself in disagreements with his loftily held predecessors on contentious issues. Nevertheless, it shows his willingness to depart from their views and form his own independent opinion, possibly in light of new political circumstances in some of the cases. In one of the fatwas, where he appears to push for a minority view on what constitutes *ahl al-kitāb*, he adopts a seemingly different position to the standard in the School. Nevertheless, he is keen on representing a unified position and attitude to questions at hand. This reveals that there is not a static linearity within the tradition, but a more nuanced dynamic between continuity and change; tradition represented by his legal *madhhab*, doctrinal affiliation and educational heritage.

In not advocating *jihād*, his positions on India's status as *dār al-Islam* and non-cooperation with the British, collectively, clearly stands him apart from other contemporaries, as he deems them religiously inexplicable or logically unwise. Although, where he sees a legitimate cause, he does 'cooperate' or show solidarity with those causes, such as raising funds for the protection of the Two Sacred Sanctuaries or assisting the Ottomans if able to do so. The principle appears to be that the actions in these cases are practicable, feasible and result in a beneficial outcome. This is to say that he is legally conservative[82] and politically pragmatic.[83]

(National Revolution 1945–9). On this, see A. Amiq, 'Two Fatwās on Jihād Against the Dutch Colonization in Indonesia: A Prosopographical Approach to the Study of Fatwa', *Studia Islamika* 5.3 (1998), 77–123.

81. It could be expected that in presenting the weak state of Muslims as a reason against *jihād*, the precedent of the 1857 rebellion might be given.
82. In so far as adherence to the texts and sometimes adopting the stricter view, as in the case of *ahl al-kitāb*.
83. There might be a tension between the two, as is the case of non-cooperation with both Hindus and Christians; his opponents saw a political advantage in uniting with Hindus, whereas he remains theologically consistent (while also believing that unity with Hindus is actually harmful politically too).

Instead of *jihād*, he encourages alternative resistance methods, beginning with the self, especially as they do not have the means to resist physically and financially.[84] Knowledge and cognisance of religion, and putting that into practice, is more pertinent than physical *jihād* at the present moment. Knowledge[85] functions as the foundation for a physical struggle against oppression and the key to preparing for it. He conceptualises the struggle in British India in legal–theological, moral and even spiritual terms. Potentially, some lessons from his thought may be drawn on by activists for contemporary liberation struggles similar to Gandhi's non-violent resistance *satyāgraha*.[86] With the current demonstrations in India in response to the discrimination and violence against Muslims, the words of Aḥmad Riżā Khān rejecting calls for Muslim–Hindu unity and the realisation of Muhammad Ali Jinnah (1876–1948) and Muhammad Iqbal that the rights of Muslims would not be protected and their identity put to peril under a Hindu-majority India, which led to the creation of Pakistan, are perhaps ringing true in the ears of the protestors. Some of the 'creative' responses are bearing this out.[87]

Aḥmad Riżā Khān demonstrates with his own creativity: if the means to resist physically are elusive, then one may protest and 'resist' by turning the queen on her head, even if on a stamp.

84. The 1920 migration/*jihād* 'failure' demonstrates the unpreparedness of the Muslims.
85. His emphasis on knowledge is opposed to the Western education promoted by Sir Sayyid Aḥmad Khān (1817–98).
86. See, for example (a critical engagement with Gandhi among a growing trend of critical work), N. Finkelstein, *What Gandhi Says: About Nonviolence, Resistance and Courage* (New York/London, 2012); R. Yassin-Kassab, 'Non-Violence? Finkelstein and Gandhi', *Palestine Chronicle*. Available at http://www.palestinechronicle.com/non-violence-finkelstein-and-gandhi/.
87. One of the chants among the protestors is 'say it on the barricade *lā ilāha illā Allah*, say it on the *lāṭhī* (baton) charge *lā ilā-ha illā Allah*, say it in the tear gas *lā ilā-ha illā Allah*' and other protest anthems, such as '*tērā mērā rishta kyā* (what is my relation with you?) *lā ilāha illā Allah*.' 'There is no god but Allah' is the fundamental declaration of Muslim creed that is followed by 'Muhammad is His Messenger'. It is recited with repetition in Sufi rituals. Here it is an expression of the Muslim religious identity that is under attack by the government and its institutions. See 'Say It On the Barricade! LA ILAHA ILALLAH #RejectCAA', *YouTube*. Available at: https://www.youtube.com/watch?v=lld_IozAEdI. 'Best solgans | tera mera rishta kya "la-ilaha il-lallah"', *YouTube*. Available at: https://www.youtube.com/watch?v=Hks8Y7W85nU.

CHAPTER

6

A TALIBAN LEGAL DISCOURSE ON VIOLENCE

*Jan-Peter Hartung**

PRELIMINARIES**

In the autumn of 1996, some Afghan Taliban (*Ṭālibān*)[1] proclaimed the Islamic Emirate of Afghanistan (*Də Afghānistān Islāmī Imārat*); they ran this Emirate centrally until 2001, and since then, it has continued in a decentralised and territorially patchy form. An investigation into the various legal discourses on 'violence' of these Afghan Taliban is highly challenging for a number of reasons. Principal amongst these is the fact that they only became a focus of proper attention after the US political and military establishment mounted the so-called 'Operation Enduring Freedom'. That operation was in retaliation for the *al-Qāᶜida* attacks on targets of high symbolic value on the US East Coast on 11 September 2001. This new-found interest in the Taliban led to the emergence of literature that is, unfortunately, only partly helpful for serious research on the group.

* University of Goettingen.

** Disclaimers: (1) I am most grateful to everybody who has read and critically commented upon earlier drafts of this chapter and other related works of mine, without which I would most certainly have misrepresented various aspects of this complex matter.

(2) The romanisation of the Arabic script in this chapter follows a slightly modified pattern, necessitated by the use of Arabic, Urdu, Persian/Dari and Pashto alike. By and large, I follow here the respective ALA-LC standard for each of these languages. To avoid confusion between aspirated consonants in Urdu and the velar and dental fricatives of Arabic, however, the former are marked by an 'ħ'.

1 To emphasise the difficulty of confining the notion of 'Taliban' to one distinct representation, I have chosen to use the term here without any diacritics throughout.

The limited utility of this literature, unfortunately, is symptomatic of much academic writing on contemporary Afghanistan: the academic lens has been defined by the geopolitical constellations of the Cold War which had escalated in the coup d'état of the Soviet-backed *People's Democratic Party of Afghanistan* (PDPA) in April 1978, followed by the invasion of the Soviet Army in December 1979 and the subsequent armed resistance of prominently Islamist organisations – financially and logistically supported by chief stakeholders in the Cold War. After the defeat and withdrawal of the Soviet Army after ten years of military occupation, the victorious Islamist organisations ran for the capital Kabul, unleashing a civil war of extreme brutality in their desire to replace the PDPA government. Meanwhile, as the Cold War ended with the fall of most regimes of the Eastern Bloc, international attention shifted away from Afghanistan – only to be rekindled in 2001, when the country had regained its geopolitical significance for the nations of the 'Global North'.[2]

This said, we need to acknowledge that scholarship on the country had for some time been informed by political agendas of one kind or other, resulting in rushed and sometimes spectacular publications which – perhaps for lack of alternatives – obtained almost instantly the status of major references.[3] With regard to the Taliban, this is certainly the case with the book titled simply *Taliban* by Pakistan-born investigative journalist Ahmed Rashid, which was first published in 2000 and since been reprinted repeatedly by various publishers (academic and non-academic alike), and translated into over twenty languages.[4] I myself acknowledge that, for quite a while, my own perspective was strongly informed by the narrative of 'expert' Rashid and hence I am highly sensitive to the distortions such rushed and glossed jobs can cause. A more serious academic engagement with the Taliban is needed, which remains detached from the short-lived and rather arbitrary political agendas which lead to publishers promoting insufficiently digested research with an eye to sales figures.

2 I have deliberately opted for this term instead of the perhaps more widespread and colloquial 'West' with all its derivatives, as, firstly, 'West' seems to reciprocate the essentialisation of the 'East', or 'Orient', as has rightly been the focus of critique of the 'Orientalism' debate in the 1980s and 1990s. Instead, 'Global North/South' divide, although conceptually devised largely also in European and North-American academic circles, is defined by structural (predominantly economic) imbalance and systemic inequalities. For a diligent discussion, see Manuela Boatcă, *Global Inequalities Beyond Occidentalism* (Farnham and Burlington, VT, 2015).

3 See M. Jamil Hanifi, 'Vending Distorted Afghanistan Through Patriotic "Anthropology"', *Critique of Anthropology* 31.3 (2011), pp. 256–70.

4 See Ahmed Rashid, *Taliban: The Power of Militant Islam in Afghanistan and Beyond* (London, 2008, rev. ed.).

In fact, it shall be contended here that we still do not know who 'The Taliban' were, and are, apart from the nomenclature of the Islamic Emirate of Afghanistan. It is certainly possible to focus on these actors as emblematic representatives of the Taliban, while leaving aside the gross of those who call themselves Taliban, or identify in part or whole with whatever that label represents. This would include those whom social anthropologist David B. Edwards aptly calls 'Talifans'.[5] After the ousting of the government of the Islamic Emirate of Afghanistan from Kabul in December 2001 by the USA-led military coalition, the Bonn Agreement and the subsequent installation of the Ḥāmid Karzay government, the Taliban in Afghanistan were reduced to 'insurgents', while across the borderline in Pakistan 'New' or 'Neo-Taliban' are said to have emerged, eventually manifesting themselves in the *Taḥrīk-i Ṭālibān-i Pākistān* (TṬP).[6] Are they all separate entities? If so, what are the delineating criteria? Moreover, what makes them all 'Taliban'? It appears that we still need careful and patient research to even approximate answers to these questions.[7]

The complexities outlined here in a woodcut-like manner only, as well as the formal constraints that an edited volume puts on an author, require informed limitations of the topic. First, the 'Taliban' here will refer to those who ran the Islamic Emirate of Afghanistan between 1996 and 2001 centrally from Kabul. The later permutations will therefore only play an occasional role. Moreover, even then the 'Taliban' need to be confined further, foremost to their formal leadership, defined by their membership in the Kandahar-based Supreme Council (*ᶜālī shūrā*) and the Kabul-based Cabinet (*kābīnah*) of the Islamic Emirate.[8]

5 See David B. Edwards, *Caravan of Martyrs: Sacrifice and Suicide Bombing in Afghanistan* (Oakland, CA, 2017), pp. 173–7. A quite similar point had already been made a few years earlier by James Caron, 'Review of 'Poetry of the Taliban' by Alex Strick van Linschoten and Felix Kuehn', *jadaliyya.com*, 27 May 2012. URL: www.jadaliyya. com/Details/26082/Poetry-of-the-Taliban. For access dates of online resources, see the Bibliography and the accompanying note, p. 366.

6 See Antonio Giustozzi, *Koran, Kalashnikov and Laptop: The Neo-Taliban Insurgency in Afghanistan* (London and New York, 2007); Giustozzi (ed.), *Decoding the New Taliban: Insights from the Afghan Field* (London and New York, 2009); Sana Haroon, 'Public Visibility of Women and the Rise of the Neo-Taliban Movement in Khyber-Pakhtunkhwa, 2007–9', in *Beyond Swat: History, Society and Economy along the Afghanistan-Pakistan Frontier*, ed. Benjamin D. Hopkins and Magnus Marsden (London and New York, 2013), pp. 193–205, 318f. (notes and references).

7 This, in fact, I have begun to undertake as a first investigation of the genesis of Taliban as a discursive tradition in a *longue durée* perspective, resulting in my recent book manuscript *The Pashtun Borderland in Uproar: A Religious and Cultural History of (the) Taliban* (forthcoming).

8 For one list of the persons involved, see Mawlavī Vakīl Aḥmad 'Mutavakkil', *Afghānistān*

The second reason why an investigation into the legal universe of the Taliban is so challenging is that most academic research into the Taliban to date has been limited to geopolitical and security studies, with a special interest in *al-Qāʿida* rather than the Taliban.[9] This also explains the relative lack of serious research into the wider religious and legal universe of the Taliban,[10] especially with regard to the possibly numerous legal traditions they were inhabiting. This, in fact, will be the subject matter of my next major research. Therefore, a disclaimer seems well in place that all which is presented here must be regarded as tentative for it covers only one of numerous possible legal discourses on violence among the Taliban, even if we restrict our notion of 'Taliban' drastically.

aw Ṭālibān (Mayvand, [1384sh], 2nd ed.), pp. 38–43; for another, see S. Fida Yunas, *Afghanistan: Organization of the Peoples* [sic] *Democratic Party of Afghanistan/Watan Party, Governments and Biographical Sketches (1982–1998)*, vol. 2 (Peshawar, 1998), pp. 771–3.

9 Besides Rashid's above-mentioned journalistic account, see, for example, William Maley (ed.), *Fundamentalism Reborn? Afghanistan and the Taliban* (London, 1998); on the nexus between Arab volunteers and the network around Jalāl al-Dīn Ḥaqqānī (killed *c.* 1435/2014) in the Loyah Paktiya region of eastern Afghanistan, see Vahid Brown and Don Rassler, *The Haqqani Nexus and the Evolution of al-Qa'ida* (West Point, NY, 2011); Brown/Rassler, *Fountainhead of Jihad: The Haqqani Nexus, 1973–2012* (London, 2013); Anne Stenersen, *Al-Qaida in Afghanistan* (Cambridge, 2017).

10 Works of this type, which have been considered standard readings (despite falling considerably short on the development of the Taliban religious worldview) include Maley, *Fundamentalism*, and M. J. Gohari, *The Taliban: Ascent to Power* (Karachi et al., 2000). The latter contains a rather weak chapter on 'The Taliban's Islamic Theology' (pp. 26–43). David B. Edward's excellent article 'Summoning Muslims: Print, Politics and Religious Ideology in Afghanistan', *Modern Asian Studies* 52.3 (1993), pp. 609–28, on the religious vision of the Islamist *Ḥizb-i islāmī* faction led by Gulbuddīn Ḥikmatyār (b. 1366/1947) in the 1980s has so far not been supplemented by a similar work on the much more complex Taliban. Works like Farhat Taj, *Taliban and Anti-Taliban* (Newcastle, 2011) are a cause for cautious optimism; my own work in the last few years had been pointedly devoted to closing this apparent gap in the research: see Jan-Peter Hartung, 'Between a Rock and a Hard Place: The *Ṭālibān*, Afghan Self-Determination, and the Challenges of Transnational Jihadism', *Die Welt des Islams* 56.2 (2016), pp. 125–52; 'The Praiseworthiness of Divine Beauty – The 'Shaykh al-Hind' Maḥmūd al-Ḥasan, Social Justice, and Deobandiyyat', *South Asian History and Culture* 7.4 (2016), pp. 346–69; 'Of Pious Missions and Challenging the Elders: A Genealogy of Radical Egalitarianism in the Pashtun Borderscape', *Geopolitics* 24.2 (2019), pp. 308–43; '«He's Just a Man!» – Pashtun Salafists and the Representation of the Prophet', *Die Welt des Islams* 60.2–3 (2020), pp. 170–204; 'Taking Lessons from the Prophet in Times of War: Muḥammadan Images during the Afghan Resistance, ca. 1978–1992', in *Heirs of the Prophet: Authority and Power in Early Modern and Contemporary Islam*, ed. Rachida Chih, David Jordan and Stefan Reichmuth, (Leiden and Boston, MA, forthcoming); *The Pashtun Borderland in Uproar.*

A starting point shall therefore serve the wide-spread – though not that easily sustainable – view that, religiously, the Taliban originate and belong predominantly in the learned tradition of 'Deobandiyyat'[11] as it manifested itself in the linguistic and cultural space that I have framed as 'Pashtun Borderland'. This "borderland" can be the loosely defined belt around the colonial and post-colonial borderline between Afghanistan and British India (and then Pakistan as a successor state of the latter), topographically defined by the Hindukush mountains in the north and Registan and Dasht-i Margo deserts in the south. Alongside the quite valid hypothesis of the Taliban as representatives of a certain type of 'Deobandiyyat', which is even attributed to a small choice of *dīnī madāris* in Pakistan's province of Khyber-Pakhtunkhwa (formerly North-West Frontier Province), I discuss below the alternative hypothesis that much of the Taliban's actual legal and administrative practices are rather derived from Pashtun customary law, commonly presented by the quite colourful term 'paẍtūnvalī'.

Third and finally, we need to confine the broad term 'violence', in order to further specify the scope of this present investigation. After all, 'violence' in general can take many forms, ranging from what feminist philosopher Judith Butler has labelled 'hate speech' to various forms of physical exertion of power, either against individuals, as in sexual assault, or collectives, as in military combat.[12] Any form of 'violence' can procure religious legitimisation, for which the mere existence of heresiography writings, or the legal and theological debates on gender relations, provide ample evidence.[13] With regard to the Taliban, the gender issue almost forces itself upon us, given its broad and sometimes rather lurid media coverage.[14] In line with the overall theme of the present volume, however, the 'violence' in the Taliban legal discourse that is investigated in this chapter shall be confined mainly to two of its manifestations: religiously sustained warfare (*jihād*) and physical punishment (*ta^{c}zīr*). It will become clear that

11 I wish to refrain here from using rather static and, moreover, monolithic terms like 'Deoband school' or 'Deoband(ī) tradition'; instead, I argue for a more diverse and context-bound notion, expressed in the idea of 'Deobandiyyat' as an ideological bare minimum of claimed adherence. See Hartung, 'Praiseworthiness', pp. 346–69.

12 See Judith Butler, *Excitable Speech: A Politics of the Performative* (New York and London, 1997); Pierre Bourdieu, *Le sens pratique* (Paris, 1980); Bourdieu, *La domination masculine* (Paris, 1998), 215–22 et passim.

13 See, for example, Ralph E. S. Tanner, *Violence and Religion: Cross-Cultural Opinions and Consequences* (New Delhi, 2007).

14 See, for example, US Department of State, Bureau of Democracy, Human Rights and Labor, 'Report on the Taliban's War on Women', 17 November 2001. URL: https://2009-2017.state.gov/j/drl/rls/6185.htm; even more ghastly in Rashid, *Taliban*, pp. 105–16.

the gender-related violence exerted by the Taliban ties well into both forms an overall discourse on religiously sustained warfare.

Of course, one needs to acknowledge a disparity between theoretically substantiated ethical and legal thought, and sociopolitical praxis. While the theoretical aspect refers to normative expectations with as little space as possible for negotiation, a legal practice is informed much more by the realities of ever-changing contexts, even more so in the case of the Taliban after the end of their central government. The focus here shall nonetheless remain first and foremost on the religious legitimisation or de-legitimisation of warfare as a manifestation of 'violence', and will therefore stay mainly within the realm of theology and *fiqh*, occasionally juxtaposed with references to the Taliban governing practice before 2001.

We begin with an examination into the 'Deobandiyyat' of the Taliban and trace its impact on their legal interpretation. To do so, we first need to go back further to the foundation of the *Dār al-ᶜulūm* in North-Indian Deoband in response to the establishment of direct British colonial rule over the Subcontinent after 1857.

FROM DEOBAND TO AKOṚAH KHAṬṬAK

When the Taliban finally established their central government in Kabul, Mawlānā Samīᶜ al-Ḥaqq (assassinated 1440/2018), then principal of the *Dār al-ᶜulūm ḥaqqāniyyah* in Akoṛah Khaṭṭak near Peshawar, hastened to claim that it was his institution that served as the sole cradle for the new rulers over Afghanistan.[15] In the aftermath of the *al-Qāᶜida* attacks in the USA on 11 September 2001, journalists, policy makers and academics alike rushed to the *Ḥaqqāniyyah*, successfully seeking confirmation by speaking to Samīᶜ al-Ḥaqq without paying too much attention to the agenda behind this scholar-cum-politician's claim.[16] Notwithstanding this, the *Ḥaqqāniyyah* is undeniably one of the largest *dīnī madāris* in Pakistan, which, along with those in Karachi, and also situated in

15 See Samiul Haq [*sic*], *Afghan Taliban: War of Ideology. Struggle for Peace* (Islamabad, 2015). As proved by a random Google search on 11 November 2020, the international community appears to have bought into Samīᶜ al-Ḥaqq's narrative: in the international media coverage of his assassination on 2 November 2018, presumably for his affirmative position on polio vaccination by an adherent of the opposing TṬP, the scholar was alternately labelled 'godfather of the Taliban', 'father of the Taliban', 'spiritual father of the Afghan Taliban', credited with 'having trained most of the Taliban leaders'.

16 See, for example, Rashid, *Taliban*, 90f.; Tribune 24/7, 'Kirsten Seymour interviews Mullah Omar's teacher, Maulana Sami ul Haq [*sic*]', 31 July 2011. URL: www.youtube.com/watch?v=6SL2cnUgBT8.

the Pashtun Borderland, have, at least, a strong affinity to the Taliban.[17] It is then a chief representative of institutionalised 'Deobandiyyat' in the region, and while I contend that the religious and, subsequently, legal universe of the Taliban is locally informed also by other, including proto-Salafī, traits in the Pashtun Borderland,[18] 'Deobandiyyat' in various local modifications remains perhaps the dominant one, with the *Ḥaqqāniyyah* as one of its major representatives. It is thus feasible to start by investigating its institutional approach to *fiqh* in general, and legal views on 'just warfare' (*jihād*) in particular. Pivotal in this endeavour is Samīᶜ al-Ḥaqq's father ᶜAbd al-Ḥaqq Akoṛavī (d. 1409/1988), who had himself graduated from the *Dār al-ᶜulūm* at Deoband and, upon his return to Akoṛah Khaṫṫak in 1947, had founded the *Ḥaqqāniyyah* there. At Deoband, ᶜAbd al-Ḥaqq studied with the renowned Ḥusayn Aḥmad Madanī (d. 1377/1957),[19] who, as one of the closest disciples of the 'Shaykh al-Hind' Maḥmūd al-Ḥasan (d. 1339/1920), had a history of activity in the Pashtun Borderland himself: the Shaykh al-Hind and his circle of retainers had relocated to territories on the fringes of the British Crown Colony, using them as their operational basis for religiously sustained anti-imperialist agitation.[20]

ᶜAbd al-Ḥaqq, alongside associates of a similar background, established the *Ḥaqqāniyyah* on the tenets of the 'Deobandiyyat' that he had received from his teachers, and thereby contributed substantially to this current (*maslak*) of South Asian Muslim scholarship in the Pashtun Borderland.[21] This, at least, is what the institutional narrative promotes, supported by the label 'Second Deoband' – a name allegedly bestowed upon the *Ḥaqqāniyyah* by the then-principal of the *Dār al-ᶜulūm* at Deoband, Qārī Muḥammad Ṭayyib (d. 1403/1983), during a visit in

17 See the special issue on the Taliban of the in-house monthly *al-Ḥaqq* 31.12 (1417/1996), as well as the documentation of the interaction between the leadership of the *Ḥaqqāniyyah* and that of the Taliban in Mawlānā Samīᶜ al-Ḥaqq (ed.), *Mashāhīr bi-nām-i Mawlānā Samīᶜ al-Ḥaqq ṣāḥib*, 6 vols (Akoṛah Khaṫṫak, 1433/2012), VI, 308–431.

18 See Hartung, '«He's Just a Man!»', pp. 187–94; Hartung, 'Of Pious Missions', pp. 314–18; Hartung, 'Praiseworthiness', pp. 359–61.

19 See Shaykh al-Ḥadīs̱ Ḥaẕrat Mawlānā ᶜAbd al-Ḥaqq [Akoṛavī], *Fatāvā-yi ḥaqqāniyyah*, ed. Mawlānā Muftī Mukhtārallāh Ḥaqqānī, 6 vols (Akoṛah Khaṫṫak, 1422/2002), I, pp. 82–90. On Madanī, see Hartung, *Viele Wege und ein Ziel: Leben und Wirken von Sayyid Abū l-Ḥasan ᶜAlī Ḥasanī Nadwī (1914–1999)* (Würzburg, 2004), pp. 239–43; Barbara D. Metcalf, *Husain Ahmad Madani: The Jihad for Islam and India's Freedom* (Oxford, 2009). For a (not exceptionally exciting) Ḥaqqānī perspective on Madanī, see ᶜAbd al-Qayyūm Ḥaqqānī, *Savāniḥ-i shaykh al-islām ḥaẕrat Sayyid Ḥusayn Aḥmad Madanī* (Khāliqābād, 1425/2004).

20 See Hartung, 'The Praiseworthiness', pp. 355–9.

21 See Ajmal Khaṫṫak, *Qīṣṣah zamā də adabī žvand* (Chārsaddah, 2005), pp. 92–4, 139–44.

the mid-1970s.[22] Assuming that this institutional narrative is correct, what would that mean for the *fiqh* that is taught, studied and practised at the *Ḥaqqāniyyah* and its network of affiliated smaller *madāris*? An answer to this requires an examination of the foundational period of 'Deobandiyyat'. This was strongly shaped by the directives of its two founding figures, Rashīd Aḥmad Gangohī (d. 1323/1905) and Muḥammad Qāsim Nānawtavī (d. 1297/1877), as well as its first student, the above-mentioned Shaykh al-Hind Maḥmūd al-Ḥasan, teacher and spiritual guide of ᶜAbd al-Ḥaqq Akoṛavī's own teacher Ḥusayn Aḥmad Madanī.[23]

LEGAL INTERPRETATION IN TIMES OF INFESTATION AND CHAOS: THE ANTECEDENTS

Unlike the earlier *Ahl-i ḥadīs̱*, who emerged as the nucleus for an indigenous Proto-Salafī Islam,[24] the early scholars at Deoband remained clearly within the legal universe of the Ḥanafī *madhhab*, theologically supported by its adherence to the Māturīdī creed. It is this combination which, since around the eleventh century CE, constituted the theological and jurisprudential mainstream in the wider Muslim central and south asian nexus,[25] including those territories that would eventually emerge as the distinct political entity 'Afghanistan'.[26] This was even explicitly enshrined in the Afghan constitutions of 1931, 1952 and 1964.[27]

22 See Samīᶜ al-Ḥaqq, *Khuṭbāt-i ḥaqq*, ed. Mawlānā Muftī Mukhtārallāh Ḥaqqānī (Akoṛah Khaṭṭak, n.d.), pp. 52f.

23 Meanwhile, the body of academic works on 'Deobandiyyat' has grown considerably. Yet, the standard work still remains Metcalf, *Islamic Revival in British India: Deoband, 1860–1900* (Princeton, 1982).

24 See Philipp Bruckmayr and Hartung, 'Introduction: Challenges from 'The Periphery'? – Salafī Islam Outside the Arab World. Spotlights on Wider Asia', *Die Welt des Islams* 60.2–3 (2020), pp. 137–69, here pp. 139–44.

25 For a thorough historical overview of the spread of the Ḥanafiyya in Muslim Central Asia, see Yusuf Ziya Kavakcı, *XI. ve XII. asırlarda Karahanlılar devrinde Māvāra' al-Nahr* [sic] *İslâm hukukçuları* (Ankara, 1976); on the spread of the Māturīdiyya, see Bruckmayr, 'The Spread and Persistence of Māturīdi [*sic*] Kalām and Underlying Dynamics', *Iran and the Caucasus* 13.1 (2009), pp. 59–92; Bruckmayr, 'Güney ve Güneydoğu Asya'da Mâturîdîlik'in Geçmiş ve Bugünkü Yönleri/Past and Present Aspects of Māturīdısm [*sic*] in South and Southeast Asia', in *Uluğ Bir Çinar İmâm Mâturîdî Uluslararası Sempozyum Tebliğler Kitabı*, ed. Ahmet Kartal (Istanbul, 2014), pp. 115–31.

26 On the Ḥanafiyya in Afghanistan since the centralisation reforms of the Barakzay Amīr ᶜAbd al-Raḥmān (r. 1880–1901), see Hasan Kawun Kakar, *Government and Society in Afghanistan: The Reign of Amir ʾAbd* [sic] *al-Rahman Khan* (Austin, TX and London, 1979); Asta Olesen, *Islam and Politics in Afghanistan* (Richmond, 1995), pp. 65–8.

27 See Mohammad Hashim Kamali, *Law in Afghanistan: A Study of the Constitutions,*

It appears that in the 1830s, that is before the abolition of nominal Muslim rule in India, the question of legal authority became increasingly debated, owing to the acceleration of the hermeneutical controversy over religious interpretative authority at the hand of the 'proto-Salafī Islam' of Sayyid Aḥmad Barelvī and Shāh Ismāᶜīl Dihlavī (both killed 1246/1831).[28] The matter was of great importance, because Shāh Ismāᶜīl was, after all, a grandson of the celebrated Shāh Walīullāh Dihlavī (d. 1176/1762) who would himself emerge as a pivotal reference figure for any kind of religious reform endeavour after the establishment of direct British colonial rule. Among the fierce opponents to the proto-Salafī legal hermeneutics of Sayyid Aḥmad and Shāh Ismāᶜīl was the last Grand Mufti of the Mughals, Ṣadr al-Dīn Dihlavī, better known by his penname 'Āzurdah' (d. 1285/1868) – he himself had studied with renowned members of the Shāh Walīullāh family. In one of his *fatāwā*, Āzurdah appears to be the first to use a term that would become a defining feature in Deobandi legal hermeneutics: *taqlīd shakhṣī*.[29]

Very much in line with Āzurdah's promulgation of *taqlīd shakhṣī* as a necessity, the co-founder of the *Dār al-ᶜulūm* at Deoband, Rashīd Aḥmad Gangohī, stated:

> *Taqlīd* is a general [*muṭlaq*] duty. For a person, there are two ways of *taqlīd*. The first one is person-specific [*shakhṣī*], in as far as all issues have inevitably to

Matrimonial Law and the Judiciary (Leiden, 1985), pp. 27–35, 231–4. The passage 'The religion of Afghanistan is the sacred religion [*dīn-i muqaddas*] of Islam, the orientation in rite and social practice [*mazhab-i rasmī va ᶜumūmī*] is that of the elevated Ḥanafī; the king of Afghanistan is to hold firm to this orientation', forming the first article of the 1931 constitution, had been taken over almost verbatim into the constitution of 1963. See Markaz-i farhangī-yi nivīsandagān-i Afghānistān (ed.), *Matn-i kāmil-i qāvānīn-i āsāsī-yi Afghānistān: az 1301 tā 1372sh* (Qum, 1374 SH), pp. 170, 183.

28 See Hartung, '«He's Just a Man!»', pp. 176–87. The controversy referred to here dates back to the eighteenth century, pivoting on the primacy of either reason (*ᶜaql*) or adherence to tradition (*naql*) as mode of cognition. As a matter of academic research, it has figured much in the investigation of standardisation processes of Islamic learning: prominently, see Jamal Malik, *Islamische Gelehrtenkultur in Nordindien: Entwicklungsgeschichte und Tendenzen am Beispiel von Lucknow* (Leiden, New York and Cologne, 1997); Francis Robinson, *The 'Ulama of Farangi Mahall and Islamic Culture in South Asia* (New Delhi, 2001); critically Hartung, 'Abused Rationality? – On the Role of *maᶜqūlī* Scholars in the Events of 1857/8', in *Mutiny at the Margins: New Perspectives on the Indian Uprising of 1857. Vol. 5: Muslim, Dalit and Subaltern Narratives*, ed. Crispin Bates (New Delhi, Thousand Oaks, CA and London, 2014), pp. 135–55.

29 See Mawlavī Ghulām Qādir Baniyānī Kalkattavī (ed.), *Tanbīh al-ḍāllayn wa-hidāyat al-ṣāliḥayn* (Lahore, n.d.), pp. 40f.

> be solved according to the response of one particular scholar. The second is not person-specific [*ghayr shakhṣī*]; here one is at liberty to realise, or not realise, the solution as suggested by a particular scholar. In times of tribulation and chaos [*fitna va fasād*], however, the non-person-specific *taqlīd* is prohibited [*ḥarām*] and the person-specific compulsory [*wājib*].[30]

Such an uncompromising ruling did, of course, not go uncontested, even more so, as Gangohī could quote neither from Qurʾān nor Prophetic *ḥadīth* in order to back up the particulars of his response. Apparently, the issue stands and falls with how the phrase 'people of the remembrance' (*ahl al-dhikr*) in Q16:43 is understood. To explain his own understanding, Gangohī referred to the circumstances in which the Qurʾān had been standardised under Caliph ᶜUthmān b. ᶜAffān. At that time, he argued, the increasing variety of Qurʾānic readings had become a serious concern for the integration of the Muslim *umma*, a cause for chaos (*fasād*), which could only be overcome by the authoritative caliphal decree over the exclusively binding recension of the Qurʾān.[31] In Gangohī's view, the obedience of this decree by the Muslim *umma* constituted a precedential *taqlīd shakhṣī* which has therefore always to come into play whenever the integrity of the *umma* is in danger. Clearly, the mushrooming of all kinds of increasingly institutionalised reformist approaches (*masālik*) in Islamic hermeneutics after the end of nominal Muslim rule in India constituted, for him, a situation quite similar to the case of Caliph ᶜUmar. However, no proper argument was put forward why anyone should follow a scholar from Deoband instead of, say, a scholar from the *Ahl-i ḥadīs̱*.

It is here where the spiritual pedigree comes forcefully to the fore, a fact that helps to understand why only one of the second generation of students at the *Dār al-ᶜulūm* of Deoband, ᶜUbaydallāh Sindhī, devotes much energy to establishing the institution as the true reflection of the teachings of Shāh Walīullāh Dihlavī. The eighteenth century scholar, however, while developing his view on *taqlīd* from Q16:43 (as Gangohī also did), concluded that those who 'do not know' (*lā taᶜlamūna*) are not restricted by the adherence to any single one of the canonical *madhāhib fiqhiyya*, but may ask for guidance from any *ahl al-dhikr,* regardless of the person's affiliation to any legal or theological tradition.[32] What distin-

30 Ḥaẕrat Mawlānā al-Ḥājj al-Ḥāfiẓ Rashīd Aḥmad Gangohī, *Fatāvā-yi rashīdiyyah: mubavvab bi-ṭarz-i jadīd* (Delhi, 1987), pp. 235.

31 See Gangohī, *Fatāvā-yi rashīdiyyah*, pp. 234f.

32 See Shāh Waliyallāh Aḥmad b. ᶜAbd al-Raḥīm al-Fārūqī al-Dihlawī, *ᶜIqd al-jīd fī aḥkām al-ijtihād wa'l-taqlīd*, ed. Muḥammad ᶜAlī al-Ḥalabī al-Atharī (Sharjah, 1415/1995), pp. 75–84.

guishes Gangohī here is his emphasis on 'times of tribulation and chaos' which require those who 'do not know' to stick to the legal views of one person only; this person, in turn, is also bound by the obligation to perform *taqlīd shakhṣī* in these circumstances; in the end, it is the confines of the *madhhab fiqhī* which determines the limits of religious authority.

Gangohī's student Maḥmūd al-Ḥasan, the 'Shaykh al-Hind', followed his teacher's line: in his early *Adillah-yi kāmilah*, one of his few extant writings, he staunchly defended the binding obligation for *taqlīd shakhṣī* against the polemical intervention of the rival *Ahl-i ḥadīs̱*. Interestingly, Maḥmūd al-Ḥasan did not tie its necessity explicitly to specific circumstances, but rather to the idea of obedience (*ṭāᶜa*), derived from Q4.59, and decreed that 'those among you in command' (*ulū 'l-amr minkum*) are nowadays the *ᶜulamāʾ*.[33] This is a detail of quite some significance, because it justifies not only their demand for obedience in all religious matters, but also the *ᶜulamāʾ's* claims for political leadership, which one sees forcefully resurfacing again towards the end of the twentieth century with the Taliban.

Given the nature of Maḥmūd al-Ḥasan's treatise as a religious polemic rather than a formal legal text, the absence of references to 'times of tribulation and chaos' is explicable. Still, as an undercurrent, the theme is still detectable in references to the sectarian tendencies (*tafrīq*) within the Indo-Muslim scholarship as a manifest *fitnah*. Either scholars at the time reject the authority of the *ḥadīth* altogether (*Ahl-i qurʾān*), or the consensus of the *ṣaḥāba* and analogous reasoning (*Ahl-i ḥadīs̱*); this ultimately results in the disrespectful vilification of the Medinese Caliphs as religious innovators (*mubtadiᶜūn*).[34] By this, they risk causing severe confusion among the common Muslims, leading to disorientation and, ultimately, to the disintegration of the Muslim *umma* along sectarian lines.

Fast forward and the Taliban operated in the very same semantic universe: the Afghan Civil War since April 1992 caused by the various Islamist militias – formerly involved in the armed resistance to the Soviet military presence, but now their greed for political power had let them cynically ignore the Afghan civilian population and its need for some degree of infrastructure. This was clear proof, for the Taliban, of 'tribulation and chaos'. In the words of the then-Foreign Minister of the Islamic Emirate of Afghanistan, Vakīl Aḥmad b. ᶜAbd al-Ghaffār 'Mutavakkil' (b. *c.* 1391/1971):

33 See Maḥmūd al-Ḥasan Ṣāḥib Deobandī, *Adillah-yi kāmilah, yaᶜnī ghayr-muqallidoṇ ke das suʾālāt awr unke taḥqīqī javābāt*, ed. Muḥmmad Amīn Pālanpūrī (Karachi, 1410 AH [1294 AH]), pp. 80f.

34 See Maḥmūd al-Ḥasan, *Adillah-yi kāmilah*, pp. 86f.

> After the capture of Kabul, the interim government of the *mujāhidīn* with a rotational presidency gained some kind of popularity. After the victory, people had high hopes that under an Islamic government in the country their wishes would come true. Very soon, however, internal rivalries [*khpal manźī raqābtūnah*] turned into war [*jagṛah*]. [...] Disorder and rudeness [*be naẓməy aw nā khvāle*] climaxed, [and] the seeds for the breakdown of a formerly integrated homeland were sown.[35]

That the Taliban emerged in such a situation is no surprise against the backdrop of the early Deobandi stance on legal, and subsequently political, authority outlined above. As indicated by Maḥmūd al-Ḥasan – even before the turn to the twentieth century – it is no longer the *umarāʾ* who constitute the *ulū ʾl-amr* of Q4.59, but the *ᶜulamāʾ*. it is they who are therefore tasked with the duties formerly held by the successors to the Prophet in the leadership of the Muslim community, both politically and spiritually.[36] Foremost among those duties is the proclamation of armed *jihād* for the defence of the 'Lands of Islam' and the Muslim *umma*.[37] The aspirations of Deobandi *ᶜulamāʾ* found their institutional expression in 1919, when some leading scholars, including ᶜAbd al-Ḥaqq Akoṛavī's teacher Ḥusayn Aḥmad Madanī, established the *Jamᶜiyyat al-ᶜulamāʾ-i Hind* (JUH) and took an active part in the anti-colonial political struggle of the increasingly vocal Indian Independence Movement. The justification for the Muslim aspiration to political leadership in the subcontinent was again derived from a claim to be the sole true heir of Shāh Walīullāh's thoughts, which were then politically framed by the above mentioned ᶜUbaydallāh Sindhī (who held the epithet 'Imām-i inqilāb').[38] The chain of learned authority established in this way, very much in the sense of Hobsbawm's 'invented traditions',[39] was considerably reinforced by the practice of *taqlīd shakhṣī*, which in turn was boosted by strong Sufi patterns of allegiance that prevailed in 'Deobandiyyat'.[40]

35 Mutavakkil, *Afghānistān aw Ṭālibān*, pp. 10f. Also, see Mullā ᶜAbd al-Salām Ẓaᶜīf, *Ṭālibān lah Kandahārah tar Mazārah* (Kabul, 1396 SH/2018), pp. 6–10.

36 See Patricia Crone, *Medieval Islamic Political Thought* (Edinburgh, 2004), pp. 21–3.

37 For a prominent classical reference, invoked across the canonical *madhāhib fiqhiyya*, see Abū ʾl-Ḥasan ᶜAlī al-Māwardī, *Kitāb al-Aḥkām al-sulṭāniyya* (Beirut, 1422/2002), pp. 35–54.

38 See ᶜUbaydallāh Sindhī, *Shāh Valīyallāh awr unkī siyāsī taḥrīk* (Lahore, 1942).

39 See Eric Hobsbawm, 'Introduction: Inventing Traditions', in *The Invention of Tradition*, ed. Eric Hobsbawm and Terence Ranger (Cambridge, 1983), pp. 1–14, esp. pp. 9f.

40 See [Akoṛavī] *Fatāvā*, II, pp. 243–86; Muftī Rashīd Aḥmad Ludhiyānavī, *Aḥsan al-fatāvā*, 10 vols (Karachi, 1425 AH, 11th ed.), I, pp. 542–54.

In fact, these strong personal dependencies turned out to be Janus-faced, as allegiances to opposing scholars within the realm of 'Deobandiyyat' provoked dissent and, finally, internal schism. This discord was, ironically, precisely what *taqlīd shakhṣī* was originally meant to prevent. While one group went in the same direction with regards to piety and sharing the hermeneutical approach to religious knowledge, dissent in core political issues caused the eventual fractioning of Shabbīr Aḥmad ᶜUs̱mānī (d. 1369/1949) and his retainers from the anti-Partition JUH, and the establishment of the pro-Pakistan *Jamᶜiyyat al-ᶜulamāʾ-i islām* (JUI) in 1945.[41] While the JUH remained in the Indian Union after 1947 and soon ceased to play any significant political role, the JUI made political aspirations a central part of Deobandi identity in Pakistan. One of its early leading representatives has been ᶜAbd al-Ḥaqq Akoṛavī, who repeatedly served in what had, in the meantime, become a formal political party in the National Assembly of Pakistan.[42] He, as well as his son and successor Samīᶜ al-Ḥaqq, would consequently represent the one current of Deobandi scholarship that, allegedly, advocated an active involvement of the *ᶜulamāʾ* in politics, epitomised in ᶜAbd al-Ḥaqq's teacher Ḥusayn Aḥmad Madanī.[43] At the opposing end stood scholars for whom 'politics never became a vocation, nor an integral component of their religious practice and mission, nor did they view the realisation of their religious aims to be predicated on success in the political arena, although they did favor a state in which Muslims could live according to Islamic law'.[44] The epitome of this current is identified by Nasr as Ashraf ᶜAlī Tħānavī (d. 1362/1943), another student of the 'Shaykh al-Hind' Maḥmūd al-Ḥasan,[45] and it seems that here Sufi patterns of allegiance trumped those of students to their teachers as envisaged

41 See Sayyid A.S. Pirzada, *The Politics of the Jamiat Ulema-i-Islam* [sic] *Pakistan: 1971–1977* (Karachi, 2000), pp. 5–13. On ᶜUs̱mānī, see Sayyid Maḥbūb Riẕvī, *Tārīkh-i Dār al-ᶜulūm Deoband*, 2 vols (Deoband, 1414/1993, 2nd ed.), II, pp. 98–102.

42 See the lists of members of the fifth to seventh National Assembly at URL: www.na.gov.pk/en/content. php?id=121.

43 See Seyed Vali Reza Nasr, 'The Rise of Sunni Militancy in Pakistan: The Changing Role of Islamism and the Ulama in Society and Politics', *Modern Asian Studies* 34.1 (2000), pp. 139–80.

44 Nasr, 'Rise of Sunni Militancy', pp. 170f. Nasr's typology had been criticised for being too static by Muhammad Qasim Zaman, *The Ulama in Contemporary Islam: Custodians of Change* (Princeton, 2002), pp. 133f. While Zaman is certainly right with regard to the complex reality of the tendencies under discussion, I contend that Nasr's typology, however crude, still carries some currency, especially for the case at hand here.

45 On Tħānavī, see prominently Zaman, *Ashraf 'Ali Thanawi: Islam in Modern South Asia* (Oxford, 2008); Ali Altaf Mian, *Surviving Modernity: Ashraf 'Alī Thānvī* [sic] *(1863–1943) and the Making of Muslim Orthodoxy in Colonial India* (unpublished PhD dissertation, Duke University, 2015).

under *taqlīd shakhṣī*. The one who represents this in our context here was Rashīd Aḥmad Ludĥiyānavī (assassinated 1422/2002),[46] leading jurisconsult (*muftī*) at his own *Dār al-iftāʾ wa'l-irshād*, or *Jāmiᶜah al-rashīd*, in Karachi.[47] Despite his Punjabi ethnicity, Ludĥiyānavī became an explicit reference point for the later Taliban; some have even made the – uncorroborated – claim that he was teacher of their first supreme leader, Mullā Muḥammad ᶜUmar (d. *c.* 1434/2013).[48]

Their references to the two jurisconsults ᶜAbd al-Ḥaqq Akoṛavī[49] and Rashīd Aḥmad Ludĥiyānavī, be they explicit or implicit, are quite revealing of the religious, legal and political universe of both the Taliban leadership and – to an extent – its troopers. First, they defy Samīᶜ al-Ḥaqq's above claim that it was the *Dār al-ᶜulūm ḥaqqāniyyah* that served as cradle and most important

46 In fact, they are complemented by yet another Deobandi scholar, Muftī Niẓām al-Dīn Shāmzay (assassinated 1425/2004), originally from Swat and active out of the *Jāmiᶜah fārūqiyyah* and later the *Jāmiᶜat al-ᶜulūm* of Binori Town in Karachi. It was he who, in a *fatwā* dated 18 September 2001, declared armed resistance against the looming US-American counterstrike against the Islamic Emirate of Afghanistan as individual religious obligation (*farẓ ᶜayn*): see URL: https://sadaehaqq.wordpress.com/2013/11/14/مفتی-شامزئی-رحمہ-اللہ-کا-فتویٰ-جس-کی-بنا/). Still, neither his *fatāwā* nor his relevant writings on legal matters are available to me, which is why I leave him out of my discussion here. His impact, however, will be covered in some detail in my above-mentioned forthcoming work *The Pashtun Borderland in Uproar*, ch. 4.3.

47 See Ludĥiyānavī, *Anvār al-rashīd: amīr al-mutakallimīn, imām al-ᶜārifīn, sayf allāh al-maslūl ḥaẓrat-i aqdas Muftī Rashīd Aḥmad Ṣāḥib Ludĥiyānavī ke naṣīḥat-i āmūz va baṣīrat-i afrūz-i ḥālāt va irshādāt*, 3 vols (Karachi, 1424 AH), II, pp. 153–72.

48 See, for instance, Bernt Glatzer, 'Zum politischen Islam der afghanischen Taliban', in *Sendungsbewußtsein und Eigennutz: Zu Motivation und Selbstverständnis islamischer Mobilisierung*, ed. Dietrich Reetz (Berlin, 2001), pp. 173–82, here p. 181. While there is no evidence for Mullā ᶜUmar having studied with Ludĥiyānavī, solid proof, however, exists for their frequent meetings in Kandahar, in which Ludĥiyānavī provided his counsel to the Taliban commander-in-chief.

49 Already before the establishment of the *Ḥaqqāniyyah*, ᶜAbd al-Ḥaqq held traditional study circles in Akoṛah Khaṫṫak, attended, among others, by Jalāl al-Dīn Ḥaqqānī (see above, note 8) Muḥammad Yūnus Khāliṣ (d. 1427/2006) – military commander of his own faction of the *Ḥizb-i islāmī* during the Soviet occupation, later retainer of the Taliban in his native Nangrahar province, and facilitator of both Usāma b. Lādin (after his return to Afghanistan in 1996) and Sayyid Shīr ᶜAlī Shāh Madanī (d. 1437/2015): see Mawlānā ᶜAbd al-Qayyūm Ḥaqqānī, *Ṣuḥbate bā ahl-i ḥaqq: ifādāt-i muḥaddiṡ-i kabīr Shaykh al-ḥadīṡ Mawlānā ᶜAbd al-Ḥaqq – raḥmat allāh ᶜalayhi* (Khāliqābād, 1419/1998), pp. 201–3, 358–93; Zāhidī Aḥmadzay, *Khāliṣ Bābā: də hidāyat pah lor* (Peshawar, 1385 SH), p. 5; Shīr ᶜAlī Shāh al-Madanī, 'al-Sīra al-dhātiyya li'l-shaykh al-Duktūr Shīr ᶜAlī Shāh al-Madanī', in *Yād: Shaykh al-tafsīr va'l-ḥadīṡ Mawlānā Ḋākṫar Shīr ᶜAlī Shāh Madanī – rḥ: ḥayāt va khidmāt*, ed. Muḥammad Asrār Madanī (Akoṛah Khaṫṫak, 1437/2016), pp. 17–19, here p. 17.

cadre-factory of the Taliban.[50] More importantly, however, if, for the time being, we accept Nasr's above mentioned typology, we are very well able to account for Islamist 'governance-oriented' leanings of the Taliban, as well as their strong 'guidance-orientation'.[51] After all, it is the latter that represents the subaltern variety of 'Deobandiyyat' especially in the Pashtun Borderland that resonates very well with those commonly deprived of socio-political and economic capital. This form of religiosity is firmly rooted in anti-elitist, egalitarian and pietist ideology, reflected in strong eschatological leanings which form the theological backdrop to legal interpretation.

While such eschatological awareness is certainly detectable also in ᶜAbd al-Ḥaqq's thinking, short-term political pragmatics prevailed with his son and heir Samīᶜ al-Ḥaqq. He considered himself member of the societal elite and went on to even establish his own splinter branch of the JUI reflecting his distinct agenda. In contrast was Rashīd Aḥmad Ludĥiyānavī, who also trained at the *Dār al-ᶜulūm* at Deoband under the tutelage of Ḥusayn Aḥmad Madanī. Ludĥiyānavī's unconditional allegiance shifted toward ᶜAbd al-Ghanī Pĥūlpūrī (d. 1383/1963), a renowned adept of Ashraf ᶜAlī Tĥānavī.[52] Pĥūlpūrī's spiritual guidance was strongly shaped by what Christian Lange had aptly labelled 'salvation anxiety',[53] which combined strong roots in eschatological thinking with subaltern humility with the unconditional zeal to fulfil one's religious obligations as meticulous as any possible. This ultimately included a readiness to defend Muslim territory and interests with the sword.[54]

THEOLOGICAL UNDERPINNINGS: PRIORITISING AL-ĀKHIRA

Eschatological rhetoric that pivots on unconditional willingness to sacrifice one's life and worldly possessions in *jihād* was not exclusive to subaltern Borderland 'Deobandiyyat'. With the onset of Islamically sustained armed resistance to the PDPA–Soviet nexus in 1979, it was equally embraced by various Islamist

50 See Glatzer, 'Zum politischen Islam'.

51 For the two ideal-typical categories 'governance-orientation' and 'guidance-orientation', and the conceptual history behind them, see, for instance, Bruckmayr/Hartung, 'Introduction', p. 165f.

52 See Ludĥiyānavī, *Aḥsan*, I, pp. 7–28.

53 See Christian Lange, 'Introducing Hell in Islamic Studies', in *Locating Hell in Islamic Traditions*, ed. Christian Lange (Leiden and Boston, MA, 2016), pp. 1–28, here pp. 9–11.

54 See Ludĥiyānavī, *Anvār*, I, pp. 77–114; also, Shāh ᶜAbd al-Ghanī Pĥūlpūrī, *Barāhīn-i qāṭiᶜah dar barā-yi tawḥīd, risālat, qiyāmat*, ed. Shāh Ḥakīm Muḥammad Akhtar (Karachi, n.d.), pp. 29–41, 144–95.

organisations.[55] Yet, it seems that the rhetoric was first and foremost strategically employed for recruitment purposes; eschatology did otherwise not figure greatly in governance-oriented Islamist systematics. There, the term *jihād* was rather used to assign righteous legitimacy to the opposition to any manifestation of 'ignorance' (*jāhiliyya*), that is, any socio-political perspective not ideologically grounded in the Islamic *dīn*.[56] Be that as it may, it certainly explains why governance-oriented Deobandi scholars in the Pashtun Borderland, like ᶜAbd al-Ḥaqq Akoṛavī, had employed a *jihād*-centric rhetoric already in the mid-1960s, if not even earlier. The developments since 1979 have therefore only added momentum to this trend. Theologically, however, the discussion of all things *jihād* by more guidance-oriented Deobandi scholars like Rashīd Aḥmad Ludhiyānavī and his associates (particularly his former student and spiritual heir Muftī Abū Lubābah Shāh Manṣūr [b. unknown]) adopted a consistent eschatological dimension. Since the Taliban received inspiration, if not counsel, from both sets of scholars, they are discussed here together, despite their substantial differences.

What emerges clearly from statements on the matter by both scholars is that the Hereafter is ascribed a higher degree of reality than the empirical world; such a soteriological perspective computed rather well with the subaltern mindset prevalent in the Taliban, and thereby helped to further shape the universe of their religious thought. Consequently, the concept of *jihād* is firmly embedded here, as is indicated by ᶜAbd al-Ḥaqq Akoṛavī's adoption of Ibn Ḥajar's interpretation of the sound Prophetic *ḥadīth*: 'Good will remain in the foreheads of horses until the Day of Resurrection' (*al-khaylu maᶜqūdun fī nawāṣīhā al-khayru ilā yawmi 'l-qiyāma*).[57] According to Ibn Ḥajar, 'the *jihād* will last until the Day of Resurrection' (*al-jihād māḍin ilā yawmi 'l-qiyāma*),[58] and is thus assigned the quality of an ongoing process that continues as long as this world exists.

55 See, for example, the relevant articles in the many periodicals published by each of the Islamist organisations in the 1980s, discussed in Hartung, 'Taking Lessons'. The important contribution by Simon Wolfgang Fuchs, 'Glossy Global Leadership: Unpacking the Multilingual Religious Thought of the *Jihad*', in *Afghanistan's Islam: From Conversion to the Taliban*, ed. Nile Green (Oakland, CA, 2017), pp. 189–206, 299–307 (notes and references), has clearly a different focus of interest. More along the line of my argument here is Edwards, *Caravan of Martyrs*, pp. 57–66, although the author probably takes his conclusions too far.

56 On the conceptual cornerstones of Islamist ideology, see Hartung, *A System of Life: Mawdūdī and the Ideologisation of Islam* (London and New York, 2013), pp. 61–192.

57 See *Ṣaḥīḥ al-Bukhārī, kitāb al-jihād wa'l-sayr, bāb al-jihād māḍin ᶜalā 'l-barr wa'l-fājir*, no. 1 (2,852).

58 See [Akoṛavī], *Daᶜvat-i ḥaqq*, ed. Samīᶜ al-Ḥaqq, 2 vols (Akoṛah Khaṭṭak, 2000), II, pp. 394–6 (Friday sermon, dated Muḥarram 1383/May 1965), here p. 394; compare

This notion has two major implications. First, *jihād* becomes the permanent individual duty (*farḍ ᶜayn*) of working selflessly on one's 'obedience [*iṭāᶜat*] to Islam' by all possible means. Second, this duty requires the sacrifice of everything, including wealth and even physical integrity, for the cause. It is therefore hardly surprising that all expositions on *jihād* are coupled with a lengthy rhetoric of martyrdom, aimed at igniting in those who listen a desire for death, or, in other words, a qualification for the higher reality of the Hereafter.[59] The *epitome* of such a view is perhaps Ludhiyānavī's statement that 'the root of life is the life in the Hereafter'[60].

Given this, numerous controversial activities of the Taliban, especially in the field of material culture, appear quite consistent. Why, for example, would one want to acknowledge the significance of cultural goods in this world when they are meant to perish alongside the temporal world anyway? When such a position is assumed, then to work uncompromisingly for one's own 'obedience to Islam', as well as that of others clearly takes priority over anything else.

The radical eschatological visions underlying such a soteriologically charged ontology are not necessarily rooted in deep legal and theological thought, but rather, to a substantial extent, in common conspiracy theories prevalent in contemporary politicised Muslim circles. Of quite some influence in this regard was, and still is, Ludhiyānavī's already mentioned former student and associate Abū Lubābah Shāh Manṣūr. Highly instrumental in covertly financing religious militancy in Afghanistan and beyond by way of the 'al-Rashīd Trust' (ART), a charity established by Ludhiyānavī in February 1996,[61] Abū Lubābah has an even greater significance for openly disseminating his 'Deobandiyyat'

Aḥmad b. ᶜAlī b. Ḥajar al-ᶜAsqalānī, *Fatḥ a-bārī sharḥ ṣaḥīḥ al-Bukhārī*, ed. ᶜAbd al-ᶜAzīz b. ᶜAbdallāh b. Bāz, 13 vols (Beirut, 1379 AH), VI, pp. 56f.

59 See, for example, [Akoṛavī], *Daᶜvat-i ḥaqq*, II, pp. 106–29, esp. 120–9 (on *maḥabbat-i mawt*), 396–400, esp. 397f. (on martyrdom as the source for salvation [*shahādat sharīᶜah-yi najāt*]). Interestingly, this view runs counter those held by Shāh ᶜAbd al-ᶜAzīz b. Walīullāh Dihlavī (d. 1239/1823), after all one of those claimed as progenitors of the Deobandī *maslak*: see Mawlānā Shāh ᶜAbd al-ᶜAzīz Muḥaddiṣ-i Dihlavī, *Fatāvā-yi ᶜazīzī*, 2 vols (Deoband, 1321 AH), I, p. 41.

60 Ludhiyānavī, *Aḥsan*, VI, p. 22.

61 While there are plenty of websites on the ART, none of them appears entirely reliable, which is why its alleged direct personal and financial relations with Usāma b. Lādin must remain open to dispute, even more so as no primary literature could be found for corroboration. Be that as it may, in its resolution no. 1,267 from 15 October 1999, the UN Security Council lists a 'Mufti Rashid Ahmad Ladehyanoy' (i.e. Rashīd Aḥmad Ludhiyānavī) under the reference number QI.L.30.01 as one of the individuals to be subject to penal sanctions for their affiliation to *al-Qāᶜida*. Only on 11 September 2013, his name was deleted from that list: see URL: www.un.org/press/en/2013/sc11117.doc.htm.

that revolves around promoting 'in the common people as well as the elite the fear of the Last [Judgment] Day'.[62] Abū Lubābah's own writings in Urdu, which have also gained some prominence among South Asian Muslims in the 'Global North', are a vivid expression of this eschatological drift: his bestselling three-volume *Dajjāl* carries the well-worn stereotype of the Masonic–Zionist world conspiracy, shrouded in apocalyptic language, and culminating in the assertion that the Hour is indeed near.[63] More than a decade earlier, Ludhiyānavī portrayed the state of affairs in similar colours, though refraining from the populism of Abū Lubābah's writings.[64]

On the basis of an understanding of the temporality of the physical world, there was a bleak eschatological appraisal of its current state – that is one of 'infestation and chaos' as pointed out already by Gangohī more than a century earlier. In this, soteriology shifted to occupy an ever more central place within the Taliban worldview, manifesting itself not least in a significantly lowered inhibition to sacrifice one's own life on the Path to Salvation.[65] While this has already been the case with the Afghan Islamist organisations, the attitude here was quite different: it was not a self-perceived urban elite who used a discourse on martyrdom as a way to reel in subaltern 'human resources' for their own political ends, but subalterns conversing among themselves, thus moving within the very same discursive universe.

Also, in this light we may be better able to appreciate the radicality of their views on *jihād*, as they emerge also from the legal literature produced by Taliban-related *ᶜulamā'*, most prominently ᶜAbd al-Ḥaqq Akoṛavī and Rashīd Aḥmad Ludhiyānavī. While both scholars had clearly been conscious of the spiritual dimension of the term as upheld in Sufi circles, militancy became

62 Cited in Ved Prakash, *Encyclopaedia of Terrorism in the World*, 5 vols (Delhi, 2011), I, p. 195.

63 See Muftī Abū Lubābah Shāh Manṣūr, *Dajjāl: kawn? kahaṇ? kab?* (Karachi, 1430/2009), pp. 210–35; Abū Lubābah, *Dajjāl 2: ᶜālamī dajjālī riyāsat, ibtidā' se intihā tak* (Karachi, 1431/2010), pp. 226–30; Abū Lubābah, *Dajjāl 3: dajjālī dastāvīz, dajjāl ke ham'navā, dajjālī ᶜalāmāt, Isrā'īl kī kahānī, mashriq va maghrib ke likhāriyoṇ kī zabānī* (Karachi, 1432/2011). For similar statements, see his many articles in the ART-Urdu daily *Ẓarb-i mu'min*.

64 See Ludhiyānavī, *Khuṭbāt al-rashīd*, 7 vols (Karachi, 1425 AH), III, pp. 223–32, VI, pp. 23–41, VII, pp. 331–80.

65 A vivid expression are the numerous poems composed by and in praise of Taliban fighters throughout the Pashtun Borderland, most likely by those Edwards calls 'Talifans': see Alex Strick van Linschoten and Felix Kuehn (eds), *The Poetry of the Taliban* (London and New York, 2012), for example, pp. 57–60, 73–5, 92f., 138, 140f., 144f., 147, 196f., 211f. For a critical discussion of the provenance of these poems, see Caron, 'Review'.

increasingly regarded as the most effective tool of *jihād* under the present conditions. In a *fatwā* dated 15 Ṣafar 1423 (28 April 2002), for example, Ludhiyānavī defined *jihād* unequivocally and exclusively as 'killing on the Path of God' (*qitāl fī sabīl allāh*),[66] backing up his view with a quote from Abū Bakr al-Kasānī's (d. 587/1191) rather little-cited twelfth-century Ḥanafī compendium *Badāʾiᶜ al-ṣināʾiᶜ*.[67] While not disregarding all other derivatives of the verbal root *j-h-d*, he was nonetheless emphatic that there is a clear distinction between them, similar to the semantic difference between *ṣalāt* and *duᶜāʾ*; *jihād* can therefore have only this one specific meaning.

To what extent such a distinct notion of *jihād* in the legal literature produced by some intellectual progenitors of the Taliban was also fostered by its compatibility with notions of Pashtun tribal customary law, the legendary *pax̌tūnvalī*, is, of course, difficult to ascertain. This point we nonetheless have to address below, as it may help to better delineate the Taliban's legal discourses and, moreover, to assess them against the backdrop of a highly complex sociopolitical praxis.

For the moment, however, we shall return to the legal opinions of the scholars of Akoṛah Khaṫṫak, collectively published under the aegis of Samīᶜ al-Ḥaqq as late as January 2002,[68] where such considerations of etymology and semantics as undertaken by Ludhiyānavī above appear largely absent. The reasons for this may be manifold, including the fact that the published *fatāwā* are not individually dated and therefore do not always indicate the concrete circumstances to which they respond. Yet, the content of the questions posed by the various *mustaftiyūn* suggest that most of these available *fatāwā* appeared during the Soviet military

66 For the reasons why I have decided to translate 'qitāl' not, as is quite common, as 'fighting', but more pointedly as 'killing', see Hartung, 'A Subtle Difference: On Ending One's Own Life in Muslim Religious Thought', *Journal of the Royal Asiatic Society* 28.1 (2018), pp. 1–22, here p. 3 n.9.

67 See Ludhiyānavī, *Aḥsan*, VI, p. 29, compare Imām ᶜAlāʾ al-Dīn Abū Bakr b. Masᶜūd al-Kasānī, *Badāʾiᶜ al-ṣanāʾiᶜ fī tartīb al-sharāʾiᶜ*, ed. al-Shaykh ᶜAlī Muḥammad Muᶜawwaḍ and al-Shaykh ᶜĀdil Aḥmad ᶜAbd al-Mawjūd, 10 vols (Beirut, 1424/2002), IX, p. 379: 'In legal custom, [*jihād*] denotes the devotion of one's capability for the killing on the Path of God [*wa-fī ᶜurf al-sharᶜ yastaᶜmal fī badhl al-wusᶜ wa'l-ṭāqa bi'l-qitāl fī sabīl allāh*]'.

68 The timing of the publication of the *Fatāvā-yi ḥaqqāniyyah*, although coinciding with the overthrow of the central government of the Islamic Emirate of Afghanistan, seems significant. After all, the reputation of the *Ḥaqqāniyyah* was boosted by the rise of the Taliban in Afghanistan, in conjunction with Samīᶜ al-Ḥaqq's above discussed claim that it was his institution alone that provided both their main ideological stimulus and the bulk of the Taliban's human resources. Thanks to this enhanced notoriety, Samīᶜ al-Ḥaqq might have seen accelerated publishing activities as a way to gain some competitive advantage over other important religious seminaries in Pakistan, primarily those in Karachi.

occupation of Afghanistan – that is, between 1979 and 1989. Mostly practical in nature, they do not delve into the variety of actions that could all potentially fall under *jihād*. Instead, the notion of *jihād* as '*qitāl fī sabīl allāh*' appears widely accepted, and the questions revolve therefore only around the details of religious warfare. They include: comparisons with the situations for Muslims in Kashmir, Bosnia and Myanmar; the question of who, in the absence of a religio–political leader, would be qualified to call for *jihād*; whether one requires parental permission to go to war; whether one should offer the Soviet occupational troops the opportunity to embrace Islam before submitting to physical action; and how to deal with Muslim collaborators, especially when they belong to one's own family.[69]

When asked about the permissibility of actively seeking martyrdom, however, both ᶜAbd al-Ḥaqq and Ludħiyānavī were, outwardly, very careful.[70] This rather cautious stance, which differs significantly from the above indicated stress on that matter in poetry, public speeches and sermons, is not surprising, as it reflects the considered position on this matter shared by scholars of all canonical legal traditions. These opinions refer to the fact that it remains entirely in God's hand to accept or not accept someone's death as martyrdom.[71] Indeed, ᶜAbd al-Ḥaqq and Ludħiyānavī both argue from within this context, as is clearly indicated by the almost identical references provided in their *fatāwā*, all of which are classical works of Ḥanafī *fiqh*, common commentaries on the *Ṣiḥāḥ* and classical Qurᵓānic commentaries. These references are quite significant, because they actually point to a major cornerstone of the Taliban legal discourse, which they themselves had confirmed: the central administration of the Emirate was bound by the stipulations of 'the radiant Muḥammadan *sharīᶜah* and the Ḥanafī jurisprudence (*kih muṭābiq-i sharīᶜat-i gharrā-yi muḥammadī va fiqh-i ḥanafī*)'.[72] It is therefore certainly useful to take a closer look into the framework of reference employed by our select intellectual progenitors of the Taliban, which can be pointedly labelled as 'Proto-Taliban'.

69 See [Akoṛavī], *Fatāvā*, V, pp. 285–310.

70 See [Akoṛavī], *Fatāvā*, V, pp. 298f.; Ludħiyānavī, *Aḥsan*, VII, pp. 213f.

71 See Hartung, 'A Subtle Difference', pp. 15–19.

72 Muḥammad Riẓā Ḥājj-i Bābāyī (ed.), *Qavānīn-i Mullā ᶜUmar: majmūᶜah-yi qavānīn va āyīn'nāmah'hā-yi Ṭālibān dar Afghānistān* (Tehran, 1382 SH), p. 9. This edition contains the Persian text of a collection of legal decrees first published in the Legal Gazette of the Islamic Emirate of Afghanistan (*Də Afghanistān islāmī imārāt də ᶜadlaye vizārat: rasmī jarīdah*) mainly in 1997 in both Pashto and Dari.

THE ḤANAFĪ LEGAL UNIVERSE OF THE 'PROTO-TALIBAN'

Besides al-Kasānī's *Badāʾiᶜ al-ṣināʾiᶜ*,[73] the work most frequently cited in the section on *jihād* in both collections of *fatāwā* under review, (namely, the *Fatāvā-yi ḥaqqāniyyah* and Rashīd Aḥmad Ludhiyānavī's *Aḥsan al-fatāvā*) is the *Radd al-muḥtār*, the well-known, nineteenth-century commentary of the Syrian–Ottoman *faqīh* Muḥammad Amīn b. ᶜĀbidīn (d. 1258/1842) on the *Durr al-mukhtār* by Muḥammad ᶜAlāʾ al-Dīn al-Ḥaṣkafī (d. 1088/1677), whose views are also occasionally quoted here. A closer look, however, reveals that ᶜAbd al-Ḥaqq Akoṛavī's selection from the *Radd al-muḥtār* was quite limited, as all of his references are derived from two somewhat shorter chapters regarding (1) the difference between individual and collective duties, and (2) that obedience to one's parents is an individual duty.[74] Moreover, two particular passages are cited in ᶜAbd al-Ḥaqq's responses to five and three different questions respectively – which suggests a rather limited appreciation of the more detailed discussions in Ḥanafī *fiqh*. On the other hand, since the texts of either quote are synopses of the views of the earlier Ḥanafī scholars, Muḥammad b. Aḥmad al-Sarakhsī (d. 490/1096) and Ḥusām al-Dīn al-Sighnāqī (d. 714/1314), ᶜAbd al-Ḥaqq could well claim to have embraced the classical Ḥanafī positions on the obligatory character of *jihād* and the need for parental permission to join religious warfare.[75]

Other sources of reference that ᶜAbd al-Ḥaqq Akoṛavī and Rashīd Aḥmad Ludhiyānavī had in common were the *Jāmiᶜ li-aḥkām al-qurʾān* of the Mālikī

73 According to Ya'akov Meron, 'The Development of Legal Thought in Hanafi Texts', *Studia Islamica* 30 (1969), pp. 73–118, here pp. 82f., al-Kasānī had a rather limited impact on the development of classical Ḥanafī *fiqh* and thus did not become a dominant source in Muslim South Asia, at least after the late seventeenth century. This is evident in the famous *Fatāwā hindiyya*, or *ᶜālamgīriyya*: see Mawlānā al-Shaykh Niẓām [al-Burhānfūrī] et al., *al-Fatāwā al-hindiyya, al-maᶜrūfa bi'l-Fatāwā al-ᶜālamkīriyya fī madhhab al-imām al-aᶜẓam Abī Ḥanīfa al-Nuᶜmān*, ed. ᶜAbd al-Laṭīf Ḥasan ᶜAbd al-Raḥmān, 6 vols (Beirut, 1421/2000).

74 See [Akoṛavī], *Fatāvā*, V, pp. 285–310; compare Muḥammad Amīn Ibn ᶜĀbidīn, *Radd al-muḥtār ᶜalā al-durr al-mukhtār sharḥ tanwīr al-abṣār*, ed. al-Shaykh ᶜĀdil Aḥmad ᶜAbd al-Mawjūd and al-Shaykh ᶜAlī Muḥammad Muᶜawwaḍ, 12 vols (Riyadh, 1423/2003), VI, pp. 200–6, esp. pp. 201f., 204–6.

75 See [Akoṛavī], *Fatāvā*, V, pp. 289–91, 299; compare Ibn ᶜĀbidīn, *Radd al-muḥtār*, VI, p. 201. The reference here is made to the *Nihāya*, the earliest standard commentary on Marghinānī's *al-Hidāya* by Ḥusām al-Dīn Ḥasan b. ᶜAlī al-Sighnāqī. For the second quote, see [Akoṛavī], *Fatāvā*, V, pp. 296–8; compare Ibn ᶜĀbidīn, *Radd al-muḥtār*, VI, p. 202. The reference there is made to al-Sarakhsī's commentary on the *Kitāb al-siyar al-kabīr* of Muḥammad b. al-Ḥasan al-Shaybānī (d. 189/805).

Abū ᶜAbdallāh Muḥammad al-Qurṭubī (d. 671/1273) and the *ᶜUmdat al-qārī* – a commentary on the *Ṣaḥīḥ* of al-Bukhārī by the Ḥanafī Badr al-Dīn Muḥammad b. Maḥmūd al-ᶜAynī (d. 855/1451) – both much-cited commentaries on Qurᵓān and *ḥadīth* respectively.[76] Other than these, both *muftī*s drew on two different sets of reference works: while ᶜAbd al-Ḥaqq confined his selection exclusively to Ḥanafī works, including three earlier collections of *fatāwā*,[77] Ludḣiyānavī's list appears to be much more eclectic, as it also includes references to classical Imāmī and Ḥanbalī legal works, as well as much more contemporary South Asian works on Shīᶜī and Sunnī *ḥadīth*. In particular, the references to Imāmī works are somewhat revealing, as they are not used here, despite some disagreement, for anti-Shīᶜī polemical purposes, but rather in support of critical responses to Islamist views on the Shīᶜī notion of religious and political leadership.[78] The

76 See [Akoṛavī], *Fatāvā*, V, pp. 301f.; Ludḣiyānavī, *Aḥsan*, VI, p. 30 (*fatwā* dated 27 Jumādā II 1398h, i.e. 22 May 1978). The references to Qurṭubī and ᶜAynī on explaining Islamic rulings on spies of the enemy (*jawāsīs*) during military confrontations between Muslims and non-Muslims are identical: see Abū ᶜAbdallāh Muḥammad al-Qurṭubī, *al-Jāmiᶜ li-aḥkām al-qurᵓān wa'l-mubīn lamā taḍammanahu min al-sunna wa-āy al-qurᵓān*, ed. ᶜAbdallāh b. ᶜAbd al-Muḥsin al-Turkī, 24 vols (Beirut, 1427/2006), XX, p. 399 (relating to the interpretation of Q60:1); and Badr al-Dīn Abū Muḥammad b. Maḥmūd al-ᶜAynī, *ᶜUmdat al-qārī sharḥ ṣaḥīḥ al-Bukhārī*, ed. ᶜAbdallāh Maḥmūd Muḥammad ᶜUmar, 25 vols (Beirut, 1421/2001), XIV, p. 356 (relating to *Ṣaḥīḥ al-Bukhārī, kitāb al-jihād wa'l-siyar, bāb al-jāsūs*).

77 Compare the references to the *Hidāya* of Marghinānī (d. 593/1197) in [Akoṛavī], *Fatāvā*, V, pp. 304f., 307, with al-Imām Burhān al-Dīn al-Marghinānī, *al-Hidāya sharḥ bidāyat al-mubtadī, maᶜa sharḥ al-ᶜAllāma ᶜAbd al-Ḥayy al-Laknawī*, ed. Naᶜīm Ashraf Nūr Aḥmad, 8 vols (Karachi, 1417 AH), IV, pp. 224, 227–9. The standard commentary *Fatḥ al-qadīr* on the *Hidāya* by Ibn Humām (d. 861/1457) is referred to in [Akoṛavī], *Fatāvā*, V, p. 293; compare Kamāl al-Dīn b. Humām al-Ḥanafī, *Sharḥ fatḥ al-qadīr ᶜalā al-hidāya sharḥ bidāyat al-mubtadī*, ed. ᶜAbd al-Razzāq Ghālib al-Mahdī, 10 vols (Beirut, 1424/2003), V, p. 417. For the references to the *Baḥr al-rāᵓiq* of Ibn Nujaym (d. 970/1562) compare [Akoṛavī], *Fatāvā*, V, pp. 294, 304, 309, with al-Shaykh Zayn al-Dīn b. Nujaym al-Miṣrī, *al-Baḥr al-rāᵓiq sharḥ kanz al-daqāᵓiq*, 7 vols (Beirut, n.d.), V, p. 82. For the references to the *Fatāwā kāmiliyya* of al-Ṭarābulusī (d. 1315/1897) compare [Akoṛavī], *Fatāvā*, V, pp. 306–8, with Muḥammad Kāmil al-Ṭarābulusī, *al-Fatāwā al-kāmiliyya fi'l-ḥawādith al-ṭarābulusiyya* (Cairo, 1313/1895), pp. 250f. Finally, compare the references to the *Fatāwā hindiyya*, in [Akoṛavī], *Fatāvā*, V, p. 285, with Niẓām [al-Burhānfūrī] et al., *al-Fatāwā al-hindiyya*, II, p. 209; and the references to the *Fatāwā tātārkhāniyya* in [Akoṛavī], *Fatāvā*, V, p. 309, with al-ᶜAllāma ᶜĀlim b. ᶜAlāᵓ al-Anṣārī, *Fatāwā tātārkhāniyya*, ed. al-Qāḍī Sajjād Ḥusayn, 5 vols (Hyderabad, 1407/1987), V, p. 172.

78 More classical Imāmī works on *fiqh* and *ḥadīth* referred to by Rashīd Aḥmad Ludḣiyānavī are the *Kitāb al-iḥtijāj* of Abū Manṣūr Aḥmad al-Ṭabarsī (d. 599/1202) and the apparently more contemporary *Jāmiᶜ al-fawāᵓid fī asrār al-māqāṣid* of Ḥabīb b. Mūsā al-Riḍā

references to Ḥanbalī works – prominent amongst which are the *Mughnī* of Ibn Qudāma al-Maqdisī (d. 620/1223) and the *Iqtiḍāʾ al-ṣirāṭ al-mustaqīm* of Taqī al-Dīn b. Taymiyya (d. 728/1328) – are really citations of citations, as they figure as references in the *Iʿlāʾ al-sunan* of the Deobandi *faqīh* Ẓafar Aḥmad ʿUs̱mānī Tĥānavī (d. 1397/1974). Ludĥiyānavī quoted at length from this extensive work when discussing the curtailment of public religious expression of non-Muslims in the *dār al-islām*.[79] The referrals to Ibn Qudāma's *Mughnī*, however, are particularly significant for the matter at hand, because it is used as a standard classical legal reference work in contemporary circles of Muslim radicals on the issue of *jihād*.[80]

These and other differences in establishing an exegetical tradition by referencing earlier works begs an explanation of the comparative lack of eschatological references in the legal thought of ʿAbd al-Ḥaqq Akoṛavī. A quite possible explanation might be rooted in the different ethnic background of the two 'Proto-Taliban' *muftī*s who, after all, belong to the same generation of graduates from the *Dār al-ʿulūm* at Deoband. In this context, we may recall the formative spiritual impact of Rashīd Aḥmad Gangohī and ʿAbd al-Ghanī P̄hulpūrī on the religious worldview of the ethnically Punjabi Rashīd Aḥmad Ludĥiyānavī. These influences can, in fact, well account for Ludĥiyānavī's *fiqh* being steeped in a grim assessment of the political situation of the day as 'times of infestation and chaos' through the normative prism of Islamic eschatology; this is also manifest in the legal obligation for every righteous Muslim to engage in fighting the 'False, or Deceptive Messiah' (*al-masīḥ al-dajjāl*), the eschatological figure

al-Afshārī al-Najafī, while further reference was made to the *Tajalliyāt-i ṣadāqat* of the Pakistani Imāmī cleric Muḥammad Ḥusayn Najafī (b. 1351/1932). Compare Ludĥiyānavī, *Aḥsan*, VI, pp. 14f., 17; with Abū Manṣūr Aḥmad b. ʿAlī b. Abī Ṭālib al-Ṭabarsī, *al-Iḥtijāj*, ed. Muḥammad Ṣādiq al-Kattabī, 2 vols (Najaf, 1380 AH), II, pp. 8f.; and al-Shaykh Muḥammad Ḥusayn Najafī, *Tajalliyāt-i ṣadāqat bi-javāb-i aftāb-i hidāyat* (Sargodhā, 1982), p. 492. The position against which Ludĥiyānavī argued here was that of Abū 'l-Aʿlā Mawdūdī (d. 1399/1979) and his *Jamāʿat-i islāmī*, which Ludĥiyānavī claimed to have had more comprehensively refuted in his *Mawdūdī ṣāḥib awr takhrīb-i islām* (see Ludĥiyānavī, *Aḥsan*, VI, p. 14). Unfortunately, a copy of this work is not available to me. It needs to be stressed, though, that Ludĥiyānavī was by no means sympathetic towards the Shīʿa, as clearly emerges from his *Ḥaqīqat-i shīʿah* (Karachi, n.d.).

79 Compare Ludĥiyānavī, *Aḥsan*, VI, pp. 18–20, with Mawlānā Ẓafar Aḥmad al-ʿUthmānī al-Tĥānawī, *Iʿlāʾ al-sunan*, ed. Muḥammad Taqī ʿUthmānī, 18 vols (Karachi, 1418 AH), XII, pp. 515–21, 523. Ludĥiyānavī's quotations appear to be a patchwork of various passages from Ẓafar Aḥmad ʿUs̱mānī's work, in places without indication.

80 See, for example, ʿAbd al-Qādir b. ʿAbd al-ʿAzīz, *al-ʿUmda fī iʿdād al-ʿudda li'l-jihād fī sabīl allāh taʿālā* (Amman, 1419/1999), pp. 97f., 100 (on the necessity and significance of *sharīʿa* legislation in the *dār al-islām*).

that appears towards the end of times as the spreader of unbelief. The undisputable obligation for *jihād* against all forces of evil in this modern world at the brink of termination was complimented with an anxious observance of all other ritual obligations (*ᶜibādāt*) and the literal conformity with the stipulations of the *sharīᶜa* in all matters of *muᶜāmalāt*.

For the ethnic Pashtun scholars of Akoṛah Khaṭṭak, the loosely defined norms and values that underlie traditional conflict management in Pashtun tribal communities may – at least implicitly – have informed their legal interpretation to a much greater extent than they would probably like to admit. In his foreword to the *Fatāvā-yi ḥaqqāniyyah*, Samīᶜ al-Ḥaqq at least alluded to the impact of 'societal, communal and customary conditions' (*maᶜāsharatī awr samājī va ᶜurfī ḥālāt*)[81] as significant to the pursuit of *iftāʾ* in a manner equal with the conditions of the modern era. This, in turn, could well have played a decisive role in the Taliban's legal discourse on violence, including its practice, during the days of their central government of the Islamic Emirate of Afghanistan.[82] It appears somewhat at odds with the careful and considerate Ḥanafī arguments discussed above. In their practice of law enforcement, the Taliban seem to have strongly been guided also by moral values subsumed under the luminous label 'paẍtūnvalī'. Yet, while earlier authors have claimed that the legal universe of the Taliban was, and still is, a combination of the Islamic *sharīᶜa* and (more often than not) conflicting Pashtun customary law, I contend that this dichotomy of two distinct legal frameworks is, in fact, difficult to maintain. This, in my view, is rooted in a rather distorted perception of customary law in Muslim societies in general and those of the Pashtuns in particular; some disenchantment is required before we can possibly proceed.

UMMA VERSUS KIN? – THE ROLE OF PASHTUN CUSTOMARY LAW

It may well be argued that culturally specific beliefs and values, when utilised for the legitimisation of violence of whatever form, are hardly ever exclusively rooted in rational legal discourse.[83] Rather, such legal arguments seem in the first

81 Samīᶜ al-Ḥaqq in [Akoṛavī], *Fatāvā*, I, p. 3.

82 The material basis for the reconstruction of the Taliban legal discourses is still rather thin. Besides the few available and non-consecutive copies of the Legal Gazette of the Islamic Emirate of Afghanistan, we have, so far, only the predominantly Pashto *Farāmīn-i amīr al-muʾminīn* (n.p., 2000), and Bābāyī (ed.), *Qavānīn*, at our disposal.

83 See, Benedicte Grima, *The Performance of Emotion among Paxtun Women: 'The Misfortunes Which Have Befallen Me'* (Austin, TX, 1992); Grima, *Secrets from the Field: An Ethnographer's Notes from Northwest Pakistan* (Karachi, 2005); also, although on a

place to serve a rationalisation of strongly emotionally charged, distinct cultural values, such as the dichotomous concepts of 'honour' and 'shame', and their relation to individual physical and collective social bodies. Notions such as the essential individuality of *jihād* and its persisting character until the end of times, as emerges from the *fatāwā* of ᶜAbd al-Ḥaqq Akoṛavī, are thus easily traced back to core elements of the above mentioned *paǩtūnvalī*. Yet, I would strongly argue that, before embracing such explanations, a somewhat closer look into this 'Pashtun tribal code of conduct' and its application in practice is required, as it will help to disentangle the somewhat idealised and stereotypical concept from the actual socio-legal practices.[84]

The concept, which still dominates the social-anthropological imagination, is conceived as a relatively fixed catalogue of norms, pivoting indeed on the conceptual binary of 'honour', or 'dignity' (*nang*), and 'shame' (*sharm*).[85] The first Pashtun who appears to have extensively treated *paǩtūnvalī* in this way was the nationalist urban intellectual Qiyām al-Dīn Khādim (d. 1358 SH/1979) in his book titled simply *Paǩtūnvalī* published in the early 1950s.[86] He had appropriated, it seems, an earlier British colonial imaginary:[87] about a decade earlier, Khādim had been a leading member of the leftist *Vīǩ Zalmiyān* movement, one of the chief promoters of Pashtun nationalism in Afghanistan,[88] and against this ideological backdrop it does not seem surprising that the term *paǩtūnvalī* translates literally

linguistically distinct community, Are Knudsen, *Violence and Belonging: Land, Love and Lethal Conflict in the North-West Frontier Province of Pakistan* (New Delhi, 2009).

84 The following thoughts on the relationship of Pashtun tribal legislation and ethnic identity were first been developed in my keynote lecture at the *26th International Pakistan History Conference*, held at the University of Peshawar, 9–14 October 2017.

85 A prominent case in point here is still Willi Steul, *Paschtunwali: Ein Ehrenkodex und seiner rechtliche Relevanz* (Wiesbaden, 1981); for an excursion into the history of anthropological research on that matter see also Glatzer, 'Zum Pashtunwali als ethnisches Selbstportrait', in *Subjekte und Systeme: Soziologische und anthropologische Annäherungen. Festschrift für Christian Sigrist zum 65. Geburtstag*, ed. Günter Best and Reinhart Kößler (Frankfurt/M., 2000), pp. 93–102; Glatzer, 'The Pashtun Tribal System', in *Concept of Tribal Society* [sic], ed. Georg Pfeffer and D. K. Behera (New Delhi, 2002), pp. 265–82, for information on the supposed location of *paǩtūnvalī* in the Pashtun 'tribal system'.

86 See Qiyām al-Dīn Khādim, *Paǩtūnvalī* (Kabul, 1331 SH).

87 See, in particular, Mountstuart Elphinstone: *An Account of the Kingdom of Caubul and its Dependencies in Persia, Tartary and India, Comprising a View of the Afghaun Nation and a History of the Dooraunee Monarchy* [sic], 2 vols (London, 1815), I: 295–301.

88 On the *Vīǩ Zalmiyān*, see Faridullah Bezhan, 'Nationalism, not Islam: The 'Awaken Youth' Party and Pashtun Nationalism', in *Afghanistan's Islam: From Conversion to the Taliban*, ed. Nile Green (Oakland, CA, 2017), pp. 163–85, 293–9 (notes and references).

as 'Pashtunhood'. In this light, the hierarchical listing of concepts such as unconditional hospitality (*melmastiyā*, or *melmah pālənah*), the granting of sanctuary (*nanavātay*), (blood-)revenge (*badal*), the defence of honour (*nāmūs*), or courage (*tūrah*) reflects the attempt to conceptualise Pashtuns as a distinct 'people'. This 'people' likewise possesses of a clearly defined uniform legal system that is enforced and applied in the tribal communities by the – somewhat similarly stereotyped – institution of the council of elders (*jirgah*). With regard to *jirgah*, social anthropologists appear to have followed the precedent of the British colonial administration in the Pashtun-dominated tribal belt around the borderline between the Emirate-cum-Kingdom of Afghanistan and British India, designed in 1893 by civil servant Henry Mortimer Durand (d. 1924). As the British had derived their understanding of *jirgah* predominantly from socio-economic tribal elites, oblivious to their delicate inner-communal power plays, later social anthropologists appear to have moved predominantly in highly Persianate urban spaces and relying on the information of its intellectuals, while equally overlooking their respective interests.[89] The conceptualisation of *paẋtūnvalī* claimed academic objectivity and has subsequently helped to solidify this understanding. It has become a colloquial reference in Pashtun communities on either side of the national borderline that is still identical with the Durand Line.

While I am, of course, acknowledging the practical effect that the inclusion of this notion into colloquial discourse (and which would certainly be worthwhile to investigate), here we need to disenchant the static concept of *paẋtūnvalī*, fortified by social-anthropology, because only after having done this will we be able to assess the validity of the claim that the Taliban were, and are, employing it alongside their Ḥanafī *fiqh*. In fact, I am identifying three fundamental flaws in the prevalent notion of *paẋtūnvalī*, two of them systematic, and one methodological.

The first systematic flaw consists in identifying an ethnic identity with the observance of rules pertaining to action alone: this, however, appears to cover only one aspect of 'Pashtunhood' which is usually conceptualised by 'Doing Pashto' (*paẋto kaval*). Still, besides this there exists (at least!) two further verbal composites that express 'Pashtunhood': 'Speaking Pashto' (*paẋto vāyal*) and 'Having Pashto' (*paẋto laral*). The first points to the ability to handle the Pashto language in an accomplished manner – which necessitates a deep familiarity with its poetic universe. The second refers to one's conscious placement within one of the various tribal genealogies. Depending on one's preference and in concrete

89 See the convincing arguments regarding leading US-American social anthropologist and adviser to various US-government bodies, Thomas J. Barfield (Boston University), by Hanifi, 'Vending Distorted Afghanistan', p. 257.

situations, these three fundamental determinations appear to be played off against one another, as indicated, for example, by the popular proverb 'A Pashtun is not he who speaks Pashto, but he who has Pashto' (*Paxtūn haghah nah dəy čih paxto vāyī, magar haghah čih paxto larī*). Methodologically, this first systematic intervention points to the imperative of paying close attention to the respective context in which a statement is made, as an integral part of 'discursive formations'[90] in which a great diversity of actors negotiate Pashtun ethnic identity.

The second systematic flaw – and here we are slowly returning to the topic of this chapter – comprises of the maintenance of a strong and unshakeable dichotomy of Islamic and local customary law: this is clearly reflected in the frequent repetition of this binary in much of the literature on the Taliban. Investigations into the relationship between these two legal frameworks, however, have made a convincing case for the dichotomy being unconvincing. Even with the ideologically grounded objective to enforce the Islamic *sharīᶜa* in all public and even private domains, as explicitly espoused not least by the Taliban, we would be well advised to distinguish between normative universalistic claims, local contexts and the pragmatics necessary to negotiate both.[91] In the case of Dagestan in the Caucasus, Kemper has demonstrated the fruitfulness of a contextual understanding of the local positions on value and order when dissolving the firm dichotomy of Islamic and local customary law. Since local religious functionaries are usually involved in communal legal procedures, legal decisions with precedent value can quite frequently manifest themselves in Islamicate language and thus break down the strict separation of *sharīᶜa* law and local customary regulations.[92]

In the regional context of what I am call elsewhere the 'Pashtun Borderland',[93] individual and almost exclusively male ideas of 'honour' or 'dignity', and 'shame' (and advice on how to preserve the former and avoid the latter)[94] have to be somewhat levelled to maintain community cohesion to a large an extent

90 This useful term I borrow from Siegfried Jäger, *Kritische Diskursanalyse: Eine Einführung* (Münster, 2004, 4th ed.), pp. 133–57, who in turn presents this as his own rendering of Foucault's famous 'proliferation of discourses' (see Michel Foucault, *Histoire de la sexualité I: La volonté de savoir* [Paris, 1976], pp. 50–67).

91 See, for example, Michael Kemper, *Herrschaft, Recht und Islam in Daghestan: Von den Khanaten und Gemeindebünden zum ǧihād-Staat* (Wiesbaden, 2005), esp. pp. 23–6; also, Kemper and Maurus Reinkowski (eds), *Rechtspluralismus in der Islamischen Welt: Gewohnheitsrecht zwischen Staat und Gesellschaft* (Berlin and New York, 2005).

92 See Kemper, *Herrschaft, Recht und Islam*, pp. 317–53.

93 See my forthcoming *The Pashtun Borderland in Uproar*, ch. 2.

94 See Glatzer, 'Schwert und Verantwortung: Paschtunische Männlichkeitsideale', in *Krieg und Kampf: Die Gewalt in unseren Köpfen*, ed. Erwin Orywal, Aparna Rao and Michael Bollig (Berlin, 1996), pp. 107–20, here pp. 111–17.

as possible. This is where community representatives (which both conflicting parties agree to be trustworthy) try to mediate and work out a compromise. This compromise leaves the individual ideas of 'honour' and 'shame' intact: the former – even when violated – maintains the stability and cohesion in the community. If a compromise cannot be achieved and the conflict thus threatens to exceed the immediate confines of the community, further attempts are made on increasingly trans-communal levels until the conflict is settled and communal stability reaffirmed. The dependence on the ever-changing conflicting parties and their need to agree on trustworthy arbitrators defies already the idea of *jirgah* as something more permanent than an ad hoc congregation. Nonetheless, the British colonial engagement with these local practices of mediating conflict had a lasting impact on the local understanding of social justice. They saw a *jirgah* as some kind of semi-permanent assembly of tenured representatives of the local socio-economic and political elite, quite similar to a court of law, and the outcome of their deliberations were viewed as positive 'law'. Now, representatives of a *jirgah* of the British imaginary saw themselves increasingly as legislators and less as arbitrators, increasingly working towards the codification of regionally valid precedents (*narkhūnah*) into eventually binding legal decrees (*prekṛe*).[95] At the very same time, *jirgah*s as decision-making bodies were established in Afghanistan, all the way up to its supreme manifestation, the Grand Assembly (*loyah jirgah*), or parliament.[96]

However, a major constituent of Pashtun society and, in Afghanistan, also of non-Pashtun communities, remains reflected in all these various decision-making bodies: that of (adult) male dominance and the severe curtailment of female agency that results from it. In contrast to the problematic works on *paxtūnvalī*, in this area, social anthropologists have produced valuable studies and accounts that clearly demonstrate the severe gender imbalance. At times, it goes so far as to use females as material commodities – for example, in paying off financial debts or settling instances of blood revenge.[97] So deeply ingrained is the

95 See, for example, Ali Wardak, '*Jirga*: Power and Traditional Conflict Resolution in Afghanistan', in *Law after Ground Zero*, ed. John Strawson (London, Portland, OR and Coogee, 2004, 2nd ed.), pp. 187–204, here pp. 193–5. For the two technical terms *narkh* and *prekṛah*, see M. Ibrāhīm ᶜAṭāyī, *Də Paxtanī qabīlo də ḥuqūqī, jazāyī, taᶜāmulī iṣṭilāḥāto qāmūs* (Kabul, 1357 SH), pp. 35f., 273–5.

96 See Christine Noelle-Karimi, 'The Loya Jirga – An Effective Political Instrument? A Historical Overview', in *Afghanistan – A Country Without a State?*, ed. Christine Noelle-Karimi, Conrad Schetter and Reinhard Schlagintweit (Frankfurt/M. and London, 2002), pp. 37–50.

97 See Nancy Tapper, *Bartered Brides: Politics, Gender and Marriage in an Afghan Tribal Society* (Cambridge, 1991); Grima, *The Performance of Emotion*; Grima, *Secrets*.

patriarchal patterns of the social, economic, political and also religious fabric of Afghanistan (and also in the Pashtun majority settlement areas in Pakistan) that it is reflected even in the social values of highly educated urban elites.[98] This is vividly illustrated by the constant placing of obstacles in the way of duly elected female members of parliament in Afghanistan after 2001.[99]

It appears that these transregional socio-cultural dispositions, without the need for constant reiteration, strongly inform the local sets of values that underpin legal decision-making in the various communities of the Pashtun Borderland and beyond into other parts of Afghanistan and Pakistan. Bearing this in mind it will not surprise one to learn that, for instance, the much-publicised harsh treatment of females by the Taliban was actually quite in line with the general attitude towards women in large parts of the rural Pashtun Borderland and so needed little legal support.[100] This, however, was quite different in urban spaces, especially in Kabul, where women had been comparatively empowered under the governments of Muḥammad Dāvūd Khān and the communist PDPA between 1973 and 1992. Once again, it was this focus on the urban centres which informed the emotionally charged imaginary of the Taliban by journalists, NGO workers and politicians. They portrayed the Taliban as extremely misogynist;[101] and in response, the government of the Islamic Emirate of Afghanistan required Islamically sustained legal justifications for their strict curtailment of female movement and severe public persecution of women found guilty of having violated the legal stipulations.

Such justification rarely came as elaborate legal arguments, as we have seen in the case of the *fatāwā* issued from the Deobandi *Dār al-ᶜulūm ḥaqqāniyyah* at Akoṛah Khaṭṭak. Rather, only general references were made to the Islamicity

98 See, for instance, Anoosh Wisal Khan, *Contesting Subjectivities, Negotiating Agency, and Re-Defining Boundaries: The Ideological Subject Formation and Positioning of Pakhtun Women* (unpublished PhD dissertation, American University, Washington, DC, 2012); Ṣiddīqah Bakhtiyārī, *Muhājirat va taghayyir-i mafhūm-i mardānigī: sankh'shināsī mafhūm-i mardānigī dar miyān mardān-i muhājir-i Afghānistān dar Īrān va muqāyisah bā mardān ghayr-muhājir dar Afghānistān*, unpublished M.A. dissertation, Dānish'gāh-yi Tihrān, Dānish'kadah-yi ᶜulūm-i ijtimāᶜī, Grūh-yi jāmiᶜah'shināsī, 1393 SH).

99 See, for instance, Hafizullah Emadi, 'Establishment of Afghanistan's Parliament and the Role of Women Parliamentarians: Retrospect and Prospects', *Internationales Asienforum* 39.1–2 (2008), pp. 5–19.

100 See, for instance, the works of Grima (above, note 83), who is one of the very few social anthropologists from outside Afghanistan to have actually spent prolonged periods among women in rural communities across the Pashtun Borderland.

101 See, for example, Rashid, *Taliban*, pp. 105–16, who uses very emotive and disparaging language in his narrative of the Taliban's gender policies.

of legal decrees, not least by employing an Islamic legal terminology, starting with renaming the Ministry of Justice (*də ᶜadlaye vizārat*) to the 'Ministry for Enjoining the Commendable and Preventing the Reprehensible' (*də amr bi'l-maᶜrūf va nahy ᶜan al-munkar vizārat*), This ministry 'as part of the central administration of the Emirate, is tasked with establishing the commendable and preventing all that is reprehensible in accordance with the brilliant Muḥammadan *sharīᶜah* and the Ḥanafī jurisprudence throughout the land'.[102] Yet, the demand that women cover fully when moving in public is not supported by religious reference, and it calls first upon the male members of a household to ensure the observance of these public rules. In case of the violation of these norms, appropriate punitive measures will be applied to the men.[103]

This, in fact, is just one vivid illustration of the Taliban's approval of local cultural values: the rules of social engagement in most rural spaces are shrouded in a loose Islamic garb. Conflict, in turn, did occur in those spaces only rarely: women were almost non-existent in public anyway; men would traditionally congregate in the village mosque for communal prayer, sporting longish full beards and wear turbans. Responsibility for all public affairs fell exclusively to men; the difference now was simply that it was not only the village community that would shame a man for his inability to control the women in his household, but a political actor that would apply legal measures as representation of the state's monopoly of the law. I contend here that universalistic religious ideas played less of a role in shaping the Taliban's legal discourses than some maintain. This is reflected in the fact that the Taliban had at no point in time aspired to expand beyond Afghanistan or, in the case of the TṬP, Pakistan. Rather, the Taliban's legal discourse was informed by general social and cultural values shared across the rural communities, values that transcend more concrete local arrangements as enshrined in *narkh*, or locally valid precedent. At the core of these values lies the extended family as the chief reference point for all things social, economic and political in a tribal setting – it resonates quite well with the setting of the Arabian Peninsula in the formative period of the Muslim *umma.* In the tribal context, it is only your kin, not some overarching political structure, that provides one with the necessary protection and provisions in times of need. In a country like Afghanistan, where – not least due to its long-term strategic

102 Bābāyī (ed.), *Qavānīn*, p. 9.

103 See Bābāyī (ed.), *Qavānīn*, pp. 10–14. Interestingly, Rashid, *Taliban*, pp. 247–9, provides 'a sample of Taliban decrees relating to women and other cultural issues, after the capture of Kabul, 1996', allegedly translated 'from Dari and handed to Western agencies to implement' (p. 247), makes explicit reference to the Islamicity of their rulings on women that I was so far not able to find elsewhere.

geopolitical situation – a state with its central institutions existed only at certain points in time and in a very limited spatial extent, these basic social mechanisms remained a necessity for survival.[104] This remained by and large the case even during the first years of the government of the so-called *mujāhidīn*. These *mujāhidīn* were urbanite Islamist militias with a strong sense for statehood and central governmental institutions,[105] for which they fought fiercely in the Civil War between 1992 and the Taliban's capture of Kabul in September 1996. Being themselves overwhelmingly of rural and tribal background, the Taliban appears to have replaced the *umma*-centric rhetoric of the various Afghan Islamist organisations with one in which kinship relations played a much more pronounced role.

Having now firmly engaged with at least two of the cornerstones of the Taliban legal hermeneutics (viz, the Ḥanafī interpretation of the Islamic *sharīʿa* and 'shariatised' elements of Pashtun local customs of conflict resolution), we shall finally take a little closer look into how these two ideational threads finally played out in the Islamic Emirate of Afghanistan during its central government between September 1996 and December 2001.

LEGAL PRACTICE IN TIMES OF TRIBULATION AND CHAOS – THE TALIBAN CONTEXT

The element linking legal theory to legal practice is a careful assessment of the actual circumstances, something that later militant legal theorists – many of whom had at times substantial exposure to the Taliban during exactly the period under review here – have eventually conceptualised this as 'jurisprudence of reality' (*fiqh al-wāqiʿa*).[106] Militant Arab Salafists, prominently among

104 In this regard we need to acknowledge that the ethnically Pashtun dynasties of the Durrānī and Barakzay since the eighteenth century were also highly urbanised and Persianised and, thus, largely detached from the majority of Pashtun tribal communities that they regarded as their subjects: see the important historiographical intervention by Hanifi, 'Vending Distorted Afghanistan', pp. 264f. The narrative of the Pashtun 'tribal state' which ran on tenets of *paxtūnvalī*, had seemingly been coined by British colonial officers, like Mountstuart Elphinstone (d. 1859) and Henry Walter Bellew (d. 1892). Since then, it has shaped the perspective of social anthropologists and historians alike: for evidence, see the otherwise excellent work of Olesen, *Islam and Politics*, pp. 20–36, 61–4.

105 See Hartung, 'Taking Lessons'.

106 Scholars have noted this term for the first time in legal considerations of members of the Egyptian *Jamāʿa islāmiyya* (JIM): prominently, see Kamāl al-Saʿīd Ḥabīb, *al-Ḥaraka al-islāmiyya min al-muwājaha ilā al-murājaʿa* (Cairo, 2002), 78; Issam Fawzi and Ivesa

them leading *al-Qāʿida* ideologue Sayyid Imām al-Sharīf, a.k.a. 'Dr Faḍl', a.k.a. "ʿAbd al-Qādir b. ʿAbd al-ʿAzīz' (b. 1369/1950), would employ this concept to justify their declaration of militant *jihād* and the practice of pronouncing a fellow Muslim an apostate (*takfīr*) as non-negotiable individual religious obligations (*farāʾiḍ ʿayn*) under the present circumstances.[107]

The scenario painted by these Arab authors reflects very well that of the Taliban, which, in turn, seems to constitute just an aggravation of the early Deobandi assessment of the present as 'times of infestation and chaos' that we had prominently encountered in Rashīd Aḥmad Gangohī, Maḥmūd al-Ḥasan and Rashīd Aḥmad Ludhiyānavī. Indeed, the Qurʾānic term *fasād* – chaos, or corruption – had emerged as a core concept in the Taliban's picture of the present realities in Afghanistan, sharing a semantic field with *ẓulm* (injustice, oppression), to which, after December 2001, the concept (*bahrānī*) *ishghāl* ([foreign] occupation) was added. The latter, interestingly, would not only apply to the US-led military forces and the subsequent foreign military presence under UN mandate, for whom also the common Salafist rhetorical term 'crusader' (*ṣalībiyūn*) would be applied, but also for the more recent muscling in of the *Islamic State* (*al-Dawla al-islāmiyya*).[108]

This portrayal of the current realities corresponds well with the above outlined eschatological underpinnings. The widespread 'unbelief' especially in the urban centres of Afghanistan, viewed by conservative rural Pashtuns as abodes of immorality for quite a long time, clearly reads as one of the Greater Signs of

Lübben, 'Die ägyptische *jama'a al-islamiya* [*sic*] und die Revision der Gewaltstrategie', *DOI-Fokus* 15 (2004), pp. 1–43, here pp. 20f.; Quintan Wiktorowicz, 'Anatomy of the Salafi Movement', *Studies in Conflict & Terrorism* 29 (2006), pp. 207–39, here p. 224; Roel Meijer, 'Commanding Right and Forbidding Wrong as a Principle of Social Action: The Case of the Egyptian al-Jama'a al-Islamiyya', in *Global Salafism: Islam's New Religious Movement*, ed. Roel Meijer (London and New York, 2009), pp. 189–220, here p. 213. Numerous members of the soon to be persecuted JIM, led by Ṭalʿat b. Fuʾād b. Qāsim, a.k.a. 'Abū Ṭalāl al-Qāsimī' (killed 1416/1995), and calling themselves the *al-Murābiṭūn* group, found refuge in Afghanistan during the 1980s and early 1990s. Here, they served as an interface between Arab militant Salafists, including leading ideologues of *al-Qāʿida*, and Afghan actors who would soon surface in the closer orbit of the *Taliban*: see Hartung, *The Pashtun Borderland in Uproar*, ch. 4.5.

107 See Justyna Nedza, Takfīr *im militanten Salafismus: Der Staat als Feind* (Leiden and Boston, MA, 2020), pp. 196–200.

108 For the Taliban rhetoric of the ISAF forces as 'crusaders', see Samīʿ al-Ḥaqq, *Ṣalībī dahshat'girdī awr ʿālam-i islām: Ṭālibān-i Afghānistān ke tanāẓur meṇ*, ed. ʿAbd al-Qayyūm Ḥaqqānī (Akoṛah Khaṭṭak, 1425/2004); for the application of the 'foreign occupation' trope to the IS in Afghanistan, see Hartung, 'Between a Rock and a Hard Place'.

the End Times: that is, the almost unimpeded roaming of the Great Deceiver, the *masīḥ al-dajjāl*, which Karachi-based Muftī Abū Lubābah had pinned down to the devastating influence of Zionism and Freemasonry. For the Taliban, however, deeply rooted in the tribal and rural context of the Pashtun Borderland, these rather abstract perpetrators were of lesser importance. More relevant for them appeared to be the 'enemy within' – that is, members of their own local communities who, due to their conduct and appearance, prove severely disruptive for the integrity and consequently for the survival of these distinct social units.

The epitome of such a person in the Taliban worldview is the 'spy' (*jāsūs*), who appears to represent someone whose loyalties are not to his own community, but rather to some outside force. Consequently, in the so-called *Code of Conduct for the Taliban*, one of the last documents officially endorsed by Mullā ᶜUmar, the 'spy' is cast as an 'originator of chaos' (*sāᶜī bi'l-fasād*) and has therefore, as a consequence, to face his execution (*važəl*) as the appropriate penalty.[109] Consideration should be paid to the ethnographic work dealing with how these rural and tribal communities deal with offences by individual members; these offences threaten community cohesion and, thus, persistence. A correspondence can clearly be stated between this person and a spy, and in this light, the elucidation of the appropriate legal process in the persecution of a spy is highly interesting, as reflecting the origins of the Taliban in this very socio-cultural space. In the document it is stipulated that 'the prerogative [*ṣalāḥiyyat*] for ordering the execution of an apprehended spy lies with the Imam, his deputy and the provincial judge. However, in case there is no judge, the [provincial] governor alone is entitled to order his execution'.[110]

This already appears to constitute a departure from the classical Ḥanafī position, according to which a spy, although to be severely punished, is not to be killed.[111] Yet, the case is not as straightforward, because it all changes with the notion that a spy from among one's own is an 'originator of chaos': ᶜAbd al-Ḥaqq Akoṛavī refers in this matter to al-Ḥaṣkafī by way of Ibn ᶜĀbidīn's commentary on the *Durr al-mukhtār*, Ibn al-Nujaym, and the *Fatāwā hindiyya*. He confirms that, by consensus of the *fuqahā*ᵓ across all the canonical *madhāhib fiqhiyya*, such a person is to be executed.[112] Rashīd Aḥmad Ludhiyānavī follows

109 See Də Afghānistān Islāmī Imārat, *Də Mujāhidīno lapārah lā*ᵓ*iḥah* (n.p., 1431/2010), p. 20.

110 Də Afghānistān Islāmī Imārat, *Lā*ᵓ*iḥah.*

111 See al-Imām Muḥammad b. Aḥmad al-Sarakhsī, *Sharḥ kitāb al-siyar al-kabīr li'l-imām Muḥammad b. al-Ḥasan al-Shaybānī*, ed. Abū ᶜAbdallāh Muḥammad Ḥasan al-Shāfiᶜī, 5 vols (Beirut, 1417/1997), V, pp. 229–31.

112 See [Akoṛavī], *Fatāvā*, V, p. 165; compare Ibn ᶜĀbidīn, *Radd al-muḥtār*, VI, p. 109;

suit and adds the elaborations of Ibn ᶜĀbidīn on Ḥaṣkafī's position to support his ruling.[113] Neither scholar, however, explicitly applies this ruling to the act of spying;[114] the reason it that for this, a certain degree of governmentality is required, which in the 1980s was not as manifest as it would be a decade later. It is therefore of little surprise that, for example, *al-Qāᶜida* ideologues, like prominently Muḥammad ᶜAbd al-Majīd Ḥasan Qāʾid, a.k.a. 'Abū Yaḥyā al-Lībī' (killed 1433/2012), could build on their personal experience of the Taliban's Islamic Emirate of Afghanistan and take a much more pronounced position on violations of the Qurʾānic injunction not to spy on other Muslims.[115]

However, there is more to the Taliban legal procedure for the persecution of a spy, expressed in the context of the exposition of four rules of taking evidence, culminating in dealing with its circumstantial variety. It is in this final instance where, after all, we can clearly discern a confluence of Ḥanafī *fiqh* with the local mechanisms of conflict resolution in the Pashtun Borderland:

> Of course, not everyone is permitted to rule over such indications [*ᶜalāme*]. In case a court of law exists, it will be the judge who assesses the strengths and weaknesses of the circumstantial evidence [*qarīne*], in case of its absence, it is a pious and religious [*mudabbir aw mutadayyin*] person/elder.[116]

This clearly is a reference to the above discussed impromptu tribal council (*jirgah*), although here less reflecting its reality (as shaped by the outlined colonial and post-colonial state intervention since the middle of the nineteenth century), but rather its idealised origin. The decisive criterion is not economic wealth or political status, but rather a distinctly religious inner disposition that allows for passing judgements in view of the 'common good' (*maṣlaḥah*) as the ultimate benchmark. What it means to be 'pious and religious', and therefore just

al-Miṣrī, *al-Baḥr al-rāʾiq*, V, p. 70; [al-Burhānfūrī] et al., *al-Fatāwā al-hindiyya*, II, p. 185.

113 See Ludhiyānavī, *Aḥsan*, V, pp. 517f. (*fatwā* dated 10 Ṣafar 1407 AH, i.e. 8 December 1981); compare Ibn ᶜĀbidīn, *Radd al-muḥtār*, VI, pp. 107–11.

114 See above, note 76: there, the matter of discussion is confined to spies of the (unbelieving) enemy during war, 'while, according to Imām Abū Ḥanīfa and some others, the death sentence is not to be pronounced over a Muslim spy' ([Akoṛavī], *Fatāvā*, V, p. 301).

115 See Abū Yaḥyā al-Lībī Ḥasan Qāʾid, *al-Muᶜallim fī ḥukm al-jāsūs al-muslim* (n.p., 1430/2009). The relevant Qurʾānic passage prohibiting spying within the Muslim community is Q49:12: 'And do not spy, nor backbite one another' (*wa-lā tajassasū wa-lā yaghtab baᶜḍukum baᶜḍan*).

116 Də Afghānistān Islāmī Imārat, *Lāʾiḥah*, p. 21.

(*nyāvī* or *ᶜādil*), is finally linked back to the eschatological dimension that is so dominant in the Taliban religious worldview: 'A person is called 'just' if they are exceptionally egalitarian [*inṣāf'dār*] and unbiased [*taᶜaṣṣub larūnkī nah vī*], and if they abstain from the major sins [*kabāʾir*] and remain upright in view of the lesser sins [*ṣaghāʾir*]'.[117] While reference to the two sets of sins is found also in classical Ḥanafī literature on this matter, and links thus the legal argument to its theological underpinnings,[118] I contend here that this kind of eschatological thinking, especially the fear for the severe consequences in the Hereafter that result from committing any one of the *kabāʾir*,[119] is exceptionally strong in the rural setting of the Pashtun Borderland.

Urban spaces, in turn, hardly work along the mechanisms of the predominantly rural and tribal Pashtun Borderland. Cosmopolitanism is pitted against the ideal of uniform community cohesion; a much more mundane attitude towards reality rides on individualistic expression and pursuit of happiness. Thus a sense for competition as a generally desirable social mechanism is strengthened. The competitive attitude and a corresponding unadorned utilitarianism are strongly manifest in the various Afghan Islamist organisations and their leadership, played out most dramatically in their race for political power between 1992 and 1996.[120] The Taliban, in fact, represented a counter-draft to this, reflected in their own foundation myth: at the core was Mullā Muḥammad ᶜUmar and a numerically inferior group of Taliban. They hastened to successfully rescue two girls from Mullā ᶜUmar's own village who had reportedly been abducted, humiliated and abused by some district commander, then under direct orders of the controversial warlord Muḥammad Shāfiq 'Gul Āghā' Sherzay (b. 1954).[121] Clearly, the

117 Də Afghānistān Islāmī Imārat, *Lāʾiḥah*, p. 22.

118 See, for example, Muḥammad b. ᶜAlī al-Ḥaṣkafī, *al-Durr al-mukhtār sharḥ tanwīr al-abṣār wa-jāmiᶜ al-baḥār*, ed. ᶜAbd al-Munᶜim Khalīl Ibrāhīm (Beirut, 1423/2002), p. 316; more elaborate Ibn ᶜĀbidīn, *Radd al-muḥtār*, VI, p. 110.

119 See Lange, 'Introducing Hell', p. 7; Hartung, 'A Subtle Difference', p. 12.

120 The personality who perhaps represents this disposition in its most extreme form is Gulbuddīn Ḥikmatyār, at least since the death of Yūnus Khāliṣ supreme leader of the *Ḥizb-i islāmī*: beyond a smokescreen of Islamist rhetoric, Ḥikmatyār would make and unmake strategic alliances with just about anybody who appears useful at any given point in time to further his own position of power. See Olesen, *Islam in Afghanistan*, pp. 268, 292 and 295; Edwards, *Before Taliban: Genealogies of the Afghan Jihad* (Berkeley, Los Angeles and London, 2002), passim; Hartung, *The Pashtun Borderland in Uproar*, chs. 4.2–4.4.

121 It needs to be emphatically stressed that this story, prominently circulated by Rashid, *Taliban*, 25, lacks substantial corroboration. On the concept of 'warlord' as a useful analytical category for the Afghan context, see Dipali Mukhopadhyay, *Warlords, Strongman Governors, and the State in Afghanistan* (Cambridge and New York, 2014);

successful rescue of the girls and the punishment of the commander, allegedly by hanging him from a tank canon as would be commonly done in the ensuing years, was ample proof of God's benevolence for those who are 'pious and religious' (i.e. the Taliban). The punishment also demonstrates God's wrath against those who sought worldly gains and, by pursuing these, would create 'chaos and infestation'. These, of course, will not go away voluntarily:

> The enemy will infiltrate this noble movement [i.e. the Taliban] with its agents, which will create misunderstanding and [mutual] suspicion. The enemy will try to take advantage of some people's weakness, their lack of tolerance and their prejudice. Using those who do not even have a moderate level of honesty or understanding of the *dīn*, they will try to exploit their cowardice and spread dissent [*fitnah*].[122]

Rashīd Aḥmad Ludĥiyānavī's words, quoted here, presumably reflect an early point in the period of the central government of the Islamic Emirate of Afghanistan. Backed by numerous Qurʾānic references to prove the malintent of the unbelieving enemy, the Karachi-based scholar gathered all the righteous believers under the command of Mullā ᶜUmar, proclaimed 'Commander of the Faithful' (*amīr al-muʾminīn*) by his retainers in April 1996.[123] He was seen by Ludĥiyānavī as the sole guarantor of unity in what appeared to the salvation-anxious Taliban as the End of Times. There is a classical legal argument attached to this which merges with a more popular assertion: first, according to classical Islamic political theory, it is incumbent on the commander of the faithful to declare the individual duty (*farḍ ᶜayn*) for active efforts (*jihād*) in defence of the Lands of Islam – including warfare (*qitāl*).[124] Second, armed *jihād* and any

for a discussion of Gul Āghā Sherzay during his tenure as governor of Nangrahar province between 2005 and 2009, see Mukhopadhyay, *Warlords*, pp. 166–242.

122 Ludĥiyānavī, *Ṭālibān: mujāhidīn-i lashkar-i nabavī-yi aḥkām-i ᶜāliyyah: iṭāᶜat-i amīr* (Karachi, 1421 AH), p. 4. This booklet, frequently reprinted and allegedly translated into Pashto and Dari on behalf of the Taliban leadership itself, is now banned in Pakistan under the Anti-Terrorism Act of 1997 (XXVII/1997), its possession subject to imprisonment of up to seven years.

123 That Mullā ᶜUmar did not proclaim himself *amīr al-muʾminīn* is highly significant, because, according to Ludĥiyānavī (see Ludĥiyānavī, *Ṭālibān*, p. 30), *imāra* is 'not given to him who asks for it or to anyone who covets it'. The quote is *Ṣaḥīḥ Muslim, kitāb al-imāra, bāb nahy ᶜan ṭalabi 'l-imāra wa'l-ḥirṣi ᶜalayhā, ḥadīth* 3 (no. 4,821): *lā nuwallī … aḥadan saʾalahu wa-lā aḥadan ḥaraṣa ᶜalayhi.* Alongside Q28.83, Ludĥiyānavī comprehensively quotes here all the accepted *aḥādīth* on this matter.

124 See, again, al-Māwardī, *al-Aḥkām*, pp. 35–64.

resulting martyrdom (*istishhād*) is, according to the popular understanding of Q9.111, the *sole* means to fulfil their side of the bargain (*bay*ᶜ*a*) with God and to enter Paradise.

Ludħiyānavī, whose strong eschatological views we have already encountered above, did indeed declare armed *jihād* the 'supreme act of worship'[125] and a natural disposition of the righteous Muslim, who 'should be anxious to attain the sublime level of martyrdom and to risk [their] life, like a fish out of water'.[126] Indeed, with the aggravation of the external circumstances since the US-led military invasion in December 2001, the legal, the popular and the more theologically grounded arguments for the continuation of armed *jihād* against the forces of unbelief were explicitly invoked again and again.[127] In some way, the successful overthrowing of the Taliban's central government by military forces of the 'Global North', following the distinctly Christian apocalyptic rhetoric of then US president George W. Bush (in office 2001–9), and its various Afghan collaborators, provided clear proof, for the Taliban, of the roaming of the Dajjāl. On the other, however, it constituted a *fitna* in the theological sense – a divinely decreed test for the believer to prove themselves worthy of salvation. For the adherents of the decentralised Islamic Emirate of Afghanistan, it is the foreign military forces, the Afghan government institutions and even civilians in urban spaces that are, from the perspective of religiously conservative rural Pashtuns, creating chaos and infestation. It is not least for that reason that the armed activities of the Taliban continue.[128]

125 Ludħiyānavī, *Ṭālibān*, p. 12.

126 Ludħiyānavī, *Ṭālibān*, p. 33.

127 Of special significance here are the various periodicals officially published by the Islamic Emirate of Afghanistan in Arabic (*al-Ṣumūd*), Pashto (*Morčal* and *Ćrak*), Urdu (*Sharī*ᶜ*at*) and Dari (*Ḥaqīqat*), found on its official website (hosted by changing domains, currently under https://alemarahpashto.com). There are also official primers, such as Mawlavī ᶜAbd al-Ḥalīm Aḥmadī, *Də mujāhid tūrah: də jihād shar*ᶜ*ī masā*ʾ*il* (n.p., 1392 SH/1434 AH), pp. 23–30, 116–21.

128 A graphic case was certainly the attack on the American University of Afghanistan in Kabul on 24 August 2016. Although the Islamic Emirate had not explicitly claimed responsibility, the event was somewhat foreshadowed by Mawlavī ᶜAbd al-Hādī 'Mujāhid', *Fikrī pohānah* (Peshawar, 1389 SH/2010, 2nd ed.), pp. 297–351.

PART III

. . .

JUSTIFYING VIOLENCE

CHAPTER

7

BU'ITHTU BI'L-SAYF: *JIHĀD*, MONOLATRY AND THEONOMY IN MODERN SALAFISM

*Daniel Lav**

INTRODUCTION

This chapter will attempt to shed light on how modern radical *salafī*s conceive of the aim and meaning of *jihād*. It will do so through an examination of the relation, in their system of thought, between the commandment of *jihād* and two other topics, monolatry and theonomy. These topics will be explored more fully in the course of the chapter, but a preliminary definition of terms can be given as follows: I use monolatry (Gr. *monos*, sole + *latreia*, worship) to mean the exclusive worship of one God; it stands in contradistinction to monotheism, defined as exclusive belief in one God. By theonomy (Gr. *theo*, God + *nomos*, law) I mean the belief that rule by God's law is a sine qua non of faith, and the corresponding notion that other forms of rule, and democracy in particular, are inherently polytheistic (or, more accurately, polylatric); this tenet is often called *ḥākimiyya* in Arabic. It will be argued that a tight correlation exists in *salafī jihādī* thought between monolatry and theonomy on the one hand, and, on the other hand, between both these concepts and *jihād*. It will further be argued that this nexus of conceptions was formed from the confluence of the premodern *salafī* tradition, which already associated between monolatry and *jihād*, and the writings of Mawdūdī and Quṭb, which lent this association a theonomic inflection. It is this nexus of conceptions that undergirds the *salafī jihādī* belief that it is proper to employ violence to enforce exclusive servitude to God in both the ritual and (especially) the legal–political spheres.

* Hebrew University of Jerusalem

WAS THE PROPHET SENT WITH THE SWORD?

A good entry point into our discussion of these topics is a recent dispute over the authentication of a *ḥadīth* (Prophetic report). The *ḥadīth* in question reads as follows:

> The Prophet said: I was sent (before Judgment Day) with the sword so that Allah alone be worshiped without partner. My sustenance was placed under my spear, and those who contravened my command were humiliated and laid low. And one who resembles a people is one of them.[1]

The modern *ḥadīth* scholar Shuᶜayb al-Arnaᵓūṭ, a Syrian of Albanian extraction who lived his last decades in Jordan, declared this *ḥadīth* to be weak in the following words:

> [The *ḥadīth*'s] chain of transmission is weak due to an objectionable element in one of its expressions (*ᶜalā nakāratin fī baᶜḍ alfāẓihi*). The evaluators of transmitters of *ḥadīth* (*al-mujarriḥīn waᵓl-muᶜaddilīn*) have differing views on Ibn Thawbān, that is, ᶜAbd al-Raḥmān b. Thābit b. Thawbān. Some regarded him as a strong transmitter, and some as a weak one, and he changed [for the worse] toward the end of his life. The upshot regarding him is that he is a good transmitter (*ḥasan al-ḥadīth*) when he is not the sole line of transmission for something objectionable. Imām Aḥmad [b. Ḥanbal] noted that among his *ḥadīth*s are some that are objectionable, and this is one of them.[2]

Nearly fifteen years later, in a treatise dated 17 Rabīᶜ II 1432 (22 March 2011), the *salafī jihādī* scholar Abū Dharr al-Samharī al-Yamānī took issue with al-Arnaᵓūṭ's negative appraisal of the *ḥadīth*. Al-Yamānī faults al-Arnaᵓūṭ for not mentioning other, more positive evaluations of Ibn Thawbān, including differing evaluations all related to the name of Aḥmad b. Ḥanbal, which al-Yamānī argues, should be taken into account.[3] Nonetheless, al-Yamānī's technical assessment of Ibn Thawbān is close to that of al-Arnaᵓūṭ: both agree that, in general, his

1. Shuᶜayb al-Arnaᵓūṭ (ed.), *Musnad al-imām Aḥmad* (Beirut, 1416/1997), IX, pp. 123–6, 478.
2. *Musnad al-imām Aḥmad* XI, p. 123, footnote 1.
3. Abū Dharr al-Samharī al-Yamānī, *Ibhāj ahl al-ṣināᶜa bi-dirāsat ḥadīth buᶜithtu bil-sayf bayna yaday al-sāᶜa*, http://www.tawhed.ws/dl?i=23041129, 1432/2011, pp. 5–6, 19. For accessed dates of online resources, see the Bibliography and the accompanying note, p. 366.

transmissions should be accepted unless there exists a specific reason to doubt them. They differ on the question of whether this is one of those cases. Al-Yamānī argues that al-Arnaʾūṭ's negative evaluation of the *ḥadīth* is really based on content (*matn*) criticism rather than criticism of the chain of transmission, since al-Arnaʾūṭ only considered Ibn Thawbān objectionable as a transmitter in this instance due to the supposedly objectionable element in the *ḥadīth*'s content.

Al-Yamānī writes that content criticism in itself is an accepted practice, and correctly notes that Ibn Qayyim al-Jawziyya, the famous student of Taqī al-Dīn b. Taymiyya and an important authority for *salafī*s in his own right, engaged in it himself.[4] He adds, however, the following comment: '[T]he words in [al-Arnaʾūṭ's] evaluation "due to an objectionable element in one of its expressions" – I do not know on what basis this was said. What is the supposed objectionable element in the *ḥadīth*??? . . .'[5]

Al-Arnaʾūṭ and al-Yamānī adhere to different currents of Islamic thought. Al-Arnaʾūṭ, while respected by Salafis for his hadith scholarship, was not (or not fully) in the Salafi camp, whereas al-Yamānī served on the Sharīʿa Council of Minbar al-Tawḥīd waʾl-Jihād (www.tawhed.ws), which for several years was the most important religious authority for the radical *salafī jihādī* school.[6] Although *ḥadīth* criticism is conceived of as a practice guided by technical criteria and an ethos of objectivity, the affiliations of the two scholars are germane to our case, since they appear to be at the root of their disagreement over this *ḥadīth* and whether or not it contains an objectionable element.

Al-Yamānī goes on to write that another scholar (and then fellow member of the Minbar's Sharīʿa Council), Abū Humām Bakr al-Atharī, was told by al-Arnaʾūṭ over the telephone that 'the objectionable element in the body of the *ḥadīth* is that the Prophet was sent with mercy, and not with the sword'.[7] Al-Yamānī objects to this argument on a number of grounds, all of which come back to the basic principle that there is nothing at all objectionable in the description

4. See Ibn Qayyim al-Jawziyya, *al-Manār al-munīf fīʾl-ṣaḥīḥ waʾl-ḍaʿīf*, ed. Yaḥya b. ʿAbdallāh al-Thumālī (Mecca, 1428 AH)
5. Al-Yamānī, *Ibhāj*, p. 18.
6. On the significance of the Minbar's *lajna sharʿiyya*, see Joas Wagemakers, 'Protecting *Jihād*: The Sharia Council of the Minbar al-Tawhid wa-l-*Jihād*', *Middle East Policy* 18.2 (2011), 148–62.
7. Al-Yamānī, *Ibhāj*, p. 18. This Abū Humām is none other than Turkī al-Binʿalī, the Bahraini scholar who subsequent to this exchange became the chief religious authority for the Islamic State. On his parting of ways with the Minbar website and his former mentor Abū Muḥammad al-Maqdisī; see: Abū Sufyān Turkī b. Mubārak al-Binʿalī, *Shaykhī al-asbaq hādhā firāq baynī wa-baynaka*, https://twitter.com/turky_albinali/status/475360106717413376, 2014/1435.

of the Prophet as wielding the sword in promotion of *tawḥīd*, and that this does not contradict his having been sent with mercy.[8]

While al-Yamānī does not mention it anywhere in his treatise, al-Arnaʾūṭ's judgment on the *ḥadīth* had entered public discourse not so much due to the influence of his edition of Aḥmad b. Ḥanbal's *Musnad*, but rather by way of another scholar with a far larger media platform, the Muslim Brotherhood-affiliated Yūsuf al-Qaraḍāwī. Unlike al-Arnaʾūṭ, whose criticism of the *ḥadīth*'s content was vaguely worded, al-Qaraḍāwī quite explicitly states that he rejects the *ḥadīth* as unacceptable because, in his view, *jihād* in Islam is purely for defensive purposes, and because the *ḥadīth* contradicts Qurʾānic verses stating that the Prophet was sent with guidance and mercy:

> All these verses, which are [from both the] Meccan and the Medinan [periods], in their differing wordings, offer manifest proof that the noble Prophet was sent only with guidance, truth, preaching (*tabshīr*), admonishment (*indhār*), explanation (*bayān*), healing of hearts, and general mercy to the worlds, and he was not sent with the sword or the spear as the *ḥadīth* says.[9]

This ostensibly technical dispute on *ḥadīth* authentication thus actually serves as a vehicle for a dispute that could be called ideological: is it or is it not proper to conceive of Islam as a religion that uses violence in order to bring humans to the worship of Allah alone, as the *ḥadīth* implies? In what follows we will examine the theological roots of the radical *salafī*s' affirmative response to this question.

MONOLATRY AND *JIHĀD*

Radical *salafī*s conceive of themselves as textual originalists, but they likewise (and perhaps more importantly) are heirs to a specific theological tradition that guides their views, including those relating to the aims and significance of *jihād* in Islam. In order to understand this tradition, we need to return to the medieval

8. This same argument was made implicitly by the spokesman for the Islamic State of Iraq and Syria, Abū Muḥammad al-ʿAdnānī al-Shāmī, in the words with which he used to open his public statements: . . . *waʾl-ṣalāt waʾl-salām ʿalā man buʿitha biʾl-sayf raḥmatan liʾl-ʿālamīn*. See e.g. *Fa-qtulūhum innahum mushrikūn*, https://archive.org/details/Qatelohom.Adnani, 15 June 2013; and *Mā kāna hādhā manhajanā wa-lan yakūna* https://www.youtube.com/watch?v=roUKoO1-3hc, 17 April 2014.
9. Yūsuf al-Qaraḍāwī, *Fiqh al-jihād: dirāsa muqārana li-aḥkāmihi wa-falsafatihi fī ḍawʾ al-qurʾān waʾl-sunna* (Cairo, 1430/2009), I, pp. 325–6.

thinker whom modern *salafī*s claim as their forbearer, the Mamlūk-era Syrian scholar Taqī al-Dīn Aḥmad b. Taymiyya (d. 1328 CE).

Ibn Taymiyya's impact on modern radical *jihād* theory is not a new topic of investigation. All the major studies of Sunni radicalism published in the 1980s noted the use made by modern radicals, such as Sayyid Quṭb and ᶜAbd al-Salām Faraj, of Ibn Taymiyya's anti-Mongol fatwas. The central radical argument here was as follows: Ibn Taymiyya had declared the Ilkhanid Mongols unbelievers, and enjoined *jihād* against them, even though they had converted to Islam and pronounced the *shahāda*, since they ruled by their own law code – the *yāsā* – rather than the *sharīᶜa*. Likewise, while modern rulers claim to be Muslims, they are actually apostates due to ruling by modern law codes, and consequently must be deposed by force.[10]

Ibn Taymiyya's impact on modern militancy is not, however, limited to this historical precedent. Here, I will attempt to briefly trace the outlines of a broader development by which a central topic in Ibn Taymiyya's theology, *tawḥīd al-ulūhiyya*, was transformed by modern radical *salafī*s into a theo-political doctrine and made into the overarching aim of, and justification for, *jihād*.

Standard *salafī* theology today proclaims that there are three parts to *tawḥīd*: *tawḥīd al-ulūhiyya*, *tawḥīd al-rubūbiyya* and *tawḥīd al-asmāʾ waʾl-ṣifāt*.[11] This division derives from Ibn Taymiyya, but in his own works is usually not presented as a fixed formula. The central distinction for Ibn Taymiyya was, in fact, between *tawḥīd al-ulūhiyya* and *tawḥīd al-rubūbiyya*, which I posit might be best understood as 'monolatry' and 'monotheism' respectively, the latter meaning belief in one God to the exclusion of others, and the former worship of one God to the exclusion of others.[12] This distinction was by no means a simple

10. Emmanuel Sivan, *Radical Islam: Medieval Theology and Modern Politics* (New Haven and London, 1990), pp. 94ff; Gilles Kepel, *Muslim Extremism in Egypt: The Prophet and the Pharaoh* (Berkeley and Los Angeles, 2003), pp. 194ff; Johannes J. G. Jansen, *The Neglected Duty: The Creed of Sadat's Assassins and Islamic Resurgence in the Middle East* (New York, 1986), pp. 4, 8. In Ibn Taymiyya's fatwas themselves, this issue is only one of many justifications presented for fighting against the Mongols: see Taqī al-Dīn Aḥmad b. Taymiyya, *Majmūᶜat al-fatāwā* (al-Manṣūra, 1426/2005), XXVIII, pp. 274–301. Direct focus on the issue of legal obedience was, however, already a feature of Ibn Kathīr's comments on the Mongols: see ᶜImād al-Dīn Abū al-Fidāʾ Ismāᶜīl b. ᶜUmar b. Kathīr al-Dimashqī, *Tafsīr al-qurʾān al-ᶜaẓīm* (Beirut, 1419/1998), III, p. 119.
11. See Bernard Haykel, 'On the Nature of Salafi Thought and Action', in *Global Salafism: Islam's New Religious Movement*, ed. R. Meijer (New York, 2009), pp. 33–57, especially p. 39. For an example of the Islamic State of Iraq and Syria catechising children in the three kinds of *tawḥīd*, see the video *Rasāʾil min arḍ al-malāḥim 15* (Muʾassasat al-Furqān, https://archive.org/details/risala-15, 2013).
12. The term monolatry is most frequently employed in biblical scholarship, where it is

division of *tawḥīd* into two equal parts. It was, more than anything, a means of arguing that the heart of Islam is monolatry, and that 'mere' monotheism is not sufficient to make one a Muslim.

The *rubūbiyya* aspect of *tawḥīd*, derived from the noun *rabb* ('lord'), refers in Ibn Taymiyya's writings to Allah as Creator and Sustainer of the cosmos. It expresses what could be called the objective aspect of Allah's divinity, and above all, His omnipotence. In contrast, the *ulūhiyya* aspect of *tawḥīd* refers to Allah as the sole (rightful) object of worship, and thus expresses what could be called the relational aspect of Allah's divinity. Ibn Taymiyya terms this aspect *ulūhiyya* (also *ilāhiyya*), based on a traditional etymology glossing *ilāh* as *maᶜbūd*[13] – an object of worship. At times, he uses the terms *tawḥīd al-ᶜibāda* or *ᶜubūdiyya* in the same meaning.

Ibn Taymiyya writes on this topic in many different modalities, at times employing parallel terminologies,[14] depending on the context and aim of the argument. He also co-opts the Aristotelian/Avicennan language of causality to his framework, identifying the *rubūbiyya* aspect with Allah's role as efficient cause of the cosmos (i.e. that which gives the cosmos its existence) and the *ulūhiyya* aspect with Allah's role as final cause or *telos* of the cosmos (i.e. the aim and purpose of existence).[15] His standard proof-text for the argument that monolatry is the *telos* of existence is Q51:56: 'I only created the *jinn* and humans in order that they worship Me.'[16] For our purposes, however, we will restrict ourselves here to the simpler modes of exposition, as these are the ones with the most obvious influence on later *salafī* thought.

normally used to refer to a pre-monotheistic stage of ancient Israelite religion in which only one God was worshipped while other gods were still acknowledged to exist. My use of the term with regard to Ibn Taymiyya, however, is close to the view of Yehoshua Amir, who argued that monolatry was not merely a stage of religious development destined to be superseded, but rather remained the true core even of 'monotheistic' Biblical faith. Yehoshua Amir, 'Die Begegnung des biblischen und des philosophischen Monotheismus als Grundthema des jüdischen Hellenismus', *Evangelische Theologie* 38 (1978), 2–19; see p. 4.

13. Ibn Taymiyya, *Majmūᶜat al-fatāwā* II, p. 15. For the etymological derivation, see, for example, Ismāᶜīl b. Ḥammād al-Jawharī, *al-Ṣiḥāḥ* (Beirut, 1399/1979), VI, pp. 2223–4.
14. On the language of *ḥaqīqa kawniyya* and *ḥaqīqa dīniyya*, see Roelof Willem van Diffelen, *De Leer der Wahhabieten* (Leiden, 1927), p. 11. For *irāda khalqiyya* and *irāda sharᶜiyya*, see Jon Hoover, *Ibn Taymiyya's Theodicy of Perpetual Optimism* (Leiden and Boston, MA, 2007), p. 73.
15. See Hoover, *Ibn Taymiyya's Theodicy*, pp. 28–9. For examples, see Ibn Taymiyya, *Majmūᶜat al-fatāwā* II, p. 29; and at length in idem., 'Faṣl fīʾl-tawḥīd' in *Jāmiᶜ al-masāʾil* (Mecca, 1422/[2001–2]), VI, pp. 87–129.
16. Ibn Taymiyya, *Majmūᶜat al-fatāwā* I, p. 7; II, p. 10; X, p. 91; *Jāmiᶜ al-masāʾil* VI, p. 45.

The simplest mode of exposition is perhaps Ibn Taymiyya's argument that it was *ulūhiyya*, and not *rubūbiyya*, that was the issue in dispute between the Prophet and the *mushrikūn*.[17] Pointing to Qur'ānic verses in which the *mushrikūn* acknowledge that Allah is Creator and Master of the cosmos,[18] Ibn Taymiyya argues that the call of the prophets and of the revealed scriptures is simply that humans devote exclusive worship to this same deity that they themselves acknowledge.[19] In Ibn Taymiyya's terminology, the argument is thus: the *mushrikūn* acknowledged *tawḥīd al-rubūbiyya*, but lacked *tawḥīd al-ulūhiyya*. The former is clearly not sufficient, then, to make one a Muslim, and it follows that the constitutive feature of Islam is really *tawḥīd al-ulūhiyya*, or exclusivity of worship. In essence, Ibn Taymiyya's contention is that the heart of Islam is really monolatry, and not 'mere' monotheism, which everyone, believer or unbeliever, more or less acknowledges.[20] This emphasis can also be seen clearly in a concise formula that Ibn Taymiyya reiterates quite often: 'Islam is built on two foundations. The first: that we worship Allah alone, without any partner; and the second: that we worship Him as He decreed on the tongue of His Prophet.'[21] This formula is entirely a statement of monolatry, and says nothing about belief or what one would normally consider to be 'creed'. It goes without saying that creedal '*rubūbiyya*' issues were, in fact, of great importance to Ibn Taymiyya, but they were nonetheless secondary to the issue of monolatry.

In Ibn Taymiyya's own expositions of *tawḥīd al-ulūhiyya*, he does not usually dwell on *jihād* as such, but when he does mention it the connection between the two issues is clear. In one passage, for example, after citing Qur'ānic verses suggesting that the *tawḥīd* with which the prophets were sent was monolatry, Ibn Taymiyya cites the *buʿithtu bi'l-sayf* tradition in order to buttress this contention: people are to be fought until Allah alone be *worshipped* [viz. and not just acknowledged] without partner (*ḥatta yuʿbada llāhu waḥdahu lā sharīka lahu*). He then follows this with his argument that Quraysh, 'about whose *shirk*

17. Ibn Taymiyya, *Majmūʿat al-fatāwā* I, p. 71 (*wa-hādhā huwa alladhī qātala ʿalayhi rasūl Allāh mushrikī al-ʿarab li-annahum ashrakū fī'l-ulūhiyya . . . wa-ammā al-rubūbiyya fa-kānū muqirrīna bihā*); and I, p. 117 (*wa'l-mushrikūn min Quraysh wa-ghayrihim . . . kānū muqirrīna bi-anna llāha waḥdahu khalaqa al-samāwāt wa'l-arḍ*).
18. Ibn Taymiyya, *Majmūʿat al-fatāwā* I, pp. 71, 117.
19. Ibn Taymiyya, *Majmūʿat al-fatāwā* II, p. 15.
20. See, for example, Ibn Taymiyya, *Majmūʿat al-fatāwā* II, p. 29: the basic principle (*aṣl*) of *tawḥīd al-rubūbiyya* is 'not disputed by anyone, and they have only disputed some of its details . . . but as for *tawḥīd al-ilāhiyya*, it is [the area of] the general and prevalent *shirk*, in which various kinds of *mushrikūn* have fallen, who [nonetheless] affirm that there is no Creator but Allāh and no Lord but Him . . .'
21. Ibn Taymiyya, *Majmūʿat al-fatāwā* I, pp. 63, 140, 218, 231, 248, 251, 260.

the Qurʾān informed [us], and whose blood and property . . . the Prophet made licit', acknowledged that Allah alone was the Creator (i.e. the *rubūbiyya* aspect); they were nonetheless deemed *mushrikūn*, who must be fought because they worshipped those they believed to be intercessors (*shufaᶜāʾ*) with Allah.[22] We find the same notion in Ibn Taymiyya's comment on the *ḥadīth* in which the Prophet said: 'I was commanded to fight people until they testify that there is no *ilāh* but Allah . . .' He writes that what was required (viz. for cessation of hostilities and immunity of blood and property) was both affirmation (*iqrār*) of Allah and exclusive worship of Him, because the Prophet required that they testify that there is no '*ilāh*' but Allah, and not that there is no '*rabb*' but Allah, and an *ilāh* is an object of worship.[23] In other words, the Prophet's *casus belli* against Quraysh was monolatry, and not just monotheism.[24]

The connection between monolatry and *jihād* is elaborated further in a treatise by another Ḥanbalī scholar, Ibn Rajab (d. 1393 CE).[25] The treatise, titled *al-Ḥikam al-jadīra biʾl-idhāᶜa min qawl al-nabī buᶜithtu biʾl-sayf bayna yaday al-sāᶜa*, is (as its title indicates) devoted to a commentary on the *buᶜithtu*

22. Ibn Taymiyya, *Majmūᶜat al-fatāwā* I, pp. 116–17.
23. Ibn Taymiyya, *Majmūᶜat al-fatāwā* II, p. 15.
24. It should be noted that modern proponents of the idea that *jihād* is purely defensive in nature sometimes argue that Ibn Taymiyya likewise held this view; see, for example, al-Qaraḍāwī, *Fiqh al-jihād*, pp. 335–6. The authenticity of the treatise cited in support of this contention, published as *Qāᶜida mukhtaṣira fī qitāl al-kuffār wa-muhādanatihim wa-taḥrīm qatlihim li-mujarrad kufrihim*, is disputed. See, for example, Muḥammad b. ᶜAbd al-Raḥmān al-Qāsim (ed.), *Fatāwā wa-rasāʾil samāḥat al-shaykh Muḥammad bin Ibrāhīm bin ᶜAbd al-Laṭīf Āl al-Shaykh* (Mecca, 1399 AH), VI, pp. 200–1; and Sulaymān b. ᶜAbd al-Raḥmān b. Ḥamdān, *Dalālat al-nuṣūs waʾl-ijmāᶜ ᶜalā farḍ al-qitāl liʾl-kufr waʾl-difāᶜ* (Amman, n. d.).
25. The question of the relation between Ibn Rajab and the neo-Ḥanbalī school has yet to be fully explored. Ibn Rajab was (briefly) a student of Ibn Taymiyya's closest student, Ibn Qayyim al-Jawziyya, and he was clearly an admirer of Ibn Taymiyya; see Livnat Holtzman, 'Ibn Qayyim al-Jawziyya', in *Essays in Arabic Literary Biography*, eds J. E. Lowry and D. Stewart (Wiesbaden, 2009), pp. 202–23; see p. 208; and ᶜAbd al-Raḥmān b. Aḥmad b. Rajab, *al-Dhayl ᶜalā ṭabaqāt al-ḥanābila* (Riyadh, 1425/2005) IV, pp. 491–529 (no. 531). (For a differing assessment, however, of Ibn Rajab's *tarjama* of Ibn Taymiyya, see: Caterina Bori, 'Ibn Taymiyya *wa-Jamāᶜatuhu*: Authority, Conflict and Consensus in Ibn Taymiyya's Circle', in *Ibn Taymiyya and His Times*, eds Yossef Rapoport and Shahab Ahmed (Karachi, 2010), pp. 23–52; see pp. 34–6. In legal disputes between the 'Taymiyyans' (*al-taymiyyūn*) and their opponents, Ibn Ḥajar reports that Ibn Rajab at first upheld, then retracted, the Taymiyyan position on some rulings, and was not a member of either camp; Ibn Ḥajar al-ᶜAsqalānī, *Inbāʾ al-ghumr bi-anbāʾ al-ᶜumr* (Beirut, 2nd edn, 1406/1987), III, p. 176.

bi'l-sayf tradition.[26] While the treatise does not employ the Taymiyyan language of *tawḥīd al-ulūhiyya*, it does seem to bear a neo-Ḥanbalī imprint in its emphasis on monolatry. In his exegesis of the tradition's words 'so that Allah alone be worshipped without partner', Ibn Rajab writes: 'This is the supreme aim of the Prophet's mission, and indeed of the mission of the prophets before him . . . and indeed it is the aim of the creation and existentiation of created beings . . .'[27] As noted above, this presentation of monolatry as the *telos* of existence is characteristically Taymiyyan, as is the Qur'ānic verse Ibn Rajab cites here as evidence (51:56): 'I only created the jinn and humans in order that they worship Me.'[28] Likewise, Ibn Rajab writes (using the language of the *buʿithtu* tradition) that the Prophet Muhammad's 'sole aim was that Allah alone be worshipped without partner',[29] and this was, thus, the sole reason why he fought.[30] In essence, Ibn Rajab conceptualises military *jihād* as simply *daʿwa* by other means. At the beginning on his commentary on the first words of the tradition, *buʿithtu bi'l-sayf*, he writes:

> This means that Allah sent him (the Prophet) as a caller to *tawḥīd* through the sword, after having called to *tawḥīd* through [verbal] proof. Whoever did not respond favorably to the call to *tawḥīd* through the Qur'ān, verbal proof and explanation, was then called [to it] through the sword.[31]

This conception of monolatry (as opposed to monotheism) as the *casus belli* for *jihād* found its real-world expression in the early Wahhābī movement in central Arabia. It would not be much of an oversimplification to say that *tawḥīd al-ulūhiyya* was the *raison d'être* of the early Wahhābī movement, and was the

26. Zayn al-Dīn Abī al-Faraj ʿAbd al-Raḥmān b. Aḥmad b. Rajab al-Ḥanbalī, *Majmūʿ rasā'il al-ḥāfiẓ Ibn Rajab al-Ḥanbalī* (Cairo, n. d.), I, pp. 225–55.
27. *hādhā huwa al-maqṣūd al-aʿẓam min baʿthatihi ṣallā llāh ʿalayhi wa-sallama bal min baʿthat al-rusul min qablihi . . . bal hādhā huwa al-maqṣūd min khalq al-khalq wa-ījādihim . . .* Ibn Rajab, *Majmūʿ rasā'il* I, p. 231.
28. Ibn Rajab, *Majmūʿ rasā'il* I, p. 231.
29. *mā maqṣūd al-nabī ṣallā llāh ʿalayhi wa-sallama illā an yuʿbada llāh waḥdahu lā sharīka lahu*; Ibn Rajab, *Majmūʿ rasā'il* I, p. 237.
30. *wa-kāna ṣallā llāh ʿalayhi wa-sallam innamā yuqātilu ʿalā dukhūl al-nās fī'l-tawḥīd*; Ibn Rajab, *Majmūʿ rasā'il* I, p. 238. That *tawḥīd* here should be understood as monolatry seems clear from the preceding part, especially from his identification of monolatry as the sole aim of the Prophet Muḥammad's mission.
31. *qawluhu ṣallā llāh ʿalayhi wa-sallama buʿithtu bi'l-sayf yaʿnī anna llāha baʿathahu dāʿiyyan ilā tawḥidihi bi'l-sayf baʿda duʿā'ihi bi'l-ḥujja fa-man lam yastajib ilā al-tawḥīd bi'l-qur'ān wa'l-ḥujja wa'l-bayān duʿiya bi'l-sayf*; Ibn Rajab, *Majmūʿ rasā'il* I, p. 227.

reason why they famously viewed their contemporaries as *mushrikūn* who must be fought.

While presented in simplified form for didactic purposes, Muhammad b. ᶜAbd al-Wahhāb's doctrine of *tawḥīd al-ulūhiyya* was clearly taken from Ibn Taymiyya.[32] Monolatry is stated to be the purpose of the creation of humans and created beings in general, with Q51:56 often adduced on this score.[33] Like Ibn Taymiyya, Ibn ᶜAbd al-Wahhāb insists that the meaning of *ilāh* is *maᶜbūd* – that which is worshipped or one to whom supplication is made[34] – and thus that the *shahāda* is a statement of monolatry (*tawḥīd al-ulūhiyya*) rather than monotheism (*tawḥīd al-rubūbiyya*): its meaning is that there is nothing worthy of worship apart from Allah.[35] Ubiquitous as well is the Taymiyyan argument that the

32. This point is not as clear from the secondary literature as it ought to be. A fine early treatment can be found in van Diffelen, *De leer der Wahhabieten*, op. cit. Henri Laoust did not devote much space to *tawḥīd al-ulūhiyya* in either his discussion of Ibn Taymiyya himself or in his discussion of this scholar's influence on the Wahhābīs: Henri Laoust, *Essai sur les doctrines sociales et politiques de Taḳī-d-Dīn Aḥmad b. Taimīya* (Cairo, 1939), pp. 472, 525, 531–3. Esther Peskes has called into question the identity between the two *tawḥīd al-ulūhiyya* doctrines: *Muḥammad b. ᶜAbdalwahhāb (1703–92) im Widerstreit: Untersuchungen zur Rekonstruktion der Frühgeschichte der Wahhābīya* (Beirut, 1993), p. 21, n. 33.
33. ᶜAbd al-Raḥmān b. Muḥammad b. Qāsim (ed.), *al-Durar al-saniyya fīʾl-ajwiba al-najdiyya*, 6th edn (1417/1996), I, pp. 126, 137–8, 144, 147, 152; II, pp. 6, 23, 32, 36, 66, 102. In addition to the clear emphasis here on monolatry, it appears that Ibn ᶜAbd al-Wahhāb was likewise consciously following Ibn Taymiyya in the very statement that Allāh created for a purpose, *pace* Ashᶜarī voluntarism. He was certainly aware of the issue: cf. *Durar* I, p. 179, *wa-mā ẓannū annahu khilaf al-ḥikma qālū lā yafᶜalu li-ḥikma bal li-mashīʾa* (the phrasing here perhaps influenced by Ibn Qayyim al-Jawziyya, *al-Kāfiya al-shāfiya fīʾl-intiṣār liʾl-firqa al-nājiya* (Mecca, 1428 AH), I, p. 64). On this issue in Ibn Taymiyya, see Hoover, *Ibn Taymiyya's Theodicy*, pp. 70–102. See also the adduction of Q51:56 at the very opening of Ibn ᶜAbd al-Wahhāb's *Kitāb al-tawḥīd*: ᶜAbd al-ᶜAzīz Zayd al-Rūmī et al. (eds), *Muʾallafāt al-shaykh al-imām Muḥammad bin ᶜAbd al-Wahhāb* (Riyadh, n. d.), I, p. 7; in *masʾala* no. 1 thereon (1: 9), which reads '*al-ḥikma fī khalq al-jinn waʾl-ins*', the word *ḥikma* should be understood in the Taymiyyan sense as 'purpose'.
34. ᶜAbd al-Raḥmān b. Muḥammad (ed.), *Durar* I, pp. 112, 114 (including polemic against the Ashᶜarī gloss of *ilāh* as *qādir*), p. 138; II, pp. 32, 41, 73, 103, 127.
35. See ᶜAbd al-Raḥmān b. Muḥammad (ed.), *Durar* II, pp. 103–4: When Ibn ᶜAbd al-Wahhāb is asked to explain why he was displeased with the statement 'I testify that there is no god but Allāh alone, without partner in His will and volition', he expresses surprise that the questioner needs any clarification on this topic, and explains simply that the *shahāda* is about *ulūhiyya*, whereas the statement in question turned it to *tawḥīd al-rubūbiyya*, which the unbelievers also affirm (*fa-ᶜajab kayfa yakhfā ᶜalayka hādhā liʾl-ulūhiyya waʾl-madhkūr fīʾl-khuṭba tawḥīd al-rubūbiyya alladhī aqarra bihi al-kuffār*).

Qurʾānic *mushrikūn* professed *tawḥīd al-rubūbiyya* – that is, they knew Allah and acknowledged that He alone was the Creator and Sustainer – and what they lacked was *tawḥīd al-ulūhiyya*. Thus, the *shirk* for which they are condemned in the Qurʾān was less polytheism than polylatry: the appeal to, and worship of, others as intercessors with Allah.[36]

Needless to say, Ibn ᶜAbd al-Wahhāb's interest in the nature of the Qurʾānic *mushrikūn* was not an antiquarian one: it was a means of clarifying the true nature of the opposition between *tawḥīd* and *shirk* for contemporary purposes.[37] He believed that many or most of his contemporaries in Najd were *mushrikūn*, and this for one root cause: like their Qurʾānic counterparts, they did not know, or refused to accept and implement, the *tawḥīd* that is monolatry, and only upheld the *tawḥīd* that is 'mere' monotheism.[38] In consequence, like the original Qurʾānic *mushrikūn*, they engaged in polylatric practice, first and foremost through their supplication of deceased holy men:

> Most people, though they know this religion [i.e. its true meaning], hear the *ᶜulamāʾ* in [the towns of] Sudayr and al-Washm, and others saying: "We fulfill *tawḥīd* of Allah. We know that no one benefits or harms but Allah, and that the righteous [to whom we appeal] do not benefit and do not harm". [When you hear this] you know that the only *tawḥīd* they know is the *tawḥīd* of the unbelievers, *tawḥīd al-rubūbiyya* . . .[39]

There is, then, nothing mysterious about why Ibn ᶜAbd al-Wahhāb believed his contemporaries to be unbelievers: this belief was grounded in Ibn Taymiyya's distinction between monotheism and monolatry.

See also ᶜAbd al-Raḥmān b. Muḥammad (ed.), *Durar* I, pp. 69–70, 114, 130, 138, 153; II, pp. 87, 102–3.

36. ᶜAbd al-Raḥmān b. Muḥammad (ed.), *Durar* I, pp. 59–60, 65–9, 106, 137, 145, 159; II, pp. 24, 27–8, 33–4, 37–8, 40–1, 63–5, 67, 72–3, 76–7, 104–5, 107, 117–18, 125–6.
37. For the basic principle cf. ᶜAbd al-Raḥmān b. Muḥammad (ed.), *Durar* I, pp. 107: 'No one knows *tawḥīd* who does not know *jāhiliyya*', and the verses at the opening of *Masāʾil al-jāhiliyya*: *faʾl-ḍidd yuẓhiru ḥusnahu al-ḍidd / wa-bi-ḍiddihā tatabayyanu al-ashyāʾ*; ᶜAbd al-ᶜAzīz Zayd al-Rūmī et al. (eds), *Muʾallafāt al-shaykh al-imām* I, p. 333. For the substantive conclusion that 'it is worship that is *tawḥīd*, because the dispute between the prophets and the nations was over this', see ᶜAbd al- Raḥmān b. Muḥammad (ed.), *Durar* II, pp. 66–7, and similar language in the opening chapter of *Kitāb al-tawḥīd*: ᶜAbd al-ᶜAzīz Zayd al-Rūmī et al. (eds), *Muʾallafāt al-shaykh al-imām* I, p. 9.
38. ᶜAbd al-Raḥmān b. Muḥammad (ed.), *Durar* II, p. 67: *waʾl-aṣl al-thānī wa-huwa tawḥīd al-ulūhiyya fa-huwa alladhī waqaᶜa fīhi al-nizāᶜ fī qadīm al-dahr wa-ḥadīthihi* . . .
39. ᶜAbd al-Raḥmān b. Muḥammad (ed.), *Durar* II, p. 77.

In consequence, Ibn ᶜAbd al-Wahhāb saw monolatry as the aim of, and justification for, *jihād*. At the outset of his *Masāʾil al-jāhiliyya* he writes that exclusivity of worship was the greatest point of dispute between the Prophet and the people of the *jāhiliyya*; it was what led people to split into Muslims and unbelievers, was the cause of hostility between them and was the reason for which *jihād* was ordained (*wa-li-ajlihā shuriᶜat al-jihād*).[40] This contention that the Prophet's *casus belli* was his contemporaries' polylatry appears frequently in Ibn ᶜAbd al-Wahhāb's writings;[41] that it was polyatry rather than polytheism that served as the *casus belli* almost goes without saying, since like Ibn Taymiyya he viewed the Qurʾānic *mushrikūn* as monotheists in matters of *rubūbiyya*.[42] And just as Ibn ᶜAbd al-Wahhāb's insistence on the nature of *shirk* in the *jāhiliyya* was always aimed at denouncing the recurrence of this *shirk* in his own day, so, too, is his insistence on that *shirk*'s function as a *casus belli* aimed at justifying his own movement's wielding of the sword for the sake of monolatry: 'This is what we call people to, and what we fight them over, after having presented them with proof.'[43]

THE THEONOMIC SHIFT: MAWDŪDĪ AND QUṬB

Among modern radical *salafī*s, the heritage of monolatric *jihād* just described has been refocused on the issue of theonomy – that is, the theological imperative of establishing a government of rule by Allah's law, and abolition of government based on man-made law. *Salafī jihādī*s generally claim that this focus is simply an application of the traditional *salafī* concern for *tawḥīd* to a newly arisen form of *shirk*.[44] In terms of historical development, however, this theonomic

40. Ibid., p. 132.
41. See, for example, ᶜAbd al-Raḥmān b. Muḥammad (ed.), *Durar* II, pp. 68–9: *wa-ᶜarafta anna al-tawḥīd alladhī jaḥadūhu huwa tawḥīd al-ᶜibāda . . . wa-ᶜarafta anna rasūl Allāh qātalahum ᶜalā dhālika . . .*
42. ᶜAbd al-Raḥmān b. Muḥammad (ed.), *Durar* II, pp. 144–5: Quraysh's affirmation of Allāh as the sole Creator and Sustainer [i.e. *tawḥīd al-rubūbiyya*] did not suffice to immunise them from attack.
43. ᶜAbd al-Raḥmān b. Muḥammad (ed.), *Durar* I, p. 87, and likewise I, pp. 95–6.
44. These old and new forms of *shirk* are sometimes termed respectively *shirk al-qubūr* (viz. tomb-centered worship) and *shirk al-quṣūr* (with *quṣur* – 'palaces' – as metonymy for political regimes); see, for example, Abū Muḥammad al-Maqdisī, *Tabṣīr al-ᶜuqalāʾ bi-talbīsāt ahl al-tajahhum waʾl-irjāʾ* (http://www.tawhed.ws/r?i=2mianrha), p. 18; idem., *Ḥiwār al-shaykh Abī Muḥammad al-Maqdisī maᶜa majallat al-ᶜaṣr* (http://www.tawhed.ws/dl?i=j37307wg, 1423 AH), p. 1; Abū Baṣīr al-Ṭarṭūsī, *Ḥukm al-Islām fīʾl-dīmuqrāṭiyya waʾl-taᶜaddudiyya al-ḥizbiyya* (http://www.abubaseer.bizland.com/books/read/b1.doc, 1410/1990,), p. 448.

shift in modern radical Salafism is largely due to the influence of two twentieth-century thinkers, Abū al-Aᶜlā Mawdūdī and Sayyid Quṭb,[45] whose own relation to Salafism is a matter of controversy.[46] Thus, in order to understand theonomy's grounding in premodern monolatry on the one hand, and its relation to *jihād* on the other, it will be necessary to address these issues first in the writings of these two thinkers.

The term employed by Mawdūdī and Quṭb for what I call here theonomy is *ḥākimiyya*. The basic principle of *ḥākimiyya* is that sovereignty is an exclusive prerogative of Allah;[47] it follows that human sovereignty is thus usurpation of a divine attribute. The usurper is a false god, and those who accept such a usurper as sovereign are idol worshippers. The rather striking juxtaposition of the political and the religious in this doctrine has given rise to much debate. Some influential *ᶜulamāᵓ* have argued that the doctrine is a departure from, and politicised reduction of, traditional Islam;[48] and these arguments have been adduced in academic research in support of the claim that *ḥākimiyya* is a distinctively modern political theory with few roots in premodern Islamic thought.[49] While Mawdūdī's and Quṭb's formulation of the *ḥākimiyya* doctrine is certainly novel, in what follows I will attempt to show that it bears close structural parallels to the specifically *salafī* doctrine of monolatry.[50] Structurally speaking, theonomy

45. On *salafī* Jihadism's 'salafisation' of Quṭb, see Daniel Lav, *Radical Islam and the Revival of Medieval Theology* (New York, 2012), pp. 168–9; and Joas Wagemakers, *A Quietist Jihādi: The Ideology and Influence of Abu Muhammad al-Maqdisi* (Cambridge, 2012), pp. 35, 38, 66–7.
46. Cf. Stéphane Lacroix, *Les islamistes saoudiens: une insurrection manqué* (Paris, 2010), pp. 67–8, 105, 128–9, *inter alia*; Lav, *Radical Islam*, pp. 126–9.
47. Mawdūdī used *ḥākimiyya* simply as an Urdu equivalent of the English 'sovereignty', a gloss that he sometimes gives himself in parentheses; for example, Mawlānā Sayyid Abū al-Aᶜlā Mawdūdī, *Qurᵓān kī chār bunyādī iṣṭilāḥēñ* (New Delhi, 2011), p. 58. Elsewhere, he explicitly refers to *ḥākimiyya* as a term taken from the field of political science: Mawdūdī, *Islāmī riyāsat* (Lahore 2008), p. 334.
48. For example, Abū al-Ḥasan al-Nadwī, *al-Tafsīr al-siyāsī liᵓl-islām fī mirᵓāt kitābāt al-ustādh Abī al-Aᶜlā al-Mawdūdī waᵓl-shahīd Sayyid Quṭb* (Cairo, 1980); and Muḥammad Manẓūr Nuᶜmānī, *Mawlānā Mawdūdī kē sāth mērī rafāqat kī sar-guzasht awr ab mērā mawqif* (Karachi, [n. d.]).
49. For example, Seyyed Vali Reza Nasr, *Mawdudi and the Making of Islamic Revivalism* (New York and Oxford, 1996), pp. 58–9; Irfan Ahmad, 'Genealogy of the Islamic State: Reflections on Maududi's Political Thought and Islamism', *Journal of the Royal Anthropological Institute* 15 (2009), pp. 145–62; p. 156.
50. Ahmad, 'Genealogy', p. 156, notes that Mawdūdī (*apud* Nuᶜmānī, *Mawlānā Mawdūdī*, p. 90) cited Ibn Taymiyya as the closest precedent for his understanding of *lā ilāha illā llāh*. Ahmad's point, however, is to show how little precedent Mawdūdī could muster, and he does not follow up on the issue. Nadwī likewise devotes some effort to demon-

can be understood as simply the transposition of monolatry onto a legal–political register.

Like Ibn Taymiyya, both Mawdūdī and Quṭb regularly emphasise a conceptual distinction between two aspects of divinity, one of which could be termed objective or cosmic, and the other relational. They argue that the central flaw of modern-day society, including in (putatively) Muslim countries, is that it acknowledges only the cosmic objective aspect, and fails to acknowledge and act in accordance with the relational aspect. Much like Ibn Taymiyya's polemics against those who recognise only *tawḥīd al-rubūbiyya*, Mawdūdī essentially views this restrictive conception of divinity and its prerogatives as a reversion to a pre-Islamic conception of divinity – that of the *mushrikūn* – who acknowledged only the cosmic or objective aspect, that is, Allah's existence and His aspect as Creator and Sustainer.[51] And like Ibn Taymiyya, Mawdūdī adduces the Qurʾān's testimony that the *mushrikūn* acknowledged this aspect as proof that the dispute between them and the prophets was only over the relational aspect of divinity, acknowledgment of which then must be the constitutive element of Islam.[52]

In line with this analysis of the nature of divinity, our two twentieth-century authors, like Ibn Taymiyya, understand Islam to be first and foremost monolatry, and its opposite – *shirk* – first and foremost as polylatry. If one considers Mawdūdī's depiction of the 'central idea' of the Qurʾān, before addressing the manner in which he (re-)defines his terms, it, in fact, reads like a rather straightforward statement of Islam-as-monolatry: 'Allah is *rabb* and *ilāh*; no one apart from Allah has *rubūbiyya* and *ilāhiyya*; thus worship (*ʿibāda*) needs to be to Him; and religion (*dīn*) needs to be exclusively (*khāliṣatan*) for Him.'[53] He and Quṭb did not, however, interpret this imperative as relating primarily to ritual monolatry (though they did, of course, endorse it in principle).[54] The move from monolatry to theonomy, and from the ritual to the political, hinges on the definition of worship: this is why Mawdūdī places *ʿibādat* as the third of his 'four basic

strating differences between Ibn Taymiyya's understanding of *ilāh* and *ʿubūdiyya* and Mawdūdī's: Nadwī, *al-Tafsīr al-siyāsī*, pp. 81ff. This is a polemical strategy somewhat reminiscent of anti-Wahhābī literature, and suggests that Mawdūdī may have been more influenced by Ibn Taymiyya than is generally recognised. This question, however, deserves a fuller inquiry than is possible here, and my aim for the time being is simply to point out structural parallels between the two systems of thought.

51. See, for example, Mawdūdī, *Qurʾān kī chār bunyādī iṣṭilāḥēñ*, pp. 37–8 (*qawm* Nūḥ), pp. 40–1 (ʿĀd and Thamūd), p. 42 (*qawm* Ibrāhīm), p. 66 (the *mushrikūn* of Muḥammad's time).
52. Mawdūdī, *Qurʾān kī chār bunyādī iṣṭilāḥēñ*, p. 66 (citing Q23:84–90).
53. Ibid., p. 7.
54. Ibid., pp. 87–90; Sayyid Quṭb, *Maʿālim fīʾl-ṭarīq* (Beirut and Cairo, 1399/1979), p. 85.

Qur'ānic terms', after *ilāh* and *rabb*,[55] and why he refers to it as the fundamental concept underlying all religion.[56] If we understand worship primarily in a ritual sense, then a strict monolatry would look something like the Wahhābī movement. Mawdūdī argues, however, that the term, properly understood, means obedience (*iṭāʿa*) and servitude (*bandagī*) as well as ritual devotion (*parastish*); to restrict its meaning solely to the latter is an error that diminishes the true scope of the Qur'ān's message.[57] This then lays the foundation for Mawdūdī's discussion of the fourth term, *dīn*: Islam is not merely a 'religion' (*madhhab*) – that is, a collection of beliefs and rituals – but rather a comprehensive way of life to be followed, including the social, political and legal organisation of society, in accordance with the rule of a supreme power.[58] Obedience to Allah and His law is Islam, and obedience to another and his law is *shirk*.

The formal rationale behind Mawdūdī's characteristically 'political' take on Islam can thus be restated as follows: Islam is a monolatry, and monolatry – when the true meaning of 'worship' is understood – mandates theonomy. This same rationale is readily apparent in Quṭb's writings as well: for example, he writes that the foundation of the political system needs to be exclusive *ʿubūdiyya* to Allah, and this means that the political system must take its laws solely from Allah.[59] Once again, this is simply theonomy based on monolatry.

Mawdūdī's 'political' interpretation of Islam is thus clearly grounded in his theology. When Mawdūdī explains why human government is evil, he asks rhetorically: who created the land, the humans who dwell on it and the means required for their subsistence – God or another? He then continues: if the answer to this question is God, then how can it be that another reign over a realm that is God's? How can the subjects in this realm be ruled by another's law, or by a

55. Mawdūdī, *Qur'ān kī chār bunyādī iṣṭilāḥēñ*, p. 5.
56. Abū al-Aʿlā Mawdūdī, 'Islām mēñ ʿibādat kā taṣawwur', in *Tafhīmāt* (Lahore, 2004), I, p. 46.
57. Mawdūdī, *Qur'ān kī chār bunyādī iṣṭilāḥēñ*, p. 98. Such a conception of *ʿibāda* is not itself without precedent in premodern monolatry. Ibn Taymiyya by no means restricted it to ritual devotion: he considered *ʿibāda* to be 'a term that comprises every speech and act, interior or exterior, that Allāh loves and is pleased with'; *Risālat al-ʿubūdiyya* in *Majmūʿat al-fatāwā* X, p. 91. And cf. *Majmūʿat al-fatāwā* I, p. 101: 'All that Allāh orders the servant, whether as an obligatory or recommended [act] – performance of it is *ʿibāda* to Allāh.' Stress on obedience (*ṭāʿa*) and observance of prohibition and permission as elements of *tawḥīd al-ulūhiyya* is common in his intra-Ṣūfī polemics; e.g. *Majmūʿat al-fatāwā* II, p. 276. Similar themes are found in Ibn ʿAbd al-Wahhāb's writings as well, but in practice the Wahhābīs' principal concern was with violations of ritual monolatry.
58. Mawdūdī, *Qur'ān kī chār bunyādī iṣṭilāḥēñ*, p. 109.
59. Quṭb, *Maʿālim fī'l-ṭarīq* (Beirut and Cairo, 1399/1979), p. 64; see also Quṭb, *Maʿālim fī'l-ṭarīq*, p. 62 for the characterisation of submission to law as *al-ʿubūdiyya al-kubrā*.

law of their own invention, when they are God's subjects? This is clearly against what is right, and is the root of the evil.[60] In other words, Mawdūdī argues that acknowledgment of Allah's cosmic aspect as Creator and Sustainer, without recognition of His relational aspect and action in accordance with it, is the root of evil in the world; his argument is, in essence, the same one that he characterises as the message of all the prophets: 'These two aspects of *rubūbiyya*, which due to *jāhiliyya* you separated one from another, are in truth [both] necessary [aspects] of, and particular to, divinity';[61] and '*rubūbiyya* is indivisible (*nā qābil-i taqsīm*)'.[62]

As a necessary aside, it must be noted that Mawdūdī and Quṭb's understanding of the terms *rabb* and *ilāh* are not consistent with Ibn Taymiyya's; in the passages just cited, for example, Mawdūdī subsumes both the cosmic and the relational aspects under *rubūbiyya*. While Mawdūdī's interpretation of the nature of divinity is grounded in his understanding of the terms *rabb* and *ilāh*, they do not correspond neatly to the two different aspects of divinity in his analysis. Ibn Taymiyya had viewed only the term *ilāh* and the issue of *ulūhiyya*, which he identified with the relational aspect of divinity, as having become corrupted from their original meanings; in contrast, Mawdūdī argues that the understanding of *rabb* as denoting only an omnipotent being who provides sustenance (*parwardagār*) is itself a later corruption.[63] Rather than contrasting the terms *rubūbiyya* and *ulūhiyya*, he views both – but *rubūbiyya* in particular – as comprising the relational aspect of divinity, alongside the cosmic objective one. As for Quṭb, he appears inconsistent in his use of the terms, and at times even employed them in precisely inverse fashion from Ibn Taymiyya – i.e. with *ulūhiyya* as the cosmic or objective aspect of divinity that was acknowledged by the people of the *jāhiliyya*, and *rubūbiyya* as the relational aspect that ought to govern human action, and that was the point of contention between the prophets and their opponents.[64] These divergences of terminology have the effect of obscuring somewhat the structural parallels noted above between Ibn Taymiyya's monolatry and the *ḥākimiyya* doctrine. This complication arises only with regard to Mawdūdī

60. Abū al-Aᶜlā Mawdūdī, *Khuṭbāt* (New Delhi, 2005), p. 271.
61. Mawdūdī, *Qurʾān kī chār bunyādī iṣṭilāḥēñ*, p. 74.
62. Ibid., p. 73.
63. Ibid., p. 9.
64. This point did not escape the notice of *salafī* critics of Quṭb: see Rabīᶜ b. Hādī ᶜUmayr al-Madkhalī, *Aḍwāʾ islāmiyya ᶜalā ᶜaqīdat Sayyid Quṭb wa-fikrihi* (Cairo, 1428/2007), pp. 49–52; and ᶜAbdallāh b. Muḥammad b. Aḥmad al-Dawīsh, *al-Mawrid al-zulāl fīʾl-tanbīh ᶜalā akhṭāʾ al-ẓilāl* (= *Majmūᶜat muʾallafāt al-shaykh ᶜAbdallāh al-Dawīsh*, III; Burayda, 1411/1990), pp. 95–6, 103–6.

and Quṭb themselves; the *salafī jihādī*s who later incorporated *ḥākimiyya* into their own doctrine employ the Taymiyyan terminology in consistent fashion, as we will see shortly.

Thus far we have commented on the monolatric grounding of the doctrine of *ḥākimiyya*; now we will turn to the relation between the issues of *ḥākimiyya* and *jihād* in the writings of Mawdūdī and Quṭb. In the chapter on *jihād* in Mawdūdī's *Khuṭbāt*, we can see the great extent to which theonomy has occupied the structural position held by ritual monolatry in the premodern *salafī* tradition and how it has replaced monolatry as the direct aim of *jihād*. Mawdūdī writes that the ritual commandments of pilgrimage, fasting, prayer and *zakāt*, dealt with in previous chapters of *Khuṭbāt*, were simply commanded as a kind of preparation of the individual towards the true aim of Islam and the great work it requires. This aim is to establish God's government over humans by obliterating government of humans over humans, and to stake one's life for this aim is the great work that is known as *jihād*.[65] *Jihād*, for Mawdūdī, is thus the human exertion and struggle by means of which the supreme aim of existence is achieved: Allah's rule over humans, as expressed through government by His laws.[66] The centrality of *jihād* in his thought is due to its direct connection with theonomy.

This same conception of *jihād* is the guiding theme of both Mawdūdī's essay 'Jihād fī sabīl Allah' and the identically titled chapter of Sayyid Quṭb's *Maᶜālim fīʾl-ṭarīq* (*Milestones*), which is clearly patterned after it.[67] The principal topic of these essays is thus not really *jihād* per se, but rather the nature of Islam itself as a project to deliver humans from servitude to humans and bring them to exclusive servitude to Allah. For Mawdūdī, the upshot of Islam's 'revolutionary call' is simply (Q2:21): 'Oh people, worship your Lord who created you' (*yā ayyuhā al-nās uᶜbudū rabbakum alladhī khalaqakum*);[68] i.e. the same divinity who created you (in His cosmic aspect) is the only one worthy of worship and obedience (in His relational aspect). Likewise, when Quṭb states that the aim of, and justification for, *jihād* is the liberation of humans from *ᶜubūdiyya* to other humans, he cites the verse (Q43:84) 'And it is He who is *ilāh* in heaven and *ilāh* on earth' (*wa-huwa alladhī fīʾl-samāʾ ilāh wa-fīʾl-arḍ ilāh*);[69] i.e. Allah is

65. Mawdūdī, *Khuṭbāt*, p. 267.
66. Ibid., p. 274.
67. This is one of the chapters of *Maᶜālim* that was adapted from his Qurʾān commentary, *Fī ẓilāl al-qurʾān*. For more on Quṭb's indebtedness to Mawdūdī on the issue of *jihād*, see Jan-Peter Hartung, *A System of Life: Mawdūdī and the Ideologisation of Islam* (London, 2013), pp. 209–13.
68. Abū al-Aᶜlā Mawdūdī, *Tafhīmāt* (Lahore, 2004), I, p. 81.
69. Sayyid Quṭb, *Maᶜālim*, pp. 59–60.

not just the cosmic divinity, but must also be the sole one to whom *ᶜubūdiyya* is devoted on earth, including and especially that 'greatest *ᶜubūdiyya*' that is obedience to law.[70]

Jihād is, then, an intrinsic and necessary element of Islam for these two thinkers. They both condemn the apologetic characterisation of *jihād* as solely defensive in nature, a view they see as stemming from modern Muslims' misunderstanding of *dīn* as merely a religion or creed, rather than a universal monolatric–theonomic imperative.[71] There is no need to seek justification for *jihād* in external conditions such as enemy aggression, since 'delivering people from *ᶜubūdiyya* to humans, and to *ᶜubūdiyya* to Allah alone without partner, is itself sufficient' justification for *jihād*;[72] this is an 'inherent justification found in the nature of this *dīn* itself'.[73]

Neither Quṭb nor Mawdūdī themselves translated this conception into violent revolution against the political regimes of their countries.[74] Their conception of theonomy as the aim and justification of *jihād* was, however, to become a major influence, several decades later, on the nascent *salafī jihādī* movement.

JIHĀD AND THEONOMY IN *SALAFĪ JIHĀDĪ* THOUGHT

Salafī jihādism emerged as a discrete school in the 1980s and 1990s, the period in which its first generation of scholars, such as Abū Muhammad al-Maqdisī, Abū Qatāda al-Filasṭīnī and Sayyid Imām al-Sharīf, authored their major works. A central feature of the *salafī jihādī* school is its salafisation of the *ḥākimiyya* doctrine of Mawdūdī and (especially) Quṭb – that is, the reformulation of this doctrine in a form more in keeping with traditional *salafī* discourse.[75] In particular, the *salafī jihādīs* conceived of *ḥākimiyya* as a derivative of *tawḥīd al-ulūhiyya*,[76] thus taking the ostensibly modern issue of theonomy and insisting that it is really none other than that same issue of monolatry championed by Ibn Taymiyya and the Wahhābī movement. As we have seen, this monolatric grounding of theonomy was already a structural feature of Mawdūdī's and Quṭb's writings, and

70. Ibid., p. 62.
71. Mawdūdī, *Tafhīmāt* I, pp. 75–6, and I, pp. 92–3; Quṭb, *Maᶜālim*, pp. 58–60, 65.
72. Quṭb, *Maᶜālim*, p. 74.
73. Ibid., p. 75.
74. Quṭb may have been trying, but he was only briefly out of prison before being executed in 1966. On the discrepancy between Mawdūdī's belligerent theory and moderate practice as head of the Jamāᶜat-i Islāmī in Pakistan, see Nasr, *Mawdudi*, pp. 69ff.
75. Lav, *Radical Islam*, pp. 168–9; Wagemakers, *A Quietist Jihādi*, pp. 35, 38 and 66–7.
76. As noted in Haykel, 'On the Nature', p. 50; for a similar argument in the writings of Muḥammad Quṭb, see Lacroix, *Les islamistes saoudiens*, pp. 67–8.

in this sense it is quite natural that the *ḥākimiyya* doctrine would lend itself to 'salafisation' under the rubric of *tawḥīd al-ulūhiyya*. In today's *salafī* jihādism this conception of the issue is a staple of orthodoxy: for example, a credo published by Jabhat al-Nuṣra, formerly al-Qāᶜida's Syrian affiliate, opens with the standard *salafī* tripartite division of *tawḥīd*, and then lists *tawḥīd al-ḥākimiyya* as one of the subdivisions of *tawḥīd al-ulūhiyya*, directly after ritual monolatry (*tawḥīd al-nusuk*).[77]

The interrelation of *jihād* with theonomy likewise carried over from Mawdūdī and Quṭb to the *salafī jihādī*s and was reinserted into the traditional *salafī jihād*–monolatry conjunction. A good example thereof is Abū Qatāda al-Filasṭīnī's *Li-mādhā al-jihād* ('Why *jihād*?'). The treatise opens with a description of the *telos* of human life as monolatry: all things were created to serve humans, and humans were created for the worship of Allah, as stated in Q51:56. Allah willed that some of humanity would deviate from this aim, and sent prophets and revealed scriptures to bring them back to exclusive worship of Him.[78] In similar manner to Ibn Rajab's treatise, Abū Qatāda conceives of this prophetic mission as comprising both verbal proof and the use of force, both the Book and the Sword, and it is in this context that he, like Ibn Rajab, cites the *buᶜithtu biʾl-sayf* tradition:

> His Book guides to the truth, and iron rectifies those who depart from it. Only thus are people put right . . . as the Prophet said, 'I was sent with the sword before Judgment Day so that Allah alone be worshiped without partner'. This was the inheritance [he bequeathed] to his nation: The Book that guides and the sword that defends and rectifies.[79]

Abu Qatāda's answer to the question 'why *jihād*?' thus begins much as it did for Ibn Rajab: it is for the sake of monolatry.

From the continuation of the treatise, however, it becomes clear that Abū Qatāda uses this basis primarily as an argument for a theonomic *jihād* orientation. He argues that *jihād* is to be waged first and foremost against those who have apostatised 'due to their replacement (*tabdīlihim*) of the Merciful One's *sharīᶜa* and their allegiance (*muwālātihim*) to the Jews, Christians, and Communists . . .'[80] In his exposition of why the replacement of the *sharīᶜa* by man-made law

77. Jabhat al-Nuṣra, *Nubdha ᶜammā naᶜtaqiduhu wa-nadīnu llāha bihi* (al-Manāra al-Bayḍāʾ, https://twitter.com/JabhtAnNusrah/status/438393864190033920, 2014), pp. 3–4.
78. ᶜUmar b. Maḥmūd Abū ᶜUmar (Abū Qatāda al-Filasṭīnī), *Li-mādhā al-jihād* (http://www.tawhed.ws/dl?i=yrvjtyr8), p. 1.
79. Ibid., p. 4.
80. Ibid., p. 9.

is apostasy, Abū Qatāda makes full use of the monolatric basis he introduced earlier in the treatise. He, like Ibn Taymiyya, interprets the meaning of *ilāh* as *maᶜbūd* (an object of worship). He then equates worship with obedience, and argues that '[exclusive] worship (*al-ᶜubūdiyya*) is based on obedience and compliance with command, and it is not valid without compliance with the command of the commanding Master, who is the object of worship (*al-maᶜbūd*).' It follows that anyone who arrogates to himself the right to command and forbid, and to rule over others through legislation, has, by making himself an object of obedience, made himself an *ilāh* to be worshiped.[81] The obligation to fight against the rulers is subsequently presented simply as an evident consequence of this *takfīr*.[82] We see that what Abū Qatāda meant by the question 'why *jihād*?' was really 'why *jihād* against the rulers?', and the answer is provided by a conception of theonomy that is heavily indebted to Taymiyyan monolatry.

Another example of this nexus of *jihād*, monolatry and theonomy is to be found in Sayyid Imām al-Sharīf's *al-ᶜUmda fī iᶜdād al-ᶜudda* (1987), an important early *salafī jihādī* work on the topic of *jihād* that was used as a manual in al-Qāᶜida training camps in Afghanistan.[83] Imām opens this work with an exposition of *tawḥīd al-rubūbiyya* and *tawḥīd al-ulūhiyya*, and writes of the latter that it 'requires compliance with the command of [Allah], may He be praised, and with His law (*sharᶜ*) that He sent with His prophets', the last of whom was Muhammad, who brought the final, comprehensive *sharīᶜa*.[84] This is precisely the same emphasis that we saw in Abū Qatāda's treatise on obedience and compliance with law as a fundamental aspect of monolatry. It follows that to adopt the legal determinations (*ḥukm*) of someone else in preference to those of Allah is to take that someone as an *ilāh*. Sayyid Imām, again like Ibn Taymiyya, defines

81. Ibid., p. 9, and cf. p.13.
82. Ibid., pp. 15–16.
83. This work has recently been the subject of a thorough and nuanced study: Simon Wolfgang Fuchs, *Proper Signposts for the Camp: The Reception of Classical Authorities in the Ǧihādī Manual al-ᶜUmda fī Iᶜdād al-ᶜUdda* (Würzburg, 2011); and Simon Wolfgang Fuchs, 'Do Excellent Surgeons Make Miserable Exegetes? Negotiating the Sunni Tradition in the *ǧihādī* Camps', *Die Welt des Islams* 53.2 (2013), pp. 192–237. In the latter article, Fuchs argues (p. 237) that '[n]arrow, clear-cut paths of reception in the vein of Ibn Taimīya/Ibn ᶜAbd al-Wahhāb/Saiyid Quṭb do not hold up to close scrutiny' in the case of Sayyid Imām's treatise. I share Fuchs' concern for combating reductionist conceptions of the relation between modern radicalism and the Islamic tradition, but it would perhaps be helpful to differentiate between jurisprudential writing, into which category most of the *ᶜUmda* falls, and core theological issues of the kind discussed here. On this difference, cf. Haykel, 'On the Nature', pp. 41–2.
84. ᶜAbd al-Qādir b. ᶜAbd al-ᶜAzīz [=Sayyid Imām al-Sharīf], *Risālat al-ᶜumda fī iᶜdād al-ᶜudda liʾl-jihād fī sabīl Allāh taᶜālā* (http://www.tawhed.ws/dl?i=f8ro5d45), p. 3.

ilāh as an object of worship (*ma*ᶜ*būd*); and like Sayyid Quṭb, he cites Q43:84 – 'And it is He who is *ilāh* in heaven and *ilāh* on earth' – in order to buttress the point that worldly affairs also fall under the mandate of exclusivity of worship.[85]

This monolatry-based theonomy is employed by Sayyid Imān to explain the proper aim of *jihād*:

> From this you understand, brother, that the invented human systems – man-made laws, democracy, socialism, communism, and so forth . . . are all outright unbelief (*kufr bawāḥ*). And you understand likewise that the rule (*ḥukm*) of the *ṭawāghīt* that is based in many Muslim countries on these systems is a flagrant aggression against Allah the Exalted's *ulūhiyya* over His creation on this earth . . . This is the enemy against whom the Muslims must rise up in order to defend the *ulūhiyya* of their Lord, may He be praised . . . and this, in the language of the *shar*ᶜ, is what is called *jihād fī sabīl Allah.*[86]

It seems clear that Sayyid Imām's use of the term *ulūhiyya* here ought to be taken in the technical Taymiyyan sense, and the imperative of defending Allah's *ulūhiyya* as the defense of His exclusive right to worship and obedience against those who would usurp it. It is only natural, then, that we find the following reflection on the relationship between *jihād* and *tawḥīd* at the end of the introduction:

> I had already begun to publish a series of books titled 'The Call (*Da*ᶜ*wa*) to *Tawḥīd*' series. I made this treatise [viz. *al-*ᶜ*Umda*] an installment in this series, and it is appropriate that it should be so. How could it be otherwise? *Jihād* was only commanded (*shuri*ᶜ*a*) in order to spread the call to *tawḥīd*, and to champion it and protect it. Did the Prophet not say: 'I was commanded to fight people until they testify that there is no *ilāh* but Allah and that Muhammad is the Prophet of Allah . . .'? And he said: 'I was sent with the sword before Judgment Day so that Allah alone be worshiped without partner.' *Tawḥīd* is the aim (*ghāya*), and *jihād* is one of the means for its realization.[87]

We can now see why *salafī jihādī* scholars are so keen to defend the authenticity of the *bu*ᶜ*ithtu bi*ᵓ*l-sayf* tradition against the charge that it contains an

85. ᶜAbd al-Qādir b. ᶜAbd al-ᶜAzīz, *al-*ᶜ*Umda*, p. 4.
86. Ibid., p. 4.
87. Ibid., p. 7. See also the section titled 'Maᶜālim asāsiyya fīᵓl-jihād' (pp. 278ff.), which returns to the same themes, and likewise makes extensive use of Ibn Taymiyya's distinction between Allāh's ontological will and His legislative will, on which, see Hoover, *Ibn Taymiyya's Theodicy*, pp. 122–9.

'objectionable element'. The proper use of the sword, in their view, is precisely to bring humanity to the exclusive worship of, and obedience to, Allah – in particular, through the establishment of theonomy.[88] They do, of course, recognise the propriety of other forms of *jihād*, such as fighting in order to repel foreign invasion (*dafᶜ al-ṣāʾil*),[89] but *jihād* in its most meaningful sense is for them a means to the realisation of *tawḥīd* on earth through the establishment of exclusive adherence to Allah's law. This conception is pithily encapsulated in Abū Muhammad al-Maqdisī's definition of *al-salafiyya al-jihādiyya* as:

> [A] current that joins between *daᶜwa* to *tawḥīd* in all its comprehensiveness, and *jihād* for that aim at one and the same time. Or one could say that it is a current that strives to achieve *tawḥīd* by means of *jihād* against the idol-rulers (*taḥqīq al-tawḥīd bi-jihād al-ṭawāghīt*).[90]

As a final example, we can cite the first public *khuṭba* (sermon) of Abū Bakr al-Baghdādī, the first 'Caliph' of the Islamic State. In this *khuṭba*, al-Baghdādī proclaims that monolatry is the purpose for which humans were created, citing Q51:56 as a proof-text. He then directly relates the commandment of *jihād* to this aim of creation: 'And Allah the Exalted, may He be blessed, commanded us to fight His enemies and to wage *jihād* for His sake (*fī sabīlihi*) in order to achieve this and to establish the *dīn*.' Al-Baghdādī then explains that this aim is only achieved through the establishment of the rule of Allah's law:

> Oh people, the *dīn* of Allah the Exalted, may He be blessed, is only established, and this aim for which Allah created us is only realized, with the enforcement (*taḥkīm*) of Allah's law, and submission to it in judgment (*waʾl-taḥākum ilayhi*).[91]

In this *khuṭba* we can thus see the same nexus of conceptions as in the previous

88. The author of the treatise in defense of the '*buᶜithtu*' *ḥadīth*, Abū Dharr al-Samharī al-Yamānī, is also the author of a treatise declaring the state of Yemen apostate on theonomic grounds: *Maᶜālim al-wathaniyya fīʾl-dawla al-yamaniyya* (http://www.tawhed.ws/dl?i=22031001, 1431 AH [2010 CE]).
89. See, for example, Abū Muḥammad al-Maqdisī's introduction to Abū Qatāda al-Filāsṭīnī, *Juʾnat al-muṭayyabīn* (http://www.tawhed.ws/dl?i=y06fitvm), p. 8
90. *Ḥiwār maᶜa al-shaykh Abī Muḥammad al-Maqdisī sanat 1423* (http://www.tawhed.ws/dl?i=j37307wg), p. 1.
91. *Taghṭiya khāṣṣa li-khuṭba wa-ṣalāt al-jumᶜa fīʾl-jāmiᶜ al-kabīr bi-madīnat Mawṣil* (Muʾassasat al-Furqān, https://twitter.com/al_e3tisam/status/485410559139909632, 5 July 2014), 07:28 – 08:30.

examples: monolatry is the *telos* of existence, *jihād* was ordained for the achievement of monolatry, and monolatry mandates theonomy. Al-Baghdādī's exposition is thus far true to the *salafī jihādī* vision. In what follows, however, he goes on to present the newly proclaimed caliphate as the very instrument by which this aim of existence is realised.[92] This exclusivist claim, which identifies the *salafī jihādī* project on the whole with one single entity which would then command the obedience of all, is currently a matter of fierce dispute within the *salafī jihādī* movement.

CONCLUSION

This chapter has attempted to demonstrate the connection between, on the one hand, *salafī jihādīs*' formulation of *tawḥīd* in terms of monolatry and (especially) theonomy, and on the other, their understanding of *jihād* and its aim. As self-professed heirs to the Taymiyyan tradition, the *salafī jihādīs* view the heart of Islam as monolatry – that is, exclusive worship of Allah, rather than mere belief in Allah. Largely due to the influence of Sayyid Quṭb and Mawdūdī, they interpret the imperative of monolatry as mandating theonomy: the establishment of exclusive obedience to Allah through adherence to His law, and the rejection of all systems of government founded on human law. Finally, drawing on both these influences, they see the aim of *jihād* as being identical to the *telos* of existence itself: to bring humanity to the exclusive worship of, and obedience to, Allah.

This nexus of conceptions is shared by the *salafī jihādī* movement as a whole and differentiates it from other currents in contemporary Islam. How this understanding of *jihād* is implemented on the ground is, however, often a matter of disagreement within the movement. Such disputes are beyond the purview of the present study, but perhaps these observations on the conception of *jihād* common to radical *salafīs* may provide a useful basis for further research into internal divergences as well.

92. See also IS spokesman Abū Muḥammad al-ᶜAdnānī al-Shāmī's statement that in the territories under the Islamic State's control 'religion has become entirely Allāh's' (*wa-ṣāra bi-faḍli llāh al-dīn kulluhu lillāh*; cf. Q8:39). *Hādhā waᶜd Allāh* (Muʾassasat al-Iᶜtiṣām, https://twitter.com/al_e3tisam/status/483263714700054528, 29 June 2014).

CHAPTER

8

AL-QĀʿIDA'S POST-ARAB SPRING JIHAD: CONFIRMATION OR RE-EVALUATION?

*Joas Wagemakers**

INTRODUCTION

In recent years, many publications have focused on (new) social movements, which can be defined as 'distinct social process[es] consisting of the mechanisms through which actors engaged in collective action: are involved in conflictual relations with clearly identified opponents; are linked by dense informal networks; [and] share a distinct collective identity'.[1] Such movements are increasingly global in character and try to mobilise their resources and make use of political opportunities and constraints to achieve their goals.[2] Apart from these factors, however, ideas play a role too. In social movement theory terms, these are usually dealt with by looking at how movements 'frame' their beliefs and ideas to attract new followers or keep those they have already got.[3]

Although ideology is somewhat different from other resources that social movements can use (money, access to politicians, experience, etc.), it is similarly shaped by the political opportunities and constraints that movements exist

* Associate Professor of Islamic and Arabic Studies, Utrecht University, The Netherlands

1. Donatella Della Porta and Mario Diani, *Social Movements: An Introduction* (Malden, MA, 2006 [1998]), p. 20.
2. See, for example, Donatella Della Porta and Sidney Tarrow (eds), *Transnational Protest & Global Activism: People, Passions, and Power* (Lanham, 2005); Kevin McDonald, *Global Movements: Action and Culture* (Malden, MA, 2006); Sidney Tarrow, *The New Transnational Activism* (Cambridge, 2005).
3. See, for example, Hank Johnston and John A. Noakes (eds), *Frames of Protest: Social Movements and the Framing Perspective* (Lanham, 2005).

in. Tarrow has pointed out, for example, that the American invasion of Iraq in 2003 not only provided Islamist militants with an opportunity to wage jihad in a country that had previously been closed to them, but it also allowed them to reinforce their image of the West as a 'Crusader' enemy.[4] Moreover, it was also partly because of the war in Iraq and the violent attacks against Shīᶜite civilians there that some jihadi ideologues became more introspective and started criticising the practices that they considered excessive.[5]

In short, events and contexts can (and often do) change ideas. This is presumably also the case with al-Qāᶜida's ideology in response to the series of uprisings and revolutions since 2010, collectively known as the 'Arab Spring'. Since al-Qāᶜida is precisely the type of global social movement described above, it tries to make use of the opportunities and constraints that the Arab world offers and – it may be assumed – also adjusts its ideas somewhat to these changing circumstances.[6] Several publications have focused on how al-Qāᶜida has responded to the Arab Spring,[7] and some have argued that the uprisings in the Arab world – with their calls for freedom and democracy – are (or at least could be) a distinct blow to the jihadi narrative of al-Qāᶜida, which is geared towards founding an (explicitly undemocratic) Islamic state based on strict religious principles.[8] Others, however, have pointed out that the Arab Spring could also act

4. Tarrow, *New*, p. 128.
5. See, for instance, Joas Wagemakers, 'Protecting Jihad: The Sharia Council of the Minbar al-Tawhid wa-l-Jihad', *Middle East Policy* 18.2 (2011), 148–62; Joas Wagemakers, 'Reclaiming Scholarly Authority: Abu Muhammad al-Maqdisi's Critique of *Jihadi* Practices', *Studies in Conflict & Terrorism* 34.7 (2011), 523–39.
6. Following Burke, I divide al-Qāᶜida into three circles: a core around Ayman al-Ẓawāhirī, a broader circle of scholars and activists who are not organisationally linked to the former but who certainly sympathise with him, and an even broader circle that represents the al-Qāᶜida 'worldview'. This paper focuses on the first and particularly the second circles. See Jason Burke, *Al-Qaeda: The True Story of Radical Islam* (London and New York, 2004), pp. 8–14.
7. William McCants, 'Al Qaeda's Challenge: The Jihadists' War with Islamist Democrats', *Foreign Affairs* 90.5 (2011), 20–32; Nelly Lahoud, 'Ayman al-Zawahiri's Reaction to Revolution in the Middle East', *CTC Sentinel* 4.4 (2011), 4–7; Joas Wagemakers, 'Salafi's en politieke participatie sinds de Arabische Lente', *ZemZem: Tijdschrift over het Midden-Oosten, Noord-Afrika en islam* 8.2 (2012), 27–35.
8. Anno Bunnik and Peter B. M. Knoope, 'Geweldloze opstand in de Arabische wereld bevestigt bankroet van Al Qaeda', *Internationale Spectator* 65.4 (2011), 167–9; Daveed Gartenstein-Ross and Tara Vassefi, 'Perceptions of the "Arab Spring" Within the *Salafi-Jihadi* Movement', *Studies in Conflict & Terrorism* 35.12 (2012), 831; Donald Holbrook, 'Al-Qaeda's Reponse to the Arab Spring', *Perspectives on Terrorism* 6.6 (2012), 4–5; Nelly Lahoud, 'Revolution in Tunisia and Egypt: A Blow to the Jihadist Narrative?' *CTC Sentinel* 4.2 (2011), 4–5; Alex S. Wilner, 'Opportunity Costs or Costly Opportunities?

as an opportunity for al-Qāᶜida instead of a constraint, given the fact that dictators repressing radical Islamism have disappeared. Moreover, these authors also argue that the whole experiment with democracy might well end in disappointment, perhaps causing al-Qāᶜida to claim that they had predicted this all along.[9]

This chapter contributes to this debate by dealing not so much with the question of whether the Arab Spring so far has been an opportunity or a constraint for al-Qāᶜida's actions, but rather with the question of whether the new opportunities and constraints provided by the uprisings and their aftermath have caused al-Qāᶜida to reconsider its ideology. More specifically, this chapter deals with an applied version of a question posed by Nelly Lahoud: 'Why jihad and not democracy?'[10] Al-Qāᶜida clearly sees jihad as the (main) way towards Islamic rule and rejects democracy as a way to express its contention. One could argue that this was partly because of ideology and partly because of the lack of true democratic means. With the possible emergence of (more) democratic means in several Muslim countries in the aftermath of the Arab Spring, the main question of this chapter is: has the Arab Spring led al-Qāᶜida to a confirmation or a re-evaluation of its views on jihad and democracy as different and perhaps opposing means of contention?

Based largely on an extensive reading of the international Arabic discourse of Jihadi–Salafi[11] scholars that forms al-Qāᶜida's ideology (as expressed in books, articles, communiqués and fatwas published since the advent of the Arab Spring), this chapter first deals with al-Qāᶜida's initial response to the uprisings and its attempts to appropriate them. It then moves on to the practical ideas expressed about jihad in the context of the revolts in Tunisia, Egypt, Yemen, Libya and Syria. Finally, this chapter discusses if, and how, al-Qāᶜida ideologues

The Arab Spring, Osama bin Laden, and al-Qāᶜida's African Affiliates' *Perspectives on Terrorism* 5.3/4 (2011), 55–6.

9. Gartenstein-Ross and Vassefi, 'Perceptions', p. 831, 838–9; Holbrook, 'Al-Qaeda's', pp. 5–7; Floor Janssen and Joas Wagemakers, 'Is al-Qa'ida echt failliet?', *Internationale Spectator* 65.7–8 (2011), 393–6; Floor Janssen and Joas Wagemakers, 'Luidt de Arabische lente de winter van al-Qaida in?', *ZemZem: Tijdschrift over het Midden-Oosten, Noord-Afrika en islam* 7.1 (2011), 40–5; Philip Mudd, 'How the Arab Spring Could Embolden Extremists', *CTC Sentinel* 4.4 (2011), 7–9; Wilner, 'Opportunity', pp. 56–8; Aaron Y. Zelin, Daveed Gartenstein-Ross and Andrew Lebovich, 'Al-Qa'ida in the Islamic Maghreb's Tunisia Strategy', *CTC Sentinel* 6.7 (2013), 22, 23.
10. Nelly Lahoud, *The Jihadis' Path to Self-Destruction* (New York, 2010), pp. 147–93.
11. I define Jihadi–Salafism as the branch of Salafism whose adherents believe jihad is not only a legitimate means to deal with non-Muslim countries that attack Muslim lands, but also a justified tool within Muslim countries themselves, primarily to overthrow the supposedly un-Islamic leaders that rule them. See also Joas Wagemakers, *A Quietist Jihadi: The Ideology and Influence of Abu Muhammad al-Maqdisi* (Cambridge, 2012), pp. 7–10.

have re-evaluated their ideas on the various aspects of democracy after 2010. This chapter argues that, although the changing context in the Arab world has led some Jihadi–Salafi scholars to re-evaluate parts of their ideology, most of their ideas have been confirmed by the Arab Spring.

APPROPRIATING THE ARAB SPRING

The so-called Arab Spring started when a Tunisian fruit vendor called Muḥammad al-Būᶜazīzī, frustrated by the confiscation of his products by, and harassment suffered at the hands of, Tunisian officials, set himself on fire on 17 December 2010. This incident sparked an increasing number of protests that called for – and ultimately succeeded in achieving – the toppling of the Tunisian regime about a month later. The protests in Tunisia, in turn, led to similar uprisings in Egypt, Libya, Yemen, Bahrain and Syria with mixed results. While the Libyan leader Muᶜammar al-Qadhdhāfī was removed and killed in 2011 and his Egyptian counterpart Ḥusnī Mubārak stepped down in the same year, the Yemeni situation was murkier, with President ᶜAlī ᶜAbdallāh Ṣāliḥ being replaced by his vice-president ᶜAbd Rabbihi Manṣūr al-Hādī. In Bahrain and Syria, meanwhile, the old rulers are still in place, although Syria is still mired in a civil war between its regime and mostly Islamist militias. The situation was further complicated by the 2013 army coup against the Muslim Brotherhood-led government in Egypt, which had been elected to replace Mubārak and his regime. All of this caused the initial enthusiasm across much of the world for what seemed like a wave of democracy washing over the Middle East in 2011 to cool somewhat after the transition from dictatorship to democracy turned out to be more difficult than expected.

AL-QĀᶜIDA'S 'ABSENCE' EXPLAINED

One actor that was entirely absent from the initial stages of the Arab Spring, being mostly led by ordinary citizens fed up with their regimes rather than radical Islamists, was al-Qāᶜida. As several scholars have pointed out, this did not stop al-Qāᶜida from trying to appropriate the Arab Spring as something they had wanted and called for all along.[12] Al-Qāᶜida's Egyptian leader Ayman al-Ẓawāhirī, for example, clearly wanted to give the impression that the recent uprisings were merely the latest phase of a struggle that he and other radical

12. Gartenstein-Ross and Vassefi, 'Perceptions', pp. 834–5; Holbrook, 'Al-Qaeda's', pp. 7–9; Wilner, 'Opportunity', pp. 55–6.

Islamists have been part of for decades. In fact, referring to the place where most of the anti-Mubārak protests in Cairo took place, he points out that he himself was among the protesters in Tahrir Square in 1971, demonstrating 'against the regimes of corruption and tyranny (*anẓimat al-fasād wa-l-ṭughyān*)', thus portraying himself as a forerunner of the current revolutionaries.[13] It is therefore not surprising that al-Ẓawāhirī calls on his followers to continue the uprisings,[14] which is echoed by the Syrian–British Abū Baṣīr al-Ṭarṭūsī, who asks all Syrians to join 'join the caravan of jihad (*qāfilat al-jihād*)'[15] and to stop paying taxes to the regime.[16]

Al-Qāᶜida ideologues also stimulated those engaged in the uprisings to continue by further criticising the regimes against which these revolts were directed. In the case of Egypt, this was mostly limited to reminding readers how repressive the regime was – for example, by pointing to the army's physical action against women.[17] With regard to Syria, however, perhaps the most important accusation was related to the sectarian nature of the Syrian regime. The Mauritanian radical scholar Abū al-Mundhir al-Shinqīṭī, for example, claims that the ᶜAlāwī beliefs of Syrian President Bashār al-Asad are quite deviant from a Sunni point of view, which is one reason why he states that ᶜAlāwīs (or Nuṣayrīs, as he calls them) have always been loyal to other religions against Islam.[18] Muslims therefore have a duty, al-Shinqīṭī says, to fight not only the Syrian regime, but anti-Sunnī hostile ᶜAlāwīs in general.[19] Such views are echoed particularly often by al-Ṭarṭūsī, who almost constantly refers to the sectarian background of the Syrian regime, although he does distinguish it more

13. Ayman al-Ẓawāhirī, *Risālat al-Amal wa-l-Bishr li-Ahlinā fī Miṣr 6* (www.tawhed.ws/dl?i=30081130, 2011), p. 5. See also Ayman al-Ẓawāhirī, *Risālat al-Amal wa-l-Bishr li-Ahlinā fī Miṣr 11* (www.tawhed.ws/dl?i=24041317, 2012), pp. 3–4. For accessed dates of online resources, see the Bibliography and the accompanying note, p. 366.
14. Ayman al-Ẓawāhirī, *Risālat al-Amal wa-l-Bishr li-Ahlinā fī Miṣr 5* (www.tawhed.ws/dl?i=30081129, 2011), p. 17; Ayman al-Ẓawāhirī, *Ilā l-Amām Yā Usūd al-Shām* (www.tawhed.ws/dl?i=12041233, n. d.), p. 3.
15. Abū Baṣīr al-Ṭarṭūsī, *Bayn Nuṣra wa-Taʾyīd li-Iᶜlān Shurafāʾ wa-Abṭāl ᶜAshāʾir Dayr al-Zūr* (www.abubaseer.bizland.com/hadath/Read/hadath%2084.doc, 2011).
16. Abū Baṣīr al-Ṭarṭūsī, *Fatwā ilā Ahl Sūriya* (www.abubaseer.bizland.com/hadath/Read/hadath%2083.doc, 2011).
17. Abū al-Mundhir al-Shinqīṭī, *Lā Nisāʾ fī Mīdān al-Taḥrīr!* (www.tawhed.ws/r?i=20121101, 2011), pp. 1–2.
18. Abū al-Mundhir al-Shinqīṭī, *Qitāl al-Nuṣayriyya Farḍ ᶜAyn ᶜalā l-Muslimīn* (www.tawhed.ws/dl?i=24041384, 2012), pp. 1–10. See also Abū Saᶜd al-ᶜĀmilī, *Aḍwāʾ wa-Bayānāt Sharᶜiyya ḥawla l-Thawratayni l-Lībiyya wa-l-Sūriyya 2: Al-Thawra al-Sūriyya* (www.tawhed.ws/dl?i=28111103, 2011), pp. 2–7.
19. Al-Shinqīṭī, *Qitāl*, pp. 11–13.

clearly from other ᶜAlāwīs.[20] Al-Ṭarṭūsī also frequently directs his readers' attention to the repressive acts of the Syrian regime,[21] including in a scrapbook[22] and a short-lived magazine.[23] Interestingly, he also accuses the Syrian regime of acting as a guardian for Israel, defending that country's borders and looking out for its interests.[24]

THE CONNECTION WITH THE WEST

This latter accusation points to another way al-Qāᶜida-affiliated ideologues tried to appropriate the Arab Spring – namely, by framing it as closely related to their own fight against the West.[25] In fact, Ayman al-Ẓawāhirī describes the revolutions as 'the beginning of the fall of [America's] agents', which he claims is the fourth 'disaster' that has happened to the United States over the last decade, following the terrorist attacks of 11 September 2001 and the US's 'defeat' in the wars in Iraq and Afghanistan.[26] To underline the relevance of the West to the Arab Spring, al-Qāᶜida leaders point to American support for the dictators in Egypt and Yemen, French ties with the Tunisian regime,[27] Western 'crimes'

20. See, for instance, Abū Baṣīr al-Ṭarṭūsī, *Mā lā Yaᶜrifuhu l-Nās ᶜan al-Niẓām al-Sūrī al-Ṭāʾifī* (www.tawhed.ws/r?i=30081109, 2011), pp. 1, 3–4.
21. al-Ṭarṭūsī, *Mā lā Yaᶜrifuhu*, pp. 2–3; Abū Baṣīr al-Ṭarṭūsī, *Kalimāt Akhuṣṣu bi-hā l-Ṭāʾifa al-Nuṣayriyya al-Musammāt bi-l-ᶜAlawiyya'* (www.abubaseer.bizland.com/refutation/read/F%20102.doc, 2011); Abū Baṣīr al-Ṭarṭūsī, *Al-Istiᶜmār al-Qarmaṭī al-Bāṭinī li-Sūriya wa-Sharᶜiyyat al-Difāᶜ ᶜan al-Nafs* (www.tawhed.ws/r?i=30081101, 2011), pp. 1–2.
22. Abū Baṣīr al-Ṭarṭūsī, *Daftar al-Thawra wa-l-Thuwwār* (www.abubaseer.bizland.com/books/read/b&2040.doc, 2011/12). For more on this scrapbook, see Joas Wagemakers, 'Al-Qaida Advises the Arab Spring: Abu Basir's Scrapbook', Jihadica.com, posted 28 July 2012, www.jihadica.com/al-qaida-advises-the-arab-spring-abu-basirs-scrapbook/.
23. This magazine, with frequent articles by al-Ṭarṭūsī, can be accessed at http://tartosi.blogspot.nl/search/label/%D8%A7%D9%84%D9%85%D8%AC%D9%84%D8%A9.
24. Al-Ṭarṭūsī, *Daftar*, p. 15; Abū Baṣīr al-Ṭarṭūsī, *Li-Mādhā Samaḥa l-Niẓām al-Sūrī bi-ᶜUbūr baᶜḍ al-Mutaẓāhirīn Ḥudūd al-Jawlān maᶜa Dawlat Isrāʾīl?* (www.abubaseer.bizland.com/hadath/Read/hadath%2082.doc, 2011). For a similar argument, see Ayman al-Ẓawāhirī, *ᶜIzz al-Sharq Awwaluhu Dimashq* (www.tawhed.ws/dl?i=30081124, 2011), p. 4.
25. See also Gartenstein-Ross and Vassefi, 'Perceptions', pp. 835–7.
26. Al-Ẓawāhirī, *Risalat 6*, pp. 23–4.
27. Abū Yaḥyā al-Lībī, *Ilā Ahlinā fī Lībiyā* (www.tawhed.ws/dl?i=30081117, 2011), pp. 10–11.

in Syria[28] and the allegedly dominating role of US interests in the region.[29] Unsurprisingly, al-Qāᶜida ideologues not only blame Western powers for their previous relations with Arab autocrats, but they are also suspicious of their cutting these ties. The Western attacks on Libya to help oust al-Qadhdhāfī in 2011, for example, are described as being launched by 'the Crusader NATO' against 'the Muslims of Libya' in order to 'fight their religion'.[30] Muslims should therefore not mistake the supposed Western change in policies – from supporting dictators to supporting the people – for a genuine change of heart among American politicians. Instead, this development in US foreign policy is 'a direct result of the blessed raids on New York, Washington and Pennsylvania [of September 2001]'[31] and only seeks token changes to give people the impression that things have improved instead of real reform.[32]

So al-Qāᶜida ideologues see the Arab Spring as a good thing that they themselves inspired, but they also want to 'protect' it from Western influence and dominance. As others have pointed out, their objective in appropriating the Arab Spring is not only to claim it as their own idea, but also to use the space that the fall of the dictators has created to implement Islamic law (*sharīᶜa*).[33] This 'Islamic Spring' could act as a first step towards 'liberating' Jerusalem under an Islamic banner,[34] but most importantly could – in the words of al-Qāᶜida leader Abū Yaḥyā al-Lībī – lead to the Arab peoples' 'true happiness and their pure welfare and freedom (*saᶜādatahā l-ḥaqīqiyya wa-rakhāʾahā wa-ḥuriyyatahā l-ṣāfiya*)', as a result of a 'serious and real return' to the *sharīᶜa*.[35] This sentiment is echoed by al-Ẓawāhirī, who frequently calls on the Arab peoples to

28. Abū Yaḥyā al-Lībī, *Maʾāsī l-Shām bayna Ijrām al-Nuṣayriyya wa-Makāʾid al-Gharb* (www.tawhed.ws/dl?i=24041307, 2012).
29. Ayman al-Ẓawāhirī, *Risālat al-Amal wa-l-Bishr li-Ahlinā fī Miṣr 7* (www.tawhed.ws/dl?i=30081131, 2011), pp. 6–7.
30. Abū al-Ḥasan Rashīd al-Bulaydī, *Risāla Maftūḥa ilā l-Muslimīn fī Lībiyā* (www.tawhed./dl?i=28111118, 2011), p. 4.
31. Ayman al-Ẓawāhirī, *Risālat al-Amal wa-l-Bishr li-Ahlinā fī Miṣr 4* (www.tawhed.ws/dl?i=30081128, 2011), p. 3. See also Ayman al-Ẓawāhirī, *Risālat 5*, p. 2; Ayman al-Ẓawāhirī, *Risālat al-Amal wa-l-Bishr li-Ahlinā fī Miṣr 9* (www.tawhed.ws/dl?i=12041225, 2012), p. 4.
32. Ayman al-Ẓawāhirī, *Risālat al-Amal wa-l-Bishr li-Ahlinā fī Miṣr 3* (www.tawhed.ws/dl?i=30081127, 2011), p. 4.
33. Gartenstein-Ross and Vassefi, 'Perceptions', pp. 833–4, 839–40; Holbrook, 'Al-Qaeda's', pp. 9–16.
34. Abū ᶜUbayda Yūsuf al-ᶜUnnābī, *Bi-Ḥadd al-Ḥussām.. Tataḥarraru l-Shām* (www.tawhed.ws/dl?i=12041219, 2012), p. 4; al-Ẓawāhirī, *Risālat 11*, p. 3.
35. Al-Lībī, *Ilā*, p. 7.

apply Islamic law,[36] warning particularly Tunisians not to return to the secularist system of their former regime.[37]

VIOLENT CONTENTION: *JIHĀD*

Al-Qāᶜida's appropriation of the Arab Spring and its wish to turn it into an Islamic one inevitably leads to the question of how to achieve the latter. In 2011, several dictators had left the scene, leaving uncertainty and disarray in their wake. One of the shaykhs who increasingly dismissed peaceful protests and took a more aggressive approach is the aforementioned al-Shinqīṭī, who issued hundreds of fatwas throughout the period of the Arab Spring on behalf of the Sharīᶜa Council of the biggest online library of radical Islamist literature, the Minbar al-Tawḥīd wa-l-Jihād. As such, he has been – more than any other radical scholar – responsible for shaping the ideological details behind jihad since 2010.[38]

DUTIES AND OBSTACLES

One topic related to jihad that frequently reoccurs in the advice al-Shinqīṭī gives his readers is the existence of possible obstacles to joining a war against any of the regimes in the Arab world. Among these is the presence of debts and loans among possible *jihād* fighters (*mujāhidūn*), which – in classical Islamic legal sources – could be a reason why someone was not allowed to go and wage an offensive jihad, which is a duty incumbent only upon the number of Muslims necessary to fight (*farḍ kifāya*).[39] Al-Shinqīṭī argues, however, that the conflicts in the countries affected by the Arab Spring are all forms of defensive jihad, which is a duty incumbent upon every Muslim (*farḍ ᶜayn*), making the presence of debts and loans a minor obstacle that should preferably be overcome, but that cannot be an impediment to *jihād*.[40] For the same reason, al-Shinqīṭī dismisses

36. See, for example, al-Ẓawāhirī, *Risālat 9*, p. 5.
37. Ayman al-Ẓawāhirī, *Yā Ahl Tūnis Unṣirū Sharīᶜatakum* (www.tawhed.ws/dl?i=24041354, 2012).
38. For more on this Sharīᶜa Council, see Wagemakers, 'Protecting'.
39. Wael B. Hallaq, *Sharīᶜa: Theory, Practice, Transformations* (Cambridge: Cambridge University Press, 2009), p. 326.
40. Abū al-Mundhir al-Shinqīṭī, *Maᶜa Ayy al-Jamāᶜāt Nuqātilu fī Sūriyā?.. Wa-Hal Yajibu l-Khurūj Dūna Idhn al-Waladayni wa-Aṣḥāb al-Dayn?*, no. 6080 (www.tahwed.ws/FAQ/pr?qid=6080, 2012); Abū al-Mundhir al-Shinqīṭī, *Hal Yaḥtāju l-Ikhwa fī Sūriyā ilā Sawād? Wa-Hal Yataᶜayyanu l-Nafīr ilayhim ᶜalā Kull Aḥad?*, no. 6889 (www.tawhed.ws/FAQ/pr?qid=6889, 2012); Abū al-Mundhir al-Shinqīṭī, *Hal Yataᶜayyanu l-Jihād ᶜalā Man ᶜalayhi Dayn?*, no. 6926 (www.tawhed.ws/FAQ/pr?qid=6926, 2012);

parents who object to their sons waging jihad – which, in classical Islamic law, could also be an obstacle to offensive warfare[41] – and states that *mujāhidūn* should convince their parents of the justness of their desire for combat or, if this does not work, go and fight anyway.[42]

Al-Shinqīṭī is similarly dismissive of arguments such as not having any money,[43] wanting to get married[44] or fear[45] as reasons not to wage jihad. While he urges his readers to ensure their needy family members (ill parents, pregnant wives, etc.) are taken care of, he emphasises that *mujāhidūn* can leave them behind[46] or take them with them when they leave for jihad.[47] The only reason for delaying jihad that al-Shinqīṭī accepts and finds legitimate in general is the pursuit of knowledge or the acquiring of skills that will be helpful to jihad once

Abū al-Mundhir al-Shinqīṭī, *Hal Ākhudhu Ahlī maᶜī ilā Arḍ al-Jihād?*, no. 6921 (www.tawhed.ws/FAQ/pr?qid=6921, 2012); Abū al-Mundhir al-Shinqīṭī, *Majmūᶜat As'ila Ḥawla l-Nafīr (2)*, no. 7081 (www.tawhed.ws/FAQ/pr?qid=7081, 2013); Abū al-Mundhir al-Shinqīṭī, *Majmūᶜat As'ila Ḥawla l-Nafīr (4)*, no. 7157 (www.tawhed.ws/FAQ/pr?qid=7157, 2013); Abū al-Mundhir al-Shinqīṭī, *Majmūᶜat As'ila Ḥawla l-Nafīr (5)*, no. 7098 (www.tawhed.ws/FAQ/pr?qid=7098, 2013); Abū al-Mundhir al-Shinqīṭī, *ᶜAlayya Dayn li-Kāfir Lā Astaṭīᶜu Sadādahu l-Ān, fa-Hal lī An Anfura li-l-Jihād?*, no. 7376 (www.tawhed.ws/FAQ/display_question?qid=7376&pageqa=1&i=, 2013).

41. Hallaq, *Sharīᶜa*, p. 326.
42. Abū al-Mundhir al-Shinqīṭī, *Maᶜa Ayy al-Jamāᶜāt*; Abū al-Mundhir al-Shinqīṭī, *Mā Ḥukm al-Jihād al-Yawm fī Sūriyā li-Waḥīd Wālidatihi?*, no. 6392 (www.tawhed.ws/FAQ/pr?qid=6392, 2012); Abū al-Mundhir al-Shinqīṭī, *Urīdu al-Dhahāb li-l-Jihād wa-Abawāya Yuᶜāriḍāni.. Fa-Mādhā Afᶜalu?*, no. 6942 (www.tawhed.ws/FAQ/pr?qid=6942, 2012); Abū al-Mundhir al-Shinqīṭī, *Majmūᶜat As'ila Ḥawla l-Nafīr (1)*, no. 7033 (www.tawhed.ws/FAQ/pr?qid=7033, 2013); Abū al-Mundhir al-Shinqīṭī, *Majmūᶜat* (2); Abū al-Mundhir al-Shinqīṭī, *Majmūᶜat As'ila Ḥawla al-Nafīr (3)*, no. 7166 (www.tawhed.ws/FAQ/pr?qid=7166, 2013); al-Shinqīṭī, *Majmūᶜat (4)*; al-Shinqīṭī, *Majmūᶜat (5)*.
43. Al-Shinqīṭī, *Majmūᶜat (4)*.
44. Al-Shinqīṭī, *Urīdu*; Abū al-Mundhir al-Shinqīṭī, *Majmūᶜat (3)*.
45. Abū al-Mundhir al-Shinqīṭī, *Kayfa Yakūna Ikhlāṣ al-Niyya li-llāh fī l-Jihād? Wa-Hal Yaᶜtabiru l-Mujāhid alladhī Qutila fī l-Maᶜraka wa-Huwa Khā'if min al-Mawt Shahīd?*, no. 7006 (www.tawhed.ws/FAQ/pr?qid=7006, 2013).
46. Abū al-Mundhir al-Shinqīṭī, *Hal Anfuru ilā Sūriya wa-Wālidatī fī Muddat al-ᶜIdda?*, no. 6990 (www.tawhed.ws/FAQ/pr?qid=6990, 2012); Abū al-Mundhir al-Shinqīṭī, *Hal Yajūzu al-Tashaffī bi-Mu'ayyidī al-Niẓām al-Sūrī lladhīna Yuṣābūna bi-l-Maṣā'ib? Wa-Mā Ḥukm al-Takhalluf ᶜan Arḍ al-Jihād li-Mutābaᶜat Shu'ū* [sic], no. 7110 (www.tawhed.ws/FAQ/pr?qid=7110, 2013); al-Shinqīṭī, *Majmūᶜat (2)*; al-Shinqīṭī, *Majmūᶜat (3)*; al-Shinqīṭī, *Majmūᶜat (4)*; al-Shinqīṭī, *Majmūᶜat (5)*.
47. Abū al-Mundhir al-Shinqīṭī, *Hal Ākhudhu Ahlī*; Abū al-Mundhir al-Shinqīṭī, *Hal Uᶜayyilu Wālidī wa-Ahlī am Atrukuhum wa-Ujāhidu?*, no. 6909 (www.tawhed.ws/FAQ/pr?qid=6909, 2012); al-Shinqīṭī, *Majmūᶜat (1)*.

the reader in question has finished his studies.[48] As he points out in his response to one reader:

> As for the specialisation that you study, if it is among the fields that are important to jihad, there is no harm in delaying jihad until you have finished it because you will be of greater use to the *mujāhidūn* at that time.[49]

CHOICES AND TARGETS

It is clear from the Sharīᶜa Council's fatwas that jihad, according to al-Shinqīṭī, is incumbent upon all able-bodied Muslim men with the right intentions in the countries directly affected by the Arab Spring. As I have pointed out elsewhere,[50] however, the Sharīᶜa Council was probably partly founded to guide *mujāhidūn* in their pursuit of jihad and during its 'proper' execution, which means that numerous fatwas were issued on where and how to fight as well. The first question – where to fight – was clearly influenced by the gravity of the conflict in Syria. Nowhere else were so many Muslims being killed by a regime that was so widely reviled, both for its brutality and for its 'apostate' ᶜAlāwī leaders. Al-Shinqīṭī's fatwas therefore generally stress the importance of Syria, because the conflict there

> is among the conflicts of Islam that may have a major role in setting the characteristics of the future of the Muslim community (*waḍᶜ malāmiḥ mustaqbal al-umma*). Victory in this conflict may be the prelude to victory in many new conflicts (*al-maᶜārik allatī ᶜalā l-abwāb*).[51]

Still, he does take his questioners' personal circumstances into account, advising one Western reader not to go to Syria if his absence will cause significant

48. Abū al-Mundhir al-Shinqīṭī, *Hal Yajūzu lī Sharᶜan An Uʾakhkhira al-Nafīr ilā An Atakhaṣṣaṣa fī Majāl Muᶜayyan?*, no. 7005 (www.tawhed.ws/FAQ/pr?qid=7005, 2013); al-Shinqīṭī, *Majmūᶜat (5)*.
49. Abū al-Mundhir al-Shinqīṭī, *Majmūᶜat (2)*.
50. Wagemakers, 'Protecting', pp. 152–3.
51. Abū al-Mundhir al-Shinqīṭī, *Hal Yajibu al-Nafīr ilā l-Shām ᶜalā Kull Qādir?*, no. 6837 (www.tawhed.ws/FAQ/pr?qid=6837, 2012). See also Abū al-Mundhir al-Shinqīṭī, *Hal Astaʾdhinu Aḥadan fī al-Nafīr min Miṣr ilā Sūriyā?*, no. 6479 (www.tawhed.ws/FAQ/pr?qid=6479, 2012); Abū al-Mundhir al-Shinqīṭī, *Hal al-Ūlā l-Jihād fī Sūriyā am al-Daᶜwa fī Arḍ Tūnis wa-Qad Katharat fīhā al-Fitan?*, no. 7141 (www.tawhed.ws/FAQ/pr?qid=7141, 2013).

damage to the missionary activities (*da^cwa*) in his home country,[52] and he allows others to continue their jihad in Libya[53] or the Gaza Strip[54] if the need for them is greater there than in Syria.

Once fatwas turn to the question of how to fight, which boils down to military tactics and targets and is therefore a matter of life and death, al-Shinqīṭī's anwers become even less clear-cut. Although he supports suicide attacks (*ᶜamaliyyāt istishhādiyya*, 'martyrdom operations') in principle, he emphasises that the rules of such operations must always be observed among *mujāhidūn*. A case in point is the question of whether pregnant women are allowed to commit suicide attacks. Al-Shinqīṭī prohibits this if the foetus is viable and, in any case, at any stage during the pregnancy later than four months. Although he recognises that there are reasons for such operations to be permitted for women who have been pregnant for less than four months, he still advises them to not to do it and calls on men to make sure no women are needed for this task.[55]

Al-Shinqīṭī displays a similar reluctance towards targeting civilians of any religion or sect. Although he disagrees with Abū Baṣīr al-Ṭarṭūsī's statement that a visa for foreigners can be considered an insurance of protection (*amān*) against jihad,[56] he advises against targeting Syrians who do not assist their regime and warns that *mujāhidūn* should always be careful to avoid civilian casualties.[57] He specifically mentions that Christians should not be collectively held accountable for the actions of some of them,[58] that crosses on their churches should be left undisturbed[59] and that ᶜAlāwīs who do not aid the regime should also be left alone.[60] This is significant, since al-Shinqīṭī is unapologetically negative about

52. Abū al-Mundhir al-Shinqīṭī, *Hal Uhājiru li-l-Jihād am Abqā fī Bilād al-Gharb wa-Ujāhidu fīhā?*, no. 7128 (www.tawhed.ws/FAQ/pr?qid=7128, 2013).
53. Abū al-Mundhir al-Shinqīṭī, *Mā Ḥukm al-Khurūj li-l-Jihād Khārij Lībiyā bi-l-Nisba li-l-Ikhwa fī Lībiyā?*, no. 6339 (www.tawhed.ws/FAQ/pr?qid=6339, 2012).
54. al-Shinqīṭī, *Majmūᶜat (2)*.
55. Abū al-Mundhir al-Shinqīṭī, *Mā Ḥukm Qiyām al-Ḥāmil bi-ᶜAmaliyya Istishhādiyya?*, no. 7176 (www.tawhed.ws/FAQ/pr?qid7176, 2013).
56. Abū al-Mundhir al-Shinqīṭī, *Hal Ifshāʾ al-Salām ᶜalā al-Kāfir li-Ḍarūra Yaᶜtabiru Amān?*, no. 7467 (www.tawhed.ws/FAQ/display_question?qid=7467, 2013).
57. Abū al-Mundhir al-Shinqīṭī, *Mā Ḥukm Istihdāf al-Ṭawāʾif ghayr al-Muslima al-Musālima fī Sūriyā?*, no. 6360 (www.tawhed.ws, 2012).
58. Abū al-Mundhir al-Shinqīṭī, *Hal Yajūzu lanā Qatl Ayy Naṣrānī fī Baladatinā li-Anna Aḥadahum Qatala Musliman minnā?*, no. 7076 (www.tawhed.ws/FAQ/pr?qid=7076, 2013).
59. Abū al-Mundhir al-Shinqīṭī, *Amaranā Amīrunā Fī Sāḥat al-Jihād bi-Tark al-Ṣulbān fī l-Kanāʾis.. Fa-Hal Nuṭīᶜuhu?*, no. 7101 (www.tawhed.ws/FAQ/pr?qid=7101, 2013).
60. Abū al-Mundhir al-Shinqīṭī, *Hal Taᶜtabiru l-Asliḥa allatī Naʾkhudhuhā min al-Nuṣayriyyīn*

Shīᶜites in general[61] and ᶜAlāwīs in particular (and so are his fellow radical scholars, as we have seen earlier), yet he still warns against causing Shīᶜite civilian casualties when attacking the pro-Syrian Lebanese militant Ḥizbullāh organisation.[62] Al-Shinqīṭī further limits the number of legitimate targets by pointing out that even those who support their regimes verbally may do so to hide their true feelings out of fear (*taqiyya*) and should therefore not automatically be attacked.[63] The same caution even applies to men being trained as soldiers for the regime. According to al-Shinqīṭī, these men are not soldiers yet and may therefore not be seen as helpers of the regime's alleged apostasy.[64]

GROUPS AND CONFLICTS

Because several Arab countries witnessed revolts in the past few years and so many al-Qāᶜida-affiliated militants decided to wage jihad against their regimes, it was almost inevitable that numerous jihadi groups would come into existence and that they would not always be on good terms with one another. The conflicts between these groups were partly reflected in the positions taken by various radical scholars. This was, and is, particularly the case in Syria, where groups such as the Free Syrian Army, Aḥrār al-Shām and especially the al-Qāᶜida-affiliated Jabhat al-Nuṣra and its main rival ISIS (the Islamic State of Iraq and Shām) fight amongst each other for influence. Since disagreements in this conflict are still ongoing and highly detailed, therefore requiring more space than this chapter affords me, I will not go into that issue here.[65]

One of the problems with choosing one of the many groups available is that

Ghanīma? Wa-Hal Yajūzu Qatl al-Aṭfāl wa-l-Nisāʾ al-Nuṣayriyyīn?, no. 7167 (www.tawhed.ws/FAQ/pr?qid=7167, 2013).

61. See, for example, Abū al-Mundhir al-Shinqīṭī, *Hal Yajūzu Qatl al-Rawāfiḍ al-ghayr Muqātilīn mimman Yaṭᶜunūna fī al-Ṣaḥāba wa-Yasīʾūna ilā Ahl al-Sunna?*, no. 6845 (www.tawhed.ws/FAQ/pr?qid=6845, 2012).
62. Abū al-Mundhir al-Shinqīṭī, *Hal Yajūzu lī An Anfadha ᶜAmaliyya Istishhādiyya fī Tajammuᶜāt Ḥizb Allāh al-Rāfiḍī?*, no. 7485 (www.tawhed.ws/FAQ/pr?qid=7485, 2013).
63. al-Shinqīṭī, *Hal Yajūzu l-Tashaffī.*
64. Abū al-Mundhir al-Shinqīṭī, *Hal Yajūzu lanā An Nastahdifa Madrasa Yarᶜāhā l-Niẓām li-Tajnīd Ṭalabatihā li-l-Dukhūl li-Jayshihi baᶜda An Yanhū Dirāsatahum?*, no. 7618 (www.tawhed.ws/FAQ/display_question?qid=7618&pageqa=1&i=, 2013).
65. For brief but good accounts of the conflicts between these groups, see Cole Bunzel, 'The Islamic State of Disobedience: Al-Baghdadi's Defiance', Jihadica.com, posted 5 October 2013, www.jihadica.com/the-islamic-state-of-disobedience-al-baghdadis-defiance/; Cole Bunzel, 'Caliphate Now: Jihadis Debate the Islamic State', Jihadica.com, posted 25 November 2013, www.jihadica.com/caliphate-now-jihadis-debate-the-islamic-state/ (accessed 15 April 2014); Cole Bunzel, 'The Islamic State of Disunity: Jihadism

it is more or less expected of a *mujāhid* to swear an oath of fealty (*bayᶜa*) to the leader of a group (*amīr*),[66] which presumably increases group loyalty and thereby also the chance of stronger negative feelings towards other organisations. However, more important perhaps have been the ideological differences over the conduct of some groups. The Yemeni al-Qāᶜida-affiliate Anṣār al-Sharīᶜa is a case in point.[67] In a brotherly epistle, Abū Baṣīr al-Ṭarṭūsī – who, as we have seen above, expressed dissenting opinions before[68] – chides this group for deviating from the *sharīᶜa* in their behaviour (despite their name), because of their supposedly excessive violence, their continued jihad after Yemeni President ᶜAlī ᶜAbdallāh Ṣāliḥ had already left and, as such, their deviation from the goals of the revolution in Yemen.[69] The Bahraini radical scholar Abū Humām al-Atharī takes a rather mild approach to refute al-Ṭarṭūsī's criticism of Anṣār al-Sharīᶜa, stating that 'what we have learned from [al-Ṭarṭūsī] and the benefit we have derived from him is greater than what we dispute about him and what we criticise'.[70] Out of a sense of reverence, al-Atharī therefore respectfully points out that applying the *sharīᶜa* should be the goal, not just the removal of a president, and that as long as the former has not happened, Anṣār al-Sharīᶜa's fight is justified.[71] Similarly, the Jordanian scholar Abū Muḥammad al-Maqdisī,

Divided', Jihadica.com, posted 30 January 2013, www.jihadica.com/the-islamic-state-of-disunity-jihadism-divided/; Joas Wagemakers, 'Al-Qaida Advises the Arab Spring: The Case for al-Baghdadi', Jihadica.com, posted 21 September 2013, www.jihadica.com/al-qaida-advises-the-arab-spring-the-case-for-al-baghdadi/.

66. Abū al-Mundhir al-Shinqīṭī, *Hal Yumkinu An Ujāhidu maᶜa l-Mujāhidīn dūna al-Iltizām bi-l-Bayᶜa?*, no. 6304 (www.tawhed.ws/FAQ/display_question?qid=6304&pageqa=1&i=, 2012). See also Abū al-Mundhir al-Shinqīṭī, *Fuṣūl fī al-Imāma wa-l-Bayᶜa* (www.tawhed.ws/dl?i=28121305, 2013), for more on the concept of *bayᶜa* from a Jihadi–Salafi point of view.
67. For more on this dispute, see Cole Bunzel, 'Jihadism's Widening Internal Divide: Intellectual Infighting Heats Up', Jihadica.com, posted on 29 January 2013, www.jihadica.com/jihadism's-widening-internal-divide-intellectual-infighting-heats-up/; Joas Wagemakers, 'Al-Qaida Advises the Arab Spring: Yemen', Jihadica.com, posted on 5 June 2012, www.jihadica.com/al-qaida-advises-the-arab-spring-yemen/.
68. In al-Ṭarṭūsī's case, this is rooted in a longer history of what I refer to as 'nuanced radicalism'. See Joas Wagemakers, 'Between Purity and Pragmatism? Abu Basir al-Tartusi's Nuanced Radicalism', in *Jihadi Thought and Ideology*, ed. Rüdiger Lohlker (Göttingen, 2013), pp. 16–37.
69. Abū Baṣīr al-Ṭarṭūsī, *Ilā al-Ikhwa Anṣār al-Sharīᶜa fī Yaman* (www.abubaseer.bizland.com/hadath/Read/hadath%2092.doc, 2012), pp. 1–2.
70. Abū Humām Bakr b. ᶜAbd al-ᶜAzīz al-Atharī, *Al-Ijābāt al-Sarīᶜa fī al-Intiṣār li-Anṣār al-Sharīᶜa* (www.tawhed.ws/dl?i=12041206, 2012), p. 2.
71. al-Atharī, *Al-Ijābāt al-Sarīᶜa*, pp. 2–6.

who is also on good but sometimes critical terms with Abū Baṣīr,[72] praises Anṣār al-Sharīᶜa, but also advises it to remain true to the unity of God (*tawḥīd*), thereby implying that he may perhaps agree with al-Ṭarṭūsī to a certain extent.

Other scholars are less friendly in their response to al-Ṭarṭūsī's criticism. While the radical scholar Abū l-Zubayr al-ᶜUbab wonders whether Abū Baṣīr has perhaps left Jihadi–Salafism but nevertheless answers him rather neutrally,[73] al-Shinqīṭī accuses him openly of slandering the *mujāhidūn* and their jihad in a way that is not based on arguments. He asks Abū Baṣir if he does not believe the Yemeni government is an apostate one and calls his descriptions of Anṣār al-Sharīᶜa 'disgusting'.[74] Although such conflicts are based on slight ideological differences on how to wage jihad, they had mostly lain dormant when few of al-Qāᶜida's ideas could be implemented. Now that the Arab Spring provided al-Qāᶜida ideologues with an entirely new opportunity to comment on jihad on a scale not seen before in recent times, these differences came to the surface. This was underlined by their treatment of a possible alternative to their Islamic state achieved through jihad: democracy.

DEMOCRACY

Al-Qāᶜida-affiliated ideologues have long rejected democracy for three main reasons: firstly, they believe that sovereignty and the responsibility to make laws should ultimately not lie with the people – as in a democracy – but with God; secondly, they believe that decision-making should not be based on what the majority of the people want, but simply on what is the right thing to do; thirdly, they claim that democracies grant their citizens equality and rights that are at odds with Islamic law. Although association with the West is also a powerful reason for some radical scholars to reject democracy,[75] the three reasons given above form the basic ideological underpinning of most Jihadi–Salafi arguments against democracy. As such, al-Qāᶜida-affiliated scholars also reject more

72. See Joas Wagemakers, 'An Inquiry into Ignorance: A Jihādī-Salafī Debate on *Jahl* as an Obstacle to *Takfīr*', in *The Transmission and Dynamics of the Textual Sources of Islam: Essays in Honour of Harald Motzki*, eds Nicolet Boekhoff-van der Voort, Kees Versteegh and Joas Wagemakers (Leiden, 2011), pp. 314–25.
73. Abū al-Zubayr ᶜĀdil al-ᶜUbab, *Halā Taraktum lī Shaykhanā Abā Baṣīr al-Ṭarṭūsī?!* (www.tawhed.ws/dl?i=12041247, 2012).
74. Abū al-Mundhir al-Shinqīṭī, *Al-Inḥirāfāt al-Shanīᶜa li-Muntaqid Anṣār al-Sharīᶜa* (www.tawhed.ws/dl?i=28051208, 2012).
75. For an example of this sentiment expressed during the Arab Spring, see Abū al-Mundhir al-Shinqīṭī, *Al Ḥukm al-Qurʾān fī Duwaylāt al-Ikhwān* (www.tawhed.ws/dl?i=12041202, 2012), pp. 29–36.

moderate Islamists who are willing to work within the systems of their countries – particularly the Muslim Brotherhood – as deviant believers who twist Islam to fit their political needs, but, ironically, without any real political results after decades of trying.[76] Such attitudes could partly be explained, however, by pointing to the closed and dictatorial systems in the Arab world that, however one viewed democracy, were not going to allow real opposition anyway. In other words, radical Islamists could easily adopt negative yet principled attitudes towards democracy, knowing that their beliefs would not be put to the test. All of this changed with the Arab Spring, of course, which saw the overthrow of some of the biggest obstacles to democracy and suddenly offered Islamists of all stripes a chance to translate their popularity into real political power. What effect did this have on al-Qāᶜida affiliated ideologues?

NEW REGIMES: MORE OF THE SAME?

Several of the new regimes in the Arab world assumed a distinctly Islamist flavour after parliamentary and presidential elections were held, most prominently in Egypt and Tunisia, where the Muslim Brotherhood and the Islamist al-Nahḍa party came to power, respectively. Naturally, this raised questions among Jihadi–Salafis, who realised that these organisations were not properly Islamic according to their own standards, yet who were also uneasy about treating the new regimes as if nothing had changed. Seeing pious Muslims in their countries who actively strive to give Islam – even if it is a 'deviant' form of Islam – a greater role in politics and society was a new phenomenon, leading some to wonder what to do. Al-Shinqīṭī states that it is all right to be happy about the Muslim Brotherhood's victory in the Egyptian elections because their organisation is 'the lesser of two evils' (*akhaff al-ḍararayn*).[77] Yet he also states that in the end, the Brotherhood adheres to an inconsistent and deviant form of Islam that allows all kinds of things that clash with Islamic law and is more interested in its own power and good ties with the West than in applying the *sharīᶜa*.[78] Al-

76. For a detailed overview of radical Islamists' views on democracy and democrats, see Joas Wagemakers, '"The *Kāfir* Religion of the West": *Takfīr* of Democracy and Democrats by Radical Islamists', in *Accusations of Unbelief in Islam: A Diachronic Perspective on Takfīr*, eds Camilla Adang, Hasan Ansari, Maribel Fierro and Sabine Schmidtke (Leiden, 2015), pp. 327–53.
77. Abū al-Mundhir al-Shinqīṭī, *Hal Yashraᶜu Taʾyīd Mursī fī al-Qarārāt al-Dustūriyya al-Akhīra?*, no. 6938 (www.tawhed.ws/FAQ/pr?qid=6938, 2012).
78. Abū al-Mundhir al-Shinqīṭī, *Ḥukm al-Qurʾān*, pp. 5–12, 16–18, 25–6; Abū al-Mundhir al-Shinqīṭī, *Mā Huwa l-Mawqif al-Sharᶜī min Najāḥ Mursī fī Miṣr?*, no. 6535 (www.tawhed.ws/FAQ/pr?qid=6535, 2012).

Shinqīṭī therefore does not see the fact that the Muslim Brotherhood in Egypt had to take the views of the military[79] and those of other non-Islamists into account as an excuse for supposedly not applying the *sharī^ca*.[80] Instead, radical scholar Ḥussām ^cAbd al-Ra^ʾūf points out that the revolution in Egypt should continue until there is a 'constitution that God and his Messenger are satisfied with and [that] restores the truth to its proper place (*yu^cīdu al-ḥaqq ilā niṣābihi*)'.[81]

The same conclusion is drawn with regard to the Tunisian al-Nahḍa party, which is blamed for wanting democracy and women's rights and for merely adhering to what it refers to as the principles (*mabādi^ʾ*) of Islam, without ever talking about the application of Islamic law (*taṭbīq al-sharī^ca al-Islāmiyya*).[82] Moreover, al-Shinqīṭī accuses al-Nahḍa of waging a war against Jihadi–Salafis by preventing them from getting their message out and repressing them.[83] Given this criticism of the new regimes, it is understandable that any cooperation with them (in the form of government-related jobs, for example) should be extremely limited and should not entail any involvement with man-made laws.[84] Still, it is clear that al-Qā^cida-affiliated scholars do not see the Islamist governments that came to power through the Arab Spring as simply more of the same, as if nothing had changed since the overthrow of their predecessors. This became particularly clear in 2013, when a military coup overthrew the Muslim Brotherhood-led government in Egypt. Al-Maqdisī and his Jordanian countryman Iyād Qunaybī underline the army's strong cooperation with Israel and their adherence to

79. For al-Shinqīṭī's views on the Egyptian military ('the army of the idol (*ṭāghūt*) and the protectors of man-made laws'), see Abū al-Mundhir al-Shinqīṭī, *Mā Ḥukm al-^cAsākir al-Miṣriyyīn?*, no. 6344 (www.tawhed.ws/FAQ/pr?qid=6344, 2012); Abū al-Mundhir al-Shinqīṭī, *Mā Ra^ʾyukum bi-khtiṭāf al-Junūd fī Miṣr?*, no. 7461 (www.tawhed.ws/FAQ/pr?qid=7461, 2013). The words cited in this note are from the former fatwa.
80. Abū al-Mundhir al-Shinqīṭī, *Hal Ya^ctabiru Muḥammad Mursī Ma^cdhūr li-Annahu lā Yastaṭī^cu An Yuṭabbiqa l-Sharī^ca?*, no. 7344 (www.tawhed.ws/FAQ/pr?qid=7344, 2013).
81. Ḥussām ^cAbd al-Ra^ʾūf, *Law Kuntu Makān Mursī wa-Qa^cadtu ^calā al-Kursī* (www.tawhed.ws/dl?i=24041354, 2012), p. 3.
82. Al-Shinqīṭī, *Ḥukm al-Qur^ʾān*, pp. 13–14.
83. Abū al-Mundhir al-Shinqīṭī, *Jarā^ʾim al-Nahḍa fī Tūnis.. ilā Matā?* (www.tawhed.ws/dl?i=28011302, 2013), p. 6.
84. Abū al-Mundhir al-Shinqīṭī, *Hal Yashra^cu li-l-Ikhwa fī Lībiyā l-Inḍimām ilā Wizārat al-Dākhiliyya wa-Tawallī Wizārāt Ukhrā bi-Ḥujjat ^cadam Taslīmihā li-l-Mufsidīn wa-l-Mur* [sic], no. 6341 (www.tawhed.ws/FAQ/pr?qid=6341, 2012); Abū al-Mundhir al-Shinqīṭī, *Mā Ḥukm al-^cAmal Mudarris Jughrāfiyā aw Muhandis Zirā^cī ^cinda Dawlat Bashār?*, no. 6393 (www.tawhed.ws/FAQ/pr?qid=6393, 2012); Abū al-Mundhir al-Shinqīṭī, *Mā Ḥukm al-Inḍimām ilā Ri^ʾāsat al-Arkān bi-Lībiyā bi-Ḥujjat Akhdh al-Māl ^cIlman Annahu Yalzamu Baytahu wa-Lā Yaḥḍuru?*, no. 7116 (www.tawhed.ws/FAQ/pr?qid=7116, 2013).

man-made laws.[85] Both men also reprimand other Jihadi–Salafis who were apparently quite happy about the Egyptian coup because it meant a drawback for the Muslim Brotherhood. Although al-Maqdisī and Qunaybī were no friends of the Brotherhood either, they point out that one should not equate that organisation with secularists and that the military regime is even worse.[86] This is confirmed by the reluctance of al-Qāᶜida ideologues to apply excommunication (*takfīr*) to Islamist leaders. While calling men such as Mubārak apostates (*murtaddūn*) and unbelievers (*kuffār*) was a basic part of Jihadi–Salafi ideology, al-Shinqīṭī is clearly more careful with men such as Muslim Brother and former Egyptian President Muḥammad Mursī and al-Nahḍa leader Rāshid al-Ghannūshī and even more so with their supporters. Although al-Shinqīṭī condemns their governments as engaged in unbelief (*kufr*), he clearly stops short of saying this about the entire Muslim Brotherhood.[87]

'WE TOLD YOU SO!'

While al-Qāᶜida-affiliated ideologues do not excuse the Islamist governments for their alleged unwillingness to apply the *sharīᶜa*, they do make clear that the circumstances in the countries directly affected by the Arab Spring do not allow for Islamism to take root, or at least not without a drastic overhaul of the entire system. This is particularly clear in radical scholars' treatment of the new constitutions in countries such as Egypt, Libya and Tunisia. Although al-Ṭarṭūsī did not reject the new Libyan constitution outright but was willing to accept it with (substantial) changes here and there, other Jihadi–Salafi ideologues dismissed the new constitutions out of hand. According to various radical scholars, they are not necessarily all bad, but they clearly give the people the

85. Abū Muḥammad al-Maqdisī, *Aḥdhiyat al-Mūsād [2]* (www.tawhed.ws/dl?i=02111301, 2013 (accessed 6 November 2013)), pp. 1–3; Iyād Qunaybī, *Mawqif baᶜḍ Mashāyikh al-Salafiyya min al-Jaysh* (http://twitmail.com/email/532700952/157/, 2013).
86. Abū Muḥammad al-Maqdisī, *Al-Inṣāf Ḥillat al-Ashrāf wa-l-Ashrāf Aqall al-Aṣnāf* (www.tawhed.ws/r?i=23101301, 2013), pp. 1, 3, 5; Iyād Qunaybī, *Daᶜwat Muᶜāriḍī Muḥammad Mursī ilā Ittiḥād Mawqif Sharīf min Khiṭāb al-Sīsī* (http://twitmail.com/email/532700952/156/, 2013).
87. Abū al-Mundhir al-Shinqīṭī, *Kayfa Yanbaghī li-l-Ikhwa fī Tūnis al-Taṣarruf maᶜa Niẓām al-Ḥukm al-Jadīd?*, no. 6370 (www.tawhed.ws/FAQ/pr?qid=6370, 2012); Abū al-Mundhir al-Shinqīṭī, *Mā Taᶜlīqātukum ᶜalā Kalām al-Shaykh ᶜAbd al-Qādir b. ᶜAbd al-ᶜAzīz fī Qanāt al-Jazīra?*, no. 7275 (www.tawhed.ws/FAQ/pr?qid=7275, 2013); Abū al-Mundhir al-Shinqīṭī, *Suʾāl Ḥawla Qawla li-Mursī: Mafīsh* [sic] *Farq bayna ᶜAqīdat al-Masīḥiyya wa-ᶜAqīdat al-Islāmiyya* [sic], *Kull Yaᶜtaqidu bi-Man Yashāʾu*, no. 6931 (www.tawhed.ws/FAQ/pr?qid=6931, 2013).

right to legislate and therefore go against the absolute sovereignty and unity of God, making them at least partly products of *kufr* and polytheism (*shirk*),[88] which further expresses itself in their respect for equal rights and citizenship for non-Muslims.[89] Non-al-Qāᶜida-affiliated scholars who are in favour of the new constitutions as 'the lesser of two evils' (i.e. less bad than the constitutions they replaced) are therefore criticised as taking this principle too far. With people or parties, this rule can apply, but according to radical scholars, one cannot compromise with the outright unbelief and polytheism found in these constitutions.[90] As such, the people who apply these constitutions are seen as clear apostates.[91]

The problem is deeper than just these new constitutions, however. One scholar points to the history of the Egyptian constitution and laws, indicating that the whole system is dictated by principles (such as the president's duty to uphold the constitution) that are fundamentally un-Islamic.[92] The military coup in Egypt against the Muslim Brotherhood in 2013 was clearly seen as proof of this by several radical scholars, who collectively seemed to be saying 'we told you so!'. 'If [secularists] succeed in what they want to reach', al-Shinqīṭī states, 'they will only strive for the disappearance of the *sharīᶜa*'.[93] With the odds supposedly stacked against Islamists in such a way, one gets the impression that the application of the *sharīᶜa* through democratic means was never going to succeed, which is precisely the point radical scholars want to make. Al-Maqdisī, for example, reminds his readers that he has denounced democracy all along and that the coup

88. Abū l-Ḥasan al-Azdī, *Al-Tajliya wa-l-Naqḍ li-Mudrik Qawl Majīz al-Taṣwīt li-l-Dustūr* (www.tawhed.ws/dl?i=24041368, 2012); Abū Humām Bakr b. ᶜAbd al-ᶜAzīz al-Atharī, *Al-Mukhtaṣar fī Ḥukm al-Taṣwīt ᶜalā Dustūr Maṣr* [sic] (www.tawhed.ws/dl?i=28011301, 2012), p. 2; Ḥāzim al-Miṣrī, *Al-Īḍāḥ li-Mā fī l-Dustūr al-Jadīd min al-Kufr al-Bawāḥ* (www.tawhed.ws/dl?i=24041374, n. d.), pp. 2–3.
89. Al-Miṣrī, *Al-Īḍāḥ*, p. 9.
90. Al-Azdī, *Al-Tajliya*, pp. 4–8; Abū al-Mundhir al-Shinqīṭī, *Mā Huwa Taᶜlīqukum ᶜalā Fatwā l-Shaykh al-Barrāk Ḥawla l-Dustūr al-Miṣrī?*, no. 6985 (www.tawhed.ws/FAQ/display_question?qid=6985, 2012); Abū al-Mundhir al-Shinqīṭī, *Mā Taᶜlīqukum ᶜalā Fatwā l-Shaykh ᶜAbd al-ᶜAzīz al-Ṭurayfī Ḥafaẓahu llāh fīmā Yataᶜallaqu bi-l-Ṭaswīt ᶜalā al-Dustūr al-Miṣrī?*, no. 7099 (www.tawhed.ws/FAQ/pr?qid=7099, 2013).
91. Abū al-Mundhir al-Shinqīṭī, *Mā Ḥukm man Waḍaᶜa Dustūr Miṣr?*, no. 6967 (www.tawhed.ws/FAQ/pr?qid=6967, 2013).
92. Aḥmad ᶜAshūsh, *Iᶜlām al-Muslimīn bi-Ḥaqīqat al-Dustūr wa-l-Qawānīn* (www.tawhed.ws/dl?i=24041367, n. d.); Aḥmad ᶜAshūsh, *Hidāyat al-Ḥīrān ilā Ḥurmat Sulūk Ṭarīq al-Dustūr wa-l-Barlamān* (www.tawhed.ws/dl?i=12041208, n. d.), pp. 13–68.
93. Abū al-Mundhir al-Shinqīṭī, *Mādhā Yajibu An Yakūna Mawqifunā fī al-Aḥdāth al-Mutawaqqaᶜa fī Miṣr bi-Tārīkh 30 Yūniyū al-Qādim ḍidd al-Ikhwān?*, no. 7512 (www.tawhed.ws/FAQ/pr?qid=7512, 2013).

in Egypt has made the futility of this system only more apparent, stressing that it is the Muslim Brotherhood that has failed, not Islam itself.[94] He also notes that some talked about 'the failure of the jihadi project [. . .] and that the success of some revolutions of the Arab Spring would come at the expense of their thinking', but that it has turned out to be quite the opposite.[95] Qunaybī similarly calls on Islamists to repent for the mistakes they made[96] and laments 'the insistence on democracy until death'.[97] Yet the Arab Spring was, at least at first, the quintessence of 'people power'; given the sensibility that social movements have for such trends and circumstances, did the ideologues' views on democracy remain as negative as before or did they perhaps adopt some of it as well?

REJECTING THE PHILOSOPHY BEHIND DEMOCRACY

The rejection of the Muslim Brotherhood and like-minded groups by radical scholars was a sign that al-Qāᶜida was still against democracy as a means of contention. This point of view was given more theoretical backing by several publications produced after the beginning of the Arab Spring that criticised the tenets of democracy in a way that was less directly in response to events in Egypt or Tunisia. These writings confirm two of the three main Jihadi–Salafi objections against the philosophy behind democracy – namely, that it gives sovereignty to the people instead of to God, thereby violating the *tawḥīd* and – according to some – constituting what really amounts to a new religion;[98] and that it gives rights and freedom to people who are not entitled to them, according to the *sharīᶜa*.[99] Such an 'un-Islamic' system cannot bring about the application of Islamic law, and democracy should therefore also not be equated with the early Islamic concept of *shūrā* (consultation), as many moderate Islamists

94. Abū Muḥammad al-Maqdisī, *Fawāʾid wa-ᶜIbar min al-Inqilāb ᶜalā Ṣanādīq al-Iqtirāᶜ fī Miṣr* (www.tawhed.ws/r?i=21091301, 2013), pp. 1–8.
95. al-Maqdisī, *Fawāʾid*, p. 9.
96. Iyād Qunaybī, *Ayyuhā al-Islāmiyyūn bi-Miṣr* (http://twitmail.com/email/532700952/151/, 2013).
97. Qunaybī, *Al-Iṣrār ᶜalā al-Dīmuqrāṭiyya Ḥattā l-Mawt! Durūs min Aḥdāth Miṣr 1* (http://twitmail.com/email/532700952/144/1, 2013).
98. ᶜAshūsh, *Hidāyat*, p. 6. This notion of democracy being a new religion is certainly not new and was also expressed in the early 1990s by Abū Muḥammad al-Maqdisī in his *Dīmuqrāṭiyya Dīn* (www.tawhed.ws/dl?i=mo5o2fpb, n. d.).
99. Jalāl al-Dīn Abū al-Futūḥ, *Al-Fiqh al-Dīmuqrāṭī* (www.tawhed.ws/dl?i=12041240, 2012); Abū Ayman al-Miṣrī, *Suʾāl wa-Jawāb Ḥukm Dukhūl al-Aḥzāb li-Maṣlaḥat Taṭbīq al-Sharīᶜa* (www.tawhed.ws/dl?i=08021208, 2012).

have tried to argue,[100] because whereas the latter only gives people the power to decide within the confines of the *sharīᶜa*, democracy leaves all decisions to human beings.[101] Moreover, radical scholars also disagree that the application of the *sharīᶜa* can only be done gradually through the use of democracy, as some Islamists have argued.[102]

Interestingly, because the Arab Spring made democracy such a real and concrete prospect for many Muslims, some radical scholars have also examined several aspects of democracy, such as parliamentary participation and Islamist parties. Considering the strong emphasis on the application of the *sharīᶜa* found in the writings of al-Qāᶜida ideologues and the belief among them that democracy cannot lead to this application, it is not surprising that entering parliament is utterly rejected because such legislative councils supposedly always end up making un-Islamic laws.[103] Al-Shinqīṭī states that some argue that becoming a member of parliament could enable one to stop 'un-Islamic' laws and to legislate only *sharīᶜa* compliant ones instead, but he does not believe that engaging in a system that is fundamentally polytheistic can achieve that.[104] Unsurprisingly, the idea of establishing Islamist political parties and using them to win seats in parliament is also rejected by al-Qāᶜida-affiliated scholars and those non-radical scholars who do allow this are condemned.[105] This even applies to Salafi political

100. For more on this, see Uriya Shavit, 'Is *Shura* a Muslim Form of Democracy? Roots and Systemization of a Polemic', *Middle Eastern Studies* 46.3 (2010), 349–74.
101. Al-Miṣrī, *Al-Īḍāḥ*, p. 5; al-Ẓawāhirī, *Risālat 5*, p. 17.
102. Madḥat b. al-Ḥasan Āl Farāj, *Muḥammad ᶜAbd al-Maqṣūd wa-Muᶜāraḍatuhu li-Man Yurīdu Taṭbīq al-Sharīᶜa Fawran* (www.tawhed.ws/dl?i=20081211, n. d.); al-Shinqīṭī, *Ḥukm al-Qurʾān*, pp. 19–24.
103. Aḥmad ᶜAshūsh, *Al-Ḥujja wa-l-Burhān ᶜalā Ḥurmat Dukhūl al-Barlamān* (www.tawhed.ws/dl?i=12041207, n. d.); Ṭalᶜat Fuʾād Qāsim, *Al-Adilla al-Naqliyya wa-l-ᶜAqliyya ᶜalā Ḥurmat Dukhūl al-Majālis al-Tashrīᶜiyya* (www.tawhed.ws/dl?i=20081202, 2012 [2nd edn]), pp. 5–25.
104. Abū al-Mundhir al-Shinqīṭī, *Mā Huwa Raddukum ᶜalā Shubhat al-Mushāraka fī l-Intikhābāt bi-Ḥujjat Irtikāb Akhaff al-Ḍararayn?*, no. 5829 (www.tawhed.ws/FAQ/pr?qid=5829, 2012); Abū al-Mundhir al-Shinqīṭī, *Hal Yuᶜtabaru ᶜUḍw al-Barlamān alladhī Yuᶜlinu Annahu Lan Yashraᶜu Ḥukman Mukhālifan li-l-Sharīᶜa. Hal Yuᶜtabaru Musharriᶜan min dūna allāh? Wa-Shibh* [sic], no. 6323 (www.tawhed.ws/FAQ/pr?qid=6323, 2012); Abū al-Mundhir al-Shinqīṭī, *Mā l-Radd ᶜalā Hadhihi l-Shubhāt li-ᶜAdad min al-Salafiyyīn al-Dīmuqrāṭiyyīn fī Miṣr*, no. 6331 (www.tawhed.ws/FAQ/pr?qid=6331, 2012).
105. Abū al-Mundhir al-Shinqīṭī, *Al-Radd ᶜalā Fatwā l-Shaykh Muḥammad al-Maqṣūd bi-Khuṣūṣ al-Intikhābāt*, no. 5018 (www.tawhed.ws/FAQ/pr?qid=5018, 2011). See also, however, Abū al-Mundhir al-Shinqīṭī, *Hal Yajūzu Waṣf al-Shaykhayn Muḥammad ᶜAbd al-Maqṣūd wa-Muḥammad Ḥassān bi-Mashāyikh al-Ḍalāla[?]*, no. 5098 (www.tawhed.ws/FAQ/pr?qid=5098, 2011); Abū Humām Bakr b. ᶜAbd al-ᶜAzīz al-Atharī, *Hal*

parties such as the Egyptian Ḥizb al-Nūr[106] and similar efforts by others to establish parties on the supposedly more doctrinally sound basis of Salafism.[107]

ADOPTING THE MEANS OF DEMOCRACY

The seemingly full-blown condemnation of democracy by radical ideologues makes it appear as if the Arab Spring did not change anything about these scholars' views on this subject. This is not entirely the case, however. Apart from al-Ṭarṭūsī's willingness to engage in rewriting the Libyan constitution instead of immediately rejecting it, we also saw in the previous section that only two of the three main objections against democracy frequently reoccurred. The third one – the idea of relying on a majority in elections – was rejected much less often after the Arab Spring. There are some precedents for this among al-Qāᶜida ideologues and leaders. As McCants has pointed out, both Usāma b. Lādin and Ayman al-Ẓawāhirī stated even before the Arab Spring that they were not against the principle of elections as such, as long as this would not lead to parliaments that legislate outside the boundaries of the *sharīᶜa*,[108] and they are not the only ones who, while rejecting the philosophy behind democracy, see elections as one of its positive aspects.[109] Moreover, several quietist and political Salafi scholars also stated years ago that supporting one side over the other during elections can sometimes be considered a case of 'the lesser to two evils', a concept we have seen before in this chapter.[110]

After the Arab Spring, several radical scholars began re-evaluating their old

Muḥammad Ḥassān wa-Muḥammad ᶜAbd al-Maqṣūd min Shuyūkh al-Ḍalāla?, no. 5247 (www.tawhed.ws/FAQ/pr?qid=5247, 2012).

106. Aḥmad ᶜAshūsh, *Ḥizb al-Nūr bayna al-Islām wa-l-Jāhiliyya al-Ūrubiyya* (www.tawhed.ws/dl?i=13121108, 2011); Iyād Qunaybī, *Mawqif min 'Ḥizb al-Nūr'* (http://twitmail.com/email/532700952/134/, 2013). See also Ṭalḥa Muḥammad al-Masīr, *Al-Barāʾa min al-Tanāzulāt allatī Tuqaddimuhā Salafiyyat al-Iskandariyya* (www.tawhed.ws/dl?i=24041302, n. d.).
107. Iyād Qunaybī, *Risāla li-l-Ustādh Ḥāzim Ṣalāḥ bi-Khuṣūṣ Inshāʾ Ḥizb Yumārisu l-ᶜAmal al-Barlamānī* (http://twitmail.com/fullview/331778, 2013). See also Iyād Qunaybī, *Mā Hakadhā Tunāqishu Hadhihi al-Qaḍāyā al-Maṣīriyya Yā Ustādh Ḥāzim* (http://twitmail.com/fullview/331990, 2013).
108. McCants, 'Al Qaeda's', p. 29.
109. Behnam Timo Said, 'Djihadismus nach dem Arabischen Frühling und das Vermittlungsangebot Muhammad al-Zawahiris', *Zeitschrift für Außen und Sicherheitspolitik* (2013).
110. For more on this, see William McCants, 'The Lesser of Two Evils: The Salafi Turn to Party Politics in Egypt', *Middle East Memo No. 23, Saban Center at Brookings*, May 2012.

ideas and noticed that they could stay true to their beliefs but nevertheless change their views on democracy in light of the new circumstances. None go further in this than Abū Baṣīr al-Ṭarṭūsī, who not only allows his readers to run in elections but also to found political parties, provided they do all this according to the teachings of the Qurʾān and the Sunna, do not legislate 'man-made laws' and remain loyal to Islam instead of to their parties. He even encourages his followers to take this peaceful approach, since non-violence is more likely to reap benefits in the current climate, he believes.[111] Other radical scholars do not go that far and still reject the founding of parties,[112] but do acknowledge that there is nothing wrong with elections as such,[113] and sometimes explicitly allow them in certain contexts and under conditions similar to those al-Ṭarṭūsī mentioned.[114] Al-Shinqīṭī even dedicates an entire treatise to the idea of a majority in elections, concluding that relying on a majority in itself is invalid,[115] but that it can be legitimate if it does not transgress the rules of the *sharīᶜa* or leads to 'man-made laws'.[116]

The emphasis Jihadi–Salafis place on what they see as the legislative drawbacks of democracy suggests that they would be less uncomfortable with elections for the presidency of a country. This does, indeed, seem to be the case. Again, al-Ṭarṭūsī goes furthest in this by openly endorsing the Egyptian Salafi candidate for president, Ḥāzim Abū Ismāᶜīl.[117] He justifies this not only by pointing out that Abū Ismāᶜīl is better than the alternatives, but also by stating that the presidency of Egypt is not the caliphate, and it should therefore be allowed to elect a president every few years. He even traces the term limits and indirect control by the people that elections for executive office imply to early Islam,

111. Abū Baṣīr al-Ṭarṭūsī, *Kalimāt fī al-Siyāsa al-Sharᶜiyya Akhuṣṣu bihā Ahlanā fī Tūnis wa-Miṣr* (www.tawhed.ws/r?i=30081106, 2011), pp. 1–2.
112. See, for instance, ᶜAshūsh, *Ḥizb*; Abū al-Mundhir al-Shinqīṭī, *Mā Ḥukm al-Dukhūl fī al-Aḥzāb al-Islāmiyya (al-Nūr wa-l-Faḍīla) min Ajl al-Muṭālaba bi-Inshāʾ Dustūr Islāmī?*, no. 4855 (www.tawhed.ws/FAQ/pr?qid=4855, 2012).
113. Abū Muḥammad al-Maqdisī, *Kashf al-Zukhruf wa-l-Buhtān fī Fatwā ᶜUlamāʾ al-Sulṭān* (www.tawhed.ws/dl?i=30031301, 2013), p. 3.
114. Abū al-Mundhir al-Shinqīṭī, *Mā Ḥukm al-Mushāraka fī ntikhāb al-Muʾtamar al-Waṭanī al-Lībī?*, no. 6455 (www.tawhed.ws/FAQ/pr?qid=6455, 2012); Abū al-Mundhir al-Shinqīṭī, *Mā Ḥukm al-Ṭarīqa wa-l-Taswīt wa-llatī Tamma min Khilālihimā Tashkīl Majlis Shūrā li-l-Tayyār al-Salafī al-Jihādī fī l-Urdunn?*, no. 6606 (www.tawhed.ws/FAQ/pr?qid=6606, 2012).
115. Abū al-Mundhir al-Shinqīṭī, *Bulūgh al-Amniyya fī Ḥukm al-Tarjīḥ bi-Qawl al-Aktharīyya* (www.tawhed.ws/dl?i=20081207, 2012), pp. 3–20.
116. al-Shinqīṭī, *Bulūgh al-Amniyya*, pp. 21–7.
117. Abū Baṣīr al-Ṭarṭūsī, *Al-Mawqif min Tarashshuḥ al-Ustādh 'Ḥāzim Ṣalāḥ Abū Ismāᶜīl' li-Riʾāsat Miṣr* (www.abubaseer.bizland.com/hadath/Read/hadath%2089.doc, 2011).

making them seem natural things for Muslims to engage in.[118] Interestingly, the responses by other radical scholars are not entirely negative. Al-Shinqīṭī disagrees, but more because he believes voting for Abū Ismāᶜīl will be useless and because he sees al-Ṭarṭūsī as a revisionist than for strictly ideological reasons.[119] Other scholars also treat this question with scepticism rather than rejection, acknowledging that there is, indeed, a difference between an executive and a legislative position, but nevertheless without having much hope for Abū Ismāᶜīl's chances to actually apply the *sharīᶜa*.[120]

Democracy was thus still rejected as a system of politics by Jihadi–Salafi scholars after the Arab Spring, yet some of its means were adopted within the strict confines of their conception of the *sharīᶜa*. From 2013 onwards, however, this whole discussion about democracy among radical ideologues was drowned out by news of the coup in Egypt in 2013 and the increasing violence in Syria, which led to new discussions over who to support in the latter conflict. Moreover, the instalment of a military regime in Egypt and the continued fighting in Syria made the prospect of democracy in those two countries all the more unlikely, while simultaneously increasing the prospects for jihad.

CONCLUSION

Global social movements like al-Qāᶜida mobilise the resources at their disposal and function within the opportunities and constraints that they face. Moreover, they also frame their ideas in the context of the latter. The opportunities and restraints that presented themselves through the revolts in the Arab world known as the 'Arab Spring', which began in 2010, also shaped al-Qāᶜida's ideas. Although the Arab Spring was started without the aid of al-Qāᶜida, this did not stop the movement from trying to appropriate the uprisings as simply the latest phase in a struggle it had long been engaged in. Moreover, al-Qāᶜida ideologues tried to tie the Arab Spring to their own anti-Western agenda and steer it into a more Islamist direction by calling on demonstrators to demand the application of the *sharīᶜa*. This was to be achieved by waging jihad, on which scholars advised

118. Abū Baṣīr al-Ṭarṭūsī, *Ḥattā Yakūna al-Tamthīl ᶜĀdilan wa-Shāmilan* (www.abubaseer.bizland.com/articles/read/a%20153.doc, 2011), pp. 5–22.

119. Abū al-Mundhir al-Shinqīṭī, *Mā Taᶜlīqukum ᶜalā Kalām al-Shaykh Abī Baṣīr Ḥawla Tarashshuḥ al-Shaykh Ḥāzim Abū Ismāᶜīl li-Riʾāsat al-Jumhūriyya fī Miṣr?*, no. 5624 (www.tawhed.ws/FAQ/pr?qid=5624, 2011).

120. Abū al-Mundhir al-Shinqīṭī, *Mā Ḥukm al-Mushāraka fī al-Intikhābāt bayna Mursī wa-Shafīq aw li-Ibṭāl al-Ṣawt*, no. 6442 (www.tawhed.ws/FAQ/pr?qid=6442, 2012); ᶜAshūsh, *Hidāyat*, pp. 1–2, 11–12, 55–68; al-Miṣrī, *Suʾāl*, pp. 16–18.

their followers with regard to possible obstacles, targets and what groups (not) to join. The alternative to jihad – expressing contention through democracy – was mostly treated the same as before the Arab Spring with regard to the philosophical underpinnings of this concept: scholars rejected it as a system based on people's sovereignty and 'man-made laws' that violated God's sole right to power and legislation. With regard to the means of democracy, however, the situation was slightly different. Elections (particularly for an executive office) and even the founding of political parties were not dismissed out of hand by some scholars, whereas this used to be the case before.

The opportunities provided by the Arab Spring have thus caused al-Qāᶜida to re-evaluate certain aspects of democracy as an alternative to jihad, even if the movement's ideologues still unanimously reject democracy as a system. This is not to suggest that Jihadi–Salafi scholars are about to become Jeffersonian democrats. There are, nevertheless, clear – yet small – differences in the way radical ideologues frame the means of democracy now. These small differences probably did not develop into anything bigger because of the increased constraints that the Arab Spring created: a military coup in Egypt against elected Islamists and an increasingly dominant conflict in Syria that took all attention away from democratic thinking. These constraints ensured that, in the end, al-Qāᶜida-affiliated scholars mostly confirmed their long-held ideas during the Arab Spring.

Of course, al-Qāᶜida's staunchly anti-democratic ideology itself was partly responsible for the lack of bigger changes in Jihadi–Salafi ideas too, yet we have also seen that previously almost unthinkable ideas like elections and voting for 'the lesser of two evils' became more widely accepted among radical scholars after the Arab Spring. In the future and under the right circumstances, these changes might grow into something bigger. After all, the Muslim Brotherhood was once quite sceptical of democracy too, while many of its members now embrace it. The same may apply to al-Qāᶜida, which – like the Muslim Brotherhood – is not 'trapped' inside its own ideology either, but might expand on the ideological developments witnessed in the Arab Spring to grow into a different kind of movement. One could argue that if al-Qāᶜida ever became a movement contesting elections, it would lose its *raison d'être* of jihad against the West and 'apostate' regimes in the Muslim world. I would argue, however, that their aim is not jihad, but 'true' Islamic rule in the Muslim world and a removal of Western influence in Muslim countries. Whatever one may think of this goal, a time may come when al-Qāᶜida ideologues start believing that this is less achievable through jihad than through peaceful, democratic means. That moment – if it ever comes – is still very far off for now, but if the movement ever reaches that point, its ideologues may look back on the Arab Spring as the time when the re-evaluation of their ideas began.

CHAPTER

9

THE ARAB REVOLUTIONS AND JIHADISM

*Farhad Khosrokhavar**

The uprisings of the Arab Spring marked a new period in the ups and downs of Jihadism.[1] One can divide the period extending from 2011 (Bin ᶜAlī was forced to leave Tunisia on 14 January 2011) up to March 2014 into three distinct eras in regard to Jihadism within the Arab countries. The first period marks the crisis of Jihadism: partisans of radical Islam were reduced to the role of spectators in a world where *jihād* as promoter of action was sidelined to the benefit of peaceful action within the new social upheaval. The second period that began around the end of 2011 marked the crisis of the new Arab revolutions and the return of violence on the street in many countries. Jihadists were on the defensive, but found new opportunities within the crises of the Arab societies. The third period beginning around 2013 was that of a new thriving for Jihadist organisations, due to the civil war in Syria and the failed state in some countries like Libya and Yemen.

THE FIRST PERIOD OF THE ARAB UPRISINGS

The so-called Arab Spring changed the pattern of Islamic radicalisation in the region during the first year, in 2011, and even part of 2012. The Arab revolutions advocated new values, rooted in peaceful secularised Islamic notions that were in deep opposition to the Jihadist cultural values, like the dignity of the citizen (*karāma*) and peaceful political mobilisation (*salmiyya*). Before the

* L'École des hautes études en sciences sociales (EHESS)

1. The words 'Jihadism' and 'Islamic radicalism' or 'extremism' are used here as synonyms to designate those trends within Islam that justify violence in the name of *jihād* (the holy or just war).

downfall of the Tunisian and Egyptian autocracies, the Jihadist trend within Muslim countries was on the decline. Repression against Islamic radicals, but also the utter violence of the Jihadists and their lack of any constructive project for their host societies brought down their prestige. Their attacks against tourists and Muslims in Egypt, Jordan and elsewhere made them unpopular among many Muslims.

However, the major blow was administered to them by the Arab revolutions. The 'easy' fall of Tunisia and Egypt engendered an internal crisis among Jihadist circles, based on this common sense observation: in more than two decades they had been unable to bring down any Arab regime, whereas peaceful demonstrators had overthrown two major autocracies in less than a month (respectively, 28 and 18 days in Tunisia and Egypt). The Jihadist strategy, based mainly on massive violence and a small group of activists, was questioned: peaceful street demonstrations and 'leaderless' protestors were more successful than the violent promoters of a 'holy war', who did not succeed to topple any of the Arab regimes. Ayman al-Ẓawāhirī's words – 'There is no solution except through Jihād, all other solutions are futile. Rather, other solutions would only worsen the state of dilapidation and submissiveness in which we live; [purported solutions that exclude Jihād] are equivalent to treating cancer with aspirin.'[2] – became pointless in that period.

Besides that, two major setbacks were suffered by the Jihadists: the killing of Usāma bin Lādin on 2 May 2011 by American forces in Pakistan; and the assassination of Anwār al-Awlakī, the American-turned-Jihadist and one of the editors of a Jihadist electronic journal in English, *Inspire*, on 30 September 2011 by US drones in Yemen.[3] These two killings had a large symbolic impact on Jihadist circles around the world.

The first period of the Arab Spring, which extended to the end of 2011, had a devastating effect on Jihadist attraction in the Arab world, as much because it contradicted their pattern of action (mass killings by small groups of devoted radicals) as their ideas (*jihād*, universal caliphate, intransigent Islamist values). Through the new protest movements, the Arab street learned how to

2. Ayman al-Ẓawahiri, 'Ḥaqāʾiq al-Sirāʿ bayna al-Islām wa-l-Kufr' (audio speech), cited in Nelly Lahoud (with Muhammad al-'Ubaydi), 'Jihadi Discourse in the Wake of the Arab Spring', *Combatting Terrorism Center Reports*, December 2013 (online). References in this chapter to online materials (designated by '(online)') are listed in full in the bibliography (accessed dates for all online materials are explained in a note on p. 366 below).
3. Alexander Meleagrou-Hitchens, 'As American as Apple Pie: How Anwar al-Awlaki Became the Face of Western Jihad', *International Centre for the Study of Radicalisation and Political Violence Policy Reports*, September 2011 (online).

act non-violently in order to topple autocracies that the Jihadists had been incapable of overthrowing for many decades. In the first months of the uprising, symbolic places like Tahrir Square (Cairo), Taqyir Square (Sanaa) and the Pearl Roundabout (Manama) became foci for the apprenticeships of public actions that called into question the legitimacy of the radical Islamic model, which had been comprised of small groups, motivated by violent and spectacular actions, devised in secrecy within Jihadist circles. The pattern of mobilisation within these peaceful protest movements was thus frontally opposed to the Jihadist pattern of avant-garde action by self-proclaimed Islamist elites of warriors (*mujāhidīn*, those combatants who perform *jihād*). People learned to express their grievances and demands premised on the individuals' rights, in dire opposition to the Jihadist worldview, in which the individual has no right, only religious duties summarised in martyrdom, through which one achieves the status of an Islamic hero by fighting against the worldwide disbelievers.

THE SECOND PERIOD OF THE ARAB SPRING

From the second half of 2011, many Arab authoritarian regimes began to successfully put up new strategies against the seemingly irresistible wave of street demonstrations. The latter shook, for a while, the autocratic rulers in Yemen, Syria and Bahrain, and in some monarchies it did force the kings to make minimal concessions to the public demand by introducing new constitutions. These paid lip service to the aspiration for change, as was the case in Morocco (a referendum held on 1 July 2011 approved changes within the constitution that did not call into question the king's prerogatives).

After the downfall of the Tunisian and Egyptian regimes, no others were toppled as 'painlessly' as they were in the first month of 2011. The Libyan regime fell in August 2011 after many months of fighting, by the intervention of NATO and the assistance of European and some Arab countries (Saudi Arabia and Qatar). In Syria, after more than five years of street protest civil war, the Asad regime is still resisting, its overthrow not being on the agenda, due to the Russian and Iranian support and the Jihadist groups' involvement that pushes the Western countries to a *modus vivendi* with the regime. In this second period, the shattered autocracies gave birth to 'failed states', and their loosened repressive grip on society opened up new opportunities for the Jihadists. In Yemen, al-Qāᶜida affiliated groups emerged that were able to show continuity and perceptible presence in some parts of the country, from their stronghold in the south. In Syria, Jihadist groups originating from Iraq were able to show their teeth in terrorist attacks in the cities. Ayman al-Ẓawāhirī, the head of al-Qāᶜida after the elimination of Bin Lādin, addressed Syrians and urged Muslims to fight for their

Syrian brothers as well as Syrians themselves. He asserted: 'Wounded Syria is still bleeding day after day, and the butcher (Asad) isn't deterred and doesn't stop.'[4]

The Iraqi branch of al-Qāᶜida (the al-Qāᶜida in Iraq, AQI) carried out bombings in Damascus, the capital of Syria, and was probably behind various suicide bombings. The first attack occurred on 23 December 2011, in which at least forty-four people were killed and 160 wounded, and the second, on 6 January 2012, in which twenty-six people were killed in an attack against an intelligence agency compound. The bombings came on the orders of Ayman al-Ẓawāhirī.[5] AQI began operations in Syria, finding an opportunity to expand outside Iraq due to the crisis of the Asad regime after the popular uprising in March 2011. In both Iraq and Syria, the target is 'Shīᶜite power'; in Syria, the Asad regime being regarded as a Shīᶜite deviant sect in the eyes of the Jihadist Sunnis.

In Yemen, al-Qāᶜida's strongholds are in the south, but the organisation operates in many places, with partial or full al-Qāᶜida control in the towns of Jār, Radda, Shuqrah, Zinzibār, Ḥawta, Rawḍa and Azan. The Ṣāliḥ (Saleh) government used al-Qāᶜida as a scapegoat to dissuade the Western governments from supporting the civil movement against its autocratic rule. With Yemen, the poorest Arab country, being devoid of a credible government during the year 2011, al-Qāᶜida attacks intensified and extended to many parts of the country.[6] The fragmentation of the Yemeni state thus increased al-Qāᶜida's operational capability and its geographic extension in the country.[7]

In Libya, armed militia and the lack of a centralising government led to greater disorder and a fragmented power structure that encouraged the return of the Jihadists. The fact that many Jihadists had joined Libya after their release from prison in order to fight the Qadhdhāfī regime strengthened their ranks for future attacks inside and outside that country, some of them becoming prominent in the new political structure and renouncing violence, others looking for new opportunities to promote *jihād.*

In Egypt, during Mursī's rule (Mohamed Morsi, up to June 2013), the predominantly non-repressive attitude towards the Jihadists (they were supposed to

4. Cited in Joshua Landis, 'Al-Qaida Targets Syria', *joshualandis.com*, 14 February 2014 (online).
5. Jonathan S. Landay, 'US Officials: Al Qaida Behind Syria Bombings', *mcclatchydc.com*, 10 February 2012 (online).
6. The geographic spread of al-Qāᶜida is impressive, compared to January 2010. See the map 'Yemen Crackdown', *wikipedia.com* (online).
7. Frederick W. Kagan, 'Yemen Crisis Situation Report', *Critical Threat Project Reports*, 29 June 2011 (online).

become open to dialogue if not frontally repressed) gave them some leeway for taking roots and preparing for future actions.

Turning to the Sunni/Shīᶜite relations in the wider Muslim world, their strife was heightened following the invasion of Iraq by the United States and Great Britain in 2003. Before that date, killing and maiming Shīᶜites did not occur in Iraq on a large scale. In the sectarian strife, Jihadists found new opportunities to mobilise radicalised Sunnis against Shīᶜites.

A similar picture is seen within the crisis in Syria, where the Alawites (ᶜAlawiyya), considered a heretical Shīᶜite sect by many Sunnis, have ruled the country for many decades. The civil war within Syria has increased the antagonism between the two religious groups, amplifying mutual hatred and multiplying the violent self-defence among the Sunnis. The opposite happened in Iraq: the Sunnis, under Shīᶜite rule for the first time after the demise of Saddam Hussein, felt humiliated and reacted violently to what they considered to be Shīᶜite–American complicity; and then, after the departure of the Americans, the sectarian rule of Mālikī (Nouri al-Maliki) strengthened the radical Sunnis' legitimacy.

The dynamics of the new order pushed many Shīᶜites towards radicalisation, in particular in Bahrain, where the Sunni regime, supported by Saudi Arabia, denies political freedom to the Shīᶜite majority. In many emirates Shīᶜite are considered heretical Muslims and rejected by the Arab governments as the Trojan Horse of the Islamic Republic of Iran. The democratically minded Civil Society Movement – made up of a majority of Shīᶜite in Bahrain, but also many Sunnis who rejected the autocracy of the ruling monarchy – was crushed with the direct assistance of Saudi Arabia through the Cooperation Council for the Arab States of the Gulf (GCC) army in March 2011. The movement was framed by the government as a sectarian conflict, the government taking the side of the Sunni minority against the Shīᶜite majority.

More generally, authoritarian governments endeavoured to transform the civil society movements into sectarian clashes, in order to repress them with the complicity of broader society, as is the case in Syria, where the Assad government exploited Alawite/Sunni, Christian/Muslim, and Arab/Kurd divisions, successfully breaking down the protest movement for democracy.

THE THIRD PERIOD

In 2013, the crisis deepened in most of the Arab countries, due to the resistance of the autocratic governments and the assistance of the counter-revolutionary regimes to their client states. This included Saudi Arabia economically assisting the Egyptian regime after the military coup; militarily and financially supporting

Bahrain and proposing to integrate Morocco and other North African countries into the Cooperation Council for the Arab States of the Gulf; and Iran assisting the Asad regime, Hezbollah in Lebanon and Hamas in Gaza. In addition, the disintegration of the Arab uprisings under economic hardship and the radicalisation of the activists who acted more and more violently, as was the case in Egypt and Syria, called into the question the fundamentals of the Arab uprisings (non-violence, dignity of the citizen and the like). In Egypt and Syria, radicalisation occurred through different paths. In the other countries, like Yemen and Libya, the government suffered from the predicament of many failed states; the only country in transition to a democratic status being Tunisia (on 26 January 2014 Tunisia's National Constituent Assembly ratified a new secular constitution).

In Syria, the crisis deepened into a civil war, with the Asad regime killing and indiscriminately maiming the opposition (around 140,000 people killed on both sides), alternatively losing ground and regaining it through air and chemical bombings against numerous opponents divided into three main categories: the more or less secular Free Syrian Army, the 'legitimate Jihadist groups' (recognised by al-Qāᶜida), and the other Jihadists who do not recognise the legitimacy of Ayman al-Ẓawāhirī (which became Islamic State). Syria has also become a magnet that attracts Jihadists from all over the world; from Europe, around 1,000 young people have joined the Jihadist militia there.

In Egypt, the military coup in July 2013 and the subsequent killing of the Muslim Brotherhood members in street protests (culminating in the 14 August 2013 mass killing of 638 people, including forty-three police officers, according to the Ministry of Interior) made reconciliation with them impossible. Jihadist groups that had lost legitimacy in the first period of the Egyptian revolution vindicated the appropriateness of *jihād* in this period, due to the failure of the Muslim Brotherhood (MB) to remain in power: since moderate Muslims (the MB) were ousted from the government by the military, there was no other way than revolutionary violence sanctioned by Allah to establish Islamic rule. Jihadism attracted part of the MB youth, disappointed by the 'passive' attitude of the MB hierarchy towards the repression by the army. In particular, daily clashes with the security forces in Sinai carried on for many months after the military coup.

In Egypt and Tunisia, and in Libya and Yemen also, the changes introduced by the uprisings involved the freeing of many Jihadists from prison, either legally (being pardoned) or illegally (escaping during the period of turmoil). They joined, in some cases, the non-Jihadist forces for Islamisation from below (namely, the Salafis) or for changes through peaceful means (the MB), but a large number went either to other countries to promote *jihād* (primarily Libya and Syria) or remained home in order to build up new cells and prepare for the future violent action. The justification was that Egypt and Tunisia had become lands of proselytising and calling (*da*ᶜ*wā*), not *jihād*, during the rule of Ennahda (al-Nahda, in Tunisia) and MB (in Egypt). That was regarded as the second step in accordance with the Prophet's pattern of action, beginning with a call to join the ranks of the Muslims and followed by a war against the infidels. After the overthrow of Morsi's government in Egypt by the military and the toughening in Tunisia following the murder of two major political figures in 2013 by the Jihadists, the situation of mutual tolerance gave way to a new attitude on the part of the governments. In Tunisia, many people in the street demonstrations and in the security forces advocated military action against the radical Islamists. In Egypt, under Morsi's rule, the attacks on the security forces in Sinai were followed by military reprisal. After the coup, the military adopted a much tougher line against the Jihadists – in particular, in the Sinai desert – not hesitating to bomb their headquarters and kill their sympathisers.

YEMEN AS THE CASE OF A FAILED STATE AND ITS IMPACT ON JIHADISM

The Yemeni case can illustrate the failed state situation and the manner in which Jihadists exploit it. In this country, Islamist militants, directly linked to al-Qāᶜida, became much more active than before, in part due to the complacency of the Ṣāliḥ regime that intended to frighten the West and push it to their side by agitating the scapegoat of radical Islam, and in part due to the uprising in Yemen as part of the Arab revolutions. On 27 May 2011, around 300 Islamist militants attacked and captured the city of Zinjibār. They killed seven army personnel. The fighting with the army left a toll of around 800 people during the entire year.[8] On 4 March 2012, Jihadists launched an attack against the army on the outskirts of Zinjibār, killing 187 soldiers and wounding some 135 others, with thirty-two Jihadists being killed in the battle. The group called itself Anṣār al-Sharīᶜā, a new brand name for 'al-Qāᶜida in the Arabian Peninsula' (AQAP). The city of Lawdar was attacked by the Jihadists in early April. The army launched a massive military operation at the end of the same month, reaching the centre of Zinjibār after several days of intense fighting, with around fifty militants being killed, and eighty-five soldiers being captured by the Jihadist group.[9]

8. 'Suspected al Qaeda Militants Seize Yemeni Town', *france24.com*, 29 May 2011 (online); 'Eight Dead in South Yemen Violence: Security Officials', *news.egypt.com*, 27 May 2011 (online); 'AQAP Claims Responsibility for Yemen Attacks', *edition.cnn.com*, 8 March 2012 (online).
9. 'Huge Death Toll Doubles in Yemen "Slaughter"', *edition.cnn*, 14 May 2012; 'Heavy Yemeni Troop Losses Reported in Raid', *Aljazeera.com*, 8 March 2012 (online); 'Al-

After the departure of Ṣāliḥ in February 2012 and his replacement by ^{c}Abd Rabbih Manṣūr Hādī, new trends underlined the resiliency of the Yemen organisations tied to al-Qā^{c}ida. The city of Zinjibār was divided *de facto* into two parts: the Jihadists holding the western part of the city, while the army controlled the east of the city. The number of people displaced due to the fighting was estimated at around 97,000. On 31 March 2012, Islamist militants attacked an army checkpoint in Lāhīj governorate, killing twenty soldiers and capturing heavy weapons and at least two tanks.[10]

On 9 April, a group of Jihadists attacked Lawdar, with ninety-four people being killed in the attack, and the militants being driven out with the assistance of the local population. This was the third assault in recent months: two similar attacks in March had left more than 130 soldiers dead and seventy becoming prisoners of the al-Qā^{c}ida groups.[11] On 10 April, the fighting raised the number of dead to 124 in two days, including 102 militants, fourteen soldiers and more than eight civilians. Among the Jihadists dead there were twelve Somalis and some Saudis, demonstrating the transnational character of the Anṣār al-Sharī^{c}a. Planes bombed the areas near Lawdār and the road to Zinjibār, with fifty-one people being killed, most of them from al-Qā^{c}ida.[12] On 13 April, the fighting was still raging around the city, spreading to Mudiyya, the only town apart from Lawdār that the Jihadists did not control in the area.[13] Fighting resumed on 18 April, with many cases of suicide car bombing being reported; the government responding with air strikes and shelling.[14] In other parts of Yemen, a checkpoint was assaulted in Aden, killing four soldiers, and with eight attackers dying in the event. The town of Radda, south of the capital Sanā^{c}a, was briefly occupied by the Jihadists, before being taken back by the government forces a week later. On 21 May 2012, a soldier detonated a suicide bomb in a crowd of military personnel gathered together for a rehearsal for the Unity Day Parade in Sanā^{c}a, killing ninety-six people and wounding more than 200. AQAP claimed responsibility

Qaida Says It Captures 70 Yemeni Soldiers in Abyan's Battle', *chinadaily.com.cn*, 5 March 2012 (online).

10. Mohammed Mukhashaf, 'Qaeda-Linked Militants Kill at Least 20 Yemeni Soldiers', *reuters.com*, 31 March 2012 (online).
11. Ahmed Al-Haj, 'Yemen: 44 Killed in Clashes With al-Qā^{c}ida Fighters', *washingtontimes.com*, 9 April 2012 (online).
12. '133 Killed in Qaeda Violence in Yemen', *khaleejtimes.com*, 10 April 2012.
13. 'Toll Hits 200 in Battle With Qaeda for Yemen Town', *france24.com*, 13 April 2012 (online).
14. Ahmed Al-Haj, 'South Yemen Violence Kills 2 Children, 6 Militants', *newsok.com*, 18 April 2012 (online).

for the attack.[15] On 12 December 2013, the fighting between the Hūthīs (Houthis, a dissident Shīᶜite group) and the radical Sunnis in the north left forty people dead after the Salafis took over a Houthi stronghold in the strategic area close to Saudi Arabia.[16] On 16 January 2014, Jihadists killed ten Yemeni soldiers in three simultaneous attacks in Rada, with eight militants being killed.[17] The US drone attacks on the Jihadists began in November 2002, with the approval of the Yemen government. Like all the drone attacks, the 'collateral damage' sometimes benefitted the radical groups. In May 2014, a drone attack against the al-Qāᶜida members in Wadī ᶜAbīda killed five people, among them the deputy governor of the province, who was mediating between the government and the Jihadists. His killing angered his tribesmen, the Shabwānīs, who attacked the government security forces and the oil pipeline in Maᶜārib.[18] As in Pakistan and Afghanistan, in spite of the government complicity, the Yemeni government demanded the suspension of the drone attacks. Suspected drone attacks on April 2012 in Shabwa and Abyān provinces, predominantly under the control of the Jihadists, were launched by the US, killing at least nine militants.[19] On 30 September 2011, Anwār al Awlakī, the prominent American–Yemeni al-Qāᶜida member, was killed by a US drone strike. It killed him and another significant Jihadist figure, Samīr Khān, as well as few other militants who were in the same car.

The Yemeni case demonstrates the complex nature of the Jihadists' action within a society where the tribal order, the government's clientelist structure and the ambitions of a leader are all in the mix (President Ṣālih reluctantly gave up power in February 2012, after having weakened the government through his multiple manipulations). Added to this are the geopolitics of *jihād* involving the US and the Saudi governments and the capacity for renewal of the Jihadists. AQAP changed its name to Anṣār al-Sharīᶜa, probably in order to attract the pious rural population of Yemen, exploiting the government weakness due to the protest movements during the Arab uprising by establishing themselves in a few towns for longer periods of time. By doing this, they marked their capacity to be more than mere fighting groups; they were able to dominate both urban areas and their rural hinterland for many months.

15. 'Al-Qaeda Claims Deadly Yemen Suicide Blast', *aljazeera.com*, 21 May 2012 (online).
16. 'Sectarian Clashes Kill at Least 40 in Yemen', *ahram.org*, 12 December 2013 (online).
17. 'Militants Kill 10 Soldiers in Central Yemen', *arabamericannews.com*, 17 January 2014 (online).
18. 'Drones Spur Yemenis' Distrust of Government and U.S.', *reuters.com*, 27 October 2010 (online).
19. '"US Drone Strike" Kills 5 Qaeda Militants in Yemen', *dailynewsegypt.com*, 17 April 2012 (online).

2013 AS A SEMINAL YEAR FOR JIHADISM

On the whole, 2012 and, more significantly, 2013 were propitious years for al-Qāᶜida and other Jihadist groups, due to the deep ongoing crisis of the Arab revolutions. In Iraq, Jihadist violence attained the highest levels since 2007. In northern Syria, some cities fell under their control. Jailbreaks were successful in three countries in less than two weeks. On 21 July 2013, 500 prisoners from the notorious Abu Ghraib prison were freed, with many Jihadists amongst them. On 28 July, 1,117 inmates from Benghazi's Kuafiya prison in Libya were freed, as a result of a Jihadist attack, according to Interpol. On 30 July, in Pakistan (a non-Arab country where al-Qāᶜida is powerful), around 250 prisoners escaped in a prison break, among them many Jihadists.[20]

Following the killing of two prominent political figures by Jihadists in Tunisia, the fight was exacerbated between the security forces and the Jihadists – despite denials of involvement by Anṣār al-Sharīᶜa. Eight Tunisian soldiers were killed by the Jihadists in an ambush in July 2013.

In Egypt, Jihadist networks like al-Furqān Brigades, Anṣār Bayt al-Maqdis and al-Jamal network increased their activities after the military coup in July 2013. From a land of *daᶜwā* (proselytising and appeal to join the Muslim militants peacefully), Egypt became a land of active *jihād*. Jihadist veterans, freed from jail after the demise of Mubārak or escaping through jailbreaks in recent years in the other Arab countries, appear to have flocked to Sinai, many from Yemen, Somalia, Algeria and Libya.[21] Crossing the borders became easier for them as the intelligence services had almost collapsed in many Arab countries after the uprisings. Prison escape and the freeing of the veteran Jihadists filled the vacuum between two generations of Islamist militants, the more experienced ones coming to the assistance of the younger recruits, and then acting as magnets to attract new candidates. For example, Ramzī Muwāfī, an Egyptian physician close to Bin Lādin, and Muḥammad Jamal al-Kāshif were captured by the Egyptian security forces in 2012. Some of the Muslim Brotherhood, particularly the younger elements of the movement, desperate at the sight of the military repression against them, joined the Jihadists, with Sinai becoming a major battleground, due to its closeness to the Israeli border and because it is inhabited by poor Bedouins, resistant to the central government.

20. David Gartenstein-Ross, 'A Momentous Month', *Atlantic Council*, 5 August 2013 (online).
21. Jamie Dettmer, 'Egypt's Newest Jihadists: The Jamal Network', 1 November, *thedaily beast.com*, 13 January 2013 (online).

THE SECTARIAN STRIFE AND THE RENEWAL OF JIHADISM

The Arab revolutions reactivated the Jihadist trend through three main factors. First and foremost, some countries suffered the predicament of the failed states: Libya, Yemen and Syria. The latter became also a major theatre of a bloody civil war, claiming the lives of around 140,000 people in the first two years. The second factor was the turmoil caused by the Arab revolutions; the crisis of power made possible many Jihadists' escape or the remission of their sentences by the authorities. In Tunisia, Egypt and Libya, many hundreds of Jihadists were set free, galvanising the radical Islamist movements that were joined by the experienced persons who had field experience and could fight efficiently on the ground. At the same time, the Muslim Brotherhood style governments that took the reins of power in Tunisia (Ennahda) or in Egypt (Muslim Brotherhood) believed that Jihadists could be convinced to join their moderate view of Islam and that they would renounce violence if given the opportunity to act legally within the prevailing framework. Therefore, there was a *de facto* tolerance of them; Jihadists used this indulgence in order to take root in many areas or bolster their base. This is what happened in Tunisia, where they firmly established themselves in the poor districts around Tunis and in the poor areas (mainly the centre and south) of Tunisia.

The third factor was revival of sectarianism through the opposition between the Sunnis and the Shīᶜites. It began long before the Arab uprisings, after the invasion of Iraq by the American and English armies in 2003. Before that date, there was no major sectarian strife in Iraq. The overthrow of Saddam Hussein and the handover of power to Shīᶜites pushed the Sunnis towards the Jihadists. General Petraeus' policy of buying a Sunni clientele and opposing it to the Jihadists partially worked, until the American army pulled out and Nuri al-Maliki was elected as the prime minister in May 2006. The latter alienated many Sunnis and rekindled the Jihadists' legitimacy among them. Since then, the al-Qāᶜida in Iraq (AQI) and its recent incarnation, the Islamic State of Iraq and Syria (ISIS) or the Islamic State of Iraq and the Levant (ISIL), rose not so much in opposition to America, as opposing Maliki's policies of excluding the Sunnis from power. It also resulted in the partial domination of the Jihadists in some districts of the cities of Fallujah and Ramadi in 2014.[22]

In Syria, the Asad regime, rooted in the Alawite community – a dissident Shīᶜite minority (constituting around 12 per cent of the population) – harshly

22. Anthony H. Cordesman, 'The "Rise" of Al Qaeda in Iraq and the Threat from Prime Minister Maliki', *Center for Strategic and International Studies Comment*, 13 January 2014 (online).

repressed the protesters, treating them as Sunni terrorists allied to the Jihadists. They did not, at the beginning, assert any Sunni identity, their main slogan being: 'Neither Sunni, nor Shīᶜite, only Syrian!'. Geopolitics played a role in this situation: Saudi Arabia came to the defence of the Sunnis; Qatar to the Muslim Brotherhood; Iran to the Shīᶜites; Russia sided with the Asad regime; the West provided assistance to the non-Islamist opposition to Asad (mainly the so-called Free Syrian Army). The civil strife took on multiple dimensions: sectarian (Sunni versus Shīᶜite), ethnic (Kurd versus Arab), secular versus Jihadist (Free Syrian Army versus Jihadist groups like Jabhat al-Nuṣra (JN), among others) and inter-Jihadist fighting (warring between radical Salafist factions like ISIS on the one hand, Aḥrār al-Shām and JN on the other). The last of these factors has developed into one of the most violent clashes between the Jihadists – in particular, in Deir al-Zour (Dayr al-Zūr) and al-Hasāka, and on a smaller scale in rural Aleppo and Raqqa (in January 2014), with a toll of many hundreds dead.[23] Zawāhirī took sides and condemned ISIS, ordering its withdrawal to Iraq, but they took no notice.

In Yemen, with the weakening of the government, AQAP emerged over the past few years as the most active group, claiming allegiance to Ayman al-Ẓawāhirī. The group has its origins before the Arab uprisings, beginning in 2009, when the Yemeni and the Saudi branches of al-Qāᶜida merged.[24]

Jihadism in Egypt resulted in the presence of hundreds of Egyptians in Syria, a major battlefield where Islamic extremism is thriving. Those who choose to fight in Syria do so for sectarian reasons: fighting against the 'heretical' regime of (Shīᶜite) Asad, rather than declaring *jihād* in their own homeland. Some have become 'professional revolutionaries', like Abū Aḥmad, in his early thirties, who fought the Mubārak regime in Egypt and then was drawn to the holy war in Syria.[25]

On the whole, the crisis of the Arab uprisings contributed to the internationalisation of *jihād*; many people flocked towards those Arab countries where the fight against the 'impious' governments could be launched by the militants.

23. Daniel Abdallah, 'Inter-Rebel Fighting Enters a New Phase as Salafists Declare Open War on ISIS', *joshualandis.com*, 14 February 2014 (online).
24. 'Profile: al Qaeda in the Arabian Peninsula', *aljazeera.com*, English, 9 May 2012.
25. Mohamed Fadel Fahmy, 'Egyptian Fighters Join "Lesser Jihad" in Syria', *al-monitor.com*, 17 April 2013 (online).

THE INVIGORATION OF THE WESTERN JIHADISM UNDER THE IMPACT OF THE ARAB CRISIS

The civil war in Syria had an unexpected consequence: the influx of many young Muslims from the West and particularly Europe into Syria, to fight under the banner of the radical Islamist groups against the Asad regime. The numbers are uncertain, but in January 2014, according to the French authorities, some 250 Frenchmen fought in Syria, more than twenty of them having perished in the combat zones. According to Belgian experts, more than 200 nationals were involved in *jihād* in Syria, more than twenty of them having died in the battle zones. From Germany, more than 270 were fighting in Syria, fifteen of them having died there. At least 200 British fighters were involved in *jihād* in Syria. Two Jihadist groups, JN and ISIS, are the major recipients of the young European Jihadists.[26] On the whole, according to the International Centre for the Study of Radicalisation, an estimated number of between 3,300 to 11,000 foreign fighters were in Syria by the end of 2013, the majority on the side of the Jihadist groups.[27] The major difference between the Western Jihadists in Syria and those who perpetrate violence in Europe is that the former have, at the outset, a strong 'humanitarian' urge, coupled with a strong view of the Asad regime in terms of sectarianism (Shīᶜite and therefore not legitimate Muslims). Once on the spot in Syria, they are indoctrinated by the radical Islamist groups in order to become staunch Jihadists. Those who operate in Europe consider their native country (or those in which they have grown up) as heretical and anti-Islamic, and their violence is directed towards their home country and not outside it. The young people, Muslims or converts, who go to Syria do not at first consider Europe as a battlefield for *jihād*, and their ire is directed towards the 'infidel' regime of Asad, who kills genuine Muslims (Sunnis) and belongs to a fake Muslim sect (the Alawites).

Many young men from France,[28] Germany,[29] Denmark,[30] England[31] and North Africa fight in Syria. Journalists have described their adventures and given

26. See the numbers based on the AFP report of Pierre-Marie Giraud, 'Swelling Ranks of European Fighters in Syria Sparks Concern', *yourmiddleeast.com*, 23 January 2014.
27. ICSR, 'Up To 11000 Foreign Fighters in Syria: Steep Rise Among Western Europeans', *International Centre for the Study of Radicalisation and Political Violence*, 17 December 2013 (online).
28. Christophe Cornevin, 'L'inquiétant profil des djihadistes français en Syrie', *lefigaro.fr*, 13 September 2013 (online).
29. Kurt Pelda, 'Fodder for the Front: German Jihadists on Syria's Battlefields', *spiegel.de*, 30 April 2013 (online).
30. 'Danish Jihadist Reportedly Killed in Syria', *cphpost.com*, 13 January 2014 (online).
31. Tom Porter, 'UK Jihadists Join Fight in Iraq', *ibtimes.com*, 12 January 2014.

sometimes a more or less romanticised picture of their fighting, thereby alerting the authorities, but also unintentionally pushing other young men to choose the Jihadist pathway. Besides Europeans, around 1,000 young men from Tunisia, some of them with ties in France, are fighting the holy war in land of 'Sham' (Syria).

European Jihadists find themselves in national brigades, the English together as well as the French or the Germans, due to the linguistic problems (most of them do not master Arabic).[32] This togetherness during the war strengthens their ties, and their friendship can be put at the service of *jihād* once back home.

The return of the European Jihadists to Europe will pose many problems, besides the trauma of the war zone, their ideological tenet and their capacity to fabricate bombs and their general military capability giving them a major role in the *jihād*, in comparison to the so-called 'homegrown Jihadists', who mostly behave in an amateurish fashion in terms of making bombs or technical devices.

CONCLUSION

Broadly speaking, at its outset the Arab Spring marginalised the Jihadist trend in the Arab world. Even before the demise of Bin ᶜAlī in Tunisia and Mubārak in Egypt, radical Islam had undergone a visible decline, due to repression by Western and Muslim countries, but also because of their lack of any positive project that might go beyond the mere violence of the 'enemy'. Besides that, Jihadists had shown their willingness to put to death fellow Muslims, and the number of Muslims killed by them was by far greater than non-Muslims in their terrorist attacks.

The Arab revolutions brought a whole new set of ideological concepts based on secular values, such as 'the dignity of the citizen' and 'peacefulness'. These became significant values, in contradiction to the violence-prone radical Islam and the denial of the citizen's rights in the name of a rigid Islamic community (the *neo-Ummah*), cherished by the Jihadists.

The values of the new generations and their cultural tendencies were in absolute contradiction to radical Islam. But the crisis of the new revolutionary movements opened up new opportunities for Jihadist groups. Failed states like the Ṣāliḥ regime in Yemen or the weakened dictatorships initiating civil war like the Asad regime in Syria made it possible for radical Islamists to develop new

32. Stuart Ramsey, 'Syria: Sky News Gains Access to UK Jihadists', *news.sky.com*, 18 December 2013 (online); Benjamin Weinthal, 'The German Jihadists' Colony in Syria', *longwarjournal.org*, 19 December 2013 (online); Paule Gonzales, 'Le recrutement de jeunes djihadistes pour la Syrie, c'est l'usine', *lefigaro.com*, 17 January 2014 (online).

strategies, using the power vacuum or state crises as a ground for their violent action. Jihadists also found a vindication of their violent strategy through the military coup in Egypt that signalled, according to them, the denial of Islamic rule, even a peaceful and democratic one, by the secular people under the spell of the 'Crusaders' (the Western imperialists) and the 'Zionists' (Israel and all those who support it). The rule of the Muslim Brotherhood and Ennahda benefitted the Jihadists as well, who were sometimes tempted or forced by the governments to join the ranks of the non-violent Islamists. Jihadism found a major opportunity in Syria through the civil war, as hordes of Jihadists from all over the world, and in particular Europe, joined the radical Islamist groups for the sake of fighting the infidel regime of Asad.

At its beginnings, the Arab uprisings pushed Jihadism to the sidelines. The deepening crisis of many Arab countries in the following years changed the relationship to Jihadism; late 2012 and, more pronouncedly, 2013 were the years when fortunes changed: the latter prospered on the ruins of the Arab revolutions, opening up a new phase in the tortuous pathways of the Islamic holy war in the world at large.

CHAPTER

10

THE LOGIC OF THE CONQUEST SOCIETY: ISIS, APOCALYPTIC VIOLENCE AND THE 'REINSTATEMENT' OF SLAVE CONCUBINAGE

*Omar Anchassi**

INTRODUCTION[1]

> Thumāma b. Ashras . . . held that taking women from the Abode of Unbelief as slave-concubines is unlawful, and that whoever has sex with such a captive woman is a fornicator, any [resultant] child illegitimate (*walad zinā*).[2]
>
> Abū l-Muẓaffar al-Isfarayīnī (d. 471/1078)

> . . . precisely in such epochs of revolutionary crisis they anxiously conjure up the spirits of the past to their service, borrowing from them names, battle slogans, and costumes in order to present this new scene in world history in time-honoured disguise and borrowed language.[3]
>
> Karl Marx (d. 1300/1883)

The past is an interminable source of legitimation. It is invoked, appealed to and mobilised to confute competing claims and to demonstrate the correctness of

* University of Edinburgh

1. Most of the research for this chapter was undertaken during a stint as a postdoctoral researcher at the University of Exeter on the USPPIP (Understanding Sharīᶜa: Past Perfect, Imperfect Present) Project, funded by a grant from HERA. I thank Professor Rob Gleave for his exemplary mentorship during (and beyond) this period of my career.

2. Abū al-Muẓaffar al-Isfarayīnī, *al-Tabṣīr fī l-dīn wa tamyīz al-firqa al-nājiya ᶜan al-firaq al-hālikīn* ed. Majīd al-Khalīfa (Beirut, 1429/2008), p. 269.
3. Karl Marx, *The Eighteenth Brumaire of Louis Bonaparte*, (marxists.org/archive/marx/works/1852/18th-brumaire/ch01.htm, accessed 2 June 2020). For accessed dates of online resources, see the Bibliography and the accompanying note, p. 366.

one's own. In writing to justify the revival of slave concubinage, Turkī al-Binᶜalī (d. 1438/2017), the chief jurisconsult of ISIS and the author of a treatise on the subject, dismissed alternative views as opposed to 'the Qurʾān, the *Sunna*, and consensus'. He charged that the only people to entertain the unlawfulness of the institution were 'some Modernists (*baᶜḍ al-ᶜaṣrāniyyīn wa l-ḥadāthiyyīn*)'.[4] The counter-example of Thumāma (d. 213/828), then, ought to give one pause. We do know of premoderns who despised slavery *qua* slavery;[5] is it conceivable that this *éminence grise* of the Maʾmūnid court objected to the sexual use of female captives? On inspection, it turns out that he was nothing if not a rigorist: the Ashᶜarite theologian ᶜAbd al-Qāhir al-Baghdādī (d. 429/1037–8) reports that Thumāma refused to recognise the legitimacy of the 'Abode of Islam', owing to the prevalence of unbelief therein (rendering it a *dār shirk*).[6] Al-Isfarayīnī points to this as the cause of his idiosyncratic take on the question. Slavery and the closely related institution of concubinage were ubiquitous in early Islamic society, so this absence of condemnation from Thumāma is hardly surprising. He himself, the heresiographers acerbically note, was the outcome of such a union. Van Ess observes that his patrilineal Arab descent was, in remote Khurāsān, a source of personal pride, obviously emphasised in self-defence.[7]

The excavation of past opinion, the example of Thumāma notwithstanding,

4. *Al-Sabī: aḥkām wa masāʾil* (Dīwān al-buḥūth wa l-iftāʾ, 1435/2014), p. 6. On the biography of al-Binᶜalī, see Cole Bunzel, 'Wahhabism, Saudi Arabia, and the Islamic State: 'Abdullah Ibn Jibrin and Turki al-Bin'ali', in *Salman's Legacy: The Dilemmas of a New Era in Saudi Arabia*, ed. Madawi al-Rasheed (London, 2018), pp. 183–313 (pp. 190–3). See also Bunzel, 'The Caliphate's Scholar-in-Arms' (www.jihadica.com/the-caliphate's-scholar-in-arms/). On the infighting that led to the marginalisation of al-Binᶜalī, see Bunzel, 'Ideological Infighting in the Islamic State', *Perspectives on Terrorism* 13.1 (2019), 13–22 (esp. pp. 16–17). For two other well-known justifications of slavery in the ISIS literature, see 'The Revival of Slavery Before the Hour', *Dabiq* 4 (Dhū l-Ḥijja 1435), 14–17 and 'Slave-Girls or Prostitutes?', *Dabiq* 9 (Shaᶜbān 1436), 44–9.
5. For example, Gregory of Nyssa (d. 394), who argued that it was immoral to so treat those made in the *imago Dei*: Jonathan A. C. Brown, *Slavery and Islam* (Oxford: Oneworld, 2019), p. 188.
6. ᶜAbd al-Qāhir al-Baghdādī, *Al-Milal wa l-niḥal*, ed. Albert Nader (Beirut, 1986), p. 123. See also the discussion in Josef van Ess, *Theology and Society in the Second and Third Centuries of the Hijra: Volume 3* (Leiden, 2018), pp. 180–1. Van Ess has compiled much of the material on Thumāma's views (except for the sources cited here) in *Theologie und Gesellschaft im. 2. Und 3. Jahrhundert Hidschra: Band V* (Berlin, 1993), pp. 345–52.
7. Van Ess, *Theology and Society: Volume 3*, p. 173. ᶜAbd al-Qāhir uses the customary term of abuse, referring to Thumāma as a *hajīn* or 'mixed race' person (*al-Milal*, p. 123). Al-Isfarayīnī, probably drawing on ᶜAbd al-Qāhir, denounces this doctrine as a 'confession of his bastardy': *iqrār minhu bi-annahu min walad al-zinā* (*al-Tabṣīr*, p. 269). He claims that Thumāma was a non-Arab client (*mawlā*) of the Numayrids.

is more than an exercise in antiquarianism, especially where ISIS is concerned. The deployment of precedent was very much part of the ideological fabric of the short-lived, self-proclaimed caliphate. Useful work has been done on tracing elements of this purported continuity.[8] Numerous commentators have also called attention to the importance of apocalypticism as part of the movement's 'brand', a phenomenon with a very long history in Islamdom.[9] As Marx would recognise, however, continuity – while important – can conceal great rupture. Danton, Robespierre and other revolutionaries, he writes, 'performed the task of *their* time' (emphasis mine), as it were, though garbed 'in Roman costumes' and making use of 'Roman phrases'.[10] It would clearly be a mistake to ignore the significant divergences between the revolutionary propaganda of, say, the Hāshimites in the second/eighth century and the highly choreographed public appearance of Abū Bakr al-Baghdādī (d. 1441/2019) in his inaugural sermon of July 2014. One should recognise these departures, while remaining sensitive to the evocativeness of the wardrobe (ᶜAbbāsid black)[11] and rhetoric (the first caliphal *khuṭba* reported of Abū Bakr, d. 13/634) of Ibrāhīm ᶜAwwād al-Badrī, Abū Bakr al-Baghdādī. Even his name, the adoption of a *kunya* (teknonym) and *nisba* (affiliation), is emblematic of this evocatory style: neither of these retain any legal significance in modern Middle Eastern states.[12] They are carefully cultivated archaisms.

8. Including David J. Wasserstein's *Black Banners of ISIS: The Roots of the New Caliphate* (New Haven, 2017). On the place of ISIS in the genealogy of Wahhābism generally, see Cole Bunzel, 'From Paper State to Caliphate: The Ideology of the Islamic State', Brookings Foundation: U.S. Relations with the Muslim World, No. 19, March 2015, available online at www.brookings.edu/research/from-paper-state-to-caliphate-the-ideology-of-the-islamic-state/.
9. This element is emphasised in Graeme Wood's *The Way of the Strangers: Encounters with the Islamic State* (London, 2017), pp. 246–69 (esp. pp. 249–64). See also William McCants, *The ISIS Apocalypse: The History, Strategy and Doomsday Vision of the Islamic State* (New York, 2015), pp. 99–120, also pp. 142–7, 163–81.
10. www.marxists.org/archive/marx/works/1852/18th-brumaire/ch01.htm.
11. Hilāl al-Ṣābiʾ, *Rusūm Dār al-Khilāfah: The Rules and Regulations of the ᶜAbbāsid Court*, trans. Ellie A. Salem (Beirut, 1975), p. 73. The use of black banners features prominently in premodern apocalyptic literature – for example, the *Kitāb al-Fitan* of Nuᶜaym b. Ḥammād al-Marwazī (d. 228/843–4), recently translated by David Cook. I cite this in preference to the existing Arabic editions as it is properly critical, being based on the three published editions and one manuscript. See *'The Book of Tribulations': The Syrian Muslim Apocalyptic Tradition, An Annotated Translation* (Edinburgh, 2019), pp. 155, 174–80. See also McCants, *The ISIS Apocalypse*, pp. 25–7.
12. Wasserstein notes this occurs much more commonly as a given name (*ism*) than a teknonym in biographical dictionaries, see Wasserstein, *Black Banners*, p. 221.

This article attempts to strike a balance between a number of concerns – namely, what one is to make of ISIS's 'reinstatement' of slave concubinage; and what, if anything, this owes to the past. We begin with some remarks on warfare and the social logic of slave concubinage in pre- and early Islamic society to establish a context for comparative purposes. We then devote some attention to exploring the relevance of apocalypticism in ISIS propaganda, along with its strategic deployment of symbolic violence. After a brief excursus on ISIS's regulation of slave concubinage, we turn to address the treatise *al-Sabī: aḥkām wa masāʾil* ('Slave concubinage: rulings and [legal] issues') at length, exploring its sources and the author al-Binᶜalī's engagement with the premodern juristic tradition.

I. WARFARE AND SLAVE CONCUBINAGE IN PRE- AND EARLY ISLAMIC SOCIETY

They did not give us – the [men of Ṭayy] – their daughters in marriage;
But [rather,] we wooed them against their wills with our swords.[13]

Intertribal violence was a fact of life in pre-Islamic Arabia. This often took the form of raiding for booty, prominently womenfolk. Sexual abduction (*ghaṣb*) was an alternative to contracting marriage by payment of a dowry (*nikāḥ*). A captive woman found her existing marital ties dissolved and she became a *sabīya*, liable to redistribution among the men of the victorious tribe.[14] One notes, incidentally, that the jurists were divided on whether the pre-existing marriages of couples seized together remained intact.[15] In any case, reference to the enslavement of women in raids is found throughout the *Ayyām al-ᶜarab* ('Battle-days of the Arabs') corpus, with the suggestion that the resulting offspring became part of the dominant group. As ᶜAmr b. Kulthūm proclaims: 'How often shalt thou see among us the son of a captive bride:/who staunchly thrusts

13. The *muᶜallaqa* of ᶜAmr b. Kulthūm, cited by Hina Azam, *Sexual Violation in Islamic Law: Substance, Evidence, and Procedure* (New York, 2015), p. 55. It also occurs in *al-Sabī*, p. 3. On the appropriation of pre-Islamic poetry by militant groups, see Elisabeth Kendall, 'Jihadist Propaganda and its Exploitation of the Arab Poetic Tradition', in *Reclaiming Islamic Tradition: Modern Interpretations of the Classical Heritage*, eds Elisabeth Kendall and Ahmad Khan (Edinburgh, 2018), pp. 223–46 (at pp. 229–30).
14. Azam, *Sexual Violation*, pp. 54–5.
15. See the discussion in *al-Sabī*, pp. 22–4, according to which the Ḥanafites and Ḥanbalites maintain these marriages intact, while the Mālikites and Shāfiᶜites (among others) hold them to be dissolved by virtue of captivity.

through heroes when he meets them in the fight'.[16] Ironically, then, the children of enslaved womenfolk contributed to the fighting strength of the tribe, augmenting its power and prestige. Beginning in the Prophet's lifetime, this and related practices of war came to be reshaped by the new religious ethos. The notion of *nuṣra* ('mutual support'), for example, lost much of its purely tribal character and was increasingly associated with religiously inspired solidarity: 'if they seek your aid for the sake of religion (*istanṣarūkum fī l-dīn*), then it is your duty to help them . . . (*fa ʿalaykum al-naṣr*, Q8:72)'.[17] Goldziher notes more broadly the 'strong and unreconcilable [sic] difference in respect of the social order between the attitude of Arab paganism and the teachings of Islam'.[18]

Much scholarship has tracked the transformation of Jāhilī institutions in the early Islamic period. Increasingly, efforts have been directed towards situating these developments in their Late Antique context.[19] *Ghazw* (raiding), previously aimed at despoiling the tribal enemy and integrating captive womenfolk into one's kinship group, grew into the more ambitious and evidently confessional warfare of the *jihād*, 'one of the best attested facts in early Muslim history'.[20] There is very little, indeed, to commend the thesis of Juan Cole that the Conquests represent a perversion of the Prophet's teaching.[21] As the

16. Azam, *Sexual Violation*, p. 55.
17. M. M. Bravmann, *The Spiritual Background of Early Islam: Studies in Ancient Arabian Concepts*, intro. Andrew Rippin (Leiden, 2009), pp. 66–72. Al-Ṭabarī (d. 310/923) glosses the phrase *fī l-dīn* 'that is, if they invoke your help by virtue of belonging to your religion (*bi-annahum min ahli dīnikum*), against your mutual enemies among the pagans': *Tafsīr al-Ṭabarī*, ed. Bashshār Maʿrūf and ʿIṣām al-Ḥarastānī (Beirut, 1415/1994), IV, p. 68.
18. *Muslim Studies*, trans. C. R. Barber and S. M. Stern (New Brunswick, NJ, 2006 repr. of vol. I), p. 45.
19. One excellent recent example of the former is Nurit Tsafrir, *Collective Liability in Islam: The ʿĀqila and Blood-Money Payments* (Cambridge, 2020), pp. 1–4, 10–17. For the latter, as it relates to the question of violence specifically, see Thomas Sizgorich, *Violence and Belief in Late Antiquity: Militant Devotion in Christianity and Islam* (Philadelphia, 2011), pp. 153–6, 161–7.
20. Khalid Blankinship, *The End of the Jihād State: The Reign of Hishām Ibn ʿAbd al-Malik and the Collapse of the Umayyads* (Albany, 1994), p. 11. His summary of the doctrine and its implications remains the best in the literature: pp. 11–19. On the religious elements of *Jāhilī* warfare, see Reuven Firestone, 'Divine Authority and Territorial Entitlement in the Hebrew Bible and the Qur'an', in *Twenty-First Century Jihad: Law, Society and Military Action*, eds Elisabeth Kendall and Ewan Stein (London, 2015), pp. 45–69 (at pp. 54, 57).
21. Juan Cole, *Muhammad: Prophet of Peace Amid the Clash of Empires* (New York, 2018), pp. 199–205. Cole's scepticism is arbitrary, leading him to reject as fabricated whatever elements of the *sīra-maghāzī* tradition undermine his argument. As Fred Donner has pointed out: 'The Islamic conquest cannot be viewed . . . as something separate from the

Caliphate came to dominate much of the known world shortly after the death of the Prophet, the Arab Muslims formed a conquest elite, settled for the most part in newly established garrison cities (*amṣār*) and living off the stipends garnered from the tribute of subject populations. The conquest elite constituted a tiny minority of the population of the Near East,[22] but they were soon joined by others; peasants fleeing poverty, non-Muslims of elite status, and slaves in great profusion. These persons' integration into Muslim society, such as it was, took place through conversion, clientage and, no less importantly, the institution of the *umm al-walad* (literally, 'mother of the child'– that is, the slave mother of the master's child). After some fierce debate that has left its traces in the earliest legal literature, Sunnī jurists more or less agreed by the close of the formative period that these 'mothers of children' (*ummahāt al-awlād*) could not be sold.[23] This made it a much more secure (if slow) form of emancipation than *mukātaba* (contractual release in exchange for payment), and to a lesser extent *tadbīr* (manumission on the master's death).[24] The prohibition on the sale of *ummahāt al-awlād*, like many an Islamic innovation, is often attributed to ᶜUmar b. al-Khaṭṭāb (d. 23/644), which may be why (as with the prohibition of *mutᶜa*) Twelver jurists dissented.[25] Though the children of these unions did encoun-

career of Muḥammad the Apostle . . . it must be seen as an organic outgrowth from the Prophet's teachings and their impact on Arabian society': *The Early Islamic Conquests* (Princeton, 1981), p. 90. For an illuminating discussion of the earliest non-Muslim sources and how they might be utilised to reconstruct early Islamic doctrine on this point, see Sean W. Anthony, *Muhammad and the Empires of Faith: The Making of the Prophet of Islam* (Oakland, CA, 2020), pp. 42–54.

22. This has been emphasised by Jack Tannous, *The Making of the Medieval Middle East: Religion, Society, and Simple Believers* (Princeton, 2018), p. 350.
23. Ibn Kathīr (d. 774/1373) documents eight opinions on the question in his *Juzʾ fī bayᶜ ummahāt al-awlād*, ed. ᶜUmar b. Sulaymān al-Ḥafyān (Beirut, 1427/2006), ranging from categorical prohibition (pp. 46–8) to categorical permissibility (i.e. *jawāz bayᶜ ummahāt al-awlād muṭlaqan*, pp. 93–4). For a discussion of this essay, see Younus Mirza, 'Remembering the Umm Walad: Ibn Kathir's Treatise on the Sale of the Concubine', in *Concubines and Courtesans: Women and Slavery in Islamic History*, eds Matthew S. Gordon and Kathryn A. Hain (Oxford, 2017), pp. 297–323. For other forms of enslavement that some early jurists permitted (self-dedition, debt slavery and the enslavement of foundlings), only for these views to be marginalised by the later alleged consensus, see Irene Schneider, 'Freedom and Slavery in Early Islamic Time [sic] (1st/7th – 2nd/8th Centuries)', *al-Qanṭara* 28 (2007), pp. 353–82.
24. As noted by Jan Hagedorn, *Domestic Slavery in Syria and Egypt 1200–1500* (Bonn, 2020), p. 163. Various Sunnī jurists held that the *mukātaba* agreement could be unilaterally revoked by the master. Other jurists held that the *mudabbar* slave was released from the third of the deceased's estate that could be disposed of as a bequest (*waṣiyya*).
25. The argument is sometimes made that ᶜUmar's endorsement suffices to overrule alterna-

ter prejudice (including the apocalyptically inflected kind), they quickly made important contributions to the cultural and intellectual life of the community, and so were ultimately recognised as Muslims in good standing.[26] Prosopographical study has shown that, while slave concubinage had been known among the pre-Islamic Arabs, it had not been '. . . widely practiced among the pre-Islamic Quraysh . . . [and it] was not a practice known to other peoples of the Late Antique Near East either'.[27] The integration of massive numbers of outsiders through this institution therefore appears to be, at least in its immediate temporal and geographic context, without precedent.

Evidently, the incentives to join the conquest elite were numerous, even more so following the ᶜAbbāsid revolution; and 'rarely', Crone observes, 'have imperial powers set the bar to membership of their own favoured ranks so low'.[28] Though much ink has been spilled on the subject of motivations for conversion, usually to suggest they were of the mercenary sort, this is somewhat misguided.

tive opinions, a view refuted by Ibn Kathīr, *Juzʾ fī bayᶜ*, pp. 73–4. On the Twelver view, see Elizabeth Urban, *Conquered Populations in Early Islam: Non-Arabs, Slaves and the Sons of Slave Mothers* (Edinburgh, 2020), p. 117. Urban's view needs to be qualified, as the evidence suggests that Twelver jurists generally permitted these sales in only a few cases, e.g. debt. See, for example, Shaykh al-Ṭāʾifa al-Ṭūsī (d. 460/1067), *al-Istibṣār fī mā ukhtulifa min al-akhbār* (Beirut, 1326/2005), p. 680 (reconciling this view with other reports permitting their sale without condition). At al-Ṭūsī, *al-Istibṣār*, pp. 680–1, one finds the view that *ummahāt al-awlād* are assigned to the inheritance share of their child/ren, leading to their manumission. This is not the only dimension of slave concubinage on which Twelver jurists disagree with their Sunnī counterparts. For the opinion that masters can 'lend out' their slave women to others for sexual use – an opinion the author acknowledges as scandalous to Sunnī jurists – see al-Ṭūsī, *al-Istibṣār*, pp. 537–8. One finds this view amply attested in other Twelver *ḥadīth* compilations – e.g. *al-Kāfī* (Beirut, 1328/2007), V, pp. 282–4. For another example of 'sexual hospitality', see Ibn al-Mundhir, *al-Awsaṭ min al-sunan wa l-ijmāᶜ wa l-ikhtilāf*, ed. Muḥammad ᶜAbd al-Salām (al-Fayyūm, 2009), VIII, p. 402.

26. On the dynamics of this integration, see Urban, *Conquered Populations in Early Islam*, pp. 106–39. On apocalyptically inflected prejudice: pp. 122–3. See also Patricia Crone, *The Nativist Prophets of Early Islamic Iran: Rural Revolt and Local Zoroastrianism* (New York, 2012), pp. 9–11. For a rejoinder to the overemphasis on the pre-eminence of the *mawālī* (more generally) in scholarship, see Harald Motzki, 'The Role of Non-Arab Converts in the Development of Early Islamic Law', *Islamic Law and Society* 6.3 (1999), pp. 293–317. Majied Robinson has argued that, while prejudice against the *hujanāʾ* existed, we cannot assume it was the norm: *Marriage in the Tribe of Muhammed A Statistical Study of Early Arabic Genealogical Literature* (Berlin, 2020), p. 122.
27. Robinson, *Marriage*, p. 107. The novelty of the institution receives further emphasis on pp. 110–11: it 'contrasted with the prevailing norms of every major Near Eastern religious practice of the conquest era, including that of the pre-Islamic *Ḥijāz*'.
28. Crone, *The Nativist Prophets*, p. 16.

> The fact that conversion enabled people to change their lives for the better in material terms in no way implies they converted insincerely: it is after all a good deal easier to believe in the truth of ideas that work wonders than it is to deny their truth while still accepting that they have wondrous effects.[29]

Not all such forms of membership were voluntary, of course. But even enslavement, which radically deracinated people and admitted them to a new society ultimately contributed to the process of integration. It is not without reason that various *ḥadīths* speak of persons being 'dragged to paradise in chains'. As Ibn Ḥajar (d. 852/1449) explains, citing a variant report, they are 'a non-Arab people (*ᶜajam*) captured by the *muhājirūn* (emigrants), who enter them into Islam forcibly': in eschatological terms, the captives' embrace of Islam, whatever its original circumstances, ultimately leads them to felicity.[30] In short, *jihād* and the related practice of slave concubinage functioned (to use a phrase coined in another context) as a 'massive assimilation machine'.[31] *Jihād* redirected the energies previously expended on intertribal raiding *outwards*, organising this no longer primarily on the basis of kinship, but on confession. The tribe became the *Umma*, or as Watt so felicitously put it, the 'super-tribe'.[32] At least in principle, loyalty was reorganised along the same lines: the believers are meant to be 'unyielding towards the unbelievers, full of mercy among themselves (Q48:29)'. Donner has emphasised, in this vein, how 'members of the *umma* were to sever ties with the tainted society of pagans, even if they were one's close kinsmen'.[33] Alongside this new vision of the confessionally organised society came an 'apocalyptic eschatology . . . [as part of which] the Believers would literally inherit the Earth from the sinful, just as the followers of earlier prophets had'.[34]

29. Ibid., p. 14.
30. *Fatḥ al-bārī bi-sharḥ Ṣaḥīḥ al-Bukhārī*, ed. Muḥammad Fuᵓād ᶜAbd al-Bāqī et al (Cairo: al-Maktaba al-salafiyya, n. d.), VI, p. 145. See also 'Slave-Girls or Prostitutes?', p. 49. Note that the term *muhājir* is used here in its original sense of migrant to the garrison cities to participate in the *jihād*, as argued by Crone in 'The First-Century Concept of "Hiǧra"', *Arabica* 41.3 (1994), 352–87 (at p. 367). See also Patricia Crone and Michael Cook, *Hagarism: The Making of the Islamic World* (Cambridge, 1977), p. 130.
31. For this phrase, see Sean W. Anthony, 'Muḥammad, the Keys to Paradise, and the *Doctrina Iacobi*: A Late Antique Puzzle', *Der Islam* 91.2 (2014), 243–65 (at p. 261).
32. *Muhammad: Prophet and Statesman* (Oxford, 1974), p. 95. Admittedly, fighting units were organised on the basis of (supposed) kinship, and early settlement in the garrison cities followed similar patterns.
33. Donner, *The Early Islamic Conquests*, p. 57. See also pp. 75–6.
34. Fred Donner, *Muhammad and the Believers: At the Origins of Islam* (Harvard, 2010), pp. 81–2. For a work that puts even greater emphasis on the apocalyptic element in

II. APOCALYPTIC, SYMBOLIC VIOLENCE, SLAVE CONCUBINAGE AND *DAWLA*

> . . . [W]e dug Sulayman ibn Abd al-Malik up out of the soil in Dabiq, but we found only his spine, his ribs and his skull, so we burnt them. And we did the same to other members of that family.[35]

There is no better way to inaugurate a new political order (*dawla*) than through violence. Examples are legion, including the ᶜAbbāsid desecration of Umayyad tombs. This violence can also have apocalyptic overtones, and undoubtedly much of the related *ḥadīth* material was put into circulation by propagandists and popular preachers or storytellers (*quṣṣāṣ*), eager to attract or retain an audience.[36] Scepticism about this material is also attested very early.[37] ISIS counted the restoration of slave concubinage as a harbinger of the eschaton, one of their more significant achievements as self-declared revivers of the *Umma*:

> . . . [T]hey have restored the religion in its entirety, levying the poll-tax on the People of the Book and enjoining upon them the terms of ᶜUmar (*al-shurūṭ al-ᶜumariyya*); and they have enslaved the women and children of the unbelievers.[38]

Enslavement and the imposition of the *dhimma* on non-Muslim populations are forms of symbolic violence.[39] The latter represents the subversion of what Ussama Makdisi has termed the 'ecumenical frame', an attempt to retrieve a

the Prophet's teaching, see Stephen J. Shoemaker, *The Death of a Prophet: The End of Muhammad's Life and the Beginnings of Islam* (Philadelphia, 2012), pp. 118–96.

35. ᶜUmar b. Hāniʾ, as reported in Muḥammad b. Munᶜim al-Ḥimyarī, *al-Rawḍ al-miᶜṭār fī khabar al-aqṭār*, ed. Iḥsān ᶜAbbās (Beirut, 1974), p. 231, cited in Wasserstein, *Black Banners*, p. 178.
36. For concern that apocalyptic material was being foisted on the Prophet (under the rubric of *malāḥim* or *fitan*), see, for example, Ibn al-Jawzī, *Kitāb al-Mawḍūᶜāt*, ed. ᶜAbd al-Raḥmān ᶜUthmān (Manṣūra, 1388/1968), III, pp. 189–99. For a revisionist view of the role of the *quṣṣāṣ*, see Lyall Armstrong, *The* Quṣṣāṣ *of Early Islam* (Leiden, 2016).
37. For one early example, see Ḍirār b. ᶜAmr (d. c. 200/815), *Kitāb al-Taḥrīsh*, ed. Hüseyin Hansu and Mehmet Keskin (Istanbul, 2014), pp. 121–3. For a somewhat later critique, see Abū ᶜAlī al-Jubbāʾī (d. 303/915–16, attrib.), *Kitāb al-Maqālāt*, ed. Özkan Şimşek, A. İskender Sarıca and Yusuf Arıkaner (Istanbul, 2020), p. 360.
38. *Al-Sabī*, p. 3. See also 'The Revival of Slavery Before the Hour'.
39. Jurists debated how to exact the *jizya*, with some insisting on demeaning the payee. Much of this hangs on the well-known controversy about the interpretation of the phrase *ᶜan yadin* in Q. 9.29. For one interpretation, see M. J. Kister, '*ᶜAn Yadin* (Qurʾān IX: 29): An Attempt at Interpretation', *Arabica* 9 (1964), 272–8.

political order in which Islam was hegemonic.[40] Other revolutionary movements, perhaps more heavily invested in the chiliastic enterprise, did away with the toleration of non-Muslims altogether.[41] There is, in any case, clearly no ignoring the prominence of eschatological themes in ISIS propaganda. The former title of their English-language magazine, *Dabiq*, itself proclaims this, as the reported site of apocalyptic clashes.[42] Similarly, *ḥadīth* about the prevalence of *ummahāt al-awlād* – mothers 'giving birth to their masters' in the end times – loomed large in their literature. Younus Mirza has demonstrated that, while appealing to such tropes, the act of appropriation often shores up their understandings in the premodern tradition, according to which 'eschatological ḥadīths should not legislate'.[43] Medieval commentators did not generally recognise these reports as a mandate for increasing the number of enslaved persons; they merely indicated the religious entropy and disorder that would mark the end of the world. The 'giving birth to their masters' element is suggestive of the upending of social norms. It is likely that, when first put into circulation, these *ḥadīth* reflected the conquest elite's concerns about challenges to their status posed by the offspring of slave concubines. These so-called *hujanāʾ* ('mixed race' persons), some variant reports mention, would figure among the followers of the Antichrist (*Dajjāl*), alongside 'Turks, weavers, magicians, Uzbeks . . . and all the lowest type of people'.[44]

Another significant and highly publicised element of ISIS's redemptive violence was the systematic destruction of tombs. This does not seem to have possessed the same apocalyptic resonances as the reinstatement of slave concubinage, though in the Shīʿī *ḥadīth* corpus one does find reports on the Mahdī's desecration of the graves and bodies of the enemies of the Imāms.[45] This practice instead draws on the strictures against tomb construction and veneration found

40. Ussama Makdisi, *Age of Coexistence: The Ecumenical Frame and the Making of the Modern Arab World* (Oakland, CA, 2019), pp. 6–11.
41. Most famously, the Almohads, who compelled non-Muslim residents of their territories to convert to Islam. For possible explanations of their motives in doing so (the most convincing of which links this to Ibn Tūmart's status as *Mahdī*), see Maribel Fierro, 'The Religious Policy of the Almohads', in *The Oxford Handbook of Islamic Theology*, ed. Sabine Schmidtke (Oxford, 2016), pp. 679–92 (at pp. 684–5).
42. Wasserstein, *Black Banners*, Chapter 7.
43. Younus Mirza, '"The Slave Girl Gives Birth to Her Master": Female Slavery from the Mamlūk Era (1250–1517) to the Islamic State (2014–)', *Journal of the American Academy of Religion* 85.3 (2017), 577–99 (at p. 594).
44. David Cook, *Studies in Muslim Apocalyptic* (Princeton, 2002), p. 99.
45. For example, Muḥammad Bāqir al-Majlisī, *Biḥār al-anwār* (Beirut, n. d.), XXII, p. 232.

in numerous *ḥadīth*s attributed to the Prophet.[46] Postclassical Islam was, like late medieval Catholicism, a veritable 'cult of the living in the service of the dead', with tombs serving as the confluence of the divine and terrestrial realms, places where one sought healing, sanctuary and intercession. These sites enjoyed the esteem of both commoners and learned elite, as emphasised by Christopher S. Taylor.[47] By the sixth/twelfth centuries their location in a sacred geography and their patronage by rulers could be taken for granted: the construction of lavish tomb complexes typically indicated rulers' particular religious sympathies, as in the case of the Ottomans and Ibn ᶜArabī (d. 638/1240).[48] There were often objections from the learned elite to certain excesses at these sites (e.g. mingling of the sexes), but more categorical condemnation seems to have been muted. Violence and demolition on these lines was, in the ordinary course of affairs, exceedingly rare.[49] Ibn ᶜAbd al-Wahhāb (d. 1206/1792) – a figure of no little influence on the theology of ISIS – engaged in this sort of behaviour, famously levelling the domed edifice on the supposed grave of Zayd b. al-Khaṭṭāb (d. 11/632).[50] He also reinstated the punishment of lapidation for adultery, in much the same way as ISIS would later proclaim.[51] The chronicler ᶜUthmān b. Bishr (d. 1290/1873) observes that Ibn ᶜAbd al-Wahhāb's stoning of an adulteress (subsequent to the tomb demolition) marked a turning point in his career: 'following this his affair became great, his fortune (*dawla*) increased and the recognition of God's unicity (*tawḥīd*) spread'.[52] Without necessarily recalling the end times or the millennium, then, acts of symbolic violence signal the advent of a new order, or *dawla*. While the use of symbolic violence is neither novel nor distinctively Muslim – think of the narratives of founding violence in nationalist historiography – ISIS's

46. Some of the more well-known ones are listed by Ondřej Beránek and Pavel Ťupek in their *The Temptation of Graves in Salafi Islam: Iconoclasm, Destruction and Idolatry* (Edinburgh, 2018), pp. 21–2.
47. Christopher S. Taylor, *In the Vicinity of the Righteous:* Ziyāra *and the Veneration of Muslim Saints in Late Medieval Egypt* (Leiden, 1998). See also Beránek and Ťupek, *The Temptation of Graves*, pp. 36–7.
48. Mustafa Tahrali, 'A General Outline of the Influence of Ibn ᶜArabi on the Ottoman Era', ibnarabisociety.org/influence-of-ibn-arabi-on-the-ottoman-era-mustafa-tahrali/.
49. For exceptions, see, for example, Beránek and Ťupek, *The Temptation of Graves*, p. 74.
50. ᶜUthmān b. Bishr al-Najdī, *ᶜUnwān al-majd fī tārīkh najd*, ed. ᶜAbd al-Raḥmān b. ᶜAbd al-Laṭīf Āl al-Shaykh (Riyadh, 1402/1982), I, p. 39.
51. It is worth noting that polling indicates widespread support for the stoning of adulterers in parts of the Muslim-majority world (particularly MENA and South Asia): www.pewforum.org/2013/04/30/the-worlds-muslims-religion-politics-society-beliefs-about-sharia/.
52. ᶜUthmān b. Bishr, *ᶜUnwān al-majd*, p. 39.

emphasis on apocalypticism seems to have differentiated it from other modern Sunnī militant groups.

According to the Arabist and lexicographer Edward William Lane (d. 1293/1876), a *dawla* signifies 'a turn, mutation, change or vicissitude of time, or fortune . . . from an unfortunate and evil, to a good and happy state or condition'.[53] The word features in apocalyptic texts, effectively as a synonym for the ᶜAbbāsids and their revolution. In the *Kitāb al-Fitan* of Nuᶜaym b. Ḥammād (d. 228/843–4), Ibn ᶜAbbās, the progenitor of the dynasty, asks ᶜAlī (the forbear of their ᶜAlid rivals): '[W]hen will our turn (*dawla*) be, O Abū l-Ḥasan?'[54] Elsewhere in the text, Muᶜāwiya asks anxiously when that turn will come, only to be told it will emerge in the end of days (*ākhir al-zamān*) at the hands of the ᶜAbbāsids' Khurāsānī supporters.[55] Other apocalyptic references to those clad in black, the regime's colour, are decidedly negative.[56] Both detractors and supporters of ISIS similarly invoked these reports for and against their causes, including a figure no less influential than the former Muftī of Egypt, Ali Gomaa.[57] Evidently, much was at stake in the interpretation of these tumultuous events.

III. LEGALISED VIOLENCE AND SLAVE CONCUBINAGE IN THE CONQUEST SOCIETY

> The Islamic State in northern Iraq from 2014 attempted to restore a conquest society but it was horrible in new ways because its context was so different. Max Weber observed that modern conditions are not conducive to saintliness.[58]

The reinstatement of a conquest society looks decidedly odd in a world of nation-states. Insofar as the state-sanctioned repression of minorities occurs in the modern period, it is meant to be the outcome of properly bureaucratic norms, Arendt's 'banality of evil'. We do know that ISIS kept meticulous records and

53. Edward William Lane, *An Arabic-English Lexicon* (Cambridge, 1984 repr.), I, p. 934.
54. *The Book of Tribulations*, p. 100.
55. Ibid., p. 101.
56. In one report, the Prophet says pointedly: 'What do I have to do with the ᶜAbbāsids? They have divided my community, forced them to wear black clothes, so may God force them to wear clothes of fire!' (*The Book of Tribulations*, p. 101).
57. Citing the *Kitāb al-Fitan*, see 'Mutfī of Egypt: ᶜAlī b. Abī Ṭālib warned against Dāᶜish', gerasnews.com/print/160291. On ISIS and religious authority, see the article by Sohaira Siddiqui, 'Beyond Authenticity: ISIS and the Islamic Legal Tradition', www.jadaliyya.com/details/31825/beyond-authenticity-isis-and-the-islamic-legal-tradition.
58. Christopher Melchert, *Before Sufism: Early Islamic Renunciant Piety* (Berlin, 2020), p. 194.

furnished all manner of official certification for procedures, including manumission.[59] This state-building dimension of the ISIS enterprise distinguished it in important ways from other militant organisations such as al-Qāᶜida. Admittedly, ISIS owed much to the playbook of al-Qāᶜida strategist Abū Bakr Nājī – namely, the 2004 *Idārat al-tawaḥḥush* ('Management of Savagery').[60] This work envisions the establishment of a caliphate in three phases, beginning with coordinated violence against sites such as oil facilities and tourist resorts in weak states. After many such attacks, the target state would be crippled, the breakdown of law and order permitting the emergence of rudimentary militant-operated alternatives. Once these solidify, the third and final stage would ensue, with the forcible unification of pre-existing militias under a single banner, the establishment of public services and the proclamation of a new order.[61] The US-led invasion achieved the first objective, crippling Iraq's infrastructure; sectarian violence and regime incompetence accomplished much of the rest. In line with Nājī's strategy, ISIS quickly consolidated their rule and established ministries (using the deliberately archaic *dīwān* in preference to *wizāra*),[62] including one devoted to the spoils of war. They 'set up . . . a detailed bureaucracy of sex slavery, including sales contracts notarized by its Islamic courts'.[63] The Yezidis found themselves on the business end of this bureaucratic and military machine in 2014.

The offer of terms by ISIS to local Christian populations – namely, the choice between conversion and payment of the poll tax – was not extended to Yezidi communities.[64] This was on the grounds that the Yezidis as non-Scriptuaries (*ghayr kitābīs*) were not entitled to state protection, one of several mainstream views in classical *fiqh*, particularly associated with the Shāfiᶜites (and sundry

59. On this theme, see Mara Revkin, *The Legal Foundations of the Islamic State*, Brookings Foundation: U.S. Relations with the Muslim World, No. 26, July 2016, available online at www.brookings.edu/wp-content/uploads/2016/07/brookings-analysis-paper_mara-revkin_web_v2.pdf.
60. On this work, see, for example, Fawaz Gerges, *ISIS: A History* (Princeton, 2017), pp. 36–42. See also McCants, *The ISIS Apocalypse*, pp. 82–4. See also Lawrence Wright, 'ISIS's Savage Strategy in Iraq', *The New Yorker*, 16 June 2014, www.newyorker.com/news/daily-comments/isiss-savage-strategy-in-iraq.
61. Abū Bakr Nājī, *Idārat al-tawaḥḥush*, pp. 19–20, 23–4, etc. Available online at noor-book.com/كتاب-إدارة-التوحش-pdf.
62. Wasserstein, *Black Banners*, p. 59. See, alternatively, McCants, *The ISIS Apocalypse*, p. 21.
63. Gerges, *ISIS: A History*, p. 31. See also McCants, *The ISIS Apocalypse*, pp. 111–14.
64. For a translation of the terms offered to the Christians of al-Raqqa, closely modelled on the 'Pact of ᶜUmar', see Wasserstein, *Black Banners*, pp. 153–5.

jurists from other schools).[65] Under Ottoman rule – good Ḥanafites theoretically tolerant of non-Arab pagans – Yezidis had not been considered *dhimmīs* and their religion 'was not protected in any way until the Tanzimat'.[66] Even after the emergence of the ecumenical frame in the mid-nineteenth century, Yezidis remained subject to official persecution, including punitive expeditions and forcible conversion under the pious ᶜAbd al-Ḥamīd II (r. 1293/1876 – 1327/1909).[67] Persecution no doubt owed much to the perception of the Yezidis of Mt Sinjar as an obstreperous tribal population who resisted integration into the modernising Ottoman state, including conscription into its army. But it may also owe something to the religious conceptualisation of the group; syncretic religions identified as quasi-Islamic would not necessarily have been indulged by jurists as liable to pay the *jizya*.

Though not identifying as Muslims today, the status of Yezidis historically is somewhat mysterious. They are first apparently referred to in sources from the sixth/twelfth century as devotees of the Umayyad Yazīd b. Muᶜāwiya (r. 60/680 – 64/683), but this identification seems less than certain. Other authors, such as Ibn Kathīr (d. 774/1373), mention Kurdish groups who 'had forgotten their ancient religion, Magism [sic], and begun to accept another religion, a hybrid with Islam'.[68] Açıkyıldız concludes that this is a case of 'syncretism between Sufi Islam and ancient Iranian religions', a view essentially shared by ISIS.[69] This makes the Yezidis comparable to other such groups in the Middle East,

65. Wasserstein, *Black Banners*, p. 31. See also 'The Revival of Slavery Before the Hour', pp. 14–15. For a valuable summary of the divergent views on the question, see Yohanan Friedmann, *Tolerance and Coercion: Interfaith Relations in the Muslim Tradition* (Cambridge, 2003), pp. 54–86. For a list of religious groups entitled (or otherwise) to tolerance, see the Shāfiᶜite ᶜAbd al-Qāhir al-Baghdādī's *Kitāb Uṣūl al-dīn* (Istanbul, 1346/1928), pp. 324–8. Zoroastrians, though not strictly speaking Scriptuaries, were generally afforded protection by the jurists based on various *ḥadīth*.
66. Yohanan Friedmann, 'Minorities', in *Islamic Political Thought: An Introduction*, ed. Gerhard Bowering (Princeton, 2015), pp. 123–34 (at p. 129).
67. On ᶜAbd al-Ḥamīd's policies towards the Yezidis, see Nelida Fuccaro, 'Communalism and the State in Iraq: the Yazidi Kurds c. 1869–1940', *Middle Eastern Studies* 36.2 (1999), 1–26 (at pp. 3–6).
68. Birgül Açıkyıldız, *The Yezidis: The History of a Community, Culture and Religion* (London, 2014), p. 38. For the origins and history of the community generally, see Chapter 1. The term *majūs* was often used to denote pagans generally. See also 'The Revival of Slavery Before the Hour', p. 15.
69. Açıkyıldız, *The Yezidis*, p. 37. Yezidis are described as monotheists believing in the deity *Xwêde*, though they direct their prayers to an angel–demiurge, *Tawûsî Melek*, whence their association by some observers with devil worship: pp. 71, 73–8.

most prominently the Nuṣayrī-ᶜAlawīs, also the subjects of repeated persecution.[70] Unlike the Nuṣayrī-ᶜAlawīs and the Twelvers, however, the Yezidis were not denounced as apostates, but as non-Scripturaries or pagans.[71] The evidence suggests that this view was operationalised on the ground. In one early encounter near the northern Iraqi village of Kocho in August 2014, an ISIS commander met with the local Yezidi headman (*mukhtār*) to demand that the residents embrace Islam. After nearly a fortnight of negotiation, by which point it was obvious that conversion was not forthcoming, residents were herded into a school building where the men and pubescent boys were separated from the others. After the seizure of some property, they were transported a few hundred metres away from the village and shot *en masse*. The women and remaining children were later taken elsewhere to be sold.[72]

The sale of Yezidi women and girls as slave concubines attracted international media, as well as scholarly, attention beginning in August 2014.[73] A number of ISIS documents were subsequently published online that articulated the juristic argument for enslavement. Some of these were translated in abridged form into English, attracting further comment from the news media and human rights NGOs.[74] This is not the place for an analysis of these journalistic and NGO

70. On the Nuṣayrī-ᶜAlawīs, see Meir Bar-Asher and Aryeh Kofski, *The Nuṣayrī-ᶜAlawī Religion: An Enquiry into its Theology and Liturgy* (Leiden, 2002). See also Yaron Friedman, *The Nuṣayrī-ᶜAlawīs: An Introduction to the Religion, History and Identity of the Leading Minority in Syria* (Leiden, 2010).
71. A point emphasised in 'The Revival of Slavery Before the Hour', where they are described as 'a pagan minority existent for ages in the regions of Iraq and Shām', p. 14.
72. Valeria Cetorelli and Sareta Ashraph, 'A Demographic Documentation of ISIS's Attack on the Yazidi Village of Kocho', LSE Middle East Reports, 2019, esp. pp. 8–13, http://eprints.lse.ac.uk/101098/. See also Donatella Rovera, 'Testimonies from Kocho: The Village ISIS Tried to Wipe Off the Map', www.amnesty.org/en/latest/news/2014/08/testimonies-from-kocho-the-village-isis-tried-to-wipe-off-the-map/. Further information on the logistics of enslavement can be found in Nadia al-Dayel, Andrew Mumford and Kevin Bales, 'Not Yet Dead: The Establishment and Regulation of Slavery by the Islamic State', *Studies in Conflict and Terrorism* (2020), doi.org/10.1080/1057610x.2020.1711590. See also McCants, *The ISIS Apocalypse*, pp. 112–13.
73. Some of the more widely circulated pieces include Rukmini Callimachi's 'ISIS Enshrines a Theology of Rape', nytimes.com/2015/08/14/world/middleeast/isis-enshrines-a-theology-of-rape.amp.html, Graeme Wood's 'What ISIS Really Wants', theatlantic.amp/article/384980/, and Kecia Ali's insightful 'Redeeming Slavery: The "Islamic State" and the Quest for Islamic Morality', www.mizanproject.org/journal-post/redeeming-slavery/.
74. For example, 'The Culture of Rape Within ISIS, and the Questions That Arise', nytimes.com/2016/03/20/world/middleeast/the-culture-of-rape-within-isis-and-the-questions-that-arise.html. See also Kenneth Roth, 'Slavery: The ISIS Rules', www.hrw.org/news/2015/09/05/slavery-isis-rules.

interventions, which has already been undertaken very ably by others. Instead, we propose to analyse the most comprehensive ISIS publication on the question, the aforementioned *al-Sabī: aḥkām wa masāʾil*. It is not clear exactly when in 1435/2014 the document was first published, though one presumes this took place shortly after the attack on Sinjar, beginning in early August. We do know that ISIS field commanders had already solicited a *fatwā* on the treatment of Yezidis in advance of the campaign from the relevant bureau, *Dīwān al-Buḥūth wa l-Iftāʾ*.[75] This suggests there may have been plans to enslave the Yezidis some time before the assault.

IV. SLAVE CONCUBINAGE IN A POST-ABOLITION WORLD

> The use of scriptural sources and history is not only important for religiously legitimizing their actions, it also promotes their overall objectives. In other words, they subject scripture and history for their own political and religious motivations . . . [ISIS] often steps away from the literal meaning of texts where necessary.[76]

A perusal of the voluminous literature produced by ISIS demonstrates that they engaged very closely with the Islamic legal tradition: this is certainly the case for slave concubinage.[77] The argument that this engagement was shaped by strategic needs, while well-taken, can and has been directed meaningfully at some of their detractors. The condemnatory 'Open Letter to Baghdadi', signed by a galaxy of leading Sunnī *ʿulamāʾ* in September 2014, is, in the words of Kecia Ali, a document that 'makes a hash of both history and the classical tradition, with its ahistorical declarations and simplistic proclamations'.[78] Her broader goal here is to emphasise that Islam is a living, dynamic religion that cannot

75. 'Prior To the Taking of Sinjar', according to 'The Revival of Slavery Before the Hour', p. 14. See also al-Dayel, Mumford and Bales, 'Not Yet Dead', p. 3.
76. Sohaira Siddiqui, 'Experts Weigh In (Part 2): How Does ISIS Approach Islamic Scripture?', www.brookings.edu/blog/markaz/2015/03/26/experts-weigh-in-part-2-how-does-isis-approach-islamic-scripture/amp/.
77. For analysis, see Brown, *Slavery and Islam*, pp. 256–8. See also Bernard K. Freamon, *Possessed by the Right Hand: The Problem of Slavery in Islamic Law and Muslim Cultures* (Leiden, 2019), pp. 465–78.
78. 'ISIS and Authority', www.feminismandreligion.com/2015/02/24/isis-and-authority-by-kecia-ali.amp/. For the text of the letter, see lettertobaghdadi.com. McCants makes the point that 'anyone who reads and acts on scripture' engages with it tendentiously (*The ISIS Apocalypse*, p. 150).

be reduced to its textual heritage, a point that surely bears repeating.[79] Ali calls attention to the ways in which 'consensus' is invoked to marginalise not just violent fringe groups, but those advocating, for example, greater gender equality. In a thoughtful addition to her now-classic *Sexual Ethics and Islam*, Ali further adds that while 'grotesque and violent', the ISIS literature on the subject seems quixotically 'sincere . . . [it] contemplates the integration of slaves into a new sort of society – or rather, a very old one, harking back to (an imagined) Muslim community'.[80] Examination bears these observations out.

Al-Sabī is a carefully researched treatise comprised of eight sections (e.g. 'the command to treat captives and slave women well'). The text begins with a discussion of technical terms, before proceeding to explore the licitness of slave concubinage, the need for good treatment of those so enslaved (*al-amr bi-l-iḥsān li-l-sabāya*) and whether slave women of various confessional backgrounds (Scriptuaries, pagans and apostates) can be used sexually. The text ends with a section on miscellaneous issues, including such questions as the dissolution of captives' marriages. The treatise is introduced by the head (*raʾīs*) of the relevant ISIS bureau, Turkī al-Binʿalī, whose authorship has been assumed here. Given his role as ISIS's star jurist, it seems reasonable to assume that he played the dominant role in writing and researching it. The possibility that *al-Sabī* may be a collective enterprise cannot, however, be ruled out.

Al-Sabī is best characterised as a sober and scholarly exercise reflecting a high degree of juristic acumen. Accompanying frequent reference to the teachings of the four Sunnī legal schools, to whom due respect is afforded, are the typical concerns for careful definition of terms, both legal and lexical.[81] Al-Binʿalī evinces a decided fondness for jurists who are known for their relative independence from school doctrine, particularly Ibn al-Qayyim (d. 751/1350), his *shaykh* Ibn Taymiyya (d. 728/1328), Ibn Qudāma (d. 620/1223) and (on one particularly controversial point) al-Shawkānī (d. 1250/1834), as well as others of a textualist bent. These are highly regarded for their embodiment of the value of *taḥqīq* ('verification').[82] *Al-Sabī* is by no means a work that eschews the cumulative

79. This has been emphasised in the second edition of her important *Sexual Ethics and Islam: Feminist Reflections on Gender, Hadith, and Jurisprudence* (Oxford, 2016), Chapter 3 (esp. pp. 67–71).
80. Ali, *Sexual Ethics and Islam*, p. 70.
81. *Al-Sabī*, for example, p. 4 (on the definition of *sabī* and the typology of spoils of war).
82. On this point (omitting Ibn Qayyim and Ibn Qudāma for contextual reasons), see Ahmed El Shamsy, *Rediscovering the Islamic Classics: How Editors and Print Culture Transformed an Intellectual Tradition* (Princeton, 2020), pp. 55–60. On the modern appropriation of Ibn Taymiyya, see El Shamsy, *Rediscovering the Islamic Classics*, pp. 182–91.

Sunnī legal tradition in favour of a *de novo* engagement with scriptural texts, however. Departures from the teachings of the *madhāhib* are exceptional, and are always conscientiously indicated. Al-Binᶜalī is invested in the pluralism of classical *fiqh*: for his arguments to 'work', they need only reflect the teaching of one of the four schools, or at the very least scholars of stature. *Ḥadīths* are for the most part not cited directly, but only as they occur in the writings of others (in twenty-two of thirty-four cases, 'embedded' citations, below). The same is true, incidentally, of the Qurʾān. Page and volume references are scrupulously furnished. As far as one is able to tell, material is quoted faithfully, without any distortion of its original sense.[83] The table below hopefully conveys a sense of the range and depth of al-Binᶜalī's engagement with the premodern tradition. Further comments on method may be found in the appendix to this chapter.[84]

What is one to make of the seemingly low proportion of the total (26.8 per cent) attributable directly to al-Binᶜalī? In part, this is a function of authority. The author is aware that his opinions bear no weight in themselves and are only compelling to the extent that they can be demonstrated to belong to the tradition. Secondly, this pattern of textual deployment is familiar to anyone knowledgeable of the literature (presumably, his audience). As Merlin Swartz observes of the *Kitāb al-Quṣṣāṣ wa l-mudhakkirīn* of Ibn al-Jawzī (d. 597/1200): '[S]omewhat more than three-quarters of the work is taken from other, and for the most part earlier, sources'.[85] This is not to repeat the claim that either lack originality, which can be exercised through choice and arrangement of material.[86] As will shortly become clear, furthermore, authors' agency is at work in their arbitration between existing opinions, something al-Binᶜalī does with some flair. The diversity of sources used (thirty-six in total) indicates both facility with the tradition and the 'wide' reading practices noted by Ahmed El Shamsy in his outstanding recent study of Arabic print culture. The Internet (together with other factors)

83. A random sampling of references to premodern legal texts was cross-checked to verify accuracy. The author does not indicate which editions were used, but many of the relevant works have been digitised and are available in searchable form online.
84. For the counting words to establish relative importance, see Antonia Bosanquet's valuable 'Minding their Place: Space and Religious Difference in Ibn al-Qayyim's *Aḥkām ahl al-dhimma*', unpublished PhD dissertation, Freie Universität, Berlin, 2016, p. 72. The method used to collect the data above is explained in the appendix to this chapter.
85. Ibn al-Jawzī's *Kitāb al-quṣṣāṣ wa 'l-mudhakkirīn* (Beirut, 1971), p. 70. I thank Reyhan Durmaz for kindly (and very promptly) providing me with the page number.
86. We still await a scholarly treatment of the notion of plagiarism in Islamic scholarly culture. A number of studies have been addressed to the question of theft of verse (*sariqa*), but this is irrelevant here. For some useful preliminary remarks, see Joel Blecher, *Said the Prophet of God: Hadith Commentary Across a Millennium* (Berkeley, 2018), pp. 57–63.

Table 1 Citations of scholars in *al-Sabī: aḥkām wa masāʾil*

Authority/Text Cited	Citations (Embedded)	Words	%
Turkī al-Binᶜalī (d. 1438/2017): author	–	1,669	26.8
Ibn al-Qayyim (d. 751/1350): various works, Ḥanbalī	8	1,462	23.5
Muslim b. al-Ḥajjāj (d. 261/875): *Ṣaḥīḥ*	9 (7)	530	8.5
Ibn Taymiyya (d. 728/1328): various works, Ḥanbalī	10	414	6.7
Al-Bukhārī (d. 256/870): *Ṣaḥīḥ*	7 (2)	358	5.8
Ibn Qudāma (d. 620/1223): *al-Mughnī*,: Ḥanbalī	7	313	5
Qurʾān	26 (22)	264	4.2
Abū Isḥāq al-Shirāzī (d. 476/1083): *al-Muhadhdhab*, Shāfiᶜī	4	155	2.5
Ibn ᶜAbd al-Barr (d. 463/1071): various works, Mālikī	2 (2)	152	2.4
Al-Shawkānī (d. 1250/1834): *Nayl al-awṭār*, independent	3	148	2.4
Abū Yūsuf (d. 181/798): *Kitāb al-Kharāj*, Ḥanafī	2	141	2.3
Aḥmad b. Ḥanbal (d. 241/855): *Musnad*	9 (5)	132	2.1
Al-Qurṭubī (d. 621/1273): *Tafsīr*, Mālikī	2	103	1.7
Ibn Kathīr (d. 774/1373): *Tafsīr*, Shāfiᶜī	1	100	1.6
Abū Dāwūd al-Sijistānī (d. 275/889): *Sunan*	6 (2)	85	1.2
ᶜAbd al-Razzāq al-Ṣanᶜānī (d. 211/827): *Muṣannaf*	6 (2)	56	0.9
Al-Tirmidhī (d. 279/892): *Sunan*	5 (3)	49	0.8
Al-Naḥḥās (d. 338/950): *Maᶜāni al-Qurʾān*	1 (1)	46	0.7
Al-ᶜAdawī (d. 1189/1775): *Ḥāshiyya*, Mālikī	1	42	0.7
Al-Ṭabarī (d. 310/923): *Tafsīr*	2 (1)	41	0.7
Ibn Manẓūr (d. 711/1311): *Lisān al-ᶜarab*	2	32	0.5
Al-Shāfiᶜī (d. 204/820): *Kitāb al-Umm*	1	31	0.5
Ibn al-Humām (d. 861/1457): *Fatḥ al-qadīr*, Ḥanafī	1	29	0.5
Al-Māwardī al-Shāfiᶜī (d. 450/1058): *al-Aḥkām al-sulṭāniyya*	1	28	0.4
Al-Wāqidī (d. 207/823): *Kitāb al-Maghāzī*	2	23	0.4
ᶜAmr b. Kulthūm (d. 584 CE): *Muᶜallaqa*	1	10	0.2
Al-Kāsānī (d. 587/1191): *Badāʾiᶜ al-ṣanāʾiᶜ*, Ḥanafī	3	0	0
Abū Yaᶜlā al-Ḥanbalī (d. 458/1066): *al-Aḥkām al-sulṭāniyya*	2	0	0
Al-Mawṣūᶜa al-fiqhiyya al-kuwaytiyya (general reference work)	1	0	0
Al-Fayrūzabādī (d. 817/1415): *al-Qāmūs al-muḥīṭ*	1	0	0
Al-Maqqarī (d. 770/1368): *al-Miṣbāḥ al-munīr*	1	0	0
Al-Nasāʾī (d. 303/915): *Sunan*	1 (1)	0	0
Ibn ᶜĀbidīn (d. 1252/1836): *Radd al-muḥtār*, Ḥanafī	1	0	0
Al-Khurashī (d. 1090/1679): *Sharḥ al-Khurashī ᶜalā l-Khalīl*, Mālikī	1	0	0
Al-Ābī (d. 1335/1916): *al-Thamar al-dānī*, Mālikī	1	0	0
Al-ᶜAbdarī (d. 897/1492): *al-Tāj wa l-iklīl*, Mālikī	1	0	0
Shams al-Dīn al-Ramlī (d. 1004/1596): *Nihāyat al-muḥtāj*, Shāfiᶜī	1	0	0
Shams al-Dīn al-Maqdisī (d. 682/1283): *Sharḥ al-Kabīr*, Ḥanbalī	1	0	0
TOTAL	**134 (50)**	**6,223**	**103**[87]

87. For an explanation of this figure, see the appendix.

has been responsible for 'a revolution in the availability of edited texts . . . the opportunity for a comprehensive engagement with the Islamic tradition has been diffused to the level of the individual almost anywhere in the world'.[88] This unprecedented availability has proven destabilising. To any specialist, the 'Open Letter to Baghdadi' does not do at all well by comparison. It is almost as though the collective prestige of the signatories was expected to outweigh the careless, slipshod and fundamentally misrepresentative – if well-intentioned – nature of the work.[89]

V. RELATING SLAVE CONCUBINAGE TO THE TRADITION: TWO CASE STUDIES

To demonstrate the nature of *al-Sabī*'s relationship to the Islamic legal tradition, two particularly important issues will be dissected here. The first, that of the taking of non-Scriptuaries (in this case, Yezidis) as slave concubines, represents a departure from the agreement of the four Sunnī schools, a departure al-Bin^{c}alī freely acknowledges.[90] The second is concubinage with apostates; here, the author sides with most of the jurists against the Ḥanafites, deploying a very creative historical argument to discredit the dissenting view.[91]

In the first (2006) edition of her *Sexual Ethics and Islam*, Kecia Ali hinted that classical views restricting concubinage to 'Christian and Jewish (and perhaps Sabean or Zoroastrian) captives' may have overlaid earlier practice on this point.[92] This is an important insight. Further research highlights the extent to which early jurists were at pains to equate the rules on licit marriage partners with those on slave concubines. The Qur'ān explicitly forbids *nikāḥ* with pagans (*wa lā tankiḥū l-mushrikāt*, Q2:221), while apparently permitting marriage to Scriptuary women (Q5:5). Much, of course, hinges on the interpretation of the word *nikāḥ* in the first verse; does it suggest marriage, or sexual intercourse (including concubinage) more generally? Similarly, does *mushrikāt* refer solely to female non-Scriptuaries, or does it encompass 'People of the Book' – Q5:5

88. El Shamsy, *Rediscovering the Islamic Classics*, p. 242.
89. One of the more egregious of many examples is the claim about the longstanding consensus against slavery. Many of the signatories come from countries where it has only very recently been abolished, as noted by McCants, *The ISIS Apocalypse*, pp. 112 (on Mauritania).
90. 'As for sex with non-Scriptuary concubines (*wathaniyyāt*) . . . this has been forbidden by the great majority [of jurists] from the four schools and others; the opposite view [permitting this] has even been characterised as erratic (*shādhdh*)!', *Al-Sabī*, p. 15.
91. *Al-Sabī*, pp. 20–1. See also 'The Revival of Slavery Before the Hour', p. 15.
92. Ali, *Sexual Ethics and Islam*, p. 50.

notwithstanding – whom the Qurʾān also charges with *shirk* (e.g. Q9:31)? The relevant point for our purposes in this article is the relationship between marriage and slave concubinage. A number of early figures are said to have made explicit the analogy between the two – viz. whichever religious group it is prohibited to marry are likewise prohibited for purposes of concubinage. Saḥnūn (d. 240/854) attributes this formula to the Companion ᶜAmmār b. Yāsir (d. 37/657), an ascription that strikes one as anachronistic.[93] We are on firmer ground with al-Shāfiᶜī (d. 204/820), who makes the connection similarly explicit:

> Any category (*ṣinf*) of unbelievers whose free women are licit to marry, are likewise permissible by virtue of ownership (*ḥall waṭʾ imāʾihim bi l-milk*) . . . it is not permissible to have sexual intercourse with a pagan woman (*mushrika ghayr kitābiyya*) by virtue of ownership, just as it is not permissible to marry their free-women.[94]

The need for systematisation and the desire for doctrinal consistency evidently drove jurists to exclude the possibility that marriage with pagans was prohibited, while concubinage with them was licit.[95] This impulse seems to have affected jurists known for their textualist inclinations, no less than those who found *raʾy* more congenial. The great Ibn Ḥanbal (d. 241/855), who similarly upholds the prohibition, turns sheepish when questioned about the (obviously pagan) captives of the Battle of Awṭās (8/630), to which many of the *ḥadīth*s on slave concubinage are linked.[96] Abū ᶜUbayd al-Qāsim b. Sallām (d. 224/838), of similar textualist bent, is less embarrassed by these difficulties, but adopts the same conclusion: concubinage with pagans is prohibited, and the captives of Awṭās must have converted.[97]

93. *Mā ḥarram Allāh min al-ḥarāʾir shayʾan illā ḥarrama mithlahū min al-īmāʾ:* Saḥnūn, *al-Mudawwana al-kubrā* (Riyadh, n. d.), IV, p. 157. This report is presented without an *isnād*. Al-Shāfiᶜī does furnish us with one for a comparable report: *Kitāb al-Umm*, ed. Rifᶜat Fawzī ᶜAbd al-Muṭṭalib (al-Manṣūra, 1422/2001), VI, p. 5. The same formula is also attributed to Ibn Masᶜūd (*al-Umm*, p. 6).
94. Al-Shāfiᶜī, *al-Umm*, VI, p. 21.
95. Kecia Ali has noted the contribution of inter-jurist polemics to this increased systematisation. See *Marriage and Slavery in Early Islam* (Boston, MA, 2010), p. 1, etc.
96. Queried about the tribe of Hawāzin ('were they not pagans?'), Aḥmad concedes that he is not sure. 'I do not know if they converted or not' (*lā adrī kānū aslamū am lā*). Put on the spot by a relevant *ḥadīth*, he feebly responds: 'I do not know . . . perhaps they converted'. Al-Khallāl, *Aḥkām ahl al-milal*, ed. Sayyid Ḥasan (Beirut, 1414/1994), p. 168.
97. Abū ᶜUbayd al-Qāsim b. Sallām, *al-Nāsikh wa l-mansūkh*, ed. Muḥammad b. Ṣāliḥ al-Mudayfar (Riyadh, n. d.), p. 98.

Al-Binᶜalī makes no claim to originality in permitting the taking of *mushrikāt ghayr kitābiyyāt* as concubines, leaving Ibn al-Qayyim and al-Shawkānī to do the hard work for him. The latter is cited as invoking common sense to make his point: '[N]o sane person can hold that great numbers like those of the female captives of Awṭās all embraced Islam simultaneously of their own accord'.[98] To transcend the authority of the school–jurists, al-Binᶜalī adduces the views of a number of the early Muslims (*salaf*) as evidence too.[99] The case is, as Ali suggests, not without its merits.

The question of taking apostates as concubines forms an interesting contrast to that of the Yezidis. The label 'apostate' is applied rather widely in ISIS literature to encompass rival Muslim groups, including not only the 'heterodox' Twelver–Shīᶜa and Druze, but also Sunnīs opposed to their caliphate.[100] ISIS possessed both the means and (presumably) the incentive to adopt the Ḥanafite view (shared by Ibn Taymiyya) permitting the taking of apostates as slave concubines. Somewhat surprisingly, however, al-Binᶜalī sides with the majority (*jumhūr*). It is the way in which he does this that deserves comment. To invalidate the Ḥanafite argument that ᶜAlī b. Abī Ṭālib (d. 29/661) took a woman from the apostate tribe of the Banī Ḥanīfa as a concubine, al-Binᶜalī reaches creatively for the history books. Al-Wāqidī (d. 207/823) reports that the woman in question was black, and 'blackness is rare among the Arabs'.[101] The accuracy of this claim notwithstanding, the suggestion is that the woman was a slave of the Banī Ḥanīfa, rather than a member of the tribe, and therefore not an apostate. That al-Binᶜalī reaches this conclusion suggests that *al-Sabī: aḥkām wa masāʾil* is more complex than a cynical appeal to tradition. The same pattern of serious engagement of the juristic literature is evident in other ISIS publications.[102]

98. *Al-Sabī*, p. 18.
99. Ibid., p. 17.
100. In their fondness for declaring other Muslims unbelievers (*takfīr*), they are much like certain of the early Muᶜtazila. See Maher Jarrar (in collaboration with Sebastian Günther), *Doctrinal Instruction in Early Islam: The Book of the Explanation of the Sunna by Ghulām Khalīl (d. 275/888)* (Leiden, 2020), p. 117. On *takfīr* generally, see Camilla Adang, Hassan Ansari and Maribel Fierro (eds), *Accusations of Unbelief in Islam: A Diachronic Perspective on Takfīr* (Leiden, 2015).
101. *Al-Sabī*, p. 21.
102. Including the responsa (*fatāwā*) of al-Binᶜalī himself. Some of these are available as recordings at www.archive.org/details/alsulami2/فتاوى+عبر+الاثير+الشيخ+تركي+البنعلي+الحلقة+التاسعة.mp3.

CONCLUSION

If Danton and Robespierre established modern bourgeois society while garbed in Roman costume, as it were, they did not do so in circumstances of their own making. The emergence of ISIS, similarly, was more than anything an outcome of the American invasion and occupation of Iraq, rampant sectarianism and decades of brutalisation by a despotic regime. But it is doubtful that these circumstances would have given rise to anything comparable had they so complemented each other half a century ago. The advent of a neo-Wahhābī conquest polity owes much to transnational elements that have only become relevant in the intervening decades, including Jihadist networks and ideology. It is within those constraints that men, Marx might say, make their own history. The example of (Lebanese) Tripoli is instructive. 'In the late sixties', Bernard Rougier writes, 'it was the scene of intense militancy . . . an amalgam of Marxist references, slogans backing the Palestinian cause, and a desire for social reform shaped the political discourse of the period'.[103] Only slightly more than ten years later, with Lebanon in the throes of a civil war and an Israeli invasion, a 'zeal for militant Islamism' along Iranian lines arose. The *Ḥarakat al-Tawḥīd al-Islāmī* militia established de facto control over a few Tripolitan neighbourhoods and began 'forbidding alcohol and imposing strict Islamic rules on the population'. One local Emir executed twenty-eight communist militants on charges of apostasy. Shortly thereafter, the Syrian army made short work of the militants.[104] It is against this backdrop of endemic violence, failed states and kleptocratic rule that ISIS's appeal to the premodern juristic tradition must be understood. Within such constraints, it is possible to exercise one's agency, to make history. The 'reinstatement' of slave concubinage, taking place in the radically altered conditions of the twenty-first century, is a case in point. In choosing to retrieve dormant aspects of the tradition, Turkī al-Binᶜalī (and others, no doubt) were making an interpretive choice. And, ultimately, people bear responsibility for their interpretive choices.[105]

103. *The Sunni Tragedy in the Middle East: Northern Lebanon from al-Qāᶜida to ISIS* (Princeton, 2015), p. 3.
104. Rougier, *The Sunni Tragedy*, pp. 10–11.
105. In her review of *Sexual Ethics and Islam*, Laury Silvers remarks (in this vein) that Ali 'calls on contemporary Muslims to take responsibility for their own engagement of the intellectual tradition.' See *Journal of Middle East Women's Studies* 4.3 (2008), 134–6 (at p. 135).

APPENDIX: METHODS USED IN ANALYSING THE SOURCES OF *AL-SABĪ*

Counting the words attributed to different sources in *al-Sabī* is less straightforward an exercise than it seems. After some deliberation, it was decided that *ḥadīth* compilations and other works cited in secondary fashion (e.g. Ibn al-Qayyim's frequent resort to the *Ṣaḥīḥ*s) would be considered as independent sources. This is because such materials do not typically acquire their authoritativeness by virtue of citation, but are probative in and of themselves. This may give the misleading impression of broader engagement with the tradition than is actually the case – a risk we have chosen to take. Additionally, one will notice the percentage for total citation coming to 103 per cent; this reflects the rounding up of figures and the decision to count *ḥadīth*s attributed to multiple collections separately. In order to preclude any potential skewing of the data, the number of citations is noted. This conveys a sense of the importance of particular sources to the author's argument, even when their word count remains modest. The supreme example of this is the Qurʾān, frequently but only ever economically deployed – often only part of a verse – and enjoying an epistemic status far above other sources. Additionally, al-Binʿalī often provides references for the reader to follow up without these texts being quoted: these are the zero-word count entries.

Authors have been listed in order of word count and, where this is the same, in order of appearance in *al-Sabī*. Though *madhhab*-affiliation has been mentioned in cases where legal texts are referenced, this is not to suggest that jurists are reducible to their legal school. Ibn Taymiyya's complex relationship with the Ḥanbalīs is well known. Similarly, among Mālikīs, Ibn ʿAbd al-Barr is remarkable for his textualist bent, a fact that makes him congenial to ISIS, belonging as they do to the highly textualist Wahhābī–*salafī* legal tradition.

CHAPTER

11

'NAY, WE OBEYED GOD WHEN WE BURNED HIM': DEBATING IMMOLATION (*TAḤRĪQ*) BETWEEN THE ISLAMIC STATE AND AL-QĀʿIDA

*Mathias Ghyoot**

INTRODUCTION[1]

This chapter will study how the self-proclaimed caliphate calling itself the 'Islamic State' (henceforth by the acronym IS) justified burning to death the captured fighter pilot Muᶜādh al-Kasāsba in 2015. Specifically, the chapter will study a legal work by IS's foremost *salafī jihādī* propagandist Aḥlām al-Naṣr who – contrary to a long-established prohibition on immolation (*taḥrīq*) – permitted immolation as retribution for the fiery bombardment wrought by al-Kasāsba. Aḥlām al-Naṣr's position will be demonstrated in a four-part study, beginning with delineating the scholarly campaign launched by IS in February 2015 to justify burning al-Kasāsba. Secondly, we will, in a close reading of her work, demonstrate how Aḥlām al-Naṣr (1) presented the punishment of retribution (*qiṣāṣ*) as a defensive measure; (2) argued that IS did not burn a Muslim; and (3) bypassed the prohibition on immolation by arguing that the punishment did not impinge upon the sanctity of immolation, that the prohibition was never consensual and that public interest (*maṣlaḥa*) was ensured by burning al-Kasāsba. Thirdly, we will explore how the legality of immolation was debated within the *salafī jihādī* scholarly community by looking first at how the punishment was explained within IS, and secondly how immolation was debated between IS and al-Qāᶜida. Fourthly, and in conclusion, we will argue that Aḥlām al-Naṣr's work

* University of Copenhagen

1. I would like to thank Daniel Lav, Christian Lange, Cole Bunzel and Nathan French who all read an earlier version of this chapter and provided me with valuable comments and suggestions.

may ultimately be seen as a critique of the position on violence in contemporary Islamic law that to IS is considered to be nothing but an appeasement to the West.

'WHAT IS THE RULING FOR BURNING AN INFIDEL TO DEATH?'

Captured on 24 December 2014 after performing an emergency landing in the Euphrates, Muᶜādh al-Kasāsba was, in a film released by IS on 3 February 2015, theatrically paraded past a bombarded district in IS's de facto capital al-Raqqa. Dressed in an orange jumpsuit reminiscent of imprisoned *jihādī*s at Guantánamo and Abu Ghurayb, al-Kasāsba was placed inside an iron cage and made to watch as 'a commander of one of the districts (*qawātiᶜ*) bombed by the crusading coalition' set alight a petrol-doused trail leading to the cage, consequentially burning al-Kasāsba to death.[2] Finally, as the film was brought to an end, a bulldozer was seen covering al-Kasāsba's charred body with debris to the sound of a *nashīd* (hymn) singing: '[T]he bullets will ragingly burn, for retribution (*qiṣāṣ*) has come; where then may mortals find an escape from the sparks (*sharār*)?'.[3] Al-Kasāsba's immolation immediately sparked outrage across the Muslim world, and from the religious institution al-Azhar in Egypt to the clerical establishment in Saudi Arabia, scholars unanimously declared immolation unfounded in Islam. Yūsuf al-Qaraḍāwī (b. 1926), the influential exiled Azharī scholar, issued a *fatwā* that strongly rejected immolation, owing to the prophetic precept that 'if you shall kill, then kill in a kind manner (*idhā qataltum fa-aḥsinu al-qitla*)'.[4] Similarly, when interviewed on the official call-in-and-get-a-*fatwā* programme *Yastaftūnak* (*They Seek Your Counsel*), a member of the prominent Council for Senior Scholars in Saudi Arabia, Saᶜd al-Shathrī (b. 1967), assured the viewers

2. Muʾsassat al-Furqān, 'Shifaʾ al-ṣudūr', https://archive.org/details/islamicstate93_2015 1228_2339, 14:40–19:35. According to an article published in IS's magazine *Dābiq* in December 2014, Kasāsba was captured on 24 December 2015. This information was provided in a published transcript of the interrogation of Kasāsba shown in the videotaped execution – thereby suggesting that this recording (and possibly even the execution) occurred prior to the publication of the magazine in late-December 2014; see 'The Capture of a Crusader Pilot', *Dābiq* (1436/2014), 6, p. 34.
3. This is an excerpt from IS's famous hymn *Qarīban qarībā*; see Muʾsassat al-Ajnād, 'Qarīban qarībā', https://archive.org/details/Qariba-234, 2015 (accessed 10 June 2020). For accessed dates of online resources, see the Bibliography and the accompanying note, p. 366.
4. 'al-Qaraḍāwī yunaddid bi-qatl al-Kasāsba', https://www.eremnews.com/news/arab-world/201323, 2015, p. 1.

that IS was not allowed to justify immolation by 'picking a proof out of thin air' (*lā yantiqū ᶜan al-hawāᵓ*) from either the Qurᵓān or the Sunna.[5]

This condemnation was even echoed within the *salafī jihādī* scholarly community when Abū Muḥammad al-Maqdisī (b. 1959) – a scholar from Jordan historically aligned with al-Qāᵓida[6] – denounced the act of immolation as an 'evil custom' (*sunna sayyiᵓa*) invented by IS:

> Yesterday, you [IS] were in the Baᶜath Party, torturing and slaughtering Muslims. And today, you are leading a caliphate? Yet, what kind of caliphate is this? [. . .] Every day they invent another reprehensible innovation (*bidaᶜ*): first the innovation of slaughter, and now, immolation. I say that this has nothing to do with Islam [. . .] How could they do this when the Prophet Muhammad, may God's prayer and peace be upon him, explicitly said: 'None may punish with fire except the Lord of Fire' (*lā yuᶜadhdhib bi-l-nār illā rabb al-nār*)? [. . .] Also, they ranked the word of a man, the *shaykh al-islām* [an epithet for Taqī al-Dīn b. Taymiyya], above that of the Prophet Muḥammad, may God's prayer and peace be upon him. Is this what they call Salafism?[7]

Speaking on national television on 6 February 2015, al-Maqdisī referred to al-Kasāsba's videotaped execution that had ended with a quote by the medieval Ḥanbalī polymath Taqī al-Dīn Ibn Taymiyya (d. 728/1328), who equated exemplary retaliation (*al-tamthīl al-shāᵓiᶜ*) with implementing the divinely prescribed penalties (*ḥudūd*) and waging *jihād*.[8] However, al-Maqdisī not only decried that IS had invoked a statement by a fallible scholar to the detriment of a Sunnaic

5. 'Taᵓlīq maᶜālī al-shaykh Saᶜd al-Shatharī ᶜạlā ḥarq Muᶜādh al-Kasāsba', https://www.youtube.com/watch?v=qPMDw6Gtsu4, 2015, 3:53–7. For a survey of the opinions of establishment clergy in Saudi Arabia on IS, see Raihan Ismail, 'Reclaiming Saudi Salafism: The Saudi Religious Circles and the Threat of ISIS', *Journal of Arabian Studies* 9.2 (2020), 164–81.
6. For the authoritative study on al-Maqdisī, see Joas Wagemakers, *A Quietist Jihadi: The Ideology and Influence of Abu Muhammad al-Maqdisi* (Cambridge, 2012).
7. 'Liqāᵓ ḥaṣarī li-qanā Ruᵓyā maᶜ Abū Muḥammad al-Maqdisī', https://www.youtube.com/watch?v=XFh6gMKSGmA&t=2s, 2015, 5:11–7:33.
8. For the unabridged statement, see Taqī al-Dīn Ibn Taymiyya, *Majmūᶜ al-fatāwa* (Beirut, 2011) III, pp. 223–4. Ibn Taymiyya elsewhere explicitly addressed immolation, saying: 'Many a jurist has said that if a person murders by immolation, drowning, strangulation or the like that person must be exposed to what he did himself, although not by an act that in itself is prohibited, such as drinking alcohol or anal penetration. Among them are also some who say that there is no retaliation (*qawd*) except by the sword. However, the first opinion is more resembling (*ashbah*) of justice, the Book, and the Sunna'; see Ibn Taymiyya, *Majmūᶜ*, III, pp. 28:381.

commandment not to 'punish with fire', but consequentially partook in a punishment the right to which was reserved exclusively for God. Thus, without explicitly saying it, al-Maqdisī alluded to IS's major transgression: a crime of *shirk* (association) by equalling itself with God.

Shortly after al-Maqdisī's televised rebuttal, IS responded with a refutation penned by the young *salafī jihādī* scholar Turkī al-Binᶜalī (d. 2018) – a former protégé of al-Maqdisī's who had shifted allegiances and was heading IS's official Council for Research and Fatwās (Diwān al-Buhūth wa-l-Iftāᵓ).[9] Writing under the pseudonym Abū Khuzayma al-Muḍarī,[10] al-Binᶜalī reprimanded al-Maqdisī for slighting al-Kasāsba's 'blatant infidelity', asking him why – 'when denouncing slaughter and immolation' – al-Maqdisī had not denounced the anchorman's attribution of martyrdom (*shahīd*) on al-Kasāsba.[11] Apparently more concerned with refuting al-Maqdisī's 'seniority' than justifying immolation, al-Binᶜalī simply asserted that immolation was a 'penalty of reciprocity' (*al-muᶜāqaba bi-l-taḥrīq mumāthalatan*) in return for al-Kasāsba burning the townsfolk of al-Raqqa.[12] IS was, however, acutely aware that immolation was a matter of controversy, and so in an attempt to supress criticism, on 4 February 2015 released a film endeavouring to show the everyday man's contentment with burning al-Kasāsba. Thus, filming a crowd of onlookers watching the execution on a screen in downtown al-Raqqa, one man explained to the camera:

> Look, [the pilot] launched missiles against children and lands of the Muslims, and so the method of execution (*ṭarīqat al-qatl*) must be immolation (*ḥarq*). This is more complaisant (*hādhā yusā'yir akthar*) [with God].[13]

9. Abu Usāma al-Gharīb, *al-Mukhtaṣar al-jalī bi-sīrat shaykhnā Turkī al-Binᶜalī*, https://archive.org/details/almokhtasar.algali.high, 2013, p. 2.
10. Abū Khuzayma al-Muḍarī was identified as Turkī al-Binᶜalī by ᶜAbdullāh b. Aḥmad al-Ḥusaynī, *Wa-lā yawm al-ṭīn*, http://www.ilmway.com/site/maqdis/MS_7665, 2015, p. 6.
11. Quoted in al-Ḥusaynī, *Wa-lā yawm al-ṭīn*, p. 8.
12. Ibid., p. 28. ᶜAbdullāh b. Aḥmad al-Ḥusaynī, who himself was a member of al-Maqdisī's Shariᶜa Council on the latter's website Minbar al-Tawḥīd wa-l-Jihād, rebutted al-Binᶜalī by correcting him that the position that 'retaliation should not be sought except with the sword' (*lā qawad illā bi-l-sayf*) had been authorised by the Ḥanbalīs and Ḥanafīs; see al-Ḥusaynī, *Wa-lā yawm al-ṭīn*, p. 28.
13. al-Maktab al-Iᶜlāmī, 'Farḥat al-muslimīn bi-ḥarq al-ṭayyār al-ᵓurdunī', https://archive.org/details/oma_222_mail_050, 2015, 1:38–1:50. IS released a similar video on 12 February 2015, yet this time from Homs, where a young man displayed satisfaction with the punishment of immolation by simply reciting: 'If you have to respond to an attack, make your response proportionate, but it is best to stand fast' (Q16:126); see al-Maktab al-Iᶜlāmī

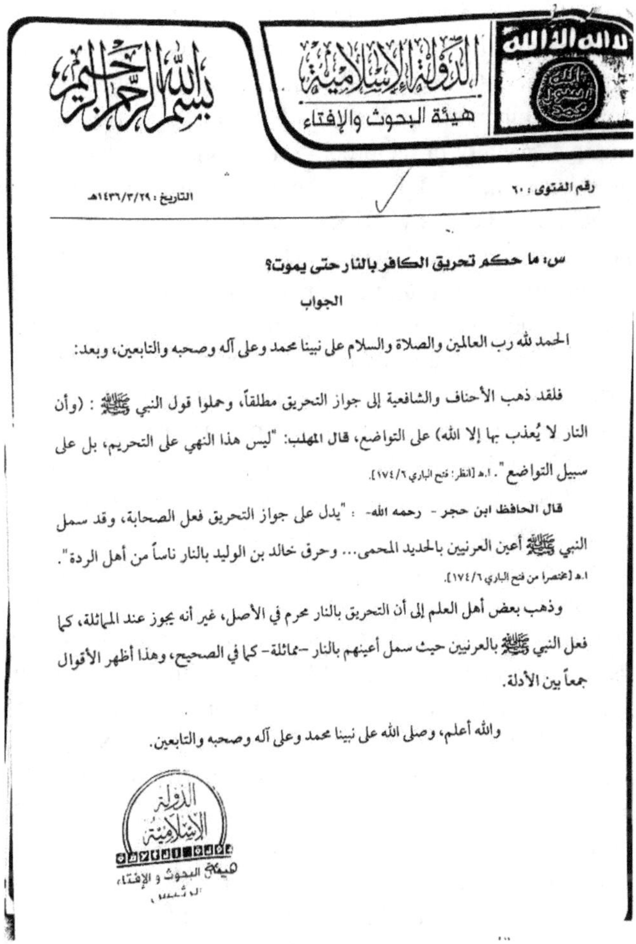

بسم الله الرحمن الرحيم

الدولة الإسلامية

هيئة البحوث والإفتاء

رقم الفتوى : ٦٠

التاريخ : ١٤٣٦/٣/٢٩هـ

س: ما حكم تحريق الكافر بالنار حتى يموت؟

الجواب

الحمد لله رب العالمين والصلاة والسلام على نبينا محمد وعلى آله وصحبه والتابعين، وبعد:

فلقد ذهب الأحناف والشافعية إلى جواز التحريق مطلقاً، وحملوا قول النبي ﷺ : (وأن النار لا يُعذب بها إلا الله) على التواضع، قال المهلب: "ليس هذا النهي على التحريم، بل على سبيل التواضع". ا.هـ [انظر: فتح الباري ٦/١٧٤].

قال الحافظ ابن حجر - رحمه الله- : "يدل على جواز التحريق فعل الصحابة، وقد سمل النبي ﷺ أعين العرنيين بالحديد المحمى... وحرق خالد بن الوليد بالنار ناساً من أهل الردة". ا.هـ [مختصرا من فتح الباري ٦/١٧٤].

وذهب بعض أهل العلم إلى أن التحريق بالنار محرم في الأصل، غير أنه يجوز عند المماثلة، كما فعل النبي ﷺ بالعرنيين حيث سمل أعينهم بالنار -مماثلة- كما في الصحيح، وهذا أظهر الأقوال جمعاً بين الأدلة.

والله أعلم، وصلى الله على نبينا محمد وعلى آله وصحبه والتابعين.

الدولة الإسلامية

هيئة البحوث والإفتاء

Figure 1 *Fatwā* justifying immolation issued by IS's Council for Research and Fatwas and distributed by IS in Syria and Iraq (photo by author)

IS had, however, even prior to the execution, been concerned with the legality of immolating al-Kasāsba. Thus, in a series of leaked legal documents (see Figure 1) dated two weeks prior to al-Kasāsba's immolation, a *fatwā* was unveiled (most likely authored by al-Binᶜalī) answering the inquiry: '[W]hat is the ruling for burning an infidel (*taḥrīq al-kāfir bi-l-nār*) to death?'. It concluded that

'Arā' al-muslimīn bi-ḥarq al-ṭayyār al-urdunī', https://archive.org/details/w.homs.araa.mouslimen.harq.tayyar.original.quality, 2015, 2:11–2:19.

'some scholars considered immolation principally prohibited, yet permitted in the case of reciprocity (*al-mumāthala*)'.[14] Explaining how the punishment had not breached the sanctity of immolation, al-Binᶜalī adduced a story relating how the Prophet Muḥammad gouged out the eyes of a group of tribesmen from ᶜUrayna in a 'penalty of reciprocity', and importantly so with 'fire-heated iron' (*bi-l-ḥadīd al-muḥammi*). Despite being repeated verbatim by IS's official magazine *Dābiq* on 12 February 2015,[15] al-Binᶜalī's analogy was, however, not enough to allay concerns that IS had violated the sanctity of immolation. Thus, within the coming month IS's unofficial publishing house al-Ghurabaᵓ li-l-Iᶜlām launched a major scholarly campaign to justify burning al-Kasāsba.

A dozen works (see Figure 2) written by some of IS's foremost ideologues were released; one work, however, was surprisingly penned by a young woman by the name Shaymāᵓ Haddād (b. 1992), yet known more commonly by her pseudonym Aḥlām al-Naṣr. Published online on 13 February 2015, the work entitled *Nay, We Obeyed God When We Burned Him, You Slaves of the Luxurious Life (Bal ᵓaṭᶜanā allāh idh aḥraqanāhu ya ᶜabīda al-rafāhiyya)* became IS's lengthiest *apologia* ever written for burning al-Kasāsba.[16] Rejecting the accusation that IS had transgressed a prohibition by burning al-Kasāsba, Aḥlām al-Naṣr posited a tripartite ruling stating that (1) retribution (*qiṣāṣ*) was a defensive measure; (2) that al-Kasāsba was not a Muslim; and (3) that burning him was nothing short of applying *qiṣāṣ* in return for al-Kasāsba's incendiary bombardment of IS. Aḥlām al-Naṣr's work aptly represented the legal reasoning permeating the campaign, and therefore serves as a proper point of departure for us for studying how IS justified burning al-Kasāsba.

Aḥlām al-Naṣr's scholarly profundity was, however, not incidental. Born into a family of religious learning in Damascus in 1992, Aḥlām al-Naṣr's grandfather, Muṣṭafā al-Bughā (b. 1938), was a prominent jurist in the Syrian Arab Republic who had taught at the Faculty of Sharīᶜa at the University of Damascus before being appointed to the governmental Higher Council for Fatwās.[17] Aḥlām

14. Hayᵓat al-Buhuth wa-l-Iftaᵓ, 'Mā ḥukm taḥrīq al-kāfir bi-l-nār hatā yamūt?', 2015 (see Figure 1), p. 1.
15. 'The Burning of the Murtadd Pilot', https://jihadology.net/2015/02/12/al-ḥayat-media-center-presents-a-new-issue-of-the-islamic-states-magazine-dabiq-7/, 2015, pp. 5–8.
16. For a translation of this work, see my forthcoming chapter, 'Aḥlām al-Naṣr and the Islamic State's Justification for Execution by Burning', in *Islamic Law in Context: A Primary Source Reader*, eds Omar Anchassi and Robert Gleave (Cambridge, forthcoming).
17. Thomas Pierret and Mériam Cheikh, '"I Am Very Happy Here": Female Jihad in Syria as Self-Accomplishment', *Hawwa: Journal of Women of the Middle East and the Islamic World* 13.2 (2015), 241–69, here p. 248. Aḥlām al-Naṣr also signed *Nay, We Obeyed God When We Burned Him* with the pseudonym Umm Usāma al-Dimashqiyya, suggesting that

Figure 2 Some works justifying the legality of immolation released by al-Ghurabāʾ li-l-ʿIlām and al-Wafāʾ; the top first from the right being Aḥlām al-Naṣr's (photo by author)

al-Naṣr's mother, Īmān al-Bughā, also received a doctoral degree in Syria, but had moved to Saudi Arabia to teach *fiqh* at the University of Dammām prior to joining IS in October 2014, taking up a judicial position alongside al-Binᶜalī.[18] Aḥlām al-Naṣr, who accompanied her mother to al-Raqqa, soon became something of a court scholar with more than a dozen apologetic works released by IS in the period between 2014–19 – most notably a major compilation of poetry entitled *ᶜUwār al-ḥaqq* (*The Blazing Truth*).

Nay, We Obeyed God When We Burned Him was to become, however, Aḥlām al-Naṣr's most legally oriented work published to date, and so even though not conforming to the scholarly scrupulousness typical of classical *fiqh*, the work certainly suggested a legal prowess beyond that expected of a lay Muslim.[19] Likely authored in al-Raqqa,[20] the work confidently – albeit somewhat rudimentarily – engaged in a series of legal debates that were crucial in formulating criminal law in the medieval Muslim world. Aḥlām al-Naṣr's scholarly jargon, however, often turned polemical to the point of threatening to burn infidel children at a 'barbecue party' (*hafla shawā*).[21] Yet, this combination of a coarse methodology and a vulgar rhetoric may indeed be the defining character, if not strength, of Aḥlām al-Naṣr's legal reasoning; a reasoning that in the end empowered her to surmount even the most adamant scholarly opposition – not least the prohibition on immolation, to which we now turn.

THE BEST DEFENCE IS . . . REVENGE!

Aḥlām al-Naṣr introduced her work by praising how IS had restored Islam according to 'the methodology of its ancestors' (*man nahaja abnāʾahu*) who – continuing her argument – 'neither slept from injustice nor accepted shame or

she was born in Damascus and had given birth or aspired to do so to a son named Usāma – likely in honour of the late leader of al-Qa'ida, Usāma b. Lādin (d. 2011). For more on Muṣṭafā al-Bughā, see Thomas Pierret, *Religion and State in Syria: The Sunni Ulama from Coup to Revolution* (Cambridge, 2013), p. 45.

18. Diwān al-Daᶜwa wa-l-Masājid, 'Qissat mujāhid: al-duktūra Īmān Muṣṭafā al-Bughā', http://www.aymennjawad.org/19132/the-archivist-stories-of-the-mujahideen-unseen, 2016, p. 1.
19. Īmān al-Bughā emphasised her daughter's erudition, explaining how Aḥlām al-Naṣr was 'born with a dictionary in her mouth'; see Robyn Creswell and Bernard Haykel, 'Poetry in Jihadi Culture', in *Jihadi Culture: The Art and Social Practices of Militant Islamists*, ed. Thomas Hegghammer (Cambridge, 2017), p. 24.
20. This was suggested by a rare first-hand report describing how Aḥlām al-Naṣr saw people in al-Raqqa rejoice when IS burned al-Kasāsba; see Aḥlām al-Naṣr, *Bal ʾaṭᶜanā allāh*, p. 22.
21. Aḥlām al-Naṣr, *Bal ʾaṭᶜanā allāh idh aḥraqanāhu ya ᶜabīda al-rafāhiyya*, https://justpaste.it/je3o, 1436/2015, p. 33.

humiliation'.[22] Aḥlām al-Naṣr readily identified the ancestors with 'those believers' (*li-lladīna āmanū*) intimated at in Q42:39, and 'who when stricken with insolence defended themselves'.[23] Having demonstrated that the act of defending oneself (*intiṣār*) was integral to ancestral methodology – albeit without specifying what precisely 'insolence' (*baghy*) meant – Aḥlām al-Naṣr proceeded to quote an array of early and medieval exegetical authorities to establish that *intiṣār* was a retributive act of self-defence meant to dissuade the enemy from attacking Muslims. Aḥlām al-Naṣr, for example, quoted the early Ḥanafī jurist Abū Bakr al-Jaṣṣāṣ (d. 370/942) who argued that: '[T]he preponderant meaning (*ẓāhir*) of the verse suggests that retribution (*intiṣār*) is preferable in this circumstance. Do you not see how He compared [retribution] to performing the prayer and obeying God the Exalted?'.[24] While equating retribution with the obligation to perform the daily prayer, Aḥlām al-Naṣr took pain to clarify that *intiṣār* was not an act of aggression, but of self-defence. Aḥlām al-Naṣr quoted the Shāfiʿī scholar Ismāʿīl b. Kathīr (d. 774/1373), who argued that the believers in Q42:39 'were neither weak nor humiliated, but able to seek retaliation (*inṭiqām*)'. Aḥlām al-Naṣr's wish to prove *intiṣār*'s violent qualification became abundantly clear when she quoted the early Meccan jurist ʿAbd al-Mālik b. Jurayj (d. 150/767) for saying that Q42:39 referred to none other than the Prophet Muḥammad, 'who defended himself with the sword (*yantaṣir bi-l-sayf*)'.[25] Aḥlām al-Naṣr concluded the commentary on Q42:39 by stating that retribution should 'not be sought in doltish peacefulness, self-abasement, or tears', asking who dared be 'so sharp-witted to say by the sword, but not by fire (*bi-l-nār*)?'.[26] Before we return to the question of how to legally carry out retribution, we must, however, first take a look at the idea of retaliatory punishment (*qiṣāṣ*) in Islamic law.

Despite being mentioned as early as in the Code of Hammurabi (dating to the First Babylonian Dynasty),[27] the lex talionis was famously uttered by Moses (Exod. 2:23–5), and was much later – as acknowledged by Aḥlām al-Naṣr – paraphrased in Q5:45.[28] Defined in classical *fiqh* as a punishment of death or

22. Ibid., p. 5.
23. Q42:39's relative pronoun *alladhīna* (who) refers back to Q42:36's mention of 'those who believe and trust in their Lord'.
24. Aḥlām al-Naṣr, *Bal ʾaṭʿanā allāh*, p. 6.
25. Ibid. This was quoted from Jalāl al-Dīn al-Suyūṭī, *al-Durr al-manẓūr fī tafsīr bi-l-maʾthūr* (Riyadh, 2015), VII, p. 358.
26. Aḥlām al-Naṣr, *Bal ʾaṭʿanā allāh*, p. 6.
27. David P. Wright, *Inventing God's Law: How the Covenant Code of the Bible Used and Revised the Laws of Hammurabi* (Oxford, 2009), pp. 180–2.
28. This similarity between the Hebrew Bible and the Qurʾān was noted by Aḥlām al-Naṣr, *Bal ʾaṭʿanā allāh*, p. 10.

bodily harm dealt against an offender in a manner equivalent to that suffered by the offended, the medieval scholarly community was divided on the question of how *qiṣāṣ* should be applied if the offender had murdered a person in an unlawful mode of slaying – e.g. by sodomy or drowning the victim in alcohol.[29] Thus, was the executioner himself to indulge in unlawful anal penetration or intoxication in order to faithfully carry out the punishment? Muwaffaq al-Dīn Ibn Qudāma (d.620/1223), the revered medieval Ḥanbalī jurist, was a purveyor of the majority opinion that the offender was always to be 'slain by the sword' and advanced the same prophetic precept as did al-Qaraḍāwī – namely, that 'if you shall kill, then kill in a kind manner'.[30] Yet, a minority, represented by the Andalusian jurist Abū Muḥammad b. Ḥazm (d. 456/1064), argued that if one had murdered in an unlawful mode of slaying, the offender ought to be slain in a mode *as equal as possible* (e.g. by a rock or an arrow), albeit never unlawful.[31] But what about immolation? What if the offender was a fighter pilot who had burned townsfolk in flames issuing from modern-day missiles? While we shall later return to this question, for now keep in mind that though carrying out *qiṣāṣ* in an unlawful mode of slaying was considered forbidden across the scholarly spectrum, what precisely constituted the unlawful still remained a disputed question. Holding on to that thought, we may return to Aḥlām al-Naṣr's work.

Although demonstrating that defensive retribution is a legal obligation on par with the daily prayer imposed on IS, Aḥlām al-Naṣr had not yet equated *intiṣār* (or *intiqām*) with *qiṣāṣ* nor established that the punishment was reciprocal. Thus, in order to do this, Aḥlām al-Naṣr proceeded to interpret the sequential verse, Q42:40:

> Let evil be requited by an equal evil (*wa-jazāʾu sayyiʾatin sayyiʾatun mithluhā*), [though anyone who forgives and puts things right will get a reward from God. Surely, He does not like those who do wrong].

Failing to mention the bracketed part of the verse, Aḥlām al-Naṣr instead quoted an interpretation by the Mauritanian *salafī* scholar Muḥammad al-Amīn

29. Mahfodz Mohamed, 'The Concept of Qisas in Islamic Law', *Islamic Studies* 22.2 (1982), 80; see also Rudolph Peters, *Crime and Punishment in Islamic Law: Theory and Practice from the Sixteenth to the Twenty-First Century* (Cambridge, 2007), pp. 38–9.
30. Muwaffaq al-Dīn b. Qudāma, *al-Mughnī* (Riyadh, 2013), XI, pp. 532–3.
31. Abū Muḥammad b. Ḥazm, *al-Muḥallā bi-l-āthār fī sharḥ al-mujallā bi-l-ikhtiṣār* (Beirut, 2016), XV, p. 245. For more on this debate, see Mohamed, 'The Concept of Qisas in Islamic Law', pp. 82–4.

al-Shinqīṭī (d.1973), who in the 1960s authored one of the most widely read commentary works (*tafsīr*) in the modern Muslim world.[32] Al-Shinqīṭī was quoted commenting on Q42:40, which – faithful to the commentary work's intertextual methodology – was explained with reference to Q2:194. Aḥlām al-Naṣr – as will we – quoted al-Shinqīṭī at length:

> God commanded that an 'evil be requited by an equal evil' [Q42:40], but *qiṣāṣ* is not an evil (*ma*ᶜ *anna al-qiṣāṣ laysa bi-sayyiʾa*) as He also said: 'If anyone commits aggression against you, attack him as he attacked you' [Q2:194]. As is apparent (*kamā huwa ẓāhir*), *qiṣāṣ* dealt against an aggressor can never in itself be an act of aggression (*i*ᶜ*tidaʾ*) as suggested by the resemblance between the wordings (*lafẓayn*) in [Q2:194 and Q42:40].[33]

Aḥlām al-Naṣr now skilfully transformed *qiṣāṣ* from a discretionary punishment to a form of defensive war by appropriating al-Shinqīṭī's link between Q40:42's emphasis on reciprocal evil and the call to defend oneself in Q2:194.

This transformation became even more obvious when Aḥlām al-Naṣr argued – contrary to the position in classical *fiqh* – that *qiṣāṣ* was not meant as a mechanism to restrict the harm dealt against an offender, but to pre-emptively deter him, or in her own words: '[T]o repel through chastisement and disciplinary punishment'.[34] Aḥlām al-Naṣr substantiated this assertion by quoting Ibn Kathīr, who explained that 'if a murderer knows he is about to proceed with a murder, yet abstains from the act, there is life to be saved for mankind in this [very act of abstinence]'[35] – a reference to the qurʾānic injunction that 'there is life for you in *qiṣāṣ*' (Q2:179). Similar to Aḥlām al-Naṣr's portrayal of *qiṣāṣ* as an instrument of defensive war, Soheil Hashmi has explained how al-Qāᶜida was always careful to portray their 'war' as a defensive *jihād* in order to relax any legal restraint imposed on the classical expansionist *jihād* – e.g. the obligation to prevent collateral damage or the prohibition on suicidally 'rushing into combat'.[36] Thus, by repeatedly

32. Muḥammad al-Amīn al-Shinqīṭī's commentary work *ᶜAdwāʾ al-bayān fī īdāḥ al-Qurʾān bi-l-Qurʾān* was published sequentially in nine volumes between March 1963 and September 1976 in Cairo. For a study on this work and al-Shinqīṭī, see my article in preparation, 'From Mauritania to Medina: Muḥammad al-Amīn al-Shinqīṭī (d. 1973) and the Search for a Salafī Hermeneutics'.
33. Aḥlām al-Naṣr, *Bal ʾaṭᶜanā allāh*, p. 7. This was quoted from al-Shinqīṭī, *ᶜAdwāʾ al-bayān fī ʾidāḥ al-Qurʾān bi-l-Quʾrān* (Beirut, 2013), II, p. 955.
34. Aḥlām al-Naṣr, *Bal ʾaṭᶜanā allāh*, p. 12.
35. Ibid. This was quoted from Ismāᶜīl b. Kathīr, *Tafsīr al-Qurʾān al-ᶜazīm* (Dammam, 2019), I, p. 212.
36. Soheil Hashmi, '9/11 and the Jihad Tradition', in *Terror, Culture, Politics: Rethinking*

emphasising how immolation was 'less than he deserved' (*aqall mā yastaḥiqquhu*) and carried out in 'a reduced manner' (*bi-shakl muṣaghghar*), Aḥlām al-Naṣr similarly widened IS's legal window of action, and allowed herself to completely overlook the thorny question of how to treat prisoners of war – the subject of which is a major concern in both medieval and modern Islamic law.[37] Moreover, although the requirement of the defendant's admission of guilt was fulfilled by al-Kasāsba's published (yet likely forced) confession in *Dābiq* in December 2014,[38] nowhere did Aḥlām al-Naṣr mention the classical stipulation that either a pardon or a payment of blood money (*diyya*) could have absolved al-Kasāsba.[39] This latter possibility was even explicitly discarded by a fellow propagandist with the pseudonym ᶜAhd, who in a work entitled *Muᶜādh's Burning Under the Microscope (Ḥarq Muᶜādh taḥt al-mijhar)* argued that al-Kasāsba's immolation exonerated IS from the accusation of 'taking lightly the blood of the Muslims'.[40] Thus, rather than portraying al-Kasāsba as a lapsed believer who had committed a punishable crime, Aḥlām al-Naṣr – as we shall now see – was more concerned with convincing the reader that IS had not burned a Muslim.

FORMULATING A RADICAL THEOLOGY OF FAITH

Daniel Lav has demonstrated that what makes a Muslim truly a Muslim has been, and still remains, a defining question in contemporary Jihadism. Thus, questions concerning the indivisibility of faith, whether acts are required for belief, and if so, whether *takfīr* (excommunication) may be pronounced on a Muslim who has committed a sin (minor or major) or act of unbelief, have pitted the *salafī jihādī* community against itself since the 1960s.[41] Similarly, the sheer

9/11, eds Daniel J. Sherman and Terry Nardin (Bloomington, 2006), p. 154. This was also an interpretive strategy employed by al-Maqdisī; see Wagemakers, *A Quietist Jihadi*, p. 71.

37. For the profundity of this issue, see Muhammad Munir, 'Debates on the Rights of Prisoners of War in Islamic Law', *Islamic Studies* 49.4 (2010), 463–92; and Lena Salaymeh, 'Early Islamic Legal-Historical Precedents: Prisoners of War', *Law and History Review* 26.3 (2008), 521–44. As pointed out to me by Nathan French, the concern for the principle of *a maiore ad minorus* – from the greater to the lesser – also greatly affected the radical *salafī* scholar Ḥamūd al-Shuᶜaybī (d. 2001), who would explain how the 'modern' variety of martyrdom-seeking (such as suicide bombing) was *a lesser* form of violence than that used in the medieval period; see Nathan French, *And God Knows the Martyrs: Martyrdom and Violence in Jihadi-Salafism* (Oxford, 2020), pp. 168–9.
38. 'The Capture of a Crusader Pilot', p. 34.
39. Peters, *Crime and Punishment in Islamic Law*, pp. 44–6.
40. ᶜAhd, *Ḥarq Muᶜādh taḥt al-mijhar*, 2015, p. 6.
41. Daniel Lav, *Radical Islam and the Revival of Medieval Theology* (Cambridge, 2012), p. 4.

space devoted to delineating al-Kasāsba's apostasy betrays Aḥlām al-Naṣr's awareness of the sensitivity of the subject. Thus, one might ask, why bother excommunicating al-Kasāsba? Why not simply charge him for murder – that is, as a *compos mentis* Muslim? To me, the answer quite simply is that it was easier for Aḥlām al-Naṣr to justify burning an infidel than a Muslim. As we shall see, Aḥlām al-Naṣr claimed that al-Kasāsba's enrolment in an infidel army consequentially transformed him into an infidel himself, thereby pigeonholing him with the excommunicated Āl al-Salūl. This historical designation was ultimately Aḥlām al-Naṣr's justification for arguing that IS did not burn a Muslim, but rather a descendent of the archetypical *murtadd*-cum-*kāfir*, ᶜAbdullāh b. Salūl (d.9/631). Aḥlām al-Naṣr's exegetical starting point was, however, somewhat different, and began with a commentary on Q5:51:

> You who believe, do not take the Jews and Christians as allies (*awliyāʾ*). They are allies only to each other. Anyone who takes them as an ally becomes one of them (*wa-man yatawalla-hum min-kum fa-innahu min-hum*). Surely, God does not guide the wrongdoers.

Q5:51 had historically posed three exegetical questions to the scholars of the medieval Muslim world: (1) who are the Jews and Christians that a Muslim must not take as *awliyāʾ*; (2) what does the pronoun *awliyāʾ* actually mean; and (3) what are the legal ramifications for a Muslim who had *yatawallā* with a Jew or a Christian? These were also the very three questions that directed Aḥlām al-Naṣr's exegesis, and for that reason we will, in the following, make Aḥlām al-Naṣr answer each question in turn.

As part of the effort to identify the Jews and Christians whom a Muslim may not take as *awliyāʾ*, Aḥlām al-Naṣr turned to al-Jaṣṣās, who in a commentary on Q5:51 argued that God:

> prohibited in these verses allying oneself with the infidels (*kuffār*) and showing hospitality to them. He commanded that they be affronted and humiliated just as He prohibited the act of seeking help from them in any matter concerning the Muslims.[42]

Aḥlām al-Naṣr did not comment upon the quotation, suggesting that she was in agreement with al-Jaṣṣās, who – writing in the tenth century Abbasid

42. Aḥlām al-Naṣr, *Bal ʾaṭᶜanā allāh*, p. 15. This was quoted from Abū Bakr al-Jaṣṣās, *Ahkām al-Qurʾān* (Beirut, 1992), IV, p. 293.

Caliphate – held that Jews and Christians were infidels, and for that simple reason prohibited allying with, showing hospitality to, or seeking help from a Jew or a Christian. Yet what Aḥlām al-Naṣr neglected to mention was that al-Jaṣṣās's exposition was part of a larger effort to delimit the circumstances under which Christians and Jews could actually live *amicably* alongside Muslims in medieval Baghdad.[43] Mohammad Khalil has accordingly noted how IS would often promote a minority opinion, albeit in an 'incomplete or misleading manner', to the status of consensus in order to claim a spot for their peripheral opinion in Islam.[44] Similarly, by decontextualising al-Jaṣṣās's interpretation, Aḥlām al-Naṣr conveniently avoided the question of whether Q5:51 referred generically to all Jews and Christians (regardless of time and place), or solely to those Jews and Christians inimical to the Prophet Muhammad when Q5:51 was revealed to him in Medina.

Aḥlām al-Naṣr decided to strengthen her ahistorical interpretation by turning to a familiar ally, and so al-Shinqīṭī was once again summoned to comment on Q5:51:

> [God] in this beneficent verse said that any Muslim who takes Jews or Christians as allies will due to allying with them become one of them. He also clarified in another place that some actually did take them as allies, which was the cause for the infinite duration of torment [they would receive in their graves] and the displeasure of God. They even took them as allies after having turned Muslims as the Exalted said: 'You see many of them allying (*yatawallawn*) with those who have disbelieved (*alladhīna kafarū*)' [Q5:80].[45]

Although quoting al-Shinqīṭī might seem like an odd option considering the latter's proximity to the clerical establishment in Saudi Arabia – whose royal family has frequently been declared infidel by IS[46] – this, on closer scrutiny, is not necessarily odd at all. Simon Wolfgang Fuchs, for example, noted how the *jihādī* scholar Sayyid Imām al-Sharīf's (b. 1950) broad reading of the scholarly tradition was an attempt to position himself squarely within the bounds of

43. Aḥlām al-Naṣr, *Bal ʾaṭʿanā allāh*, p. 15.
44. Mohammad Hassan Khalil, *Jihad, Radicalism, and the New Atheism* (Cambridge, 2017), p. 86.
45. Aḥlām al-Naṣr, *Bal ʾaṭʿanā allāh*, p. 15. This was quoted from al-Shinqīṭī, *ʿAdwāʾ al-bayān*, I, p. 412.
46. Cole Bunzel, 'Wahhabism, Saudi Arabia, and the Islamic State: 'Abdullah Ibn Jibrin and Turki al-Bin'ali', in *Salman's Legacy: The Dilemmas of a New Era in Saudi Arabia*, ed. Madawi Al-Rasheed (London, 2018), p. 195.

orthodoxy.[47] Likewise, for al-Qāᶜida, 'the credibility of the source and context is less important than the nature of the message being pinpointed', with the result that they could paraphrase a medieval alcohol-consuming poet in a work on modest behaviour.[48] Similarly, one could say, by appropriating the opinion of 'a pay-roll scholar' like al-Shinqīṭī, Aḥlām al-Naṣr was able to prove to the reader – and herself, one may add – that IS's interpretation was shared by a scholar who, by many in the *salafī* movement, is regarded as a foremost authority in the Muslim world.

Moving on to the second question, Aḥlām al-Naṣr glossed that the verb *yatawallā* did not merely mean fighting on behalf of infidels, but indeed any act of 'serving or pleasing them'.[49] Johanna Pink has shown that despite the widely held belief that the Jews and Christians mentioned in Q5:51 were infidels, a majority of scholars in the modern period still held that the verse did not call for hostility against non-Muslims.[50] Although never mentioning the relation, Aḥlām al-Naṣr's discussion of *yatawallā* was also semantically and ideationally related to the concept of *al-walāᵓ wa-l-barāᵓ* (loyalty and disavowal) that had been transformed by al-Maqdisī, who shifted the emphasis from condemning wrongful *walāᵓ* to apply violent *barāᵓ* against infidel rulers of the Muslim world.[51] However, contrary to both mainstream and radical scholarship, Aḥlām al-Naṣr did not distinguish between the different forms of interaction that could occur between an infidel and a Muslim. Nāṣir al-Fahd (b. 1968), a *salafī* scholar from Saudi Arabia aligned with al-Qāᶜida, by contrast distinguished between permissible interaction (*muᶜāmala jāᵓiza*), assistance (*muwālat*) and alliance (*tawallī*), while arguing that only the latter qualified as unbelief (*kufr*).[52] This graduation

47. Simon Wolfgang Fuchs, 'Do Excellent Surgeons Make Miserable Exegetes? Negotiating the Sunni Tradition in the *gihadi* Camps', *Die Welt des Islams* 53.2 (2013), pp. 192–237, 202. This is not much different from how al-Binᶜalī in a study of the legality of man-made law favoured an opinion made by the former Grand Mufti in Saudi Arabia, Muḥammad b. Ibrāhīm (d. 1969); see Bunzel, 'Wahhabism, Saudi Arabia, and the Islamic State', p. 195. This trend was also noted by Michael Cook, *Ancient Religions, Modern Politics: The Islamic Case in Comparative Perspective* (Princeton, 2014), pp. 385–6.
48. Elisabeth Kendall, 'Jihadist Propaganda and its Exploitation of the Arab Poetic Tradition', in *Reclaiming Islamic Tradition: Modern Interpretations of the Classical Heritage*, eds Elisabeth Kendall and Ahmad Khan (Edinburgh, 2016), p. 233.
49. Aḥlām al-Naṣr, *Bal ᵓaṭᶜanā allāh*, p. 15.
50. Johanna Pink, 'Tradition and Ideology in Contemporary Sunnite Qur'anic Exegesis', *Die Welt des Islams* 50.1 (2010), pp. 3–59, here p. 44.
51. Wagemakers, 'The Transformation of a Radical Concept: *al-wala' wa-l-bara'* in the Ideology of Abu Muhammad al-Maqdisi', in *Global Salafism: Islam's New Religious Movement*, ed. Roel Meijer (London, 2009), pp. 95–7.
52. Justyna Nedza, 'The Sum of its Parts: The State as Apostate in Contemporary Saudi

was not specified by Aḥlām al-Naṣr, who merely posited that the act of *yatawallā* was categorical: '[A] person is either a believer or an infidel (*fa-l-nās immā muʾmin wa-immā kāfir*)'.[53]

Having answered the first and second question, Aḥlām al-Naṣr proceeded to answer the third: what are the legal ramifications of allying oneself with an infidel? Historically, scholars in the medieval period were acutely aware that Q5:51's phrase 'becomes one of them' (*min-kum fa-inna-hu min-hum*) could *literally* mean that a Muslim became either Jew or Christian. Al-Jaṣṣāṣ accordingly favoured that Q5:51 be read metaphorically, and so rather than enjoying the protected status granted to Jews and Christians, a Muslim who had allied with an infidel became an apostate (*murtadd*) apart from the protected 'People of the Book' (*ahl al-kitāb*).[54] Aḥlām al-Naṣr was equally determined to prove that al-Kasāsba had not *literally* turned into a Jew or a Christian – thereby becoming an infidel by birth (*kāfir aṣli*) – but instead turned into something much worse: an infidel by choice. However, in order to concludingly answer the third question, Aḥlām al-Naṣr proceeded to present the *sabab al-nuzūl* (occasion for revelation) material that occasioned Q5:51.

Aḥlām al-Naṣr quoted a report attributed to the companion ᶜUbāda b. Ṣāmit (d. 34/656), explaining why, how and when Q5:51 was revealed. This report told the story of the controversial companion ᶜAbd Allāh b. Ubayy (d. 9/631) – derogatorily referred to by the maternal *nasab* Salūl[55] – who despite claiming allegiance to the Prophet Muḥammad was accused of cooperating with the Jews in Medina. Thus, when another companion went to the Prophet Muḥammad to disclaim association with the very Jews whom Salūl cooperated with, Q5:51 was purportedly revealed to the Prophet Muḥammad.[56] Due to the lip-service paid to the latter, Salūl was to become the *munāfiq* (hypocrite) par excellence in the

Militant Islamism', in *Accusations of Unbelief in Islam: A Diachronic Perspective on Takfir*, eds Camilla Adang et al. (Leiden, 2015), p. 314. This position was also favoured by Jordanian *salafi-jihādī* scholar Abū Qatāda al-Filasṭīnī (b. 1960); see Lav, *Radical Islam and the Revival of Medieval Theology*, pp. 180–1. For a biography of Nāṣir al-Fahd, see Thomas Hegghammer, *Jihad in Saudi Arabia: Violence and Pan-Islamism since 1979* (Cambridge, 2010), pp. 87–9.

53. Aḥlām al-Naṣr, *Bal ʾaṭᶜanā allāh*, p. 10.
54. al-Jaṣṣās, *Aḥkām al-Qurʾān*, IV, p. 100.
55. Naming according to one's maternal *nasab* (lineage) rather than paternal one was traditionally perceived as patronising, merely adding to the choice of Aḥlām al-Naṣr's derogatory designation; see Patricia Crone, *God's Rule: Government and Islam* (New York, 2004), p. 159.
56. Aḥlām al-Naṣr, *Bal ʾaṭᶜanā allāh*, p. 16. This was quoted from al-Suyūtī, *al-Durr al-manthūr*, III, p. 98.

medieval scholarly tradition, and so Aḥlām al-Naṣr readily adduced the derogatory label, Āl al-Salūl. This was, however, inarguably a synonym for the scholarly establishment in Saudi Arabia, whose loyalty to the royal family – known as Āl Saᶜūd – was a frequent subject of scorn for Aḥlām al-Naṣr:

> What's the matter with you, Family of Salūl, you who pretend to possess wisdom! All you do is brag and falsely claim to speak the truth! Why did you not cry before [we burned al-Kasāsba]? Why did you not bemoan the crimes of your tyrant rulers, you, Family of Salūl?[57]

Pigeonholing al-Kasāsba together with the Āl al-Salul, Aḥlām al-Naṣr seemed to argue that when you nominally appear to be a Muslim, yet at the same time neglect the very community to which you hypocritically claim to belong, you qualify as a member of the Āl al-Salūl.

Aḥlām al-Naṣr was certainly not the first *salafī jihādī* scholar to put forth this contention, but was indebted to an argument of causality connecting hypocrisy (*nifāq*) with apostasy (*ridda*) that had a particularly violent intellectual history in contemporary Jihadism. Justyna Nedza, who studied the novel idea of *takfīr* directed at a non-singular entity – e.g. a state or institution – noted that al-Fahd in the 1990s worked according to a chain of causality in which 'hypocrisy leads to non-permissible association with the unbelievers (*tawallī*) which in turn leads to apostasy'.[58] Thus, the only remedy against apostasy was, according to al-Fahd, to shun hypocrisy and remain faithful to Islam. But, while one could do so by, for example, purifying one's creed or avoiding public employment, the only way to steer clear of hypocrisy according to Aḥlām al-Naṣr was to 'show hostility towards the infidels'.[59] Thus, in contrast to the position favoured by al-Fahd, Maqdisī[60] and Safar al-Ḥawālī[61] (b. 1960) – to mention but a few – Aḥlām al-Naṣr's uncompromising requirement of hostility was a product of a radical theology of faith that emerged during al-Qāᶜida's heyday in Iraq.

Thus, when the Taliban (Ṭālibān) Movement in the 1990s decided to form a wider fighting coalition in Afghanistan, their political (not to mention theological) pragmatism had sparked a heated debate within the burgeoning *salafī jihādī* community in Jordan. Abū Musᶜab al-Zarqāwī (d. 2006), the late leader of al-Qāᶜida in Iraq, favoured the minority position of declaring any member of the

57. Aḥlām al-Naṣr, *Bal ᵓaṭᶜanā allāh*, p. 20.
58. Nedza, 'The Sum of its Parts', p. 319.
59. Aḥlām al-Naṣr, *Bal ᵓaṭᶜanā allāh*, p. 17.
60. Wagemakers, *A Quietist Jihadi*, p. 154.
61. Safar al-Ḥawālī, *Ẓāhirat al-irjāᶜ fī-l-fikr al-islāmi* (Cairo, 1417/1996), I, pp. 299–302.

pragmatist Taliban non-Muslim, while al-Zarqāwī's former teacher, al-Maqdisī, represented the majority position that the Taliban could not afford to apply 'a pure theology, unmediated by jurisprudence' in the bid to rule Afghanistan.[62] Furthermore, claiming that faith (*imān*) was a single entity – either entirely present or entirely absent – was, according to the *salafī jihādī* scholar Abū Qatāda al-Filasṭīnī (b. 1960), akin to reviving the heretical dogma of the zealous *khawārij*, who in the period following the death of the Prophet Muḥammad forcefully argued that the negation or affirmation of a part entailed the negation or affirmation of the whole – such as the belief in Islam.[63] This was also why al-Maqdisī safely interpreted Q5:51 to refer to a state – and not an individual – thereby allowing himself to declare an infidel ruler an 'idol of infidelity' (*ṭāghūt al-kufr*), while concomitantly arguing that the 'idol's helper' (*nāṣir al-ṭāghūt*) – e.g. a government employee or conscript – was still truly a Muslim.[64]

Aḥlām al-Naṣr was, however, no doubt heir to al-Zarqāwī's minority position and was for this reason unconcerned with delineating penal differentiation – e.g. the right to repent (*istiṭāba*), the prerequisite of having good faith (*ḥusn al-islām*) prior to one's apostasy, or the stipulation that punishment should be contingent on whether the apostate poses a societal threat – that historically caused jurists to suspend judgement on cases of apostasy.[65] Similar to the application of law by Ḥarakat al-Shabāb al-Mujāhidīn in Somalia, Aḥlām al-Naṣr could be said to 'overlook the strict traditional rules of evidence and procedural requirements' in the belief that enforcing punishment was more religiously rewarding than abiding by the classical 'canon of doubt' that demanded one to avoid punishment in the slightest presence of doubt.[66] In light of this observa-

62. Lav, *Radical Islam and the Revival of Medieval Theology*, pp. 178–9.
63. Abū Qatāda al-Filasṭīnī, *Thiyāb al-khalīfa, https://archive.org/details/thiyab-alkhalifa*, 1435/2014, p. 25. For more on the rhetorical appropriation of the *khawārij*, see Jeffrey T. Kenney, *Muslim Rebels: Kharijites and the Politics of Extremism in Egypt* (Oxford, 2006), and Wagemakers, '"Seceders" and "Postponers"? An Analysis of the "Khawarij" and "Murji'a" Labels in Polemical Debates Between Quietist and Jihadi-Salafis', in *Contextualising Jihadi Thought*, eds Jevan Deol and Zaheer Kazmi (London, 2012).
64. Wagemakers, *A Quietist Jihadi*, pp. 92–3.
65. This is evident in the dearth of reported death penalties against apostates in the medieval and modern period, despite the dominant legal position that the punishment for apostasy is death; see David Cook, 'Apostasy from Islam: A Historical Perspective', *JSAI* 31 (2006), 248–88, here p. 255; and Rudolph Peters and Gert de Vries, 'Apostasy in Islam', *Die Welt des Islams* 17.1 (1976/7), 1–25, here pp. 5, 13. Apart from the sinner's right to repent, Safar al-Ḥawālī also mentioned the requirement that a sinner must be aware of having committing a sin prior to being declared an apostate; see al-Ḥawālī, *Ẓāhirat al-irjāʿ fī-l-fikr al-islāmī*, II, pp. 627–8.
66. Michael Skjelderup, 'Ḥudūd Punishments in the Forefront: Application of Islamic

tion, Aḥlām al-Naṣr was simply more concerned with passing judgement and convincing the reader that al-Kasāsba was not a Muslim. Then, having claimed IS's right to defend itself by *qiṣāṣ* and apostatised al-Kasāsba, Aḥlām al-Naṣr was now ready to circumvent the last major impediment: the prohibition on immolation.

'ONLY GOD MAY PUNISH WITH FIRE'

Humankind has, whether on earth or in the hereafter, throughout *Heilsgeschichte* been threatened with the punishment of fire by God. Thus, when Aaron's sons, Nadab and Abihu, sacrificed 'alien fire' to YHWH they were punished as 'fire came forth from YHWH and consumed them; thus they died at the instance of YHWH' (Lev. 10:2). Similarly, the Qurʾān abounds with descriptions of fiery punishment, including how those who dwell in Hell (*aṣḥāb al-nār*, literally 'the people of fire') will burn on Judgement Day (Q104) – a motif that has also frequently been brought up in the eschatological literature reproduced by IS.[67] However, despite being described in medieval *fiqh* manuals as a mode of slaying reserved exclusively for God, the divine prerogative of immolation did not always deter mankind from partaking in the punishment of God.[68] Hence, not only is immolation attributed to the early caliphs Abū Bakr al-Ṣiddīq (d. 13/634) and ʿAlī b. Abī Ṭālib (d. 21/661),[69] but immolation was also intermittently practiced

Criminal Law by Harakat al-Shabab al-Mujahideen', *Journal of Law and Religion* 29.2 (2014), pp. 317–29, here p. 327; for a historical study of the 'doubt canon', see Intisar A. Rabb, *Doubt in Islamic Law: A History of Legal Maxims, Interpretation, and Islamic Criminal Law* (Cambridge, 2015), particularly pp. 258–9.

67. For similar examples, see Q4:30, Q9:6, Q25:14 and Q40:71–2. For more on immolation in the hereafter, see Christian Lange, *Paradise and Hell in Islamic Traditions* (Cambridge, 2015), pp. 46–7; and Nerina Rustomji, *The Garden and the Fire: Heaven and Hell in Islamic Culture* (New York, 2013), pp. 79–83. For IS's employment of the eschatological imagery of fire, see Bronislav Ostranský, *The Jihadist Preachers of the End Times: ISIS Apocalyptic Propaganda* (Edinburgh, 2019), p. 104.
68. While there is no mention of the punishment of immolation being carried out by people in the Qurʾān, immolation was mentioned as a capital punishment for adultery and sacrilege in the Hebrew Bible (see Gen. 38:24, Lev. 21:9 and Lev. 20:14). For a study on immolation in ancient Israel, see Shaul Bar, 'The Punishment of Burning in the Hebrew Bible', *Old Testament Essays* 25.1 (2012), 27–39. Even earlier, immolation was likely a punishment in ancient Egypt; see Anthony Leahy, 'Death by Fire in Ancient Egypt', *Journal of the Economic and Social History of the Orient* 27.2 (1984), 199–206.
69. For a survey of incidents of immolation in the Rashidūn Caliphate, see Joel L. Kraemer, 'Apostates, Rebels, and Brigands', *Israel Oriental Studies* 10.1 (1980), 34–74, here pp. 44–6; and Lange's entry 'Immolation', *EI3* (Leiden, 2017), p. 149.

as a capital punishment in the Umayyad and later Saljuq period, continuing well into thirteenth century Iraq and Khurāsān and even the Ottoman Empire.[70]

Yet around the early medieval period we begin to see the contours of an *ijmā*ᶜ (scholarly consensus) prohibiting immolation in the Muslim world. Thus, even while condoning immolation as 'the right of [the ruler] (*fa-lahu dhālika*)', the Ḥanbalī polymath Ibn Qayyim al-Jawziyya (d. 751/1359) still sensed the otherworldliness of the punishment, describing how homosexuals 'had tasted the heat of fire on earth before the hereafter' when burned by Abū Bakr al-Ṣiddīq.[71] Averroes (d. 595/1198), the acclaimed Andalusian polymath, summarised the nascent *ijmā*ᶜ, observing that while a minority considered immolation permitted – 'if the perpetrator had initiated the act' – a majority counted immolation prohibited with reference to the very same *ḥadīth* cited at the outset by al-Maqdisī.[72] Averroes explained:

> This is the reason for the disagreement: a general rule standing in opposition to a particular rule (*mu*ᶜ*āraḍat al-*ᶜ*umūm li-l-khuṣūṣ*). About the general rule the Exalted said, 'wherever you find the idolaters (*al-mushrikīn*), kill them' [Q9:5], without precluding any mode of slaying. However, a particular rule was established when the Messenger of God, may God's prayer and peace be upon him, told someone: 'When you find a person, kill him, but do not burn him. None may punish with fire except the Lord of Fire' (*fa-innahu lā yu*ᶜ*adhdhib bi-l-nār* ᵓ*illā rabb al-nār*).[73]

70. Andrew Marsham, 'Attitudes to the Use of Fire in Executions in Late Antiquity and Early Islam', in *Violence in Islamic Thought: From the Qur'an to the Mongols*, eds Robert Gleave and István Kristó-Nagy (Edinburgh, 2015), pp. 117–18; and Lange, *Justice, Punishment, and the Medieval Muslim Imagination* (Cambridge, 2008), pp. 68–9. Lange noted how one public executioner performing immolation in Iṣfahān in 494/1101 was nicknamed Mālik in reference to the mythical guardian angel in Hell (see Q39:71); see Lange, 'Where on Earth is Hell? State Punishment and Eschatology in the Islamic Middle Period', in *Public Violence in Islamic Societies*, eds Christian Lange and Maribel Fierro (Edinburgh, 2009), pp. 162–3. Fernando R. Mediano recounted how a Jew was executed by stoning and immolation as late as 1595 in Morocco; see Fernando R. Mediano, 'Justice, Crime and Punishment in 19th/16th-Century Morocco', in *Public Violence in Islamic Societies*, eds Lange and Fierro, p. 187.
71. Shams al-Dīn b. Qayyim al-Jawziyya, *al-Ṭuruq al-ḥukumiyya fī-l-siyāsa al-shar*ᶜ*iyya* (Mecca, 2007), p. 38.
72. Averroes (Abū al-Walīd b. Rushd), *Bidāyat al-mujtahid wa-l-nihāyat al-muqtaṣid* (Beirut, 1990), II, pp. 743–4.
73. Averroes (Abū al-Walīd b. Rushd), *Bidāyat al-mujtahid wa-l-nihāyat al-muqtaṣid*, XII, pp. 339–40.

Averroes was paraphrasing the famous *ḥadīth* on the prohibition on immolation reported by the companion Abū Hurayra (d. 59/678), who recounted how:

> [T]he Messenger of God, may God's prayer and peace be upon him, once dispatched us on a mission saying: 'When you find so-and-so (*fulānan wa-fulānan*), burn them.' But when we eventually departed the Messenger of God, may God's prayer and pace be upon him, said: 'I ordered you to burn so-and-so, but none may punish with fire except for God, and so when you find them, just kill them'.[74]

Aḥlām al-Naṣr easily sensed the problem posed by Abū Hurayra's *ḥadīth* that had served as proof for the consensual prohibition since at least the time of Averroes.[75] Aḥlām al-Naṣr accordingly advanced three arguments in a bid to permit immolation, each of which we will look at in turn: (1) that immolation did not breach any sacrosanctity (*ḥurma*); (2) that the prohibition was never consensual; and (3) that public interest (*maṣlaḥa*) was ensured by burning al-Kasāsba.

Advancing the first argument, Aḥlām al-Naṣr presented an exegetical opinion attributed to the Andalusian authority on Muḥammad al-Bukhārī's (d. 256/870) canonical *ḥadīth* compilation, al-Muhallab b. Abī Ṣufra (d. 435/1044), who was quoted saying that the Prophet Muḥammad:

> [D]id not forbid immolation in the sense of prohibition (*ᶜalā maᶜnā al-taḥrīm*), but rather for the sake of showing humility to God (*ᶜalā sabīl al-tawāḍuᶜ li-llāh*), and so as not to mimic His wrath (*lā yatashabbah bi-ghaḍabihi*) when punishing people.[76]

While I will later comment upon the important distinction between prohibition and disapproval, here it suffices to say that Aḥlām al-Naṣr was determined to clarify that IS had not conflated temporal with divine modality when burning Kasāsba, and so rather than mimicking God's punishment in Hell, emphasised that IS merely – and to a lesser degree – imitated the advanced weaponry wielded by the West. Aḥlām al-Naṣr accordingly asked whether 'the crusading coalition' had not already 'burned people with incendiary bombs (*qanābilahum al-ḥāraqa*) and caused disfigurements in countless generations to come' – a reference to America's use of napalm during the Vietnam War. Aḥlām al-Naṣr continued:

74. This *ḥadīth* is found in a variety of renditions, however, the one cited is from al-Bukhāri, *al-Jāmiᶜ al-ṣaḥīḥ*, 56:225.
75. Aḥlām al-Naṣr, *Bal ᵓaṭᶜanā allāh*, p. 26.
76. Ibid., p. 25.

> Those who primarily concern themselves with the details of the immolation neither see the act accurately nor in the wider perspective. Thus, the caliphate did not merely capture and burn [Kasāsba]. Rather, they placed him in a cage and set him on fire before covering him with gravel and rubble, pouring rocks over him, and mixing his flesh with the dirt. But, why did the caliphate do this, and why in such detail?[77]

Aḥlām al-Naṣr readily replied:

> This they did to present a miniature picture to the world of what happens every time a missile descends upon the heads and homes of Muslims. This is – around the clock – a recurrent picture: [Muslims] surrounded with nowhere to escape. You burn their bodies beyond recognition to the point where no one may distinguish one from the other. Was the pain of burning [al-Kasāsba's] body greater than this? Did the pilot had to watch his own child, son, or family member burn in front of him? That is the greatest pain! Thus, when houses collapse upon their heads, and their purified bodies mix with the dirt, who may remain alive? Yet again, some even get a taste of both [the collapse and the dirt] until they reach a point where they can barely escape from underneath the rubble and may only continue their life handicapped, amputated, and broken! Thus, all the pain brought by the infidel bombardment has been suffered by Muslims. Yet, we can also tell you about the rest of the tragedies that are taking place in the inward-looking, narcissist, self-worshipping, and self-glorifying sheikhdoms in the East and West. Here, [the Muslims] are silent and dead, not able to move a single finger despite the sweet smell of grilled Muslim flesh filling up the air! Thus, to kill Muslims has become an ordinary and most natural matter – has hostility towards us not become like drinking a sip of water?[78]

Parading the 'hypocrisy' of those who overlook the use of incendiary weaponry while decrying immolation, Aḥlām al-Naṣr shifted the argument from a theological discussion of the potential of anthropomorphism to a political statement on modern arms control. Aḥlām al-Naṣr, however, not only limited herself to questioning whether the laws of war applied equally to everyone, but also raised doubts about whether the consensual prohibition was, indeed, consensual.

77. Ibid., p. 27.
78. Ibid., p. 28.

'For the sake of argument', Aḥlām al-Naṣr proceeded, 'let us forget that we live in an age where every weapon spews fire until death (*kull al-asliḥa fī-hi ḥāraqa hattā al-mawt*), and instead imagine that we lived in an age before [the invention of] these weapons'.[79] While ridiculing the antiquated spirit of the consensual prohibition – deemed out of touch with the technological advancement of modern weaponry – Aḥlām al-Naṣr mentioned five incidents where immolation had been practised or condoned by the Prophet Muḥammad or the Companions. Paying no regard to the provenance or soundness of the transmitted reports,[80] Aḥlām al-Naṣr confidently proclaimed that the Companions 'never prohibited immolation, though some disapproved of it and others permitted it' with the approval of the Prophet Muḥammad. After all, the Prophet Muḥammad 'would never do something prohibited', and so Aḥlām al-Naṣr assured the reader that the Prophet Muḥammad sanctioned immolation by gouging out the eyes of the tribesmen of ᶜUrayna.[81] Contrary to the classical commentary tradition, which posited that Q5:33–4 was revealed in order to 'restrict the scope of punishment' dealt against the tribesmen of ᶜUranya,[82] Aḥlām al-Naṣr intimated that their punishment not only sanctioned immolation, but also excessive violence, as the tribesmen never burned their victim, but merely 'killed the herd'.[83] Thus, while never explicitly expressed by Aḥlām al-Naṣr, the fellow *salafī jihādī* scholar Abū al-Ḥārith al-Anṣārī would later admit that the immolation was 'an extra punishment (*ᶜuqūba zāʾida*) [. . .] exceeding the mere *qiṣāṣ*' dealt against the tribesmen of ᶜUranya.[84]

79. Ibid., p. 25.
80. Aḥlām al-Naṣr only at one point added that a report about the tribesmen of ᶜUrayna was a 'true story (*qiṣṣa ṣaḥīḥa*)'; see Aḥlām al-Naṣr, *Bal ʾaṭᶜanā allāh*, p. 6.
81. Ibid., p. 25.
82. This was pointed out to me by Christian Lange; see Lange, 'Crime and Punishment in Islamic History (Early to Middle Period): A Framework of Analysis', *Religion Compass* 4.11 (2010), 694–706, here p. 696.
83. This *ḥadīth* is found in a variety of renditions, yet the one transmitted by the traditionist Muḥammad al-Bukhārī (d. 256/870) reads: 'Qatāda reported to me from Ānas that some men from ᶜUrayna once came to Medina. Then, the Messenger of God, may God's prayer and peace be upon them, allowed them to pay a visit to the camels – as a gesture of charity – to drink their milk and urine. However, they killed the herd and chased [the camels] away, and so the Messenger of God, may God's prayer and peace be upon him, went in their pursuit. When they were brought to him, [the Messenger of God] cut off their hands and legs, gouged out their eyes, and abandoned them in al-Ḥarra to die [literally, to hold on to or bite the rocks (*yaᶜḍḍun al-ḥijāra*)]'; see Muḥammad al-Bukhārī, *al-Jāmiʾ al-ṣaḥīḥ* (Cairo, 2012) XXIV, p. 102.
84. Abū al-Ḥārith al-Anṣārī, *Li-llāh daruk yā dawlat al-islām*, https://top4top.io/downloadf-top4top_3d8b657fc31-pdf.html, 2015, pp. 7–8.

Almost every work published in the campaign by al-Ghurabāʾ li-l-ᶜIlām fervently rejected that the Prophet Muḥammad had prohibited immolation and delegated the punishment to God, and so did everything in their power to discredit the formation of a consensual prohibition by highlighting instances of immolation at the hands of the Companions. Thus, in one such work, the *salafī jihādī* scholar Abū ᶜUbayda al-Shinqīṭī compared al-Maqdisī's reliance on Abū Hurayra's *ḥadīth* to the Muᶜtazila's erroneous belief in the unsighting of God on Judgement Day. Thus, like the Muᶜtazila's dependency on Q2:143 – 'He said you will not see Me' – Abū ᶜUbayda interestingly reversed the critique commonly levelled against IS by arguing that al-Maqdisī's reading of 'none may punish with fire' was *too literalist* and needed to be contextualised by the custom of the Companions.[85] Mirza Younus has, in a study on IS's justification of female slavery, similarly demonstrated how IS neglected mentioning scholarly disagreement (*ikhtilaf*) in order to stifle opposition – much in the same vein opposition to immolation was downplayed by Aḥlām al-Naṣr.[86] However, contrary to female slavery, immolation was not presented as a mere timeless repetition of prophetic custom, but as a necessary evil in a modern world where 'fire-spewing weaponry' *(al-asliḥa fī-hi ḥāraqa)* – e.g. missiles, napalm and cluster bombs – had become the preferred weapon in the war against Islam. Thus, paraphrasing Joel Blecher, even though IS has often been caricatured for calling for a return to a timeless medieval order, we interestingly see how *timeliness* – not timelessness – was key to Aḥlām al-Naṣr's justification for burning al-Kasāsba.[87]

Finally, we reach the third and last argument, and as though Aḥlām al-Naṣr forgot she was living in a 'state', she only now proceeded to bring forth the overarching authority of the self-declared caliph, Abū Bakr al-Baghdādī (d. 2019). Aḥlām al-Naṣr began by explaining how 'the law had been revealed to uphold justice (*ᶜadl*) and safeguard the purposes of the law (*maqāṣid al-sharīᶜa*)', proceeding to mention four such purposes – pride, strength, justice and dignity (*al-ᶜazza wa-l-quwwa wa-l-ᶜadāla wa-l-karāma*) – none of which were included

85. Abū ᶜUbayda al-Shinqīṭī, *Ḥarq Muᶜādh al-Kasāsba bayna tadāᶜiyyat al-sharᶜ wa-l-wāqiᶜ*, 2015, p. 9.
86. Mirza Younus, '"The Slave Girl Gives Birth to Her Master": Female Slavery from the Mamluk Era (1250–1517) to the Islamic State (2014–)', *Journal of the American Academy of Religion* 83.3 (2017), 577–99. This argument was also put forth by Rosalind Gwynne in her study of Usāma b. Lādin's interpretation of the Qurʾān, 'Usama bin Ladin, the Qur'an and Jihad', *Religion* 36.2 (2006), 61–90.
87. Joel Blecher, *Said the Prophet of God: Hadith Commentary Across a Millennium* (Berkeley and Los Angeles, 2017), p. 187.

in the original five proposed by Abū Ḥāmid al-Ghazālī (d. 505/1111).[88] Quite the contrary, al-Ghazālī had foreseen the dangerous attraction to this powerful discretionary tool, and accordingly cautioned the legal utilisation of the *maqāṣid al-shariᶜa* to the point of deeming them 'illusory sources' (*usūl mawhūma*) in the derivation of law.[89] Paying no heed to this warning, Aḥlām al-Naṣr argued that whenever the 'public interest' (*maṣlaḥa*) was found, 'one must specify how to implement [that interest]'[90] – a rewording of the Azharī reformer 'Abd al-Wahhāb Khallāf's (d. 1956) famous dictum that 'wherever the *maṣlaḥa* is found, so is God's law'.[91] However, failing to properly delimit the extent of the *maṣlaḥa*, Aḥlām al-Naṣr simply stipulated that concerning the treatment of prisoners (*asrā*), 'a leader (*imām*) may rule according to what the latter himself considers to carry the greatest weight in the *maṣlaḥa* of Islam and the Muslims'.[92] Abū Bakr al-Baghdādī was then practically awarded full discretionary powers to determine the *maṣlaḥa* and thereby the fate of the imprisoned al-Kasāsba.

Aḥlām al-Naṣr was, however, keenly aware of the critique that a weak and unchecked definition of *maṣlaḥa* could result in the dilution and even irrelevance of Islamic law. Thus, while al-Khallāf's definition certainly 'enlarged the area of rulings validly based on an unattested *maṣlaḥa*', this reformed notion of *maṣlaḥa* was never meant to impinge upon 'those matters in scripture that [. . .] were unequivocally stated'[93] – such as the prohibition on immolation. Anticipating the critique of stretching the concept of *maṣlaḥa* beyond recognition, Aḥlām al-Naṣr warned the reader that 'neither one's desires nor those of a breastfed child may ever replace the *maṣlaḥa*'.[94] Aḥlām al-Naṣr decried how IS had been portrayed as 'madmen', 'dumb' and 'maniacs' – implored to 'act rationally and consider the *maṣlaḥa* of the country' – when burning al-Kasāsba was about nothing else than 'upholding God's law'.[95] Thus, according to what *maṣlaḥa* – Aḥlām al-

88. Abū Ḥāmid al-Ghazālī established these respectively as religion (*dīn*), life (*nafs*), intellect (*ᶜaql*), progeny (*nasl*) and property (*māl*), while progeny and property was sometimes substituted with honour (*ᶜird*); see Felicitas Opwis, *Maṣlaḥa and the Purpose of the Law: Islamic Discourse on Legal Change from the 4th/10th to 8th/14th Century* (Leiden, 2010), pp. 67, 100.
89. Opwis, *Maṣlaḥa and the Purpose of the Law*, p. 77.
90. Aḥlām al-Naṣr, *Bal ʾaṭᶜanā allāh*, p. 29.
91. ᶜAbd al-Wahhāb Khallāf, *Maṣādir al-tashrīᶜ al-islāmi fī-mā lā naṣṣ fī-hi* (Cairo, 1954), pp. 90, 101, 160.
92. Aḥlām al-Naṣr, *Bal ʾaṭᶜanā allāh*, p. 29.
93. Opwis, 'Maslaha in Contemporary Islamic Legal Theory', *Islamic Law and Society* 12.2 (2005), 182–223, here p. 213.
94. Aḥlām al-Naṣr, *Bal ʾaṭᶜanā allāh*, p. 30.
95. Ibid., p. 14.

Naṣr pointedly asked – 'should we give into gratefulness and thank al-Kasāsba for burning and killing Muslims?'.[96]

Al-Maqdisī, on 7 February 2015 – a week prior to the publication of *Nay, We Obeyed God When We Burned Him* – released a letter online addressed to Abū Bakr al-Baghdādī in which al-Maqdisī rejected any 'defiant interest' (*maṣlaḥa nikaʾiyya*) IS hoped to safeguard by burning al-Kasāsba. Proposing instead a prisoner exchange between al-Kasāsba and Sājida al-Rishāwī (d. 2015) – a woman arrested on 9 November 2005 after a failed attack on the Radisson Hotel in Amman – al-Maqdisī explained that the only purpose (*maqṣūd*) for implementing *qiṣāṣ* was the protection of life as mentioned in Q2:179:

> [S]hould the *qiṣāṣ* you demand for [al-Kasāsba] cost the life of this pure sister, then [the punishment of immolation] cannot be justified as it opposes its own purpose and contradicts the *maṣlaḥa* for which it was stipulated.[97]

Clearly aware of the proposal, Aḥlām al-Naṣr concludingly launched an attack against the so-called 'shaykh-pretender' (*mutamashaykh*) – a designation reserved exclusively for al-Maqdisī. Portrayed as nothing but 'a ball between the tyrant's legs', Aḥlām al-Naṣr scolded al-Maqdisī for being puppeteered by an infidel government 'to do a predetermined job', and claimed that even 'an ordinary subject' in al-Raqqa knew more about law than al-Maqdisī.[98] Al-Maqdisī was, however, not the only *salafī jihādī* scholar to openly critique the punishment of immolation, and so within a year of the publication of Aḥlām al-Naṣr's work, the *salafī jihādī* community found itself embroiled in a heated debate not merely about the legality of immolation, but about the very raison d'être of Islamic law. In the remainder of this chapter, I will replay these discussions as they unfolded within and between IS and al-Qāʿida.

DEBATING IMMOLATION IN THE ISLAMIC STATE

Aside from the punishment of *qiṣāṣ*, which was frequently mentioned as a justification – or exemption from the prohibition – of immolation, the principle of *maṣlaḥa* was the most oft-repeated justification for burning al-Kasāsba in the scholarly campaign launched by al-Ghurabāʾ li-l-Iʿlām. Thus, the self-styled

96. Ibid., p. 7.
97. Abū Muḥammad al-Maqdisī, 'Risāla ʾilā amīr dawlat al-ʿirāq wa-l-shām al-islāmiyya al-shaykh Abū Bakr al-Baghdādī', https://alghad.com/,نص-رسالة-المقدسي-للبغدادي-حول-الكساسب 2015.
98. Aḥlām al-Naṣr, *Bal ʾaṭʿanā allāh*, p. 24.

scholar Abū Bakr al-Atharī had, contrary to Aḥlām al-Naṣr, undoubtedly read al-Ghazālī, and so in a work entitled *Or Do They Have Locks on Their Hearts (Am ᶜalā qulūb aqfālu-hā)* correctly identified the original *maqāṣid al-shariᶜa*, and argued that immolation was an even more justified reason than *qiṣāṣ* for burning al-Kasāsba.[99] This concern for the public interest was echoed in another work released in the campaign that – written by an anonymous 'distinguished sister' – urged the reader to 'go see the frontlines for yourselves, taste the blazing flame (*saᶜīr*) of the aircrafts, and watch children turn to ashes!'.[100] Avoiding discussing the legality of immolation herself, the 'distinguished sister' instead referred the reader to a study on immolation by Aḥmad b. Nāsir al-Ghāmidī, an assistant professor at the Umm al-Qurā University in Mecca. Having been deleted from the university's website sometime in February 2015, the study was reprinted by al-Ghurabāᵓ li-l-Iᶜlām under the title *The Forbidden Word (al-Kalima al-mamnūᶜa)* and the conclusion summarised by al-Ghāmidī:

> Immolation is not permitted except by the order of the ruler (*sulṭān*) if the latter deem the public interest to demand either harming [the enemy] (*nikāyatan*) or treating [a perpetrator] in a reciprocal manner (*muᶜāmilatan bi-l-mithl*). However, immolation is also permitted for one who has committed a prohibited act as well as for burning wood. However, as for the animal, immolation is forbidden because there is no benefit to be derived from mutilating or tormenting it, except if the infidels have employed [that animal] in an act of military aggression against the Muslims.[101]

Thus, even though al-Ghāmidī explicitly upheld Islam as 'the religion of mercy' (*dīn al-raḥma*) and admonished 'killing in a kind manner' (*bi-iḥsān al-qitla*), IS could easily show how the opinion of a payroll scholar in Saudi Arabia 'agreed with the action of the *mujāhidīn*' to burn al-Kasāsba.[102]

Around the time al-Maqdisī released the letter to Abū Bakr al-Baghdādī, al-Ghurabāᵓ li-l-Iᶜlām published another work, written this time by the *salafī jihādī* scholar Ḥusayn b. Maḥmūd. Published online on 4 February 2015, the work entitled *On the Question of Burning (Masᵓalat al-ḥarq)* lamented how

99. Abū Bakr al-Atharī argued that immolation served as 'a deterrence for killing lives (*nufūs*) and annihilating progeny (*nasal*)'; see *Am ᶜalā qulūb aqfāluha*, 2015, pp. 19–21. This title was a reference to Q47:24.
100. Afdī Dawlat al-Khilāfa, *Ḥawl iḥrāq al-ḥāriq!*, https://islamicstatecaliphate.blogspot.com/2015/03/blog-post_46.html, 2015, p. 6.
101. Aḥmad b. Nāsir al-Ghāmidī, *al-Kilma al-mamnūᶜa*, 2015, p. 22.
102. Ibid., pp. 3–4.

'numbskulls, imposters, and infiltrators' even cared to 'research the legality of burning a soldier (*rajul ḥarbī*) who had not only carried the banner of the cross, but thrown burning charcoals (*yaqdhif ḥumam al-nār*) on children of Muslims'.[103] This was not the first time Ibn Maḥmūd debated the subject of immolation as the latter had already discussed Sarāyā al-Mujāhidīn's threat to burn three hostages from Japan in Iraq back in 2004. Thus, on 11 April 2004, Ibn Maḥmūd released a short text titled *Nay, You Have in Immolation a Precedent (Bal la-kum fī-l-ḥarq salaf)*, asking rhetorically: '[W]hy the *mujāhidīn* should not treat [the hostages] in a manner equal (*bi-l-mithl*) [. . .] to the incendiary cluster bombs, heavy rockets, and radioactive materials that Americans had thrown on Muslims?'.[104] However, despite condoning immolation, Ibn Maḥmūd still cautioned that there was 'no consensus on the matter', and so admonished Sarāyā al-Mujāhidīn to instead 'kill them with the sword or in a quick manner so as to avoid opposition and kill kindly (*yuḥassinū al-qitla*)'.[105]

While we do not know exactly what – more than ten years after – prompted him to change his opinion, Ibn Maḥmūd now contended that 'the guardians of the children have a legal right (*ḥaqq*) to burn [al-Kasāsba]'. Thus, confident that a permission on immolation had existed at the time of the Prophet Muḥammad, Ibn Maḥmūd adduced a report about the companion Khālid b. al-Walīd (d. 50/642):[106]

> Khālid b. al-Walīd once wrote to Abū Bakr after discovering that two men had performed intercourse (*yankuḥ*) in the way you have intercourse with a woman in a region controlled by Arabs. [Abū Bakr] sought counsel from the Companions of the Prophet – among them ᶜAlī [b. Abī Ṭālib] – who said that 'burning them is a command by God' [. . .] Abū Bakr then wrote Khālid b. al-Walīd and ordered him to burn [the two men].[107]

103. Ḥusayn b. Maḥmūd, *Masʾalat al-ḥarq*, https://justpaste.it/j9fp, 1436/2015, p. 1. Maḥmūd excommunicated al-Kasāsba by analogy to an opinion by Aḥmad Shākir (d. 1958), a late professor at al-Azhar, who was quoted as saying: 'As for cooperating with the British [in Egypt] – in any form whether extended or minimal – this is an act of recalcitrant apostasy (*ridda jāmiḥa*) and blatant infidelity for which there is no excuse'; see Ḥusayn b. Maḥmūd, *Masʾalat al-ḥarq*, p. 2.
104. Ibn Maḥmūd, *Bal la-kum fī-l-ḥarq salaf*, https://justpaste.it/j8bt, 1425/2004, p. 1. This work was later republished by IS in February 2015 as part of the campaign launched by al-Ghurabāʾ li-l-ᶜIlām.
105. Ibn Maḥmūd, *Bal la-kum fī-l-ḥarq salaf*, p. 5.
106. Ibn Maḥmūd, *Masʾalat al-ḥarq*, p. 4.
107. Ibid., p. 7.

Ibn Maḥmūd described how Ibn Qayyim explained that with the exemption of anal penetration (*lūṭiyya*) and drowning by alcohol, 'what is done to a culprit must be equal to what was done to the victim [. . .] such as being burned, thrown off a high building, or strangulated'.[108] Describing how some scholars had even circumvented the problem of anal penetration by instead 'inserting a stick in the anus until death', Ibn Maḥmūd quoted the prominent *salafī* scholar Muḥammad b. Ṣāliḥ al-ᶜUthaymīn (d. 2001) for ruling that 'smashing, stabbing, electrocution, and burning are all permitted if the perpetrator did so himself'.[109] Relating a story from the famous *jihādī* scholar Abū ᶜUmar al-Sayf (d. 2005) from Chechnya, the latter in addition explained how while fighting in Afghanistan in the 1980s, al-ᶜUthaymīn had issued him with a *fatwā* blanketly permitting mutilating the enemy 'for the sake of causing terror to enter their hearts'.[110] Terror, so it seemed, was a sufficient reason to permit immolation according to Ibn Maḥmūd.

Aḥlām al-Naṣr's work may reasonably be considered an expansion of the work by Ibn Maḥmūd, which in March 2015 was followed by another work justifying immolation, produced by IS's unofficial publishing house al-Wafāʾ. This work was written by Musāᶜid b. Bashīr (b. 1944), a famed traditionist from Sudan who had studied with Muḥammad Abū Khubza (d. 2020) and Muḥammad Nāṣir al-Dīn al-Albānī (d. 1999) in Morocco and Saudi Arabia, respectively, before pledging allegiance to IS on 24 June 2014. Thus, rather than a legal exposition, Ibn Bashīr's work resembled a traditional *ḥadīth* compilation in which reports were plainly reproduced to prevail upon the reader that immolation was practised by the Prophet Muḥammad. Thus, we only catch a brief glimpse of Bashīr's own opinion when, in conclusion, Bashīr justified immolation in the case of *qiṣāṣ*, since 'we do not possess neither the oxide nor the fiery and chemical substances (*al-uksīd wa-l-mawād al-ḥāriqa wa-l-kīmāwiyya*) with which the victims were wronged'.[111] Echoing the argument made by Ibn Maḥmūd, Ibn Bashīr moreover justified the cruelty of the punishment by arguing how al-Kasāsba's execution had 'imprinted itself on the mind and left a profound impression that', continuing

108. Ibid., p. 8.
109. Ibid., p. 11. Abū Sulaymān al-Ṣūmālī, whom we shall later encounter, similarly creatively argued that rather than punishing a person by drowning him in alcohol, one should drown the convicted in 'a fluid like vinegar, water, or something bitter'; see *Nasb al-manjanīq li-naqḍ risālat al-Taḥqīq fī ḥurmat al-taḥrīq*, https://archive.org/details/nasb_al-mnjnq, 1436/2015, p. 73.
110. Ibn Maḥmūd, *Masʾalat al-ḥarq*, p. 13.
111. Musāᶜid b. Bashīr, *Masʾalat al-taḥrīq bi-l-nār*, https://www.noor-book.com/كتاب-مساله-التحريق-بالنار-pdf, 1436/2015, p. 8.

the argument, 'will work as a suppression of criminality (*zajr*) and an instrument of deterrence (*radᶜ*)'.[112]

Ibn Bashīr and Ibn Mahmūd's argument was once again reiterated when an obscure *salafī jihādī* scholar from Gaza by the name Abū al-Zahrāʾ al-Atharī on 16 August 2015 released a work that too justified burning al-Kasāsba. Relying on the scholarship of both al-Hawālī and the late Grand Mufti of Saudi Arabia, ᶜAbd al-ʾAzīz b. Bāz (d. 1999), Abū al-Zahrāʾ claimed that Q5:51 proved that al-Kasāsba had committed 'the worst likely violation (*nāqiḍ min nawāqiḍ*) against the faith', and for this single reason was entitled to suffer a pain 'equal to the injury caused by the torment of fire' (*tusūmu-hum sūʾ al-ᶜadhāb bi-l-nār*) inflicted on the people in Syria.[113] However, contrary to both Ibn Bashīr, Ibn Mahmūd and Aḥlām al-Naṣr, Abū al-Zahrāʾ fully acknowledged that immolation was principally prohibited in Islamic law. However, in order to avoid brandishing the punishment as an innovation (*ibtidāʾ*), Abū al-Zahrāʾ compared immolation to the act of consuming pork, which though *principally* forbidden was permitted 'if anyone is forced to eat such things out of hunger' (Q2:173). Adducing the legal theorem 'to every rule is an exemption' (*li-kull qāᶜida istithnāʾ*), Abū al-Zahrāʾ simply explained that immolation was a mode of slaying exempted by *qiṣāṣ*, and so IS was absolved from blame by having burned al-Kasāsba.[114] Yet, even when admitting that 'burning infidels is principally forbidden unless they burn us first',[115] Abū al-Zahrāʾ still lamented how some *salafī jihādī* scholars not only categorically prohibited immolation, but even went as far as publicly reproofing IS.[116] Abū al-Zahrāʾ's scorn was, however, reserved for one very particular scholar: Abū al-Mundhir al-Shinqīṭī.

112. Ibid., pp. 8–9.
113. Abū al-Zahrāʾ al-Atharī, *al-Taḥqīq fī jawāz al-taḥrīq muᶜāmalatan bi-l-mithl*, https://justpaste.it/tahqiqtahrq, 1436/2015, pp. 3, 5. Abū al-Zahrāʾ also signed the work with the name Taqī al-Dīn b. Aḥmad al-Ghazī al-Atharī.
114. Ibid., p. 5.
115. Abū al-Zahrāʾ also permitted immolating a murderer to death even if the murderer had burned – yet not killed – a victim with reference to a (undocumented) ruling by the eponymous Mālik b. Anas (d. 179/795); see al-Atharī, *al-Taḥqīq fī jawāz al-taḥrīq muʾāmalatan bi-l-mithl*, p. 7.
116. Abū al-Zahrāʾ explicitly mentioned Abū Mundhir al-Shinqīṭī; see al-Atharī, *al-Taḥqīq fī jawāz al-taḥrīq muʾāmalatan bi-l-mithl*, pp. 7–8. Abū al-Zahrāʾ was referring to Abū al-Mundhir's earlier work (see below) *al-Hadī al-samaḥ fī ṭuruq al-qatl wa-l-dhabḥ*, https://justpaste.it/alhady, 1436/2014.

A RESPONSE FROM AL-QĀʿIDA

Though likely born in Mauritania,[117] not much else is known about the shadowy online persona Abū al-Mundhir. Appointed to the Shari^{c}a Council on al-Maqdisī's popular website, Minbar al-Tawḥīd wa-l-Jihād, in 2009,[118] Abū al-Mundhir was a prolific *salafī jihādī* scholar aligned with al-Qā^{c}ida who, for example, justified al-Qā^{c}ida's attack on the US Ambassador to Libya in 2012, and urged *jihādī* groups to establish theonomy in Egypt, Tunisia and Syria during the Arab Spring.[119] However, with IS's establishment in Syria, allegiances suddenly shifted, and so in the period between April 2013 and January 2014, Abū al-Mundhir authored a series of articles that not only stated that IS had a claim to 'a general oath of allegiance' (*bay^{c}ā ^{c}āmma*), but were even published by al-Ghurabā$^{\circ}$ li-l-I^{c}lām.[120] However, when Abū Bakr al-Baghdādī on 4 July 2014 ascended the pulpit in the al-Nūrī Mosque in Mosul to declare the establishment of the caliphate, Abū al-Mundhir suddenly reversed the opinion on IS. As noted by Cole Bunzel, Abū al-Mundhir had in May 2013 already concluded that pledging allegiance to the founder of the Ṭālibān in Afghanistan, Muḥammad ^{c}Umar (d. 2013), was a duty bestowed on each capable Muslim.[121] Thus, given that Muḥammad ^{c}Umar had been the effective caliph since 1996, Abū al-Mundhir on 18 July 2014 issued a *fatwā* disputing Abū Bakr al-Baghdādī's claim to the caliphal seat, practically denouncing IS's raison d'être in Syria.[122]

Having been removed from Minbar al-Tawḥīd wa-l-Jihād in 2013, Abū al-Mundhir was now welcomed back by al-Maqdisī, who once again began to

117. This is solely based on Abū al-Mundhir's kinship attribution (*nisba*) to Shinqīṭ (located in northern Mauritania).
118. Wagemakers, 'Protecting Jihad: The Sharia Council of the Minbar al-Tawhid wa-l-Jihad', *Middle East Policy* 18.2 (2011), 148–62, here p. 153. Wagemakers also noted Abū al-Mundhir's personal and ideological affinity with al-Maqdisī; see Wagemakers, 'Protecting Jihad', p. 154.
119. Daveed Gartenstein-Ross and Tara Vassefi, 'Perceptions of the "Arab Spring" within the Salafi-Jihadi Movement', *Studies in Conflict and Terrorism* 35.12 (2012), 831–48, here pp. 839–40; and Aaron Y. Zelin, *Your Sons Are at Your Service: Tunisia's Missionaries of Jihad* (New York, 2020), pp. 130, 164.
120. Abū al-Mundhir al-Shinqīṭī, *Raf^{c} al-malām ^{c}an junūd dawlat al-islām*, https://www.jihadica.com/wp-content/uploads/2014/07/1رفع-الملام-عن-جنود-دولة-الإسلام.pdf, 1435/2013, p. 23.
121. Cole Bunzel, *From Paper State to Caliphate: The Ideology of the Islamic State* (Washington, DC, 2015), p. 34.
122. Abū al-Mundhir al-Shinqīṭī, *^{c}Ilān al-khilāfa fī-l-mīzān al-shar$^{\circ}$ī*, https://www.jihadica.com/wp-content/uploads/2014/07/إعلان-الخلافة-في-الميزان-الشرعي.pdf, 2014, see, in particular, pp. 6–7.

publish the former's work – beginning with a book denouncing the use of violence by IS. Published on 9 October 2014, the lengthy work entitled *The Right Conduct for Modes of Slaying and Slaughter (al-Hudā al-samaḥ fī ṭuruq al-qatl wa-l-dhabḥ)* argued that the prophetic precept to 'kill in a kind manner' had been 'prescribed' (*kutiba*) as an obligation on each and every Muslim.[123] Thus, in addition to prohibiting execution by beheading, beating the facial region, slicing the neck and removing a decapitated head from the body, Abū Mundhir also addressed the legality of immolation that, according to him, had been abrogated by the Prophet Muḥammad. Abū al-Mundhir explained that even though the Prophet Muḥammad had threatened to burn houses belonging to 'those who did not attend the congregational prayer' (*al-mutakhallifīn ᶜan al-ṣalāt*), the threat was uttered 'in a period of legality before being abrogated' by Abū Hurayra's *ḥadīth* that 'none may punish with fire except for God'.[124] As noted by Nathan French, Abū al-Mundhir had already addressed the subject of immolation back in 2011 when – in response to a street vendor setting himself on fire on 17 December 2010 in Tunisia, effectively launching the Arab Spring – Abū al-Mundhir prohibited self-immolation (*ashᶜal al-nār fī nafsihi*) as an act of suicide meant only 'to escape divinely appointed suffering for this life'.[125] However, appalled by al-Kasāsba's immolation, Abū al-Mundhir raised a renewed critique against IS, consequentially prompting perhaps the most intriguing contribution to the discussion of immolation since Aḥlām al-Naṣr.

Published on 4 September 2015 by Nukhbat al-Fikr – a media network engaged in rebranding Minbar al-Tawhīd wa-l-Jihād – Abū al-Mundhir's work entitled *A Study on the Sanctity of Immolation (al-Taḥqīq fī ḥurmat al-taḥrīq)* directly addressed IS's immolation of Kasāsba. Denouncing the *fatwā* written by al-Binʾalī, Abū al-Mundhir castigated him as a 'young student who cannot possibly claim the competency of a scholar'.[126] Abū al-Mundhir criticised al-Binʾalī for misquoting the position of the Shāfiʾīs and the Ḥanafīs, who according to Abū al-Mundhir upheld the prohibition (*ḥurma*) on immolation with reference to the *ḥadīth* reported by Abū Hurayra. Citing the medieval Shāfiʾī jurist Abū Zakariyyā al-Nawawī (d. 676/1277), Abū al-Mundhir acknowledged

123. al-Shinqīṭī, *al-Hudā al-samaḥ fī ṭuruq al-qatl wa-l-dhabḥ*, p. 8.
124. Ibid., p.11.
125. Nathan S. French, *And God Knows the Martyrs*, pp. 107–8. Abū Mundhir's *fatwā* was entitled *Ḥukm al-muntaḥir ashᶜal al-nār fī nafsihi*, http://www.ilmway.com/site/maqdis/FAQ/MS_6354.html, 2011.
126. Abū al-Mundhir al-Shinqīṭī, *Taḥqīq fī ḥurmat al-taḥrīq*, https://jihadology.net/2015/09/04/majmuah-nukhbat-al-fikr-presents-a-new-release-from-shaykh-abu-al-mundhir-al-shinqiti-the-investigation-into-the-sanctity-of-burning, 1436/2015, p. 9.

that the Prophet Muḥammad immolated the tribesmen of ᶜUrayna, yet argued that the penalty occurred before the revelation of Q5:33–4 detailing the *ḥudūd*, and so had been derived solely by the independent reasoning (*ijtihād*) wielded by the Prophet Muḥammad.[127] Thus, acknowledging the apparent contradiction (*taᶜāruḍ*) between the mutilation of the tribesmen of ᶜUrayna, and the Prophet Muhammad's prohibition on immolation as reported by Abū Hurayra, Abū al-Mundhir reminded the reader of the legal maxim that 'the prophetic word always takes precedence over prophetic action'.[128] Additionally, contrary to Aḥlām al-Naṣr's argument that immolation was frequently performed by the Companions, Abū al-Mundhir categorised these reports as 'unusual and contradictory' and confidently declared that 'no such thing was reported during the time of the Prophet'.[129] Moreover, and similar to the sanctity of immolation, God had, according to Abū al-Mundhir, proclaimed the inviolability of such attributes as 'pride' and 'majesty' by stating that: '[P]ride is My cloak and majesty My robe, and whoever competes with Me in either of them shall be thrown in the Hellfire'.[130] Thus, wondered Abū al-Mundhir, what audacity had driven IS to perform the punishment of immolation, consequentially entering into a competition with God?

Abū al-Mundhir effectively made safeguarding sanctity the overarching argument for prohibiting immolation, since 'God the Exalted permitted [immolation] for no one but Himself' (*allah taᶜāla jaᶜala dhālika li-nafsihi wa-lam yajaᶜaluhu li-aḥad*) – much like the *ḥudūd* that were traditionally considered penalties for violating the rights (*ḥuqūq*) not of men but of God.[131] Categorising immolation as 'one of the greatest sins' (*min al-kabāʾir*), Abū al-Mundhir implicitly critiqued Aḥlām al-Naṣr for misleadingly presenting as consensual the peripheral opinion

127. However, with reference to the medieval Shāfiᶜī traditionist Abū Bakr al-Bayhaqī (d. 458/1066) and the Ḥanafī scholar Muḥammad b. ᶜĀbidīn (d. 1836), Abū al-Mundhir conceded that the Shafiᶜīs and Ḥanafīs permitted the punishment of immolation in the case of infidels resisting surrender (*imtināᶜ*), albeit immolation was strictly prohibited in captivity; see al-Shinqīṭī, *Taḥqīq fī ḥurmat al-taḥrīq*, pp. 4–5, 12.

128. Abū al-Mundhir attributed this maxim to the Mālikī jurist Abū Isḥāq al-Shāṭibī (d. 790/1388); see al-Shinqīṭī, *Taḥqīq fī ḥurmat al-taḥrīq*, p. 14.

129. Ibid., p. 18. Abū al-Mundhir, for example, argued that the report on immolation attributed to Khālid b. al-Walīd and mentioned by Ibn Maḥmūd was not even transmitted by the famed traditionist ᶜAbd al-Razzāq al-Ṣanᶜānī (d. 211/827); see al-Shinqīṭī, *Taḥqīq fī ḥurmat al-taḥrīq*, p. 23. Moreover, in the case of burning houses of those who did not attend the congregational prayer, this punishment was subsumed under the prohibition on immolation in captivity; see al-Shinqīṭī, *Taḥqīq fī ḥurmat al-taḥrīq*, p. 24.

130. Ibid., p. 18.

131. Ibid., p. 11; and Peters, *Crime and Punishment in Islamic Law*, p. 7.

that mere 'disapproval' of immolation had not prohibited the Companions from practising immolation in Medina. Correcting that this opinion was solely held by al-Muhallab, Abū al-Mundhir clarified that the consensual position entailed that the permission of immolation was abrogated due to a concern for violating the prohibition (*ḥurma*) on immolation – an opinion represented by the pre-eminent traditionist Shahāb al-Dīn b. Ḥajar al-ᶜAsqalānī (d. 852/1449).[132] Aḥlām al-Naṣr could, moreover, neither claim the existence of a consensual permission on immolation, since this process had been invalidated by the companion ᶜAbd Allāh Ibn ᶜAbbās's (d. 68/687) opposition as reported by al-Bukhārī:

> ᶜAlī [b. Abī Ṭālib] burned a group of people who had apostatized from Islam. However, when the news reached Ibn ᶜAbbās he said: 'If it had been I, then I would not have burned them, for the Messenger of God, may God's prayer and peace be upon him, said: "Do not punish with the punishment of God" (*lā tuᶜadhdhibū bi-ᶜadhāb allāh*). As for myself, I would merely have killed them as the Prophet, may God's prayer and peace be upon him, said: "As for the person who changes his religion, kill him".'[133]

Abū al-Mundhir thus strongly rejected immolation as a mode of slaying (*wasīlat al-qatl*), reiterating that the ratio legis (*ᶜilla*) for the prohibition was that 'lighting fire' (*al-kayy bi-l-nār*) was considered 'a prerogative' (*min khaṣāᵓiṣ*) of God. Relying on the opinion of the premodern jurist Muḥammad al-Shawkānī (d. 1839), Abū al-Mundhir contended that robbing God of the right to burn was tantamount to 'disobeying and rebelling against Him'.[134] Deploring how the principle of reciprocity was grossly exceeded in the punishment dealt against al-Kasāsba, Abū al-Mundhir concluded the work by repeating that immolation was not merely disapproved, but considered a blasphemous breach of the sacrosanctity that shrouded God.[135]

It was not long before a radical *salafī* scholar from Somalia known widely as Abū Sulaymān reacted to the criticism raised by Abū al-Mundhir. Presently a teacher at the religious institution Dār al-Ḥadīth in Nairobi, Abū Sulaymān in 2015 released a series of apologetic treaties favourable to IS. This support was, for example, evident when Abū Sulaymān on 19 January 2015 published a work entitled *Providing Counsel (Badhal al-nuṣḥ)* that served as a commentary on Abū al-Mundhir's aforementioned *The Right Conduct for Modes of Slaying*

132. Ibid., pp. 6–8.
133. Ibid., p. 20. This *ḥadīth* is found in al-Bukhārī, *Jāmiᶜ al-ṣaḥīḥ*, LVI, p. 226.
134. al-Shinqīṭī, *Taḥqīq fī ḥurmat al-taḥrīq*, p. 29.
135. Ibid., p. 32.

and Slaughter. Even though *Providing Counsel* was released a week prior to al-Kasāsba's published execution on 3 February 2015, Abū Sulaymān still devoted a paragraph to discussing the subject of immolation first addressed by Abū al-Mundhir. Claiming that 'killing infidels in any manner possible is a righteous and kind deed', Abū Sulaymān directly opposed Abū al-Mundhir's mantra to 'kill in a kind manner', explaining how ᶜAlī b. Abī Ṭālib had even trampled a group of apostates to death with his own feet in the condoning presence of the Companions.

Thus, contrary to Abū al-Mundhir's argument that kindness was 'prescribed' (*kutiba*) as an obligation on humankind, Abū al-Sulaymān contended that kindness was rather a 'predestined prescription' (*katab qadrī*) beyond human control, meaning that one could only act kindly if such an act was predestined by God.[136] Proceeding to the question of immolation, Abū Sulaymān protested that the opposing opinion attributed to Ibn ᶜAbbās had invalidated the consensual permission on immolation – a consensus established when Abū Bakr and ᶜAlī b. Abī Ṭālib reportedly 'immolated homosexuals' (*ḥarq al-lūṭiyya*) in Medina – since Ibn ᶜAbbās at that time was 'too young to partake in a consensus'.[137] Abū Sulaymān's most damning reproof was, however, directed at Abū al-Mundhir's belief in the sanctity of immolation, favouring instead that a solid majority had argued that immolation was merely disapproved, but never prohibited by the Prophet Muḥammad.[138]

This point was briefly raised by Aḥlām al-Nasr[139] and was important, since disapproval (*karāha*) as a legal category included 'that for which an aversion is felt' – like divorce or swearing – 'even though it is thought to be in all probability permissible'.[140] Thus, claiming that the encouragement to fight 'the infidels' (*al-kāfirīn*) in Q2:191 was 'a command to kill them in any way, shape, or form', Abū Sulaymān explained that:

136. Abū Sulaymān al-Ṣūmālī, *Badhal al-nuṣḥ fī-l-taʾlīq ᶜala al-Hudā al-samaḥ fī ṭuruq al-qatl wa-l-dhabḥ*, https://www.noor-book.com/كتاب-بذل-النصح-في-التعليق-علي-الهدي-السمح-في-طرق-القتل-والذبح-pdf, 1436/2015, pp. 12, 14.
137. Abū Sulaymān argued that the Prophet Muḥammad burned those who did not attend the congregational prayer 'without excusing himself' (*min ghayr ᶜadhar*); see al-Ṣūmālī, *Badhal al-nuṣḥ*, pp. 94, 99.
138. Abū Sulaymān more specifically argued that the Companions of the Prophet Muḥammad 'agreed that [immolation] was permitted before any mention of a prohibition because they cited "disapproval" (*karāha*) before the argument for abrogation (*naskh*)'; al-Ṣūmālī, *Badhal al-nuṣḥ*, p. 94.
139. Aḥlām al-Naṣr, *Bal ʾaṭᶜanā allāh*, p. 25.
140. Bernard G. Weiss, *The Search for God's Law: Islamic Jurisprudence in the Writings of Sayf al-Dīn al-Āmidī* (Salt Lake City, 2010), pp. 98.

> [T]he majority favoured that [immolation] was disapproved rather than abrogated since the argument for abrogation was annulled and invalidated by the majority's opposition (*khilāf*) to this argument. Rather, they favoured that [Q2:191] commanded them to burn as this was merely one among many ways to slaughter infidels. However, [the Prophet Muḥammad] still abstained from [immolation] for the sake of disassociating himself from the image of partaking in the punishment of fire and to strengthen the role of the Lord.[141]

This argument was reiterated when Abū Sulaymān on 28 September 2015 once again confronted Abū al-Mundhir by releasing a commentary titled *Raising the Catapult (Nasb al-manjanīq)* on Abū al-Mundhir's *A Study on the Sanctity of Immolation*. Arguing that Abū al-Mundhir's preference for the sanctity of immolation was 'a matter of personal belief (*iᶜtiqādiyya*), not of reality', Abū Sulaymān repeated that 'the general command to kill [infidels] precipitated the command to employ every means of slaughter' (*bi-jamiᶜ ālāt al-qatl al-mukhtalifa*).[142] Reacting to Abū al-Mundhir's argument that 'pride' and 'majesty' were also reserved for God, Abū Sulaymān countered that the two attributes 'are still permitted for some citizens (*muwāṭin*)'[143] – like rulers or shaykhs – adding that:

> [I]f every form of punishment is a punishment reserved by God, then every punishment in existence should be forbidden (*muḥarram*) – not merely disapproved (*makrūh*) – since [these punishment] are prerogatives (*min khaṣāʾiṣ*) of God.[144]

God, in other words, was simply so omnipotent that any attempt to mimic Him was deemed not only ludicrous, but outright impossible, according to Abū Sulaymān. Yet although having conceded to the argument that immolation was disapproved in *Providing Counsel*, Abū Sulaymān now completely discarded the position on disapproval, claiming that 'neither the emigrants (*muhājirīn*) nor the helpers (*anṣār*) disapproved of [immolation] when they saw or performed it' during the era of the Prophet Muḥammad.[145] Disapproval was similarly rejected as an argument by Abū Bakr al-Atharī, who instead stated that

141. al-Ṣūmālī, *Badhal al-nuṣḥ*, p. 94.
142. al-Ṣūmālī, *Nasb al-manjanīq li-naqḍ risālat al-Taḥqīq fī ḥurmat al-taḥrīq*, pp. 18, 22.
143. Abū Sulaymān similarly argued that since God was not angry when mankind began to address one another by the title 'lord' (*sayyid*) – potentially stripping God of the titular synonym 'Lord' (*rabb*) – the punishment of immolation could neither be considered a breach of the sanctity (*taḥrīm*) on immolation; see al-Ṣūmālī, *Nasb al-manjanīq*, pp. 63, 95.
144. al-Ṣūmālī, *Nasb al-manjanīq*, p. 60.
145. Ibid., p. 54.

the exclamation not to 'punish with fire' was 'a consideration, not an absolute command (*wa-lakin tamahhalū fa-laysa al-amr ͨalā iṭlāqi-hi*)' on the part of the Prophet Muḥammad.[146] Furthermore, given that the Prophet Muḥammad permitted cautery, branding animals and burning corpses – all acts that required kindling fire – Abū Sulaymān held that there was no reasonableness in permitting merely 'a small portion of immolation' and prohibiting a large one.[147] Reflecting the binary thinking that permeated Abū Sulaymān's work, immolation – whether minor or major – was, according to him, either performed absolutely or not performed at all. Thus, if one was permitted to brand an animal or burn down a building without breaching the sanctity of immolation, how could burning a human being reasonably be said to breach the hallowed prerogatives of God?[148]

CONCLUSION: 'ISLAM IS THE RELIGION OF THE SWORD, NOT PACIFISM'

Even though Abū Sulaymān's *Raising the Catapult* was the last major contribution to appear in IS's scholarly campaign to justify immolation, Muͨādh al-Kasāsba was not the last victim to be immolated by IS. Having established a legal precedence, IS on 31 August 2015 released a video depicting the immolation of four conscripts of the Popular Mobilization Forces, who were strung up, suspended from a swing and roasted alive over a bonfire in al-Anbār in western Iraq. Claimed as retaliation for an incident on 31 May 2015, where members of the Popular Mobilization Front burned a young man to death in al-Anbār, the executioner spoke directly to the camera saying: '[R]etribution (*qiṣāṣ*) has come, for today, we attack them in proportion (*bi-mithl*) to how they attacked our brothers.'[149] Later, on 22 December 2016, IS released yet another video recording the immolation of two servicemen from Turkey, who, tied to the ground with dog collars, were burned alive in Aleppo. As they writhed in agony on the ground, flames devouring them, the executioner poured petrol over them while shouting to the camera: 'Now, we have avenged the blood (*akhadnā bi-thaʾr*) of the Muslims.'[150] However, in contrast to al-Kasāsba, neither servicemen had

146. al-Atharī, *Am ͨalā qulūb aqfāluha*, p. 16.
147. al-Ṣūmālī, *Nasb al-manjanīq*, p. 61.
148. Ibid., p. 38.
149. al-Maktab al-Iͨlāmī, 'Fa-ͨāqabū bi-mithl mā ͨawqabtum bi-hi', https://archive.org/details/jamalalqudsy_yahoo_20160618_1529, 2015, 04:17–04:30. This video's title referred to Q16:126.
150. al-Maktab al-Iͨlāmī, 'Dirͨ al-ṣalīb', https://archive.org/details/goolf_printf_20190228_0622, 2016, 17:31–17:34.

ever piloted an aircraft, and so IS now seemed to extend the purview of *qiṣāṣ* to include anyone associated with an enemy military wielding an air force. Deterring the enemy through creative displays of ever more excessive violence was, so it seemed, more important than abiding by the detailed rules governing Islamic law.

Flicking through the pages of the seventh instalment of the glossy magazine *Dābiq* published immediately after al-Kasāsba's execution, one article held that Islam's consonantal root *s-l-m* did not entail peace (*salām*), but rather submission to the eschatological inevitability that 'the sword will continue to be drawn, raised, and swung until ᶜĪsā (Jesus) kills the Dajjāl (the Antichrist) [. . .] and justice will prevail on the entire Earth'.[151] Lamenting how so-called 'palace scholars [. . .] who visit the White House and claim to represent Islam' nullify *jihād* and abandon the duty of terrorising the enemy, the article's anonymous author claimed that 'the religion of the sword', not pacifism, was the most apt description of Islam.[152] This dual concern (1) for reviving the violent pedigree in Islam and (2) denouncing the clerical establishment's attempt to pacify religion in subservience to the West also permeated the work by Aḥlām al-Naṣr.

Charged with 'drinking coffee on your plush couches in the West and the Gulf',[153] Aḥlām al-Naṣr directly attacked the clerical establishment – interchangeably called 'quietists' (*sākitiyyin*), 'naïve', 'over-sensitives' (*ᶜātifiyyīn*) or simply monkeys[154] – for softening, abrogating and explaining away even the slightest mention of violence in Islamic law – a law that instead had become nothing but an appeasement to the West:

> [. . .] [N]o sound jurist ever proposed that if infidels think badly of our religion, we ought to explain the law to them, clarify what prompted our actions, and do what they wish with the result of appearing as foolish humanitarians, rationalists, or madmen! Nor have we ever been obliged to halt a legal ruling if godless people become mad or begin to cry in order to prevent their tears from falling or their nerves from breaking down since this might harm their health![155]

151. 'Islam is the Religion of the Sword, not Pacifism', https://jihadology.net/2015/02/12/al-ḥayat-media-center-presents-a-new-issue-of-the-islamic-states-magazine-dabiq-7/, 2015, pp. 23–4.
152. 'Islam is the Religion of the Sword, not Pacifism', pp. 20, 22.
153. Aḥlām al-Naṣr, *Bal ᵓaṭᶜanā allāh*, p. 15.
154. Ibid., pp. 8–9, 11, 13.
155. Aḥlām al-Naṣr, *Bal ᵓaṭᶜanā allāh*, pp. 29–30. Aḥlām al-Naṣr at one point specifically referred to the Danish Cartoon Controversy, wondering how scholars at that time could rule that the *maṣlaḥa* 'obligated us (*tūjib ᶜalaynā*) to ridicule the mockers' when Islamic law clearly stipulated that 'whoever harms the Prophet Muḥammad should be killed'; see Aḥlām al-Naṣr, *Bal ᵓaṭᶜanā allāh*, p. 13.

Mirroring a critique that has often been levelled at IS, Aḥlām al-Naṣr effectively blamed the clerical establishment for reading scripture *selectively* in order to downplay or abrogate any element deemed too violent, bigoted or unbefitting for their relationship with the West. Thus, rather than mankind being the judge of whether an action is 'kind' or 'evil', Aḥlām al-Naṣr, in a display of a radical voluntarism, intimated that an action was simply kind if commanded by God. This meant that any endeavour to pacify religion by, for example, prohibiting immolation ironically served only to 'strip the revealed law of that kindness and guidance (*bi-samāḥati-hi wa-hadyi-hi*)' already granted by God.[156]

Aḥlām al-Naṣr's concern for reviving the violent pedigree in Islam was also shared by some of the other scholars who partook in IS's campaign to justify burning al-Kasāsba. Thus, in a work published by al-Ghurabāʾ li-l-Iʿlām entitled *For God It Was an Accomplishment, Oh State of Islam (Li-llāh daruk yā dawlat al-islām)*, Abū al-Ḥārith decried how:

> [W]e have surrendered our minds to be conquered by 'the semi-shaykhs' (*anṣāf al-mashāyikh*) who portray Islam as a religion of mercy, compassion, sympathy, and affection – which is correct – but only for Muslims.[157]

Failing to accept that Islam must show hostility to infidels and mercy to Muslims, Abū al-Ḥārith reproofed the clerical establishment for 'repeating the technical terms and concepts of infidels such as human rights [. . .] in the search for an Islam that pleases the infidel West'.[158] This reproof was echoed by Abū ʿUbayda, who in a work released on 5 February 2015 rebutted how the clerical establishment – termed 'sensitive humanists' – had made the word 'humanism' (*insāniyya*) to stand in opposition to Islam.[159] Proposing an array of heinous penalties like 'tearing a head apart and cooking it [. . .] or eating the flesh of an

156. Aḥlām al-Naṣr, *Bal ʾaṭʿanā allāh*, p. 8. This argument was echoed by Ibn Maḥmūd, who not only accused the scholarly establishment for having 'invented a pragmatist approach (*wasaṭiyya*)', but effectively asked 'the infidels and apostates for mercy in return for softening the religion (*bi-tamyīʾ al-dīn*) and fabricating lies about God'; see Ibn Maḥmūd, *Masʾalat al-ḥarq*, p. 14.
157. al-Atharī, *Li-llāh daruk yā dawlat al-islām*, p. 4.
158. Ibid., p. 5.
159. al-Shinqīṭī, *Ḥarq Muʿādh al-Kasāsba bayna tadāʿiyyat al-sharʿ wa-l-wāqiʿ*, p. 11. Akin to the voluntarist critique raised by Aḥlām al-Naṣr, Abū ʿUbayda argued that legal rulings did not necessarily have to 'agree with [human] temper' in order to be just, and one should instead calmly 'surrender to the godly command; the epitome of religious obligation (*taklīf*) and worship (*ʿabūdiyya*)'; see al-Shinqīṭī, *Ḥarq Muʿādh al-Kasāsba bayna tadāʿiyyat al-sharʿ wa-l-wāqiʿ*, p. 8.

infidel women', Abū ᶜUbayda commended IS for creatively reviving the punishment of immolation, arguing that 'originality, not innovation' (*ibdāᶜ wa-laysa bi-ibtidāᶜ*) was the key to deter the West.[160]

This violent excessiveness was exactly what Abū al-Mundhir warned against when cautioning that the punishment of *qiṣāṣ* must never exceed (*lā yuzād ᶜalayhi*) the crime committed.[161] Abū al-Mundhir's concern for popular discontent with violence was, however, reminiscent of an even older debate about the public display of violence between al-Zarqāwī and the current leader of al-Qāᶜida, Ayman al-Ẓawāhirī (b. 1951) – a discussion that was sparked by the former's videotaped beheading of the abducted journalist Nicholas Berg (d. 2004). Conceding that 'victory' would not be complete until 'a caliphal state [build] upon the prophetic methodology' (*dawlat al-khilāfa ᶜalā minhāj al-nubuwwa*) was established in Iraq, al-Ẓawāhirī, in a personal letter dated 9 July 2005, explained that 'the strongest weapon' (*aqwā silāḥ*) in the hands of al-Zarqāwī was 'the popular support shown by the masses of the Muslims in Iraq'.[162] Admonishing that al-Qāᶜida 'must avoid any action that the masses do not understand or approve', al-Ẓawāhirī implored al-Zarqāwī to stop showing 'scenes of slaughtering hostages' (*mashāhid dhabḥ al-rahāʾin*), elaborating that:

> [W]e are in a battle, and more than half of this battle is occurring on the media battlefield. Thus, we find ourselves in a media battle in a race for the hearts and minds of our religious nation (*umma*). But, however far our capabilities reach, they will never equal the thousand capabilities of the Kingdom of Satan waging war on us. We do, however, possess the capability to kill prisoners by bullets; [a mode of slaying] that would fulfil the goal (*al-murād*) without opening the gates on ourselves to [endless] questions and doubts – let us spare the people from this.[163]

Given the increasingly violent atrocities committed by IS, al-Ẓawāhirī's apprehensiveness continues to reverberate in today's scholarly *salafī jihādī* community that continues to discuss not only the utility and extent of violence, but the very raison d'être of Islamic law.

160. al-Shinqīṭī, *Ḥarq Muᶜādh al-Kasāsba bayna tadāᶜiyyat al-sharᶜ wa-l-wāqiᶜ*, p. 21.
161. al-Shinqīṭī, *Taḥqīq fī ḥurmat al-taḥrīq*, p. 32.
162. Ayman al-Ẓawāhirī, 'al-Akh al-karīm al-fāḍil Abū Muṣᶜab', https://ctc.usma.edu/wp-content/uploads/2013/10/Zawahiris-Letter-to-Zarqawi-Original.pdf, 2005, p. 5.
163. Ayman al-Ẓawāhirī, 'al-Akh al-karīm al-fāḍil Abū Muṣᶜab', pp. 12–13.

PART IV

. . .

COMMUNICATING VIOLENCE

CHAPTER

12

VIOLENCE AND POLITICAL MOBILISATION IN THE DISCOURSE OF MUQTADĀ AL-ṢADR

*Sarah Elibiary**

I. INTRODUCTION

Ever since the events of 9/11, Islamist militant discourses have occupied the world's centre stage and have been paralleled with an increase in self-proclaimed experts on Islam and Islamic law.[1] This has resulted in a flood of material in the media, and academic and non-academic publications addressing violence and terrorism and their association with Islamic thought and practice. Amidst the plethora of literature, explanations and intellectual deliberations proliferated in attempt to answer a number of questions; namely: the different underpinnings of this 'upsurge' in radicalism and Islamist violence, its basis and justification in Islamic thought, the different situations in which violence is deemed legitimate and/or illegitimate, and whether or not justifications legitimating violence constitute a continuity of themes in traditional Islamic thought. The answers have not been as straightforward as those deliberating them had hoped for them to be.

Some scholars attributed the rise of militancy and Islamist radicalism to social, political and economic grievances, and the failures of Arab regimes.[2] These scholars argued that political Islam has strengthened over the ruins of

* School of Law, SOAS, London

1. Khaled Abou El Fadl, *Great Theft*: *Wrestling Islam from the Extremists* (New York, 2007), p. 29.
2. Gilles Kepel, *Jihad: The Trail of Political Islam*, trans. Anthony F. Roberts (London, 2002), pp. 213–17; Gilles Kepel, *The Roots of Radical Islam* (London, 2005), pp. 15–16; B. Milton-Edwards, *Islamic Fundamentalism Since 1945* (London & New York, 2005), pp. 49, 51–4, 65.

the 'secular-Arab-nationalist project'.[3] Islamists, therein, capitalise on, and respond to, such grievance by rationalising the failures as a 'natural' result of the abandonment of an Islamic political alternative.[4] Halliday argues that 'the Islamist sentiment and Islamist movements have developed as a cultural and nationalist response to very real contemporary problems facing these societies'.[5] Kepel furthers this claim, of relevance to the chapter here, stating that 'militants had found some early resonance amongst the radicalised youth and the urban poor'.[6] Others argue that Islamism has not replaced any ideology, nor has it risen on grievances, but has built on something of great appeal – that is, religious sentiment. Religion for Muslims and in the Muslim world maintains a pre-eminent appeal and profound resonance that has not diminished; Esposito, in this respect, affirms that 'both in Muslim belief and in Muslim history, Islam has occupied an important place in the ideology of the state and in the conduct of Muslim politics'.[7] Hence, appropriating a religious discourse would more likely than not garner an audience and sympathy for whatever cause it propagates. Unfortunately, this blind sentimental religiosity has seen many Muslim youth, from the Muslim world and around the globe, drawn to committing acts of violence in the name of the duty of *jihād* and defence of religion.

This leads to another issue in the current deliberations among scholars, which is the 'silent distance' that is maintained by the official or establishment Muslim scholars. This anomalous stance has caused a vacuum in religious authority which arguably gave way to the rise of violent Islamism. As most lucidly described in the words of a prominent Egyptian journalist, referring to the absent role of al-Azhar:

> The waning role of al-Azhar and its message as a beacon of Islamic moderation and enlightenment – caused by the enforced restriction of resources and the reduction of its role to that of just another mosque – gave way to the proliferation of terrorism at the hands of radical militants. Groups that champion slogans of

3. Kepel, *Jihad*, pp. 213–17; Kepel, *Roots*, pp. 15–16; Milton-Edwards, *Islamic*, pp. 49, 51–4, 65.
4. Fred Halliday, *Islam and the Myth of Confrontation* (London, 2003), pp. vii–xv; Kepel, *Roots*, pp. 9, 15–16; Milton-Edwards, *Islamic*, pp. 33, 58–60, 65–6.
5. Halliday, *Islam*, p. 128 (and generally, pp. 1, 118–28).
6. Kepel, *Roots*, p. 15.
7. John L. Esposito *et al.*, *Voices of Resurgent Islam* (New York, 1983), p. 3; see Glen E. Robinson, 'The Battle for Iraq: Islamic Insurgencies in Comparative Perspective', *Third World Quarterly* 28 (2007), 262–9; Thomas Hegghammer, 'Global Jihadism After the Iraq War', *Middle East Journal* 60 (Winter, 2006), pp. 12–13.

> ‘excommunication and immigration’ (*takfīr wa-hijra*) only to spread corruption and sedition in the name of Islamic revivalism.[8]

Abou El Fadl has attributed this ‘vacuum’ in religious authority to the nationalisation of religious establishments.[9] Others like Bonney, and Cook and Allison have blamed this vacuum on the apologist discourse adopted by Muslim scholars. For them, the apologist discourse is yet another assertion of the lack of a thorough legal assessment of the militant Islamist doctrine and the insufficient body of academic and ‘unapologetic’ Muslim scholarship that rigorously addresses the radical Muslim discourses from within the Islamic law tradition.[10] Cook and Allison, rightly, highlight a gap in literature through their critique of the discourses of Muslim scholars opposing suicide attacks:

> All too often reading Muslim opponents of suicide attacks, one has the strong feeling that they either do not know that much about Islamic tradition or they are obscuring these truths from their non-Muslim readership. Instead of endlessly emphasizing the humane aspects of Islam, they should be confronting the problematic aspects. Until this problem is confronted squarely and honestly, radical Muslims will continue to control the discourse, intimidate their more moderate opponents and feel free to inflict suicide attacks [and other terrorizing actions in the name of religion] whenever they wish, justifying these attacks using basic Islamic texts.[11]

The ‘vacuum’ highlighted above presents a predicament for Muslim lay believers, as they are confronted with two opposing discourses. On one side, a relentless ‘emancipatory’ rhetoric that emphasises religious ‘legitimacy’ by appropriating the ethos of Islamic law (the radical/militant rhetoric); and on the other, a silent non-confrontational religious establishment, which long ago ‘lost’ its legitimacy because of its image as submitting to the dictates of governments. Unfortunately, this situation is compounded when the religious establishment decides to break this silence in their attempt to confront the militant discourses legitimating acts of

8. Makram Muḥammad Aḥmad, ‘Ḥadīth fī al-ᶜUmq Maᶜa Shaykh al-Azhar’, *al-Ahrām*, 10 July 2010.
9. Abou El Fadl, *Great Theft*.
10. See Abou El Fadl, *Great Theft*; Richard Bonney, *Jihād: From Qur’ān to Bin Laden* (Basingstoke, 2004); David Cook and Olivia Allison, *Understanding and Addressing Suicide Attacks: The Faith and Politics of Martyrdom Operations* (Westport, Conn, 2007).
11. Cook and Allison, *Understanding and Addressing*, p. 16.

violence. Rather than beginning to confront the problem with a project of juristic re-evaluation and reform, the establishment adopts a stance of an unexplained rejection of violent discourses as simply ignorant, erroneous or un-Islamic.

The continued deliberations of scholars and the general intellectual activity questioning legitimate and illegitimate violence in Islamic thought and the causes behind violence in general has, broadly speaking, concluded that a 'simple', straightforward explanation that fits all contexts is not possible. This conclusion is only a reaffirmation of the complexity of the questions and, more importantly, a reaffirmation of the highly complex, nuanced and non-deterministic nature of Islamic thought, legal tradition and juristic activity.

This chapter hopes to contribute to the developing intellectual deliberations on the topic of 'Islam and violence'. The contribution here is based on a larger research inquiry into classical and modern-day Shīᶜī *Ithnā ᶜAsharī* (Twelver).[12] The research focused on the central themes constituting the discourse(s) of the Islamist insurgencies operating in Iraq between 2003 and 2008 and, befitting of the ongoing deliberations, questioned the extent to which Islamic law supports or detracts from such discourses.[13]

The chapter here offers a brief analysis of the themes of violence and political mobilisation in the discourse of Muqtadā al-Ṣadr, the leader of the al-Ṣadr movement and its military faction *Jaysh al-Mahdī* ('the Mahdi Army'). As stated above, the analysis here also covers the period between 2003 and 2008 during the war when Muqtadā al-Ṣadr's deployment of violent speech and political mobilisation was at its peak. For the purpose of this analysis, a multi-pronged methodology to data collection was employed. This involved web research, archive research and semi-structured and unstructured interviews conducted during fieldwork in London, Tehran and Qum.[14] Firstly, to identify the central themes of Muqtadā al-Ṣadr's discourse, his Friday sermons at the al-Kūfa Grand Mosque are reviewed, in addition to the Ṣadrists' weekly newspaper, *Anṣār al-Mahdī*

12. 'Classical' here refers to fourth to thirteenth century AH/tenth to nineteenth CE 'Modern' refers to twentieth/twenty-first centuries CE.
13. This chapter is based on the author's PhD research: Sarah Elibiary, 'Islamic Jurisprudential Discourses on the Conduct of Hostilities: Embracing Pragmatism' (Unpublished PhD dissertation, University of London, School of Oriental and African Studies, 2012).
14. The fieldwork and interviews were conducted in line with SOAS, University of London, guidelines on fieldwork ethics. Prior to conducting the interviews (a total of twenty-three in Iran and London), interviewees were informed as clearly as possible about the topic of the research and its aims. Whatever questions they had were answered and clarified, their requests to either not be recorded or to maintain anonymity has been taken into account. Also, the interviewees were provided with interview consent forms, which they were requested to sign (on file with author).

('Supporters' or 'Endorsers' of al-Mahdi), Muqtadā al-Ṣadr's published communiqués, and interviews with the media and public meetings. It should be noted here that, because of the insufficiency of hard sources, collection of data relied primarily on the media and the web (which has emerged as a major arena for Islamist insurgent groups and militant groups in general).[15] Following the identification of the central themes of Muqtadā al-Ṣadr's discourse, research into the discourses of classical and modern-day Shīᶜī juristic literature was carried out. This investigation was to determine whether or not Muqtadā al-Ṣadr's themes constitute a departure from tradition by mapping the patterns of continuities and/or discontinuities between the three discourses – the classical, modern-day and al-Ṣadr's.

As a result, it is argued here that al-Ṣadr's rhetoric is not that of an isolated eccentric; nor, in the context of Ithnā ᶜAsharī thought, is his terminology alien. In fact, al-Ṣadr's discourse presents a continuation of themes that are found in both classical and modern-day Ithnā ᶜAsharī thought and jurisprudential literature. This argument is illustrated through examining the two main themes central to Muqtadā's discourse, focusing primarily on his rhetoric during the war.

In view of this, the chapter is divided into four parts. Part II presents a very brief background on the war and the subsequent Iraqi Shīᶜī insurgency led by Muqtadā al-Ṣadr and his movement. Part III addresses the first of the two themes discussed here – violence – and argues that in spite of the wide rejection and ridicule, al-Ṣadr's rhetoric of 'violence' –and specifically his call for jihād, defence (*difāᶜ*) and martyrdom (*shahāda*), his legitimation of roadside bombs and improvised explosive devices (IEDs), and his distinction between resistance and terrorism – symbolise an extension and a continuity of themes discussed in classical juristic texts regulating conduct of hostilities. Part IV subsequently examines themes of political mobilisation in al-Ṣadr's rhetoric, illustrating how these themes represent yet another continuity but, this time, of modern-day activist Ithnā ᶜAsharī thought. Of particular significance to the illustration of the argument here is his emphasis on an active role of the *marjaᶜiyya* and the *ḥawza* (seminary; a vocal or 'speaking' seminary or *al-ḥawza al-nāṭiqa*). Finally, Part V takes the reader forward to current post-war Iraq and concludes with a few observations and speculations on Muqtadā al-Ṣadr's current stance and possible future role on the religio-political scene in Iraq – a role that has come into question recently by his recent widely publicised withdrawal from the political scene.

15. Even though they may be envisaged as unreliable sources, the media and the web (to a greater extent) represented one of the very few avenues into the world of the insurgent groups.

II. BACKGROUND

The war in Iraq started on 19 March 2003 with the United States of America's invasion. It took the US troops three weeks to win their battle against the Iraqi Army and to fully occupy Baghdad.[16] Yet, soon after the collapse of the former Iraqi regime, the US's control of the situation began to wane against an emerging strong Islamist 'insurgency'.[17] By autumn 2003, armed attacks were escalating rapidly, and the US administration then declared that it was confronted with an 'unforeseen', intense and resilient insurgency that was incessantly launching attacks targeting the coalition forces, non-governmental organisations and Iraqi civilians working with the coalition.[18]

16. For literature on policies in the aftermath of 9/11, the war on terrorism, the causes and consequences of the war on Iraq, the discourses of terrorism and policies of counterterrorism, see David J. Barron and Martin S. Lederman, 'The Commander in Chief at the Lowest Ebb – Framing the Problem, Doctrine, and Original Understanding', *Harvard Law Review* 121 (January, 2008), 689–804; James Bovard, *Terrorism and Tyranny: Trampling Freedom, Justice and Peace to Rid the World of Evil* (New York, 2003); Alejandro Colās and Richard Saull (eds), *War on Terror and the American Empire After the Cold War* (London, 2006); Daim bin Zainuddin, *War of Deception – The Facts and Fallacies About the War in Iraq* (Subang Jaya, 2004); Helen Duffy, *The 'War on Terror' and the Framework of International Law* (Cambridge, 2005); Laura K. Donohue, 'Terrorism and the Counter-terrorist Discourse', in *Global Anti-Terrorism Law and Policy*, eds Michael Hor, Yew Meng, Victor Vridar Ramraj and Kent Roach (Cambridge, 2005), pp. 13–36; Rick Fawn and Raymond A. Hinnebusch (eds), *The Iraq War: Causes and Consequences* (Boulder, 2006); Christine D. Gray, *International Law and the Use of Force* (Oxford; New York, 2004).
17. The groups are commonly referred to across war scholarship as 'insurgent' groups active in Iraq. The usage of a value-laden term such as 'insurgency' to refer to the armed groups in Iraq may inadvertently attach ideological or political biases to this chapter – similar to the case if, for instance, the terms 'resistance' or 'terrorist' groups were to be used instead of more neutral yet infrequently used terms, such as 'non-state armed groups' or 'armed militias'. Therefore, to remove any doubts about biases or ideological affiliations, after reviewing several of the definitions and categorisations of what constitutes an insurgency, this chapter adopts John Thackrah's definition and defines insurgent groups as groups who 'seek through violent means to separate themselves from existing arrangements and to establish a separate political community'. See John Richard Thackrah, *Dictionary of Terrorism* (London, 2004), p. 127.
18. Colin H. Kahl, 'Is There a Future for Counter-insurgency?', *Foreign Affairs* 86 (November/December 2007), 169–76; Brian Knowlton, 'Powell Says, We Are Still in Conflict: US Surprised in Iraq by Insurgents' Fight', *International Herald Tribune*, 27 October 2003, http://www.iht.com/articles/2003/10/27/policy_ed3_.php. For accessed dates of online resources, see the Bibliography and the accompanying note, p. 366.

Estimates of the exact numbers of insurgents varied over the years. The same inconsistency is found in accounting for the existing groups, their names, ideological affiliation, their leaders and the nationalities of those involved. This is partly because groups have constantly changed names, merged, split up or became inactive. Since the outbreak of the war, estimates of the number of active groups reached up to thirty groups, of which only twenty-three were steadily covered in the media and in war literature.[19] In one of the most extensive studies on insurgency and counter-insurgency in Iraq, Ahmed Hashim identifies twenty-five active groups segregated and classified as eleven nationalist (including Baᶜth Party loyalists, tribalists and non-partisan nationalist resistance) and fourteen religion-based (eight of which are Arab–Sunnī, four Shīᶜī and two Kurdish–Sunnī).[20]

However, background research for this chapter revealed that there were only two main Shīᶜī groups operating in post-2003 Iraq.[21] The *Jaysh al-Mahdī*, analysed here, is one of these two. The other being *Faylaq Badr* (Badr Brigade) – the military branch of the Supreme Council of the Islamic Revolution in Iraq (SCIRI), which changed its name in May 2007 to the Islamic Supreme Council of Iraq (ISCI).

II.1. The 'Anti-American' Cleric

Often referred to in Western media as an anti-American cleric, Muqtadā al-Ṣadr (b. August 1973), the leader of the al-Ṣadrist Movement and its military branch *Jaysh al-Mahdī*, is envisaged by some as representing 'one of the most dramatic turns in Iraqi Shīᶜism since the 19th century Usuli-Akhbari clashes in Najaf'.[22]

19. For example, generally, see Anthony H. Cordesman, 'Iraq's Sunni Insurgents: Looking Beyond Al Qa'ida', *Center for Strategic & International Studies* 2 (16 July 2007); Ahmed Hashim, *Insurgency and Counter-Insurgency* (London, 2006); Bruce Hoffman, *Insurgency and Counterinsurgency in Iraq* (Santa Monica, CA, 2004).
20. Hashim, *Insurgency and Counter-Insurgency*; reviewed by Professor Charles Tripp of SOAS as 'the most authoritative account yet of the insurgency in Iraq' (dust jacket). Ahmed Hashim is a Professor of Strategic Studies at the US Naval War College. He has authored two extensive studies on the insurgency in Iraq.
21. Other than Badr Brigade and the Mahdi Army, there are many, much smaller Shī'ī militias such as: *ḥizb allāh fī al-ᶜIrāq* and *ᶜaṣāʾib ahl al-ḥaqq* (which has a number of militias named after the different infallible imams, like *katāʾib al-Imām al-Kāẓim, katāʾib al-Imām al-Hādī*); see Aparisim Ghosh, 'The Face of Brutality', *Time Magazine*, 4 December 2006, pp. 36–9; Scott Johnson, 'A New Enemy Emerges: 'The Shīᶜite Zarqawi', *Newsweek Magazine*, 13 November, 2006, p. 10; Ali A. Allawi, *The Occupation of Iraq: Winning the War, Losing the Peace* (New Haven: 2007), p. 139.
22. Faleh A. Jabar, *The Shīᶜite Movement in Iraq* (London, 2003), p. 25.

A scion of a renowned family of active clerics, Muqtadā al-Ṣadr has inherited the legacy of political activism from his father, the first leader of the al-Ṣadr Movement –Muḥammad Muḥammad Ṣādiq al-Ṣadr (assassinated along with his two sons in 1999); and his father's cousin – the renowned and revered reformist scholar (ᶜ*ālim*), Muḥammad Bāqir al-Ṣadr, known as al-Ṣadr al-Awwal (executed in 1980).[23] It is often argued that any popularity that Muqtadā al-Ṣadr may garner, especially among the Iraqi Shīᶜī populace, is not really for his person or an ideology he projects. It is this legacy and the popularity of al-Ṣadrs with the Shīᶜī disadvantaged masses of Iraq that has acquired Muqtadā al-Ṣadr wide support among the general Iraqi Shīᶜī populace.[24]

Notwithstanding his family's reputable longstanding legacy or his current popularity and wide support, Muqtadā al-Ṣadr has been subject to a lot of criticism, not only in the West, but also within Shīᶜī circles, as well as in Iraq generally.[25] As is widely known, since surfacing on the Iraqi scene in 2003, al-Ṣadr's religious credentials and overall proficiency in issuing accurate opinions on the rulings of Sharīᶜa have been undermined by both the learned and the laity. His relations with the institution or the 'seat' of religious authority (*marjaᶜiyya)* and the religious seminary (*ḥawza*) have been, to say the least, unamiable. His actions and general narrative has been considered disrespectful to the

23. Literature covering al-Ṣadr al-Awwal and al-Ṣadr al-Thānī includes: Faleh A. Jabar, *Shīᶜite Movement*; Chibli Mallat, 'Religious Militancy in Contemporary Iraq: Muhammad Baqer as-Sadr and the Sunni-Shia Paradigm', *Third World Quarterly* 10.2 (April 1988), 699–729; Chibli Mallet, *The Renewal of Islamic Law: Baqer as-Sadr, Najaf and the Shīᶜi International* (Cambridge, 1993); John Walbridge, 'The Search for New Foundations', in *The Most Learned of the Shi'a*, ed. Linda Walbridge (Oxford, 2001), pp. 131–9; Sajjad Rizvi, 'Political Mobilization and Shīᶜi Religious Establishment (*marja'iyya*)', *International Affairs* 86.6 (2010), 1302–5; Ṣadr al-Dīn Qabbānjī, *al-Jihād al-Siyāsī liʾl-Shahīd al-Ṣadr* (n. p. (Iraq), 1983); 'Abd al-Jabbār Rifā'ī, *Manhaj al-Shahīd al-Ṣadr fī Tajdīd al-Fikr al-Islāmī* (Qum, 1998); Husayn Baraka al-Shāmī, *al-Ṣadr al-Thānī: Dirāsāt fī Fikrihi wa-Jihādihi* (London, 2002); Fā'iq Shaykh 'Alī, *Ightiyāl Shaᶜb* (London, 2000); ᶜAdel Ra'ūf, *Muḥammad Muḥammad Ṣādiq al-Ṣadr: Marjaᶜiyyat al-Maydān: Mashrūᶜ ᶜahu al-Taghyīrī wa Waqāᶜiᶜ al-Ightīyāl* (Damascus, 1999); ᶜAdel Ra'ūf, *al-'Amal al-Islāmī fī al-'Irāq Bayn al-Marja'iyya waʾl-Hizbiyya: Qirā'a Naqdiyya li-Masīrat Niṣf Qarn* (Damascus, 2000). *Muʾassasat al-Ṣadr liʾl-Dirāsāt al-Istrātījiyya*, http://www.alsadrain.com/.
24. Bonney, *Jihād*, pp. 264–5; Patrick Cockburn, *Muqtada al-Sadr and the Fall of Iraq* (London, 2008); Juan Cole, 'The United States and Shīᶜite Religious Factions in Post-Ba'thist Iraq', *Middle East Journal* 57.4 (Autumn, 2003), 79–80; Nimrod Raphaeli, 'Understanding Muqtada al-Sadr', *Middle East Quarterly* (Fall 2004), 34–5.
25. The group's website was last accessed on 11 April 2009, http://www.manhajalsadren.com/. Muqtadā al-Ṣadr's new website, is operational (January 2020) http://jawabna.com.

longstanding conventions of clerical traditions of seniority, rank, knowledge-based recognition and scholarly achievements. As described by Shīᶜī scholars, 'he is nowhere near qualified. He has just initiated his *ḥawza* training.'[26] In addition to this, al-Ṣadr's general rhetoric – whether religious or political – has often been described as erratic, ignorant, inconsistent and lacking a clear vision.[27]

II.2. Highlights on Discourse

It should be noted that apart from the two main themes, which are consistent in Muqtadā's discourse, his pronouncements and decisions have at times seemed arbitrary and even contradictory. This arbitrariness is evident, for instance, in his intermittent and usually sudden declarations of ceasefire, only to follow these with a call for *jihād* or another sudden declaration abandoning the ceasefire. Not only that, but at times al-Ṣadr's messages seemed confused and disorderly. For example, in one sermon, he called for 'violent struggle against the root causes of oppression', expounding to his audience the merits of sacrificing lives and relinquishing all material possession in defence of Islam. He then ended the sermon with a call for peaceful non-violent resistance.[28] In another seemingly contradictory communiqué issued in November 2003, al-Ṣadr declares that 'for the sake of stability of a new liberated and democratic Iraq abandoning armed struggle

26. This statement was the recurring response of most interviewees to questions citing quotes from al-Ṣadr's sermons. Dr ᶜAlī ᶜAllāwī, interview by author, 10 November 2008, London, United Kingdom, tape recording (interviewee consent forms for all interviews on file with author); Al-Sayyid ᶜAbd al-Hādī Fāḍil, interview by author, 26 June 2009, Qum, Iran, tape recording; Ghānim Jawād, interview by author, 7 October 2008, London, tape recording; Dr Nāṣir Qurbān-Nia, interview by author, 18 May 2009, Qum, Iran, tape recording; Sayyid Muḥammad Mahdī al-Rabbānī, interview by author, 20 June 2009, Qum, Iran, tape recording; Ayatollah al-Shaykh Ḥasan Muḥammad Taqī al-Jawāhirī, interview by author, 22 June 2009, Qum, Iran, tape recording; Ayatollah Dr Sayyid Muṣṭafa al-Muḥaqiq al-Dāmād, interview by author, 10 June 2009, Tehran, Iran, tape recording. Muqtadā al-Ṣadr has since completed significant portions of his scholarship.
27. Faleh Abdul Jabar, 'Worldly Roots of Religiosity in Post-Saddam Iraq', *Middle East Report* 227 (Summer, 2003), 17; Emirates Centre for Strategic Studies, *Iraq: Reconstruction and Future Role* (2004), p. 80; Edmund Ghareeb, *Historical Dictionary of Iraq* (Lanham, 2005), p. 201; Dr Adam Goodman, 'Informal Networks and Insurgency in Iraq', *Defence Academy of the United Kingdom, Advanced Research and Assessment Group* (April, 2008), 8; International Crisis Group, 'Iraq's Muqtada al-Sadr: Spoiler or Stabilizer?', *Middle East Report* 55 (11 July 2006), 6–8; J. Cole, 'Iraq's Shīᶜites Under Occupation', *Middle East Briefing* (9 September 2003), 16.
28. International Crisis Group, 'Iraq's Muqtada', p. 9.

against the American troops'; and in the very same communiqué, he calls upon the US troops to embrace Islam.[29] The seeming contradiction here arises from his calling on the troops to embrace Islam, which, in theory, is a measure taken before launching an offensive jihād, which, according to the majority Shīᶜī jurists – with the notable exception of al-Khūʾī – is obsolete in the era of occultation.[30] Another example of apparent confusion within his statements is in his communiqué declaring the renewal of ceasefire, which seems to carry forward two messages: one calling for relinquishing armed activity and another of praise for those who are sustaining armed activity. In the communiqué al-Ṣadr urges his followers to conform with fulfilling and commanding the good and abstaining from the 'evil' through submitting to his declaration to ceasefire, which he declares as a gesture of commanding good and forbidding evil *(al-amr biʾl-maᶜrūf wal-nahy ᶜan al-munkar)*. At the end of the communiqué he praises the *mujāhidīn* from amongst his followers for their 'patience, sustained *jihād* against apostasy and the infidels and continuous love of piety and the pious, Islam and the Muslims, Iraq and the Iraqis'.[31]

Yet, beyond his dubious orations and all the resulting criticism and ridicule, eleven years after the war, al-Ṣadr was still able to amass the largest following of Iraqi Shīᶜas. Furthermore, he is recognised as one of the key players in contemporary Iraqi politics and, by some, as the most powerful politician in Iraq today.[32] Eric Davies observes, with assertion, that Muqtadā al-Ṣadr has been able 'to build a powerful political coalition, which has become a core element of all political coalitions since 2006', arguing that he has, in fact, become 'kingmaker' on the Iraqi political scene.[33] Beyond attributing his popularity to the legacy of his family, ironically some analysts have attributed it to his rhetoric and charismatic oratory skills. He champions a revolutionary emancipatory rhetoric raising popular Shīᶜī messianic fervour and at the same time is highly inflammatory, which successfully rallies followers and galvanises his enthused audience into a highly charged event of slogan chanting.[34] This is not to say that his speech is

29. *Jaysh al-Mahdī* newspaper, *Anṣār al-Mahdī* 14 Ramaḍān 1424/8 November 2003.
30. Abū al-Qāsim al-Mūsawī al-Khūʾī, *Minhāj al-Ṣāliḥīn* (Qum, 1990), I, pp. 359–62.
31. Muqtadā al-Ṣadr, *Tajmīd Jaysh al-Mahdī*, 22 February 2008, http://www.manhajalsadren.com/almakalat/2008/02/030.htm.
32. Eric Davis, 'Is Muqtada al-Sadr the New Kingmaker in Iraqi Politics?', *The New Middle East Blogspot*, 31 July 2012, http://new-middle-east.blogspot.co.uk/2012/07/is-muqtada-al-sadr-new-kingmaker-in.html.
33. Ibid.
34. For an example of the messianic fervour and nationalist slogan chanting in Muqtadā's speech, see Muqtadā al-Ṣadr, 'Speech: al-ᶜImāra', online video clip, http://www.youtube.com/watch?v=-oLwlNdKS8Y.

devoid of any substantive political and religious content. Al-Ṣadr had his own cadre of devoted young clerics, such as, *inter-alia*, Shaykh Hādī al-Khalīṣī, Ḥasan al-Zarqānī and Ṣalāḥ al-ᶜUbaydī, to assist him with his speeches and with matters and questions of religion, as they may arise, at least at the beginning of his public appearances. His Friday sermons at al-Kūfa Grand Mosque (*al-Masjid al-Aᶜẓam*) combined notions of populism, nationalism and, of course, religious rhetoric.[35]

The notions of populist nationalism are reflected in al-Ṣadr's projection of the Ṣadrist Movement. He presented the movement and the services that it extends to belong to all Iraqis regardless of religion, sect or ethnicity.[36] The movement has been described as one with a nationalist populist ideology whose primary aim is to extend and secure services to the disadvantaged segments of Iraqi society. It is composed of three branches: clerics, formed mostly of loyalists to al-Ṣadr's father (henceforth, al-Ṣadr al-Thānī), so this element may be referred to as the 'advisory' committee or the 'legislative' committee; the second branch consists of the networks of services and charities – already formed and consolidated under al-Ṣadr al-Thānī; and the third and last branch is the Mahdi Army.[37]

Whether the source of al-Ṣadr's popularity and wide support is his family's legacy, the services that the Ṣadrist Movement secures or his charismatic fiery speeches is all secondary. He has been able to successfully carve a niche for himself on the Iraqi arena and a far-reaching popularity, especially with the masses. As Etherington observes:

> [Muqtadā al-Ṣadr] successfully fashioned a personal platform comprising a muscular re-imposition of Islamic tenets, nationalism and intellectual opposition to the occupation. This . . . found real resonance among the poor and disaffected of Iraq, particularly the young . . . [the aspects which widened the gap] between the followers of Sistani and Sadr.[38]

35. Hashim, *Insurgency and Counter-Insurgency*, pp. 253–4.
36. Muqtadā al-Ṣadr, Thirty-Fifth Sermon, delivered at al-Kūfa Grand Mosque, al-Kūfa, 19 December 2003. (Transcripts for all sermons cited here on file with author).
37. Hashim, *Insurgency and Counter-Insurgency*, pp. 348, 252–5; International Crisis Group, 'Iraq's Muqtada', pp. 7–11; International Crisis Group, 'Iraq's Shīᶜite', p. 3; Jabar, *The Shīᶜite Movement*, pp. 24–7.
38. Mark Etherington, *Revolt on the Tigris: The Sadr Uprising and the Governing of Iraq* (Ithaca, New York, 2005), p. 89.

III. VIOLENCE

Al-Ṣadr's affiliation with violence stems from his leadership of the powerful *Jaysh al-Mahdī*, which he founded in 2003 to challenge the occupation forces in Iraq generally and especially in al-Najaf and other holy cities.[39] His discourse on violence centred on two main themes: a call for jihād that is coupled with readiness for martyrdom and legitimation of the usage of roadside bombs and IEDs with an emphasis on the distinction between resistance and terrorism.

III.1. Jihād, Defence and Martyrdom

Jihād, defence (*difāᶜ*) and martyrdom (*shahāda*) are recurring themes in almost all of al-Ṣadr's Friday sermons.[40] In the first part of the Friday sermon delivered on 12 Muḥarram 1425/3 March 2004, less than a year after the invasion, al-Ṣadr expressed strong disapproval of what he considered to be signs of support for the presence of foreign occupation in Iraq. He lashed out at Shīᶜī clergyman who 'recount the benefits of the occupation' as essential for a peaceful transition.[41]

Al-Ṣadr often expressed his readiness for martyrdom and willingness to sacrifice his life for Iraq, presenting himself as 'the shield for all Iraqis', reiterating that Islām 'grows' through sacrifice and martyrdom.[42] Like al-Ṣadr al-Thānī before him, Muqtadā al-Ṣadr wore a white shroud whilst delivering his sermons during the years of occupation as a symbol connoting a declaration of jihād (defensive) and readiness for martyrdom.[43] Al-Ṣadr's discourse of glorifying

39. Al-Ṣadr, Sixty-Fourth Sermon, al-Kūfa, 9 July 2004; Hashim, *Insurgency and Counter-Insurgency*, p. 257.
40. Note in Shīᶜī legal thought, offensive *jihād* (*al-jihād al-ibtidāʾī or hujūmī or al-ṭalab*) as opposed to defensive *jihād* (*difāᶜ or jihād al-dafᶜ*) is rendered obsolete in the era of occultation – by the great majority of Shīᶜī jurists. Therefore, any initiation of armed activity is not sanctioned during the era of occultation, and thus the topic of *jihād* as signifying the 'initiation' of an armed struggle is obsolete in both the classical and modern-day juristic discourses. However, there is an established consensus obligating the fight in defence of Islam, of oneself and of *bayḍat al-Islām* (the power base of Islam, the abode of Islam) against an advancing enemy. Unlike in Sunnī treatises, Shīᶜī treatises of *furūᶜ* do not refer to a defensive jihād as *jihād al-dafᶜ*, but as just defence or *difāᶜ*. Jurists are very cautious to refer to any conduct of hostilities during the era of occultation as *difāᶜ*. This is with the exception of two, as mentioned earlier – al-khūʾī – and from the classical – eighteenth-/nineteenth-century jurist Jaᶜfar Kashif al-Ghitā, addressed later in this chapter.
41. Al-Ṣadr, Forty-Sixth Sermon, al-Kūfa, 5 March 2004.
42. Al-Ṣadr, Twenty-Seventh Friday Sermon, al-Kūfa, 24 October 2003.
43. Muḥammad Muḥammad Ṣādiq al-Ṣadr, Excerpt of Last Sermon, al-Kūfa, online video

martyrdom, self-sacrifice and particularly his emphasis on struggling against all forms of tyranny and oppression (whether this tyranny is in the form of a despotic rule or a foreign invasion) and responding to the grievances of the oppressed and dispossessed mirrors traditional historical Shīᶜī narratives. As part of this rhetoric al-Ṣadr often evokes the historical narratives; al-Ḥusayn Ibn ᶜAlī's martyrdom during the Battle of Karbalāᵓ in 680 CE is constantly evoked as an example worthy of emulation in the fight against tyranny and oppression, which is embodied in Iraq by the presence of an occupation.[44]

In his call for a defensive jihād and emphasis that in fighting the occupation, members of the 'resistance' should not be concerned over the military superiority of the occupier, al-Ṣadr addressed (seemingly 'archaic') themes such as fleeing and steadfastness (*al-firār and al-thabāt*), which are central to the classical juristic discussions on regulations in battle.[45] Hence, al-Ṣadr called upon his followers to trust in God's Qurᵓānic 'promise' to overcome the enemy as expounded in the Qurᵓānic verse: '. . . How often a small force has defeated a large army with God's permission . . .'[46] He continuously urged his followers to remain ready and 'steadfast', even if weapons and resources are scarce. Reverberating the opinion of al-Najafī and other jurists, cited hereunder, he stated that 'fleeing' battle in the presence of an advancing army is amongst the prohibitions set by God and tantamount to the gravest sins (*kabāᵓir*). Al-Ṣadr, of course, supported his opinion by citing Q8:46, commanding believers to '. . . Be steadfast: God is with the steadfast', in order to emphasise the imperativeness of steadfastness (*al-thabāt*) when confronted with a transgressor.[47]

Al-Ṣadr's narrative, above, affirmed a continuity and an extension of themes that are central to classical jurisprudential discourses regulating war and conduct of hostilities. Classical jurists' consensual opinion holds that defence of the

clip, https://www.youtube.com/watch?v=_BnGw23Xsk4; cf. Muqtadā al-Ṣadr, Friday Sermon, al-Kūfa, online video clip, http://www.youtube.com/watch?v=GuorfcqfqHg.

44. Al-Ṣadr, Forty-Fifth Sermon, al-Kūfa, 27 February 2004; Al-Ṣadr, Seventieth Sermon, al-Kūfa, 20 August 2004. The martyrdom of al-Ḥusayn is commemorated annually by all Shīᶜī denominations on 10th Muḥarram and is referred to as *yawm ᶜāshūrāᵓ*. The events of commemoration are highly charged with emotional expressions of profound grief for the suffering and tragic death of the grandson of the Prophet and in reflection of veneration guarded for al-Ḥusayn's cause and for his martyrdom.
45. Al-Ṣadr, Thirty-Fifth Sermon, al-Kūfa, 19 December 2003; Al-Ṣadr, Seventy-Fourth Sermon, al-Kūfa, 17 September 2004.
46. Muḥammad S. ᶜAbdel Haleem, *The Qur'ān* (Oxford, 2004): Q2:249; Q47:7; Al-Ṣadr, Seventy-Fourth Sermon, al-Kūfa, 17 September 2004.
47. Q8:46; Al-Ṣadr, Seventy-Third Sermon, al-Kūfa, 10 September 2004; Al-Najafī, *Jawāhir* XXI, pp. 46–9.

abode of Islam (*bayḍat al-Islam*) is obligatory, even if alongside an unjust ruler (*al-ḥākim al-jāʾir*).[48] However, capacity is not to be considered in a situation of transgression, where defence becomes obligatory.[49] With regards to fleeing (*al-firār*), al-Najafī, also known as Ṣāḥib al-Jawāhir, (d. 1266 AH/1849 CE), generalises and does not mention the condition he earlier made on permitting defence alongside the *jāʾir* only if 'Islām and its rituals are at risk'.[50]

Moreover, al-Ṣadr emphasised that 'resistance is a rationally and consensually justifiable and righteous cause that aims to achieve independence, liberation, peace, democracy, defence of shrines and holy sites'.[51] He considered it as an individual duty to 'actively defend Islam and pre-empt any attacks on its holy sites'.[52] Al-Ṣadr's conceptualisation here seems to resonate with that of the eighteenth-/nineteenth-century jurist Kāshif al-Ghiṭāʾ (d. 1228 AH/1813 CE), who maintained that the defence of the abode of Islam does not just signify the territory of Islam, but also extends to signify the protection of Muslims and the protection of the subsistence and the performance of Islamic rituals.[53]

Current jurists have expressed their rejection of al-Ṣadr's call for defence, basing their opinion on his lack of credentials and lack of 'official' capacity to assume such a responsibility.[54] For instance, al-Sīstānī asserted his rejection of the formation of Islamic armed militias.[55] Moreover, al-Sīstānī's office issued a memo in October 2003 declaring that upon receiving Muqtadā al-Ṣadr, representatives of al-Sīstānī urged him to cease all armed activities, to hand over

48. Abī Ja ᶜfar Muḥammad ibn Manṣūr ibn Aḥmad Ibn Idrīs al-Ḥillī, *Kitāb al-Sarāʾir al-Ḥāwī li-Taḥrīr al-Fatāwī* (Qum, 1990), II, p. 4; Jaᶜfar ibn al-Ḥasan al-Ḥillī [al-Muḥaqqiq], *al-Mukhtaṣar al-Nāfiᶜ fī Fiqh al-Imāmiyya* (Qum, 1990), p. 109; Al-ᶜAllāma, *Taḥrīr* II, p. 132; Al-Ḥasan ibn Yūsuf ibn al-Muṭahhar al-Ḥillī [al-Allāmah], *Thadhkirat al-Fuqahāʾ* (Qum, 1993), IX, p. 37; Jaᶜfar Kāshif al-Ghiṭāʾ, *Kashf al-Ghiṭāʾ ᶜan Mubhamāt al-Sharīᶜa al-Gharrāʾ* (Isfahān, n. d.), II, p. 382.
49. Al-Najafī, *Jawāhir* XXI, pp. 46–9.
50. Ibid.
51. Al-Ṣadr, Sixty-Fourth Sermon, al-Kūfa, 9 July 2004.
52. Ibid.
53. Kāshif al-Ghiṭāʾ, *Kashf* II, p. 382.
54. Dr Al-Sayyid Muṣṭafa Mīrmuḥammadī, interview by author, 20 May 2009, Qum, Iran, tape recording; Al-Sayyid Muḥammad Mahdī al-Rabbānī, interview by author, 20 June 2009, Qum, Iran, tape recording; Al-Jawāhirī, interview: Qum, 22 June 2009; Nobahār, interview: Tehran, 14 June 2009; Ayatollah Dr al-Sayyid Muṣṭafa al-Muḥaqiq al-Dāmād, interview by author, 10 June 2009, Tehran, Iran, tape recording; Qurbān-Nia, interview: Qum, 18 May 2009; Abdul Jabar, *Shīᶜite Movement*, pp. 25–6; Abdul Jabar, 'Worldly Roots', p. 17.
55. Questions put by Fox News to al-Sayyid al-Sīstānī, 23 October 2003, http://www.sistani.org/local.php?modules=extra&eid=2&sid=22.

weapons and to submit to the rule of the national law enforcement agencies,[56] a request that seemed to go unheeded.

However, al-Ṣadr's initiative also finds support in Kāshif al-Ghiṭā'ʾs opinion. The nineteenth-century jurist holds that defence of the abode of Islam is obligatory, notwithstanding the absence of the Imām, his deputy or the *mujtahid*.[57] Moreover, Kāshif al-Ghiṭāʾ maintained that in the absence of the Imām and his deputy, it becomes the role of the *mujtahid*s to launch jihād in the four situations of defence that he set out in his treatise (amongst them being defending the abode of Islam).[58] Not only that, he asserts that in the case that the extant *mujtahids* are unable to launch or participate in defence or *jihād*, it then becomes mandatory upon anyone else who has the capacity to launch it. In the situation where it becomes incumbent on people to obey this particular individual leader of defence, failure to comply, according to Kāshif al-Ghiṭāʾ, would be tantamount to disobeying the Imām.[59]

III.2. Roadside Bombs and IEDs

Al-Ṣadr's justification for the use of improvised explosive devices (IEDs) and roadside bombs in Iraq was an example of drawing on longstanding notions in Islamic legal thought and treatises on *furūᶜ* ('positive law' compendiums). In his quest to justify their use, al-Ṣadr drew upon classical juristic opinions permitting attack in situations of *tatarrus* (the usage of 'non-combatant' shields, specifically Muslim) and have exonerated the resulting 'homicide' as collateral damage.[60]

For example, al-Ṣadr explicitly justified the use of roadside bombs in civilian populated areas as a means to combat the foreign occupation in Iraq. In one sermon he declared that:

56. Ḥāmid al-Khaffāf, *al-Nuṣūṣ al-Ṣādira ᶜan Samāḥat al-Sayyid al-Sīstānī* (Beirut, 2007), p. 209.
57. Kāshif al-Ghiṭāʾ, *Kashf* II, p. 38. Kāshif al-Ghiṭāʾ explains that whilst the presence of the *mujtahid* is not required in defence, his permission is *awlā* (preferred).
58. Ibid., pp. 381–2.
59. Ibid., p. 382.
60. It should be noted here that there was no formal conceptualisation of a civilian in any of the classical literature reviewed for this research. Therefore, for purposes of accuracy and consistency with the resources, it is more 'accurate' to refer to what in modern day would be considered a 'civilian' as 'non-combatant'. In Islamic juristic discourses, the criteria for a legitimate target is not whether they are a 'civilian' or not, but it is their involvement in battle or capacity to be involved in combat, and hence 'non-combatant' is more accurate in our context here.

> The occupation forces intentionally use our civilians as shields when they decide to drive their tanks through civilian populated areas . . . attacking with all available means will not be hampered by the presence of civilians.[61]

Al-Ṣadr here illustrated that in a state of war or in battle, all means and devices are legitimate in order to overcome the enemy, irrespective of casualties amongst Muslims or non-Muslims and regardless of whether or not they were considered to be combatants. His reference to the use of 'civilians' as shields echoed the opinions of both Sunnī and Ithnā ᶜAsharī classical jurists. It should be noted here, as would be evident to any researcher of classical Islamic laws of war, that in spite of their different historical trajectories, classical Sunnī and Ithnā ᶜAsharī jurisprudential discourses regulating war and conduct of hostilities bear more similarities than they do differences. The literature shows that the majority of Muslim jurists, as discussed below, concur that during times of war forsaking the lives of a few for securing and protecting the lives of the larger community is permissible if necessity requires it.

Hence, al-Ṣadr's rationalisation above could be seen as an extension of opinions of eminent classical Ithnā ᶜAsharī jurists, such as al-Allāma al-Ḥillī (d. 726/1325), al-Shahīd al-Thānī (d. 966/1558) and al-Najafī. These jurists, among many others, who cannot be cited here given the limited scope of this chapter, permit attacking the enemy on the basis of necessity, even in situations where the enemy is using Muslims as human shields. This permission is granted, especially in situations during the collision of forces or in the heat of battle (*iltiḥām al-ḥarb*), and if conquest and/or overcoming the enemy is subject to killing a shield – Muslim or not.[62] This permission is granted on the condition that avoiding Muslim civilian shields – or non-combatants shields, to be more accurate – is attempted, if possible.[63] In the case that a Muslim shield is killed in a Muslim attack, al-Shahīd al-Thānī held the view that a *kaffāra* (reparation or penance) would be necessary.[64]

As stated at the outset of this chapter, al-Ṣadr's rhetoric is not that of an isolated eccentric; nor, in the context of Ithnā ᶜAsharī thought, is his terminology

61. Al-Ṣadr, Seventy-Fourth Sermon, al-Kūfa, 17 September 2004.
62. Al-Ḥasan ibn Yūsuf ibn al-Muṭahhar al-Ḥillī [al-ᶜAllāmah], *Thadhkirat al-Fuqahā'* (Qum, 1993), IX, pp. 72, 74–5; Zayn al-Dīn al-ᶜĀmilī [al-Shahīd al-Thānī], *Masālik al-Afhām fī Sharḥ Sharā'iᶜ al-Islām* (Qum, 1992), III, pp. 25–6; Muḥammad Ḥasan al-Najafī, *Jawāhir al-Kalām fī Sharḥ Sharā'iᶜ al-Islām* (Beirut, 1981), XXI, p. 68.
63. For the Ithnā ᶜAsharī jurists, see, for example, al-ᶜAllāma al-Ḥillī, *Thadhkirat* IX, pp. 73–4; al-Shahīd al-Thānī, *Masālik* III, pp. 25–6; al-Najafī, *Jawāhir* XXI, pp. 68–9.
64. Al-Shahīd al-Thānī, *Masālik* III, p. 26.

alien. His rationalisation of certain acts of violence, in what he sees as a legitimate defense against an occupation, is nothing but a reiteration of the wider classical juristic discourse regulating armed activity.

In situations of war, the afore-reviewed classical jurists give priority to military necessity and guarding the *maṣlaḥa* or the overall benefit of *jihād*, which is, essentially, overcoming the enemy. As a result, all that is forbidden, reprehensible or discouraged becomes permitted (*mubāḥ* and/or *jāʾiz*) if necessity requires, and this necessity is essentially overcoming the enemy and protecting Muslims and their army.[65] For example, al-Najafī holds 'cutting trees, attacking with fire and flooding with water is reprehensible unless necessity requires it'.[66] To substantiate his premise, al-Najafī cites a number of *ḥadīth*s – for example, he quotes a *ḥadīth* on the authority of Imam Jaʿfar al-Ṣādiq averring that the Prophet commands to Muslim armies on their way to battle was continuously to 'commit no treason, nor excess, nor mutilation, and do not cut a tree *unless you are forced to do so by necessity*'.[67] Thus, in examining classical juristic texts, one will notice that at the end of almost every paragraph expounding the prohibitions during war, one will usually be confronted with a statement to the effect of 'unless overcoming the enemy requires it', 'unless it is a contingent to the success of conquest' or 'unless the protection of Muslims requires it'.[68] As is evident in this passage from Shahīd al-Thānīʾs *Masālik*:

> It is permissible in battle to besiege the enemy, to obstruct roads, use mangonels, destroy fortresses and homes, and everything else that is necessary for conquest. However, cutting trees and using fire or flooding to attack the enemy is reprehensible [*makrūh*] unless necessary. The usage of poison and like substances against the enemy is forbidden [*ḥarām*], but if conquest is contingent on its usage, then it is permissible [*jāʾiz*].[69]

III.3. Resistance vs Terrorism

For al-Ṣadr, the above legitimation of roadside bombs and IEDs and the justifications for attacking non-combatants should not to be construed as condoning terrorism. As according to him, it is imperative that a distinction be drawn between

65. Al-Najafī, *Jawāhir* XXI, pp. 65–6.
66. Ibid., p. 66.
67. Ibid.; Al-Allāma al-Ḥillī, *Thadhkirat* IX, pp. 69, 72 (emphasis added).
68. For example, see Al-Najafī, *Jawāhir* XXI, p. 68; Al-Allāma al-Ḥillī, *Thadhkirat* IX, pp. 68–9.
69. Al-Shahīd al-Thānī, *Masālik* III, p. 25.

resistance (*muqāwama*) and terrorism (*irhāb*). He defines the latter as 'actions that are carried out without any rational or justifiable reason but *for the sole aim of terrorising people*'.[70]

Al-Ṣadr's conceptualisation of what constitutes 'terrorism' is yet another extension of a concept that is treated in classical juristic literature under the crimes and punishments category of the *muḥāribūn* (*sing. muḥārib* brigands or modern-day 'terrorists'). This, broadly speaking, could be considered as the classical juristic conceptualisation of 'terrorism', under which acts of banditry, brigandage, highway robbery and display of weapons with the sole purpose of terrorising the peaceful public are subsumed.[71]

For instance, al-Ṭūsī (d. 1067) holds that the *muḥārib* or brigand is one who uses weapons to 'terrorise' people in a city, desert, land or sea. Al-Ṭūsī narrows his definition further, clarifying that the standard of proof or 'evidential requirement' is spreading terror.[72] On the other hand, al-Najafī proposes a more descriptive yet cryptic definition – which is similar to al-Ṣadr's – he maintains that the brigand is one who uses weapons 'with the intent of scaring people'.[73] He emphasises the importance of determining the intent of the armed individual as the evidential requirement, being a *muḥārib* or not.[74] This armed individual is not condemned or categorised as a *muḥārib* if he has no intention of instigating fear, even if, in fact, he does ultimately spread fear and terror amongst the people.[75] Alternately, al-Shahīd al-Awwal's (d. 1384) definition is not as contentious. He

70. Al-Ṣadr, Sixty-Fourth Sermon, al-Kūfa, 9 July 2004 (emphasis added).
71. Khaled Abou El Fadl, *Rebellion and Violence in Islamic Law* (Cambridge; New York, 2001). *Muḥāribūn, sing. muḥārib is one who commits an act of ḥirābah*: the etymology of the word is from *ḥarb* (war) and *yūḥārib* (to engage in war); it is the crime committed by those who 'wage war against God and His Messenger', as described in Q5:33 and 34. Islamic law: refers to crimes of highway robbery, banditry, brigandage and, generally, crimes of corrupting the earth. Literally, a fighter; as in he who 'fights' or *yūḥārib* God and His Prophet; fighting God and His Prophet is manifested in many ways other than the actual negation of Their injunctions. It includes taking up arms with the 'intent' of terrorising people, obliterating the peace, order and stability of a community (corrupting the earth), theft, murder, . . . etc. It is synonymous with a modern-day bandit or brigand.
72. Muḥammad ibn al-Ḥasan al-Ṭūsī, *al-Mabsūṭ fī Fiqh al-Imāmiyya* (Tehran, 1958), VIII, pp. 47, 50; Muḥammad ibn al-Ḥassan al-Ṭūsī, *al-Nihāya fī Mujarrad al-Fiqh wa al-Fatāwā* (Qum, n. d.), p. 720; Muḥammad ibn al-Ḥasan al-Ṭūsī, *al-Khilāf* (Qum, 2000), V, pp. 457.
73. Al-Najafī, *Jawāhir* XLI, p. 564.
74. It should be noted here that the centrality of 'expression' and 'intent' in Islamic law is too big of a topic to be addressed here and does not directly fall within the scope and purpose of this chapter.
75. Al-Najafī, *Jawāhir* XLI, pp. 566–7.

defines the *muḥārib* as anyone who carries weapons with the purpose of instigating fear in people.[76] The most straightforward of definitions is by al-Shahīd al-Thānī – that instigating fear in people is sufficient to condemn a person as *muḥārib*, regardless of whether he had the intent or not.[77]

Therefore, as per these definitions of classical jurist (with the exception of that by al-Shahīd al-Thānī), the armed activity of the Mahdi Army would not fall under the category of *ḥirāba* as their supposed intent and purpose for armed activity is not to instigate fear, but rather to resist the occupation. Hence, as al-Ṣadr may have wanted to allude to by the distinction he makes above, the activity of the Mahdi Army as per 'classical Islamic law' or, more accurately, the opinions of jurists cited here is not one that falls under the category of terrorism, but that of resistance.

As stated at the outset of this chapter, al-Ṣadr's discourse presents a continuation of themes that are found in both classical and modern-day Ithnā ᶜAsharī thought and juristic discussions. The section above illustrates how and why al-Ṣadr's discourses on armed defence, self-sacrifice and the sacrifice of the 'few' for the sake of the 'greater good' of the community and his own idea of the 'evidential requirement' of terrorism are not an anomaly, nor are they alien or detached from classical Islamic legal thought in general. On the other hand, the following section illustrates the connection between modern-day Islamic and al-Ṣadr's theme of political mobilisation.

IV. POLITICAL MOBILISATION

The main themes of al-Ṣadr's political mobilisation centre on adopting strong anti-imperialist dissenting rhetoric that is intertwined with a fervent advocacy for an active role of the *marjaᶜiyya* and the *ḥawza* – as opposed to a quietist one.[78]

76. Muḥammad ibn Jamāl al-Dīn ibn Makkī al-ᶜĀmilī [al-Shahīd al-Awwal], *al-Durūs al-Sharᶜiyya fī Fiqh al-Imāmiyya* (Qum, n. d.), II, p. 59.
77. Zayn al-Dīn al-Jabᶜī al-ᶜĀmilī [al-Shahīd al-Thānī], *al-Rawḍa, al-Bahiyya fī Sharḥ al-Lumᶜa al-Dimashqiyya* (Tehran, 1968), VI, pp. 290–1.
78. There is a significant amount of scholarship on activism and quietism of the *marjaᶜiyya*. Of most relevance here is that which has been written on the *marjaᶜiyya* of al-Najaf since the war. See, for example: Allawi, *Occupation*, pp. 209–10; Hashim, *Insurgency and Counter-Insurgency*, p. 214; Juan Cole, 'The United States and Shīᶜite Religious Factions', pp. 543–66; Cole, *The Ayatollahs and Democracy in Iraq* (Amsterdam and Leiden, 2006); Mehdi Khalaji, 'The Last Marja: Sistani and the End of Traditional Religious Authority in Shīᶜism', *The Washington Institute for Near East Policy*, Policy Focus no. 59 (September 2006); Babak Rahimi, 'The Discourse of Democracy in Shīᶜi Islamic Jurisprudence: The Two Cases of Montazeri and Sistani', *Robert Schuman Centre*

IV.1. Activism vs Quietism

For Muqtadā al-Ṣadr, like al-Ṣadr al-Awwal and al-Ṣadr al-Thānī, the *marjaᶜiyya and ḥawza* has to actively reach out to the people and engage with their needs. He carries his family's political legacy forward as he envisages politics and religion to be intertwined and inseparable.[79] Thus, according to al-Ṣadr, gone should be the days when the clerics confined themselves behind the walls of the *ḥawzah*. In this respect, to distinguish himself and his followers from quietism, he often refers to himself and addresses his audience as 'children' or disciples of the 'speaking' or vocal/active *ḥawza* (*abnāʾ al-ḥawza al-nātiqa*).[80]

He emphasises that an 'active' vocal *marjaᶜiyya* is an imperative necessity to cater for the requirements of the Iraqi people; to establish Friday prayers and deliver sermons as 'a platform from which societal concerns and people's grievances are addressed and resolved'.[81] The Friday sermon, furthermore, is to be a platform from which followers are morally and religiously guided, and reminded of the centrality of commanding good and forbidding evil.[82]

Muqtadā al-Ṣadr continues to present himself as the symbol of *al-ḥawza al-nāṭiqa* and, thus, following in the footsteps of al-Ṣadr al-Thānī, diligently upholds Friday prayers and delivers the Friday sermon in person, rarely by a proxy. Additionally, he put himself forth as the 'liberator' who was ready to sacrifice himself in the fight against the tyrannical oppressive occupier and to deliver the long-oppressed and dispossessed Iraqi people from subjugation to their freedom.[83] To achieve this objective, in October 2003, al-Ṣadr declared the establishment of what he referred to as the 'government of righteousness' (*ḥukūmat al-ḥaqq*), which he describes as 'a truly Iraqi government that represents the Iraqi people',[84] inclining towards the ideologies of both al-Ṣadr al-Awwal and al-Ṣadr al-Thānī, which legitimate for political activism towards a 'just society' that is 'emancipated' according to principles of Islam where community welfare is guarded and social justice prevails.[85] Al-Ṣadr announced his

For Advanced Studies: Mediterranean Programme Series (European University Institute, Florence, 2008); Reidar Visser, 'Sistani, the United States and Politics in Iraq: From Quietism to Machiavellianism?', *NUPI, Norwegian Institute of International Affairs* 700 (2006), 1–37.

79. Al-Ṣadr, Fiftieth Sermon, al-Kūfa, 2 April 2004.
80. Ibid.
81. Al-Ṣadr, Thirty-Third Sermon, al-Kūfa, 5 December 2003.
82. Al-Ṣadr, Fifty-Sixth Sermon, al-Kūfa, 14 May 2004.
83. Al-Ṣadr, Fiftieth Sermon, al-Kūfa, 2 April 2004.
84. Al-Ṣadr, Twenty-Sixth Sermon, al-Kūfa, 17 October 2003.
85. Talib Aziz, 'The Political Theory of Muhammad Baqir al-Sadr', in *Ayatollahs, Sufis*

reasons for establishing the 'government of righteousness' as follows: the prime objectives of the nascent government was to ensure that community welfare takes precedence over personal/individual interests, to protect and secure the Iraqi people, to fulfil their needs, and to combat corruption through commanding good and forbidding evil.[86]

Al-Ṣadr Thānī was very forceful, on many occasions – in public sermons and in interviews – in his criticism of the quietist policy of the *marja*ᶜ*iyya* in al-Najaf during his time.[87] In an interview that was widely disseminated, al-Ṣadr Thānī considered the *ḥawza* to have been negligent in fulfilling its duties towards the people, and the *marja*ᶜ*iyya* to have been 'inactive' and detached from the people. He held that:

> The *ḥawza* grew and flourished over the years while maintaining a strict traditional system of learning in the sciences of religion and jurisprudence . . . confining the *ḥawza* to just this system of education does not serve the community nor the individual and ultimately, and more importantly, fails to serve the religion . . . detaching oneself from the world and the ongoings of the community and the needs of Muslims for the purpose of studying and serving the *ḥawzah.* The righteous *marja*ᶜ*iyya* (*al-marja*ᶜ*iyya al-saliha)* is one that is in touch with the people and their needs, one that rises above personal whim and worldly or material desires . . . [88]

Similarly, al-Ṣadr al-Awwal's project of reform was built on the fundamentals of a 'non-quietist' active *marja*ᶜ*iyya*, which conducts itself 'justly', abandons *taqiyya* (precautionary dissimulation), is involved in politics and with the affairs of the people –understanding the social, political and economic conditions of its community.[89]

In line with the two Ṣadrs, Muqtadā al-Ṣadr incessantly criticised quietism for what he saw to be a misappropriation of *taqiyya*, describing the silence of

and Ideologues: State, Religion and Social Movements in Iraq, ed. Faleh Abdul Jabar (London, 2002), pp. 233–5; Faleh A. Jabar, *The Shī*ᶜ*ite Movement*, pp. 294–9.

86. Al-Ṣadr, Twenty-Sixth Sermon, al-Kūfa, 17 October 2003.
87. Muḥammad Muḥammad Ṣādiq al-Ṣadr, Excerpt of Last Sermon, al-Kūfa, online video clip, https://www.youtube.com/watch?v=_BnGw23Xsk4; Idem, excerpt from *liqā*ʾ *al-ḥanāna*, interview, online video clip, https://www.youtube.com/watch?v=jjGG U5qat0o.
88. Muḥammad Muḥammad Ṣādiq al-Ṣadr, *liqā*ʾ *al-ḥanāna*, interview, online video clip, https://www.youtube.com/watch?v=-JVxdAqU9E0.
89. Aziz, 'The Political Theory', pp. 238–9; Rizvi, 'Political Mobilization', p. 1304.

the Najaf *ḥawza* as 'nothing but cowardice',[90] and holding that the prerequisites permitting the practice of *taqiyya* are currently non-existent. In fact, he went as far as to insinuate that the absence of an 'active' or an 'involved' role of the *marjaᶜiyya* in al-Najaf was a factor which 'aided' the continued presence of the occupation.[91] In a meeting with students and professors of the al-Kūfa University, al-Ṣadr forcefully lashed out, as usual, at the policy of quietism adopted by the al-Najaf *ḥawzah*.[92] He warned his audience and followers against *taqiyya* as a sign of weakness and cowardice, and against 'remain clinging to *taqiyya* until the Jews invade the holy city of al-Najaf'.[93] His statement was in line with his adherence to the concept of *al-ḥawza al-nātiqa* and igniting people's religious emotions regarding protecting the holy cities to galvanise them in order to fight the occupation. Furthermore, on his mission to further undermine the role of the quietist *ḥawza*, to persuade the masses to his cause, al-Ṣadr goes on to assert that 'contrary to the quietist *al-ḥawza*, the vocal – which is actively engaged with the individual and the community – fulfils its religious obligation – ordained by God Almighty – of commanding good and forbidding evil'.[94] Al-Ṣadr's incessant attack on the traditional *ḥawza*, while bringing forth the virtues of *al-ḥawza al-nātiqa*, was possibly out of his sense of being on a mission to inspire his audience through advocacy and through attempting to create a 'mass revolutionary following' by which ideological change – on the conceptualisation of the *marjaᶜiyya* – may result in, and possibly be followed by an, eventual overall restructuring of the institute itself in al-Najaf – as the two Ṣadrs had previously aspired.

Therefore, his attacks against the *marjaᶜiyya* never waned during the years of war, blaming all mishaps on the absence of the 'vocal' *marjaᶜ* (*al-marjaᶜ al-nāṭiq*). Three years into the war, following the attacks on the Samarrāʾ Shīᶜī Shrines, al-Ṣadr blamed the occupation forces and what he called the 'inauspicious trio' (*al-thālūth al-mashʾūm*) – in reference to the United States, Israel and Britain – accountable for orchestrating the attacks and also held the *marjaᶜiyya* equally accountable, because had it not been for the absence of the 'activist *marjaᶜ* who, unlike the quietist, would be politically engaged and would actively defend Islam and pre-empt any attacks on its holy sites', those attacks would not have happened.[95]

90. Rizvi, 'Political Mobilization', p. 1304.
91. Ibid.
92. Ibid.
93. Ibid.
94. Al-Ṣadr, 'Meeting with Professors and Students'.
95. Muqtadā al-Ṣadr, Press release on the occasion of the bombing of the Samarrāʾ Shrines,

Al-Ṣadr's attacks on the *ḥawza* and the *marja^c^iyya* in al-Najaf were not always just verbal. It was widely believed that his antagonism and criticism instigated action when mobs of the Ṣadrist Movement were accused of involvement in attacks and acts of intimidation against the clergy in al-Najaf. The Ṣadrists have been indicted in a number of armed encounters, not least the infamous murder of ^c^Abd al-Majīd al-Khū'ī, a scion of the *marja^c^iyya*, in Najaf on 10 April 2003.[96] Immediately after al-Khū'ī's murder, supporters of al-Ṣadr surrounded the house of Sīstānī, for no declared reason. One can only speculate about the reasons. It is possible that the siege was carried out as a gesture of dissent and intimidation against the 'non-Arab', 'quietist' *marja^c^* or possibly as a gesture of protection: al-Ṣadr, at the time, had declared waging 'the revolution of the Imām Mahdī' to protect the holy cities.[97]

IV.2. Anti-imperialist Nationalism

In spite of his attacks on the *ḥawza* institutions, Muqtadā al-Ṣadr, like al-Ṣadr al-Awwal and al-Ṣadr al-Thānī, defended national integrity and generally espoused a discourse that transcends sectarian boundaries. During the war, however, he was not always very consistent in reaching out beyond sectarian divide, especially following the sectarian attacks on Shī^c^īs or their shrines. However, generally speaking, al-Ṣadr's sectarian rhetoric was seldom his norm, and one may safely say that it almost always followed an episode of sectarian attack. As stated earlier, he often projected his movement and the services as belonging to all Iraqis, regardless of ethnicity, religion or sect.

For al-Ṣadr, the Friday pulpit is not just utilised as a platform from which to command good and forbid evil or to preach the virtues of *al-ḥawza al-nāṭiqa*, but equally to launch a strong anti-imperialist, anti-Israeli and anti-American rhetoric, which usually includes very fiery slogan chanting from the crowds: 'No, No, America! No, No, Israel! No, No, Satan!' The purpose was to posit himself as the inheritor of the legacy of al-Ṣadr al-Thānī and, of course, to rally the masses to fight the occupation – the 'symbol of imperialism'.[98] In accordance with his espousal of an anti-imperialist, emancipatory discourse – in which he also,

13 June 2007 (on file with author).

96. Patrick Cockburn, *The Occupation: War and Resistance in Iraq* (London, 2006), pp. 95–9; Raphaeli, 'Understanding Muqtada', p. 36.
97. Raphaeli, 'Understanding Muqtada', p. 36.
98. Raphaeli, 'Understanding Muqtada', pp. 34–5; Rizvi, 'Political Mobilization', p. 1304; Al-Ṣadr, Speech: al-^c^Imāra, online video clip, http://www.youtube.com/watch?v=-oLwlNdKS8Y.

diligently, took on defending national integrity – al-Ṣadr frequently reiterated that Iraqis should put their differences aside and unite against the one enemy, which was the occupation and the 'inauspicious trio' (*al-thālūth al-mashʾūm*), in reference to the United States, Israel and Britain.[99]

V. CONCLUDING OBSERVATIONS

After the end of the 'imperialist occupation', al-Ṣadr took on a different 'cause' to fight for. Still a staunch defendant of national integrity, he preserves and promotes the legacy of the previous Ṣadrs. He aims to reach out to people, promoting democratic reforms, instituting governmental checks and balances, campaigning against corruption and securing government services, especially to the poor – all of which have gained him far-reaching charisma with Shīʿī masses. Muqtadā al-Ṣadr's status was at its peak at the end of the war. Besides the public causes he took upon himself to speak out for, he seemed to be consolidating his own platform as a religious authority. He currently receives requests for his religious opinion about matters (*istiftaʾāt*) and issues *fatāwā* (religious opinion) and conducts his own *halaqāt* (circles of traditional learning). Yet, his political appeal was likely to take over his religious one. The prospects of al-Ṣadr becoming a *marjaʿ aʿlā* were highly doubted within Shīʿī circles, yet he could still be a '*marjaʿ* in making'.[100]

On 16 February 2014, al-Ṣadr announced he was retiring from political life to avoid sedition, in view of the mounting tensions between him and the current political leadership in Iraq. Whether he will conform to his decision or not is unknown, only time will tell.

This chapter is a brief presentation of some examples of patterns of continuity with classical and modern notions of violence and conceptions of political mobilisation in al-Ṣadr's discourse. Even though much has been written about Muqtadā al-Ṣadr, to my knowledge, no study thus far has attempted to analyse the underpinnings of his discourse. This chapter hopes to contribute to filling this gap in scholarship.

99. Press release on the occasion of the bombing of the Samarrāʾ Shrines, 13 June 2007. (On file with author).
100. Muqtadā al-Ṣadr website, http://jawabna.com/index.php.

CHAPTER

13

MANAGING VIOLENT CONFLICT: HUDNA AND TAHDI'A, BEYOND A STRATEGIC PAUSE

*Beverley Milton-Edwards**

INTRODUCTION

In the late twentieth and early twenty-first centuries many of the territories in which Muslim adherents reside have become synonymous with war and conflict rather than peace. This is particularly true of the modern Muslim domains of the Middle East, where Muslim majority countries such as Iran, Iraq, Egypt, Syria, Lebanon, Algeria and Yemen have become engulfed in internal civil and external regional wars and conflicts. Additionally, the discourse on violence in modern Islamic thought is frequently presented myopically and as extreme by many media as the frame by which Muslim communities, Muslim politics and Muslim states should be understood.[1]

In the seventh century when the Prophet Muḥammad founded the faith of Islam, the territories of Arabia and beyond were also frequently characterised by violent dispute. Yet Islam was founded on the principles of peace. Nevertheless, the Prophet Muḥammad and his successors, like other statesmen of their time developed approaches for the management of violent internal and

* School of History, Anthropology, Philosophy and Politics, Queen's University, Belfast

1. The author is grateful to Ruud Peters and Joas Wagemakers for their insights and constructive comment on this work. See E. Elgamri, *Islam in the British Broadsheets: The Impact of Orientalism on Representations of Islam in the British Press* (Reading, 2010); D. Garland, *The Culture of Control: Crime and Social Order in Contemporary Society* (Oxford, 2001); E. S. Herman and N. Chomsky, *Manufacturing Consent: The Political Economy of the Mass Media* (New York, 1988); B. L. Nacos, *Mass-Mediated Terrorism: The Central Role of the Media in Terrorism and Counterterrorism* (Lanham, 2007).

external conflict, leaving in their wake a record of their approaches and a legacy which prompted some classical thinkers to address specific conflict management themes such as *jihād* and ceasefires (*hudna*).[2]

Hence, within Islam there has been a long-standing discourse on conflict, war, its management and cessation. The Qur°ān contains verses which address the circumstances under which warfare becomes permissible. Other verses of the Qur°ān outline the context in which offers of peace from the enemy are acceptable, including the permissibility and conditions of a truce (*hudna*) and reconciliation with an enemy (*ṣulḥ*). Over the centuries since Islam was founded, Muslim rulers have encountered dimensions of war and conflict and regulated relations with their enemies according to such rules. The legitimacy of violence, its regulation and its cessation has been incorporated into Islam and jurisprudence to create ethical boundaries for Muslim societies and state governance. Modern Islamic thinkers have also developed and contributed to discourse, legitimating acts of violence and warfare and contending that ceasefire and pause may also have a part in conflicts.[3]

In the present day such specific themes of ceasefire (*hudna*) and temporary halt to hostilities or calm (*tahdi°a*) have entered the lexicon of some modernist Islamist movements. In this chapter I address these themes and question whether they reflect examples that can go beyond a so-called 'strategic pause' as a reflection of a changed discourse and debate with respect to the place of legitimate or illegitimate violence in modern Islamic thought. I will explore this issue through a case study of the Palestinian Islamic Hamas (Ḥamās) movement and the Palestinian–Israeli conflict.

HAMAS: A DIMENSION OF MODERN MARTIAL ISLAM?

The Palestinian Islamic movement Hamas proves a useful case study in this debate. Hamas, founded in 1987, is typified in most academic literature as a broad political–socio movement that is also engaged in sustained violent conflict

2. See Ann K. S. Lambton, *State and Government in Medieval Islam: An Introduction to the Study* (New York, 1981); R. Peters, *Jihad in Classical and Modern Islam* (Princeton, 1996); Abu al-Hasan al-Marwardi, *Al-ahkam As-sultaniyyah: Translated by Asadullah Yate* (London, 1996); A. H. I. Al-Matroudi, *The Hanbali School of Law and Ibn Taymiyyah: Conflict or Conciliation* (London, 2006).
3. See M. Hatina, 'The "Ulama" and the Cult of Death in Palestine', *Israel Affairs* 12.1 (2006), 29–51, who contends that modern day scholars of Islam access historical and judicial sources to legitimate their positions on the legitimacy or otherwise of Muslim violence.

with the state of Israel (as occupier of Muslim *waqf* territory) and with its opponents in the Palestinian secular national movement of Fatah (*Fataḥ*).[4] Some studies go as far as depicting Hamas as a monolithic terrorist organisation devoid of other dimensions or features.[5] Hamas's interpretation of particular Muslim motifs, it has been contended, is ideologically predisposed to *jihād* of a particular kind.[6] Major contemporary Muslim scholars such as Shaykh Yūsuf al-Qaraḍāwī have reinforced this unique dimension of the context in which Hamas wages *jihād* against a foreign occupier and usurper of foreign lands.[7]

Much of the discourse of Hamas, including its charter (*mīthāq*), statements from its leaders and communiqués, emphasise that *jihād* is a form of resistance (*muqāwama*). While there are some scholars who contend that elements of the charter are flexible and have changed in emphasis or have become irrelevant over time, nevertheless this founding contract declares that a central goal of the movement is to wage *jihād* to wrest Palestine from Israeli hands.[8] The charter states: 'There is no solution for the Palestinian question except through Jihad . . . The Palestinian people know better than to consent to having their future, rights and fate toyed with.'[9] In more recent years there is certainly evidence that Hamas's discourse has changed by means of expressing the ways in which resistance in the name of *jihād* is strategically ordered – primarily in terms of how

4. Historical and contemporary accounts of Hamas frequently address its employment of violence. See B. Milton-Edwards and S. Farrell, *Hamas, the Islamic Resistance Movement* (Cambridge, 2010); Z. Abu-Amr, 'Hamas: A Historical and Political Background', *Journal of Palestine Studies* 22.4 (1993), 5–19; S. Mishal and A. Sela, *The Palestinian Hamas: Vision, Violence and Coexistence* (New York, 2000); Z. Chehab, *Hamas: The Untold Story of Militants, Martyrs and Spies* (London, 2007); P. Cardici, *Hamas From Resistance to Government* (New York, 2012); K. Hroub, *Hamas: Political Thought and Practice* (Washington, 2000); A. Knudsen, 'Crescent and Sword: The Hamas Enigma', *Third World Quarterly* 26.8 (2005), 1373–88; A. Tamimi, *Hamas: A History from Within* (London, 2007).
5. See M. Levitt, *Hamas: Politics, Charity, and Terrorism in the Service of Jihad* (New Haven and London, 2006); J. Schanzer, *Hamas vs. Fatah: The Struggle for Palestine* (New York, 2008).
6. See J. Wagemakers, 'Legitimizing Pragmatism: Hamas' Framing Efforts From Militancy to Moderation and Back?', *Terrorism and Political Violence* 22.3 (2010), 358–78; A. Al-Shaer, 'Islam in the Narrative of Fatah and Hamas', in *Narrative Conflict in the Middle East*, eds D. Matar and Z. Harb (London, 2013).
7. R. Ghannoushi, 'What is New About al-Qaradawi's Fiqh of Jihad?', n. p., June 2008; M. Lynch, 'Qaradawi's Revisions', www.foreignpolicy.com, 9 July 2009 (online). For accessed dates of online resources (designated in this chapter by '(online)'), see the Bibliography and the accompanying note, p. 366.
8. See Tamimi, *Hamas*, pp. 150–1.
9. 'Hamas Charter, 1988', law.yale.edu, Article 13 (online).

armed resistance is emphasised and expanded to include other forms of popular and even non-violent resistance. In the wake of the Hamas electoral victory in January 2006 and international debate, Hamas leader Khaled Meshal (Khālid Mishᶜal) signalled a discursive position on what was meant by resistance, declaring it to have a 'political and diplomatic' form.[10] Nevertheless, the *mithāq* in indicating a political reference point in the history of Hamas clearly signposts the permissibility of warfare/*jihād* against an enemy (Israel), but cautions against it in terms of its Palestinian secular opponents. Interestingly, the *mithāq* omits reference to strategic management of conflict, such as a ceasefire (*hudna*[11]) *or calm (tahdiʾa*) entirely, yet in practice the Hamas movement was compelled to confront just such issues as in the Palestinian–Israeli arena.

In terms of legitimate and illegitimate violence, Hamas, at this point in its early evolution, was defining its position in relation to its enemy (Israel) in terms of the religious legitimacy bestowed and accrued to its cause by defining its violence against Israel as *jihād*. Israel was designated as an illegitimate entity and an occupier. Hamas was not just a resistance organisation (like the PLO), but it was an Islamic resistance organisation and hence obliged (*farḍ ᶜayn*) to engage in a violent *jihād* against Israel. Hamas's charter explains the *jihād* duty:

> The day that enemies usurp part of Moslem land, Jihad becomes the individual duty of every Moslem. In face of the Jews' usurpation of Palestine, it is compulsory that the banner of Jihad be raised. To do this requires the diffusion of Islamic consciousness among the masses, both on the regional, Arab and Islamic levels. It is necessary to instil the spirit of Jihad in the heart of the nation so that they would confront the enemies and join the ranks of the fighters.[12]

Contemporary Muslim scholars in contributing to the debate about *jihād* have reinforced the legitimacy of such a posture.[13] As such, *jihād* was initially defined by Hamas according to some of the classic norms of war in Islam (including important injunctions against targeting civilians).[14] By and large, Hamas defined

10. As reported in *al-Hayat al-Jadida* (Palestinian newspaper), 22 January 2006.
11. By *hudna* here, I am referring to the classical Islamic term of a long-term truce between Muslims and their enemies. The enemy here can be both internal (a fellow Muslim) or external. In the period beginning in 628 CE, the Prophet Muḥammad called for a ten-year ceasefire, known as the Truce of Hudaybiyah, with his enemies from the Quraysh tribe. During the *hudna* the two sides were to live in peace.
12. 'Hamas Charter, 1988', law.yale.edu, Article 15 (online).
13. See Al-Shaer, 'Islam in the Narrative of Fatah and Hamas', p. 128 (n. 7).
14. Peters, *Jihad*; and Ghannoushi, 'What is New'.

its position around those Qurʾānic passages and previous historical instances in Muslim history such as Ṣalāḥ al-Dīn's war against the Crusader occupation of Jerusalem, which allowed for war to be waged under specific circumstances. As with the Qurʾān, Hamas defined its early position as one of defined and limited warfare, rather than limitless terror and violence.[15] Yet it began to give ideological import to certain dimensions of *fiqh* on *jihād* with far-reaching consequences for the ways in which it signified itself and was signified by others.[16] It is also apparent that Hamas omitted those passages of Qurʾānic, religious literature and history that addressed overtures of reconciliation, the cessation of hostilities and conclusion of peace (*ṣulḥ*) which would require ceasefires and negotiation with the enemy.

TRANSITION

By the late 1990s there is evidence that within Hamas their leadership engaged in a form of ideological transition regarding their position on the strategic management of conflict. The transition impacted both on the management of conflict with Israel and with their fellow Palestinians – particularly the PLO's major Fatah faction and the governing Palestinian Authority (PA) under the leadership of Yasser Arafat (Yāsir ᶜArafāt). Hamas leaders, including its founder Sheikh Yassin, went on public record in 1998 with an endorsement of ceasefire (*hudna*) for the first time.[17] From this point there emerges within Hamas delineated yet dynamic discourse on ceasefire and other mechanisms for strategic management of conflict. Similarly, a decade later, Hamas would engage in the same attenuated discourse over the practice of a pause or 'calm' (*tahdiʾa*) in hostilities with their enemies.

Returning to the issue of ceasefire, the leadership of Hamas appear to have introduced the idea of a ceasefire as a twofold mechanism for strategic management, rather than resolution of their conflicts. Indeed, the strategic dimension is articulated in two important ways. Firstly, the Hamas leadership designated a *hudna* as limited by a time frame (according to Islamic tradition); 'Islam permits a temporary truce for a limited period of time with the Jewish enemy

15. See B. Milton-Edwards, *Islamic Politics in Palestine* (London, 1996).
16. See I. Malik, 'Jihad and its Development and Relevance, the Meaning and Importance of Jihadi in Islamic Thought', *Palestine–Israel Journal* 1.2, 1994 (online); and N. Johnson, *Islam and the Politics of Meaning in Palestinian Nationalism* (London, 1982).
17. See Shaykh Ahmad Yasin (Shaykh Aḥmad Yāsīn), 'Interviews, Gaza Strip, October 1997 (excerpts)', *Journal of Palestine Studies* 2 (1998), 150–5. Tamimi claims that the idea of *hudna* was mooted within the movement in the mid-1990s (Tamimi, *Hamas*, p. 158.)

if necessary', stated leader Sheikh Yassin in 1998.[18] Secondly, the leadership at this point, unlike its fellow Palestinians in the PLO, was offering no compromise in its position regarding the resolution of the conflict with Israel that required recognition for permanent peace. Such issues, argued Hamas leaders, would be in the hands of others. Yet coupled to the discourse on *hudna* was an implicit recognition by the Hamas leadership of Israel delimited by the 1967 borders.[19]

REDEFINING AND CREATING HUDNA

When the second Palestinian Intifada broke out in September 2000 it was marked by an unprecedented escalation of violence on both sides, including suicide bomb attacks which targeted many Israeli civilians.[20] The extent to which civilians on both sides of the conflict ended up the target of violence exerted pressures to seek ways to manage the conflict better and reduce violence. This included proposals by the US in terms of the Tenet and Zinni plans, which called for comprehensive ceasefire, but included security coordination as well.[21] The extent to which the reduction of such violence could be perceived as an overture for conflict resolution or merely a strategic pause was difficult to discern during this phase, as Palestinian political movements such as Hamas grappled ideologically with the implications of introducing such a mechanism into their remit. Israel, and its supporters, largely dismissed arguments that Hamas's position on a ceasefire could mean anything other than a strategic pause in the conflict to rearm and regroup against Israel militarily.

Yet, it can be contested that a ceasefire has always been a flexible instrument employed in different ways by Muslim state rulers over the course of history.[22] In the case of Hamas, a similar flexible approach appears to emerge in the thinking of the leadership during the period of the second Palestinian Intifada (2000–5). As Palestinian opposition to the tactic of suicide attacks as *jihād* was increasingly challenged and deemed illegitimate, Hamas had to balance the

18. Yasin, 'Interviews'.
19. Tamimi, *Hamas*, pp. 156–9.
20. Milton-Edwards and Farrell, *Hamas*.
21. See Giora Eiland, 'The IDF in the Second Intifada', *Strategic Assessment* 13.3 (2010); and K. Shikaki, 'Palestinians Divided', *Foreign Affairs* (2002), 89–105. The Tenet and Zinni plans for ceasefire between Israel and the Palestinians did not include a monitoring mechanism.
22. Hroub, *Hamas, A Beginner's Guide* (London, 2006), p. 55; P. M. Holt, 'Qalāwūn's Treaty with Acre in 1283', *The English Historical Review* 91 (1976), 802–12; P. M. Holt, 'The Treaties of the Early Mamluk Sultans with the Frankish States', *Bulletin of the School of Oriental and African Studies* 43.1 (1980), 67–76.

fundamental rhetoric and *raison d'être* of *jihād*, as well as appear to calibrate or offer to engage in a unilateral ceasefire that would mean an end to the increasing practice of targeting Israeli civilians.[23] Hamas also needed to distinguish itself from the PLO, which had ended the option of armed resistance against Israel and entered into a ceasefire and peace negotiation. Hamas's offer of *hudna* was thus made, according to their leaders, within a specific time frame and without concessions such as 'recognition' of the enemy.

Hamas's actual participation in a ceasefire[24] would first manifest itself in the initiatives of 2001–3 and include the movement as one among other Palestinian national factions.[25] The ceasefire was a unilateral step by Palestinians and was not part of a reciprocated agreement with Israel. It was an agreement by Hamas (and other factions) to stop armed attacks on Israel and a call on the international community to leverage Israel into meeting Palestinian demands to stop violence against Palestinians (specifically targeted assassinations), to release prisoners and detainees, to halt illegal settlement activity and to protect Christian and Muslim holy places.[26] It also required Hamas and the PLO (mainly Fatah) to negotiate with each other over the terms of a ceasefire offer to Israel, revealing the internal tensions and competing objectives between the two rival movements.

23. Tamimi *Hamas* argues that the Hamas leadership argued that targeting civilians was an 'aberration', yet other Hamas leaders themselves explicitly stated that civilians could be targeted. See Mahmoud Zahar, Hamas leader, author interview, September 2002, Gaza City: 'If Israelis are killing Palestinian civilians then why we are not using the same means. An eye for an eye . . . None of them are civilians . . . they say they are a military society and in civil uniform. The second point is – that its [sic] not about civilian or military . . . is it right to accept occupation as legal or illegal. If it is illegitimate them every means to end that occupation is legitimate . . . it is justified. So don't waste your time in Europe discussing is it civilian or not . . . Discuss is it a legal occupation and for it continue since 1948 and people are looking to be liberated. This is a dirty war and then in what sense can we make these distinctions. It is a mistake of our leaders . . . of Mr Arafat who is condemning our operations and considering martyr operations as doing harm. They should tell Europe the truth.'
24. Hamas leaders had offered forms of truce or ceasefire formally to Israel in the mid- to late 1990s, but they were not made manifest.
25. In June and December 2001, Hamas temporarily abided by ceasefires called by President Yasser Arafat. In June 2002 Hamas engaged its first formal calm (*tahdi'a*), which broke down after Israel assassinated Hamas leader Saleh Shehadeh (Ṣāliḥ Shihāda) on 22 July 2002. It then re-entered a process of both internal organisation dialogue and dialogue with other parties outside the organisation to engage in further attempts to cease fire against Israeli targets.
26. See the full text of ceasefire: 'Words of Fatah, Hamas and Islamic Jihad: "Just, Lasting and Comprehensive Peace"', nytimes.com, 30 June 2003 (online).

Explaining Hamas's motivation in signing up to the 2003 ceasefire is subject to contested and varied interpretations. The decision to engage in 2003 is explained according to a number of competing explanations: prosaic resource mobilisation and political opportunity, strategic military realities in relation to the movement's relative weakness at the time – particularly with respect to the success of Israeli counterterror measures against the organisation – intra-group competition with the PLO, political bidding and legitimacy, and defining and redefining resistance. What is largely absent from such rationalisations of Hamas discourse on this matter is reference to theological positioning on *hudna*.

Thus, while authors like Gunning highlight local political developments, including changes within the Palestinian factional milieu as it related to Hamas's power and legitimacy, the necessary change in terms of religious interpretation of *hudna* and its portents is absent. Here, Hamas is portrayed in a fashion almost identical to secular nationalist factions in the Palestinian milieu.[27] Its religious character is emptied of meaning. This despite the specific employment of a portentous Islamic term: *hudna*. It is true that by 2003 the political environment had changed; Hamas (like other Palestinian factions) had felt the effect of Israel's counterterror measures and the impact of such measures on the collective public. Indeed, public opinion – key in the past to Hamas's legitimacy claims – had begun to swing against the violent tactics that it had employed against Israel. In contrast to Gunning, Hroub contends that Hamas 'bound by its religious roots . . . felt the need to justify its adoption of a controversial policy [a *hudna*] on Islamic religious grounds'.[28] This was because if forms of religious interpretation had been employed to justify violent attack (*jihād*) against Israel and successfully delineate Hamas from its Palestinian competitors, then *fiqh* limiting or ceasing such violent attacks was necessary to preserve the movement's Islamist ideological character. Hardliners within the movement remained sceptical of a ceasefire. Hamas leader Abdel Aziz Rantissi argued:[29]

> [A]s long as we are under occupation we have to continue fighting until we finish this mission. The formula is not cease-fire because we are not two states facing each other across a border. We are under occupation and we are defending ourselves. So the word ceasefire is not working here but resistance and occupation. They should stop occupation and then we will stop resistance.

27. See J. Gunning, *Hamas in Politics* (London, 2007), pp. 222–3.
28. Hroub, *Hamas*, p. 55.
29. Dr Abdel Aziz Rantissi (ᶜAbd al-Azīz Rantīsī), Hamas leader, author interview, Gaza, September 2002.

PROSAIC POLITICAL OBJECTIVES

The experience of negotiating the June 2003 *hudna* also revealed that Hamas would determine its position on prosaic political objectives linked to its rivalry and later enmity with its internal Palestinian competitor Fatah. Here, the discourse on *jihād*, *hudna* and avoidance of *fitna* (chaos) was much more ambiguous. Hamas remained consistent in its demands that the PLO leadership reform from within and loosen the reigns of leadership to accommodate Hamas on a significant basis of representation.[30] Hamas ended up negotiating with particular elements of the Fatah leadership, including Tanẓīm leader Marwan Barghouti (Marwān Bārghūtī) and the leadership in the prisons.[31] It was in the prisons that the key elements of the ceasefire were debated and agreed between Hamas and Fatah. Specifically, the prison leadership of the factions broke new ground by appearing to accept as an agreed premise that the new Palestinian State would be on the basis of the lines of 1967 (boundary between Israel and the Palestinian territories).

One dimension of the 2003 *hudna* that at least implicitly addressed jurisprudence with respect to avoiding *fitna* among Muslims was that the ceasefire statements from Palestinian emphasised 'unity' (though national rather than Islamic). Hamas leader Ismail Abu Shanab (Ismāᶜīl Abū Shanab), who was a key figure in promoting the internal decision by Hamas to engage in a ceasefire, explained the import of unity, declaring that:

> [F]irst of all we want to . . . find common ground with other groups and leave our differences aside. That's the golden rule. The common ground is: Intifada, resisting the occupation, developing better Palestinian life and reform and developing a Palestinian state and struggling towards the return of the refugees. Those are the main targets on the document that we tried to establish.[32]

Internal enemies have always arisen within Islam. Medieval jurists such as al-Ghazālī (d. 505/1111) and Ibn Taymiyya (d. 728/1328) shaped much debate on this topic and continue to inform the discourse of modern-day jurists and

30. See L. Lybarger, *Identity and Religion in Palestine: The Struggle between Islamism and Secularism in the Occupied Territories* (Princeton, 2007); Milton-Edwards and Farrell, *Hamas*.
31. Palestinian factions all maintain wings of their leadership within the Israeli detention and prison system. The Hamas leadership, for example, consists of four wings: Gaza Strip, external, prison and West Bank.
32. Ismail Haniyeh, Hamas leader, author interview, Gaza City, August 2002.

movements.[33] Al-Ghazālī addressed the threat to Muslim unity and stability engendered by internal civil conflicts and was concerned that chaos (*fitna*) be avoided. He contended that the unity of community could avoid such strife, and that politics must serve such an end.[34] Internal unity, of the kind addressed in the ceasefire to which the Palestinian factions signed up to, was a way by which the goal of protection from a foreign occupier could be better achieved. This was a goal that Hamas could feel conceptually aligned to.

Hence, it is contended that the 30 June 2003 *hudna* unilaterally declared by the Palestinians addressed Hamas's perpetual concern to remain Islamist and legitimate, both in terms of Israel, to whom it had declared a *jihād* against, and its Palestinian nationalist rivals, with whom it should avoid internal chaos or civil war with. More generally, Palestinian supporters of Hamas also reacted positively to the declaration. This constructive reaction signalled that those who had feared that a Hamas ceasefire would gravely weaken popular support if it appeared to abandon *jihād* could be mistaken. Nevertheless, some supporters of Hamas remained unconvinced that a ceasefire would provide sufficient political dividends compared to those wrought against Israel from armed violence.

This established tension in terms of the political and resistance. The Hamas political leadership, in particular, has always tacitly recognised that a political outcome was inevitable in the conflict with Israel. Moreover, there were elements of the Hamas leadership that believed that a *hudna* would set the stage for negotiations and signalled ideological pragmatism.[35] It was a signal, however, that was regarded with deep suspicion by other actors. Israel was disbelieving, with the argument circulated that Hamas's commitment to the *hudna* was tactical, 'merely inducing Hamas to stop attacks through a *hudna* or truce is not acceptable, since Hamas will simply wait to fight again another day while keeping its capabilities intact'.[36] Certainly, Israeli and other opinion regarded Hamas's position to be no more than strategic.

The ceasefire of 29 June 2003 was a failure. A unilateral act designed to achieve a pause in hostilities only lasted a month. Israeli reciprocation was limited, and its military forces still continued with targeted assassinations. Hamas responded with violence. Israel counter-responded with further targeted

33. See Anthony Black, *The History of Islamic Political Thought: From the Prophet to the Present* (New York, 2001).
34. See Lambton, *State and Government in Medieval Islam*, p. 124.
35. Meir Hatina, 'Hamas and the Oslo Accords: Religious Dogma in a Changing Political Reality', *Mediterranean Politics* 4.3 (1999), 37–55.
36. B. Ganor, 'Countering Hamas', Phase III in the War on Terrorism? Challenges and Opportunities', *Brookings Institute*, 2003 (online).

assassinations, including pro-ceasefire Hamas leader Ismail Abu Shanab.[37] The causes of the breakdown of the June 2003 *hudna* remain a source of debate. A number of lessons, however, were drawn by Hamas. Hamas leaders concluded that unilateral *hudna* would not draw Israeli reciprocation.[38] Israel did not appear to be prepared to enter into the kind of formal ceasefire arrangement that it had done previously with Hizballah in Lebanon in 1996. Some in the leadership of Hamas were unwilling to undertake further unilateral ceasefires because they disbelieved Israel's intentions, contending that Israeli violence was still perpetrated against Palestinians. Nevertheless, the challenge of the Israeli–Palestinian conflict at that time lay in how Hamas would remain responsive to its popular constituency and compete against its secular national rivals if there was a demand that armed attacks and violence against Israel be halted. One way Hamas responded to this was to change the language around *hudna*, including the introduction of new semantics in terms of the ceasefire lexicon.

A CALM (BEFORE THE STORM)

Throughout 2003–5 violence continued to punctuate Israeli–Palestinian relations, and Hamas had concluded that neither Israeli Prime Minister Ariel Sharon nor the ruling Fatah faction of the PLO were capable or serious in terms of political progress on a viable contiguous Palestinian state. The hope of another *hudna* seemed remote, but as Hamas sought to capitalise on domestic political opportunities to challenge the hegemonic institutional hold of Fatah over the Palestinian Authority, it announced that it would participate in pause/period of calm (*tahdiʾa*).

The predominance of political over military and religious streams within the movement created new opportunities to consider a pause or period of 'calm', and on this occasion would allow Hamas to participate in Palestinian local elections and, in a sense, facilitate the Israeli withdrawal from Gaza.[39] In March 2005 President Abbas (ʿAbbās) announced a *tahdiʾa* (calm) which Hamas agreed to abide by. On this occasion Hamas leaders were specific that they would agree to conditions that constituted 'calm', rather than a ceasefire (*hudna*). Hamas leader Khaled Meshal argued that the move to reduce violence against Israel

37. See B. Milton-Edwards and A. Crooke, 'Elusive Ingredient: Hamas and the Peace Process', *Journal of Palestine Studies* 33.4 (2004), 1–14.
38. The first reciprocal ceasefire between Hamas and Israel would not occur until the conflict of November 2012, codenamed by Israel operation Pillar of Defence, when an Egyptian mediated ceasefire was brokered.
39. The government of Israel withdrew from the Gaza Strip in 2005.

was an entirely legitimate element of maintaining the resistance.[40] The *tahdiʾa* endured for more than a year, and in that time Hamas capitalised on the opportunity to contest (for the first time) Palestinian local and legislative elections that resulted in victories at the ballot box for the movement.[41] The political gain was apparent, but weighed against wider ideological factors it created tension within the movement, as hardliners complained of a degree of capitulation in terms of resistance against Israel and Salafi–Jihādī elements, such as al-Qāʿida scorned and critiqued Hamas. By contesting for power in the local arena through elections, Hamas abided by its own undertakings to desist from violent attacks against Israel. Hamas gained from its decision to halt violence against Israel, and it was left relatively unhindered by Israel during this period to freely campaign and compete for votes. The outcome of the elections, though a surprise, created the opportunity for Hamas to achieve power; Hamas won seventy-four of the 132 seats in the Palestinian legislature, and many Palestinian local municipalities also became dominated by them.

Once elected, its leadership initially indicated that the possibility of a long-term truce could be back on the agenda and that it was prepared to negotiate on such terms. Khaled Meshal declared to Israel: '[I]f you are willing to accept the principle of a long-term truce, we are prepared to negotiate the terms. Hamas is extending a hand of peace to those who are truly interested in a peace based on justice.'[42] This scenario, however, was dependent on the reactions of other actors to Hamas's democratic victory, and the ways in which the offer of a ceasefire was perceived and understood. Israel continued to reject such offers and contended that they were nothing more than rhetorical statements, as Hamas exploited its ballot box gains to entrench power against its rivals in Fatah. It remained sceptical that Hamas would abide by such an agreement when it failed to incorporate recognition of Israel and an agreement to fully cease from all violence and abide by previous Palestinian–Israeli agreements. It also refused to recognise the legitimacy of the Palestinian electoral victory visited on Hamas.[43]

Nevertheless, in November 2006 Hamas announced a further *tahdiʾa* to limit violent attacks on Israel. The rationale of this move was questioned by Palestinians in the context of Hamas's substantive discourse about resistance

40. See *Al Ahram* weekly, 30 March 2005.
41. Milton-Edwards and Farrell, *Hamas*.
42. Khaled Meshal, 'We Will Not Sell Our People or Principles for Foreign Aid', theguardian.com, 31 January 2006 (online); also T. Butcher, 'Hamas Offers Deal if Israel Pulls Out', *The Telegraph*, 9 February 2006, telegraph.co.uk (online).
43. In August 2006, Hamas ended its *tahdiʾa* with Israel following the kidnap of Israeli soldier Gilad Shalit.

against Israel, the principles of *jihād* and the right to employ legitimate violence in defence from Israeli military attack. Furthermore, some argued that Hamas had become Israel's guarantor against attacks perpetrated against Israel from Gaza by other Palestinian factions. Moreover, Hamas was soon embroiled in serious internecine conflict in the West Bank and Gaza Strip. Throughout 2006–7, as inter-Palestinian violence flared, the resort to localised ceasefire was a key mechanism that was employed to try to halt and ultimately end Hamas–Fatah bloodshed. Local negotiators in Palestinian reconciliation committees along with other actors employed *tahdiʾa* agreements between the local warring factions.[44] Yet the need for such a mechanism at a local level was obviated by the Hamas takeover of the Gaza Strip in June 2007 and the rout of pro-Fatah and PA forces. Under Hamas's complete control, Gaza would also maintain its *tahdiʾa* against Israel.

By June 2008 it was announced that the Hamas leadership – through mediation by the Government of Egypt – had reached a new *tahdiʾa* with Israel. The truce would begin with Gaza and then extend to the West Bank. In Cairo for discussions were Hamas hardliners Foreign Minister Mahmoud al-Zahar and Minister of the Interior Said Siam (Saᶜīd Siyām). The key elements of this first time agreement with Israel were based on principles of reciprocation from Israel, Egyptian mediation and a graduated decline of violence from Hamas. Mahmoud Zahar outlined the calm, stating:

1. The *tahdiʾa* between Israel and Hamas in the Gaza Strip would be for a period of six months during which time Egypt would try to extend it to the West Bank.
2. The *tahdiʾa* must be reciprocal and simultaneous on the part of Israelis and Hamas. Israel must lift its blockade of the Gaza Strip and reopen all the crossing points, specifically Rafah, concurrently with the starting of the truce.
3. If Israel rejects the *tahdiʾa*, Egypt would reopen Rafah. If Israel reneges on its *tahdiʾa* commitments, Egypt would have to then keep Rafah open.
4. Egypt will play a role getting other Palestinian factions to agree to the *tahdiʾa*. Egypt will host a meeting for the factions and then mediate directly with Israel on the details.
5. Egypt has committed itself to commence contacts with Tel Aviv to discuss the terms of the *tahdiʾa* and provide essential needs to Gaza esp. fuel.[45]

44. Throughout 2006–7 local factional committees and members of the Egyptian diplomatic delegation in Gaza encouraged Hamas and Fatah to participate in a variety of ceasefire/calm agreements.
45. Mahmoud Zahar (Maḥmūd al-Zahār), Hamas leader, author interview, April 2008.

Hamas leader Mushir Masri, from Gaza, argued that the *tahdiʾa* with Israel had not compromised the movement in terms of its ideological position on *jihād*, but had, in fact, created gains for Palestinians, particularly those suffering from the Israeli-imposed blockade of the Gaza Strip. 'It' [*tahdiʾa*], argued Masri, 'was according to our terms and not Israel. We didn't give into Israel's terms on Shalit, on weapons, on forcing factions, or on power consolidation.'[46] By the summer of 2008, however, it was evident from Hamas discourse that it did not believe that Israel was keeping its side of the *tahdiʾa* bargain. Chief among Hamas's concerns was that Israel lift its blockade on the population of the Gaza Strip.

As the *tahdiʾa* progressed throughout 2008, differences within the Hamas leadership also emerged. Gaza leader Ghazi Hamad called the *tahdiʾa* 'dirty politics', conceding that it had allowed Hamas to 'jump into the political square in a very short time', but that the compromises that had been required of the movement had led to a 'contradiction between resistance, politics and ideology'.[47] Another Hamas leader put it more bluntly when he stated that despite the *tahdiʾa* with Israel, 'we [people in Gaza] are still struggling and suffering. There is a shortage of everything.' He further asserted that while the *tahdiʾa* had led to a 'drop in the number of funerals the real fruits of the ceasefire such as agriculture development, building materials, etc have not materialised. They [people] don't have faith in Israel and say its just a tactic.'[48] Hamas claimed that Israel had agreed to end its closure of Gaza, but Israeli officials disputed this. Two months into the *tahdiʾa*, the UN reported that the number of goods allowed into Gaza by Israel had actually decreased.[49] Despite some infringements, the calm lasted until 4 November 2008, when Israeli soldiers undertook an operation into Gaza and killed six Hamas members. The subsequent escalation led to Israel's major attack on Gaza in Operation Cast Lead a month later.

CONFLICT AMIDST CALM AND CEASEFIRES

The outbreak of Israeli violence against Gaza in December 2008 through to January 2009 called Operation Cast Lead[50] must be seen in the context of the

46. Mushir al Masri (Mushīr al-Maṣrī), Hamas leader, author interview, Gaza, 16 July 2008.
47. Ghazi Hamad (Ghāzī Ḥamad), Hamas leader, author interview, Gaza, 15 July 2008.
48. Ahmad Yousef (Aḥmad Yūsuf), Hamas leader, author interview, Gaza, 14 July 2008.
49. See 'Decrease in Commodities Allowed into Gaza', *The Humanitarian Monitor: Occupied Palestinian Territory*, ochaopt.org, August 2008 (online).
50. Operation Cast Lead on 27 December 2008. Israel launched Operation Cast Lead, a twenty-two day military campaign on the Gaza Strip. OCL led to some 1,400 Palestinian

failure of the *tahdi'a* from the perspective of both Israel and Hamas. The ambition of ceasefire should have been regarded as a key component of conflict management and confidence-building measures. Hamas, however, were considered as promoting a counter-agenda with a fundamental impulse to violent *jihād*. They were seen as preternaturally disposed towards violence. Hence, the participation by Hamas in *hudna* and *tahdi'a* was thus regarded with suspicion by Israel and many in the international community. Hamas leaders had signalled otherwise. 'A cease-fire is acceptable but not if we deny our rights to exist in the process. If the West deny us security and safety we have to seek it for ourselves', declared Ismail Abu Shanab.[51] By December 2008 it appeared that neither Hamas nor Israel had much incentive to sue for a ceasefire of any substance and longevity. Neither side was being seriously pushed by external actors to invest in this conflict-reduction measure. The international community, including regional Arab and Muslim actors, the EU, US and Quartet, exhibited a predisposition to perpetuate the asymmetric formulation. Moreover, it was also clear that Israel and Hamas had failed to achieve any truly reciprocal ceasefire arrangements that brought tangible benefits in terms of security, stability and confidence-building measures. This can be explained by the contention that Israel was not serious about a reciprocated arrangement with Hamas. The Israeli press had revealed that Israeli leaders had only agreed to the June 2008 *tahdi'a* in order to engage in military preparations for a strike against Gaza.[52] Hamas also failed to understand that the kind of calm or ceasefire they were offering did not predispose other actors to build on such activities in terms of confidence building. Neither Israel nor Hamas felt that they had 'their' kind of ceasefire. Israel equated a Hamas ceasefire with surrender, and Hamas with victory over Israel. The drawbacks were obvious.

In the protracted and complex mediation process[53] that led to the ceasefire of January 2009 and a halt to Operation Cast Lead, Israel demanded, once again, an arrangement which dealt with the security threat posed by Hamas's position of strength in Gaza. Hamas would have to agree to end missile attacks and maintain an exclusion zone in Israeli border areas. Israel further demanded that Hamas

and six Israeli fatalities. In the aftermath, a UN-appointed fact-finding mission found strong evidence of war crimes and crimes against humanity committed by both the Israeli military and Palestinian militias.

51. Ismail Abu Shanab, Hamas leader, author interview, August 2002.
52. S. Roy, *Hamas and Civil Society in Gaza, Engaging the Islamist Social Sector* (Princeton, 2011), p. 229
53. See 'Hamas and Diplomacy: The Pressures Mount', economist.com, 16 January 2009 (online).

end the phenomenon of the tunnels.[54] Hamas's compliance to Israeli demands was perceived evidence of its enfeeblement, which no amount of self-proclaimed victory rhetoric could cover. Hamas continued to reiterate that no deal would be possible without a minimum of open borders, external monitoring of an Israeli withdrawal and a cessation of all Israeli military actions, including the targeted assassinations of their own political and military leadership in Gaza and elsewhere. Hamas leader Ismail Haniyeh declared of past attempts:

> We've offered hudna on two occasions. A major *hudna* and interim *hudna* and they [Israel] rejected both . . . Israel continued its war against us and didn't respect the major or interim *hudna* which we offered. What, then, do they want from us?[55]

Wagemakers argues, however, that in reality Hamas were compelled to scale back on the demands it could win from Israel in return for a form of ceasefire.[56]

Amidst the ruins of Gaza, such factors were secondary when a truce was finally agreed between Hamas and Israel in January 2009. Hamas were perceived as being militarily weakened and hence ripe for agreeing to cease violence against Israel. This it did, but with little by way of compromise on other issues, such as recognition of Israel, the release of Gilad Shalit, or surrender of arms to the victor. In its statements its leaders claimed victory and contended that the war with Israel had altered the resistance and Palestinian steadfastness.[57]

There were little by way of political opportunities created by the 2009 truce for either Israel or Hamas in terms of reducing enmity. Hamas, however, attempted to capitalise on its position in the Palestinian political landscape in opposition to President Abbas and Fatah. Resistance still remained on the agenda for Hamas, alongside its claim to governance in the absence of other Palestinian rivals (which it had all but eliminated) in Gaza. Hamas began planning for Gaza recovery and reconstruction before the war had ended. It remained bounded by concerns within Gaza that were prevalent before the end of the *tahdiʾa* and which the *tahdiʾa* failed to deliver on for them. Hence, the political dimensions

54. Nicolas Pelham, 'Gaza's Tunnel Phenomenon: The Unintended Dynamics of Israel's Siege', *Journal of Palestine Studies* 41.4 (2012), 6–31.
55. Ismail Haniyeh (Ismāʿīl Haniyya), Hamas leader, author interview, Gaza, August 2002.
56. Wagemakers, 'Legitimizing Pragmatism', p. 372
57. Filastin al-Muslima, 'al-Muqāwama fī Ghazza aẓharat kafaʾa qitāliyya wa-lam tataʾaththir bil-ḍaghṭ al-ʿaskarī (Resistance in the Gaza Strip Showed High Fighting Capabilities are Unaffected by Military Pressure)', *Filastin al-Muslima*, 3 February 2009, pp. 42–3; Milton-Edwards and Farrell, *Hamas*.

of the recovery and reconstruction centred on: open borders and crossings, inter-Palestinian rivalries and tensions, the relationship with Israel and the relationship with other external regional and international actors.

Reconstruction – for Hamas – took place amidst a self-declared victory. As Hamas leader Salah Bardawil declared:

> Hamas has high flexibility and will not impede the reconstruction but it must not be politicized and we should remember that there should be direct rather than mediated relationship between those that give aid and contractors for reconstruction in Gaza.[58]

The ensuing period of early recovery and reconstruction was delicate and volatile in terms of the tender political climate that the cessation of violence had occurred in. Getting Hamas and Israel (mediated by Cairo) to agreement on a longer-term ceasefire proved difficult. Hamas had yielded much, and this had been as a result of pressure on the movement from Gaza. Hamas subsequently dedicated the energies of the organisation to maintaining legitimacy in Gaza through steering the recovery and reconstruction process, governance, indirect negotiations with Israel (via Egypt) and direct negotiations with PLO/Fatah/PA. Negotiations, indirect or otherwise, failed to manifest long-term change, and Hamas used reconstruction funding issues as a means to underscore governance, rather than resistance claims. Hamas's Said Radwan stated that the movement's priority was the establishment of a Higher Committee for Reconstruction. 'The legitimate government and the national factions [in Gaza] will supervise the reconstruction project, in addition to Arab countries who are interested in helping out . . . We want aid to go to the people who deserve it.'[59] The overriding economic challenge to bring relief, reconstruction and governance to Gaza had been factored into the recovery and reconstruction effort by Hamas.[60] Similarly, in November 2012, when Israel assassinated Hamas leader Ahmad Jabari (Aḥmad Jābarī) and launched Operation Pillar of Defence, the ensuing *tahdiʾa*, mediated by Egypt, failed to establish political opportunities for either side in terms of progressing

58. Salah Baradwil (Ṣalāḥ Bardawīl), Hamas member of the PLC and spokesman, author interview, Gaza City, 28 January 2009.
59. Said Radwan (Saʿīd Raḍwān), Hamas PLC member, author interview, Gaza City, 28 January 2009.
60. Hamas leadership addressed enabling conditions for recovery: opening of borders and crossings with Israel and Egypt, operation of the banking sector in Gaza for inward flow of funds and revival of the local economy and consolidation of the ceasefire.

to full ceasefire or negotiations for peace, but have merely regulated relations to reduce violence and win strategic concessions.[61]

CONCLUSION

This chapter has demonstrated that neither intellectual discourse within the Hamas movement or in contribution from other notable contemporary Muslim thinkers on the legitimacy of violence lends itself to the perpetuation of *hudna* or *tahdiʾa* beyond strategic pause in its conflict with Israel. Moreover, the political environment with which Hamas contends with does not support or seek to leverage ceasefire as a mechanism for conflict resolution for it would require the admission of Hamas into a diplomatic process from which it has been firmly excluded.

The movement's policies and ideological Islamist justification has oscillated in terms of ceasefire as a pause in war, but not beyond to the negotiation and conclusion of peace treaties, either with its local rivals or external enemies. Hence, in terms of its conflict with Fatah, Hamas has appeared to utilise the tool of *hudna* or *tahdiʾa* for pragmatic purposes, as and when it is politically motivated to do so. In such calculations, conflict reduction for the purposes of reducing or eliminating civilian casualties, if it figures at all, may be no more than a secondary consideration. Similarly, *hudna* for the purposes of advancing negotiation with an enemy (external – Israel or internal – Fatah) is limited in the first place by Hamas's consideration of its resistance rhetoric and the emphasis it puts on notions of legitimacy and recognition. Hence, the contention that Hamas's stance towards ceasefire can be seen to demonstrate that its pragmatism endures over ideological rigidity. What limits this pragmatism is the unwillingness of either its internal rivals or its external enemies to test Hamas beyond its rhetoric of what is often referred to as its moderation.[62]

Over the last decade, Hamas has demonstrated that it is capable of engaging with the concepts of *hudna* and *tahdiʾa*, but it does so first and foremost as a localised Palestinian resistance organisation that 'competes' with other Palestinian factions to claim the resistance for themselves and to frame and reframe it within some Islamist discourses – principally as it relates to *jihād*. Hamas appears to have discovered early on that in relation to Israel – the enemy – resilience to a negotiated ceasefire and continued policies of aggression, including targeted assassination, means that Israel would not engage in the measures that Hamas

61. See 'Text of Israel-Hamas Ceasefire Agreement', jadaliyya.com, 21 November 2012 (online).
62. Wagemakers, 'Legitimizing Pragmatism', pp. 358–78.

required from it in return for a cessation of violence. Nevertheless, Hamas continued to embark on such measures, and in large part this is explained by its desire to emerge as a significant, if not the *most* significant, Palestinian actor and to oust the PLO in terms of legitimacy and monopolies of legitimacy that the organisation has previously held and enjoyed. The theological or Islamist discourse is not as significant in terms of Hamas's calculations and its mobilising discourse and rhetoric. Does this mean that in some ways Hamas has acculturated to the nationalist environment in which it was established and still operates in? Certainly there is evidence of a dissonance between the rhetorical language of resistance (*muqāwama*)/*jihād* and its decade-long participation in a variety of *hudna* and *tahdiʾa*. Similarly, when West Bank Hamas leader Hassan Yousef (Ḥasan Yūsuf) addressed this issue in 2004, he spoke of the 'national concerns' and the reality of present-day conflict with 'the Zionist enemy'.[63] If the evidence here is that Hamas acts as a political national movement, then engaging it in terms of reality, rather than existential ideological threat, holds out the slightest hope that the *hudna* could allow the movement to move beyond a strategic pause.

63. Hassan Yousef, 'The Concept of Truce in Islam and its Impact on the Palestinian Issue', passia.org, December 2004 (online).

CHAPTER

14

NOTES ON SOME JIHADIST POEMS

*András Hámori**

The following observations address some pieces from an online collection of Saudi Jihadist poetry called *Dīwān al-ᶜizza*.[1] The authors obviously believe their version of *jihād* to be lawful under Islam, and on occasion what they say smacks of legal justification. So one poet argues, contrary to evidence, that no Muslims died when the Jihadists blew up the Muhayya complex in Riyadh (*kadhabū wa-qālū fī l-mujammaᶜi ikhwatun*, p. 6); another devotes ten lines to debating those who employ the concept of public interest (*maṣlaḥa*) to discourage or condemn violent *jihād* (*lā lan uᶜīra l-samᶜa ayya mukhadhdhilin / zaᶜama l-maṣāliḥa fī l-sukūti l-ghāshimi*, p. 12). My interest, however, lies not in legal theory, but in the emotional vindication the poems propose, that dangerous cousin to reliance on law and morality. I will touch on just two means to this: the traditional rhetoric that matches the poets' image of themselves as knights in an ancient and enduring battle, and the reveries about girls beyond the grave, a silky future that makes liveable an emotionally maimed present.

The anthology contains twenty-two pieces in classical Arabic, followed by twelve in Saudi dialect, which I do not understand. They are by militants, several of them now killed, and date from the last thirty years or so. All but one of the poems in *fuṣḥā* are in classical metres. The texts range from tracts in verse to a

* Princeton University

1. I am grateful to Professor Bernard Haykel, who, in 2011, generously drew my attention to this material. The anthology no longer has its own website, but it can be accessed at https://archive.org/details/ozaaloza_gmail_20140216. For accessed dates of online resources, see the Bibliography and the accompanying note, p. 366.

well-crafted traditional eloquence, as in a compliment addressed to Bin Laden (p. 25):

wa-sayfu ghayrika yashkū ghimdahū malalan
wa-ghimdu sayfika yashkū qaswata l-alifi

The swords of others complain that they have wearied of their sheaths; the sheath of your sword complains of its lover's unkindness (i.e. that the sword is never home).[2]

1. ECHOES OF THE CLASSICS

My first example is an elegy (p. 28, by ᶜAbd al-ᶜAzīz ibn Mushrif al-Bakrī) for Yūsuf al-ʿUyayrī, who created the infrastructure of al-Qāʿida in the Arabian Peninsula in the 1990s and was killed in 2003 by the Saudi security services. The opening is:

wa-laylin ka-layli l-jubbi ghābat nujūmuhu
wa-aẓlama fī 'aynī wa-qalbī bahīmuhu

I recall a night without stars, like the night in the well, whose gloom was unrelieved in my eyes and heart

The verse alludes to the words *ghayābat al-jubb* in Sūrat Yūsuf (12:10 and 15). Perhaps the point of the allusion is that in Joseph's career, the dark well is a setback, but only that. The next two lines pick up the terms *ᶜayn* and *qalb*. By assonance, *ᶜayn*, 'eye', leads to *'uyūn*, 'springs, fountains', in verse two:

wa-ghārat ᶜuyūnu l-shiᶜri ᶜannī kaʾannamā
aghārat ᶜalā shayṭāni shiᶜrī rujūmuhu

The fountains of verse had dried up for me, as if the missiles meant for the shaytan of my poetry had been let loose upon him.

There is *tajnīs* (paronomasia, play on words) between *ghārat* 'ebbed away' and *aghārat*, whose basic sense is 'to attack'. *Tajnīs* is a common figure of speech in

2. For the disposition of identities and antitheses, one might compare al-Mutanabbī's line: *huwa l-shujāᶜu yaᶜuddu l-bukhla min jubunin / wa-hwa l-jawādu yaᶜuddu l-jubna min bakhali. al-ᶜArf al-ṭayyib fī sharḥ dīwān Abī al-Ṭayyib* (Beirut, 1964), I, p. 36.

Abbasid poetry, and this poet in the *Dīwān al-ᶜizza* loves it. In verse three *qalb* reappears in connection with a stock figure:

wa-ᶜādhilatin lam taˀlu juhdan wa-lam uṭiᶜ
wa-qad nazaḥat bil-qalbi ᶜanhā humūmuhu

That woman wouldn't tire of chiding me, but I didn't listen because its cares had taken my heart far beyond her reach.

The censorious woman who bids moderation in grief (or in hospitality or audacity), and whose nagging the hero ignores, appears already in the Jāhiliyya. Here she is anonymous. In another elegy in the diwan, the *'ādhila* is given one of the handful of arbitrary names traditionally used in this context: *wa-talūmunī suᶜdā ᶜalā farṭi l-shajā . . .*

In verse four, the dead man is named. In verse five, the mourner cries out in a conventional phrase:

fa-lillāhi qabrun wussida l-shaykhu turbahū . . .

How excellent is the grave in whose dust the shaykh was laid . . .

To *fa-lillāhi qabrun . . .*, we may compare al-Buḥturī (d. 897):

fa-lillāhi qabrun fī khurāsāna adrakat
nawāḥīhi aqṭāra l-ᶜulā wal-ma'āthiri[3]

How excellent is the grave in Khurasan that embraces the summits of glory and memorable deeds!

Verse six:

wa-mā māta ḥattā anhaka l-arḍa ḍarbuhū . . .

He died but not before his blows wore out the earth . . .

is reminiscent of a line by Abū Tammām (d. 845):

3. Abū al-Walīd al-Buḥtūrī, *Dīwān al-Buḥturī* (Beirut, 1994), II, p. 555 (incipit: *ᶜadhīriya min ṣarfi l-layālī l-ghawādiri . . . bawātiri*).

wa-mā māta ḥattā māta maḍribu sayfihī
mina l-ḍarbi wa-ᶜtallat ᶜalayhi l-qanā s-sumru[4]

He died, but not before the edge of his sword had died from striking blows and the light brown spears' health had broken upon his body.

Verses eight and nine list al-ᶜUyayrī's feats of violence in paroxysms of *tajnīs*:

aṭāra ᶜani l-rūsi l-ruʾūsa qitāluhū
wa-awqafa zaḥfa l-rūmi ᶜammā tarūmuhu
fa-awrā bi-ahli l-kufri nāran lahā laẓan
wa-arwā dhawī l-īmāni nahlan ᶜulūmuhu

The battle he waged made Russian heads fly and stopped the Byzantine army from marching on its goal;
He lit a blazing fire among the unbelievers, and his knowledge quenched the thirst of the faithful.

Verse nine is a solid example of classical rhetoric. The contrasting sound sequences *awrā/arwā* are embedded in *ṭibāq* (antithesis), as the fire lit under the *ahl al-kufr* is contrasted with the thirst-quenching drink of the man's knowledge. These mannerisms are not playful. The traditional verbal pomp is sought because it is pomp and because it is traditional. The enemy is the 'Christian' army, hence the army of Byzantium, arch-foes of the caliphate a thousand years back. Anachronism varies in effect and intent. In the last lines of this piece, the writer speaks of 'our sword' and 'the swords of Allāh'. In another poem (p. 7), in a phrase that sounds odder than 'our sword' in English, and I think in Arabic as well, it is said of the Jihadists who were killed that 'their long spears had spoken for them' (*naṭaqat ᶜanhumu r-rimāḥu l-ᶜawālī*). This is the common manner of self-dramatisation by anachronism, meant to create an aura of historic importance. It is not limited to poetry. Compare, for example, Ayman al-Ẓawāhirī's book title: *Fawāris taḥt rāyat al-nabiyy*. The good do it too; recall the quote from Tennyson in Churchill's speech of 4 June 1940:

Every morn brought forth a noble chance
And every chance brought forth a noble knight.

4. Abū Tammām, *Dīwān Abī Tammām* (Cairo, 1965), IV, p. 80. Incipit: *kadhā fal-yajilla l-khaṭbu . . . ᶜudhru.*

But to say 'sword' for Kalashnikov is one thing. To say in one and the same line that al-ᶜUyayrī made the Russians' heads fly off and checked the progress of the Byzantines is to go beyond analogy. Headless Russians jostle Byzantines on the march because the claim is one of identity. The Jihadist outrages and the medieval battles (and skirmishes) that, say, al-Mutanabbī spins into epoch-making triumphs of Islam are, for these men, scenes in a single war. In another poem (p. 5), we come upon the boast *ḍarabū bilāda l-rūmi fī manhātanin*, 'in Manhattan they struck the land of Rūm'. The line cannot be literally translated without producing, despite the horror of the crime, the ludicrous effect of a mixed metaphor. No less confused are the metaphors in another poem (p. 24):

wa-fī manhātanin dusnā ᶜulāhā
wa-dakkaynā l-maᶜāqila wal-ḥuṣūnā

In Manhattan we trampled their glory and smashed their strongholds and fortresses . . .

For the jihadis, *bilād al-rūm* and the fortresses of Manhattan are not really metaphors at all. 'The centuries blend and blur.' There is no distancing the past.[5]

Verse thirteen speaks of al-ᶜUyayrī, the theoretician, author of a treatise called *al-Mīzān li-ḥarakat ṭālibān*:

dafaᶜta bi-mīzānin ani l-ṭālibāni idh
taʾazzafa min jayshi l-ṣalībi hujūmuhu
wa-bayyanta ḥukma llāhi fī l-fitnati llatī
idhā mā raʾāhā l-shaykhu ḍallat ḥulūmuhu

In the *Mizan* you defended the Taliban as the crusader army came to attack;
You made clear God's judgment when strife could make a man of ripe years stray from his even temper.

The phrase about the *shaykh* who could not remain calm and collected is an old cliché, especially in love poetry. In verse eighteen, with *fa-balligh ṭawīla l-ᶜumri fī l-kufri nāyifan*, the poem turns to *hijāʾ*: mockery and menace, hurled at Prince Nayef, the police minister. In medieval poetry (but also in twentieth-century

5. The first sentence of an article on the blowing up of the Muhayya complex boasts that on that day 'the squadrons of Truth boldly leveled the crusaders' fortresses', *sārat katāʾib al-ḥaqq wa-aqdamat tadukku maᶜāqil al-ṣalībiyyīn*. (http://www.ilmway.com/site/maqdis/MS_16199.html).

Nabati poetry), such a message commonly starts, as here, with formulas like *balligh!* or *man mublighun?* In verse nineteen, we are told, in a manner that the Umayyad poets Jarīr and al-Farazdaq would recognise, that Nayef has been forever dishonoured by his wife, 'and there's no good in a man whose women are fair game for the public' (*wa-lā khayra fī-man yustabāḥu ḥarīmuhu*). This would be Nayef's wife, Maha al-Sudairy. I do not know which of her adventures this refers to – perhaps appearing in a Florida court in an orange prison jumpsuit for pushing her maid down the stairs? The poem ends (lines twenty to twenty-two) with:

fa-lasta lanā niddan wa-in kunta marta^can
li-asyāfinā yadhwī ^calayhā hashīmuhu
wa-inna suyūfa llāhi ta^crifu darbahā
ilayka wa-yadrī bil-gharīmi gharīmuhu
taqaddamanā fa-^clam ilayka wa^cīdunā
wa-yasbiqu wadqa l-muthqalāti hazīmuhu

You are no match for us, though you are pasturage for our swords, whose grass wilts at their coming.
The swords of God know their path to you, and those to whom the debt is owed do not lose sight of the debtor!
Our threat, make no mistake, has reached you before we will, but so does the roar of thunder precede the downpour from the encumbered clouds.

'Our threat' is not tantamount to 'all the grim speeches we have been making'. It refers specifically to the threat in lines twenty to twenty-one. The same kind of self-reference occurs at the end of another poem in the *Dīwān al-^cizza* (p. 6): *fa-suyūfunā ^cashiqat ^cināqa riqābikum / wal-shi^cru yā ṭāghūtu jā^ɔa muḥadhdhiran*, 'Our swords' passion is to embrace your necks! The verse, O tyrant, has come to warn.' Such final references to the poem itself are frequent in *qaṣīdas* of the classical period.[6] Similarly common is the use of a gnomic statement, *ḥikma*, as final cadence.

* * *

In another poem (p. 10, by Usāma al-Khālidī) a dead Jihadist, now in Paradise, comforts his mother. I wonder if it is related in layout to a well-known poem

6. Often introduced by the formula *dūnakahā*, 'take it!'.

Abū Firās (d. 968) wrote from Byzantine captivity to his mother in Manbij.[7] The poems are fourteen and fifteen verses long. Both are marked by the recurrence of a kind of name. In the Jihadist poem, *ayā ummāhu* comes in lines one, five, seven, ten and fourteen. In Abū Firās's poem, the place name Manbij, which has a close and, at times, metonymic relation to 'mother', is spoken only three times, but also in lines one, five and ten. The endings may add confirmation. In our poem we read:

fa-ṣabran fī sabīli llāhi ṣabran
ayā ummāhu fal-dunyā thawānī

Patience in God's path, patience
O mother, for this world is a matter of seconds.

Abū Firās signs off with:

ūṣīki bil-ṣabri l-jamī-
li fa-innahū khayru l-waṣiyyah

I bid you endure in patience – for this is the best of counsels.

Both lines start with an exhortation to *ṣabr* and end with a timeless judgment: 'To counsel patient endurance is the best of counsels', and 'This world is a matter of seconds.' Al-Khālidī adapts a verse from a very famous poem by the Kharijite leader Qaṭarī ibn Fujā'a, which runs: *fa-ṣabran fī majāli l-mawti ṣabran / fa-mā naylu l-khulūdi bi-mustaṭāᶜi.*[8] The first half-line keeps very close to the model. The gnomic response in the second echoes Qaṭarī's, only in more pious language.[9] As I have said, the poem is very famous, but one source would practically guarantee that a well-read Jihadist saw it as pertinent. It is cited in a *faḍāʾil al-jihād* book much admired by modern Jihadists (Awlaki, for example): the *Mashāriᶜ al-ashwāq ilā maṣāriᶜ al-ᶜushshāq* by Ibn al-Naḥḥās (d. 814/1411 or 12).[10] In its original form, *fa-ṣabran fī majāli l-mawti ṣabran*, the half-line

7. Abū Firās al-Ḥamdānī, *Dīwān Abī Firās al-Ḥamdānī* (Damascus, 1944), III, pp. 433–4.
8. *Shiᶜr al-khawārij* (Beirut, n. d.), p. 43.
9. The first half-line, manipulated in the same way (reading *fa-ṣabran fī sabīli llāhi ṣabran*), appears in several poems online. No such variant is recorded in the edition by Iḥsān ᶜAbbās.
10. Abū Zakariyyā Aḥmad b. Ibrāhīm al-Dimashqī al-Dumyāṭī, known as Ibn al-Naḥḥās:

is used in a poem (beginning *taᶜālat ṣarkhatu l-īmāni fīnā*; widely accessible online) by a major Jihadist figure, Abū Yaḥyā al-Lībī (killed in 2012).

If in al-Khālidī's poem the adaptation of a classical verse is extremely probable, there is in the *Dīwān al-ᶜizza* an example (p. 34) where it is certain. It comes from an elegy for another Jihadist (ᶜAmīr al-Shihrī), who was shot to death in al-ᶜArījā, a suburb of Riyadh:

kaʾanna l-ᶜarījā lam yaṭaʾ qaṭṭu arḍahā
anīsun wa-lam yasmur bihā qaṭṭu sāmiru

It is as if no friend had trodden the ground of al-ᶜArījā; as if no one had ever spent the night in conversation there . . .

The verse derives from a frequently cited line (as, for example, in the Sirah[11]) addressed, so we are told, to a man of Jurhum centuries before Islam, after his tribe had been driven from Mecca. Al-Ḥajūn and al-Ṣafā are place names:

kaʾan lam yakun bayna l-ḥajūni ilā l-ṣafā
anīsun wa-lam yasmur bi-makkata sāmiru.

2. THE GIRLS TO COME

The Jihadists' poetry is bleakly masculine. Apart from the stock figure of the censorious woman, in these poems mothers and houris are the only female characters. A very impressionistic comparison between the *Dīwān al-ᶜizza* on the one hand and the *Mashāriᶜ al-ashwāq* and the citations in the historical study *Shīᶜr jihād al-Rūm*[12] on the other suggests that the houris turn up in this diwan more often, per verse, than in classical poetry.

In the dead Jihadist's letter to his mother, they are a source of tenderness. After assurances that he is now in Paradise because he shunned the delights of this world, 'answered the call' and chose honour over abasement, the speaker eyes his mangled limbs with gusto and announces that his violent death is the *mahr*, the bridewealth, of the houris. No canonical *ḥadīth* says that death in *jihād* is their *mahr*, but it is an old idea. After the violence comes solace (verses 10–12):

Mashāriᶜ al-ashwāq ilā maṣāriᶜ al-ᶜushshāq (Beirut, 1990), I, p. 579. The attribution is *qāla baᶜḍ al-shujᶜān*, as if Ibn al-Naḥḥās were reluctant to acknowledge a Kharijite chief.

11. Ibn Hishām, *Sīrat al-nabiyy* (Cairo, 1937), I, p. 126.
12. By ᶜAbd Allāh ibn Ṣālih al-ʿArīnī (Riyadh, 2002).

ayā ummāhu qad ulbistu tājan
wa-uskintu l-quṣūra maᶜa l-ghawānī
maᶜa l-ḥawrāᵓi tuṭribunī bi-laḥnin
wa-tusqīnī bi-aṭrāfi l-banāni
abītu wa-qad ḍamamtu ilayya ṣadran
wa-qalban qad ḥawā kulla l-ḥanāni

Mother, a crown has been set upon my head; I was made to dwell in palaces with lovely young girls;
With a houri who sings to me and lifts the cup to my mouth with her fingertips.
I spend the night pressed against a breast and heart containing all tenderness.[13]

The crown of dignity, the palatial halls, the chanting houris are all promised by *ḥadīth*. The jewelled cup in the houri's fingers is prominently mentioned (for example) in al-Muḥāsibī's (d. 243/857) delicately ecstatic pages on the delights of Paradise.[14] Verse twelve is remarkable. One's allotted houris are certainly ladies of feeling; they love their fiancé and grow faint with desire as he approaches. As al-Muḥāsibī puts it: '[T]hey are on the lookout for your face to appear and for their long yearning and intense desire for you to be appeased' (*fa-yaskun ṭūl ḥanīnihinna wa-shiddat shawqihinna ilayka*).[15] In our poem the emphasis has shifted to *ḥanān*, a solicitous tenderness. The *Lisān al-ᶜarab* defines *ḥanān* as *raḥmah*, then as 'compassion and caring affection', *raḥmah wa-ᶜaṭf*. The modern sense is not far different. A look at the web will turn up popular topics ranging from *ḥanān al-umm* through to a wife's need for *ḥanān al-zawj* (which consists in his being caring and attentive to her feelings and psychological needs) and all the way to the tender affection that keeps the husband from heart attacks: *ḥanān al-zawja yaqī al-rijāl min al-azamāt al-qalbiyyah*. This houri's heart is filled not with the passion of *ᶜishq* or *shawq*, but with *ḥanān*. It would be tactless, of course, to treat the grieving mother to X-rated scenes on the celestial couch, but the dream of a sweet (maternal?) tenderness functions on its own as emotional justification, a counterweight to the relish for violent death.

We also have in the *Dīwān al-ᶜizza* a piece of soft-core erotica (pp. 26–7), where the tenderness is sexual. Its inspiration probably comes from a story in the

13. It is always light in Paradise, but the commentators infer from the Qurᵓānic phrase *lahum rizquhum fīhā bukratan wa-ᶜashiyyan* (Q19:62) that the inhabitants can distinguish the times of day.
14. Ḥārith b. Asad al-Muḥāṣibī, *Kitāb al-tawahhum* (Cairo, 1937), pp. 46–7. *Fa-tawahham al-ka's min al-yāqūt wal-durr fī banānihā*, etc.
15. Muḥāṣibī, *Kitāb al-tawahhum*, p. 40.

*Mashāri*ᶜ *al-ashwāq*. In that story the *kuffār* threaten the frontier regions, and a *khaṭīb* urges the Basrans to take up arms and confront them. Promoting martyrdom, he recites a poem (sixteen lines are quoted), picturing the beauty of the houris. At once, a certain Umm Ibrāhīm al-Hāshimiyyah, for whom no girl has been good enough, wants her son to go to war, be killed and marry one of these spectacular creatures. In this project she is successful.

In the poem in the *Dīwān al-'izza*, after an introduction about honour and self-abasement and a few didactic lines about the seven favours shown to the martyr, the poet's fantasy takes off as he imagines himself dead and collecting the heavenly reward:

wal-ḥūru tarqubu fi shtiyāqin muqbalī
yā qiblatan hiya dāʾiyā wa-dawāʾiyā
ṭarfu l-ᶜuyūni li-wajnatayhā jāriḥun . . .

The houris await my approach with yearning – O qibla that is my sickness and my remedy!
The glance of an eye would wound her cheek . . .

This is the time-honoured language of love poetry. The punning phrase 'my sickness and my remedy' goes far back, but one cannot make too much of this: we can hear *nasiytu dā'ī ḥīna jāʾa dawāʾī* in a pop song accessible on YouTube. On the other hand, *ṭarfu l-ᶜuyūni li-wajnatayhā jāriḥun* is a version of an image common from a very early period, and it is paralleled in the verses in the story of Umm Ibrāhīm:[16]

yakādu khtilāsu l-laḥẓi yajraḥu khaddahā . . .

A stolen glance at her would wound her cheek . . .

The houri is supremely beautiful, but so is he. She reassures him: 'I've never set eyes on anything so splendid (*mā qad raʾat ᶜaynāya mithlaka bāhiyā*).'[17] They lock fingers; they embrace; he begins to undress her. In the green clothes of Paradise she is like a pearl hidden among emeralds. Then modesty supervenes:

ḍaḥikat fa-usdila wajhuhā bi-jadāʾilin
min baᶜdi iṭrāqi l-ḥayāʾi li-fiᶜliyā

16. Ibn al-Naḥḥās, *Mashāri*ᶜ I, p. 217.
17. That his beauty matches hers is a standard topic in descriptions of life in Paradise.

She laughed and her tresses veiled her face as she turned bashful at what I was doing.

The rhyme is not edifying, but it pleased Abbasid poets too to imagine the demure letting down of a cataract of hair.[18]

Then, as soon as one houri is satisfied, another approaches.[19] This goes well beyond the poem quoted in the *Mashāriᶜ*, but both texts are self-professed recruitment devices. Toward the end of our poem, the writer says: 'Lord, forgive what I wrote – my goal was to spur men's resolve to turn from the fleeting vanities of this world', adding that he has never written poems to pretty earth girls. 'What do they and I have to do with one another (*mā lahunna wa-mā liyā*)?' And indeed, the dream of heavenly tenderness flows from an emotional mutilation here on earth, an appalled (and appalling) disgust that is perhaps consciously inculcated:

lawlā l-taṭahhuru wal-taᶜaṭṭuru mā danā
minhā l-rijālu wa-mā taghannā ghāniyā
wal-lāhi law wuḍiᶜat bi-aḥlā ḥilyatin
la-hya llatī fīhā l-adhā mutakhaffiyā

Were it not for [ritual] cleansing and the use of perfume, no man would come near them and none would get married![20]

18. As in the poem about the bather observed, whose black locks must shield her nakedness: *raᵓat shakhṣa l-raqību ᶜalā tadānin / fa-asbalati l-ẓalāma ᶜalā l-ḍiyāᵓi*. The poem is probably by Ibn al-Muᶜtazz, to whom al-Abshīhī ascribes it: *al-Mustaṭraf* (Beirut, 1996), II, p. 37. The *Dīwān Ibn al-Muᶜtazz* (Beirut 1995), I, p. 134, prints *arsalat* in place of *asbalat*). Not all editions of the diwan of Ibn al-Muᶜtazz include the poem. It is at times ascribed to Abū Nuwās, but is not found in Ewald Wagner's critical edition. The houris hair is long and luxuriant, as it must be: *ghaṭṭayna badanaka wa-jallalnahu bi-dhawāᵓibihinna* (al-Muḥāṣibī, *Kitāb al-Tawahhum*, p. 43).
19. Hadith no. 8877, transmitted by al-Ṭabarānī, tells us that the man who has gained admission to Paradise will 'go from wife to wife'. While savouring happiness with one houri, he will hear another one call: 'Hey, friend of God, don't I get a turn (*yā waliyy Allāh a-mā lanā fīka dawlah*)?', Sulaymān b. Aḥmad al-Ṭabarānī, *al-Muᶜjam al-awsaṭ* (Cairo, 1995), VIII, p. 362. Al-Ṭabarānī comments that 'only Saᶜīd ibn Zarbī transmits this hadith from Thābit'. Al-Haythamī, who copies the *ḥadīth*, considers Saᶜīd ibn Zarbī to be *ḍaᶜīf* (Nūr al-Dīn ᶜAlī al-Haythamī, *Majmaᶜ al-zawāᵓid* (Beirut, 1992), X, p. 774), while Ibn Ḥajar al-ᶜAsqalānī (*Tahdhīb al-tahdhīb* (Beirut, 1996)) says he is *ṣaḥīḥ*. The *Kitāb al-tawahhum*, p. 51, adds a charming pictorial detail: *fa-baynā antumā qad maliᵓtumā faraḥan wa-surūran idh nādatka ukhrā min qaṣr min quṣūrika: yā waliyy Allāh a-mā lanā fīka dawlah?*
20. I am not sure of the last three words, but can't imagine what else they might mean. Lane

By God, if she were adorned with the finest jewels she would still be one in whom filth lay hidden.[21]

Unlike the poem to the mother, in this piece the dowry of the houris is not mentioned. But in the likely prototype, the story of Umm Ibrāhīm al-Hāshimiyya, the dowry takes the form of 10,000 dinars she spends on Ibrāhīm's weaponry and horse. She also gives him a shroud and the embalming ointment, *ḥanūṭ*.[22] The

gives 'he took a wife' as a meaning of *ghaniya*, and the Qāmūs confirms *al-ghinā=al-tazwīj*. *Taghannat al-marʾa*, 'the woman got married', is not problematic, but I don't know whether *taghannā* can be predicated of a man in the same sense. I assume that *ghāniyā* stands for *ghānin*, by poetic license (as in W. Wright, *A Grammar of the Arabic Language Translated from the German of Caspari and Edited with Numerous Additions and Corrections by W. Wright* (London, 1875), II , para. 379B, but even more boldly).

21. The word *al-adhā* (with the letter *dhāl*) comes, ultimately, from Q2:222: *wa-yasʾalūnaka ʿani l-maḥīḍi qul huwa adhan*. Since our author is expressing disgust, his understanding of *adhan* must be something like al-Ṭabarī's, who says of menstrual blood: *wa-huwa fī hādhā al-mawḍiʿ yusammā adhan li-natan rīḥihi wa-qadharihi wa-najāsatihi*. (Or as Ibn al-Jawzi puts it: *al-adhā yaḥṣul lil-wāṭiʾ bil-najāsah wa-natan al-rīḥ*). It should be noted that the Jihadist poet's generalised revulsion has nothing particularly Islamic about it. In many of the classical commentaries to Q2:222, the point is made that while men are enjoined from having sexual intercourse with women during their menstrual period, in all other respects, contrary to Jewish custom, they can interact with them normally, physical expressions of affection included. al-Bukhārī records a *ḥadīth* (*Kitāb al-ḥayḍ, Bāb mubāsharat al-ḥāʾiḍ*) in which Aisha says: 'When I had my period, the Prophet used to tell me to put on a waist-wrapper and then he would caress me' (*kāna yaʾmurunī fa-attaziru fa-yubāshirunī wa-ana ḥā'iḍ*). Ibn Kathīr cites a *ḥadīth* transmitted by Aḥmad b. Ḥanbal, Abū Dāwūd, al-Tirmidhī and Ibn Mājah, in which the Prophet is asked, 'what part of my wife is it lawful for me to touch (*mā yaḥillu lī min imraʾatī*) while she is menstruating?', and he replies, 'what is above the waist' *mā fawqa l-izār*. A modern summary of the schools' opinions, together with these reports and their references, concerning this issue may be found on islamweb.net, by searching for *aqwāl al-aʾimmah al-arbaʿah fī mā yalzam man jāmaʿa imraʾatahu al-ḥāʾiḍ*. In the poem, the human female in need of cleansing is implicitly contrasted with the *azwāj muṭahhara* mentioned in the Qurʾān (Q2:25, Q3:15, Q4:57) and usually taken to be the *ḥūr al-ʿayn*. The purity of the *azwāj muṭahhara* is commonly understood to be physical. To Q2:25, Ibn Kathīr's commentary cites Ibn ʿAbbās's discreet explanation 'pure from filth and *adhā*', *muṭahhara min al-qadhar wal-adhā*, as well as Mujāhid's comprehensive list of exemptions from offensive bodily functions, starting with freedom from menstruation. Many modern websites echo this (see the reference above). But Ibn Kathīr also cites Qatāda's more nuanced conception: 'pure from *adhā* and sin', *muṭahhara min al-adhā wal-maʾtham*.

22. Ibn al-Naḥḥās, *Mashāriʿ* I, p. 218. Traditional opinions differ as to whether martyrs are to be shrouded, but the symbolism is ineradicable. A Jihadist song, mentioned in another

dead Ibrāhīm appears to her, crown on his head, and says *yā ummāh! abshirī fa-qad qubila l-mahr wa-zuffat al-ᶜarūs*, 'Rejoice, mother, for the *mahr* has been accepted and the bride presented to the groom.' The world is whole again. The tale has been told; it ends with a wedding. And the lust for death goes on.

poem in the *Dīwān al-ᶜizza* (p. 14), offers the update *bārūdatī bi-yadī wa-bi-jaᶜbatī kafanī*.

CHAPTER

15

THE 'OTHER' IN THE DISCOURSE OF HAMAS AND HIZBULLAH

*Atef Alshaer**

INTRODUCTION

All identities, as all discourses, are premised on distinction from an 'Other',[1] which more often than not, leads to an 'Othering', a process of opposition with potential for violence. Such distinction is multilayered and is better understood through focus on the ideological, as well as the contextual underpinnings of what constitutes an 'Other' and 'Othering'. In this respect, it is understood that there is no static 'Othering'. Othering and its implications are embedded within ideological and contextual factors that nuance and sometimes add to Othering or cancel some previous elements of it. Each political group is built on a particular identity and, by implication, ideological markers through which it identifies itself and opposes an array of Others, some of which belong to its own ethnic groups and share similar ethnic elements, such as language and culture, and others are outside the national boundaries of the ethnic in-group. The political landscape of the Middle East offers notable examples of Othering that show the dynamics of in-group as well as out-group aspects of Othering; the latter being an active process of otherness with sociopolitical, economic and existential consequences.

This chapter will shed light on two prominent and active Islamic movements in the Middle East – namely, the Palestinian Islamic Resistance Movement Hamas and the Lebanese Islamic Resistance Movement of Hizbullah. In

* University of Westminster, London

1. See D. Macdonell, *An Introduction: Theories of Discourse* (Oxford, 1989).

particular, it will refer to their treatment of the Other within, as well as outside, their national boundary and constituency. In particular, the chapter will use the writings of two prominent leaders of these movements, in order to highlight the points in question – namely, Naim Qassem of Hizbullah and Mushīr al-Maṣrī of Hamas. The reason for choosing these two authors lies in the fact that they have been at the forefront of providing theoretical and political treatises and positions that explain the rationale behind the actions of their movements.

Both movements, Hizbullah and Hamas, share one enemy which has come to haunt the Arab world since its foundation in 1948 – namely, Israel. Yet, they both operate within complex political settings – Lebanon and Palestine – which are intricately bound up with regional Arab regimes and their international connections and loyalties. The make-up of these movements and their dynamics are a by-product of such complex backgrounds. To this end, this chapter opens by explaining the process of Othering in the case of Hizbullah as a movement that emerged in 1982. The second part is dedicated to discussing Othering in the case of the Islamic Resistance Palestinian Movement Hamas, which came into being in 1987.

HIZBULLAH AND ITS OTHERS

The Lebanese Islamist party Hizbullah emerged in 1982 in Lebanon within a much contested field of power. Its emergence was preceded by the appearance of Amal, another Shīᶜa movement, which paved the way for Hezbullah's politics, particularly as a representative political body to the Shīᶜa community in Lebanon, then headed by the charismatic Shīᶜa leader Mūsā al-Ṣadr in 1975.[2] Therefore, Hizbullah's discourse was, from the beginning, entangled within the sectarian complexity of Lebanon, as well as the historical conditions of its Shīᶜa community. But one of the first emblems of Othering, which can be described as an 'uncompromised Othering', was directed against Israel, an enemy which the Palestinian movement Hamas and other Islamist movements share in the same way. The 'Othering' of Israel by Hizbullah as well as the Palestinian movements bear ideological as well as contextual reasons;[3] and it was sometimes expressed through violence.

2. See I. Moussawi, 'The Making of Lebanon's Hizbullah', in *Political Islam: Context Versus Ideology*, ed. K. Hroub (London, 2010), pp. 210–31.
3. On the relevance of context and ideology to Islamist movements, see K. Hroub, 'Introduction', in *Political Islam: Context Versus Ideology*, ed. K. Hroub (London, 2010), pp. 9–20.

In this respect, in 1982, the Hizbullah fighter Aḥmad Qaṣīr carried out the first attack by the movement on 11 November 1982, targeting the Israeli military headquarters in Tyre in South Lebanon. Qaṣīr is described in the discourse of Hizbullah as 'the opener of the era of martyrs through martyrdom; the Emir of Martyrs . . .'[4] Fighting the Israeli occupation in the South of Lebanon from 1982 until the liberation in 2000 was the modus operandi of Hizbullah, creating narratives of resistance, heroism, suffering, defiance and victory along the way; narratives through which it marketed itself and defined its raison d'être. The Israeli invasion of Lebanon for the stated purpose of annihilating the Palestine Liberation Organisation (PLO) from the country in July 1982 galvanised the Palestinians and the Lebanese Shīᶜa population to resist it, given that the latter has long felt marginalised in Lebanese politics and the region.[5] Thus, it is the context of marginalisation and deprivation alongside the resurgence of Iran as a major political player in the region, with its message of Islamic governance, that gave rise to, and later emboldened, Hizbullah. The Iranian revolution of 1979 abetted the Shīᶜa population in Lebanon and elsewhere to organise and be active politically. Hizbullah's early literature abounds with references to Iran and its Islamic revolution, which is perceived as glorious, righteous and long-coming. Therefore, alongside Israel, as enshrined in Zionism, which is depicted as the arch-enemy of the Islamic world, Hizbullah asserted itself within an Islamic guardianship as overseen by the Islamic Republic of Iran and its revolutionary leader Ayatollah Khomeini.[6] Iran projected a version of an authentic and uncorrupted Islam, the chief tenant of which is that it does not accept oppression or subservience to others, particularly the imperialism of the West. Hizbullah adopted this discourse and accentuated its narrative of authenticity through rootedness in the Islamic system in a way that makes an Other of the Sunni (or particularly Wahhābī) Saudi Arabia, which was seen, and by implication, vilified, as subservient to the West. The concept of resistance and rootedness in an Islamic order with imperatives of its own is very strong in the discourse of Hizbullah. Naim Qassem, the deputy secretary of Hizbullah, expresses this powerfully in his 2008 book, *The Society of Resistance: The Will to Martyrdom and the Making of Victory*:

4. Nasrallah's speech took place on 'the Day of the Martyr' (11 November 1982), which coincides with the day of Aḥmad Qāṣīr's operation. See 'Al-Sayyid Naṣrullāh Fī Takrīm Abnāʾ al-Shuhadāʾ', in *al-Muqāwama al-Islāmiyya*. Available at: http://www.moqawama.org/essaydetails.php?eid=17725&cid=142. For accessed dates of online resources, see the Bibliography and the accompanying note, p. 366.
5. L. Louër, *Transnational Shia Politics: Religious and Political Networks in the Gulf* (London, 2008), pp. 204–19.
6. Louër, *Transnational Shia Politics*, p. 153.

> Resistance is not a superficial, spontaneous reaction; it's rather an act of founding and rooting . . . As to the act of founding, it is the one within which resistance is perceived as a complete project. Weapons are not for confrontation in this project. But rather there must be mobilization based on cultural, political, media, educational and military ingredients . . . this is to be constructed with our sovereignty, independence and freedom in our country and the region in mind and within a comprehensive and complete framework to undertake this mission. As for rooting, *al-taṣīl*, it provides an exit, a way out, from the trivialisation of the act of resistance and its immediacy, towards fixing it on solid basis to achieve its continuity, as well as the benefiting from intellectual and spiritual (morale-boosting) foundations which direct and guide the long path (of our action) towards the target, *al-hadaf*'.[7]

Qassem focuses on the principle of resistance, which has not changed in the discourse of Hizbullah since its founding in 1982. By effectively rendering resistance as such an existential necessity, Hizbullah distinguished itself from a host of players in Lebanon and in the region. It adopted an identity with roots in the Shīʿa fate regarding the uncompromising nature of fighting injustice, and this was most successful when directed towards Israel, which continued to occupy South Lebanon until 2000. Hizbullah was the most effective resistance against Israel throughout the 1990s, forcing the latter out of Lebanon in 2000, and garnering Arab support along the way. However, what changed regarding Hizbullah's identity is the framing of resistance and the taking into consideration of the specific Lebanese sectarian make-up. Initially, Hizbullah spoke in authoritative terms, as Iran did, putting itself up as the vanguard of the Islamic *umma*, implicitly against the Sunni Saudi Arabia. This appeared in one of the founding documents of Hizbullah in 1985, called the Open Letter:

> We are the sons of the umma, the party of God (Hizb Allah), the vanguard of which was made victorious by God in Iran . . . [W]e do not constitute an organised closed party in Lebanon, nor a narrow political framework. Rather we are an umma linked to the Muslims of the whole world by the solid doctrinal and religious bond, namely Islam.[8]

7. See N. Qassim, *Mujtamaʿ al-Muqāwama: Irādat al-Shahāda wa-Ṣināʿat al-Intiṣār (The Society of Resistance: The Will to Martyrdom and the Making of Victory)* (Beirut, 2008), p. 79.
8. In Moussawi, 'The Making of Lebanon's Hizbullah', p. 213.

It is clear from this letter that Hizbullah defined itself in grand, as well as ambiguous, terms. It did not state its position regarding the Lebanese state and its sovereignty, and where it stands vis-à-vis its multiethnic composition, particularly in light of the Lebanese Civil War (1975–89), which settled on power sharing with equal ethnic representation. It is an 'Islamic system' that this letter suggested, with Iran as its driving actor through the newly reinvigorated doctrine of *wilāyat al-faqīh*, which gives the supreme spiritual leader the right to guide and sanction the democratic rules.[9] Thus, Islam or, perhaps more accurately, 'an Islamic discourse' continued to define and frame Hizbullah's identity. However, Hizbullah's second significant document in 1992 – when its charismatic leader Hassan Nasrallah was elected to serve as its Secretary[10] – came to practically bind itself within the sovereignty of the Lebanese state and accommodate its particularity, entering the political system which it had so far set itself apart from, through participation in the parliamentary elections. With this step, Hizbullah elaborated on its identity, which became more entrenched in Lebanese politics, and more focused on the Israeli occupation of South Lebanon. Resistance remained, throughout its history, the strongest element in its discourse; and it was resistance that meant to defend the Lebanese state and its sovereignty. Hizbullah collaborated with other sects within Lebanon at all levels, and with time adopted a nationalist Lebanese discourse that honours the sovereignty of Lebanon. However, it kept its military wing immune of serious alliances with other Lebanese nationalist groups, since its military capability gave its discourse of resistance strength and leverage, both inside and outside Lebanon. In this respect, Hizbullah's sense of Othering developed to accept the status quo of Lebanon's political system, while insisting on its identity as an Islamic resistance movement, in adherence to the celebrated sentiments of rootedness and authenticity. Naim Qassem explains the importance of the name 'Islamic resistance' to Hizbullah as follows:

> The naming of the 'Islamic resistance' was provoked, for it means belonging to Islam. And this is harmful in a sectarian country. What is required of us is to change the name and generalize it to satisfy all tastes and not to provoke any sensitivity, like calling it 'the popular resistance' or 'the nationalist resistance' and the like, but we have insisted on the naming . . . for this naming expresses content

9. H. Mavani, 'Ayatullah Khomeni's Concept of Governance (*wilayat al-faqih*) and the Classical Shīʿi Doctrine of Imamate', *Middle Eastern Studies* 47.5 (2001), 807–24.
10. D. Matar, 'The Power of Conviction: Nassrallah's Rhetoric and Mediated Charisma in the Context of the 2006 July War', *Middle East Journal of Culture and Communication* 1.2 (2008), 122–37.

> . . . we have succeeded in bestowing pragmatism on this distinction that 'Islamic resistance' became a respectable and acceptable address, embodying Jihadi, cultural and political connotations aiming to benefit the people and the homeland.[11]

There is vagueness regarding the concept of 'Islamic resistance', but Hizbullah developed a pragmatic discourse that adapted to the Lebanese political system, while remaining rooted in the Shīᶜa tradition. In this context, Joseph Alagha writes:

> The logic of operating within the bounds of the Lebanese state prevailed over the logic of the revolution. The party justifies and legitimizes its political program by resorting to Qurᵓānic and Jurisprudential bases. Significantly, the Shīᶜite religio-political heritage conferred upon Hizbullah all the authenticity it needed in order to derive from it a political program based on flexibility and pragmatism.[12]

Notwithstanding this, Hizbullah has proven to be very entrenched in its Shīᶜa doctrine, inspiring itself by resonant examples of sacrifice and struggle in order to defend its beliefs. Two quotations by Qassem, which are echoed in various outlets of Hizbullah, as well as in the discourse of the Secretary General of Hizbullah Hassan Nasrallah concerning martyrdom, are indicative of this tradition:

> Death in your life as oppressed and life in your death as oppressors.[13]

Imām 'Alī, referred to in Hizbullah's language as the Emir of the Faithful (*Amīr al-Mu'minīn*), is said to have stated in the *Nahj al-balāgha* (a source that many Hizbullah leaders reference in their writings and speeches):

> Mountains vanish but you do not vanish; so strengthen your hands; lend your skulls to God; strike your feet on the ground, direct your eyesight towards the furthest of people; and disguise your gaze, and know that victory is granted by the almighty God.[14]

Though Hizbullah has come to be a central player within the post-Taif Lebanese political system, it has remained true to its Shīᶜa roots in fighting any potential

11. See Qassem, *Mujtamaᶜ al-Muqāwama*, p. 44.
12. J. Alagha, *Hizbullah: Identity Construction* (Amsterdam, 2010), p. 60.
13. See Qassem, *Mujtamaᶜ al-Muqāwama*, p. 101.
14. Ibid., p. 102.

enemies that might threaten the core of its identity as a Shīᶜa movement for the Shīᶜa constituency in Lebanon first and foremost. Martyrdom for a cause has remained a central trope in its discourse. Though the party had garnered Arab-wide plaudits for its resistance against Israel in the 1990s, during which the party became famous and was adulated further in 2006 when it withstood Israel's thirty-three day onslaught on Lebanon, the party had come to be seen as suspect (and even condemned) when it intervened on the side of the Syrian regime as the Syrian revolution became more bloody and acquired sectarian undertones. To this end, it is possible to conclude that Hizbullah's identity as a resistance movement has been tested and proven to be entrenched within its Shīᶜa origin and vision. Its Others include all those who threaten its identity as a powerful party within Lebanon, even if this meant fighting against Sunni groups in Syria and elsewhere. From this perspective, Hizbullah's alliances with other sects in Lebanon is tactical; but its link with Iran and the Shīᶜa Syrian regime are ideological and strategic. This example demonstrates the unsettled and porous character of the nation-state system in the region that it is yet to be truly citizenship-based, but rather is overridden with sectarian and patriarchal loyalties. At various junctures of its history, Hizbullah adopted Islamism as rooted within a rebellious streak of Shīᶜism, nationalism and Arabism,[15] but it has proven to be willing to shed all these, effectively in order to preserve its identity as a Shīᶜa party loyal to its Shīᶜa alliances, including in Iran and Syria. This is unlike Hamas, which boasts a Sunni and Palestinian identity with a history of Othering of its own.

HAMAS AND ITS OTHERS

Hamas came to the Palestinian national life at an opportune time in 1987. It incorporated itself within an existing Islamist political framework long established by the Muslim Brotherhood in Egypt and elsewhere in the region, such as in the Iranian revolution of 1979. It also strengthened itself amidst ripe political conditions, with a determined Islamist leadership base in Gaza during the inspiring first Palestinian Intifada (1987–93). Hamas flourished relatively quickly, while Fatah, the other mainstream Palestinian party which had popularly spearheaded Palestinian politics and its national cause since it was founded in 1965, suffered blows of various kinds. After its forced evacuation from Lebanon in 1982 to Tunisia, Fatah lacked the influence it had once had on the imagination of

15. See L. Khatib, D. Matar and A. Alshaer, *The Hizbullah Phenomenon: Politics and Communication* (New York; Oxford, 2014).

the entire Palestinian nation. Thus, Hamas competed with Fatah at a time when the latter was relatively weaker, which it confirmed and further compounded by signing the unpopular Oslo Accords with Israel in 1993.[16] The terms of the Oslo agreement, which promised independence for the Palestinians after a short interim period lasting five years but never delivered, was used by Hamas to highlight its readiness to assume the leadership of the Palestinian people from Fatah and the PLO, who were painted as having traded the Palestinian national rights for power and subservient political cohabitation with the hegemonic politics of the US and its protégé in the region, Israel. This competition for power between Hamas and Fatah continued and intensified after Hamas won democratic and fair elections in 2006, which consolidated its legitimacy, in addition to vindicating its narrative of sacrifice, having lost many of its prominent leaders, assassinated during the second Palestinian Intifada (2000–5).[17] However, the gradual military confrontations between Hamas and Fatah ended in the former taking over Gaza in 2007 and ruling supreme there, while Fatah and the PA have continued to do the same in the West Bank ever since.

Against this background, Hamas reinforced its partisan position in Gaza, despite the debilitating siege that was forced on it following Hamas's takeover of Gaza. On its part, Fatah restricted its influence and rule to the West Bank, over which the Israeli occupation has had an overall control. Despite many meetings between Fatah and Hamas in order to reconcile and unite the Palestinian territories in the West Bank and Gaza under one authority, nothing had come to fruition. The Arab uprisings came to stoke further passion among the Palestinians for reconciliation that would redirect their energies towards resisting the ever aggressive Israeli occupation. This has yet to happen. Therefore, it is these multiple contexts and layers of the Palestinian conditions, surveyed schematically here, which define Hamas's politics. However, there are ideological elements to Hamas's discourse, as manifested in the writings of one of its leaders – namely, Mushīr al-Maṣrī – which suggest exclusivity of authority as understood through an Islamic perspective that does not in principle accommodate secular politics.[18]

16. See K. Hroub, *Hamas: Political Thought and Practice* (USA, 2000).
17. It is worthwhile to quote Loren D. Lybarger here for his 2007 study of Hamas and Fatah, and the ideological content of their competition provides an accurate observation that explains later events: '[V]ying to define and control the collective Palestinian fate, these movements and their associated socio-political milieu have so far proven incapable of overtaking or absorbing one another'. Loren D. Lybarger, *Identity and Religion in Palestine* (Princeton, 2007), p. 3.
18. Mushīr al-Maṣrī, *al-Mushārka fī al-Ḥayā al-Siyāsiyya fī ẓill Anẓimat al-Ḥukm al-Muʿāṣara* (Cairo, 2006).

In this respect, Hamas's politics rests on preserving and ultimately asserting its identity as an Islamic movement.

Al-Maṣrī's masters thesis, which has become an important reference for Islamic movements, is entitled *The Participation of Islamic Movements in Political Life in Light of the Current Governing Regimes*. It offers insight into the thinking of the Islamist movements, as well as their worldview in general. Relying on major texts from the Islamic tradition as well as modern Islamist writings, and with the use of linguistic and textual definition and analysis, al-Maṣrī reinforces the view that governance belongs to God. It should be sanctioned through religious commandments and rules, and any political programme must revolve around this basic premise, to which religious legitimacy is central. In the book, al-Maṣrī suggests that it is permissible for Islamic movements to participate in politics alongside secular movements, such as the Palestinian Fatah. But such participation seems tactical and interest driven. So long as Islamic movements do not possess enough power to unseat their secular opponents and govern in accordance with the imperatives of Islamic rule, they can join others and form coalitions. Yet, once they are in a position of power and able to preserve it, then they should not be party to a secular political structure, as secularism is grounded in man-made paradigms; whereas governance should be sanctioned by God and grounded in a system that includes appreciation of an afterlife.

Yet, like Hizbullah, contextually and pragmatically, Hamas's raison d'être is its resistance to Israel as an occupying power. Hamas has undergone the same journey that Hizbullah took earlier in 1992, as was explained above. Initially, Hamas rejected to enter into the democratic process as first undertaken by the Palestinian Authority in 1996, and adopted an Islamic discourse of a rigid nature. When it felt consolidated with its military wing, 'Izz al-Dīn al-Qassām (founded in 1992), having become more powerful, Hamas entered the political process in 2006. It then unexpectedly won the parliamentary elections. In congruence with the nationalist side of its discourse, Hamas sought to incorporate Fatah within a framework of power sharing, but the latter rejected that for a myriad of reasons. Fatah saw Hamas as fundamentally different from it ideologically, as well as the fact that some elements within Fatah were interested in seeing Hamas rule fail so that they could replace it. Thus, when the issue at hand is seen comprehensively, it is possible to argue that the ideological differences between Fatah and Hamas on fundamental strategic aspects, including the management of the conflict with Israel, the nature of Palestinian society and the struggle over its authority, caused the split between these movements. To this end, while Israel is the first 'uncompromised Other' to Hamas, Fatah is its 'in-group Other' within the nationalist and social spectrum. In effect, Hamas has proven pragmatic and has even confronted Palestinian factions in their fight against Israel when it suited its interests in maintaining and preserving its authority over Gaza, which has become very significant to Hamas's political survival and strength. In this regard, Hroub's observation is important:

> Hamas and the earlier Palestinian Islamists of the MBP have shown a great measure of context answerability. They have promoted a multi-track agenda combining social change, religious propagation, political participation and military engagement, although not necessarily with the same momentum at any given time. The flexibility of moving back and forth between these tracks and across them, speeding one up and slowing another down, while justifying all manoeuvres by religious rulings and *fatwas*, is one of the most salient conclusions of the study of Hamas's political behaviours.[19]

Following this, Mushīr al-Maṣrī stresses the importance of Islamic governance and its imperatives. He emphasises that Islam takes precedence over any other system of governance, and therefore any alliance with secularists or other movements identifying outside the Islamic model is temporary and tactical until there is a seizure of power by a movement that governs according to Islamic principles, to whose authority all must submit.[20] In his words:

> [I]n Islamic philosophy calls for the implementation of God's *sharīʿa* in all the affairs of life, and the rejection of all that breaches its principles and laws, and this necessitates the submission of all to this philosophy.[21]

One cannot overestimate the role of ideology in guiding the politics of movements that also adopt nationalist discourses and operate pragmatically in congruence with the political activity of the region, as Hizbullah and Hamas do. Both are committed nation-state orientated movements, and Hamas in particular has remained restricted to (officially) acting within the boundaries of Palestine. Yet, both have acquired military capabilities and articulate visions of an ideological kind that they protect even with the use of arms. There are contexts where their ideological character manifests itself in extreme ways, particularly when their raison d'être is threatened. At the centre of these movements' ideologies lies a basic understanding that they represent a righteous Islamic path which they

19. Khalid Hroub, 'Conflicting National Liberation and Socio-Political Change', in *Political Islam: Context Versus Ideology*, ed. Khalid Hroub (London, 2010), p. 174.
20. Al-Maṣrī's book, *al-Mushāraka fī al-Ḥayā al-Siyāsiyya fī Ẓill al-Anizma al-Muʿāṣara*, also available online: http://www.alittehad.net/vb/showthread.php?t=980.
21. See al-Maṣrī, *al-Mushāraka*.

safeguard and uphold, and that any deviation from this path incurs consequences. Therefore, in the writings of the aforementioned authors, who in general express standard political discourses of their movements, however eloquently, a basic contradictory positioning is found. On the one hand, their ideas about 'the Other' are informed by alleged firm theological roots grounded in their understanding of God's ways as interpreted by certain Islamic scholars. And on the other, they are also mindful of the political dynamics around them, in which they are central players, and of their changing imperatives. The force of this tension between ideology and pragmatism can be seen in Hamas's governance of Gaza – a place where it has the power to implement its vision (knowing that its behaviours are judged by opponents). It has still pursued a somewhat religious agenda in restricting women's activity and space in official capacities and places, suggesting the idea of Islamic lashing as punishment for perceived transgressions of *sharīᶜa*[22] *and by enforcing particular dress codes on women and even young men.*[23] *In some Hamas writings, including poetry, the Other can be totally excluded and demeaned.*[24] In one of Mushīr al-Maṣrī's well-known poems, there is no Other except that which fits within an Islamist framework, ideally one constructed by Hamas. It is noteworthy that the poem was composed within the context of the Israeli onslaught on Gaza during the second Palestinian Intifada, imbued with an ideological exclusivity that ripples with an extreme sense of self-righteousness that denigrates all others, including secular movements.

In the poem under consideration, al-Maṣrī uses intense metaphorical language to praise one of the young Hamas suicide bombers who detonated himself in a nightclub in Israel and caused several fatalities and injuries – namely, Saᶜīd al-Ḥūtarī (1979–2001). The only righteous path for Palestinian politics is the one he puts forward and represented by Hamas. Philosophically, the Other is totally excluded, the Palestinian Authority and its backbone organisation – namely, Fatah or other secular forces – are all negatively portrayed. It represents an extreme version of Islamism, which is usually associated more with al-Qāᶜida than Hamas. Throughout its history, Hamas has shown pragmatism and promulgated a nation-state discourse rather than a universalised Islamist one, as was

22. On this, see 'Tashrīᶜī Ghazza Yudrusu Iqrār ᶜUqūbat al-Jald Ḍimn Qānūn ᶜUqūbāt Jadīd' in *Falasṭīn al-Yawm*. Available at: http://paltoday.ps/ar/post/194090/.
23. See B. Milton-Edwards, 'Hamas and the Arab Spring: Strategic Shifts?', *Middle East Policy* 20.3 (2013), 63.
24. There are important figures within Hamas, such as Aḥmad Yūsuf and Ghāzī Ḥamad, who advance a civilian discourse premised on a rational basis that respects the Other and manages the conflict, whether with Israel or Fatah, through discourses of conflict and tension, rather than dogma and absolute exclusion.

previously discussed. Here, al-Maṣrī addresses the suicide bomber Saᶜīd al-Ḥūtarī in the first stanza of the poem as follows:

O, you who burn me with your pure fire
take your share from my fire
My exploding rockets had thundered upon you
and my flashes glittered
Take these shares
take them off the old debt
I am a deaf rock from the fire at the bottom of the abyss
I have rocketed the inhabitants of hell with it
with a ballista
Write down my name: (Saᶜīd)
and thousands are on the way
The daylight faded
so I do not sense sunset or sunrise
My work involves all explosives
my rights have been lost . . .[25]

Mushīr al-Maṣrī was born in 1978 in Gaza. His brother, Fāris al-Maṣrī, was assassinated by Israel during the second Palestinian Intifada. However, the poem in question should not be taken as a translation of Hamas ideology as outlined by al-Maṣrī in his aforementioned book. The poem goes beyond that in the utter gloominess of violence and narrowness it projects; yet its political context should be accounted for. After 2000, Israel employed colossal violence against the Palestinians in general, and the Gaza Strip specifically, afflicting it with a humanitarian crisis. The poem is shot with the spirit of revenge and uses base and inhumane references. The poem suggests that moments of violent intensity heightens hatred, normalises it and renders the image of the Other as less human. It confirms the dangerous one-sidedness of human emotions once the Other is totally excluded from the purview of the self, and that violence can assume a logic of its own, which, if unchecked, becomes its very own reality:

Tighten my belt which is filled with bitter death
Add ten bombs to it, for today is the day of revenge
I will grill with its fire those who have built (the Knesset) from my bones

25. For the Arabic version of the poem, see: https://www.paldf.net/forum/showthread.php?t=207053.

With this belt, the sun dawns from the deepest dark
This is my able horse . . . I pat its forehead with love
A hero who rid the earth of jinni before he was weaned
He speaks hell when he neighs amidst the herd . . . without a bridle
I will remain a ghost for ᶜIzz al-dīn . . . for he has been moulded from granite
Like a mountain, standing on the bloodsucker, the illegitimate son.[26]

There is no doubt that the Israeli occupation of Palestine has set in motion violent patterns of an absolute nature, instigating absolute returns. In this respect, Frantz Fanon describes the effects of colonial conditions on the colonised as follows:

> But it so happens that for the colonised people this violence, because it constitutes their only work, invests their characters with positive and creative qualities. The practice of violence binds them together as a whole, since each individual forms a violent link in the great chain, a part of the great organism of violence which has surged upwards in reaction to the settler's violence in the beginning. The groups recognise each other and the future nation is already indivisible. The armed struggle mobilizes the people, that is to say, it throws them in one way and in one direction.[27]

Still, the glorification of suicide bombing is absolute in this poem in a way that exalts an ideological option of a dimly indulgent nature. In effect, the poet creates an image of hell in which he wants the suicide bomber al-Ḥūtarī to consign his enemies, whereas the suicide bomber is granted Paradise with all its conceived comforts, riches and rewards. It is the sentiment of total revenge that governs the logic of the suicide bomber here, which closes any other options for resistance and struggle. The poem as a whole, with its narrowness and violent severity, violates the basic existence of the Other, in their existential sense. That suicide bombing has become one such prominent method of fighting with narrow ideological and vengeful poetry that praises it in certain parts of the Islamic world is, indeed, lamentable. In this context, it is illuminating to quote the French philosopher Levinas, who is a pioneer in writing about the concept of the Other in philosophy: 'I find myself facing the other. He is neither a cultural signification nor a simple given. He is, primordially, sense . . . because only through him can a phenomenon such as signification introduce itself, of itself, into being.'[28] It is the loss of the primary human sense towards the Other that makes this poem dark.

26. 'Taḥiyyat ilā Abṭāl al-Istishādiyyin fī Falasṭīn'.
27. F. Fanon, *The Wretched of the Earth* (London, 1963), p. 73.
28. S. Sperl, 'Crossing Enemy Boundaries: Al-Buhturi's Ode on the Ruins of Ctesiphon

CONCLUSION

The 'Other', who constitutes difference, is existentially an inescapable category, as well as an outcome of human interrelations. Yet, it is not so inescapable as to lead to inevitable conflicts with violent consequences, when coexistence is not only the better option, but also an ethical imperative. The hope is always that the Other is a source of enrichment and expansion beyond the self, whether it is a person, nation or an ethnicity. When Levinas conceived an ethical philosophy of the Other in the wake of the Second World War, he suggested, as the Polish writer Ryszard Kapuścinski puts it, that 'one must not only meet the Other, accept him and converse with him, but you must also take responsibility for him'.[29] The responsibility for the Other is displayed within Islamic heritage in clear terms, and it is a heritage to which Islamic movements refer, such as the laws of war that treat nature, animals, children and people of different faith with respect and sanctity, as proclaimed in the speech of the first Caliph of Islam, Abū Bakr (573–634), to the *umma*.[30]

Yet what is experienced in contexts of modern day Islamism are paradoxes of positioning vis-à-vis the secular Other, in particular. Though the Othering of an occupying state like Israel is to be expected, the content of this and its connotations with such a degree of ideological indulgence that herds all others, both the in-group and the out-group together, and justifies violent practices, ultimately reveals the danger of one-sided ideologies. Therefore, such paradoxes as situated within contextual as well as ideological frames, as seen in the case of Hizbullah and Hamas, highlight the fact that nation-states in the Middle East have not yet properly settled into laws and nationalist grounds that exclude ideological dangers with severe violent connotations. While Hizbullah operates within Lebanon and purports to protect and respect its sovereignty, it has involved itself in Syria in a way that suggests that the protection of its ideology and power is more important than its respect to the Lebanese state, which as a state has refused to intervene in Syria in any militaristic manner. Therefore, Hizbullah's development from an Islamist force with Islamist agendas which have developed to absorb nationalist and Arab aspirations, as in the liberation of Palestine from the Israeli occupation, retreats unto itself within its Shīᶜite identity when this identity is felt to be

Re-Read in the Light of Virgil and Wilfred Owen', *Bulletin of the School of Oriental and African Studies* 69.3 (2006), 365.

29. R. Kapuścinski, *The Other* (London; New York, 2008).
30. For this, see 'Waṣiyat Abī Bakr al-Ṣiddīq li-Junūd al-Islam Qabl Fatḥ Bilād al-Shām (12 Hijriyya)', in *Maktabat Ḥuqūq al-Insān*, available at: http://www1.umn.edu/humanrts/arab/IS-6.html.

threatened. Hamas, on the other hand, is a Palestinian Islamist and nationalist movement that developed its discourse regarding Israel and other Palestinian secular groups, accommodating both tactically. Yet, it projects another strand of discourse, where its Islamist agendas – some of which have been forced on Gaza, where it has its main base of authority – have been applied. The outcomes of such contradictions show the complexities of these movements, so the search for clarity and sound inclusion within a nation-state with citizenship-based institutions and cultural infrastructure must continue. Therefore, the Other is properly constituted within legal and ethical boundaries, rather than let loose at the mercy of unidirectional ideological impulses.

CHAPTER

16

CONCLUDING REMARKS: VIOLENCE IN ISLAMIC THOUGHT

*Robert Gleave**

Conducting academic research on Islam and violence is a political act. By bringing these two items together in a single series of publications, one is saying they should be studied together (that is, they are not unconnected). One is also effectively declaring that their relationship needs to be better understood and explained (i.e. their relationship is not fully understood, even by those who claim knowledge on this point); otherwise, why have a series looking at them at all if you have nothing new to say? As a researcher, one is announcing that more can and must be said. This may seem grandiose, but given the risks involved for academics in speaking about Islam and violence, it is worth being blunt. In this, our series *Violence in Islamic Thought* is no different from the academic study of 'Islam and gender' or 'Islam and sexuality'. To choose to study an area is to announce that more research needs to be done, and that the topic is understudied, or the topic has been ignored, marginalised or misunderstood. The three volumes in this series, then, make the political statement that the current media portrayals of Islam as intrinsically violent or inherently peaceful are totally unsatisfactory. They may be rhetorically powerful, and politicians, diplomats and commentators may enjoy the simplicity they provide. They are not, though, the results of evidence-based research. What we have tried to do in these three volumes is present the complicated relationship between violence and Islamic thought, and by doing so, we reject facile equations.

A bit of institutional context might be beneficial here. The three volumes in the EUP *Violence in Islamic Thought* series, of which this is the last, are the result of three funded research projects. First, from 2010–13, I received a 'Global

* University of Exeter

Uncertainties' fellowship as part of a collaborative research programme funded by the ESRC[1] and the AHRC[2]. That project, titled *Legitimate and Illegitimate Violence in Islamic Thought* (www.livitproject.net), was a mixed blessing: positively, it provided me with the space with which to explore these issues and recruit my friend and colleague Dr István Kristó-Nagy with whom to work. Negatively, the Global Uncertainties programme framed 'Islam' and 'Islamic Thought' as a 'global uncertainty', which carried with it the notion of Islam as a threat to stability, and this, inevitably, linked our research to security studies. This problem – of image and potentially of substance – was expressed to me on more than one occasion by fellow academics. I might have preferred to initiate this project without any connection with security studies, but that is not the nature of the UK research funding environment. The Global Uncertainties leadership fellowship I received from 2013 to 2016 was a follow-on grant for the project 'Islamic Reformulations' (www.islamicreformulations.net). That project looked at how Islamic thought was adjusting and transforming itself to the conditions of modernity, and is perhaps even more problematic if it is to be classed as a 'Global Uncertainty'. Whilst not focused on violence alone, the security studies framework once again problematised Islam in the modern world in a way with which, looking back, I should have been less comfortable. That project, though, enabled me to work with two research fellows, Dr Sarah Elibiary (a contributor to this volume) and Dr Mustafa Baig (my co-editor for this volume). It also enabled me to oversee two excellent pieces of PhD research by Dr Tayyeb Mimouni (on varieties of contemporary Salafism) and Dr Bianka Speidl (on legitimate violence in the thought of Sayyid Muḥammad Ḥusayn Faḍl Allāh). In the latter part of this volume's preparation, my time commitment has been funded through the Understanding Sharīᶜa project (www.usppip.eu) funding by HERA and a collaboration between universities in Exeter, Bergen, Gottingen and Leiden. The Exeter team's focus was on violence, and enabled me to work with Dr Omar Anchassi (now of the University of Edinburgh). I list these projects not only in recognition of the contributions of the research fellows, but to demonstrate the dynamics of research on Islam and violence in the post-9/11 environment. Undoubtedly, Islamic Studies has received a welcome boost in the last two decades, and this is in no small measure due to the subject's securitisation following the events of 9/11. The need to understand the intellectual roots of Jihadism has released funds for research into Islam more broadly, and amongst the beneficiaries has been my own work in these three volumes. It has also given

1. Economic and Social Research Council (www.esrc.ac.uk). For accessed dates of online resources, see the Bibliography and the accompanying note, p. 366.
2. Arts and Humanities Research Council (www.ahrc.ac.uk).

opportunities to emerging researchers which would not have been possible otherwise. The Islamic Studies field is, ironically, healthier today because ‘Islam’ has been perceived as a problem by the governments and the media in Europe and North America. The trick has been to use this fact to advance the field. Our priorities as Islamicists may not be those of the security services, but the large amounts of opportune funding flowing into Islamic Studies has nonetheless strengthened the field. I hope these three volumes constitute one way in which these funds might be usefully deployed for fundamental research, as well as informing wider public opinion.

One can debate the degree to which securitisation has occurred, and whether this is a detrimental or positive step. In the UK, it might be argued that the whole of the higher education system has been securitised. Since the Counter Terrorism and Security Act 2015, academics in UK universities are legally required to abide by the ‘Prevent Duty’. That is, they must ‘have due regard to the need to prevent people from being drawn into terrorism’. It is not entirely clear what ‘due regard’ means, though the advice has already been modified to mean that this duty has to be balanced by a competing duty of institutions of higher education in the UK – namely, the duty to uphold freedom of speech. The Prevent Duty still requires academics to ensure that all activities on university campuses are assessed with respect to the risk that individuals might be drawn into terrorism through an activity. Islam-related terrorism is not the only target, but it clearly is the main concern. British academics researching the relationship between Islam and violence in the context of the Prevent Duty face particular issues. Their sources (oral or text-based) are, in most instances, from individuals whose ideas could not be espoused legally in the UK. Academic researchers have, of course, a legitimate reason to be researching and teaching students about those views; but it is not yet clear whether researchers have a legal responsibility to ensure all readers (and in the classroom, students) understand some of the views being studied are ‘extremist’ and, therefore, exposure to them risks drawing an individual into terrorism. An ‘extremist view’, for the purposes of the Prevent Duty, is defined as one which is actively opposed to British values. ‘British values’ are, in turn, listed as ‘democracy, the rule of law, individual liberty and mutual respect and tolerance for those with different faiths and beliefs and for those without faith’. If it is a legal requirement for me to say this now, I am quite happy to do so: some of the views expressed by the movements and individuals studied in this volume are ‘extremist’ under this definition (though I am not, I should add, saying that this definition of extremism is either correct or useful). Representing the views of Muslim movements and individuals with honesty and intellectual integrity (that is, treating them as worthy subjects of scientific analysis) is, one might argue, a primary responsibility of any academic researcher. Some might wish to add to this responsibility the duty to expose the 'extremist' nature of their views. In the UK context, researching Islam and violence often means directly encountering the state security apparatus in a way that most other researchers would not experience.

It is important not to overplay the demands of the Prevent Duty. One may see it as an affront to academic independence, but to date there has been little restriction, in my experience, on legitimate academic activity. The legislation was put in place for reasons at a particular point in the UK's turbulent recent political history, rather than to address research-based evidence for a societal problem. The projects have experienced no official interference around what to research or how to present it in conferences and workshops. Researchers have had to inform security services that they will be engaging in this research; we were ethically required to do so, since consulting extremist material, particularly online, can raise questions, and there have been relevant legal cases against academics researching Jihadism. What the Prevent Duty (amongst other similar measures) does, though, is create an important element of the context in which research into violence in Islamic thought has taken place in the last decade. Of course, it is not a relevant context for those working outside of the UK who have participated in our volumes – they may, however, have their own context to contend with, as each set of national agencies has devised its own mechanisms for preventing extremism and terrorism. What has become clear is that something like the UK Prevent Duty would be unthinkable in comparable jurisdictions, and hence it is a peculiarity of the UK system, and comes from the political demands of successive UK governments.

Given these factors, the long view of the relationship between violence and Islamic thought appears even more important now that when we began these research projects in 2010. One would not have predicted that the most important and unrecognised global uncertainty was the fragmentation of the (apparently) stable international order. The challenge of this international fragmentation, combined with other urgent (ecological and economic) priorities reduces the appeal of a deeper, research based analysis. In this sense, the successive projects on *Violence in Islamic Thought*, and the funding which came with them, may not be possible in the future. The simplistic notion that it is extremist ideology that causes terrorist acts has been undermined in the social science literature; this removes the immediate need to understand the intellectual landscape which creates Jihadism, and with that removal, the opportunities for funding are reduced. If that is to become the new normal, then the three volumes produced in this series, we hope, demonstrate the value of *longue durée* studies not only for understanding current events, but also for a deeper engagement with the history of ideas over time.

BIBLIOGRAPHY

(A) NEWSPAPER REPORTS

'Danish Jihadist Reportedly Killed in Syria', *Copenhagen Post*, 13 January 2014.

Filastin al-Muslima, 'al-Muqāwama fī Ghazza aẓharat kafaʾa qitāliyya wa-lam tataʾaththir bil-ḍaghṭ al-ʿaskarī (Resistance in the Gaza Strip Showed High Fighting Capabilities are Unaffected by Military Pressure)', *Filastin al-Muslima*, 3 February 2009, pp. 42–3.

Ghosh, Aparisim, 'The Face of Brutality', *Time Magazine*, 4 December 2006, pp. 36–9.

Johnson, Scott, 'A New Enemy Emerges: "The Shīʿite Zarqawi"', *Newsweek*, 13 November 2006, p. 10.

Knowlton, Brian, 'Powell Says, We Are Still In Conflict: US Surprised In Iraq By Insurgents' Fight', *International Herald Tribune*, 27 October 2003.

Makram, Muḥammad Aḥmad, 'Ḥadīth fī al-ʿUmq Maʿa Shaykh al-Azhar', *al-Ahrām*, 10 July 2010.

Pelda, Kurt, 'Fodder for the Front: German Jihadists on Syria's Battlefields', *Der Spiegel*, 30 April 2013.

(B) ONLINE REFERENCES

N.B. The chapter authors accessed online resources during research; these were all checked a second time for validity by the editors in January 2020 before going to press. All references can then be taken as 'accessed 31 January 2020'. The exception to this is the crucial www.tawhid.ws website, which went defunct during the editing process. All references to www.tawhid.ws can be taken as accessed January 2017. Many of the works referenced on www.tawhid.ws are available via screengrab on www.jihadica.com. The http://www.manhajal-sadren.com/ site was replaced with the http://jawabna.com site during the editing, and so these references are no longer available as of January 2017.

1. Anonymous/No-author References

'133 Killed in Qaeda Violence in Yemen', *khaleejtimes.com*, 10 April 2012 (https://www.khaleejtimes.com/region/133-killed-in-qaeda-violence-in-yemen).

'Al-Qaeda Claims Deadly Yemen Suicide Blast', *aljazeera.com*, 21 May 2012 (https://www.aljazeera.com/news/middleeast/2012/05/201252175919491219.html).

'Al-Qaida Says it Captures 70 Yemeni Soldiers in Abyan's Battle', *China Daily*, 5 March 2012 (http://en.ce.cn/World/Middleeast/201203/05/t20120305_23129213.shtml).

'AQAP Claims Responsibility for Yemen Attacks', *edition.cnn.com*, 8 March 2012 (https://edition.cnn.com/2012/03/07/world/meast/yemen-violence/index.html).

'Best solgans | tera mera rishta kya "la-ilaha il-lallah"' (https://www.youtube.com/watch?v=Hks8Y7W85nU).

'Drones Spur Yemenis' Distrust of Government and U.S.', *reuters.com*, 27 October 2010 (https://www.reuters.com/news/picture/drones-spur-yemenis-distrust-of-governme-idUSTRE69Q36520101027).

'Eight Dead in South Yemen Violence: Security Officials', *news.egypt.com*, 27 May 2011 (http://english.ahram.org.eg/News/13087.aspx).

'Heavy Yemeni Troop Losses Reported in Raid', *Aljazeera.com*, 8 March 2012 (https://www.aljazeera.com/news/middleeast/2012/03/2012356504141349.html).

'Huge Death Toll Doubles in Yemen "Slaughter"', *edition.cnn*, 14 May 2012 (https://edition.cnn.com/2012/03/06/world/meast/yemen-violence/index.html).

'Islam is the Religion of the Sword, not Pacifism', *Dābiq* 7, 2015 (https://jihadology.net/2015/02/12/al-ḥayat-media-center-presents-a-new-issue-of-the-islamic-states-magazine-dabiq-7/).

'Kirsten Seymour interviews Mullah Omar's teacher, Maulana Sami ul Haq [*sic*]', Tribune 24/7, 31 July 2011 (www.youtube.com/watch?v=6SL2cnUgBT8).

'Lettre de l'Emir Abdelkader à Louis-Philippe (roi de France)' (http://rabahnaceri.unblog.fr/lettres-a-lire/lettre-de-lemir-abdelkader-a-louis-philippe-roi-de-france/).

'Liqā' ḥaṣarī li-qanā Ru'yā ma' Abū Muḥammad al-Maqdisī', 6 February 2015 (https://www.youtube.com/watch?v=XFh6gMKSGmA&t=2s).

'Militants Kill 10 Soldiers in Central Yemen', *arabamericannews.com*, 17 January 2014 (https://www.arabamericannews.com/2014/01/17/militants-kill-10-soldiers-in-central-yemen/).

'Mutfī of Egypt: ʿAlī b. Abī Ṭālib Warned Against Dāʿish' (Arabic) (gerasnews.com/print/160291).

'Muftī Shāmzay – raḥmat allāh [ʿalayhi] – kā fatvā jis kī banā' par unheṇ shahīd kiyā gayā', 14 November 2013 (https://sadaehaqq.wordpress.com/2013/11/14/مفتی-شامزئی-رحمہ-اللہ-کا-فتویٰ-جس-کی-بنا/)

'Open Letter to Baghdadi' (lettertobaghdadi.com).

'Profile: al Qaeda in the Arabian Peninsula', *Aljazeera.com*, 9 May 2012 (https://www.aljazeera.com/news/middleeast/2012/05/2012597359456359.html).

'al-Qaraḍāwī yunaddid bi-qatl al-Kasāsba', 4 February 2015 (https://www.eremnews.com/news/arab-world/201323).

'Say It On the Barricade! LA ILAHA ILALLAH #RejectCAA' (https://www.youtube.com/watch?v=lld_IozAEdI).

'Sectarian Clashes Kill at Least 40 in Yemen', *ahram.org*, 12 December 2013 (http://english.ahram.org.eg/News/88989.aspx).

'Slave-Girls or Prostitutes?', *Dabiq* 9 (Shaᶜbān 1436), pp. 44–9 (www.clarionproject.org/islamic-state-isis-isil-propaganda-magazine-dabiq-50/).

'South Yemen Violence Kills 2 Children, 6 Militants', *newsok.com*, 18 April 2012 (http://www.nytimes.com/aponline/2012/04/18/world/middleeast/ap-ml-yemen.html?ref=world).

'Suspected al Qaeda Militants Seize Yemeni Town', *france24.com*, 29 May 2011 (https://www.france24.com/en/20110529-suspected-al-qaeda-militants-seize-yemeni-town-zinjibar).

'Taḥiyyat ilā abṭāl al-istishādiyyin fī falasṭīn', in *Shabkat Falasṭīn lil-Ḥiwār* (https://www.paldf.net/forum/showthread.php?t=207053).

'Taᶜlīq maᶜālī al-shaykh Saᶜd al-Shatharī ᶜalā ḥarq Muᶜādh al-Kasāsba', 5 February 2015 (https://www.youtube.com/watch?v=qPMDw6Gtsu4).

'The Burning of the Murtadd Pilot', *Dābiq* 7, 2015 (https://jihadology.net/2015/02/12/al-ḥayat-media-center-presents-a-new-issue-of-the-islamic-states-magazine-dabiq-7/).

'The Capture of a Crusader Pilot', *Dābiq* 6, 2014 (https://jihadology.net/2016/07/31/new-issue-of-the-islamic-states-magazine-dabiq-6/).

'The Culture of Rape Within ISIS, and the Questions That Arise', 29 March 2016 (www.nytimes.com/2016/03/20/world/middleeast/the-culture-of-rape-within-isis-and-the-questions-that-arise.html).

'The Revival of Slavery Before the Hour', *Dabiq* 4 (Dhū l-Ḥijja 1435), pp. 14–17 (www.clarionproject.org/islamic-state-isis-isil-propaganda-magazine-dabiq-50/).

'The World's Muslims: Religion, Politics and Society' (www.pewforum.org/2013/04/30/the-worlds-muslims-religion-politics-society-beliefs-about-sharia/).

'Toll Hits 200 in Battle with Qaeda for Yemen Town', *france24.com*, 13 April 2012 (https://wikivisually.com/wiki/Al-Qaeda_insurgency_in_Yemen).

'Up to 11000 Foreign Fighters in Syria: Steep Rise Among Western Europeans', *International Centre for the Study of Radicalisation and Political Violence*, 17 December 2013 (https://icsr.info/2013/12/17/11000-foreign-fighters-syria-steep-rise-among-western-europeans/).

'"US Drone Strike" Kills 5 Qaeda Militants in Yemen', *dailynewsegypt.com*, 17 April 2012 (https://wwww.dailynewssegypt.com/author/admin/page/6/).

'Waṣiyat Abī Bakr al-Ṣiddīq li-Junūd al-Islam Qabl Fatḥ Bilād al-Shām (12 Hijriyya)', in *Maktabat Ḥuqūq al-Insān* (http://www1.umn.edu/humanrts/arab/IS-6.html).

2. *Articles and Books*

Abdallah, Daniel, 'Inter-Rebel Fighting Enters a New Phase as Salafists Declare Open War on ISIS', *joshualandis.com*, 14 February 2014 (http://warincontext.org/2014/02/14/inter-rebel-fighting-enters-a-new-phase-as-salafists-declare-open-war-on-isis/).

ᶜAbd al-Qādir b. ᶜAbd al-ᶜAzīz [=Sayyid Imām al-Sharīf], *Risālat al-ᶜumda fī iᶜdād al-ᶜudda liʾl-jihād fī sabīl Allāh taᶜālā* (http://www.tawhed.ws/dl?i=f8ro5d45).

ᶜAbd al-Raʾūf, Ḥussām, *Law Kuntu Makān Mursī wa-Qaᶜadtu ᶜalā l-Kursī*, 2012 (www.tawhed.ws/dl?i=24041354).

Abū Qatāda al-Filāsṭīnī, ᶜUmar b. Maḥmūd Abū ᶜUmar, *Juʾnat al-muṭayyabīn* (http://www.tawhed.ws/dl?i=y06fitvm).

Abū Qatāda al-Filasṭīnī, ᶜUmar b. Maḥmūd Abū ᶜUmar, *Li-mādhā al-jihād* (http://www.tawhed.ws/dl?i=yrvjtyr8).

ᶜAdnānī, Abū Muḥammad al-Shāmī al-, *Fa-qtulūhum innahum mushrikūn*, 15 June 2013 (https://archive.org/details/Qatelohom.Adnani).

ʿAdnānī, Abū Muḥammad al-Shāmī al-, *Mā kāna hādhā manhajanā wa-lan yakūna*, 17 April 2014 (https://www.youtube.com/watch?v=roUKoO1-3hc).

Ahmad, Munawar, 'Faith and Violence: The Islamic Sect Ahmadiyah Has Been Under Official Pressure and Violent Attack', *Inside Indonesia* (http://insideindonesia.org/content/view/14/29).

'Ala Hazrat Barelvi', *IstampGallery* (https://www.istampgallery.com/ala-hazrat-barelvi/).

al-Anṣārī, Abū al-Ḥārith, *Li-llāh daruk yā dawlat al-islām*, 2015 (https://top4top.io/downloadf-top4top_3d8b657fc31-pdf.html).

al-Atharī, Abū al-Zahrā, *al-Taḥqīq fī jawāz al-taḥrīq muʾāmalatan bi-l-mithl*, 16 August 2015 (https://justpaste.it/tahqiqtahrq).

Āl Farāj, Madḥat b. al-Ḥasan, *Muḥammad ʿAbd al-Maqṣūd wa-Muʿāraḍatuhu li-Man Yurīdu Taṭbīq al-Sharīʿa Fawran* (www.tawhed.ws/dl?i=20081211).

Al-Haj, Ahmed, 'Yemen: 44 Killed in Clashes with al-Qāʿida Fighters', *washingtontimes.com*, 9 April 2012 (https://www.washingtontimes.com/news/2012/apr/9/yemen-23-killed-clashes-al-qaeda-fighters/).

Al-Hayat Al-Jadida (Palestinian), 22 January 2006.

Ali, Kecia, 'ISIS and Authority', 24 February 2015 (www.feminismandreligion.com/2015/02/24/isis-and-authority-by-kecia-ali.amp).

Ali, Kecia, 'Redeeming Slavery: The "Islamic State" and the Quest for Islamic Morality', 27 September 2016 (www.mizanproject.org/journal-post/redeeming-slavery/).

ʿĀmilī, Abū Saʿd al-, *Aḍwāʾ wa-Bayānāt Sharʿiyya ḥawla l-Thawratayni l-Lībiyya wa-l-Sūriyya 2: Al-Thawra al-Sūriyya*, 2011 (www.tawhed.ws/dl?i=28111103).

ʿAshūsh, Aḥmad, *Al-Ḥujja wa-l-Burhān ʿalā Ḥurmat Dukhūl al-Barlamān* (www.tawhed.ws/dl?i=12041207).

ʿAshūsh, Aḥmad, *Hidāyat al-Ḥīrān ilā Ḥurmat Sulūk Ṭarīq al-Dustūr wa-l-Barlamān* (www.tawhed.ws/dl?i=12041208).

ʿAshūsh, Aḥmad, *Iʿlām al-Muslimīn bi-Ḥaqīqat al-Dustūr wa-l-Qawānīn* (www.tawhed.ws/dl?i=24041367).

ʿAshūsh, Aḥmad, *Ḥizb al-Nūr bayna l-Islām wa-l-Jāhiliyya al-Ūrubiyya*, 2011 (www.tawhed.ws/dl?i=13121108).

Atharī, Abū Humām Bakr b. ʿAbd al-ʿAzīz al-, *Al-Ijābāt al-Sarīʿa fī l-Intiṣār li-Anṣār al-Sharīʿa*, 2012 (www.tawhed.ws/dl?i=12041206).

Atharī, Abū Humām Bakr b. ʿAbd al-ʿAzīz al-, *Al-Mukhtaṣar fī Ḥukm al-Taṣwīt ʿalā Dustūr Maṣr* [sic!], 2012 (www.tawhed.ws/dl?i=28011301).

Atharī, Abū Humām Bakr b. ʿAbd al-ʿAzīz al-, *Hal Muḥammad Ḥassān wa-Muḥammad ʿAbd al-Maqṣūd min Shuyūkh al-Ḍalāla?*, no. 5247, 2012 (www.tawhed.ws/FAQ/pr?qid=5247).

Azdī, Abū l-Ḥasan al-, *Al-Tajliya wa-l-Naqḍ li-Mudrik Qawl Majīz al-Taṣwīt li-l-Dustūr*, 2012 (www.tawhed.ws/dl?i=24041368).

Binʿalī, Abū Sufyān Turkī b. Mubārak, *al-Shaykhī al-asbaq hādhā firāq baynī wa-baynaka*, 2014/1435 (https://twitter.com/turky_albinali/status/475360106717413376).

Al-Binʿalī, Turkī, *Fatāwā ʿabar al-athīr* (www.archive.org/details/alsulami2/فتاوى+عبر+الاثير+الشيخ+تركي+البنعلي+الحلقة+التاسعة).

Bulaydī, Abū l-Ḥasan Rashīd al-, *Risāla Maftūḥa ilā l-Muslimīn fī Lībiyā*, 2011 (www.tawhed./dl?i=28111118).

Bunzel, Cole, 'Jihadism's Widening Internal Divide: Intellectual Infighting Heats Up', *Jihadica.com*, posted 29 January 2013 (www.jihadica.com/jihadism's-widening-internal-divide-intellectual-infighting-heats-up/).

Bunzel, Cole, 'The Islamic State of Disunity: Jihadism Divided', *Jihadica.com*, posted 30 January 2013 (www.jihadica.com/the-islamic-state-of-disunity-jihadism-divided/).
Bunzel, Cole, 'The Islamic State of Disobedience: Al-Baghdadi's Defiance', *Jihadica.com*, posted 5 October 2013 (www.jihadica.com/the-islamic-state-of-disobedience-al-baghdadis-defiance/).
Bunzel, Cole, 'Caliphate Now: Jihadis Debate the Islamic State', *Jihadica.com*, posted 25 November 2013 (www.jihadica.com/caliphate-now-jihadis-debate-the-islamic-state/).
Bunzel, Cole, 'The Caliphate's Scholar-in-Arms', *Jihadica.com*, 9 July 2014 (jihadica.com/the-caliphate's-scholar-in-arms/).
Bunzel, Cole, 'From Paper State to Caliphate: The Ideology of the Islamic State', *Brookings Foundation: U.S. Relations with the Muslim World, No. 19*, March 2015 (www.brookings.edu/research/from-paper-state-to-caliphate-the-ideology-of-the-islamic-state/).
Butcher, T., 'Hamas Offers Deal if Israel Pulls Out', *The Telegraph*, 9 February 2006 (http://www.telegraph.co.uk/news/worldnews/middleeast/israel/1510074/Hamas-offers-deal-if-Israel-pulls-out.html).
Callimachi, Rukmini, 'ISIS Enshrines a Theology of Rape', 13 August 2015 (nytimes.com/2015/08/14/world/middleeast/isis-enshrines-a-theology-of-rape.amp.html).
Caron, James, 'Review of 'Poetry of the Taliban' by Alex Strick van Linschoten and Felix Kuehn', *jadaliyya.com*, 27 May 2012 (www.jadaliyya.com/Details/26082/Poetry-of-the-Taliban).
Cetorelli, Valeria, and Sareta Ashraph, 'A Demographic Documentation of ISIS's Attack on the Yazidi Village of Kocho', LSE Middle East Reports, 2019 (http://eprints.lse.ac.uk/101098/).
Cordesman, Anthony H., 'Iraq's Sunni Insurgents: Looking Beyond Al Qa'ida', *Center for Strategic & International Studies*, 16 July 2007 (https://csis-prod.s3.amazonaws.com/s3fs-public/legacy_files/files/media/csis/pubs/070716_sunni_insurgents.pdf).
Cordesman, Anthony H., 'The "Rise" of Al Qaeda in Iraq and the Threat from Prime Minister Maliki', *Center for Strategic and International Studies Comment*, 13 January 2014 (https://www.csis.org/analysis/%E2%80%9Crise%E2%80%9D-al-qaeda-iraq-and-threat-prime-minister-maliki).
Cornevin, Christophe, 'L'inquiétant profil des djihadistes français en Syrie', *lefigaro.fr*, 13 September 2013 (https://www.lefigaro.fr/actualite-france/2013/09/13/01016-20130913ARTFIG00554-volontaires-francais-en-syrie-le-casse-tete-du-renseignement.php).
Davis, Eric, 'Is Muqtada al-Sadr the New Kingmaker in Iraqi Politics', *The New Middle East Blogspot*, 31 July 2012 (http://new-middle-east.blogspot.co.uk/2012/07/is-muqtada-al-sadr-new-kingmaker-in.html/).
Al-Dayel, Nadia, Andrew Mumford and Kevin Bales, 'Not Yet Dead: The Establishment and Regulation of Slavery by the Islamic State', *Studies in Conflict and Terrorism*, 2020 (doi.org/10.1080/1057610x.2020.1711590).
Dettmer, Jamie, 'Egypt's Newest Jihadists: The Jamal Network', *thedailybeast.com*, 13 January 2013 (https://www.thedailybeast.com/egypts-newest-jihadists-the-jamal-network).
Diwān al-Daʿwa wa-l-Masājid, 'Qissat mujāhid: al-duktūra Īmān Muṣṭafā al-Bughā', 24 August 2016 (http://www.aymennjawad.org/19132/the-archivist-stories-of-the-mujahideen-unseen).
El-Tahir El-Mesawi, Mohamed, 'Religion, Society, and Culture in Malik Bennabi's Thought', in *The Blackwell Companion to Contemporary Islamic Thought*, ed. Ibrahim M. Abu-

Rabi (Blackwell Publishing, 2006), Blackwell Reference Online, 2 August 2013 (https://onlinelibrary.wiley.com/doi/10.1002/9780470996188.ch13).

Fahmy, Mohamed Fadel, 'Egyptian Fighters Join "Lesser Jihad" in Syria', *al-monitor.com*, 17 April 2013 (https://www.al-monitor.com/pulse/originals/2013/04/egyptians-lesser-jihad-syria-fighting.html).

al-Filasṭīnī, Abū Qatāda, *Thiyāb al-khalīfa*, 23 August 2016 (https://archive.org/details/thiyab-alkhalifa, 1435/2014).

Ganor, B., 'Countering Hamas', Phase III in the War on Terrorism? Challenges and Opportunities', *Brookings Institute*, 2003 (http://www.brookings.edu/~/media/events/2003/5/14middleeast/summary20030514.pdf).

Gartenstein-Ross, David, 'A Momentous Month', *Atlantic Council*, 5 August 2013 (https://www.atlanticcouncil.org/blogs/new-atlanticist/a-momentous-month/).

Ghannoushi, R., 'What is New About al-Qaradawi's Fiqh of Jihad', June 2008, (http://zulkiflihasan.files.wordpress.com/2008/06/jihad-in-islam-by-qaradawi.pdf).

al-Gharīb, Abu Usāma, *al-Mukhtaṣar al-jalī bi-sīrat shaykhnā Turkī al-Binᶜalī*, 4 October 2013 (https://archive.org/details/almokhtasar.algali.high).

Giraud, Pierre-Marie, 'Swelling Ranks of European Fighters in Syria Sparks Concern', *yourmiddleeast.com*, 23 January 2014 (https://yourmiddleeast.com/2014/page/371/).

Gonzales, Paule, 'Le recrutement de jeunes djihadistes pour la Syrie, c'est l'usine', *lefigaro.com*, 17 January 2014 (https://www.lefigaro.fr/actualite-france/2014/01/17/01016-20140117ARTFIG00245-un-expert-le-recrutement-de-jeunes-djihadistes-pour-la-syrie-c-est-l-usine.php).

Hamas Charter, 1988, Article 13 (http://avalon.law.yale.edu/20th_century/hamas.asp).

Ḥiwār maᶜa al-shaykh Abī Muḥammad al-Maqdisī sanat 1423 (http://www.tawhed.ws/dl?i=j37307wg).

al-Ḥusaynī, ᶜAbdullāh b. Aḥmad, *Wa-lā yawm al-ṭīn*, 2015 (http://www.ilmway.com/site/maqdis/MS_7665).

Ibn Bashīr, Musāᶜid, *Masʾalat al-taḥrīq bi-l-nār*, 7 May 2015 (https://www.noor-book.com/كتاب-مساله-التحريق-بالنار-pdf).

Ibn Maḥmūd, Ḥusayn, *Bal la-kum fī-l-ḥarq salaf*, 11 April 2004 (https://justpaste.it/j8bt).

Ibn Maḥmūd, Ḥusayn, *Masʾalat al-*ḥarq, 5 February 2015 (https://justpaste.it/j9fp).

International Crisis Group, 'Iraq's Shīᶜites Under Occupation', *Middle East Briefing*, 9 September 2003 (https://www.crisisgroup.org/middle-east-north-africa/gulf-and-arabian-peninsula/iraq/iraqs-shiites-under-occupation).

International Crisis Group, 'Iraq's Muqtada al-Sadr: Spoiler or Stabilizer?', *Middle East Report* 55, 11 July 2006 (https://www.crisisgroup.org/iraq-s-muqtada-al-sadr-spoiler-or-stabiliser).

Jabhat al-Nuṣra, *Nubdha ᶜammā naᶜtaqiduhu wa-nadīnu llāha bihi – al-Manāra al-Bayḍāʾ*, 2014 (https://twitter.com/JabhtAnNusrah/status/438393864190033920).

Jalāl al-Dīn Abū l-Futūḥ, *Al-Fiqh al-Dīmuqrāṭī*, 2012 (www.tawhed.ws/dl?i=12041240).

Kagan, Frederick W., 'Yemen Crisis Situation Report', *Critical Threat Project Reports*, 29 June 2011 (https://www.criticalthreats.org/briefs/yemen-situation-report/2011-yemen-crisis-situation-report-june-29).

Kaviraj, Sudipta, 'Post-colonial State' (https://criticalencounters.net/2009/01/19/the-post-colonial-state-sudipta-kaviraj/).

Khairabadi, Fazle Haq Allama, Noori Foundation (http://noorifoundation.com/index.php?option=com_content&view=article&id=131:allama-fazle-haq-convention-at-jamia-millia-islamia-university-new-delhi&catid=11:news-flashes).

Khairabadi, Fazle Haq Allama, Seminar in Bhiwandi Mumbai by MSO of India (http://sunninews.wordpress.com/2012/01/31/allama-fazle-haq-khairabadi-seminar-in-bhiwandi-mumbai-by-mso-of-india).

al-Khilāfa, Afdī Dawlat, *Ḥawl iḥrāq al ḥāriq!*, 2015 (https://islamicstatecaliphate.blogspot.com/2015/03/blog-post_46.html).

kutub jihādiyya nādira bushrā (http://www.startimes.com/?t=15346170).

Lahoud, Nelly (with Muhammad al-'Ubaydi), 'Jihadi Discourse in the Wake of the Arab Spring', *Combatting Terrorism Center Reports*, December 2013 (https://ctc.usma.edu/jihadi-discourse-in-the-wake-of-the-arab-spring/).

Landay, Jonathan S., 'US Officials: Al Qaida Behind Syria Bombings', *mcclatchydc.com*, 10 February 2012 (https://www.mcclatchydc.com/news/nation-world/world/article24723991.html).

al-Lībī, Abū Yaḥyā, *Ilā Ahlinā fī Lībiyā*, 2011 (www.tawhed.ws/dl?i=30081117).

al-Lībī, Abū Yaḥyā, *Maʾāsī l-Shām bayna Ijrām al-Nuṣayriyya wa-Makāʾid al-Gharb*, 2012 (www.tawhed.ws/dl?i=24041307).

Lynch, M., 'Qaradawi's Revisions', *Foreign Policy*, 9 July 2009 (http://www.foreignpolicy.com/posts/2009/07/09/qaradawis_revisions).

al-Maktab al-Iᶜlāmī, 'Arāʾ al-muslimān bi-ḥarq al-ṭayyār al-urdunī', 16 February 2015 (https://archive.org/details/w.homs.araa.mouslimen.harq.tayyar.original.quality).

al-Maktab al-Iᶜlāmī, 'Farḥat al-muslimīn bi-ḥarq al-ṭayyār al-urdunī', 6 May 2015 (https://archive.org/details/oma_222_mail_050).

al-Maktab al-Iᶜlāmī, 'Fa-ᶜāqabū bi-mithl mā ᶜawqabtum bi-hi', 31 August 2015 (https://archive.org/details/jamalalqudsy_yahoo_20160618_1529).

al-Maktab al-Iᶜlāmī , 'Dirᶜ al-ṣalīb', 22 December 2016 (https://archive.org/details/goolf_printf_20190228_0622).

Malik, I., 'Jihad and its Development and Relevance, the Meaning and Importance of Jihadi in Islamic Thought', *Palestine-Israel Journal* 1.2 (1994) (http://www.pij.org/details.php?id=741).

Maqdisī Abū Muḥammad al-, *Dīmuqrāṭiyya Dīn* (www.tawhed.ws/dl?i=mo5o2fpb).

Maqdisī Abū Muḥammad al-, *Ḥiwār al-shaykh Abī Muḥammad al-Maqdisī maᶜa majallat al-ᶜaṣr*, 1423 AH (http://www.tawhed.ws/dl?i=j37307wg).

Maqdisī Abū Muḥammad al-, *Aḥdhiyat al-Mūsād [2]*, 2013 (www.tawhed.ws/dl?i=02111301).

Maqdisī Abū Muḥammad al-, *Al-Inṣāf Ḥillat al-Ashrāf wa-l-Ashrāf Aqall al-Aṣnāf*, 2013 (www.tawhed.ws/r?i=23101301).

Maqdisī Abū Muḥammad al-, *Fawāʾid wa-ᶜIbar min al-Inqilāb ᶜalā Ṣanādīq al-Iqtirāᶜ fī Miṣr*, 2013 (www.tawhed.ws/r?i=21091301).

Maqdisī Abū Muḥammad al-, *Kashf al-Zukhruf wa-l-Buhtān fī Fatwā ᶜUlamāʾ al-Sulṭān*, 2013 (www.tawhed.ws/dl?i=30031301).

Maqdisī Abū Muḥammad al-, 'Risāla ʾilā amīr dawlat al-ᶜirāq wa-l-shām al-islāmiyya al-shaykh Abū Bakr al-Baghdādī', 7 February 2015 (https://alghad.com/نص-رسالة-المقدسي-للبغدادي-حول-الكساسب).

Maqdisī Abū Muḥammad al-, *Tabṣīr al-ᶜuqalāʾ bi-talbīsāt ahl al-tajahhum waʾl-irjāʾ* (http://www.tawhed.ws/r?i=2mianrha).

Marx, Karl, *The Eighteenth Brumaire of Louis Bonaparte* (marxists.org/archive/marx/works/1852/18th-brumaire/ch01.htm).

Masīr, Ṭalḥa Muḥammad al-, *Al-Barāʾa min al-Tanāzulāt allatī Tuqaddimuhā Salafiyyat al-Iskandariyya* (www.tawhed.ws/dl?i=24041302).

Meleagrou-Hitchens, Alexander, 'As American as Apple Pie: How Anwar al-Awlaki Became the Face of Western Jihad', *International Centre for the Study of Radicalisation and Political Violence Policy Reports*, September 2011 (https://icsr.info/2011/09/11/as-american-as-apple-pie-how-anwar-al-awlaki-became-the-face-of-western-jihad/).

Meshal, Khaled, 'We Will Not Sell Our People or Principles for Foreign Aid', *The Guardian*, 31 January 2006, (http://www.theguardian.com/world/2006/jan/31/comment.israelandthepalestinians).

Miṣrī, Abū Ayman al-, *Suʾāl wa-Jawāb Ḥukm Dukhūl al-Aḥzāb li-Maṣlaḥat Taṭbīq al-Sharīᶜa*, 2012 (www.tawhed.ws/dl?i=08021208).

Miṣrī, Ḥāzim al-, *Al-Īḍāḥ li-Mā fī l-Dustūr al-Jadīd min al-Kufr al-Bawāḥ* (www.tawhed.ws/dl?i=24041374).

Mukhashaf, Mohammed, 'Qaeda-linked Militants Kill at Least 20 Yemeni Soldiers', *reuters.com*, 31 March 2012 (https://www.reuters.com/article/us-yemen-militants/qaeda-linked-militants-kill-at-least-20-yemeni-soldiers-idUSBRE82U07920120331).

Muʾsassat al-Ajnād, 'Qarīban qarībā', 9 May 2015 (https://archive.org/details/Qariba-234).

Muʾsassat al-Furqān, 'Shifaʾ al-ṣudūr', 28 December 2015 (https://archive.org/details/islamicstate93_20151228_2339).

al-Naṣr, Aḥlām, *Bal ʾaṭᶜanā allāh idh aḥraqanāhu ya ᶜabīda al-rafāhiyya*, 13 February 2015 (https://justpaste.it/je3o).

Porter, Tom, 'UK Jihadists Join Fight in Iraq', *ibtimes.com*, 12 January 2014 (https://www.ibtimes.co.uk/uk-jihadists-join-fight-iraq-video-1431986).

Qāsim, Ṭalᶜat Fuʾād, *Al-Adilla al-Naqliyya wa-l-ᶜAqliyya ᶜalā Ḥurmat Dukhūl al-Majālis al-Tashrīᶜiyya*, 2012 (www.tawhed.ws/dl?i=20081202).

Qunaybī, Iyād, *Al-Iṣrār ᶜalā l-Dīmuqrāṭiyya Ḥattā l-Mawt! Durūs min Aḥdāth Miṣr 1*, 2013 (http://twitmail.com/email/532700952/144/1).

Qunaybī, Iyād, *Ayyuhā l-'Islāmiyyūn bi-Miṣr*, 2013 (http://twitmail.com/email/532700952/151/).

Qunaybī, Iyād, *Daᶜwat Muᶜāriḍī Muḥammad Mursī ilā Ittiḥād Mawqif Sharīf min Khiṭāb al-Sīsī*, 2013 (http://twitmail.com/email/532700952/156/).

Qunaybī, Iyād, *Mā Hakadhā Tunāqishu Hadhihi l-Qaḍāyā l-Maṣīriyya Yā Ustādh Ḥāzim*, 2013 (http://twitmail.com/fullview/331990).

Qunaybī, Iyād, *Mawqif baᶜḍ Mashāyikh al-Salafiyya min al-Jaysh*, 2013 (http://twitmail.com/email/532700952/157/).

Qunaybī, Iyād, *Mawqif min 'Ḥizb al-Nūr'*, 2013 (http://twitmail.com/email/532700952/134/).

Qunaybī, Iyād, *Risāla li-l-Ustādh Ḥāzim Ṣalāḥ bi-Khuṣūṣ Inshāʾ Ḥizb Yumārisu l-ᶜAmal al-Barlamānī*, 2013 (http://twitmail.com/fullview/331778).

Rahimi, Babak, 'The Discourse of Democracy in Shīᶜi Islamic Jurisprudence: The Two Cases of Montazeri and Sistani', *Robert Schuman Centre For Advanced Studies: Mediterranean Programme Series* (European University Institute Working Paper) (https://cadmus.eui.eu/handle/1814/8223).

Ramsey, Stuart, 'Syria: Sky News Gains Access to UK Jihadists', *news.sky.com*, 18 December 2013 (https://news.sky.com/story/syria-sky-news-gains-access-to-uk-jihadists-10424251).

Rasāʾil min arḍ al-malāḥim 15, 2013 (Muʾassasat al-Furqān, https://archive.org/details/risala-15).

Revkin, *The Legal Foundations of the Islamic State*, Brookings Foundation: U.S. Relations with the Muslim World, No. 26, July 2016 (www.brookings.edu/wp-content/uploads/2016/07/brookings-analysis-paper_mara-revkin_web_v2.pdf).

Roth, Kenneth, 'Slavery: The ISIS Rules', 24 September 2015 (www.hrw.org/news/2015/09/05/slavery-isis-rules).

Rovera, Donatella, 'Testimonies from Kocho: The Village ISIS Tried to Wipe Off the Map', 18 August 2018 (wwwamnesty.org/en/latest/news/2014/08/testimonies-from-kocho-the-village-isis-tried-to-wipe-off-the-map/).

Ṣādiq al-Ṣadr, Muḥammad, Excerpt of Last Sermon, al-Kūfah, (https://www.youtube.com/watch?v=_BnGw23Xsk4).

Ṣādiq al-Ṣadr, Muḥammad Muḥammad, *liqāʾ al-ḥanānah* (https://www.youtube.com/watch?v=jjGGU5qat0o).

Ṣadr, Muqtadā al-, Friday Sermon, *al-Kūfah* (http://www.youtube.com/watch?v=GuorfcqfqHg).

Ṣadr, Muqtadā al-, Speech: al-ᶜImārah (http://www.youtube.com/watch?v=-oLwlNdKS8Y).

Ṣadr, Muqtadā al-, *Tajmīd Jaysh al-Mahdī*, 22 February 2008 (http://www.manhajalsadren.com/almakalat/2008/02/030.htm).

Shinqīṭī, Abū l-Mundhir al-, *Al-Radd ᶜalā Fatwā l-Shaykh Muḥammad al-Maqṣūd bi-Khuṣūṣ al-Intikhābāt*, no. 5018, 2011 (www.tawhed.ws/FAQ/pr?qid=5018).

Shinqīṭī, Abū l-Mundhir al-, *Hal Yajūzu Waṣf al-Shaykhayn Muḥammad ᶜAbd al-Maqṣūd wa-Muḥammad Ḥassān bi-Mashāyikh al-Ḍalāla[?]*, no. 5098, 2011 (www.tawhed.ws/FAQ/pr?qid=5098).

Shinqīṭī, Abū l-Mundhir al-, *Ḥukm al-muntaḥir ashᶜal al-nār fī nafsihi*, 2011 (http://www.ilmway.com/site/maqdis/FAQ/MS_6354.html).

Shinqīṭī, Abū l-Mundhir al-, *Lā Nisāʾ fī Mīdān al-Taḥrīr!*, 2011 (www.tawhed.ws/r?i=20121101).

Shinqīṭī, Abū l-Mundhir al-, *Mā Taᶜlīqukum ᶜalā Kalām al-Shaykh Abī Baṣīr Ḥawla Tarashshuḥ al-Shaykh Ḥāzim Abū Ismāᶜīl li-Riʾāsat al-Jumhūriyya fī Miṣr?*, no. 5624, 2011 (www.tawhed.ws/FAQ/pr?qid=5624).

Shinqīṭī, Abū l-Mundhir al-, *Al-Inḥirāfāt al-Shanīᶜa li-Muntaqid Anṣār al-Sharīᶜa*, 2012 (www.tawhed.ws/dl?i=28051208).

Shinqīṭī, Abū l-Mundhir al-, *Hal Ākhudhu Ahlī*; *id.*, *Hal Uᶜayyilu Wālidī wa-Ahlī am Atrukuhum wa-Ujāhidu?*, no. 6909, 2012 (www.tawhed.ws/FAQ/pr?qid=6909).

Shinqīṭī, Abū l-Mundhir al-, *Hal Ākhudhu Ahlī maᶜī ilā Arḍ al-Jihād?*, no. 6921, 2012 (www.tawhed.ws/FAQ/pr?qid=6921).

Shinqīṭī, Abū l-Mundhir al-, *Hal Anfuru ilā Sūriya wa-Wālidatī fī Muddat al-ᶜIdda?*, no. 6990, 2012 (www.tawhed.ws/FAQ/pr?qid=6990).

Shinqīṭī, Abū l-Mundhir al-, *Hal Astaʾdhinu Aḥadan fī l-Nafīr min Miṣr ilā Sūriyā?*, no. 6479, 2012 (www.tawhed.ws/FAQ/pr?qid=6479).

Shinqīṭī, Abū l-Mundhir al-, *Hal Yaḥtāju l-Ikhwa fī Sūriyā ilā Sawād? Wa-Hal Yataᶜayyanu l-Nafīr ilayhim ᶜalā Kull Aḥad?*, no. 6889, 2012 (www.tawhed.ws/FAQ/pr?qid=6889).

Shinqīṭī, Abū l-Mundhir al-, *Hal Yajibu l-Nafīr ilā l-Shām ᶜalā Kull Qādir?*, no. 6837, 2012 (www.tawhed.ws/FAQ/pr?qid=6837).

Shinqīṭī, Abū l-Mundhir al-, *Hal Yajūzu lanā An Nastahdifa Madrasa Yarᶜāhā l-Niẓām li-Tajnīd Ṭalabatihā li-l-Dukhūl li-Jayshihi baᶜda An Yanhū Dirāsatahum?*, no. 7618, 2012 (www.tawhed.ws/FAQ/display_question?qid=7618&pageqa=1&i=).

Shinqīṭī, Abū l-Mundhir al-, *Hal Yajūzu lī An Anfadha ᶜAmaliyya Istishhādiyya fī Tajammuᶜāt Ḥizb Allāh al-Rāfiḍī?*, no. 7485, 2012 (www.tawhed.ws/FAQ/pr?qid=7485).

Shinqīṭī, Abū l-Mundhir al-, *Hal Yajūzu Qatl al-Rawāfiḍ al-ghayr Muqātilīn mimman Yaṭᶜunūna fī l-Ṣaḥāba wa-Yasīʾūna ilā Ahl al-Sunna?*, no. 6845, 2012 (www.tawhed.ws/FAQ/pr?qid=6845).

Shinqīṭī, Abū l-Mundhir al-, *Hal Yashraᶜu li-l-Ikhwa fī Lībiyā l-Inḍimām ilā Wizārat al-Dākhiliyya wa-Tawallī Wizārāt Ukhrā bi-Ḥujjat ᶜadam Taslīmihā li-l-Mufsidīn wa-l-Mur* [sic!], no. 6341, 2012 (www.tawhed.ws/FAQ/pr?qid=6341).

Shinqīṭī, Abū l-Mundhir al-, *Hal Yashraᶜu Taʾyīd Mursī fī l-Qarārāt al-Dustūriyya al-Akhīra?*, no. 6938, 2012 (www.tawhed.ws/FAQ/pr?qid=6938).

Shinqīṭī, Abū l-Mundhir al-, *Hal Yataᶜayyanu l-Jihād ᶜalā Man ᶜalayhi Dayn?*, no. 6926, 2012 (www.tawhed.ws/FAQ/pr?qid=6926).

Shinqīṭī, Abū l-Mundhir al-, *Hal Yumkinu An Ujāhidu maᶜa l-Mujāhidīn dūna l-Iltizām bi-l-Bayᶜa?*,no.6304,2012(www.tawhed.ws/FAQ/display_question?qid=6304&pageqa=1&i=).

Shinqīṭī, Abū l-Mundhir al-, *Hal Yuᶜtabaru ᶜUḍw al-Barlamān alladhī Yuᶜlinu Annahu Lan Yashraᶜu Ḥukman Mukhālifan li-l-Sharīᶜa.. Hal Yuᶜtabaru Musharriᶜan min dūna llāh? Wa-Shibh* [sic!], no. 632, 2013 (www.tawhed.ws/FAQ/pr?qid=6323).

Shinqīṭī, Abū l-Mundhir al-, *Ḥukm al-Qurʾān fī Duwaylāt al-Ikhwān*, 2012 (www.tawhed.ws/dl?i=12041202).

Shinqīṭī, Abū l-Mundhir al-, *Kayfa Yanbaghī li-l-Ikhwa fī Tūnis al-Taṣarruf maᶜa Niẓām al-Ḥukm al-Jadīd?*, no. 6370, 2012 (www.tawhed.ws/FAQ/pr?qid=6370).

Shinqīṭī, Abū l-Mundhir al-, *Maᶜa Ayy al-Jamāᶜāt Nuqātilu fī Sūriyā? Wa-Hal Yajibu l-Khurūj Dūna Idhn al-Waladayni wa-Aṣḥāb al-Dayn?*, no. 6080, 2012 (www.tahwed.ws/FAQ/pr?qid=6080).

Shinqīṭī, Abū l-Mundhir al-, *Maᶜa Ayy al-Jamāᶜāt*; *id.*, *Mā Ḥukm al-Jihād al-Yawm fī Sūriyā li-Waḥīd Wālidatihi?*, no. 6392, 2012 (www.tawhed.ws/FAQ/pr?qid=6392).

Shinqīṭī, Abū l-Mundhir al-, *Mā Ḥukm al-ᶜAmal Mudarris Jughrāfiyā aw Muhandis Zirāᶜī ᶜinda Dawlat Bashār?*, no. 6393, 2012 (www.tawhed.ws/FAQ/pr?qid=6393).

Shinqīṭī, Abū l-Mundhir al-, *Mā Ḥukm al-ᶜAsākir al-Miṣriyyīn?*, no. 6344, 2012 (www.tawhed.ws/FAQ/pr?qid=6344).

Shinqīṭī, Abū l-Mundhir al-, *Mā Ḥukm al-Dukhūl fī l-Aḥzāb al-Islāmiyya (al-Nūr wa-l-Faḍīla) min Ajl al-Muṭālaba bi-Inshāʾ Dustūr Islāmī?*, no. 4855, 2012 (www.tawhed.ws/FAQ/pr?qid=4855).

Shinqīṭī, Abū l-Mundhir al-, *Mā Ḥukm al-Khurūj li-l-Jihād Khārij Lībiyā bi-l-Nisba li-l-Ikhwa fī Lībiyā?*, no. 6339, 2012 (www.tawhed.ws/FAQ/pr?qid=6339).

Shinqīṭī, Abū l-Mundhir al-, *Mā Ḥukm al-Mushāraka fī l-Intikhābāt bayna Mursī wa-Shafīq aw li-Ibṭāl al-Ṣawt*, no. 6442, 2012 (www.tawhed.ws/FAQ/pr?qid=6442).

Shinqīṭī, Abū l-Mundhir al-, *Mā Ḥukm Istihdāf al-Ṭawāʾif ghayr al-Muslima al-Musālima fī Sūriyā?*, no. 6360, 2012 (www.tawhed.ws).

Shinqīṭī, Abū l-Mundhir al-, *Mā Huwa l-Mawqif al-Sharᶜī min Najāḥ Mursī fī Miṣr?*, no. 6535, 2012 (www.tawhed.ws/FAQ/pr?qid=6535).

Shinqīṭī, Abū l-Mundhir al-, *Mā Huwa Raddukum ᶜalā Shubhat al-Mushāraka fī l-Intikhābāt bi-Ḥujjat Irtikāb Akhaff al-Ḍararayn?*, no. 5829, 2012 (www.tawhed.ws/FAQ/pr?qid=5829).

Shinqīṭī, Abū l-Mundhir al-, *Mā Huwa Taᶜlīqukum ᶜalā Fatwā l-Shaykh al-Barrāk Ḥawla l-Dustūr al-Miṣrī?*, no. 6985, 2012 (www.tawhed.ws/FAQ/display_question?qid=6985).

Shinqīṭī, Abū l-Mundhir al-, *Mā l-Radd ᶜalā Hadhihi l-Shubhāt li-ᶜAdad min al-Salafiyyīn al-Dīmuqrāṭiyyīn fī Miṣr*, no. 6331, 2012 (www.tawhed.ws/FAQ/pr?qid=6331).

Shinqīṭī, Abū l-Mundhir al-, *Qitāl al-Nuṣayriyya Farḍ ᶜAyn ᶜalā l-Muslimīn*, 2012 (www.tawhed.ws/dl?i=24041384).

Shinqīṭī, Abū l-Mundhir al-, *Urīdu al-Dhahāb li-l-Jihād wa-Abawāya Yuᶜāriḍāni.. Fa-Mādhā Afᶜalu?*, no. 6942, 2012 (www.tawhed.ws/FAQ/pr?qid=6942).

Shinqīṭī, Abū l-Mundhir al-, *ᶜAlayya Dayn li-Kāfir Lā Astaṭīᶜu Sadādahu l-Ān, fa-Hal lī An Anfura li-l-Jihād?*, no. 7376, 2013 (www.tawhed.ws/FAQ/display_question?qid=7376&pageqa=1&i=).

Shinqīṭī, Abū l-Mundhir al-, *Amaranā Amīrunā Fī Sāḥat al-Jihād bi-Tark al-Ṣulbān fī l-Kanāʾis.. Fa-Hal Nuṭīᶜuhu?*, no. 7101, 2013 (www.tawhed.ws/FAQ/pr?qid=7101).

Shinqīṭī, Abū l-Mundhir al-, *Fuṣūl fī l-Imāma wa-l-Bayᶜa*, 2013 (www.tawhed.ws/dl?i=28121305).

Shinqīṭī, Abū l-Mundhir al-, *Hal al-Ūlā l-Jihād fī Sūriyā am al-Daᶜwa fī Arḍ Tūnis wa-Qad Katharat fīhā l-Fitan?*, no. 7141, 2013 (www.tawhed.ws/FAQ/pr?qid=7141).

Shinqīṭī, Abū l-Mundhir al-, *Hal Ifshāʾ al-Salām ᶜalā l-Kāfir li-Ḍarūra Yaᶜtabiru Amān?*, no. 7467, 2013 (www.tawhed.ws/FAQ/display_question?qid=7467).

Shinqīṭī, Abū l-Mundhir al-, *Hal Taᶜtabiru l-Asliḥa allatī Naʾkhudhuhā min al-Nuṣayriyyīn Ghanīma? Wa-Hal Yajūzu Qatl al-Aṭfāl wa-l-Nisāʾ al-Nuṣayriyyīn?*, no. 7167, 2013 (www.tawhed.ws/FAQ/pr?qid=7167, 2013).

Shinqīṭī, Abū l-Mundhir al-, *Hal Uhājiru li-l-Jihād am Abqā fī Bilād al-Gharb wa-Ujāhidu fīhā?*, no. 7128, 2013 (www.tawhed.ws/FAQ/pr?qid=7128).

Shinqīṭī, Abū l-Mundhir al-, *Hal Yajūzu lanā Qatl Ayy Naṣrānī fī Baladatinā li-Anna Aḥadahum Qatala Musliman minnā?*, no. 7076, 2013 (www.tawhed.ws/FAQ/pr?qid=7076).

Shinqīṭī, Abū l-Mundhir al-, *Hal Yajūzu lī Sharᶜan An Uʾakhkhira l-Nafīr ila An Atakhaṣṣaṣa fī Majāl Muᶜayyan?*, no. 7005, 2013 (www.tawhed.ws/FAQ/pr?qid=7005).

Shinqīṭī, Abū l-Mundhir al-, *Hal Yajūzu l-Tashaffī bi-Muʾayyidī l-Niẓām al-Sūrī lladhīna Yuṣābūna bi-l-Maṣāʾib? Wa-Mā Ḥukm al-Takhalluf ᶜan Arḍ al-Jihād li-Mutābaᶜat Shuʾū* [sic!], no. 7110, 2013 (www.tawhed.ws/FAQ/pr?qid=7110).

Shinqīṭī, Abū l-Mundhir al-, *Hal Yaᶜtabiru Muḥammad Mursī Maᶜdhūr li-Annahu lā Yastaṭīᶜu An Yuṭabbiqa l-Sharīᶜa?*, no. 7344, 2013 (www.tawhed.ws/FAQ/pr?qid=7344).

Shinqīṭī, Abū l-Mundhir al-, *Jarāʾim al-Nahḍa fī Tūnis.. ilā Matā?*, 2013 (www.tawhed.ws/dl?i=28011302).

Shinqīṭī, Abū l-Mundhir al-, *Kayfa Yakūna Ikhlāṣ al-Niyya li-llāh fī l-Jihād? Wa-Hal Yaᶜtabiru l-Mujāhid alladhī Qutila fī l-Maᶜraka wa-Huwa Khāʾif min al-Mawt Shahīd?*, no. 7006, 2013 (www.tawhed.ws/FAQ/pr?qid=7006).

Shinqīṭī, Abū l-Mundhir al-, *Mādhā Yajibu An Yakūna Mawqifunā fī l-Aḥdāth al-Mutawaqqaᶜa fī Miṣr bi-Tārīkh 30 Yūniyū al-Qādim ḍidd al-Ikhwān?*, no. 7512, 2013 (www.tawhed.ws/FAQ/pr?qid=7512).

Shinqīṭī, Abū l-Mundhir al-, *Mā Ḥukm al-Inḍimām il;a Riʾāsat al-Arkān bi-Lībiyā bi-Ḥujjat Akhdh al-Māl ᶜIlman Annahu Yalzamu Baytahu wa-Lā Yaḥḍuru?*, no. 7116, 2013 (www.tawhed.ws/FAQ/pr?qid=7116).

Shinqīṭī, Abū l-Mundhir al-, *Mā Ḥukm man Waḍaᶜa Dustūr Miṣr?*, no. 6967, 2013 (www.tawhed.ws/FAQ/pr?qid=6967).

Shinqīṭī, Abū l-Mundhir al-, *Mā Ḥukm Qiyām al-Ḥāmil bi-ᶜAmaliyya Istishhādiyya?*, no. 7176, 2013 (www.tawhed.ws/FAQ/pr?qid7176).

Shinqīṭī, Abū l-Mundhir al-, *Majmūᶜat Asʾila Ḥawla l-Nafīr (1)*, no. 7033, 2013 (www.tawhed.ws/FAQ/pr?qid=7033).

Shinqīṭī, Abū l-Mundhir al-, *Majmūᶜat Asʾila Ḥawla l-Nafīr (2)*, no. 7081, 2013 (www.tawhed.ws/FAQ/pr?qid=7081).

Shinqīṭī, Abū l-Mundhir al-, *Majmūᶜat Asʾila Ḥawla l-Nafīr (3)*, no. 7166, 2013 (www.tawhed.ws/FAQ/pr?qid=7166).

Shinqīṭī, Abū l-Mundhir al-, *Majmūᶜat As᾿ila Ḥawla l-Nafīr (4)*, no. 7157, 2013 (www.tawhed.ws/FAQ/pr?qid=7157).

Shinqīṭī, Abū l-Mundhir al-, *Majmūᶜat As᾿ila Ḥawla l-Nafīr (5)*, no. 7098, 2013 (www.tawhed.ws/FAQ/pr?qid=7098).

Shinqīṭī, Abū l-Mundhir al-, *Mā Ra᾿yukum bi-khtiṭāf al-Junūd fī Miṣr?*, no. 7461, 2013 (www.tawhed.ws/FAQ/pr?qid=7461).

Shinqīṭī, Abū l-Mundhir al-, *Mā Taᶜlīqātukum ᶜalā Kalām al-Shaykh ᶜAbd al-Qādir b. ᶜAbd al-ᶜAzīz fī Qanāt al-Jazīra?*, no. 7275, 2013 (www.tawhed.ws/FAQ/pr?qid=7275).

Shinqīṭī, Abū l-Mundhir al-, *Mā Taᶜlīqukum ᶜalā Fatwā l-Shaykh ᶜAbd al-ᶜAzīz al-Ṭurayfī Ḥafaẓahu llāh fīmā Yataᶜallaqu bi-l-Taswīt ᶜalā l-Dustūr al-Miṣrī?*, no. 7099, 2013 (www.tawhed.ws/FAQ/pr?qid=7099).

Shinqīṭī, Abū l-Mundhir al-, *Su᾿āl Ḥawla Qawla li-Mursī: Mafīsh* [sic!] *Farq bayna ᶜAqīdat al-Masīḥiyya wa-ᶜAqīdat al-Islāmiyya* [sic!], *Kull Yaᶜtaqidu bi-Man Yashā᾿u*, no. 6931, 2013 (www.tawhed.ws/FAQ/pr?qid=6931).

Shinqīṭī, Abū l-Mundhir al-,*ᶜIlān al-khilāfa fī-l-mīzān al-shar᾿ī*, 18 July 2014 (https://www.jihadica.com/wp-content/uploads/2014/07/إعلان-الخلافة-في-الميزان-الشرعي.pdf).

Shinqīṭī, Abū l-Mundhir al-, *Rafᶜ al-malām ᶜan junūd dawlat al-islām* (https://www.jihadica.com/wp-content/uploads/2014/07/1رفع-الملام-عن-جنود-دولة-الإسلام.pdf).

Shinqīṭī, Abū l-Mundhir al-, *al-Hadī al-samaḥ fī ṭuruq al-qatl wa-l-dhabḥ*, 4 November 2014 (https://justpaste.it/alhady).

Shinqīṭī, Abū l-Mundhir al-, *Taḥqīq fī ḥurmat al-taḥrīq*, 4 September 2015 (https://jihadology.net/2015/09/04/majmuah-nukhbat-al-fikr-presents-a-new-release-from-shaykh-abu-al-mundhir-al-shinqiti-the-investigation-into-the-sanctity-of-burning).

Siddiqui, Sohaira, 'Experts Weigh In (Part 2): How Does ISIS Approach Islamic Scripture?', 26 March 2015 (www.brookings.edu/blog/markaz/2015/03/26/experts-weigh-in-part-2-how-does-isis-approach-islamic-scripture/amp/).

Siddiqui, Sohaira, 'Beyond Authenticity: ISIS and the Islamic Legal Tradition', 24 February 2016 (www.jadaliyya.com/details/31825/beyond-authenticity-isis-and-the-islamic-legal-tradition).

Sīstānī, Questions: Fox News to al-Sayyid al-Sīstānī, 23 October 2003 (http://www.sistani.org/local.php?modules=extra&eid=2&sid=22).

al-Ṣūmālī, Abū Sulaymān, *Nasb al-manjanīq li-naqḍ risālat al-Taḥqīq fī ḥurmat al-taḥrīq*, 28 September 2015 (https://archive.org/details/nasb_al-mnjnq).

Taghṭiya khāṣṣa li-khuṭba wa-ṣalāt al-jumᶜa fī᾿l-jāmiᶜ al-kabīr bi-madīnat Mawṣil, 5 July 2014 (Mu᾿assasat al-Furqān, https://twitter.com/al_e3tisam/status/485410559139909632).

Tahrali, Mustafa, 'A General Outline of the Influence of Ibn ᶜArabi on the Ottoman Era' (ibnarabisociety.org/influence-of-ibn-arabi-on-the-ottoman-era-mustafa-tahrali/).

Ṭarṭūsī, Abū Baṣīr al-, *Ḥukm al-Islām fī᾿l-dīmuqrāṭiyya wa᾿l-taᶜaddudiyya al-ḥizbiyya* (http://www.abubaseer.bizland.com/books/read/b1.doc, 1410/1990).

Ṭarṭūsī, Abū Baṣīr al-, *Al-Istiᶜmār al-Qarmaṭī al-Bāṭinī li-Sūriya wa-Sharᶜiyyat al-Difāᶜ ᶜan al-Nafs*, 2011 (www.tawhed.ws/r?i=30081101).

Ṭarṭūsī, Abū Baṣīr al-, *Bayān Nuṣra wa-Ta᾿yīd li-Iᶜlān Shurafā᾿ wa-Abṭāl ᶜAshā᾿ir Dayr al-Zūr*, 2011 (www.abubaseer.bizland.com/hadath/Read/hadath%2084.doc).

Ṭarṭūsī, Abū Baṣīr al-, *Fatwā ilā Ahl Sūriya*, 2011 (www.abubaseer.bizland.com/hadath/Read/hadath%2083.doc).

Ṭarṭūsī, Abū Baṣīr al-, *Ḥattā Yakūna l-Tamthīl ᶜĀdilan wa-Shāmilan*, 2011 (www.abubaseer.bizland.com/articles/read/a%20153.doc).

Ṭarṭūsī, Abū Baṣīr al-, *Kalimāt Akhuṣṣu bi-hā l-Ṭā'ifa al-Nuṣayriyya al-Musammāt bi-l-'ᶜAlawiyya'*, 2011 (www.abubaseer.bizland.com/refutation/read/F%20102.doc).

Ṭarṭūsī, Abū Baṣīr al-, *Kalimāt fī l-Siyāsa al-Sharᶜiyya Akhuṣṣu bihā Ahlanā fī Tūnis wa-Miṣr*, 2011 (www.tawhed.ws/r?i=30081106).

Ṭarṭūsī, Abū Baṣīr al-, *Li-Mādhā Samaḥa l-Niẓām al-Sūrī bi-ᶜUbūr baᶜḍ al-Mutaẓāhirīn Ḥudūd al-Jawlān maᶜa Dawlat Isrā'īl?*, 2011 (www.abubaseer.bizland.com/hadath/Read/hadath%2082.doc).

Ṭarṭūsī, Abū Baṣīr al-, *Mā lā Yaᶜrifuhu l-Nās ᶜan al-Niẓām al-Sūrī al-Ṭā'ifī*, 2011 (www.tawhed.ws/r?i=30081109).

Ṭarṭūsī, Abū Baṣīr al-, *Al-Mawqif min Tarashshuḥ al-Ustādh 'Ḥāzim Ṣalāḥ Abū Ismāᶜīl' li-Ri'āsat Miṣr*, 2011 (www.abubaseer.bizland.com/hadath/Read/hadath%2089.doc).

Ṭarṭūsī, Abū Baṣīr al-, *Daftar al-Thawra wa-l-Thuwwār*, 2011/2012 (www.abubaseer.bizland.com/books/read/b&2040.doc).

Ṭarṭūsī, Abū Baṣīr al-, *Ilā l-Ikhwa Anṣār al-Sharīᶜa fī Yaman*, 2012 (www.abubaseer.bizland.com/hadath/Read/hadath%2092.doc).

ᶜUbab, Abū l-Zubayr ᶜĀdil al-, *Halā Taraktum lī Shaykhanā Abā Baṣīr al-Ṭarṭūsī?!*, 2012 (www.tawhed.ws/dl?i=12041247).

ᶜUnnābī, Abū ᶜUbayda Yūsuf al-, *Bi-Ḥadd al-Ḥussām.. Tataḥarraru l-Shām*, 2012 (www.tawhed.ws/dl?i=12041219).

Wagemakers, Joas, 'Al-Qaida Advises the Arab Spring: Yemen', *Jihadica.com*, 5 June 2012 (www.jihadica.com/al-qaida-advises-the-arab-spring-yemen/).

Wagemakers, Joas, 'Al-Qaida Advises the Arab Spring: Abu Basir's Scrapbook', *Jihadica.com*, 28 July 2012 (www.jihadica.com/al-qaida-advises-the-arab-spring-abu-basirs-scrapbook/).

Wagemakers, Joas, 'Al-Qaida Advises the Arab Spring: The Case for al-Baghdadi', *Jihadica.com*, 21 September 2013 (www.jihadica.com/al-qaida-advises-the-arab-spring-the-case-for-al-baghdadi/).

Weinthal, Benjamin, 'The German Jihadists' Colony in Syria', *longwarjournal.org*, 19 December 2013 (http://www.derechos.org/peace/syria/doc/syr3635.html).

Wood, Graeme, 'What ISIS Really Wants', March 2015 (www.theatlantic.amp/article/384980/).

Wright, Lawrence, 'ISIS's Savage Strategy in Iraq', *The New Yorker*, 16 June 2014 (www.newyorker.cφm/news/daily-comments/isiss-savage-strategy-in-iraq).

Yamānī, Abū Dharr al-Samharī al-, *Maᶜālim al-wathaniyya fī'l-dawla al-yamaniyya*, 1431 AH [2010 CE] (http://www.tawhed.ws/dl?i=22031001).

Yamānī, Abū Dharr al-Samharī al-, *Ibhāj ahl al-ṣināᶜa bi-dirāsat ḥadīth buᶜithtu bi'l-sayf bayna yaday al-sāᶜa*, 1432/2011 (http://www.tawhed.ws/dl?i=23041129).

Yassin-Kassab, Robin, 'Non-Violence? Finkelstein and Gandhi', *Palestine Chronicle* (http://www.palestinechronicle.com/non-violence-finkelstein-and-gandhi/).

al-Ẓawāhirī, Ayman, *Ilā l-Amām Yā Usūd al-Shām* (www.tawhed.ws/dl?i=12041233).

al-Ẓawāhirī, Ayman, 'al-Akh al-karīm al-fāḍil Abū Muṣᶜab', 9 July 2005 (https://ctc.usma.edu/wp-content/uploads/2013/10/Zawahiris-Letter-to-Zarqawi-Original.pdf).

al-Ẓawāhirī, Ayman, *ᶜIzz al-Sharq Awwaluhu Dimashq*, 2011 (www.tawhed.ws/dl?i=30081124).

al-Ẓawāhirī, Ayman, *Risālat al-Amal wa-l-Bishr li-Ahlinā fī Miṣr 3*, 2011 (www.tawhed.ws/dl?i=30081127).

al-Ẓawāhirī, Ayman, *Risālat al-Amal wa-l-Bishr li-Ahlinā fī Miṣr 4*, 2011 (www.tawhed.ws/dl?i=30081128).

al-Ẓawāhirī, Ayman, *Risālat al-Amal wa-l-Bishr li-Ahlinā fī Miṣr 5* (www.tawhed.ws/dl?i=30081129).

al-Ẓawāhirī, Ayman, *Risālat al-Amal wa-l-Bishr li-Ahlinā fī Miṣr 6*, 2011 (www.tawhed.ws/dl?i=30081130).

al-Ẓawāhirī, Ayman, *Risālat al-Amal wa-l-Bishr li-Ahlinā fī Miṣr 7*, 2011 (www.tawhed.ws/dl?i=30081131).

al-Ẓawāhirī, Ayman, *Risālat al-Amal wa-l-Bishr li-Ahlinā fī Miṣr 9*, 2012 (www.tawhed.ws/dl?i=12041225).

al-Ẓawāhirī, Ayman, *Risālat al-Amal wa-l-Bishr li-Ahlinā fī Miṣr 11*, 2012 (www.tawhed.ws/dl?i=24041317).

al-Ẓawāhirī, Ayman, *Yā Ahl Tūnis Unṣirū Sharīᶜatakum*, 2012 (www.tawhed.ws/dl?i=24041354).

(C) PUBLISHED SOURCES

ᶜAbbas, Iḥsān, *Shīᶜr al-khawārij* (Beirut: Dār al-Thaqāfa, n. d.).

ᶜAbd al-ᶜAzīz, Shāh, *Fatāwā ᶜazīzīya* (Delhi: Maṭbaᶜ-yi Mujtabāʾī, n. d.).

ᶜAbd al-Ḥaqq, *Mawlawī Marḥūm Dillī Kālij* (Delhi: Anjuman-i Taraqqī-yi Urdu Hind, 1989).

ᶜAbd Allāh ibn Ṣālih al-ʿArīnī, *Shīᶜr jihād al-Rūm* (Riyadh: n. p., 2002).

ᶜAbd al-Raḥmān b. Aḥmad b. Rajab, *al-Dhayl ᶜalā ṭabaqāt al-ḥanābila* (Riyadh: Maktabat al-ᶜUbaykān, 1425/2005).

Abdali, S. Kamal, 'Muhammad Jafar Thanesari: Kala Pani or Tavarikh-e ᶜAjib', *Annual of Urdu Studies* 26 (2011), 216–30.

Abdalla, Ulil Abshar, 'Rethinking Indigenous Islam', *Afkar* 1 (2008), 100–5.

Abdel Haleem, Muḥammad S., *The Qur'ān* (Oxford: Oxford University Press, 2004).

Abou El Fadel, Khaled, *Rebellion and Violence in Islamic Law* (Cambridge: Cambridge University Press, 2001).

Abou El Fadel, Khaled, *Great Theft: Wrestling Islam from the Extremists* (New York: Harper, 2005).

al-Abshīhī, Muḥammad b. Aḥmad, *al-Mustaṭraf* (Beirut: Dār Maktabat al-Ḥayāh, 1996).

Abu-Amr, Z., 'Hamas: A Historical and Political Background', *Journal of Palestine Studies* 22.4 (1993), 5–19.

Abu Lodeh, Lama, 'Review of the Impossible State by Wael Hallaq', *International Journal of Middle East Studies* 46.1 (2014), 216–18.

Abū Tammām, Ḥabib b. Aws, *Dīwān Abī Tammām* (Cairo: Dār al-Ma'ārif, 1965).

Afghānī, Mawlānā ᶜAbd al-Ḥaqq, *Daᶜvat-i ḥaqq*, ed. Samīᶜ al-Ḥaqq, 2 vols (Akoṛa Khaṫṫak: Muʾtamar al-muṣannifīn-i dār al-ᶜulūm ḥaqqāniyyah, 2000).

Afghānī, Mawlānā ᶜAbd al-Ḥaqq, *Fatāvā-yi ḥaqqāniyyah*, ed. Mawlānā Muftī Mukhtārallāh Ḥaqqānī, 6 vols (Akoṛa Khaṫṫak: Muʾtamar al-muṣannifīn-i dār al-ᶜulūm ḥaqqāniyyah, 1422/2002).

Afsaruddin, Asma, *Striving in the Path of God: Jihad and Martyrdom in Islamic Thought* (New York: Oxford University Press, 2013).

Ahmad, Asad, 'Logic in the Khayrābādī School of India: A Preliminary Exploration', in *Law and Tradition in Classical Islamic Thought: Studies in Honor of Professor Hossein Modarressi*, eds Michael Cook, Najam Haidar, Intisar Rabb and Asma Sayeed (Basingstoke: Palgrave Macmillan, 2012), pp. 385–92.

Ahmad, Asad, 'The *Shifāʾ* in India I', *Oriens* 40 (2012), 1–24.

Ahmad, Asad, 'Arabo-Islamic Physics in the Pre-modern Period: The *Hadiya Saᶜīdīya* of Faḍl-i Ḥaqq Khayrābādī', in *The Oxford Handbook of Islamic Philosophy*, eds Sabine Schmidtke and Khaled el-Rouayheb (Oxford: Oxford University Press, 2017), pp. 488–508.

Aḥmad, Bashīr al-Dīn, *Wāqiᶜāt-i dār al-ḥukūmat-i Dihlī* (Delhi: Urdu Academy, 1990).

Ahmad, Irfan, 'Genealogy of the Islamic State: Reflections on Maududi's Political Thought and Islamism', *Journal of the Royal Anthropological Institute* 15 (2009), 145–62.

Ahmad, Jamīl, *Ḥarakat al-taʾlīf bi-l-lugha al-ᶜarabiyya fī l-iqlīm al-shimālī al-hindī* (Karachi: Jāmiᶜat al-Dirāsāt al-Islāmiyya, n. d.).

Ahmad Khān, Sayyid, *Āsār al-ṣanādīd*, ed. Khalīq Anjum (Delhi: National Council for the Promotion of Urdu Language, 2003).

Aḥmadī, Mawlavī ᶜAbd al-Ḥalīm, *Də mujāhid tūrah: də jihād sharᶜī masāʾil* (n.p.: Hidāyat, 1392 SH/1434 AH).

Aḥmadzay, Zāhidī, *Khāliṣ Bābā: də hidāyat pah lor* (Peshawar: Amīr Kroṛ kitābtūn, 1385 SH).

Ahmed, Shahab, *What Is Islam? The Importance of Being Islamic* (Princeton: Princeton University Press, 2016).

Akhtar Miṣbāḥī, Yāsīn, *Qāʾid-i inqilāb: ᶜAllāma Fażl-i Ḥaqq Khayrābādī* (Maleagaon: Nūrī Mission, n. p., n. d.).

Alagha, Joseph, *Hizbullah: Identity Construction* (Amsterdam: Amsterdam University Press, 2010).

Alavi, Seema, *Muslim Cosmopolitanism in the Age of Empire* (Cambridge, MA: Harvard University Press, 2015).

Ali, Daud (ed.), *Invoking the Past: The Uses of History in South Asia* (Delhi: Oxford University Press, 1999).

ᶜAlī, Raḥmān, *Tadhkira-yi ᶜulamāʾ-yi Hind (Tuḥfat al-fuḍalāʾ fī tarājim al-kumalāʾ)*, ed. Yūsuf Bēg Bābāpūr (Qum: Majmaᶜ-yi ẕakhāʾir-i islāmī, 1391 Sh/2012).

Ali, Syed Ameer, *Students' Handbook of Mahommedan Law* (Calcutta: Thacker, Spink and Co., 1892).

Allawi, Ali A., *The Occupation of Iraq: Winning the War, Losing the Peace* (New Haven: Yale University Press, 2007).

Allawi, Ali A., *The Crisis of Islamic Civilization* (New Haven: Yale University Press, 2009).

Allen, Charles, *God's Terrorists: The Wahhabi Cult and the Hidden Roots of Modern Jihad* (London: Little, Brown, 2006).

Al-Matroudi, A. H. I., *Ibn Taymiyyah. Conflict or Conciliation* (London: Routledge, 2006).

Alshaer, A., 'Islam in the Narrative of Fatah and Hamas', in *Narrative Conflict in the Middle East*, eds D. Matar and Z. Harb (London: I. B. Tauris, 2013), pp. 111–33.

al-ᶜĀmilī Muḥammad ibn Jamāl al-Dīn ibn Makkī al-Shahīd al-Awwal, *al-Durūs al-Sharᶜiyyah fī Fiqh al-Imāmīyyah* (Qum: Muʾassasat al-Nashr al-Islāmī al-Tābiᶜah li'Jamiᶜat al-Mudarrissīn, n. d.).

al-ᶜĀmilī Zayn al-Dīn al-Jubᶜī al-Shahīd al-Thānī, *al-Rawḍah, al-Bahiyyah fī Sharḥ al-Lumᶜah al-Dimashqiyyah* (Tehran: Dār al-Nashr al-Islāmī, 1968).

al-ᶜĀmilī Zayn al-Dīn al-Jubᶜī al-Shahīd al-Thānī, *Masālik al-Afhām fī Sharḥ Sharāʾiᶜ al-Islām* (Qum: Muʾassasat al-Maᶜārif al-Islāmiyyah, 1992).

Amiq, Amiq, 'Two Fatwās on Jihād Against the Dutch Colonization in Indonesia: A Prosopographical Approach to the Study of Fatwa', *Studia Islamika* 5.3 (1998), 77–123.

Amir, Yehoshua, 'Die Begegnung des biblischen und des philosophischen Monotheismus als Grundthema des jüdischen Hellenismus', *Evangelische Theologie* 38 (1978), 2–19.

Anderson, Claire, *The Indian Uprising of 1857–8: Prisons, Prisoners, and Rebellion* (London: Anthem Press, 2007).

Anderson, Michael R., 'Islamic Law and the Colonial Encounter in British India', in *Institutions and Ideologies: SOAS South Asia Reader*, eds David Arnold and Peter Robb (London: Curzon Press, 1993), pp. 165–85.

Andrews, C. F., *Zaka Ullah of Delhi* (Cambridge: W. Heffer & Sons, 1929).

Anonymous, *Ḥaqīqat-i shīʿa* (Karachi: Dār al-iftāʾ wa'l-irshād).

al-Anṣārī, al-ʿAllāma ʿĀlim b. ʿAlāʾ, *Fatāwā tātārkhāniyya*, ed. al-Qāḍī Sajjād Ḥusayn, 5 vols (Hyderabad: Maṭbaʿat al-majlis dāʾirat al-maʿārif al-ʿuthmāniyya, 1407/1987).

Anṣārī, Riżā, *Bānī-yi dars-i niẓāmī ustād al-hind Mullā Niẓāmuddīn Muḥammad Farangī-Maḥallī* (Aligarh: Aligarh Muslim University, 1973).

Ansorge, D., 'Is it Essentialism to Claim that Some Religions Foster Violence – and Some Do Not?', in *Islamic Peace Ethics: Legitimate and Illegitimate Violence in Contemporary Islamic Thought*, ed. H. Shadi (Baden-Baden: Nomos Verlagsgesellschaft mbH, 2017), pp. 37–54.

Aquil, Raziuddin, and Partha Chatterjee (eds), *History in the Vernacular* (Delhi: Permanent Black, 2008).

Arnold, Thomas W., *The Preaching of Islam* (Lahore: Sh. Muhammad Ashraf, 1979).

ʿArshī, Imtiyāz ʿAlī, *Majmūʿa-yi maqālāt*, ed. Fażl-i Ḥaqq Qarshī (Lahore: Majlis taraqqī-yi adab, 1970).

Asad, Talal, *Genealogies of Religion: Discipline and Reasons of Power in Christianity and Islam* (Baltimore: Johns Hopkins University Press, 1993).

Asad, Talal, 'Reading a Modern Classic: W. C. Smith's "The Meaning and End of Religion"', *History of Religions* 40.3 (2001), 205–22.

Asad, Talal, *Formations of the Secular – Christianity, Islam, Modernity* (Stanford: Stanford University Press, 2003).

Asif, Manan A., *A Book of Conquest: The Chachnama and Muslim Origins in South Asia* (Cambridge, MA: Harvard University Press, 2016).

al-ʿAsqalānī, Aḥmad b. ʿAlī b. Ḥajjar, *Fatḥ al-bārī sharḥ ṣaḥīḥ al-Bukhārī*, ed. ʿAbd al-Azīz b. ʿAbdallāh b. Bāz, 13 vols (Beirut: Dār al-maʿārifa, 1379 AH).

al-ʿAsqalānī, Aḥmad b. ʿAlī b. Ḥajjar, *Inbāʾ al-ghumr bi-anbāʾ al-ʿumr* (Beirut: Dār al-Kutub al-ʿIlmiyya, 2nd edn, 1406/1987).

al-ʿAsqalānī, Aḥmad b. ʿAlī b. Ḥajjar, *Tahdhīb al-tahdhīb* (Beirut: Muʾassasat al-Risālah, 1996).

ʿAṭāyī, M. Ibrāhīm, *Də Paxtanī qabīlo də ḥuqūqī, jazāyī, taʿāmulī iṣṭilāḥāto qāmūs* (Kabul: Də Paxto ćeṛano naṛīvāl markaz, 1357sh).

Averroes (Abū al-Walīd b. Rushd), *Bidāyat al-mujtahid wa-l-nihāyat al-muqtaṣid* (Beirut: Dār Ibn Ḥazm, 1990).

al-ʿAynī, Badr al-Dīn Abū Muḥammad b. Maḥmūd, *ʿUmdat al-qārī sharḥ ṣaḥīḥ al-Bukhārī*, ed. ʿAbdallāh Maḥmūd Muḥammad ʿUmar, 25 vols (Beirut: Dār al-kutub al-ʿilmiyya, 1421/2001).

al-ʿAzīz, ʿAbd al-Qādir b. ʿAbd, *al-ʿUmda fī iʿdād al-ʿudda li'l-jihād fī sabīl allāh taʿālā* (Amman: Dār al-bayāriq, 1419/1999).

Aziz, Talib, 'The Political Theory of Muhammad Baqir al-Sadr', in *Ayatollahs, Sufis and Ideologues: State, Religion and Social Movements in Iraq*, ed. Faleh Abdul Jabar (London: Saqi Books, 2002), pp. 233–5.

Al-Azmeh, Aziz, 'Mortal Enemies, Invisible Neighbours: Northerners in Andalusi Eyes', in *The Legacy of Muslim Spain*, ed. Salma Jayyusi (Leiden: Brill, 1992), pp. 259–72.

Bābāyī, Muḥammad Rizā Ḥājj (ed.), *Qavānīn-i Mullā ᶜUmar: majmūᶜah-yi qavānīn va āyīn'nāmah'hā-yi Ṭālibān dar Afghānistān* (Tehran: Nigāh-i amrūz, 1382sh).
Al-Baghdādī, ᶜAbd al-Qāhir, *Kitāb Uṣūl al-dīn* (Istanbul: Maṭbaᶜat al-dawla, 1346/1928).
Al-Baghdādī, ᶜAbd al-Qāhir, *al-Milal wa l-niḥal*, ed. Albert Nader (Beirut: Dar El-Machreq, 1986).
Baig, Mustafa R. K., 'Operating Islamic Jurisprudence in Non-Muslim Jurisdictions: Traditional Islamic Precepts and Contemporary Controversies in the United States', *Chicago-Kent Law Review* 90.1 (2015), 79–110.
Baig, Mustafa R. K., 'The Non-Violent Aspects of *kitab al-jihad*', in *Twenty-first Century Jihad: Law, Society and Military Action*, eds E. Kendall and E. Stein (London: I. B. Tauris, 2015), pp. 97–111.
Bakhtiyārī, Ṣiddīqah, 'Muhājirat va taghayyir-i mafhūm-i mardānigī: sankh'shināsī mafhūm-i mardānigī dar miyān mardān-i muhājir-i Afghānistān dar Īrān va muqāyisah bā mardān ghayr-muhājir dar Afghānistān' (unpublished M.A. dissertation, Dānish'gāh-yi Tihrān, Dānish'kadah-yi ᶜulūm-i ijtimāᶜī, Grūh-yi jāmiᶜah'shināsī, 1393 SH).
Bar, Shaul, 'The Punishment of Burning in the Hebrew Bible', *Old Testament Essays* 25.1 (2012), 27–39.
Barēlvī, Ikrām, *Ḥakīm Muᵓmin Khān 'Muᵓmin': shakhṣīyat aur shāᶜirī* (Karachi: Pakistan Adab Publications, 2003).
Barkātī, Maḥmūd Aḥmad, *Fażl-i Ḥaqq Khayrābādī aur san sattāvan* (Karachi: Barkat Academy, 1987).
Barron, David J., and Martin S. Lederman, 'The Commander in Chief at the Lowest Ebb – Framing the Problem, Doctrine, and Original Understanding', *Harvard Law Review* 121 (2008), 689–804.
Bates, Crispin and Marina Carter (eds), *Mutiny at the Margins*, 7 vols (New Delhi and London: Sage Publications, 2013).
Benhabib, Seyla, *Another Cosmopolitanism* (New York: Oxford University Press, 2006).
Bennison, Amira K., *Jihad and its Interpretations in Pre-colonial Morocco: State-Society Relations during the French Conquest of Morocco* (London: Routledge, 2002).
Bennison, Amira K., 'Abd al-Qādir's Jihād in the Light of the Western Islamic Jihād Tradition', *Studia Islamica* 2 (2011), 69–90.
Bessel, R., *Violence: A Modern Obsession* (New York: Simon and Schuster, 2015).
Beyer, Peter, 'Constitutional Privilege and Constituting Pluralism: Religious Freedom in National, Global, and Legal Context', *Journal for the Scientific Study of Religion* 42.3 (2003), 333–9.
Bezhan, Faridullah, 'Nationalism, not Islam: The 'Awaken Youth' Party and Pashtun Nationalism', in *Afghanistan's Islam: From Conversion to the Taliban*, ed. Nile Green (Oakland, CA: University of California Press, 2017), pp. 163–85 and 293–9 (notes and references).
Bhattacharya, Sabyasachi (ed.), *Rethinking 1857* (New Delhi: Orient Longman, 2007).
al-Binᶜalī, Turkī, *al-Sabī: aḥkām wa masāᵓil* (Dīwān al-buḥūth wa l-iftāᵓ, 1435/2014).
Black, Anthony, *The History of Islamic Political Thought: From the Prophet to the Present* (New York: Routledge, 2001).
Blecher, Joel, *Said the Prophet of God: Hadith Commentary Across a Millennium* (Berkeley and Los Angeles: University of California Press, 2017).
Boatcă, Manuela, *Global Inequalities Beyond Occidentalism* (Farnham and Burlington, VT: Ashgate, 2015).

Bonner, Michael, *Jihad in Islamic History: Doctrines and Practice* (Princeton: Princeton University Press, 2006).

Bonney, Richard, *Jihād: From Qur'ān to Bin Laden* (Basingstoke: Palgrave Macmillan, 2004).

Bori, Caterina, 'Ibn Taymiyya *wa-Jamāʿatuhu*: Authority, Conflict and Consensus in Ibn Taymiyya's Circle', in *Ibn Taymiyya and His Times*, eds Yossef Rapoport and Shahab Ahmed (Karachi: Oxford University Press, 2010), pp. 23–52.

Bourdieu, Pierre, *Le sens pratique* (Paris: Minuit, 1980).

Bourdieu, Pierre, *La domination masculine* (Paris: Seuil, 1998).

Boutaleb, Abdelkader, *L'Emir Abd-el-Kader et la formation de la nation algérienne: De l'Emir Abd-el-Kader à la guerre de libération* (Algiers: Dahlab, 1990).

Bovard, James, *Terrorism and Tyranny: Trampling Freedom, Justice and Peace to Rid the World of Evil* (New York: Palgrave Macmillan, 2003).

Bowen, J., *Can Islam Be French?: Pluralism and Pragmatism in a Secularist State* (Princeton: Princeton University Press, 2010).

Brower, Benjamin, *A Desert Named Peace: The Violence of France's Empire in the Algerian Sahara, 1844–1902* (New York: Columbia University Press, 2009).

Brower, Benjamin, 'The Amîr 'Abd Al-Qâdir and the "Good War" in Algeria, 1832–1847', *Studia Islamica* 2 (2011), 35–68.

Brown, Vahid, and Don Rassler, *Fountainhead of Jihad: The Haqqani Nexus, 1973–2012* (London: Hurst, 2013).

Bruckmayr, Philipp, 'The Spread and Persistence of Māturīdi [*sic*] Kalām and Underlying Dynamics', *Iran and the Caucasus* 13.1 (2009), 59–92.

Bruckmayr, Philipp, 'Güney ve Güneydoğu Asya'da Mâturîdîlik'in Geçmiş ve Bugünkü Yönleri / Past and Present Aspects of Māturīdısm [*sic*] in South and Southeast Asia', in *Uluğ Bir Çinar İmâm Mâturîdî Uluslararası Sempozyum Tebliğler Kitabı*, ed. Ahmet Kartal (Istanbul: Ofis Yayın Matbaacılık, 2014), pp. 115–31.

Bruckmayr, Philipp and Jan-Peter Hartung, 'Introduction: Challenges from 'The Periphery'? – Salafī Islam Outside the Arab World. Spotlights on Wider Asia', *Die Welt des Islams* 60.2–3 (2020), 137–69.

al-Buḥtūrī, Abū al-Walīd, *Dīwān al-Buḥturī* (Beirut: Dār al-Jīl, 1994).

al-Bukhārī, Muḥammad, *al-Jāmiʾ al-ṣaḥīḥ* (Cairo: Dār al-Taʾṣīl, 2012).

Bunnik, Anno, and Peter B. M. Knoope, 'Geweldloze opstand in de Arabische wereld bevestigt bankroet van Al Qaeda', *Internationale Spectator* 65.4 (2011), 167–9.

Bunzel, Cole, *From Paper State to Caliphate: The Ideology of the Islamic State* (Washington, DC: Brookings Institution, 2015).

Bunzel, Cole, 'Wahhabism, Saudi Arabia, and the Islamic State: 'Abdullah Ibn Jibrin and Turki al-Bin'ali', in *Salman's Legacy: The Dilemmas of a New Era in Saudi Arabia*, ed. Madawi Al-Rasheed (London: Hurst, 2018), pp. 183–96.

al-Burhānfūrī, Mawlānā al-Shaykh Niẓām, and others, *al-Fatāwā al-hindiyya, al-maʿrūfa bi'l-Fatāwā al-ʿālamkīriyya fī madhhab al-imām al-aʿẓam Abī Ḥanīfa al-Nuʿmān*, ed. ʿAbd al-Laṭīf Ḥasan ʿAbd al-Raḥmān, 6 vols (Beirut: Dār al-kutub al-ʿilmiyya, 1421/ 2000).

Burke, Edmund, 'Islamic History as World History: Marshall Hodgson, "The Venture of Islam"', *International Journal of Middle East Studies* 10.2 (1979), 241–64.

Burke, Jason, *Al-Qaeda: The True Story of Radical Islam* (London and New York: I. B. Tauris, 2004).

Butler, Judith, *Excitable Speech: A Politics of the Performative* (New York and London: Routledge, 1997).
Calder, Norman, 'Al-Nawawī's Typology of *Muftīs* and its Significance for a General Theory of Islamic Law', *Islamic Law and Society* 3.2 (1996), 137–64.
Calder, Norman, 'The Limits of Islamic Orthodoxy', in *Intellectual Traditions in Islam*, ed. Farhad Daftary (London: I. B. Tauris, 2000), pp. 66–86.
Cantell Smith, Wilfred, *The Meaning and End of Religion: A New Approach to the Religious Traditions of Mankind* (New York: Macmillan, 1962).
Cardici, P., *Hamas From Resistance to Government* (New York: Seven Stories, 2012).
Carter, Stephen L., '*Must Liberalism Be Violent? A Reflection on the Work of Stanley Hauerwas*', *Law and Contemporary Problems* 75 (2012), 201–19.
Cavanaugh, William, *The Myth of Religious Violence* (New York: Oxford University Press, 2009).
Chapman, Alister, John Coffey, and Brad S. Gregory (eds), *Seeing Things Their Way: Intellectual History and the Return of Religion* (Notre Dame: University of Notre Dame Press, 2009).
Chatterjee, Nandini, 'Law, Culture and History: Amir Ali's Interpretation', in *Legal Histories of the British Empire: Laws, Engagement and Legacies of Islamic Law*, eds Shaunnagh Dorset and John McLaren (Oxford: Routledge, 2014), pp. 45–59.
Chehab, Z., *Hamas: The Untold Story of Militants, Martyrs and Spies* (London: I. B. Tauris, 2007).
Chodkiewicz, Michel, *The Spiritual Writings of Amir Abd el-Kader* (Albany: SUNY Press, 1995).
Clancy-Smith, Julia, *Rebel and Saint: Muslim Notables, Populist Protest, Colonial Encounters, Algeria and Tunisia (1800–1904)* (Berkeley: University of California Press, 1997).
Cockburn, Patrick, *The Occupation: War and Resistance in Iraq* (London: Verso, 2006).
Cockburn, Patrick, *Muqtada al-Sadr and the Fall of Iraq* (London: Faber, 2008).
Colás, Alejandro, and Richard Saull (eds), *War on Terror and the American Empire After the Cold War* (London: Routledge, 2006).
Cole, Juan, 'The United States and Shīᶜite Religious Factions in Post-Ba'thist Iraq', *Middle East Journal* 57.4 (Autumn, 2003), 543–66.
Cole, Juan, *The Ayatollahs and Democracy in Iraq* (Amsterdam and Leiden: Amsterdam University Press, 2006).
Collins, Randall, *Violence: A Micro-sociological Theory* (Princeton: Princeton University Press, 2008).
Cook, David, *Understanding Jihad* (Berkeley: University of California Press, 2005).
Cook, David, 'Apostasy from Islam: A Historical Perspective', *JSAI* 31 (2006), 248–88.
Cook, David, and Olivia Allison, *Understanding and Addressing Suicide Attacks: The Faith and Politics of Martyrdom Operations* (Westport, CN: Praeger Security International, 2007).
Cook, Michael, *Ancient Religions, Modern Politics: The Islamic Case in Comparative Perspective* (Princeton: Princeton University Press, 2014).
Creswell, Robyn, and Bernard Haykel, 'Poetry in Jihadi Culture', in *Jihadi Culture: The Art and Social Practices of Militant Islamists*, ed. Thomas Hegghammer (Cambridge: Cambridge University Press, 2017), pp. 22–41.
Crone, Patricia, *God's Rule: Government and Islam* (New York: Columbia University Press,

2004). Also published as Crone, Patricia, *Medieval Islamic Political Thought* (Edinburgh: Edinburgh University Press, 2004).

Dalrymple, William, *The Last Mughal* (London: Bloomsbury, 2006).

Dalrymple, William, *The Return of a King: The Battle for Afghanistan* (London: Bloomsbury, 2013).

Dalrymple, William, *The Anarchy: The Relentless Rise of the East India Company* (London: Bloomsbury, 2019).

Danziger, Raphael, *Abd al-Qadir and the Algerians: Resistance to the French and Internal Consolidation* (New York: Holmes & Meier, 1977).

al-Dawīsh, ᶜAbdallāh b. Muḥammad b. Aḥmad, *al-Mawrid al-zulāl fīʾl-tanbīh ᶜalā akhṭāʾ al-ẓilāl* (= *Majmūᶜat muʾallafāt al-shaykh ᶜAbdallāh al-Dawīsh* (Burayda: Dār al-ᶜUlyān, 1411/1990).

Deobandī, Maḥmūd al-Ḥasan Ṣāḥib, *Adillah-yi kāmilah, yaᶜnī ghayr-muqallidoṇ ke das suʾālāt awr unke taḥqīqī javābāt*, ed. Muḥmmad Amīn Pālanpūrī (Karachi: Qadīmī kutub'khānah, 1410 AH [1294 AH]).

de Vries, Hent, *Religion and Violence: Philosophical Perspectives from Kant to Derrida* (Baltimore: Johns Hopkins University Press, 2002).

Də Afghānistān Islāmī Imārat, *Də Mujāhidīno lapārah lāʾiḥah* (n.p.: no publ., 1431/2 010).

Deringil, Selim, 'The Invention of Tradition as Public Image in the Late Ottoman Empire, 1808–1908', *Comparative Studies in Society and History* 35.1 (1993), 3–29.

Deshpande, Prachi, *Creative Pasts: Historical Memory and Identity in Western India, 1700–1960* (New York: Columbia University Press, 2007).

Devji, Faisal, *Muslim Zion: Pakistan as a Political Idea* (London: Hurst, 2013).

van Diffelen, Roelof Willem, *De Leer der Wahhabieten* (Leiden: Brill, 1927).

al-Dihlawī, Shāh Waliyallāh Aḥmad b. ᶜAbd al-Raḥīm al-Fārūqī, *ᶜIqd al-jīd fī aḥkām al-ijtihād wa'l-taqlīd*, ed. Muḥammad ᶜAlī al-Ḥalabī al-Atharī (Sharjah: Dār al-fatḥ, 1415/1995).

al-Dimashqī (Ibn Kathīr), ᶜImād al-Dīn Abū al-Fidāʾ Ismāᶜīl b. ᶜUmar b. Kathīr, *Tafsīr al-qurʾān al-ᶜaẓīm* (Beirut: Dār al-Kutub al-ᶜIlmiyya, 1419/1998).

al-Djazā'irī, Abd al-Qādir, *Le Livre des Haltes (Kitāb al-Mawāqif)*, ed. Michel Lagarde, 3 vols (Leiden: Brill, 2000).

Donohue, Laura K., 'Terrorism and the Counter-terrorist Discourse', in *Global Anti-Terrorism Law and Policy*, eds Michael Hor, Yew Meng, Victor Vridar Ramraj and Kent Roach (Cambridge: Cambridge University Press, 2005), pp. 13–36.

Dorroll, C. (ed.), *Teaching Islamic Studies in the Age of ISIS, Islamophobia, and the Internet* (Bloomington: Indiana University Press, 2019).

Doumani, Beshara, *Rediscovering Palestine: Merchants and Peasants in Jebel Nablus 1700–1900* (Berkeley: University of California Press, 1995).

Duffy, Helen, *The 'War on Terror' and the Framework of International Law* (Cambridge: Cambridge University Press, 2005).

Edwards, David B., 'Summoning Muslims: Print, Politics and Religious Ideology in Afghanistan', *Modern Asian Studies* 52.3 (1993), 609–28.

Edwards, David B., *Before Taliban: Genealogies of the Afghan Jihad* (Berkeley, Los Angeles and London: University of California Press, 2002).

Edwards, David B., *Caravan of Martyrs: Sacrifice and Suicide Bombing in Afghanistan* (Oakland, CA: University of California Press, 2017).

Eiland, Giora, 'The IDF in the Second Intifada', *Strategic Assessment* 13.3 (2010), 27–37.

Elgamri, E., *Islam in the British Broadsheets: The Impact of Orientalism on Representations of Islam in the British Press* (Reading: Ithaca Press, 2010).
Elias, Jamal J. (ed.), *Key Themes for the Study of Islam* (Oxford: Oneworld, 2010).
Elibiary, Sarah, 'Islamic Jurisprudential Discourses on the Conduct of Hostilities: Embracing Pragmatism' (Unpublished PhD dissertation, University of London, School of Oriental and African Studies, 2012).
Elphinstone, Mountstuart, *An Account of the Kingdom of Caubul and its Dependencies in Persia, Tartary and India, Comprising a View of the Afghaun Nation and a History of the Dooraunee Monarchy* [*sic*], 2 vols (London: J. Murray, 1815).
Emadi, Hafizullah, 'Establishment of Afghanistan's Parliament and the Role of Women Parliamentarians: Retrospect and Prospects', *Internationales Asienforum* 39.1–2 (2008), 5–19.
Emirates Centre for Strategic Studies, *Iraq: Reconstruction and Future Role* (2004).
Enayat, Hamid, *Modern Islamic Political Thought* (London: Macmillan, 1982).
Esposito, John L., *Voices of Resurgent Islam* (New York and Oxford: Oxford University Press, 1983).
Etherington, Mark, *Revolt on the Tigris: The Sadr Uprising and the Governing of Iraq* (Ithaca, New York: Cornell University Press, 2005).
Fanon, Frantz, *The Wretched of the Earth* (London: Penguin Books, 1963).
Farāmīn-i amīr al-muʾminīn (n. p.: n. p., 2000).
Farooqui, Amar, *Zafar and the Raj: Anglo-Mughal Delhi c. 1800–1850* (New Delhi: Primus Books, 2013).
Foucault, Michel, *Histoire de la sexualité I: La volonté de savoir* (Paris: Gallimard, 1976).
Fawn, Rick, and Raymond A. Hinnebusch (eds), *The Iraq War: Causes and Consequences* (Boulder and London: Lynne Rienner, Eurospan, 2006).
Fawzi, Issam and Ivesa Lübben, 'Die ägyptische *jama'a al-islamiya* [*sic*] und die Revision der Gewaltstrategie', *DOI-Fokus* 15 (2004), 1–43.
Finkelstein, Norman, *What Gandhi Says: About Nonviolence, Resistance and Courage* (New York/London: OR Books, 2012).
Fox, Robin, 'The Inherent Rules of Violence', in *Social Rules and Social Behavior*, ed. P. Collett (Oxford: Blackwell, 1977), pp. 132–49.
Frémeaux, Jacques, *La France et l'Algérie en guerre: 1830–1870, 1954–1962* (Paris: Economica, 2002).
French, Nathan, *And God Knows the Martyrs: Martyrdom and Violence in Jihadi-Salafism* (Oxford: Oxford University Press, 2020).
Friend, Theodore (ed.), *Religion and Religiosity in the Philippines and Indonesia: Essays on State, Society, and Public Creeds* (Washington, DC: Southeast Asia Studies Program, School of Advanced International Studies, Johns Hopkins University, 2006).
Fuchs, Simon Wolfgang, *Proper Signposts for the Camp: The Reception of Classical Authorities in the Ǧihādī Manual al-ʿUmda fī Iʿdād al-ʿUdda* (Würzburg: Ergon Verlag, 2011).
Fuchs, Simon Wolfgang, 'Glossy Global Leadership: Unpacking the Multilingual Religious Thought of the *Jihad*', in *Afghanistan's Islam: From Conversion to the Taliban*, ed. Nile Green (Oakland, CA: University of California Press, 2017), pp. 189–206 and 299–307 (notes and references).
Fuchs, Simon Wolfgang, 'Do Excellent Surgeons Make Miserable Exegetes? Negotiating the Sunni Tradition in the *ğihādī* Camps', *Die Welt des Islams* 53.2 (2013), 192–237.

Gallois, William, 'Dahra and the History of Violence in Early Colonial Algeria', in *The French Colonial Mind* (2 vols), ed. Martin Thomas (Lincoln: University of Nebraska Press, 2012), pp. 3–25.

Gallois, William, *A History of Violence in the Early Algerian Colony* (London: Palgrave Macmillan, 2013).

Gallois, William, 'Genocide in Nineteenth-century Algeria', *Journal of Genocide Research* 15.1 (2013), 69–88.

Galtung, Johan, 'Cultural Violence', *Journal of Peace Research* 27.3 (1990), 291–305.

Gangohī, Ḥażrat Mawlānā al-Ḥājj al-Ḥāfiẓ Rashīd Aḥmad, *Fatāvā-yi rashīdiyyah. mubawwab bi-ṭarz-i jadīd* (Delhi: Darsī kutubkhānah, 1987).

Gangōhī, Muḥammad Ḥanīf, *Ẓafar al-muḥaṣṣilīn bā-aḥvāl-i muṣannifīn, yaᶜnī ḥālāt-i muṣannifīn-i dars-i niẓāmī* (Deoband: Ḥanīf Book Depot, 1996).

Garland, D., *The Culture of Control: Crime and Social Order in Contemporary Society* (Oxford: Oxford University Press, 2001).

Gartenstein-Ross, Daveed, and Tara Vassefi, 'Perceptions of the "Arab Spring" Within the *Salafi-Jihadi* Movement', *Studies in Conflict & Terrorism* 35.12 (2012), 831–48.

Geer, B., 'Training Scholars to Study Non-Scholarly Life', in *Teaching Islamic Studies in the Age of ISIS, Islamophobia, and the Internet*, ed. C. Dorroll (Bloomington: Indiana University Press, 2019), pp. 35–49.

van Gelder, G., 'Sexual Violence in Verse', in *Violence in Islamic Thought from the Qur'an to the Mongols*, eds R. Gleave and I. Kristó-Nagy (Edinburgh: Edinburgh University Press, 2014), pp. 175–90.

Gellner, Ernest, 'Rulers and Tribesmen', *Middle Eastern Studies* 15.1 (1979), 106–13.

Gellner, Ernest, 'The Stakes in Anthropology', *The American Scholar* 57 (1988), 17–30.

Ghareeb, Edmund, *Historical Dictionary of Iraq* (Lanham: Scarecrow Press, 2005).

al-Ghaṭafānī, Ḍirār b. ᶜAmr, *Kitāb al-Taḥrīsh*, eds Hüseyin Hansu and Mehmet Keskin (Istanbul: Dār al-irshād in collaboration with Ḍār Ibn Ḥazm, 2014).

Ghazi, Mahmood Ahmad, *Islamic Renaissance in South Asia 1707–1867: The Role of Shah Wali Allah and his Successors* (Islamabad: Islamic Research Institute, 2002).

Ghyoot, Mathias, 'Aḥlām al-Naṣr and the Islamic State's Justification for Execution by Burning', in *Islamic Law Reader*, eds Omar Anchassi and Robert Gleave (Cambridge: Cambridge University Press, forthcoming).

Gibb, H. A. R., 'Some Considerations of the Sunni Theory of the Caliphate', in *Studies on the Civilisation of Islam*, eds Stanford J. Shaw and William R. Polk (Boston, MA: Beacon Press, 1962), pp. 151–65.

Girard, René, *Violence and the Sacred*, trans. J. Gregory (Baltimore: Johns Hopkins University Press, 1977).

Giustozzi, Antonio (ed.), *Decoding the New Taliban: Insights from the Afghan Field* (London: Hurst / New York: Columbia University Press, 2009).

Giustozzi, Antonio, *Koran, Kalashnikov and Laptop: The Neo-Taliban Insurgency in Afghanistan* (London: Hurst / New York: Columbia University Press, 2007).

Glatzer, B., 'Schwert und Verantwortung: Paschtunische Männlichkeitsideale', in *Krieg und Kampf: Die Gewalt in unseren Köpfen*, eds Erwin Orywal, Aparna Rao and Michael Bollig (Berlin: Reimer, 1996), pp. 107–20.

Glatzer, B., 'Zum Pashtunwali als ethnisches Selbstportrait', in *Subjekte und Systeme: Soziologische und anthropologische Annäherungen. Festschrift für Christian Sigrist zum*

65. Geburtstag, eds Günter Best and Reinhart Kößler (Frankfurt/M.: IKO-Verlag, 2000), pp. 93–102.

Glatzer, B., 'Zum politischen Islam der afghanischen Taliban', in *Sendungsbewußtsein und Eigennutz: Zu Motivation und Selbstverständnis islamischer Mobilisierung*, ed. Dietrich Reetz (Berlin: Das Arabische Buch, 2001), pp. 173–82.

Glatzer, B., 'The Pashtun Tribal System', in *Concept of Tribal Society* [sic], eds Georg Pfeffer and D. K. Behera (New Delhi: Concept Publishing, 2002), pp. 265–82.

Gleave, R., 'Crimes and Against God and Violent Punishment in *al-Fatawa al-Alamgiriyya*', in *Religion and Violence in South Asia: Theory and Practice*, eds J. R. Hinnells and R. King (London: Routledge, 2007), pp. 83–106.

Gohari, M. J., *The Taliban: Ascent to Power* (Karachi: Oxford University Press, 2000).

Grandmaison, Olivier Le Cour, *Coloniser: exterminer: sur la guerre et l'état colonial* (Paris: Fayard, 2005).

Grandmaison, Olivier Le Cour, 'Conquête de l'Algérie: la guerre totale', in *Le massacre, objet d'histoire*, ed. David El Kenz (Paris: Gallimard, 2005), pp. 162–77.

Gray, Christine D., *International Law and the Use of Force* (Oxford; New York: Oxford University Press, 2004).

Grima, Benedicte, *Secrets from the Field: An Ethnographer's Notes from Northwest Pakistan* (Karachi: Oxford University Press, 2005).

Grima, Benedicte, *The Performance of Emotion among Paxtun Women: 'The Misfortunes Which Have Befallen Me'* (Austin, TX: University of Texas Press, 1992).

Gunning, J., *Hamas in Politics* (London: Hurst, 2007).

Gwynne, Rosalind, 'Usama bin Ladin, the Qurʾān and Jihad', *Religion* 36.2 (2006), 61–90.

Ḥabīb, Kamāl al-Saʿīd, *al-Ḥaraka al-islāmiyya min al-muwājaha ilā al-murājaʿa* (Cairo: Madbūlī, 2002).

Ḥālī, Alṭāf Ḥusayn, *Yādgār-i Ghālib* (Kanpur: Nāmī Press, 1898).

Hallaq, Wael B., *Authority, Continuity and Change* (Cambridge: Cambridge University Press, 2001).

Hallaq, Wael B., *Sharīʿa: Theory, Practice, Transformations* (Cambridge: Cambridge University Press, 2009).

Halliday, Fred, *Islam and the Myth of Confrontation* (London: I. B. Tauris, 2003).

al-Hamdānī, Abū Rāfir, *Dīwān Abī Firās al-Ḥamdānī* (Damascus: Institut Français de Damas, 1944).

Ḥāmid, Khwāja Muḥammad, *Imām-Bakhsh Ṣehbāʾī* (Lucknow: Bazm-i Ghālib, 1982).

al-Ḥanafī, Kamāl al-Dīn b. Humām, *Sharḥ fatḥ al-qadīr ʿalā al-hidāya sharḥ bidāyat al-mubtadī*, ed. ʿAbd al-Razzāq Ghālib al-Mahdī, 10 vols (Beirut: Dār al-kutub al-ʿilmiyya, 1424/2003).

Hanifi, M. Jamil, 'Vending Distorted Afghanistan Through Patriotic "Anthropology"', *Critique of Anthropology* 31.3 (2011), 256–70.

Hannoum, Abdelmajid, *Violent Modernity: France in Algeria* (Cambridge, MA: Harvard University Press, 2010).

Hanssen, Beatrice, *Critique of Violence: Between Poststructuralism and Critical Theory* (London: Routledge, 2000).

Haq [*sic*], Samiul, *Afghan Taliban: War of Ideology. Struggle for Peace* (Islamabad: Emel, 2015).

Haq, Syed Moinul, *The Great Revolution of 1857* (Karachi: Pakistan Historical Society, 1968).

Ḥaqqānī, Mawlānā ʿAbd al-Qayyūm, *Ṣuḥbate bā ahl-i ḥaqq: ifādāt-i muḥaddis̱-i kabīr Shaykh al-ḥadīs̱ Mawlānā ᶜAbd al-Ḥaqq – raḥmat allāh ᶜalayhi* (Khāliqābād: al-Qāsim akedimī, 1419/1998).

Ḥaqqānī, ᶜAbd al-Qayyūm, *Savāniḥ-i shaykh al-islām ḥaẓrat Sayyid Ḥusayn Aḥmad Madanī* (Khāliqābād: al-Qāsim Akedimī 1425/2004).

Ḥaqqānī, ᶜIrfān al-Ḥaqq, *Ṣalībī dahshat-gardī awr ᶜālam al-islām: Ṭālibān Afghānistān ke tanāẓur meṇ* (Akoṛa Khaṭṭak: Dār al-ᶜulūm ḥaqqāniyyah, 1425/2004).

Haroon, Sana, 'Public Visibility of Women and the Rise of the Neo-Taliban Movement in Khyber-Pakhtunkhwa, 2007–9', in *Beyond Swat: History, Society and Economy along the Afghanistan-Pakistan Frontier*, ed. Benjamin D. Hopkins and Magnus Marsden (London: Hurst / New York: Columbia University Press, 2013), pp. 193–205 and 318f. (notes and references).

Hartung, Jan-Peter, *Viele Wege und ein Ziel: Leben und Wirken von Sayyid Abū l-Ḥasan ᶜAlī Ḥasanī Nadwī (1914–1999)* (Würzburg: Ergon, 2004).

Hartung, Jan-Peter, *A System of Life: Mawdūdī and the Ideologisation of Islam* (London: Hurst / New York: Oxford University Press, 2013).

Hartung, Jan-Peter, *A System of Life: Mawdūdī and the Ideologisation of Islam* (London: Hurst, 2013).

Hartung, Jan-Peter, 'Abused Rationality? On the Role of *maᶜquli* Scholars in the Events of 1857/1858', in *Mutiny at the Margins: New Perspectives on the Indian Uprising of 1857, vol. 5*, ed. Crispin Bates (New Delhi and London: Sage, 2014), pp. 135–55.

Hartung, Jan-Peter, 'Between a Rock and a Hard Place: The *Ṭālibān*, Afghan Self-Determination, and the Challenges of Transnational Jihadism', *Die Welt des Islams* 56.2 (2016), 125–52.

Hartung, Jan-Peter, 'Of Pious Missions and Challenging the Elders: A Genealogy of Radical Egalitarianism in the Pashtun Borderscape', *Geopolitics* 24.2 (2019), 308–43.

Hartung, Jan-Peter, 'The Praiseworthiness of Divine Beauty – The "Shaykh al-Hind" Maḥmūd al-Ḥasan, Social Justice, and Deobandiyyat', *South Asian History and Culture* 7.4 (2016), 346–69.

Hartung, Jan-Peter, 'A Subtle Difference: On Ending One's Own Life in Muslim Religious Thought', *Journal of the Royal Asiatic Society* 28.1 (2018), 1–22.

Hartung, Jan-Peter, '«He's Just a Man!» – Pashtun Salafists and the Representation of the Prophet', *Die Welt des Islams* 60.2–3 (2020), 170–204.

Hartung, Jan-Peter, *The Pashtun Borderland in Uproar: A Religious and Cultural History of (the) Taliban* (forthcoming).

Hartung, Jan-Peter, 'Taking Lessons from the Prophet in Times of War: Muḥammadan Images during the Afghan Resistance, ca. 1978–1992', in *Heirs of the Prophet: Authority and Power in Early Modern and Contemporary Islam*, ed. Rachida Chih, David Jordan and Stefan Reichmuth, (Leiden and Boston, MA: Brill, forthcoming).

Hasan, Mushirul, *From Pluralism to Separatism: Qasbas in Colonial Awadh* (New Delhi: Oxford University Press, 2004).

Ḥasanī, Sayyid ᶜAbd al-Ḥayy, *Nuzhat al-khawāṭir wa-bahjat al-maṣāmiᶜ wa-l-manāẓir* (Rae Bareli: Dār ᶜArafāt, 1991).

Hashim, Ahmed, *Insurgency and Counter-Insurgency* (London: Hurst, 2006).

Hashmi, Soheil, '9/11 and the Jihad Tradition', in *Terror, Culture, Politics: Rethinking 9/11*, eds Daniel J. Sherman and Terry Nardin (Bloomington: Indiana University Press, 2006), pp. 149–64.

al-Ḥaṣkafī, Muḥammad b. ᶜAlī, *al-Durr al-mukhtār sharḥ tanwīr al-abṣār wa-jāmiᶜ al-baḥār*, ed. ᶜAbd al-Munᶜim Khalīl Ibrāhīm (Beirut: Dār al-kutub al-ᶜilmiyya, 1423/2002).

Hatina, M., 'Hamas and the Oslo Accords: Religious Dogma in a Changing Political Reality', *Mediterranean Politics* 4.3 (1999), 37–55.

Hatina, M., 'The "Ulama" and the Cult of Death in Palestine', *Israel Affairs* 12.1 (2006), 29–51.

al-Ḥawālī, Safar, *Ẓāhirat al-irjāʿ fī-l-fikr al-islāmi* (Cairo: Maktab al-Ṭayyib, 1996).

Haykel, Bernard, 'On the Nature of Salafi Thought and Action', in *Global Salafism: Islam's New Religious Movement*, ed. Roel Meijer (New York: Columbia University Press, 2009), pp. 33–57.

Hegghammer, Thomas, 'Global Jihadism After the Iraq War', *Middle East Journal* 60 (2006), 11–32.

Hegghammer, Thomas, *Jihad in Saudi Arabia: Violence and Pan-Islamism since 1979* (Cambridge: Cambridge University Press, 2010).

Herman, E. S., and N. Chomsky, *Manufacturing Consent: The Political Economy of the Mass Media* (New York: Pantheon Books, 1988).

al-Ḥillī, Abū Jaʿfar Muḥammad ibn Manṣūr ibn Aḥmad Ibn Idrīs, *Kitāb al-Sarāʾir al-Ḥāwī li-Taḥrīr al-Fatāwī* (Qum: Muʾassasat al-Nashr al-Islāmī al-Tābiʿah l-Jāmiʿat al-Mudarrissīn, 1990).

al-Ḥillī, Al-Ḥassan ibn Yūsuf ibn al-Muṭahhar al-Allāmah, *Tadhkirat al-Fuqahāʾ* (Qum: Muʾassasat āl al-Bayt li-Iḥyāʾ al-Turāth, 1993).

al-Ḥillī, Ja'far ibn al-Ḥassan al-Muḥaqqiq, *al-Mukhtaṣar al-Nāfiʿ fī Fiqh al-Imāmiyyah* (Qum: Muʾassasat al-Biʿthah, 1990).

al-Ḥimyarī, Muḥammad b. Munʿim, *al-Rawḍ al-miʿṭār fī khabar al-aqṭār*, ed. Iḥsān ʿAbbās (Beirut: Maktabat Lubnān, 1974).

Hobsbawm, Eric, and Terence Ranger (eds), 'Introduction: Inventing Traditions', in *The Invention of Tradition*, eds Eric Hobsbawm and Terence Ranger (Cambridge: Cambridge University Press, 1983), pp. 1–14.

Hobsbawm, Eric, and Terence Ranger (eds), *The Invention of Tradition* (Cambridge: Cambridge University Press, 1983).

Hoffman, Bruce, *Insurgency and Counterinsurgency in Iraq* (Santa Monica, CA: RAND, National Security, 2005).

Holbrook, Donald, 'Al-Qaeda's Response to the Arab Spring', *Perspectives on Terrorism* 6.6 (2012), 4–21.

Holt, P. M., 'Qalāwūn's Treaty with Acre in 1283', *The English Historical Review* 91.361 (1976), 802–12.

Holt, P. M., 'The Treaties of the Early Mamluk Sultans with the Frankish States', *Bulletin of the School of Oriental and African Studies, University of London* 43.1 (1980), 67–76.

Holtzman, Livnat, 'Ibn Qayyim al-Jawziyya', in *Essays in Arabic Literary Biography*, eds J. E. Lowry and D. Stewart)Wiesbaden: Harrassowitz Verlag, 2009), pp. 202–23.

Hoover, Jon, *Ibn Taymiyya's Theodicy of Perpetual Optimism* (Leiden and Boston, MA: Brill, 2007).

Hroub, K., *Hamas: Political Thought and Practice* (Washington, DC: Institute for Palestine Studies, 2000).

Hroub, K., *Hamas, A Beginner's Guide* (London: Pluto, 2006).

Hroub, K., 'Conflating National Liberation and Socio-Political Change', in *Political Islam: Context Versus Ideology*, ed. Khalid Hroub (London: Saqi, 2010), pp. 59–72.

Husain, Iqbal, 'Fazle Haq of Khairabad: A Scholarly Rebel of 1857', *Indian History Congress,*

Proceedings of the Forth-Eighth Session, Goa University, Bambolim, 1987 (Delhi, 1988), pp. 355–65.

Husain, Iqbal, *Religion and Ideology of the Rebels of 1857* (Delhi: Primus Books, 2013).

Hussain, Syed A., 'Anglo-Muhammadan Law', in *The Oxford Handbook of Islamic Law*, eds Anver M. Emon and Rumee Ahmed (Oxford: Oxford University Press, 2018), pp. 537–50.

Ibn ᶜAbd al-Wahhāb, Muḥammad, '*Kitāb al-tawḥīd*', in *Muʾallafāt al-shaykh al-imām Muḥammad bin ᶜAbd al-Wahhāb*, eds ᶜAbd al-ᶜAzīz Zayd al-Rūmī, Muḥammad Biltājī and Sayyid Ḥijāb (Riyadh: Jāmiᶜat al-Imām Muḥammad b. Suᶜūd al-Islāmiyya, n. d.), I, pp. 7–151.

Ibn ᶜĀbidīn, Muḥammad Amīn, *Radd al-mukhtār ᶜalā al-durr al-mukhtār sharḥ tanwīr al-abṣār*, eds al-Shaykh ᶜĀdil Aḥmad ᶜAbd al-Mawjūd and al-Shaykh ᶜAlī Muḥammad Muᶜawwaḍ, 12 vols (Riyadh: Dār ᶜālam al-kutub, 1423/2003).

Ibn Ḥajar, *Fatḥ al-bārī bi-sharḥ Ṣaḥīḥ al-Bukhārī*, eds Muḥammad Fuʾād ᶜAbd al-Bāqī and ᶜAbd al-ᶜAzīz Bin Bāz (Cairo: al-Maktaba al-salafiyya, n. d.).

Ibn Ḥamdān, Sulaymān b. ᶜAbd al-Raḥmān, *Dalālat al-nuṣūs waʾl-ijmāᶜ ᶜalā farḍ al-qitāl liʾl-kufr waʾl-difāᶜ* (Amman: Dār al-Ṭibāᶜa waʾl-Nashr, [n. d.]).

Ibn Ḥanbal, *Musnad al-imām Aḥmad*, ed. Shuᶜayb al-Arnaʾūṭ (Beirut: Muʾassasat al-Risāla, 1416/1997).

Ibn Ḥazm, Abū Muḥammad, *al-Muḥallā bi-l-āthār fī sharḥ al-mujallā bi-l-ikhtiṣār* (Beirut: Dār Ibn Ḥazm, 2016).

Ibn Hishām, *Sīrat al-nabiyy* (Cairo: Maktabat Muḥammad 'Alī Ṣubayḥ, 1937).

Ibn al-Jawzī, *Kitāb al-Mawḍūᶜāt*, ed. ᶜAbd al-Raḥmān ᶜUthmān (Manṣūra: al-Maktaba al-salafiyya, 1388/1968).

Ibn al-Jawzī, *Kitāb al-quṣṣāṣ wa 'l-mudhakkirīn*, ed. Merlin Swartz (Beirut: Dar el-Machreq, 1971).

Ibn Kathīr, ᶜImād al-Dīn Ismāᶜīl, *Juzʾ fī bayᶜ ummahāt al-awlād*, ed. ᶜUmar b. Sulaymān al-Ḥafyān (Beirut: Muʾassasat al-risāla, 1427/2006).

Ibn Kathīr, ᶜImād al-Dīn Ismāᶜīl, *Tafsīr al-Qurʾān al-ᶜaẓīm* (Dammam: Dār Ibn al-Jawzī, 2019).

Ibn al-Mundhir, *al-Awsaṭ min al-sunan wa l-ijmāᶜ wa l-ikhtilāf*, ed. Muḥammad ᶜAbd al-Salām (al-Fayyūm: Dār al-falāḥ, 2009).

Ibn al-Naḥḥās, Abū Zakariyyā Aḥmad, *Mashāriᶜ al-ashwāq ilā maṣāriᶜ al-ᶜushshāq* (Beirut: Dār al-Bashā'ir al-Islāmīya, 1990).

Ibn Qayyim al-Jawziyya, *al-Kāfiya al-shāfiya fīʾl-intiṣār liʾl-firqa al-nājiya* (Mecca: Dār ᶜĀlam al-Fawāʾid, 1428 AH).

Ibn Qayyim al-Jawziyya, *al-Manār al-munīf fīʾl-ṣaḥīḥ waʾl-ḍaᶜīf*, ed. Yaḥya b. ᶜAbdallāh al-Thumālī (Mecca: Dār ᶜĀlam al-Fawāʾid, 1428 AH).

Ibn Qudāma, Muwaffaq al-Dīn, *al-Mughnī* (Riyadh: Dār ᶜĀlam al-Kutub, 2013).

Ibn Rajab al-Ḥanbalī, Zayn al-Dīn Abī al-Faraj ᶜAbd al-Raḥmān b. Aḥmad, *Majmūᶜ rasāʾil al-ḥāfiẓ Ibn Rajab al-Ḥanbalī* (Cairo: al-Fārūq al-Ḥadītha, [n. d.]).

Ibn Sallām, Abū ᶜUbayd al-Qāsim, *al-Nāsikh wa l-mansūkh*, ed. Muḥammad b. Ṣāliḥ al-Mudayfar (Riyadh: Maktabat al-rushd, n. d.).

Ibn Taymiyya, Taqī al-Dīn Aḥmad, *Jāmiᶜ al-masāʾil* (Mecca: Dār ᶜĀlam al-Fawāʾid, 1422/2001–2).

Ibn Taymiyya, Taqī al-Dīn Aḥmad, *Majmūᶜat al-fatāwā* (al-Manṣūra: Dār al-Wafāʾ, 1426/2005).

Ibn Taymiyya, Taqī al-Dīn Aḥmad, *Majmūᶜ al-fatāwā* (Beirut: Dār Ibn Ḥazm, 2011).

Idinopulos, Thomas A., and Brian C. Wilson (eds), *What is Religion? Origins, Definitions, and Explanations* (Leiden: Brill, 1998).

Irwin, Robert, Dangerous Knowledge: Orientalism and its Discontents (London: Overlook, 2006).

al-Isfarayīnī, Abū l-Muẓaffar, *al-Tabṣīr fī l-dīn wa tamyīz al-firqa al-nājiya ᶜan al-firaq al-hālikīn*, ed. Majīd al-Khalīfa (Beirut: Dār ibn ḥazm, 1429/2008).

Iṣlāḥī, ᶜAbd al-Raḥmān 'Parvāz', *Muftī Ṣadr al-Dīn Āzurda: ḥayāt, shakhṣīyat, ᶜilmī aur adabī kārnāmē* (New Delhi: Maktaba-yi Jāmiᶜa, 1977).

Ismail, Raihan, 'Reclaiming Saudi Salafism: The Saudi Religious Circles and the Threat of ISIS', *Journal of Arabian Studies* 9.2 (2020), 164–81.

Jabar, Faleh A., *The Shīᶜite Movement in Iraq* (London: Al-Saqi, 2003).

Jabar, Faleh A., 'Worldly Roots of Religiosity in Post-Saddam Iraq', *Middle East Report* 227 (2003), 12–18.

Jaᶜfarī, ᶜAlī Sardār, *Nawāb Muḥammad Muṣṭafā Khān 'Shēfta'* (Lahore: Azra Publications, 1999).

Jafri, Saiyid Zaheer Husain, 'The Indigenous Discourse in the Rebels' World of 1857: An Analysis of Three Documents', in *The Great Uprising of 1857: Commentaries, Studies, and Documents*, eds Syed Najmul Raza Rizvi and Saiyid Zaheer Husain Jafri (Delhi: Anamika Publishers, 2009), pp. 81–100.

Jäger, Siegfried, *Kritische Diskursanalyse: Eine Einführung* (Münster: Unrast, 2004, 4th ed.).

Jalal, Ayesha, *The Sole Spokesman: Jinnah, the Muslim League, and the Demand for Pakistan* (Cambridge: Cambridge University Press, 1985).

Jalal, Ayesha, *Partisans of Allah: Jihad in South Asia* (Cambridge, MA: Harvard University Press, 2008).

Jalil, Rakhshanda, 'Reflections of 1857 in Contemporary Urdu Literature', in *Mutiny at the Margins. New Perspectives on the Indian Uprising of 1857 Volume I: Anticipations and Experiences in the Locality*, ed. C. Bates (New Delhi: Sage Publications, 2013), pp. 120–31.

Jansen, Johannes J. G., *The Neglected Duty: The Creed of Sadat's Assassins and Islamic Resurgence in the Middle East* (New York: Macmillan, 1986).

Janssen, Floor, and Joas Wagemakers, 'Is al-Qa'ida echt failliet?', *Internationale Spectator* 65.7/8 (2011), 393–6.

Janssen, Floor, and Joas Wagemakers, 'Luidt de Arabische lente de winter van al-Qaida in?', *ZemZem: Tijdschrift over het Midden-Oosten, Noord-Afrika en islam* 7.1 (2011), 40–5.

al-Jaṣṣās, Abū Bakr, *Ahkām al-Qurʾān* (Beirut: Dār Ibn Ḥazm, 1992).

al-Jawharī, Ismāᶜīl b. Ḥammād, *al-Ṣiḥāḥ* (Beirut: Dār al-ᶜIlm liʾl-Malāyīn, 1399/1979).

al-Jawziyya, Shams al-Dīn b. Qayyim, *al-Ṭuruq al-ḥukumiyya fī-l-siyāsa al-sharᶜiyya* (Mecca: Dār ᶜĀlim al-Fawāʾid, 2007).

Jersild, Austin, *Orientalism and Empire North Caucasus Mountain Peoples and the Georgian Frontier, 1845–1917* (Montreal: McGill-Queen's University Press, 2002).

Johnson, N., *Islam and the Politics of Meaning in Palestinian Nationalism* (London: Kegan Paul, 1982).

Johnston, Hank, and John A. Noakes (eds), *Frames of Protest: Social Movements and the Framing Perspective* (Lanham: Rowman & Littlefield Publishers, Inc., 2005).

Al-Jubbāʾī, Abū ᶜAlī (attrib.), *Kitāb al-Maqālāt*, eds Özkan Şimşek, A. İskender Sarıca and Yusuf Arıkaner (Istanbul: Endulus, 2020).

Kahl, Colin H., 'Is There a Future for Counter-insurgency?', *Foreign Affairs* 86 (2007), 169–76.

Kakar, Hasan Kawun, *Government and Society in Afghanistan: The Reign of Amir ʾAbd* [sic] *al-Rahman Khan* (Austin, TX and London: University of Texas Press, 1979).

Kalkattavī, Mawlavī Ghulām Qādir Baniyānī (ed.), *Tanbīh al-ḍāllayn wa-hidāyat al-ṣāliḥayn* (Lahore: Maṭbaᶜ Ganesh Prashād, n.d.).

Kamali, Mohammad Hashim, *Law in Afghanistan: A Study of the Constitutions, Matrimonial Law and the Judiciary* (Leiden: Brill, 1985).

Kapuścinski, Ryszard, *The Other* (London and New York: Verso, 2008).

al-Kasānī, Imām ᶜAlāʾ al-Dīn Abū Bakr b. Masᶜūd, *Badāʾiᶜ al-ṣanāʾiᶜ fī tartīb al-sharāʾiᶜ*, eds al-Shaykh ᶜAlī Muḥammad Muᶜawwaḍ and al-Shaykh ᶜĀdil Aḥmad ᶜAbd al-Mawjūd, 10 vols (Beirut: Dār al-kutub al-ᶜilmiyya, 1424/2002).

Kāshif al-Ghiṭāʾ, Jāᶜfar, *Kashf al-Ghiṭāʾ ᶜan Mubhamāt al-Sharīᶜa al-Gharrāʾ* (Isfahān: Intishārāt Mahdawī, n. d.).

Katz, Marion, *The Birth of the Prophet Muḥammad: Devotional Piety in Sunni Islam* (London: Routledge, 2007).

Kavakcı, Yusuf Ziya, *XI. ve XII. asırlarda Karahanlılar devrinde Māvāra' al-Nahr* [sic] *İslâm hukukçuları* (Ankara: Sevinç matbaası, 1976).

Kemper, Michael and Maurus Reinkowski (eds.), *Rechtspluralismus in der Islamischen Welt: Gewohnheitsrecht zwischen Staat und Gesellschaft* (Berlin and New York: de Gruyter, 2005).

Kemper, Michael, *Herrschaft, Recht und Islam in Daghestan: Von den Khanaten und Gemeindebünden zum ǧihād-Staat* (Wiesbaden: Reichert, 2005).

Kendall, Elisabeth, 'Jihadist Propaganda and its Exploitation of the Arab Poetic Tradition', in *Reclaiming Islamic Tradition: Modern Interpretations of the Classical Heritage*, eds Elisabeth Kendall and Ahmad Khan (Edinburgh: Edinburgh University Press, 2016), pp. 223–46.

Kenney, Jeffrey T., *Muslim Rebels: Kharijites and the Politics of Extremism in Egypt* (Oxford: Oxford University Press, 2006).

Kepel, Gilles, *Jihad: The Trail of Political Islam*, trans. Anthony F. Roberts. (London: I. B. Tauris, 2002).

Kepel, Gilles, *Muslim Extremism in Egypt: The Prophet and the Pharaoh* (Berkeley and Los Angeles: University of California Press, 2003).

Kepel, Gilles, *The Roots of Radical Islam*, trans. Jon Rothschild and Pascale Ghazaleh (London: Saqi, 2005).

Khādim, Qiyām al-Dīn, *Paxtūnvalī* (Kabul: Də paxto ṫolānah, 1331 SH).

al-Khaffāf, Ḥāmid, *al-Nuṣūṣ al-Ṣādirah ᶜan Samāḥat al-Sayyid al-Sīstānī* (Beirut: Dār al-Muʾarikh al-ᶜArabī, 2007).

Khalaji, Mehdi, 'The Last Marja: Sistani and the End of Traditional Religious Authority in Shīᶜism', *The Washington Institute for Near East Policy*, Policy Focus no. 59 (September 2006).

Khalil, Mohammad Hassan (ed.), *Between Heaven and Hell: Islam, Salvation and the Fates of Others* (London: Oxford University Press, 2013).

Khalil, Mohammad Hassan, *Jihad, Radicalism, and the New Atheism* (Cambridge: Cambridge University Press, 2017).

Khallāf, ᶜAbd al-Wahhāb, *Maṣādir al-tashrīᶜ al-islāmi fī-mā lā naṣṣ fī-hi* (Cairo: Dār al-Qalam, 1954).

al-Khallāl, *Aḥkām ahl al-milal*, ed. Sayyid Ḥasan (Beirut: Dār al-kutub al-ᶜilmiyya, 1414/1994).

Khān, Aḥmad Rižā, *al-ᶜAṭāyā al-nabawiyya fī al-fatāwā al-riḍawiyya* (Lahore: Rižā Foundation, 1991–2005).

Khan, Anoosh Wisal, 'Contesting Subjectivities, Negotiating Agency, and Re-Defining Boundaries: The Ideological Subject Formation and Positioning of Pakhtun Women' (unpublished Ph.D. dissertation, American University, Washington, DC, 2012).

Khān, Ḥakīm Aḥsanullāh, 'Memoirs', trans. S. Moinul Haq, *Journal of the Pakistan Historical Society* 6.1 (1958), 103–12.

Khān, Sayyid Ahmad, *Asbāb-i baghāvat-i Hind: An Essay on the Causes of the Indian Revolt* (Agra: J. A. Gibbons, 1859).

Khān, Sayyid Ahmad, *The Causes of the Indian Revolt Written by Syed Ahmed Khan Bahadur by His Two European Friends* (Benares: Medical Hall Press, 1873).

Khān, Sayyid Ahmad, *Āsār al-ṣanādīd II* (Cambridge: Cambridge University Press, 1972).

Khān, Tawqīr Aḥmad, *Muʾmin Khān 'Muʾmin'* (Delhi: Urdu Academy, 2007).

Khatib, Lina, Dina Matar and Atef Alshaer, *The Hizbullah Phenomenon: Politics and Communication* (New York and Oxford: Oxford University Press, 2014).

Khaṭṭak, Ajmal, *Qīṣṣah zamā də adabī žvand* (Chārsaddah: Riyāz būk ījansī, 2005).

Khayrābādī, Fažl-i Ḥaqq Ḥabīb al-Raḥmān Maẓāhirī, *Tadhkirat al-muṣannifīn: Dars-i niẓāmiyya aur dars-i ᶜāliyya aur tamām ᶜarabī niṣābōn mēñ shāmil jumla kutub kē muṣannifīn kā mukammal tadhkira* (n. p.: Maktaba-yi Naᶜīmiyya, n. d.).

Khayrābādī, Fažl-i Ḥaqq Ḥabīb al-Raḥmān Maẓāhirī, *Bāghī Hindustān* (Lahore: Maktaba-yi Qādirīya, 1974).

Khayrābādī, Fažl-i Ḥaqq Ḥabīb al-Raḥmān Maẓāhirī, *Imtināᶜ al-naẓīr* (Lahore: Markaz taḥqīqāt-i islāmīya, 2000).

Khayrābādī, Fažl-i Ḥaqq Ḥabīb al-Raḥmān Maẓāhirī, *Taḥqīq al-fatwā fī ibṭāl al-taghwā yā shafāᶜat-i Muḥammad*, with Urdu translation of Muḥammad ᶜAbd al-Ḥakīm Qādirī (Lahore: Mumtāz Publications, 2000).

Khodja, Hamdan, *Le Miroir: Aperçu historique et statistique sur la Régence d'Alger* (Paris: Sindbad, 1985 [1833]).

al-Khūʾī, Abū al-Qāsim al-Mūsawī, *Minhāj al-Ṣāliḥīn* (Qum: Mohr, 1990).

Kiernan, Ben, *Blood and Soil: A World History of Genocide and Extermination from Sparta to Darfur* (New Haven: Yale University Press, 2007).

King, John, 'Abd el-Kader and Arab Nationalism', in *Problems of the Middle East in Historical Perspective – Essays in Honour of Albert Hourani*, ed. John Spagnolo (Oxford: The Middle East Centre, 1996), pp. 133–49.

King, R., 'The Association of "Religion" with Violence: Reflections on a Modern Trope', in *Religion and Violence in South Asia: Theory and Practice*, eds J. R. Hinnells and R. King (London: Routledge, 2007), pp. 226–57.

Knudsen, A., 'Crescent and Sword: The Hamas Enigma', *Third World Quarterly* 26.8 (2005), 1373–88.

Knudsen, Are, *Violence and Belonging: Land, Love and Lethal Conflict in the North-West Frontier Province of Pakistan* (New Delhi: Orient BlackSwan, 2009).

Kraemer, Joel L., 'Apostates, Rebels, and Brigands', *Israel Oriental Studies* 10.1 (1980), 34–74.

Kristó-Nagy, Istvan, 'Introduction', in *Violence in Islamic Thought from the Qur'an to the Mongols*, eds R. Gleave and I. Kristó-Nagy (Edinburgh: Edinburgh University Press, 2014), pp. 1–24.

Al-Kulaynī, Muḥammad b. Yaᶜqūb, *al-Kāfī* (Beirut: Manshūrāt al-fajr, 1328/2007).

Kuper, Leo, 'Genocide: Its Political Use in the Twentieth Century', in *Genocide: An Anthropological Reader*, ed. Alexander Laban (Oxford: Blackwell, 2002), pp. 48–73.

Lacroix, Stéphane, *Les islamistes saoudiens: une insurrection manqué* (Paris: Presses Universitaires de France, 2010).

Lahoud, Nelly, *The Jihadis' Path to Self-Destruction* (New York: Columbia University Press, 2010).

Lahoud, Nelly, 'Ayman al-Zawahiri's Reaction to Revolution in the Middle East', *CTC Sentinel* 4.4 (2011), 4–7.

Lahoud, Nelly, 'Revolution in Tunisia and Egypt: A Blow to the Jihadist Narrative?', *CTC Sentinel* 4.2 (2011), 4–5.

Lal, Munshī Jīwan, *Two Native Narratives of the Mutiny in Delhi*, trans. Charles T. Metcalfe (Delhi: Seema Publications, 1974).

Lal, Vinay, *The History of History: Politics and Scholarship in Modern India* (Delhi: Oxford University Press, 2003).

Lambton, Ann K. S., *State and Government in Medieval Islam: An Introduction to the Study* (New York: Routledge, 1981).

Landau-Tasseron, Ella, 'Jihad and Just War: Overt and Covert Analogies' (forthcoming).

Lane, Max, The Unfinished Nation: Indonesia Before and After Suharto (London: Verso, 2008).

Lange, Christian, *Justice, Punishment, and the Medieval Muslim Imagination* (Cambridge: Cambridge University Press, 2008).

Lange, Christian, 'Where on Earth is Hell? State Punishment and Eschatology in the Islamic Middle Period', in *Public Violence in Islamic Societies*, eds Christian Lange and Maribel Fierro (Edinburgh: Edinburgh University Press, 2009), pp. 156–78.

Lange, Christian, 'Crime and Punishment in Islamic History (Early to Middle Period): A Framework of Analysis', *Religion Compass* 4.11 (2010), 694–706.

Lange, Christian, *Paradise and Hell in Islamic Traditions* (Cambridge: Cambridge University Press, 2015).

Lange, Christian, 'Introducing Hell in Islamic Studies', in *Locating Hell in Islamic Traditions*, ed. Christian Lange (Leiden and Boston, MA: Brill, 2016), pp. 1–28.

Lange, Christian, "Immolation", in *Encyclopaedia of Islam, THREE*, eds Kate Fleet, Gudrun Krämer, Denis Matringe, John Nawas and Everett Rowson, 2017 (http://dx.doi.org.uoelibrary.idm.oclc.org/10.1163/1573-3912_ei3_COM_32442).

Laoust, Henri, *Essai sur les doctrines sociales et politiques de Taḳī-d-Dīn Aḥmad b. Taimīya* (Cairo: L'institut Français d'archéologie orientale, 1939).

Laroui, Abdallah, *The History of the Maghrib: An Interpretive Essay* (Princeton: Princeton University Press, 1977).

Lav, Daniel, *Radical Islam and the Revival of Medieval Theology* (New York: Cambridge University Press, 2012).

Lawrence, B., *Shattering the Myth: Islam Beyond Violence* (Princeton: Princeton University Press, 1998).

Lawrence, B., 'Citizen Ahmad Among the Believers: Salvation Contextualized in Egypt and Indonesia', in *Between Heaven and Hell: Islam, Salvation and the Fates of Others*, ed. Mohammad Hassan Khalil (London: Oxford University Press, 2013), pp. 299–305.

Lawrence, B., and Aisha Karim (eds), *On Violence: A Reader* (Durham: Duke University Press, 2007).

Leahy, Anthony, 'Death by Fire in Ancient Egypt', *Journal of the Economic and Social History of the Orient* 27.2 (1984), 199–206.
Leaman, Oliver, 'Review of R. Gleave and I. Kristó-Nagy (eds), *Violence in Islamic Thought from the Qur'an to the Mongols*', *Journal of Qur'anic Studies* 18.3 (2016), 124–7.
Lelyveld, David, *Aligarh's First Generation: Muslim Solidarity in British India* (Princeton: Princeton University Press, 1978).
Levitt, M., *Hamas: Politics, Charity, and Terrorism in the Service of Jihad* (New Haven and London: Yale University Press, 2006).
al-Lībī Ḥasan Qāʾid, Abū Yaḥyā, *al-Muʿallim fī ḥukm al-jāsūs al-muslim* (n.p.: Markaz al-fajr al-iʿlām, 1430/2009).
Lilla, Mark, *The Stillborn God: Religion, Politics, and the Modern West* (New York: Vintage, 2008).
Linschoten, Alex Strick van, and Feliz Kuehn, *The Poetry of the Taliban* (London: Hurst / New York: Columbia University Press, 2012).
Llewellyn-Jones, Rosie, *The Great Uprising in India, 1857–58* (Woodbridge: Boydell Press, 2007).
Louër, Laurence, *Transnational Shia Politics: Religious and Political Networks in the Gulf* (London: Hurst, 2008).
Ludhiyānavī, Muftī Rashīd Aḥmad, *Ṭālibān: mujāhidīn-i lashkar-i nabavī-yi aḥkām-i ʿāliyyah: iṭāʿat-i amīr* (Karachi: al-Rashīd trasṫ, 1421 AH).
Ludhiyānavī, Muftī Rashīd Aḥmad, *Aḥsan al-fatāvā*, 10 vols (Karachi: H. M. Saʿīd kampanī, 1425 AH).
Ludhiyānavī, Muftī Rashīd Aḥmad, *Anvār al-rashīd*, ed. Aḥmad Nūr al-Muqtadā, 2 vols (Karachi: Kitābgaṛh, 1424 AH).
Ludhiyānavī, Muftī Rashīd Aḥmad, *Khuṭbāt al-rashīd*, 7 vols (Karachi: Kitābgaṛh, 1425 AH).
Lybarger, L., *Identity and Religion in Palestine: The Struggle between Islamism and Secularism in the Occupied Territories* (Princeton: Princeton University Press, 2007).
Maalouf, Amin, In the Name of Identity: Violence and the Need to Belong (New York: Penguin, 2000).
Macdonell, Diane, *An Introduction: Theories of Discourse* (Oxford: Blackwell, 1989).
al-Madanī, Shīr ʿAlī Shāh, 'al-Sīra al-dhātiyya li'l-shaykh al-Duktūr Shīr ʿAlī Shāh al-Madanī', in *Yād: Shaykh al-tafsīr va'l-ḥadīs̱ Mawlānā Dākṫar Shīr ʿAlī Shāh Madanī – rḥ: ḥayāt va khidmāt*, ed. Muḥammad Asrār Madanī (Akoṛah Khaṫṫak: Muʾtamar al-muṣannifīn-i dār al-ʿulūm ḥaqqāniyyah, 1437/2016), pp. 17–19.
al-Madkhalī, Rabīʿ b. Hādī ʿUmayr, *Aḍwāʾ islāmiyya ʿalā ʿaqīdat Sayyid Quṭb wa-fikrihi* (Cairo: Dār al-Āthār, 1428/2007).
Majīd, Shīma, *Shēfta: ik muṭālaʿa* (Karachi: Pakistan Writers' Cooperative Society, 2005).
Al-Majlisī, Muḥammad Bāqir, *Biḥār al-anwār* (Beirut: Muʾassasat al-wafāʾ, n. d.).
Makdisi, Ussama, and Paul A. Silverstein (eds), *Memory and Violence in the Middle East and North Africa* (Bloomington: Indiana University Press, 2006).
Maley, William (ed.), *Fundamentalism Reborn? Afghanistan and the Taliban* (London: Hurst, 1998).
Malik, Jamal, *Islamische Gelehrtenkultur in Nordindien: Entwicklungsgeschichte und Tendenzen am Beispiel von Lucknow* (Leiden, New York and Cologne: Brill, 1997).
Malik, Jamal, 'Letters, Prison Sketches and Autobiographical Literature: The Case of Fazl-e Haq Khairabadi in the Andaman Penal Colony', *Indian Economic and Social History Review* 43 (2006), 77–100.

Mallat, Chibli, 'Religious Militancy in Contemporary Iraq: Muhammad Baqer as-Sadr and the Sunni-Shia Paradigm', *Third World Quarterly* 10.2 (1988), 699–729.

Mallat, Chibli, *The Renewal of Islamic Law: Baqer as-Sadr, Najaf and the Shīᶜi International* (Cambridge: Cambridge University Press, 1993).

Manṣūr, Muftī Abū Lubābah Shāh, *Dajjāl 2: ᶜālamī dajjālī riyāsat, ibtidāʾ se intihā tak* (Karachi: al-Falāḥ, 1431/2010).

March, Andrew F., Islam and Liberal Citizenship: The Search for an Overlapping Consensus (NY: Oxford University Press, 2009).

Marçot, Jean-Louis, 'Abd el-Kader et la modernité', *Studia Islamica* 2 (2011), 281–300.

al-Marghinānī, al-Imām Burhān al-Dīn, *al-Hidāya sharḥ bidāyat al-mubtadī, maᶜa sharḥ al-ᶜAllāma ᶜAbd al-Ḥayy al-Laknawī*, ed. Naᶜīm Ashraf Nūr Aḥmad, 8 vols (Karachi: Idārat al-qurʾān wa'l-ulūm al-islāmiyya, 1417 AH).

Markaz-i farhangī-yi nivīsandagān-i Afghānistān (ed.), *Matn-i kāmil-i qāvānīn-i āsāsī-yi Afghānistān: az 1301 tā 1372sh* (Qom: Markaz-i farhangī-yi nivīsandagān-i Afghānistān, 1374Sh).

Marranci, Gabriele, *Jihad Beyond Islam* (London: Berg, 2006).

Marsham, Andrew, 'Attitudes to the Use of Fire in Executions in Late Antiquity and Early Islam', in *Violence in Islamic Thought: From the Qur'an to the Mongols*, eds Robert Gleave and István Kristó-Nagy (Edinburgh: Edinburgh University Press, 2015), pp. 106–27.

al-Marwardi, Abu al-Hasan, *Al-ahkam As-sultaniyyah* (London: TaHa Publishers, 1996).

al-Maṣrī, Mushīr, *al-Mushārkah fī al-Ḥayāh al-Siyāsiyyah fī ẓill Anẓimat al-Ḥukm al-Muᶜāṣirah* (Beirut: Dār al-Kalimah lil-nashr bil-Manṣūrah, 2006).

Massoumi, N., T. Mills and D. Miller (eds), *What is Islamophobia?: Racism, Social Movements and the State* (London: Pluto Press, 2017).

Masud, Muhammad K., 'The Obligation to Migrate', in *Muslim Travellers, Pilgrimage, Migration and the Religious Imagination*, eds D. F. Eickelman and J. Piscatori (London and Berkeley: University of California Press, 1990), pp. 29–49.

Masud, Muhammad K., 'The Significance of *Istiftā'* in the *Fatwā* Discourse', *Islamic Studies* 48.3 (2009), 341–66.

Matar, Dina, 'The Power of Conviction: Nassrallah's Rhetoric and Mediated Charisma in the Context of the 2006 July War', *Middle East Journal of Culture and Communication* 1.2 (2008), 122–37.

Mavani, Hamid, 'Ayatullah Khomeni's Concept of Governance (*wilayat al-faqih*) and the Classical Shīᶜi Doctrine of Imamate', *Middle Eastern Studies* 47.5 (2001), 807–24.

al-Māwardī, Abū 'l-Ḥasan ᶜAlī, *K. al-Aḥkām al-sulṭāniyya* (Beirut: Dār al-fikr, 1422/2002).

Mawdūdī, Abū al-Aᶜlā, *Tafhīmāt* (Lahore: Islamic Publications Ltd, 2004).

Mawdūdī, Abū al-Aᶜlā, *Khuṭbāt* (New Delhi: Markazī Maktabah-i Islāmī, 2005).

Mawdūdī, Abū al-Aᶜlā, *Islāmī riyāsat* (Lahore: Islamic Publications (Private) Limited, 2008).

Mawdūdī, Abū al-Aᶜlā, *Qurʾān kī chār bunyādī iṣṭilāḥēñ* (New Delhi: Markazī Maktabah-i Islāmī, 2011).

McCants, William, 'Al Qaeda's Challenge: The Jihadists' War with Islamist Democrats', *Foreign Affairs* 90.5 (2011), 20–32.

McCants, William, *The Lesser of Two Evils: The Salafi Turn to Party Politics in Egypt* (Middle East Memo No. 23, Saban Center at Brookings, May 2012).

McDonald, Kevin, *Global Movements: Action and Culture* (Malden, MA: Blackwell Publishing, 2006).

Mediano, Fernando R., 'Justice, Crime and Punishment in 19th/16th-Century Morocco', in *Public Violence in Islamic Societies*, eds Christian Lange and Maribel Fierro (Edinburgh: Edinburgh University Press, 2009), pp. 179–200.

Meijer, Roel, 'Commanding Right and Forbidding Wrong as a Principle of Social Action: The Case of the Egyptian al-Jama'a al-Islamiyya', in *Global Salafism: Islam's New Religious Movement*, ed. idem (London: Hurst / New York: Columbia University Press, 2009), pp. 189–220.

Meron, Ya'akov, 'The Development of Legal Thought in Hanafi Texts', *Studia Islamica* 30 (1969), 73–118.

Metcalf, B., *Islamic Revival in British India: Deoband, 1860–1900* (Princeton: Princeton University Press, 1982).

Metcalf, B., *Husain Ahmad Madani: The Jihad for Islam and India's Freedom* (Oxford: Oneworld, 2009).

Mian, Ali Altaf, 'Surviving Modernity: Ashraf 'Alī Thānvī [sic] (1863–1943) and the Making of Muslim Orthodoxy in Colonial India' (unpublished Ph.D. dissertation, Duke University, 2015).

Mickelthwaite, John, and Adrian Wooldbridge, *God is Back: How the Global Rise of Faith is Changing the World* (London: Penguin, 2009).

Mignolo, Walter, *The Darker Side of Western Modernity* (Durham: Duke University Press, 2011).

Milton-Edwards, B., *Islamic Politics in Palestine* (London: I. B. Tauris, 1996).

Milton-Edwards, B., *Islamic Fundamentalism since 1945* (London and New York: Routledge, 2005).

Milton-Edwards, B., 'Hamas and the Arab Spring: Strategic Shifts?', *Middle East Policy* 20.3 (2013), 60–73.

Milton-Edwards, B., and A. Crooke, 'Elusive Ingredient: Hamas and the Peace Process', *Journal of Palestine Studies* 33.4 (2004), 1–14.

Milton-Edwards, B., and S. Farrell, *Hamas, the Islamic Resistance Movement* (Cambridge: Polity, 2010).

Minault, G., 'Urdu Political Poetry during the Khilafat Movement', *Modern Asian Studies* 8.4 (1974), 459–71.

Minault, G., 'Sayyid Ahmad Dehlavi and the Delhi Renaissance', in *Delhi Through the Ages: Essays in Urban History, Culture and Society*, ed. R. E. Fryekenberg (New York: Oxford University Press, 1986), pp. 289–98.

Minogue, K. R., 'Method in Intellectual History: Quentin Skinner's Foundations', *Philosophy* 56.218 (1981), 533–52.

Mirza, Younus, 'The Slave Girl Gives Birth to Her Master: Female Slavery from the Mamluk Era (1250–1517) to the Islamic State (2014–)', *Journal of the American Academy of Religion* 85.3 (2017), 577–99.

Miṣbāḥī, Yāsīn Akhtar, *ʿAllāma Fażl-i Ḥaqq Khayrābādī aur 1857 kā inqilāb* (New Delhi: Dār al-qalam, 2007).

Mishal, S., and A. Sela, *The Palestinian Hamas: Vision, Violence and Coexistence* (New York: Columbia University Press, 2000).

al-Miṣrī, Ḥāzim, *Al-Īḍāḥ li-Mā fī l-Dustūr al-Jadīd min al-Kufr al-Bawāḥ* (www.tawhed.ws/dl?i=24041374, n. d.).

al-Miṣrī, al-Shaykh Zayn al-Dīn b. Nujaym, *al-Baḥr al-rāʾiq sharḥ kanz al-daqāʾiq*, 7 vols (Beirut: Shirkat ʿAlāʾ al-Dīn, n. d.).

Mohamed, Mahfodz, 'The Concept of Qisas in Islamic Law', *Islamic Studies* 21.2 (1982), 77–88.
Moinul Haq, Syed, *The Great Revolution of 1857* (Karachi: Pakistan Historical Society, 1968).
Moses, Dirk A. (ed.), *Empire, Colony, Genocide: Conquest, Occupation, and Subaltern Resistance in World History* (New York: Berghahn, 2008).
Moussawi, Ibrahim, 'The Making of Lebanon's Hizbullah', in *Political Islam: Context Versus Ideology*, ed. Khalid Hroub (London: Saqi, 2010), pp. 210–31.
Muchembled, Robert, *A History of Violence from the End of the Middle Ages to the Present* (London: Polity, 2012).
Mudd, Philip, 'How the Arab Spring Could Embolden Extremists', *CTC Sentinel* 4.4 (2011), 7–31.
Muhammad, Rāja Ghulām, *Imtiyāz-i ḥaqq: Fażl-i Ḥaqq Khayrābādī aur Ismāᶜīl Dihlavī kē siyāsī kirdār kā taqābulī jāʾiza* (Lahore: Maktaba Qādirīya, 1979).
Muḥandis-i Dihlavī, Ḥażrat Mawlānā Shāh ᶜAbd al-ᶜAzīz, *Fatāvā-yi ᶜazīzī*, 2 vols (Deoband: Kutubkhānah-yi raḥīmiyyah, 1321 AH).
al-Muḥāṣibī, Ḥārith b. Asad, *Kitāb al-tawahhum* (Cairo: Maṭba'at Lajnat al-Ta'līf wa-al-Tarjamah wa-al-Nashr, 1937).
'Mujāhid', Mawlavī ᶜAbd al-Hādī, *Fikrī pohānah* (Peshawar: Ayyūb maktabah aw islāmī kīssaṫ markaz, 1389 SH/2010, 2nd ed.).
Mukhopadhyay, Dipali, *Warlords, Strongman Governors, and the State in Afghanistan* (Cambridge and New York: Cambridge University Press, 2014).
Munir, Muhammad, 'Debates on the Rights of Prisoners of War in Islamic Law', *Islamic Studies* 49.4 (2010), 463–92.
Musaddas, Hali, *The Flow and Ebb of Islam*, trans. Christopher Shackle and Javed Majeed (Delhi: Oxford University Press, 1997).
Mushīr al-Maṣrī, *al-Mushārka fī al-Ḥayāt al-Siyāsiyya fī ẓill Anẓimat al-Ḥukm al-Muᶜāṣira* (Cairo: Maktabat Dār al-Kalima, 2006).
al-Mutanabbī, Abū al-Ṭayyib, *al-ᶜArf al-ṭayyib fī sharḥ dīwān Abī al-Ṭayyib* (Beirut: Dār Ṣādir, 1964).
'Mutawakkil', Mawlawī Wakīl Aḥmad, *Afghānistān aw Ṭālibān* (Kabul: Da Maywand khaparʾnadwiyyah ṭolannah maṭbaᶜah, 1384 SH).
al-Muᶜtazz, *Dīwān Ibn al-Muᶜtazz* (Beirut: Dār al-Kitāb al-'Arabī, 1983).
Nacos, B. L., *Mass-Mediated Terrorism: The Central Role of the Media in Terrorism and Counterterrorism* (Lanham: Rowman & Littlefield Publishers Inc., 2007).
al-Nadwī, Abū al-Ḥasan, *al-Tafsīr al-siyāsī liʾl-islām fī mirʾāt kitābāt al-ustādh Abī al-Aᶜlā al-Mawdūdī waʾl-shahīd Sayyid Quṭb* (Cairo: Dār Āfāq al-Ghad, 1980).
Naim, C. M., 'Ghalib's Delhi: A Shamelessly Revisionist Look at Two Popular Metaphors', *Annual of Urdu Studies* 18 (2003), 3–24.
al-Najafī, Muḥammad Ḥassan, *Jawāhir al-Kalām fī Sharḥ Sharāʾiᶜ al-Islām* (Beirut: Dār Iḥyāʾ al-Turāth al-ᶜArabī, 1981).
Najafī, al-Shaykh Muḥammad Ḥusayn, *Tajalliyāt-i ṣadāqat bi-javāb-i aftāb-i hidāyat* (Sargodhā: Maktabah-yi sibṭayn, 1982).
al-Najdī, ᶜUthmān b. Bishr, *ᶜUnwān al-majd fī tārīkh najd*, ed. ᶜAbd al-Raḥmān b. ᶜAbd al-Laṭīf Āl al-Shaykh (Riyadh: Maṭbūᶜāt dārat al-malik ᶜabd al-ᶜazīz, 1402/1982).
Nājī, Abū Bakr, *Idārat al-tawaḥḥush* (noor-book.com/كتاب-إدارة-التوحش-pdf).
Nandy, Ashis, 'The Politics of Secularism and the Recovery of Religious Tolerance', in

Secularism and its Critics, ed. Rajeev Bhargava (Delhi: Oxford University Press, 1998), pp. 321–44.

Narang, Gopi Chand, *Ghālib: maᶜnī-āfirīnī, jadalīyātī vażaᶜ, shunyatā aur shiᶜrīyāt* (Lahore: Sang-e Meel, 2013).

Nasr, S[eyed]. V[ali]. R[eza]., 'The Rise of Sunni Militancy in Pakistan: The Changing Role of Islamism and the Ulama in Society and Politics', *Modern Asian Studies* 34.1 (2000), 139–80.

Nedza, Justyna, 'The Sum of its Parts: The State as Apostate in Contemporary Saudi Militant Islamism', in *Accusations of Unbelief in Islam: A Diachronic Perspective on Takfir*, eds Camilla Adang, Hassan Ansari, Maribel Fierro and Sabine Schmidtke (Leiden: Brill, 2015), pp. 304–26.

Nedza, Justyna, Takfīr *im militanten Salafismus: Der Staat als Feind* (Leiden and Boston, MA: Brill, 2020).

al-Nīshāpūrī, Muhammad al-Ḥākim, *al-Mustadrak ᶜalā al-Ṣaḥīḥayn* (Beirut: Dār al-Kutub al-ᶜIlmiyya, 2002).

Nölle-Karimi, Christine, 'Die paschtunische Stammesversammlung im Spiegel der Geschichte', in *Rechtspluralismus in der Islamischen Welt: Gewohnheitsrecht zwischen Staat und Gesellschaft*, eds Michael Kemper and Maurus Reinkowski (Berlin and New York: de Gruyter, 2005), pp. 177–94.

Nuᶜmānī, Muḥammad Manẓūr, *Mawlānā Mawdūdī kē sāth mērī rafāqat kī sar-guzasht awr ab mērā mawqif* (Karachi: Majlis-i Nashriyāt-i Islām, [n. d.]).

Olesen, Asta, *Islam and Politics in Afghanistan* (Richmond: Curzon, 1995).

Opwis, Felicitas, 'Maslaha in Contemporary Islamic Legal Theory', *Islamic Law and Society* 12.2 (2005), 182–223.

Opwis, Felicitas, *Maṣlaḥa and the Purpose of the Law: Islamic Discourse on Legal Change from the 4th/10th to 8th/14th Century* (Leiden: Brill, 2010).

Ostranskỳ, Bronislav, *The Jihadist Preachers of the End Times: ISIS Apocalyptic Propaganda* (Edinburgh: Edinburgh University Press, 2019).

Özcan, Azmi, *Pan-Islamism: Indian Muslims, the Ottomans and Britain, 1877–1924* (Leiden: Brill, 1997).

Pati, Biswamoy (ed.), *The Great Rebellion of 1857 in India: Exploring Transgressions, Contests, and Diversities* (London: Routledge, 2010).

Pelham, Nicolas, 'Gaza's Tunnel Phenomenon: The Unintended Dynamics of Israel's Siege', *Institute for Palestine Studies* 41.4 (2012), 6–31.

Pennington, R., and H. Kahn, *On Islam: Muslims and the Media* (Bloomington: Indiana University Press, 2018).

Pernau, Margrit (ed.), *The Delhi College: Traditional Elites, the Colonial State, and Education before 1857* (New Delhi: Oxford University Press, 2006).

Pernau, Margrit, and Yunus Jaffrey (eds), *Information and the Public Sphere: Persian Newsletters from Mughal India* (New Delhi: Oxford University Press, 2009).

Peskes, Esther, *Muḥammad b. ᶜAbdalwahhāb (1703–92) im Widerstreit: Untersuchungen zur Rekonstruktion der Frühgeschichte der Wahhābīya* (Beirut: Franz Steiner, 1993).

Peters, Rudolph, *Islam and Colonialism: The Doctrine of Jihad in Modern History* (The Hague: Mouton, 1979).

Peters, Rudolph, *Jihad in Classical and Modern Islam* (Princeton: Marcus Weiner, 1996).

Peters, Rudolph, *Crime and Punishment in Islamic Law: Theory and Practice from the Sixteenth to the Twenty-First Century* (Cambridge: Cambridge University Press, 2005).

Phūlpūrī, Shāh ᶜAbd al-Ghanī, *Barāhīn-i qāṭiᶜah dar barā-yi tawḥīd, risālat, qiyāmat*, ed. Shāh Ḥakīm Muḥammad Akhtar (Karachi: Kitāb'khānah-yi maẓharī, n.d.).

Pierret, Thomas, *Religion and State in Syria: The Sunni Ulama from Coup to Revolution* (Cambridge: Cambridge University Press, 2013).

Pierret, Thomas, and Mériam Cheikh, '"I Am Very Happy Here": Female Jihad in Syria as Self-Accomplishment', *Hawwa: Journal of Women of the Middle East and the Islamic World* 13.2 (2015), 241–69.

Pink, Johanna, 'Tradition and Ideology in Contemporary Sunnite Qur'anic Exegesis', *Die Welt des Islams* 50.1 (2010), 3–59.

Pirzada, Sayyid A. S., *The Politics of the Jamiat Ulema-i-Islam* [sic] *Pakistan: 1971–1977* (Karachi: OUP, 2000).

Popitz, H., 'Violence', in *Phenomena of Power: Authority, Domination, and Violence*, eds A. Göttlich and J. Dreher (New York: Columbia University Press, 2017), pp. 25–51.

Porta, Donatella Della, and Mario Diani, *Social Movements: An Introduction* (Malden, MA: Blackwell Publishing, 2006).

Porta, Donatella Della, and Sidney Tarrow (eds), *Transnational Protest & Global Activism: People, Passions, and Power* (Lanham, MD: Rowman & Littlefield Publishers Inc., 2005).

Pouillon, François, 'Abd el-Kader, icône de la nation algérienne', in *La guerre d'Algérie dans la mémoire et l'imaginaire*, eds A. Dayan Rosenman and L. Valensi (Paris: Editions Bouchène, 2004), pp. 87–102.

Prakash, Ved, *Encyclopaedia of Terrorism in the World*, 5 vols (Delhi: Kalpaz, 2011).

Prigarina, Natalia, *Ghalib* (Karachi: Oxford University Press, 2000).

Qabbānjī, Ṣadr al-Dīn, *al-Jihād al-Siyāsī li'l-Shahīd al-Ṣadr* (n. p.: al-Majlis al-Aᶜlā li'l-Thawrah al-Islāmīyah fī al-'Irāq, 1983).

Qādirī, ᶜAbd al-Ḥakīm Sharaf, *Andhere se ujāle tak* (Lahore: Markazī majlis riżā, 1985).

Qādrī, Muḥammad Ayyūb, *Jang-i āzādī 1857* (Karachi: Pak Academy, 1976).

Qādrī, Muḥammad Ayyūb, 'Mawlānā Fażl-i Ḥaqq Khayrābādī: dawr-i mulāzamat', in *Mawlānā Fażl-i Ḥaqq Khayrābādī: ik taḥqīqī muṭālaᶜa*, ed. Afżal (Afḍal) Ḥaqq Qarshī (Lahore: al-Faisal, 1992), pp. 17–19.

Qamaruddīn, *Hindustān kī dīnī darsgāhēn* (New Delhi: Hamdard Education Society, 1996).

al-Qaraḍāwī, Yūsuf, *Fiqh al-jihād: dirāsa muqārana li-aḥkāmihi wa-falsafatihi fī ḍawʾ al-qurʾān waʾl-sunna* (Cairo: Maktabat Wahba, 1430/2009).

al-Qāsim, Muḥammad b. ᶜAbd al-Raḥmān (ed.), *Fatāwā wa-rasāʾil samāḥat al-shaykh Muḥammad bin Ibrāhīm bin ᶜAbd al-Laṭīf Āl al-Shaykh* (Mecca: Maṭbaᶜat al-Ḥukūma, 1399 AH).

Qasim Zaman, Muhammad, *The Ulama in Contemporary Islam: Custodians of Change* (Princeton: Princeton University Press, 2002).

Qasim Zaman, Muhammad, *Modern Islamic Thought in a Radical Age: Religious Authority and Internal Criticism* (Cambridge: Cambridge University Press, 2012).

Qassim, Naim, *Mujtamaᶜ al-Muqawamah: Irādat al-Shahādah wa-Ṣināᶜat al-Intiṣār, The Society of Resistance: The Will to Martyrdom and the Making of Victory* (n. p.: Dar Al maaref Alhijmiah, 2008).

Qidwāᶜī, Alṭāf al-Raḥmān, *Qiyām-i niẓām-i taᶜlīm* (Lucknow: Niẓāmī Press, 1924).

Qureshi, Naeem M., *Pan-Islamism in British Indian Politics: A Study of the Khilafat Movement, 1918–1924* (Leiden: Brill, 1999).

al-Qurṭubī, Abū ᶜAbdallāh Muḥammad, *al-Jāmiᶜ li-aḥkām al-qurʾān wa'l-mubīn lamā taḍammanahu min al-sunna wa-āy al-qur'ān*, ed. ᶜAbdallāh b. ᶜAbd al-Muḥsin al-Turkī, 24 vols (Beirut: Mu'assasat al-risāla, 1427/2006).

Quṭb, Sayyid, *Maᶜālim fī'l-ṭarīq* (Beirut and Cairo: Dār al-Shurūq, 1399/1979).

Rabb, Intisar A., *Doubt in Islamic Law: A History of Legal Maxims, Interpretation, and Islamic Criminal Law* (Cambridge: Cambridge University Press, 2015).

Rag, Pankaj, *1857: The Oral Tradition* (Delhi: Rupa Publications, 2010).

Rāhī, Akhtar, *Tadhkira-yi muṣannifīn-i dars-i niẓāmī* (Lahore: Maktaba-yi Raḥmāniyya, 1978).

Rahimi, Babak, 'Ayatollah Ali al-Sistani and the Democratization of Post-Saddam Iraq', *Nathan Hale Foreign Policy Society Working Paper Series* (n. d.). Republished in *Middle East Review of International Affairs* 8.4 (2004), 12–19.

Raja, Masood Ashraf, *Constructing Pakistan: Foundational Texts and the Rise of Muslim National Identity* (Karachi: Oxford University Press, 2010).

Raphaeli, Nimrod, 'Understanding Muqtada al-Sadr', *Middle East Quarterly* (2004), 33–42.

Rashid, Ahmed, *Taliban: The Power of Militant Islam in Afghanistan and Beyond* (London: I. B. Tauris, 2008).

Rassler, Don, and Vahid Brown, *The Haqqani Nexus and the Evolution of al-Qa'ida* (West Point, NY: Combating Terrorism Center, 2011).

Ra'ūf, ᶜAdel, *Muḥammad Muḥammad Ṣādiq al-Ṣadr: Marja'iyyat al-Maydān: Mashrūᶜahu al-Taghyīrī wa Waqā'iᶜ al-Ighṭīyāl* (Damascus: al-Markaz al-ᶜIrāqī li'l-Iᶜlām wa-al-Dirāsāt, 1999).

Ra'ūf, ᶜAdel, *al-ᶜAmal al-Islāmī fī al-'Irāq Bayn al-Marja'iyyah wa'l-Hizbīyah: Qirā'ah Naqdīyah li-Masīrat Niṣf Qarn* (Damascus: al-Markaz al-ᶜIrāqī li'l-Iᶜlām wa-al-Dirāsāt, 2000).

Reza Nasr, Seyyed Vali, *Mawdudi and the Making of Islamic Revivalism* (New York and Oxford: Oxford University Press, 1996).

Rifā'ī, 'Abd al-Jabbār, *Manhaj al-Shahīd al-Ṣadr fī Tajdīd al-Fikr al-Islāmī* (Qum: Mu'assasat al-Tawḥīd, 1998).

Rizvi, Saiyid Athar Abbas, *Shāh ᶜAbd al-ᶜAzīz: Puritanism, Sectarian Polemics and Jihād* (Canberra: Maᶜrifat Publishing House, 1982).

Rizvi, Sajjad, ''Political Mobilization and Shīᶜi Religious Establishment (*marja'iyya*)', *International Affairs* 86.6 (2010), 1299–313.

Riżvī, Sayyid Maḥbūb, *Tārīkh-i dār al-ᶜulūm Deoband*, 2 vols (Deoband: Idārah-yi ihtimām-i Dār al-ᶜulūm, 1992–3).

Robinson, Francis, 'Ottomans-Safavids-Mughals: Shared Knowledge and Connective Systems', *Journal of Islamic Studies* 8 (1997), 152–6.

Robinson, Francis, *The 'Ulama of Farangi Mahall and Islamic Culture in South Asia* (London: Hurst, 2001). Also published as Robinson, Francis, *The 'Ulama of Farangi Mahall and Islamic Culture in South Asia* (New Delhi: Permanent Black, 2001).

Robinson, Glen E., 'The Battle for Iraq: Islamic Insurgencies in Comparative Perspective', *Third World Quarterly* 28 (2007), 262–9.

Roy, Asim, *Islam in History and Politics: Perspectives from South Asia* (New Delhi: Oxford University Press, 2008).

Roy, S., *Hamas and Civil Society in Gaza, Engaging the Islamist Social Sector* (Princeton: Princeton University Press, 2011).

Russell, Ralph, and Islam Khurshidul, *Ghalib: Life and Letters* (New Delhi: Oxford University Press, 1994).

Rustomji, Nerina, *The Garden and the Fire: Heaven and Hell in Islamic Culture* (New York: Columbia University Press, 2013).

Said, Behnam Timo, 'Djihadismus nach dem Arabischen Frühling und das Vermittlungsangebot Muhammad al-Zawahiris', *Zeitschrift für Außen und Sicherheitspolitik* 6 (2013), 429–52.

Saᶜīdur-Raḥmān ᶜAlawī, Muḥammad, *ᶜAllāma Fażl-i Ḥaqq Khayrābādī aur jihād-i āzādī* (Lahore: Sunni Publications, 1987).

Salaymeh, Lena, 'Early Islamic Legal-Historical Precedents: Prisoners of War', *Law and History Review* 26.3 (2008), 521–44.

Samīᶜ al-Ḥaqq, *Khuṭbāt-i ḥaqq*, ed. Mawlānā Muftī Mukhtārallāh Ḥaqqānī (Akoṛa Khaṫṫak: Muᵓtamar al-muṣannifīn-i dār al-ᶜulūm ḥaqqāniyyah, n. d.).

Samīᶜ al-Ḥaqq, Mawlānā (ed.), *Mashāhīr bi-nām-i Mawlānā Samīᶜ al-Ḥaqq Ṣāḥib*, 6 vols (Akoṛah Khaṫṫak: Muᵓtamar al-muṣannifīn-i dār al-ᶜulūm ḥaqqāniyyah, 1433/2012).

Sanyal, Usha, *Devotional Islam & Politics in British India: Ahmad Riza Khan Barelwi and His Movement, 1870–1920* (Delhi: Oxford University Press, 1996).

al-Sarakhsī, al-Imām Muḥammad b. Aḥmad, *Sharḥ kitāb al-siyar al-kabīr li'l-imām Muḥammad b. al-Ḥasan al-Shaybānī*, ed. Abū ᶜAbdallāh Muḥammad Ḥasan al-Shāfiᶜī, 5 vols (Beirut: Dār al-kutub al-ᶜilmiyya, 1417/1997).

Sayhūl, Salmā, *ᶜAllāma Fażl-i Ḥaqq Khayrābādī* (Lahore: Maktaba qādirīya jāmiᶜa niẓāmīya rażavīya, 2001).

Schanzer, J., *Hamas vs. Fatah: The Struggle for Palestine* (New York: Palgrave Macmillan, 2008).

Schimmel, Annemarie, *Islam in the Indian Subcontinent* (Leiden: Brill, 1980).

Schimmel, Annemarie, *The Empire of the Great Mughals: History, Art and Culture* (London: Reaktion Books, 2004).

Sen, Amartya, *Identity and Violence* (New York: W. W. Norton, 2006).

Sen, Satadru, 'Contexts, Representation and the Colonized Convict: Maulana Thanesari in the Andaman Islands', *Crime, Histoire & Société* 8.2 (2004), 117–39.

Sessions, Jennifer E., *By Sword and Plow: France and the Conquest of Algeria* (Ithaca: Cornell University Press, 2011).

Shafīᶜ, Muftī-yi aᶜẓam-i Pākistān Muḥammad, *Fatāvā-yi Dār al-ᶜulūm Deoband*, ed. Muḥammad Riżā ᶜUs̱mānī, 2 vols (Karachi: Dār al-ishāᶜat, 1396 AH).

Al-Shāfiᶜī, Muḥammad b. Idrīs, *Kitāb al-Umm*, ed. Rifᶜat Fawzī ᶜAbd al-Muṭṭalib (al-Manṣūra: Dār al-wafāᵓ, 1422/2001).

Shāh Manṣūr, Muftī Abū Lubābah, *Dajjāl: kawn? kahaṇ? kab?* (Karachi: al-Falāḥ, 1430/2009).

Shāh Manṣūr, Muftī Abū Lubābah, *Dajjāl 3: dajjālī dastāvīz, dajjāl ke ham'navā, dajjālī ᶜalāmāt, Isrāᵓīl kī kahānī, mashriq va maghrib ke likhāriyoṇ kī zabānī* (Karachi: al-Saᶜīd, 1432/2011).

Shahābī, Intiẓāmullāh, *Maulānā Fażl-i Ḥāqq aur ᶜAbd al-Ḥaqq Khayrābādī* (Badaun: Niẓāmī Press, n. d.).

Shahābī, Intiẓāmullāh, *Ghadar kē čand ᶜulamāᵓ* (Delhi: Dīnī book depot, 1979).

al-Shāmī, Husayn Barakah, *al-Ṣadr al-Thānī: Dirāsāt fī Fikrihi wa-Jihādihi* (London: dār al-islām, 2002).

Shavit, Uriya, 'Is *Shura* a Muslim Form of Democracy? Roots and Systemization of a Polemic', *Middle Eastern Studies* 46.3 (2010), 349–74.

Shaykh 'Alī, Fā'iq, *Ightiyāl Sha'b* (London: Iraqi Centre for Strategic Researches and Studies, 2000).

'Shaykh Amad Yasin, Interviews, Gaza Strip, October 1997', *Journal of Palestine Studies* 2 (1998), 150–5.

Shikaki, K., 'Palestinians Divided', *Foreign Affairs* 81.1 (2002), 89–105.

al-Shinqīṭī, Muḥammad al-Amīn, *ᶜAdwāᵓ al-bayān fī ᵓidāḥ al-Qurᵓān bi-l-Quᵓrān* (Beirut: Dār Ibn Ḥazm, 2013).

Shīrwānī, ᶜAbd al-Shāhid Khān, 'Introduction', in Khayrābādī, *Risāla ghadarīya [al-Thawra al-Hindīya]*, trans. ᶜAbd al-Shāhid Khān Shīrwānī as *Bāghī Hindustān* (Lahore: Maktaba-yi Qādirīya, 1974), pp. 3–24.

Siddque, Soofia, 'Remembering the Revolt of 1857: Contrapuntal Formations in Indian Literature and History' (unpublished PhD dissertation, School of Oriental and African Studies, University of London, 2012).

Sindhī, ᶜUbaydallāh, *Shāh Valīyallāh awr unkī siyāsī taḥrīk* (Lahore: Kitāb'khānah-yi panjāb, 1942).

Sivan, Emmanuel, *Radical Islam: Medieval Theology and Modern Politics* (New Haven and London: Yale University Press, 1990).

Sizgorich, Thomas, *Violence and Belief in Late Antiquity: Militant Devotion in Christianity and Islam* (Philadelphia: University of Pennsylvania Press, 2009).

Skinner, Quentin, 'Meaning and Understanding in the History of Ideas', *History and Theory* 8.1 (1969), 3–53.

Skjelderup, Michael, '*Ḥudūd* Punishments in the Forefront: Application of Islamic Criminal Law by Harakat al-Shabaab al-Mujahideen', *Journal of Law and Religion* 29.2 (2014), 317–29.

Smart, Ninian, 'Religious Studies in the United Kingdom', *Religion* 18 (1998), 1–9.

Sperl, Stefan, 'Crossing Enemy Boundaries: Al-Buhturi's Ode on the Ruins of Ctesiphon Re-Read in the Light of Virgil and Wilfred Owen', *Bulletin of the School of Oriental and African Studies* 69.3 (2006), 365–79.

Spivak, G., 'Can the Subaltern Speak?', in *Can the Subaltern Speak?: Reflections on the History of an Idea*, ed. R. Morris (New York: Columbia University, 2010), pp. 21–78.

Stenersen, Anne, *Al-Qaida in Afghanistan* (Cambridge: Cambridge University Press, 2017).

Stephens, J., *Governing Islam: Law, Empire, and Secularism in Modern South Asia* (Cambridge: Cambridge University Press, 2018).

Steul, Willi, *Paschtunwali: Ein Ehrenkodex und seiner rechtliche Relevanz* (Wiesbaden: Steiner, 1981).

Stoler, Ann Laura, *Along the Archival Grain: Epistemic Anxieties and Colonial Common Sense* (Princeton: Princeton University Press, 2010).

al-Suyūṭī, Jalāl al-Dīn, *al-Durr al-manẓūr fī tafsīr bi-l-maᵓthūr* (Riyadh: Dār ᶜĀlam al-Kutub, 2015).

al-Ṭabarānī, Sulaymān b. Aḥmad, *al-Muᶜjam al-awsaṭ* (Cairo: Dār al-Haramayn, 1995).

al-Ṭabarī, Ibn Jarīr, *Tafsīr al-Ṭabarī*, eds Bashshār Maᶜrūf and ᶜIṣām al-Ḥarastānī (Beirut: Muᵓassasat al-risāla, 1415/1994).

al-Ṭabarsī, Abū Manṣūr Aḥmad b. ᶜAlī b. Abī Ṭālib, *al-Iḥtijāj*, ed. Muḥammad Ṣādiq al-Kutubī, 2 vols (Najaf: Manshūrāt al-sharīf al-raḍī, 1380 AH).

Taj, Farhat, *Taliban and Anti-Taliban* (Newcastle: Cambridge Scholars Publishing, 2011).

Tamimi, A., *Hamas: A History From Within* (London: Hurst, 2007).

Tanner, Ralph E. S., *Violence and Religion: Cross-Cultural Opinions and Consequences* (New Delhi: Concept, 2007).

al-Tanūkhī, Saḥnūn b. Saʿīd, *al-Mudawwana al-kubrā* (Riyadh: Wizārat al-shuʾūn al-islāmiyya, n. d.).
Tapper, Nancy, *Bartered Brides: Politics, Gender and Marriage in an Afghan Tribal Society* (Cambridge: Cambridge University Press, 1991).
al-Ṭarābulusī, Muḥammad Kāmil, *al-Fatāwā al-kāmiliyya fi'l-ḥawādith al-ṭarābulusiyya* (Cairo: n. p., 1313/1895).
Tarrow, Sidney, *The New Transnational Activism* (Cambridge: Cambridge University Press, 2005).
Temimi, Abdeljelil, *Le Beylik de Constantine et Hadj 'Ahmed Bey (1830–1837)* (Tunis: Publications de la Revue d'Histoire Maghrébine, 1978).
Thackrah, John Richard, *Dictionary of Terrorism* (London: Routledge, 2004).
al-Thānawī, Mawlānā Ẓafar Aḥmad al-ʿUthmānī, *Iʿlāʾ al-sunan*, ed. Muḥammad Taqī ʿUthmānī, 18 vols (Karachi: Idārat al-qurʾān wa'l-ʿulūm islāmiyya, 1418h).
Thapar, Romila, *The Future of the Indian Past* (New Delhi: Institute of Social Sciences, 2004).
Thapar, Romila, *Somnatha: The Many Voices of a History* (New Delhi: Penguin, 2004).
Tharoor, Shashi, *Inglorious Empire: What the British Did to India* (London: Hurst, 2017).
Titus, Murray T., *Indian Islam* (Oxford: Oxford University Press, 1930).
Tolan, John V., *Saracens: Islam in the Medieval European Imagination* (New York: Columbia University Press, 2002).
Touati, Houari, 'L'émir 'Abd al-Qâdir et les enjeux de la biographie', *Studia Islamica* 2 (2011), 5–34.
al-Ṭūsī, Muḥammad ibn al-Ḥassan, *al-Nihāyah fī Mujarrad al-Fiqh wa al-Fatāwa* (Qum: Intisharāt Quds Muḥammadī, n. d.).
al-Ṭūsī, Muḥammad ibn al-Ḥassan, *al-Mabsūṭ fī Fiqh al-Imāmiyyah* (Tehran: Muʾassasat al-Maʿārif al-Islāmiyyah, 1958).
al-Ṭūsī, Muḥammad ibn al-Ḥassan, *al-Khilāf* (Qum: Muʾssasat al-Nashr al-Islāmī al-Tābiʿah li'Jāmiʿat al-Mudarrissīn, 2000).
al-Ṭūsī, Muḥammad ibn al-Ḥassan, *al-Istibṣār fī mā ikhtulifa min al-akhbār* (Beirut: Muʾassasat al-aʿlamī, 1326/2005).
Umar, Muhammad, *Islam in Northern India in the Eighteenth Century* (Delhi: Munshiram Manoharlal, 1993).
US Department of State, Bureau of Democracy, Human Rights and Labor, 'Report on the Taliban's War on Women', 17 November 2001. Available at: www.state.gov/j/drl/rls/6185.htm (accessed 27 August 2013).
Vaidik, Aparna, *Imperial Andamans: Colonial Encounter and Island History* (Basingstoke: Palgrave Macmillan, 2010).
Vasalou, Sophia, 'Equal Before the Law: The Evilness of Human and Divine Lies in ʿAbd al-Jabbār's Rational Ethics', *Arabic Sciences and Philosophy* 13.2 (2003), 243–68.
Veer, Peter Van Der, *Nation and Religion* (Princeton: Princeton University Press, 1999).
Vertovec, Steven, and Robin Cohen (eds), *Conceiving Cosmopolitanism: Theory, Context, and Practice* (New York: Oxford, 2002/7).
Visser, Reidar, 'Sistani, the United States and Politics in Iraq: From Quietism to Machiavellianism?', *NUPI, Norwegian Institute of International Affairs* 700 (2006), 1–37.
Wagemakers, Joas, 'The Transformation of a Radical Concept: *al-wala' wa-l-bara'* in the Ideology of Abu Muhammad al-Maqdisi', in *Global Salafism: Islam's New Religious Movement*, ed. Roel Meijer (London: Hurst, 2009), pp. 81–106.

Wagemakers, Joas, 'Legitimizing Pragmatism: Hamas' Framing Efforts From Militancy to Moderation and Back?', *Terrorism and Political Violence* 22.3 (2010), 358–78.

Wagemakers, Joas, 'An Inquiry Into Ignorance: A Jihādī-Salafī Debate on *Jahl* as an Obstacle to *Takfīr*', in *The Transmission and Dynamics of the Textual Sources of Islam: Essays in Honour of Harald Motzki*, eds Nicolet Boekhoff-van der Voort, Kees Versteegh and Joas Wagemakers (Leiden: Brill, 2011), pp. 314–25.

Wagemakers, Joas, 'Protecting Jihad: The Sharia Council of the Minbar al-Tawhid wa-l-Jihad', *Middle East Policy* 18.2 (2011), 148–62.

Wagemakers, Joas, 'Reclaiming Scholarly Authority: Abu Muhammad al-Maqdisi's Critique of *Jihadi* Practices', *Studies in Conflict & Terrorism* 34.7 (2011), 523–39.

Wagemakers, Joas, *A Quietist Jihadi: The Ideology and Influence of Abu Muhammad al-Maqdisi* (Cambridge: Cambridge University Press, 2012).

Wagemakers, Joas, 'Salafi's en politieke participatie sinds de Arabische Lente', *ZemZem: Tijdschrift over het Midden-Oosten, Noord-Afrika en islam* 8.2 (2012), 27–35.

Wagemakers, Joas, '"Seceders" and "Postponers"? An Analysis of the "Khawarij" and "Murji'a" Labels in Polemical Debates Between Quietist and Jihadi-Salafis', in *Contextualising Jihadi Thought*, eds Jevan Deol and Zaheer Kazmi (London: Hurst, 2012), pp. 143–65.

Wagemakers, Joas, 'Between Purity and Pragmatism? Abu Basir al-Tartusi's Nuanced Radicalism', in *Jihadi Theology*, ed. Rüdiger Lohlker (Göttingen: Vienna University Press, 2013), pp. 16–37.

Wagemakers, Joas, '"The *Kāfir* Religion of the West": *Takfir* of Democracy and Democrats by Radical Islamists', in *Accusations of Unbelief in Islam: A Diachronic Perspective on Takfir*, eds Camilla Adang, Hasan Ansari, Maribel Fierro and Sabine Schmidtke (Leiden: Brill, 2015), pp. 237–53.

Walbridge, John, 'Muhammad Baqir al-Sadr: The Search for New Foundations', in *The Most Learned of the Shi'a: The Institution of the Marja' Taqlid*, ed. Linda Walbridge (Oxford: Oxford University Press, 2001), pp. 131–8.

Walton, Douglas, 'Arguing from Definition to Verbal Classification: The Case of Redefining "Planet" to Exclude Pluto', *Informal Logic* 28.2 (2008), 129–54.

Wardak, Ali, '*Jirga*: Power and Traditional Conflict Resolution in Afghanistan', in *Law after Ground Zero*, ed. John Strawson (London, Portland, OR and Coogee: Glasshouse, 2004), pp. 187–204.

Washbrook, David, 'Popular History Versus Academic History', in *Revisiting 1857: Myth, Memory, History*, eds S. Gooptu and B. Majumdar (Delhi: Roli Books, 2007), pp. 3–11.

Weiss, Bernard G., *The Search for God's Law: Islamic Jurisprudence in the Writings of Sayf al-Dīn al-Āmidī* (Salt Lake City: University of Utah Press, 2010).

Wiktorowicz, Quintan, 'Anatomy of the Salafi Movement', *Studies in Conflict & Terrorism* 29 (2006), 207–39.

Wilner, Alex S., 'Opportunity Costs or Costly Opportunities? The Arab Spring, Osama bin Laden, and al-Qāᶜida's African Affiliates', *Perspectives on Terrorism* 5.3/4 (2011), 50–62.

Wilson, Roland K., *A Digest of Anglo-Muhammadan Law* (London: W. Thacker, 1995).

Wittgenstein, L., *Philosophical Investigations* (Oxford: Blackwell, 1953).

Woerner-Powell, Tom, ''Abd al-Qādir al Jazā'irī, Migration and the Rule of Law: "A Reply to Certain Persons of Distinction"', *Studia Islamica* 2 (2011), 91–124.

Wolff, Robert, 'On Violence', *The Journal of Philosophy* 66.19 (1969), 601–16.

Wright, David P., *Inventing God's Law: How the Covenant Code of the Bible Used and Revised the Laws of Hammurabi* (Oxford: Oxford University Press, 2009).

Wright, W., *A Grammar of the Arabic Language Translated from the German of Caspari and Edited with Numerous Additions and Corrections by W. Wright* (London: Cambridge University Press, 1875).

Yacine, Kateb, *Abdelkader et l'indépendance algérienne* (Alger: S. N. E. D., 1983 [Algiers, 1948).

Yunas, S. Fida, *Afghanistan: Organization of the Peoples* [sic] *Democratic Party of Afghanistan/Watan Party, Governments and Biographical Sketches (1982–1998)*, vol. 2 (Peshawar: self-published, 1998).

Ẕaʿīf, Mullā ʿAbd al-Salām, *Ṭālibān lah Kandahārah tar Maẓārah* (Kabul: Aksos, 1396 SH/2018).

Zainuddin, Daim bin, *War of Deception – The Facts and Fallacies About the War in Iraq* (Subang Jaya: Pelanduk Publications, 2004).

Zaman, Muhammad Qasim, *Ashraf 'Ali Thanawi: Islam in Modern South Asia* (Oxford: Oneworld, 2008).

Zamir, Syed Rizwan, 'Rethinking the Academic Study of the "Ulamā" Tradition', *Islamic Studies* 53.3/4 (2014), 145–74.

Zelin, Aaron Y., Daveed Gartenstein-Ross, and Andrew Lebovich, 'Al-Qa'ida in the Islamic Maghreb's Tunisia Strategy', *CTC Sentinel* 6.7 (2013), 21–6.

Zelin, Aaron Y., Daveed Gartenstein-Ross, and Andrew Lebovich, *Your Sons Are at Your Service: Tunisia's Missionaries of Jihad* (New York: Columbia University Press, 2020).

Žižek, Slavoj, *Violence* (London: Profile Books, 2009).

Zulfiqār, Ghulām Huṣayn, *Mawlānā Ẓafar 'Alī Khān: ḥayāt, khidmāt wa-āthār* (Lahore: Sang-i mīl Publications, 2005).

INDEX

Abbas, Mahmoud (Maḥmūd ᶜAbbās), 325
Abbasid (ᶜAbbāsid) Dynasty, 113, 227, 231, 233, 236
ᶜAbd al-Azīz Dihlawī, Shāh, 82–3, 85, 106–7, 121, 139
ᶜAbd al-Ḥamīd II, 238
ᶜAbd Allāh b. Ubayy, 264
ᶜAbd al-Bārī Farangī Maḥallī, 107, 114
ᶜAbd al-Qādir al-Jazāᵓirī (ᶜAbd el Kader), 41–4, 46, 48–71, 120
ᶜAbd Rabbihi Manṣūr Hādī (Yemeni President), 189, 217
ᶜAbd al- Raᵓūf, 201
Abou El Fadl, Khaled, 293
Abū al-Ḥārith al-Anṣārī, 271, 287
Abū Bakr (First Caliph of Sunni Islam), 141, 227, 267, 268, 276, 360
Abū Bakr Nājī, 237
Abū Firās al-Hamdānī, 340
Abū Ghraib, 219
Abū Hurayra, 209, 269
Abū Khubza, Muḥammad, 277
Abū Qatāda al-Filistīnī, 180–2, 264, 266
Abū Sulaymān al-Sumālī, 282–5
Abū Tammām, 336–7
Abū ᶜUbayda al-Qāsim, 245
Abū Yūsuf (Yaᶜqūb b. Ibrāhīm al-Anṣārī), 108
Aceh, 32
Açıkyıldız, Birgül, 238
Afghan Civil War (1992–6), 133, 153
Afghanistan (Afghan), 19, 87, 106, 107, 110, 123–30, 133, 134, 139–42, 146–8, 150–4, 156–9
Africa, 18, 20, 22, 23, 24, 25, 38, 54, 57, 61; *see also* North Africa, West Africa
ahl al-kitab (People of the Book/Scripture), 67, 109–11, 114, 121; *see also* Jews/ Judiasm, Christians/Christianity
Ahlām al-Naṣr, 249–88
Ahl-i hadīs̱, 130, 132, 133; *see also* Salafī/ Salafism
Ahl-i qurᵓān, 133
Aḥmad Riżā/Rażā (Riḍā) Khān al-Baraylawī/Barēlvī, 80, 100–1, 103–6, 107–22
Ahmadiyya, 31, 85
Ahmed Bey of Constantine, 47, 61, 64, 65, 68, 71
ᶜajam (non-Arabs), 232
Akoṛah Khaṭṭak, 128–9, 136, 141, 146, 151
Akoṛavī, ᶜAbd al-Ḥaqq, 129, 130, 134, 135, 136, 138, 140, 143, 145, 147, 155
Alagha, Joseph, 353
Alawite/ Nuṣayrī, 190, 195, 214, 220, 222, 239
Albānī, Muḥammad Nāṣir al-Dīn al-, 164, 277

ᶜAlī brothers (Shawkat and Muḥammad), 106
Aligarh, 80
Aleppo, 221, 285
Algeria (Algerian), 21–3, 35, 41–71
Algerian Rebellion 1871, 49
Algerian War (First), 49
ᶜAlī b. Abī Ṭālib (First Imam of Shīᶜī Islam, Fourth Caliph of Sunni Islam), 246, 267, 276, 282, 283, 352
Ali, Syed Ameer Ali, 97, 100
Ali, Kecia, 240, 241, 244
ᶜAllāma al-Ḥillī, Ḥāsan b. Yūsuf al-, 206
Almohads, 60
Almoravids, 60
al-Qāᶜida (al-Qaeda), 123, 126, 128, 154, 156, 181–94, 197–206, 208–16, 209, 219, 237, 279, 288, 357
  Al-Qaeda in Iraq (AQI), 220
  Al-Qaeda in the Arabian Peninsula (AQIP), 217, 221
Amīr Khusraw *see* Khusraw
Anbehtavī, Khalīl Aḥmad, 105
Anṣār al-Sharīᶜa
salaf al-ṣāliḥ, al- (first three generations of pious scholars in Sunni Islam), 9; *see also* Salafī/Salafism
ᶜAmmār b. Yāsir, 245
ᶜAmr b. Kulthūm, 228
Andaman Islands/Cellular Jail (penal colony), 76, 91, 93, 97, 104
Anglo-Muhammadan Law/ Mohammaden Law, 100
Anṣār al-Sharīᶜa, 198, 199, 216, 217, 218, 219
Ansār Bayt al-Maqdis, 219
Apostate (*murtadd/ridda*), 61, 95, 96, 105, 114, 154, 167, 181, 182, 184, 195, 197, 199, 202, 203, 265
Arab(s)/Arabia, 11, 21, 28, 34, 35, 39, 40, 41, 44, 46, 48, 57, 58, 62, 85, 101, 119, 126, 152, 153, 154, 171, 187, 188, 189, 191, 192, 193, 195, 197, 199–207, 210–16, 218–21, 223–4, 226, 228–31, 246, 276, 279, 280, 291, 292, 297, 315, 318, 329, 331
Arab Spring/uprisings/revolutions, 11, 28 33, 186–209, 210–24, 354
Arnaᵓūṭ, Shuᶜayb al-, 164–6
Arafat, Yaser (Yāsir ᶜArafāt), 319
Arendt, Hannah, 21, 22, 24, 236
Asad, Bashar al- (Bashār al-Asad, Syrian President), 190, 212, 213, 215, 220–4
Asad, Talal, 5, 32
Asia, 18, 20, 23–6, 38; *see also* South Asia, South East Asia
Atharī, Abū al-Zahrāᵓ al-, 278
Atharī, Abū Bakr al-, 284
Atheists/Atheism, 25
Aurangzeb ᶜĀlamgīr, Muḥī al-Dīn Muḥammad, 102; *see also Fatāwā ᶜālamgīriyya*
Awlakī, Anwār al-, 211, 218, 340
Āzād, Abū al-Kalām, 91, 92, 106, 114
Azhar, al- (Al-Azhar), 33, 34, 35, 250, 276, 292
Āzurda, Ṣadr al-Dīn Khān, 83, 84, 87, 89, 90, 103, 131

Baghdādī, ᶜAbd al-Qāhir, 226
Baghdādī, Abū Bakr al-, 184, 185, 227, 272, 273, 274, 275, 279
Bahādur Shāh Ẓafar (Bahādur Shāh II), 79, 83, 87, 89, 103, 104
Bahrain, 165, 189, 198, 212, 214, 215
Bakrī, ᶜAbd al-ᶜAzīz al-, 335–9
Bangladesh, 19; *see also* Bengal
Bardawil, Salah (Ṣalāh Bardawīl), 331
Barēlvī/Barēlwī/Baraylawī *see* Aḥmad Riżā Khān
Barghouti, Marwan (Marwān Bārghūtī), 323
Battle of Plassey, 102
Bengal (Bengali), 14, 102
Belcher, Joel, 272
Bennabi, Malek, 21–4, 26, 35
Berg, Nicholas, 288
bidaᶜ (innovation), 28, 52, 251, 278, 288
Bihārī, Ẓafar al- Dīn, 105
Bin ᶜAlī, President of Tunisia, 210, 223
Bin ᶜAlī, Turkī, 226, 241, 242, 246, 247, 248, 252, 253, 254
Bin Bāz, ᶜAbd al-ᶜAzīz, 278

Bin Lādin, Usāma (Bin Laden), 206, 211, 212, 219, 335
Bin Uthaymīn, Muḥammad b. Ṣāliḥ, 277
Būʿazīzī, Muḥammad al-, 189
Buddhism, 28–9, 43
Bughā, Īmān al-, 256
Bughā, Muṣṭafā al-, 254
Bukhara, 119
Bukhārī, Muḥammad al-, 269
Bush, George W., 159

Cairo, 33, 36, 51, 190, 212, 327, 331
Calder, Norman, 101
Camus, Albert, 23
caste, 27, 80, 116, 117
Catholicism (Catholic(s)), 24, 29, 30; *see also* Christian
China (Chinese), 18, 28
Chinese Muslims (Hui; Uighur), 18
Christian(s)/Christianity, 6, 7, 27, 28, 29, 30, 31, 36, 37, 43, 46, 49, 54, 57, 66, 70, 94, 95, 96, 102–3, 109, 110, 111, 121, 159, 181, 196, 214, 237, 244, 261, 262, 263, 264, 321, 337; *see also ahl al-kitāb*, Catholicism
Citizenship (citizen), 23–8, 34–8, 82, 203, 210, 215, 223, 353, 361
Code of Hammurabi, 257
Cold War, 30, 124
Cole, Juan, 229
colonialism (colony; colonial; anti-colonial; post-colonial), 3, 4. 17, 18, 19, 20, 22, 23, 24, 25, 26, 39–71, 75–80, 82–4, 86–98, 99, 100–4, 106–22, 127, 128, 129, 131–4, 147, 148, 150, 153, 156
Confucian(s), 29
consensus (*ijmāʿ*), 112, 133, 155, 226, 241, 244, 268, 276, 283, 302
Constitutionalism (constitutions(s)), 24–8, 30–1, 33, 35–8, 130, 131, 201, 202, 203, 206
Coptic, 35, 37
cosmopolitanism, 23–4, 157
Crone, Patricia, 231
Crusader(s), 154, 187, 224, 192, 319, 338

Dagestan, 149
dajjāl (Anti-Christ), 140, 145, 155, 159, 234, 286
Damascus, 43, 213, 254
Danton, Georges, 227, 247
dār al-Islam (abode/lands of Islam/Muslim territory), 42, 51, 67, 100, 106–11, 114–15, 121, 134, 145
dār al-ḥarb (abode/lands of war/non-Muslim territory), 51, 83, 106–11, 114–15
dars-i niẓāmī, 84, 86, 88, 103
Davies, Eric, 300
daʿwā (calling), 171, 183, 184, 196, 216, 219
Dawwānī, Jalāl al-Dīn al-, 113
de Vries, Hent, 81
democracy, 27, 35, 163, 183, 188, 189, 199, 199–200, 201, 204–8, 209, 214, 304, 364
Deoband(is)/Deobandiyyat, 78, 79, 80, 105, 107–8, 127–39, 145, 151, 154
dialogue, 29, 30, 31, 37, 45, 214
difāʿ (defence), 295, 302–2
Delhi, 76, 77, 79, 82–91, 95, 102, 103, 104, 106, 118, 119
Delhi College, 76, 84, 93, 97
Delhi Sultanate, 102
Dhimmī/ahl al-dhimma (non-Muslim tributary), 109, 114, 238
Druze, 246
Dufferin, Viceroy Lord, 92

East India Company, 82, 83, 102, 106
Egypt, 19, 21, 24, 27, 28, 32, 33, 34, 35, 36, 37, 38, 60, 70, 188, 189, 190, 191, 200, 201, 202, 203, 204, 206, 207, 208, 209, 211, 212, 215, 216, 219, 220, 221, 223, 224, 236, 250, 279, 315, 327, 331, 353
Eichmann, Adolf, 21
El Shamsy, Ahmed, 242
Enayat, Hamid, 25
Ennahda (al-Nahḍa), 200, 201, 216, 220
Esposito, John, 292

Fanon, Frantz, 23, 359
Farazdaq, al-, 339

farḍ/wājib/taklīf (religious duty/obligation), 51, 55, 60, 66, 106, 108, 111, 113, 115, 120, 131–2, 133, 136, 137, 139, 143, 145, 146, 154, 158, 158, 182, 193, 257, 258, 259, 279, 280, 283, 287, 304, 318
Farangī Maḥall (*ᶜulamāʾ*), 107, 114
Fatah (Fataḥ), 317, 323, 325, 331, 332, 353, 355, 357
fatwa (*fatwa/fatāwā* – legal opinions/ response), 36, 66, 76, 82, 84, 89, 90, 94, 97, 99, 100, 101, 103–22, 240, 250, 252, 253, 277, 279, 280, 314, 356
Fatāwā al-ᶜālamgīriyya/al-hindiyya, al-, 10, 143, 155
Faylaq Badr (Badr Brigade), 297
Fażl-i Ḥaqq Khayrābādī *see* Khayrābādī
fiqh (jurisprudence; Islamic law), 3, 4, 7, 8, 9, 10, 11, 12, 28, 36, 45, 72, 83, 99, 100, 101, 105, 106, 107, 108, 109, 110, 111, 112, 113, 114, 116, 119, 120, 121, 123, 126, 127, 128, 129, 130, 132, 131, 132, 133, 134, 135, 136, 137, 139, 140, 142, 141, 142, 143, 144, 145, 146, 148, 149, 151, 152, 153, 155, 156, 157, 158, 159, 170, 182, 192, 193, 194, 199, 200, 201, 204, 205, 237, 242, 256, 257, 259, 266, 267, 319, 322, 256; *see also* Sharīᶜa
fitna (chaos/internal conflict), 323
Free Syrian Army, 197, 213, 221
fuqahāʾ (jurists), 6, 8, 10, 36, 75, 99, 100, 101, 103, 108, 109, 110, 111, 136, 155; *see also ᶜulamāʾ*
Fuchs, Simon Wolfgang, 189, 262

Gangohī, Rashīd Aḥmad, 108, 130, 131, 132, 133, 140, 145, 154
Gaza, 327–33, 353–9
GCC (Cooperation Council for the Arab States of the Gulf), 214
Gellner, Ernst, 20, 58
George (V), King, 112
Ghaddafi, Muammer (Muᶜammar Qadhdhāfī, Libyan President), 192, 213
Ghālib, Mirza Asadullāh Baig Khān, 76, 83–5, 87, 88, 91
Ghāmidī, Aḥmad b. Nāṣir al-, 275
Ghandi, Mahatma, 8, 113, 121
ghaṣb (abduction), 228
Ghazālī, Abū Ḥāmid al-, 113, 273, 323, 324
Ghazi Hamad (Ghazī Ḥamad), 328
Ghazna, 118
Ghaznavids, 101–2
ghazw (raiding), 229
Ghannūshī, Rāshid al-, 202
Ghurabāʾ li-l-Iᶜlām, 275, 279
Goldziher, Ignaz, 229
Golden Age, 9
Gomaa, Ali (ᶜAlī Jumᶜa), 236
Gramsci, Antonio, 5
Gulf War, 17
Gunning, Joel, 322

ḥadīth (Prophetic reports), 28, 43, 64, 82, 101, 110, 112, 113, 132, 133, 138, 144, 158, 164–6, 170, 183; *see also sunna*
ḥākimiyya (religious sovereignty), 163, 175, 178–81
Hallaq, Wael, 71, 101
Ḥālī, Alṭāf Ḥusayn, 80, 85, 99, 119
Halliday, Fred, 292
Hamas (ḤAMĀS), 11, 215, 316–33, 347, 353–61
Ḥanafī(s)/Abū Ḥanīfa, 76, 100, 101, 105, 108–9, 115, 119, 130, 131, 141, 142, 143, 144, 146, 148, 152, 153, 155, 156, 157, 238, 244, 246, 257, 280
Ḥanbalī(s)/neo-Ḥanbalī/Aḥmad b. Ḥanbal, 144, 145, 164, 166, 170, 171, 245
Hanieh, Ismail (Ismāᶜīl Haniyya), 330
Ḥaramayn (Two Sacred Sanctuaries) *see* Mecca
Ḥaqqāniyyah, 128–30, 136, 143, 146
Ḥasan, Maḥmūd al-, 24, 108, 129, 130, 133, 134, 135, 154
Hasan Yousef (Ḥasan Yūsuf), 333
Hashim, Ahmed, 297
Hāshimī Rashīd al-, 110
Hashmi, Soheil, 259
Hasyim Asy'ari (Hāshim b. Ashᶜarī), 120
Ḥawālī, Safar al-, 265
ḥawza (Shīᶜite seminary), 295, 298, 299, 309, 310–13
health, 26, 286

*hijā*ʾ (mockery), 338
hijra (emigration), 67, 70, 100, 106, 107–8, 110, 114; *see also* Hijrat Movement, *muhājirūn*
Hijrat Movement, 106
Hindu(s)/Hindusim, 8, 27, 29, 95, 102, 104, 107, 109, 114, 115, 116, 117, 118, 120, 121, 122
ḥirāba (rebellion/brigandage), 9, 309
Hizbullah (Ḥizb Allāh), 11, 197, 347, 348–53, 355
Hroub, Khaled, 356
hudna (ceasefire), 316, 324, 325, 329
ḥudūd (prescribed punishments), 9, 10, 251, 281
Ḥusayn b. ᶜAlī, 303
Ḥusayn b. Mahmūd, 275–6
Ḥutārī, Saᶜīd al-, 357, 359
Hūthīs (Houthis), 218

Ibn ᶜAbbās, 282
Ibn ᶜAbd al-Barr, 248
Ibn ᶜAbd al-Wahhāb *see* Wahhābī
Ibn ᶜĀbidīn, Muḥammad Amīn, 105, 109, 143, 155, 156
Ibn ᶜArabī, 235
Ibn al-Jawzī, 242
Ibn al-Naḥḥās, 340
Ibn al-Qayyim, 163, 170, 172, 241, 246, 248, 268, 277
Ibn Hajar al-Asqalānī, 232, 282
Ibn Ḥanbal, Amad *see* Ḥanbalīs
Ibn Ḥazm, 258
Ibn Jurayj, ᶜAbd al-Malik, 257
Ibn Kathīr, 238, 257
Ibn Qudāma, 241, 258
Ibn Rajab, 170–1
Ibn Rushd (Averroes), 268
Ibn Taymiyya, 145, 165, 167–72, 174, 176–8, 180, 182, 241, 246, 248, 251, 323
imperialism (imperial(ist); imperium), 22, 40, 41, 45, 53, 57, 68, 69, 75, 78, 89, 91, 94, 97, 129, 131, 132, 134, 135, 148
ijtihād (independent juristic reasoning), 281
imtināᶜ al-naẓīr/imkān al-naẓīr (impossibility of creating another Muhammad), 84, 103, 105
India(n); Hindustān, 27, 30, 44, 75, 78, 79, 83, 85, 86, 91, 94–8, 99–122, 127, 128
Indian Mutiny 1857 (Rebellion/Revolt/War of Independence), 75, 76, 77, 78, 79, 80, 81, 82, 83, 84, 86, 89, 90, 91, 92, 93, 94, 95, 96, 97, 101, 103, 104, 106, 120
Individualism, 27, 157
Indonesia, 19, 24, 27–32, 35, 37, 38, 120
Indonesian War of Independence, 120
Indus River, 101
Intifada (Palestinian), 320
Internet, 12, 20, 21, 23, 37
Iqbal, (ᶜAllāma) Muhammad (Muḥammad Iqbāl), 99, 122
Iran, 212, 214, 215, 221, 315, 349, 350, 351, 353
ᶜĪsā (prophet) *see* Jesus
Islamic State (IS); Islamic State in the Levant (ISIL); Islamic State in Iraq and Syria (ISIS); Daesh, 7, 11, 13, 154, 165, 166, 167, 177, 184, 185, 187, 197, 199, 215, 220, 222, 227, 228–48, 249–88
Islamia (Islāmiyya) College Lahore, 114
Islamophobia, 6, 7, 12
Ismāᶜīl Dihlawī, Shāh, 84, 85, 103, 105, 106, 131
Ismail Abu Shanab (Ismāᶜīl Abū Shanab), 323–5, 329

Jabari, Ahmad (Aḥmad Jābarī), 331
Jabhat al-Nuṣra, 181, 197, 221, 222
Jackson, Sherman, 101
Jaᶜfar al-Ṣādiq (Sixth Imam of the Twelver Shīᶜites), 307
Jāhiliyya ('pre-/non-Islamic ignorance'), 138, 173–4, 178, 229, 336
Jakarta, 28
Jāmiᶜ Masjid Delhi (Mosque), 77, 103, 104
Jamᶜiyyat al-ᶜulamāʾ-i hind, 110, 114, 134, 135
Jamia Millia Islamia, 77
Jarīr, 3, 339
Jaṣṣāṣ, Abū Bakr al-, 257, 261–2
Jesus (ᶜĪsā, prophet), 111, 258, 285, 286
Jews/Judaism, 36, 63, 109, 110–11, 181, 244, 261, 262, 263, 264, 264, 312, 318, 319; *see also ahl al-kitāb*

Jihad (*jihād*), 7–12, 13, 23, 39–71, 75–80, 82, 84, 89, 90, 91, 94, 95, 97, 100, 103, 106, 107, 110, 113–15, 120–1, 210, 211, 214, 215, 221, 223, 232, 299, 302–5, 316, 333
Jinnah, Qāʾid-i Aᶜẓam Muhammad Ali (Muḥammad ᶜAlī), 78, 122
Jilānī, Sayyid Maḥmūd al- (Mahmud al-Kilani), 66; *see also* Qādiriyya
Jizya (tribute), 238
Job (Prophet Ayyūb), 96
Jordan, 164, 198, 201, 211, 251

kāfir (infidel/unbeliever), 261, 264, 209, 283
Kākorvī, ᶜInāyatullāh Aḥmad, 92, 103
Kapuścinski, Ryszard, 360
karāma (dignity), 210
Karzay, Hamid, 125
Karachi, 128, 136, 141, 155, 158
Kāshif al-Ghiṭāʾ, Jaᶜfar, 304, 305
Kāshif, Muḥammad Jamal al-, 219
Khawārij (Kharijites, 'Seceders'), 112, 266
Kebatinan (syncretic mystical sects), 28
Kepel, Gilles, 292
Khālid b. al-Walīd, 276
Khālidī, Usāma al-, 339–41
Khalil, Mohammed, 262
Khalīsī, Shaykh Hādī al-, 301
Khallāf, ᶜAbd al-Wahhāb al-, 273
Khān, Aḥmad Riżā (Riḍā) al-Barēlwī *see* Aḥmad Riżā Khān
Khān, Sir Sayyid Aḥmad, 80, 90, 122
Khān, Ẓafar ᶜAlī Khān, 99
Khayrābādī, Fażl-i ḥaqq (Faḍl al-Ḥaqq al-), 75–8, 82–98, 103–6, 120–1
Khilafat Movement (Central Khilafat Committee), 106, 110, 112–4
Khodja, Hamdan, 47, 63, 64, 65, 68, 69, 71
Khūʾī, ᶜAbd al-Majīd al-, 313
Khūʾī, Abū al-Qāsim al-, 300
Khusraw, Amīr (Amir Khusrau), 119
kufr (unbelief), 95, 105, 108, 109, 110, 115, 183, 202, 203, 263, 266, 337
Kuwait, 19

Lahore, 114
Lake, General Lord, 106
Lav, Daniel, 260
Lawdār, 217
Lebanon, 34, 197
Levinas, Emmanuel, 359, 360
Lībī, Abū Yaḥyā al-, 156, 341
liberal/liberalism, 7, 25, 27, 30, 36, 64, 82
Libya, 188, 189, 192, 196, 202, 206, 210, 212, 213, 215, 220, 279
Ludħiyānavī, Rashīd Aḥmad, 136–46, 154, 155, 158, 159

Maᶜārib, 218
Madanī, Ḥusayn Aḥmad, 129, 130, 134, 135, 137
Madrasa-yi Raḥīmiyya, 83
Mahdi, 67
Mahdi Army (*Jaysh al-Mahdī*), 294, 297
Majūs (Magian(s)), 108
Makdisi, Usaama, 233–4
Malabar Coast, 101
Mālikī(s), 42, 143–4
Manama, 212
Manṣūr, Abū Lubābah Shāh, 138, 139, 155
maqāṣid al-sharīᶜa (the intentions of the law), 272
Maqdisī, Abū Muḥammad al-, 180, 184, 198, 201–3, 251, 265, 266, 268, 275, 279
marjaᶜiyya (Shīᶜite clerical leadership), 295, 298, 309, 310–13, 314
Marx, Karl, 225, 227, 247
maṣlaḥa (public benefit), 156, 273
Maṣrī, Fāris al-, 358
Masri, Mushir (Mushīr al-Maṣrī), 328, 354
Māturīdī, 76, 130
Mawdūdī, Abū al-Aᶜlā, 163, 174–81, 183
Mecca (Makkah/Makka)/Two Sacred Sanctuaries (including Medina (Madinah/Madīna)), 30, 51, 66, 70, 92, 102, 105, 121, 166
Meshal, Khaled (Khālid Mishᶜal), 318, 326
Mirza, Younus, 234, 272
Mohammaden law *see* Anglo-Muhammadan Law
Morocco, 53, 57, 70, 212, 215, 277
Morsi, Muhammed (Muḥammad al-Mursī), 202, 213, 216

Moses (Prophet, Mūsā), 257
Muᶜādh al-Kasāsba, 249–88
Muᶜāwiya, 236
Mubarak, Hosni (Ḥusnī Mubārak, Egyptian President), 33, 36, 189, 190, 202, 219, 223
Mudiyya, 217
Mughal, 75, 76, 79, 80, 82, 87, 89, 91, 96, 97, 98, 102, 103, 104, 113
muhājirūn (emigrants), 232
Muhallab b. Abī Ṣufra al-, 269, 282
Muḥammad b. al-Qāsim, 101
Muḥammad b. ᶜUmar, 279
Muḥammad/the Prophet, 9, 43, 44, 84, 85, 87, 88, 97, 101, 105, 110, 112, 132, 134, 138, 142, 164, 165, 166, 167, 169, 170, 171, 173, 174, 176, 178, 181, 182, 183, 216, 229, 230, 235, 251, 254, 257, 262, 264, 266, 269, 271, 272, 276, 277, 280, 281, 282, 284, 285, 307, 315, 315
Muhammadan Law *see* Anglo-Muhammadan Law
muḥārib (brigand), 308–9
Muḥāsibī, al-Hārith al-, 342
mukātāba (contractual released slave), 230
Mukhtār, ᶜUmar (Lion of the Desert), 120
Muᵓmin, Muᵓmin Khān, 83
muqāwama (resistance), 317, 333
Mūsā al-Ṣadr, 348
Musāᶜid b. Bashīr, 277–8
Muslim Brotherhood (*al-ikhwān al-muslimīn*)-, 36, 166, 189, 200, 201–4, 209, 213, 215, 219, 220, 221, 353
Mutanabbī, Aḥmad al-, 338
muᶜtazila ('Rationalists'), 112, 246, 272
Muwāfī, Ramzī, 219

Naim Qassem, 349–53
Nadwatul Ulama (Nadwat al-ᶜulamāᵓ), 108
Nahdlatul Ulama (Nahḍat al-ᶜulamāᵓ), 120
Nandy, Ashis, 30
Najaf, 312, 313
Najafī, Ṣahib al-Jawāhir Muḥammad Ḥasan al-, 303, 307
Najd, 173, 235
Napoleon I, 50
Naṣr al-Fahd, 263, 265
Nasrallah, Hassan, 351
Nationalism (nationalist(s)), 19, 29, 42, 50, 58, 59, 77, 78, 79, 118, 147, 301, 313, 353
Nation-state(s), 20, 24, 26, 27, 28, 31, 37, 39, 47, 48, 51, 78, 236, 353, 356, 357, 360, 361
NATO, 192, 212
Nānōtavī, Qāsim (Qasim Nanotawi), 107–8, 130
Nawawī, Abū Zakariyya al-, 280
Nazism/Nazis, 21
New Order 1996–8, 28–9, 31
nifāq (hypocrisy), 265
nikāḥ (sexual intercourse/marriage), 108, 111, 114, 228, 244
Noah (Prophet Nūḥ), 97
Non-Cooperation Movement (*tark-i muwālāt*), 113–17
North Africa, 22, 23, 24, 41, 46, 51, 63, 65, 222
Nuᶜaym b. Ḥammād, 236
Nuᶜmanī, Shiblī, 108

Othering, 347–61
Ottoman(s)/Empire (Turks), 52, 56, 57, 63, 64, 68, 100, 102, 106, 112, 113, 115, 118, 121, 143, 238

Pakistan, 77, 78, 84, 104, 117, 122, 124, 125, 127, 128, 135, 141, 145, 151, 152, 158, 180, 211, 218, 219
paẋtūnvalī (Pashtun tribal customary law), 141, 146–8, 150
Pancasila, 29–30, 31
Papua, 32
People's Democratic Party of Afghanistan (PDPA), 124, 137, 151
Pink, Johanna, 263
PLO (Palestinian Liberation Organisation), 321
Prevent Duty, 364–5
Protestant (Protestantism), 3, 27, 29, 30; *see also* Christians/Christianity
pluralism, 26, 27, 30, 31, 34, 41

Qādiriyya/ᶜAbd al-Qādir al-Jīlānī, 66, 105
Qāᶜida/Qaeda *see* al-Qāᶜida (al-Qaeda)
Qāʾid-i Aᶜẓam *see* Jinnah
Qaraḍāwī, Yūsuf al-, 21, 36, 166, 170, 250, 258, 317
Qaṣīr, Ahmad, 349
Qassām, ᶜIzz al-Dīn al-, 355
Qatar, 212, 221
Qaṭarī b. Fujāᶜa, 340
qiṣaṣ (retributive punishment), 249, 250, 254, 257, 258, 259, 267, 271, 274, 275, 277, 278, 285, 286, 288
Qunaybī, Iyād, 204–6
Qurʾān/Qurʾanic, 4, 8, 10, 28, 30, 36, 68, 96, 99, 107, 110, 111, 114, 115, 132, 133, 142, 143, 144, 154, 156, 158, 166, 169, 177, 179, 181, 184, 207
Quraysh, 112, 113, 169–70, 174, 231, 318
Quṭb, Sayyid, 163, 167, 175–82, 185

Radda, 217
Rangoon, 91, 104, 116
Ramadan, Tariq, 21, 26–7
Rantissi, Abdel Aziz (ᶜAbd al-ᶜAzīz al-Rantīsī), 322
Raqqa, 221, 250, 256, 274
Rashid, Ahmed, 124
Rashidun Caliphate (*al-khilāfat al-rāshida*), 9
ridda/murtadd (apostasy, apostates), 61, 95, 96, 105, 114, 265
Riyadh, 334, 341
Robespierre, Maximilien, 227, 247
Rougier, Bernard, 247

Ṣadr, Muḥammad Bāqir al- (al-Ṣadr al-Awwal), 298, 310, 313
Ṣadr, Muḥammad Muḥammad al- (al-Ṣadr al-Thānī), 298, 301, 302, 310, 313
Ṣadr, Muqtadā al-, 291–314
ṣaḥāba (companions of the Prophet), 101, 112, 133, 271, 272, 276, 281, 282, 283
Saḥnūn, 245
Said Siam (Saᶜīd Siyām), 327
Salafis/Salafism *see also* Wahhābī, 114, 163–85, 199, 206, 251
Saleh, Ali Abdullah (ᶜAlī ᶜAbd Allāh Ṣāliḥ, Yemeni President), 189, 198, 213, 216–18, 223
salmiyya (peaceful mobilisation), 210
Samarra, 312
Samīᶜ al-Ḥaqq, 128–30, 135–8, 146
Sanaa, 212, 217
Sartre, Jean-Paul, 23
Saudi Arabia (KSA), 19, 212, 214, 217, 218, 221, 250, 256, 262, 263, 265, 275, 277, 278, 334, 349, 350
Sayyid Imām al-Sharīf, 154, 180, 182, 262
secularism (secular), 23, 33–4, 36, 53, 63, 64, 117, 193, 203
September 11th attacks (9/11), 12, 13, 123, 128, 191, 192
Shabab (Ḥarakat al-Shabāb al-Mujāhidīn), 266
Shāfiᶜī(s), 29, 118, 228, 237, 280
Shāh Walīullāh *see* Walīullāh
Shāh ᶜAbd al-ᶜAzīz *see* ᶜAbd al-ᶜAzīz
Shāh Ismāᶜīl *see* Ismāᶜīl
shahāda (martyrdom), 295, 302–5
Shahīd al-Awwal, Muḥammad al-ᶜĀmilī, 308–9
Shahīd al-Thānī, Zayn al-Dīn al-ᶜĀmilī, 306, 307
Sharīᶜa, 11, 28, 34, 35, 52, 108, 109, 115, 117, 118, 119, 142, 146, 149, 152, 153, 159, 165, 167, 181, 182, 183, 192, 198, 200, 201, 202, 204, 205, 206, 207, 208; *see also fiqh*
Sharīᶜa Council of Minbar al- Tawḥīd waʾl-Jihād, 165, 193, 195, 252, 279, 280
Sharon, Ariel, 325
Shathrī, Saᶜd al-, 250
Shawkānī, Muḥammad al-, 241, 246, 282
Shaybānī, Muḥammad b. Ḥasan al-, 108, 115
Shaymāᶜ Haddād, 254
Shēfta, Nawāb Muṣṭafā Khān, 76, 83, 91
Shihrī, ᶜAmīr al-, 341
Shīᶜite (Shīᶜism), 25, 85, 144, 145, 187, 197 I
Shinqīṭī, Abū al-Mundhir al-, 190–203, 205, 207, 208, 278–81, 284, 288
Shinqīṭī, Abu ᶜUbayda al-, 272, 287–8

Shinqīṭī, Muḥammad Amīn, 258–9, 262, 263
Shirwānī, ᶜAbd al-Shāhid Khān, 91
Sindhī, ᶜUbaydullāh, 79, 132, 134
shirk (polytheism), 52, 108, 111, 169, 173, 174, 176, 177, 203, 226, 245, 252
Sistānī, ᶜAlī al-, 304, 305
Smith, Wilfred Cantell, 5
Soekarno, 29
Sorbonne, 35
South Asia, 76, 78, 79, 82, 86, 101, 143
Southeast Asia, 30
Sufi/Sufism (*ṣūfī*), 43, 66, 79, 103, 105, 122, 134, 135, 140, 177, 238
Supreme Council of the Islamic revolution in Iraq/Islamic Supreme Council of Iraq (SCIRI/ISCI), 297
Suharto (government), 29
Sultan Ali Raja (Sulṭān ᶜAlī Rājā), 102
Sunna/sunnat (Prophetic tradition), 108, 119, 207
Sunni (*ahl al-sunna*), 25, 29, 76, 101, 112–13, 119, 144, 190
Swartz, Merlin, 242
Syria(n), 13, 43, 49, 57, 105, 109–10, 143, 164, 165, 167, 181, 185, 188–91, 192, 195, 196, 197, 198, 208, 209, 210, 212, 213, 214, 215, 219, 220, 221, 222, 223, 224, 247, 253, 254, 256, 278, 279, 315, 353, 360

Tamil(s), 27
tahdiʾa (cessation of hostilities), 315–33
Tahrir Square, 190, 212
Taḥrīk-i Ṭālibān-i Pākistān (TṬP), 125, 128, 152
tajnīs (play on words), 335–6
takfīr (excommunication), 105, 260, 265
Taliban (Ṭālibān), 123–9, 133–4, 136–42, 145–59, 265
taqiyya (dissimulation), 197, 311
taqlīd (following, of legal authority), 131–6
Ṭarṭūsī, Abū Baṣīr al-, 190–1, 196, 198–9, 202, 206, 207, 208
taṣawwuf see Sufism
tawḥīd, 29, 52, 111, 163, 166–9, 171–4, 176, 180–4, 235, 238
Taylor, Christopher, 235
Tayyeb, Ahmad al-, 35
Ṭayyib, Qārī Muḥammad, 129
terrorism, 13, 65, 158, 191
Thānavī/Thanawī, Ashraf ᶜAlī, 108, 135
theologians, 6, 75, 86, 103; *see also ᶜulamāʾ*
theology, 2, 3, 4, 5, 6, 8, 13, 26, 30, 42, 44, 45, 48, 53, 76, 79, 84, 85, 86, 97, 100, 105, 113, 119, 120, 121, 127, 128, 130, 132, 137, 138, 139, 157, 159, 166, 167, 174, 177, 182
Tipu Sultan (Ṭīpū Sulṭan), Tiger of Mysore), 102
Tunisia, 53, 61, 188, 189, 191, 193, 200, 201, 202, 204, 210, 211, 212, 215, 216, 219, 220, 223, 279, 280, 353
Ṭūsī, Muḥammad b. al-Ḥasan al-, 308
Tuṣullī, ᶜAlī b. ᶜAbd al-Salām al, 48
Two Sacred Sanctuaries (*ḥaramayn*) *see* Mecca

ᶜUbāda b. Ṣāmit, 264
ᶜUbaydī, Ṣalāḥ al-, 301
ᶜUbaydullāh Sindhī *see* Sindhī
ᶜudabāʾ, 4
Ulil Abshar Abdalla, 29–30
ᶜUmar b. al-Khaṭṭāb (Second Caliph of Sunni Islam), 82, 132, 230, 233
ᶜUmar, Mullā Muḥammad, 136, 155, 157, 158
ᶜulamāʾ (Islamic/Muslim scholars), 3, 4, 78, 90, 94, 105, 106, 107, 108, 109, 111, 133, 134, 135, 140, 173, 175
umm al-walad (slave mother), 230, 234
umma (Muslim community), 20, 57, 70, 132–3, 134, 152–3, 195, 223, 232, 233
ᶜurf (customary practice), 113, 146–53, 272
ᶜUthmān b. Bishr, 235
ᶜUyayrī, Yūsuf al-, 335–9

Victoria, Queen, 112

Wahhābī/Wahhabism/Ibn ᶜAbd al-Wahhāb, Muḥammad, 44, 79, 84, 85, 87, 92, 103, 105, 171–80, 182, 227, 235, 247, 248, 349

walad zinā (child of illegitimate intercourse), 225
Walīullāh Dihlawī, Shāh, 78, 83, 85, 106, 113, 131, 132, 134
Wāqidī, al-, 246
War on Terror (counterterrorism), 13
Wazzāniyya-Tayyibiyya order, 66
West Africa, 44
Wilson, Roland, 100
Wittgenstein, Ludwig, 2, 24
World War I, 24
World War II, 18, 360

Yamānī, Abū Dharr al-Samharī, 164–6
Yazīd b. Muᶜāwiya, 238
Yemen, 188, 189, 191, 198, 199, 210, 211, 212, 213, 215, 216–22, 223, 315
Yezidis, 237–40, 244, 246

Zahar, Mahmoud (Maḥmūd al-Zahār), 321, 327
Zamīndār, 99
Zarqānī, Ḥasan al-, 301
Zarqāwī, Abū Muṣᶜab, 265, 266, 288
Ẓawāhirī, Ayman al-, 187–93, 206, 211, 212, 213, 215, 221, 288, 337
Zayd b. al-Khaṭṭāb, 235
Zinjibār, 217
Žižek, Slavoj, 81–2

EU representative:
Easy Access System Europe
Mustamäe tee 50, 10621 Tallinn, Estonia
Gpsr.requests@easproject.com

www.ingramcontent.com/pod-product-compliance
Lightning Source LLC
Chambersburg PA
CBHW051554230426
43668CB00013B/1847
* 9 7 8 1 4 7 4 4 8 5 5 1 7 *